Year	GDP*	Consumption	Investment	Government Purchases	Net Exports**	Real GDP in billions of chained 2005 dollars	Percentage Change from Previous Year		
							Real GDP	Consumer Price Index	Unemployment Rate
1970	1039	648	152	234	4	4270	0.2	5.6	4.9
1971	1127	702	178	246	1	4413	3.4	3.3	5.9
1972	1238	770	208	263	−3	4648	5.3	3.4	5.6
1973	1382	852	245	282	4	4917	5.8	8.7	4.9
1974	1500	933	249	318	−1	4890	−0.5	12.3	5.6
1975	1638	1034	230	358	16	4880	−0.2	6.9	8.5
1976	1825	1151	292	383	−2	5141	5.3	4.9	7.7
1977	2030	1278	361	414	−23	5378	4.6	6.7	7.1
1978	2294	1428	438	454	−25	5678	5.6	9.0	6.1
1979	2562	1591	493	501	−23	5856	3.2	13.3	5.8
1980	2789	1756	479	566	−13	5840	−0.2	12.5	7.1
1981	3127	1940	572	628	−13	5987	2.5	8.9	7.6
1982	3253	2076	517	680	−20	5871	−1.9	3.8	9.7
1983	3535	2289	564	733	−52	6136	4.5	3.8	9.6
1984	3931	2501	736	797	−103	6577	7.2	3.9	7.5
1985	4218	2718	736	879	−115	6849	4.1	3.8	7.2
1986	4460	2897	747	949	−133	7087	3.5	1.1	7.0
1987	4736	3097	785	999	−145	7313	3.4	4.4	6.2
1988	5100	3350	822	1039	−110	7613	4.1	4.6	5.5
1989	5482	3595	875	1101	−88	7886	3.5	4.6	5.3
1990	5801	3836	861	1182	−78	8034	1.9	6.1	5.6
1991	5992	3980	803	1236	−27	8015	−0.2	3.1	6.8
1992	6342	4237	865	1274	−33	8287	3.4	2.9	7.5
1993	6667	4484	953	1295	−64	8523	2.9	2.7	6.9
1994	7085	4751	1097	1330	−93	8871	4.1	2.7	6.1
1995	7415	4987	1144	1374	−91	9094	2.5	2.5	5.6
1996	7839	5274	1240	1421	−96	9434	3.7	3.3	5.4
1997	8332	5571	1389	1474	−101	9854	4.5	1.7	4.9
1998	8794	5919	1511	1526	−162	10,284	4.4	1.6	4.5
1999	9354	6342	1642	1631	−262	10,780	4.8	2.7	4.2
2000	9952	6830	1772	1731	−382	11,226	4.1	3.4	4.0
2001	10,286	7149	1662	1846	−371	11,347	1.1	1.6	4.7
2002	10,642	7439	1647	1983	−427	11,553	1.8	2.4	5.8
2003	11,142	7804	1730	2113	−504	11,841	2.5	1.9	6.0
2004	11,868	8285	1969	2233	−619	12,264	3.5	3.3	5.5
2005	12,638	8819	2172	2370	−723	12,638	3.1	3.4	5.1
2006	13,399	9323	2327	2518	−769	12,976	2.7	2.5	4.6
2007	14,078	9826	2289	2677	−714	13,254	2.1	4.1	4.6
2008	14,441	10,130	2136	2883	−708	13,312	0.4	0.1	5.8
2009	14,256	10,089	1629	2931	−392	12,987	−2.4	2.7	9.3

* Numbers may not add up because of rounding.
** From 1929–1937, 1942, 1954, and 1959 net exports were less than ± $0.5 billion.
Source: www.bea.gov

The McGraw-Hill Series

Economics

ESSENTIALS OF ECONOMICS

Brue, McConnell, and Flynn
Essentials of Economics
Second Edition

Mandel
Economics: The Basics
First Edition

Schiller
Essentials of Economics
Eighth Edition

PRINCIPLES OF ECONOMICS

Colander
Economics, Microeconomics, and Macroeconomics
Eighth Edition

Frank and Bernanke
Principles of Economics, Principles of Microeconomics, and Principles of Macroeconomics
Fourth Edition

Frank and Bernanke
Brief Editions: Principles of Economics, Principles of Microeconomics, Principles of Macroeconomics
Second Edition

McConnell, Brue, and Flynn
Economics, Microeconomics, and Macroeconomics
Eighteenth Edition

McConnell, Brue, and Flynn
Brief Editions: Economics, Micro-economics, Macroeconomics
First Edition

Miller
Principles of Microeconomics
First Edition

Samuelson and Nordhaus
Economics, Microeconomics, and Macroeconomics
Nineteenth Edition

Schiller
The Economy Today, The Micro Economy Today, and The Macro Economy Today
Twelfth Edition

Slavin
Economics, Microeconomics, and Macroeconomics
Tenth Edition

ECONOMICS OF SOCIAL ISSUES

Guell
Issues in Economics Today
Fifth Edition

Sharp, Register, and Grimes
Economics of Social Issues
Nineteenth Edition

ECONOMETRICS

Gujarati and Porter
Basic Econometrics
Fifth Edition

Gujarati and Porter
Essentials of Econometrics
Fourth Edition

MANAGERIAL ECONOMICS

Baye
Managerial Economics and Business Strategy
Seventh Edition

Brickley, Smith, and Zimmerman
Managerial Economics and Organizational Architecture
Fifth Edition

Thomas and Maurice
Managerial Economics
Tenth Edition

INTERMEDIATE ECONOMICS

Bernheim and Whinston
Microeconomics
First Edition

Dornbusch, Fischer, and Startz
Macroeconomics
Eleventh Edition

Frank
Microeconomics and Behavior
Eighth Edition

ADVANCED ECONOMICS

Romer
Advanced Macroeconomics
Third Edition

MONEY AND BANKING

Cecchetti and Schoenholtz
Money, Banking, and Financial Markets
Third Edition

URBAN ECONOMICS

O'Sullivan
Urban Economics
Seventh Edition

LABOR ECONOMICS

Borjas
Labor Economics
Fifth Edition

McConnell, Brue, and Macpherson
Contemporary Labor Economics
Ninth Edition

PUBLIC FINANCE

Rosen and Gayer
Public Finance
Ninth Edition

Seidman
Public Finance
First Edition

ENVIRONMENTAL ECONOMICS

Field and Field
Environmental Economics: An Introduction
Fifth Edition

INTERNATIONAL ECONOMICS

Appleyard, Field, and Cobb
International Economics
Seventh Edition

King and King
International Economics, Globalization, and Policy: A Reader
Fifth Edition

Pugel
International Economics
Fourteenth Edition

M*icroeconomics*

TENTH EDITION

Stephen L. Slavin

Union County College
Cranford, New Jersey

The New School University
New York City

Mc
Graw
Hill **McGraw-Hill**
Irwin

MICROECONOMICS

Published by McGraw-Hill/Irwin, a business unit of The McGraw-Hill Companies, Inc., 1221 Avenue of the Americas, New York, NY, 10020. Copyright © 2011, 2009, 2008, 2005, 2002, 1999, 1996, 1994, 1991, 1989 by The McGraw-Hill Companies, Inc.

Some ancillaries, including electronic and print components, may not be available to customers outside the United States.

This book is printed on acid-free paper.

1 2 3 4 5 6 7 8 9 0 QDB/QDB 1 0 9 8 7 6 5 4 3 2 1 0

ISBN 978-0-07-731718-8
MHID 0-07-731718-1

Vice president and editor-in-chief: *Brent Gordon*
Publisher: *Douglas Reiner*
Director of development: *Ann Torbert*
Senior development editor: *Christina Kouvelis*
Vice president and director of marketing: *Robin J. Zwettler*
Senior marketing manager: *Jen Saxton*
Vice president of editing, design, and production: *Sesha Bolisetty*
Project manager: *Dana M. Pauley*
Senior buyer: *Carol A. Bielski*
Lead designer: *Matthew Baldwin*
Senior photo research coordinator: *Jeremy Cheshareck*
Photo researcher: *Keri Johnson*
Lead media project manager: *Kerry Bowler*
Senior media project manager: *Ron Nelms*
Typeface: *10/12 Times*
Compositor: *Aptara®, Inc.*
Printer: *Quad/Graphics*

Library of Congress Cataloging-in-Publication Data

Slavin, Stephen L.
    Microeconomics/Stephen L. Slavin.—10th ed.
        p. cm.—(The McGraw-Hill series economics)
    Includes index.
    ISBN-13: 978-0-07-731718-8 (alk. paper)
    ISBN-10: 0-07-731718-1 (alk. paper)
    1. Microeconomics. I. Title.
    HB172.S57 2011
    338.5—dc22

                                        2010027164

About the Author

Photo credit: Leontine Temsky

Stephen L. Slavin received his BA in economics from Brooklyn College and his MA and PhD in economics from New York University. He has taught at New York Institute of Technology, Brooklyn College, St. Francis College (Brooklyn), and in the MBA program at Fairleigh Dickinson University, at the New School University in New York City, and at Union County College in Cranford, New Jersey.

He has written eight other books: *The Einstein Syndrome: Corporate Anti-Semitism in America Today* (University Press of America); *Jelly Bean Economics: Reaganomics in the Early 1980s* (Philosophical Library); *Economics: A Self-Teaching Guide, All the Math You'll Ever Need, Math for Your First- and Second-Grader, Quick Business Math: A Self-Teaching Guide* (all four published by John Wiley & Sons); *Chances Are: The Only Statistics Book You'll Ever Need* (University Press of America); and *Everyday Math in 20 Minutes a Day* (Learning-Express). He is the coauthor of four other Wiley books, *Practical Algebra, Quick Algebra Review, Precalculus,* and *Geometry.* In addition he is also the coauthor of *Basic Mathematics,* a text published by Pi r squared Publishers.

Dr. Slavin's articles have appeared in *Studies in Family Planning, Economic Planning, Journal of BioSocial Science, Business and Society Review, Bankers Magazine, Education for Business, Public Management, Better Investing, Northwest Investment Review, U.S.A. Today Magazine, Patterns in Prejudice, Culturefront,* and *Conservative Review.* In addition, he has written more than 500 newspaper commentaries on public policy, demographic economics, politics, urban economics, international trade, investments, and economics fluctuations.

Preface to the Instructor

As an undergraduate economics student, I never imagined writing a textbook—let alone one going into its tenth edition. Back in those good old days, economics texts were all stand-alone books without any supplements, and seldom cost students more than five dollars. While we certainly need to keep up with the times, not all change is for the good. Surely not when our students are paying $150 for textbooks they barely read.

Why not write a book that students would actually enjoy reading and sell it at a price they can afford? Rather than serving up the same old dull fare, why not just have a conversation with the reader, illustrating various economic concepts anecdotally?

Economics can be a rather intimidating subject, with its extensive vocabulary, complicated graphs, and quantitative tendencies. Is it possible to write a principles text that lowers the student's anxiety level without watering down the subject matter? To do this, one would need to be an extremely good writer, have extensive teaching experience, and have solid academic training in economics. In this case, two out of three is just not good enough.

Why did I write this book? Probably my moment of decision arrived more than 25 years ago when I mentioned to my macro class that Kemp-Roth cut the top personal income tax bracket from 70 percent to 50 percent. Then I asked, "If you were rich, by what percentage were your taxes cut?"

The class sat there in complete silence. Most of the students stared at the blackboard, waiting for me to work out the answer. I told them to work it out themselves. I waited. And I waited. Finally, someone said, "Twenty percent?"

"Close," I replied, "but no cigar."

"Fourteen percent?" someone else ventured.

"No, you're getting colder."

After waiting another two or three minutes, I saw one student with her hand up. One student knew that the answer was almost 29 percent—*one* student in a class of 30.

When do they teach students how to do percentage changes? In high school? In middle school? Surely not in a college economics course.

How much of *your* time do you spend going over simple arithmetic and algebra? How much time do you spend going over simple graphs? Wouldn't you rather be spending that time discussing economics?

Now you'll be able to do just that, because all the arithmetic and simple algebra that you normally spend time explaining are covered methodically in this book. All you'll need to do is tell your students which pages to look at.

The micro chapters offer scores of tables and graphs for the students to plot on their own; the solutions are shown in the book. Learning actively rather than passively, your students will retain a lot more economics.

As an economics instructor for more than 30 years at such fabled institutions as Brooklyn College, New York Institute of Technology, St. Francis College (Brooklyn), and Union County College, I have used a variety of texts. But each of their authors assumed a mathematical background that the majority of my students did not have. Each also assumed that his graphs and tables were comprehensible to the average student.

The biggest problem we have with just about any book we assign is that many of our students don't bother to read it before coming to class. Until now, no one has written a principles text in plain English. I can't promise that every one of your students will do the readings you assign, but at least they won't be able to complain anymore about not understanding the book.

Distinctive Qualities

My book has six qualities that no other principles text has.

1. **It reviews math that students haven't done since middle school and high school.**

2. **It's an interactive text, encouraging active rather than passive reading.** Students are expected to solve numerical problems, fill in tables, draw graphs, and do economic analysis as they read the text.

3. **It's a combined textbook and workbook.** Each chapter is followed by workbook pages that include multiple-choice and fill-in questions, as well as numerical problems.

4. **It costs substantially less than virtually every other text on the market.** And it has a built-in study guide.

5. **It's written in plain English without jargon.** See for yourself. Open any page and compare my writing style with that of any other principles author. This book is written to communicate clearly and concisely with the students' needs in mind.

6. **It is written with empathy for students.** My goal is to get students past their math phobias and fear of graphs by having them do hundreds of problems, step-by-step, literally working their way through the book.

Special Features

Four special features of the book are its integrated coverage of the global economy, its extra help boxes, its advanced work boxes, and its end-of-chapter current issues.

The Global Economy

Until the early 1970s our economy was largely insulated from the rest of the world economy. All of this changed with the oil price shock of 1973, our subsequent growing appetite for fuel-efficient Japanese compact cars, as well as for TVs, DVD players, cell phones, personal computers, and other consumer electronics made in Asia. As our trade deficits grew, and as foreigners bought up more and more American assets, every American became quite aware of how integrated we had become within the global economy.

The tenth edition has two chapters devoted entirely to the global economy—Chapter 19 (International Trade) and Chapter 20 (International Finance). In addition, we have integrated a great deal of material dealing specifically with the global economy throughout the text.

Here are some of the things we look at:

- Shipbreaking (Ch. 3, p. 57)
- The "Isms": Capitalism, Communism, Fascism, and Socialism (Ch. 3, pp. 63–67)
- The Decline of the Communist System (Ch. 3, p. 66)
- The Corporate Hierarchy (Ch. 10, p. 256)
- The Dango (Ch. 12, p. 291)
- European Antitrust (Ch. 13, p. 317)
- Children Living in Poverty in Various Countries (Ch. 18, p. 428)

Here are some of the topics covered in the Extra Help boxes:

- Finding the Opportunity Cost (Ch. 2, p. 36)
- How Changes in Demand Affect Equilibrium (Ch. 4, p. 76)
- How Changes in Supply Affect Equilibrium (Ch. 4, p. 78)
- Price Ceilings, Price Floors, Shortages, and Surpluses (Ch. 4, p. 82)
- Differentiating between Changes in Supply and Changes in Quantity Supplied (Ch. 5, p. 108)
- Practice Problems Finding Price Elasticity of Demand (Ch. 6, p. 128)
- Calculating Marginal Utility and Total Utility (Ch. 7, p. 158)
- Finding Marginal Cost When the Output is 0 (Ch. 8, p. 174)
- What's the Difference between Shutting Down and Going Out of Business? (Ch. 8, p. 188)
- Accounting Profit vs. Economic Profit (Ch. 9, p. 206)
- Finding the Firm's Short-Run and Long-Run Supply Curves, and Shut-Down and Break-Even Points (Ch. 9, p. 214)
- How to Find the Monopolist's Price and Output (Ch. 10, p. 243)
- Productivity and Marginal Physical Product (Ch. 14, p. 332)
- Finding the Imperfect Competitor's MRP (Ch. 14, p. 336)
- Quick Review of Calculating Percentage Changes (Ch. 16, p. 379)
- Finding the Percentage of Income Share of the Quintiles in Figure 1 (Ch. 18, p. 419)
- Interpreting the Top Line in Figure 5 (Ch. 20, p. 488)

Extra Help Boxes

Students taking the principles course have widely varying backgrounds. Some have no problem doing the math or understanding basic economic concepts. But many others are lost from day one.

I have provided dozens of Extra Help boxes for the students who need them. They are especially useful to instructors who don't want to spend hours of class time going over material that they assume should be understood after one reading.

Of course these boxes can be skipped by the better prepared students.

Advanced Work Boxes

There are some concepts in the principles course that many instructors will want to skip. (Of course, if they're not included in principles texts, this will make other instructors quite unhappy.) These boxes are intended for the better prepared students who are willing to tackle these relatively difficult concepts.

Here is a sampling of my Advanced Work boxes:

- Post-World War II Recessions (Ch. 1, p. 12)
- The Law of Increasing Costs (Ch. 2, p. 34)

- Finding Equilibrium Price and Quantity (Ch. 5, p. 113)
- Why We Don't Use a Simpler Elasticity Formula (Ch. 6, p. 127)
- Deriving the Shut-down and Break-even Points (Ch. 8, p. 191)
- Calculating a Firm's Total Loss (Ch. 9, p. 211)
- Maximizing Total Profit and Maximizing Profit per Unit (Ch. 9, p. 223)
- Perfect Price Discrimination (Ch. 11, p. 276)
- The Concept of Margin in Economic Analysis (Ch. 14, p. 331)
- Who Created the Land? (Ch. 17, p. 399)
- Usury in Ancient Times (Ch. 17, p. 401)

Current Issues

Students often ask, "How does any of this affect me?" Or, "Why do I have to study economics?" The Current Issues provide answers to those questions. Each is a practical application of at least one of the concepts covered in the chapter.

What's New and Different in the Tenth Edition?

One substantial change is the doubling of the number of practical applications, which appear at the end of each chapter. These enable your students to solve real world problems using what they have learned in each chapter.

At the end of nearly each chapter, you'll now find one or two Web activities which will reinforce what your students have learned. There's a world of information on the Web, and the key to using it effectively is knowing where to look.

A third major change is a thorough discussion of the causes and effects of the Great Recession. This takes place not just in the chapters on fiscal and monetary policy, but is integrated into most of the macro chapters as well as some of the micro chapters.

The advent of the Great Recession brought Keynesian economics back into fashion. Indeed, the massive stimulus programs enacted by the United States, China, and other leading economic powers were lifted directly from Keynes' *General Theory*. If you look back at the previous nine editions, you'll see that Slavin's *Economics* covered Keynesian analysis more extensively than any other principles text. Now, in the tenth edition, we discuss how Keynesian policy prescriptions were used to fight the Great Recession.

Finally, several new "Chapter Issues" have been added—including "The Card Check Law" (Chapter 15). This feature helps make economics more relevant to students.

Content and data updates have been made throughout the book to reflect currency. In addition, many of the examples have been updated, with a focus on examples that connect to current events such as the financial crisis and the Great Recession of 2007–2009. A more thorough listing of chapter-by-chapter changes is supplied below.

- **Chapter 1:** New Section: "The Great Recession."
- **Chapter 5:** Section: "What Causes Changes in Demand?": Added box, "Did the Cash for Clunkers Tax Credit Raise Demand for New Cars?" Section: "Individual Supply and Market Supply": Table 3 and Figure 4 are redone to reflect a future motor vehicle market supply. Section: "Graphing the Demand and Supply Curves": Tables 4 and 5, and the corresponding graphs in Figures 6 and 7, were simplified, so that the equilibrium price and quantity would be whole numbers. Section: "The Equilibrium Point": Table 6, which was derived from Tables 4 and 5, and Figure 8, which was derived from Figures 6 and 7, were simplified, so that the equilibrium price and quantity would be whole numbers. The entire section was

rewritten, making it more straightforward to beginning economics students. Section: "Shifts in Demand and Supply": This new section reviews work covered in Chapter 4 of *Economics* and *Microeconomics.*

- **Chapter 13:** Current Issue: "Pharmaceutical Fraud" replaced "The Enron Case."
- **Chapter 15:** Current Issue: Made "Will You Ever Be a Member of a Labor Union?" into a regular section of the chapter. New Current Issue: "The Card Check Law."
- **Chapter 16:** Added box, "The 10-Minute Gallon."
- **Chapter 17:** Added subsection, "Profits and Losses During the Great Recession," to the section, "Profits." Added Figure 5, "The Top Corporate Winners and Losers of 2008," and Figure 6, "Declining Fortunes: 2004–2008." Cut 7 paragraphs from Current Issue, "Subprime, Fringe, and Payday Lending."
- **Chapter 19:** Part I: "A Brief History of U.S. Trade": added section, "The Effect of the Great Recession on Our Balance of Trade." Section: "What Are the Causes of Our Trade Imbalance": Added subsection: "(6) Our Shrinking Manufacturing Base." Added second Current Issue: "Globalization."
- **Chapter 20:** Deleted Advanced Work box, "The Yuan vs. the Dollar."

The Supplement Package

The *Economics* supplement package has been streamlined and updated for the tenth edition. All supplements are available at www.mhhe.com/slavin10e. In addition to updated online quizzes, the Test Bank is tagged for Learning Objectives, AACSB categories, and Bloom's Taxonomy. Also, the PowerPoint presentations for each chapter have been revised to increase relevance and clarity.

Instructor's Manual

This provides instructors with ideas on how to use the text, includes a description of the text's special features, a chapter-by-chapter discussion of material new to the tenth edition, and a rundown of chapter coverage to help them decide what they can skip. Also found here are the answers to the workbook questions and questions for thought and discussion at the end of each chapter of the text, as well as chapter worksheets and worksheet solutions.

Mark Maier, who has used the text for several editions, took over the Instructor's Manual in the sixth edition, and has included sections on chapter objectives, ideas for use in class, and homework questions and projects (including scores of very useful websites) for each chapter.

The Instructor's Manual provides a rich source of interesting ideas of classroom activities and discussions involving concepts and issues included in the text.

Test Bank

The test bank includes over 9,000 multiple-choice questions, fill-in questions, and problems tagged to Learning Objectives, AACSB categories, and Bloom's Taxonomy. My thanks to Jerry Dunn and Ralph May from Southwestern Oklahoma State University, who have kept the test bank current, culling outdated questions and adding new ones.

Computerized Testing

A comprehensive bank of test questions is provided within a computerized test bank powered by McGraw-Hill's flexible electronic testing program EZ Test Online (www.eztestonline.com). EZ Test Online supplies instructors with the capability to create tests or quizzes in this easy to use program!

Instructors can select questions from multiple McGraw-Hill test banks or author their own, and the either print the test for paper distribution or supply it online. This user-friendly program allows instructors to sort questions by format; edit existing questions or add new ones; and scramble questions for multiple versions of the same test. You can export your tests for use in WebCT, Blackboard, and PageOut. Sharing tests with colleagues, adjuncts, TAs is easy! Instant scoring and feedback is provided and EZ Test's grade book is designed to easily export to your grade book.

PowerPoint Presentations

PowerPoint presentations are available and can be customized by the professor for length and level. Deborah M. Figart and Ellen Mutari of Richard Stockton College of New Jersey have done a great job updating and revising these presentations to highlight the most important concepts from each chapter.

Digital Image Library

All the graphs from the text are available in chapter-specific files for easy download. These images will aid in classroom presentations and the student's understanding.

Videos

A selection of videos is available to adopters, including both tutorial lessons and programs that combine historical footage, documentary sequences, interviews, and analysis to illustrate economic theory. A series of videos produced by Paul Solman, business and economics correspondent for the Lehrer News Hour and WGBH Boston, covers the core topics in economics.

Book Website
www.mhhe.com/slavin10e

Some of the text's unique qualities are incorporated in a dynamic new website. Updated online multiple-choice quizzes, emphasize the chapter Learning Objectives and offer further reinforcement of important chapter concepts.

McGraw-Hill *Connect*™ *Economics*

Less Managing. More Teaching. Greater Learning.

 McGraw-Hill *Connect*™ *Economics* is an online assignment and assessment solution that connects students with the tools and resources they'll need to achieve success.

McGraw-Hill *Connect*™ *Economics* helps prepare students for their future by enabling faster learning, more efficient studying, and higher retention of knowledge.

McGraw-Hill *Connect*™ *Economics* features

 *Connect*™ *Economics* offers a number of powerful tools and features to make managing assignments easier, so faculty can spend more time teaching. With *Connect*™ *Economics,* students can engage with their coursework anytime and anywhere, making the learning process more accessible and efficient. *Connect*™ *Economics* offers the features as described here.

Simple Assignment Management

With *Connect*™ *Economics,* creating assignments is easier than ever, so you can spend more time teaching and less time managing. The assignment management function enables you to:

- Create and deliver assignments easily with selectable end-of-chapter questions and test bank items.

- Streamline lesson planning, student progress reporting, and assignment grading to make classroom management more efficient than ever.
- Go paperless with the eBook and online submission and grading of student assignments.

Smart Grading

When it comes to studying, time is precious. *Connect*™ *Economics* helps students learn more efficiently by providing feedback and practice material when they need it, where they need it. When it comes to teaching, your time also is precious. The grading function enables you to:

- Have assignments scored automatically, giving students immediate feedback on their work and side-by-side comparisons with correct answers.
- Access and review each response; manually change grades or leave comments for students to review.
- Reinforce classroom concepts with practice tests and instant quizzes.

Instructor Library

- The *Connect*™ *Economics* Instructor Library is your repository for additional resources to improve student engagement in and out of class. You can select and use any asset that enhances your lecture.

Student Study Center

The *Connect*™ *Economics* Student Study Center is the place for students to access additional resources. The Student Study Center:

- Offers students quick access to lectures, practice materials, eBooks, and more.
- Provides instant practice material and study questions, easily accessible on the go.

Student Progress Tracking

Connect™ *Economics* keeps instructors informed about how each student, section, and class is performing, allowing for more productive use of lecture and office hours. The progress-tracking function enables you to:

- View scored work immediately and track individual or group performance with assignment and grade reports.
- Access an instant view of student or class performance relative to learning objectives.
- Collect data and generate reports required by many accreditation organizations, such as AACSB.

Lecture Capture

Increase the attention paid to lecture discussion by decreasing the attention paid to note taking. For an additional charge Lecture Capture offers new ways for students to focus on the in-class discussion, knowing they can revisit important topics later. Lecture Capture enables you to:

- Record and distribute your lecture with a click of a button.
- Record and index PowerPoint presentations and anything shown on your computer so it is easily searchable, frame by frame.
- Offer access to lectures anytime and anywhere by computer, iPod, or mobile device.
- Increase intent listening and class participation by easing students' concerns about note-taking. Lecture Capture will make it more likely you will see students' faces, not the tops of their heads.

McGraw-Hill *Connect*™ *Plus Economics*

McGraw-Hill reinvents the textbook learning experience for the modern student with *Connect™ Plus Economics*. A seamless integration of an eBook and *Connect™ Economics*, *Connect™ Plus Economics* provides all of the *Connect™ Economics* features plus the following:

- An integrated eBook, allowing for anytime, anywhere access to the textbook.
- Dynamic links between the problems or questions you assign to your students and the location in the eBook where that problem or question is covered.
- A powerful search function to pinpoint and connect key concepts in a snap.

In short, *Connect™ Economics* offers you and your students powerful tools and features that optimize your time and energies, enabling you to focus on course content, teaching, and student learning. *Connect™ Economics* also offers a wealth of content resources for both instructors and students. This state-of-the-art, thoroughly tested system supports you in preparing students for the world that awaits.

For more information, please visit www.mcgrawhill connect.com, or contact your local McGraw-Hill sales representative.

Tegrity Campus: Lectures 24/7

Tegrity Campus is a service that makes class time available 24/7 by automatically capturing every lecture in a searchable format for students to review when they study and complete assignments. With a simple one-click start-and-stop process, you capture all computer screens and corresponding audio. Students can replay any part of any class with easy-to-use browser-based viewing on a PC or Mac.

Educators know that the more students can see, hear, and experience class resources, the better they learn. In fact, studies prove it. With Tegrity Campus, students quickly recall key moments by using Tegrity Campus's unique search feature. This search helps students efficiently find what they need, when they need it, across an entire semester of class recordings. Help turn all your students' study time into learning moments immediately supported by your lecture.

To learn more about Tegrity watch a 2-minute Flash demo at http://tegritycampus.mhhe.com

McGraw-Hill Customer Care Contact Information

At McGraw-Hill, we understand that getting the most from new technology can be challenging. That's why our services don't stop after you purchase our products. You can e-mail our Product Specialists 24 hours a day to get product-training online. Or you can search our knowledge bank of Frequently Asked Questions on our support website. For Customer Support, call **800-331-5094**, e-mail hmsupport@mcgraw-hill.com, or visit www.mhhe.com/support. One of our Technical Support Analysts will be able to assist you in a timely fashion.

Assurance of Learning Ready

Assurance of learning is an important element of many accreditation standards. *Microeconomics,* 10e is designed specifically to support your assurance of learning initiatives.

Each chapter in the book begins with a list of numbered learning objectives, which appear throughout the chapter, as well as in the end-of-chapter Workbook. Every test bank question is also linked to one of these objectives, in addition to level of difficulty, Bloom's Taxonomy level, and AACSB skill area. EZ Test and EZ Test Online, McGraw-Hill's easy-to-use test bank software, along with *Connect™ Economics* allow you to search the test bank by these and other categories, providing an engine for targeted Assurance of Learning analysis and assessment.

AACSB Statement

The McGraw-Hill Companies is a proud corporate member of AACSB International. Understanding the importance and value of AACSB accreditation, *Microeconomics,* 10e has sought to recognize the curricula guidelines detailed in AACSB standards for business accreditation by connecting selected questions in the test bank to the general knowledge and skill guidelines found in the AACSB standards.

The statements contained in *Microeconomics, 10e* are provided only as a guide for the users of this text. The AACSB leaves content coverage and assessment within the purview of individual schools, the mission of the school, and the faculty. While *Microeconomics, 10e* and the teaching package make no claim of any specific AACSB qualification or evaluation, we have, within *Microeconomics, 10e* labeled selected questions according to the six general knowledge and skills areas.

Acknowledgments

Over the years since the first edition, hundreds of people have helped in large and small ways to shape this text. I especially wish to thank past editors Gary Nelson, Tom Thompson, Paul Shensa, and Doug Hughes.

Anne Hilbert, the developmental editor, saw this project through from the first reviews, the chapter-by-chapter revisions, and the dozens of deadlines that we met, to the time the book finally went into production. Anne was great at keeping all the plates spinning, dealing with a diverse group of personalities, making sure that all the pieces fit, and seeing to it that the text and the supplements were ready to go.

Project manager Dana Pauley, with whom I worked day to day, managed the copyediting, artwork, and page proofs, and saw to it that we stayed not just on schedule, but ahead of schedule. Karen Nelson did a very thorough copyediting job, finding errors and inconsistencies, some of which originated in earlier editions. Also, special thanks to proofreader Nym Pedersen for exceptional attention to detail. Matt Baldwin oversaw the design of the book from cover to cover. Rakhshinda Chishty, the project manager at Aptara Corporation delivered an attractive and accurately composed text. Lead production supervisor Carol Bielski made the printing process seamless and effortless. Senior media project manager Kerry Bowler made sure the supplement production process went smoothly.

Brent Gordon, the Vice President and Editor-in-Chief, Douglas Reiner, the executive editor, and Anne Hilbert and Christina Kouvelis, the developmental editors, were all involved from start to finish. Once the book was well into production, Anne became a sales rep in the Washington, D.C. area, so she is now selling the book she edited. In addition to making sure that the text and all the supplements were printed on schedule, Christina is looking forward to hearing suggestions from instructors using the text. Jennifer Saxton, the senior marketing manager, and

Jennifer Jelinski, the marketing specialist, have been working to help the book reach an even wider audience than the ninth edition.

Every economist knows that no product sells itself. Without major sales and marketing efforts, my text could not sell very well. Most of the credit goes to all the McGraw-Hill/Irwin sales reps for all their efforts to sell my book. And I would especially like to thank the reps in Dubuque, Iowa, who have personally accounted for about a quarter of our sales.

Thomas Parsons (Massachusetts Bay Path Community College), Ronald Picker (St. Mary of the Woods College), Tom Andrews (West Chester State University), Christine Amsler (Michigan State), Cal Tamanji (Milwaukee Area Technical College), Kelly Whealan George (Embry Riddle University), Khalid Mehtabdin (The College of St. Rose), and Jim Watson (Jefferson College) very generously provided numerous suggestions which greatly improved the text. I also want to thank Ellen Mutari for her thorough accuracy check of all the in-text problems. You may have been wondering who took that great photo of me on the author's page. The photographer is Leontine Temsky, who happens to be my sister. She also found a great website, www.zillow.com, which tells you instantly how much your house is worth. You'll find dozens of useful websites listed throughout the text.

I'd also like to thank the many reviewers who helped improve this text.

Sindy Abadie, *Southwest Tennessee Community College*

Shawn Abbott, *College of the Siskiyous (California)*

Kunle Adamson, *DeVry College of New Jersey*

Carlos Aguilar, *El Paso Community College*

Ercument Aksoy, *Los Angeles Valley College*

Rashid B. Al-Hmoud, *Texas Tech University*

Ashraf Almurdaah, *Los Angeles City College*

Nejat Anbarci, *Florida International University*

Guiliana Campanelli Andreopoulos, *William Patterson University*

Thomas Andrews, *West Chester University*

Jim Angus, *Dyersburg State Community College (Tennessee)*

Lee Ash, *Skagit Valley College*

John Atkins, *Pensacola Junior College*

Lyndell L. Avery, *Penn Valley Community College (Missouri)*

James Q. Aylsworth, *Lakeland Community College*

John Baffoe-Bonnie, *Pennsylvania State University*

Mohsen Bahmani-Oksooee, *University of Wisconsin, Milwaukee*

Kathleen Bailey, *Eastern Arizona College*

Kevin Baird, *Montgomery Community College*

Gyanendra Baral, *Oklahoma City Community College*

Patrick Becker, *Sitting Bull College*

David Bennett, *Ivy Tech (Indiana)*

Derek Berry, *Calhoun Community College*

John Bethune, *Barton College (North Carolina)*

Anoop Bhargava, *Finger Lakes Community College*

Robert G. Bise, *Orange Coast College*

John Bockino, *Suffolk County Community College*

Van Bullock, *New Mexico State University*

James Burkard, *Nashville State Community College*

Gerard A. Cahill, *Florida Institute of Technology*

Joseph Calhoun, *Florida State University*

Joy Callan, *University of Cincinnati*

Tony Caporale, *University of Dayton*

Perry A. Cash, *Chadwick University (Alabama)*

Andrew Cassey, *University of Minnesota*

Jannet Chang, *Northwestern University*

Michael Cohik, *Collin Community College*

Steve Cole, *Bethel College*

Ana-María Conley, *DeVry Institute of Technology— Decatur*

Dave Cook, *Western Nevada Community College*

James Cover, *University of Alabama, Tuscaloosa*

Andre Crawford, *Virginia Polytechnic Institute and State University*

Debra Cummings, *Fort Scott Community College (Kansas)*

Rosa Lea Danielson, *College of DuPage*

Ribhi Daoud, *Sinclair Community College*

Bill Demory, *Central Arizona College*

Craig Depken II, *University of Texas, Arlington*

Thomas O. Depperschmidt, *University of Memphis*

Sowjanya Dharmasankar, *Waubonsee Community College*

Amrik Singh Dua, *Mt. San Antonio College*

Ronald Dunbar, *MATC Truax*

Swarna Dutt, *University of West Georgia*

Faruk Eray Duzenli, *Denison University*

Angela Dzata, *Alabama State University*

Stacey Edgington, *San Diego State University*

Deborah M. Figart, *Richard Stockton College (New Jersey)*

Daniel Fischer, *University of Arizona*

Russell L. Flora, *Pikes Peak Community College*

Jack Foley, *Blinn College*

Diana Fortier, *Waubonsee Community College*

Charles Fraley, *Cincinnati State Technical and Community College*

Arthur Friedberg, *Mohawk Valley Community College*

Harold Friesen, *Friends University*

Yoshikazu Fukasawa, *Midwestern State University*

Marilyn Fuller, *Paris Junior College (Texas)*

Alejandro Gallegos, *Winona State University*

Frank Garland, *Tricounty Technical College (South Carolina)*

Eugene Gendel, *Woodbury University*

Kelly George, *Florida Community College of Jacksonville*

Kirk Gifford, *Brigham Young University, Idaho*

Adam Gifford, *Lake-Sumter Community College*

Scott Gilbert, *Southern Illinois University, Carbondale*

Michael Goode, *Central Piedmont Community College*

Jay Goodman, *Southern Colorado University*

Cindy Goodyear, *Webster University*

Mehdi Haririan, *Bloomsburg University (Pennsylvania)*

Charles W. Harrington Jr., *Nova Southeastern University (Florida)*

Virden Harrison, *Modesto Junior College; California State University, Stanislaus, Turlock*

Tina Harvell, *Blinn College*

Gail Hawks, *Miami Dade Community College*

Sanford B. Helman, *Middlesex County College*

Carol Hogan, *University of Michigan, Dearborn*

Jim Holcomb, *The University of Texas at El Paso*

Lora Holcomb, *Florida State University*

Jack W. Hou, *California State University, Long Beach*

Nancy Howe-Ford, *Hudson Valley Community College*

Calvin Hoy, *County College of Morris*

Won-jea Huh, *University of Pittsburgh*

Scott Hunt, *Columbus State Community College*

Janet Hunter, *Northland Pioneer College (Arizona)*

Robert Jakubiak, *Milwaukee Area Technical College*

Danny Jeftich, *Ivy Tech (Indiana)*

Mark G. Johnson, *Lakeland Community College*

Roger Johnson, *Messiah College*

Paul Jorgensen, *Linn-Benton Community College*

George Jouganatos, *California State University, Sacramento*

Lillian Kamal, *Northwestern University*

Brad Kamp, *University of South Florida*

Tim Kane, *University of Texas, Tyler*

Janis Kea, *West Valley College*

Elizabeth Sawyer Kelly, *University of Wisconsin, Madison*

James Kelly, *Rio Hondo College*

M. Moosa Khan, *Prairie View A&M University (Texas)*

Kenneth E. Kimble, *Sinclair Community College*

Kamau Kinuthia, *American River College*

Sara Kiser, *Judson College*

Jack Klauser, *Chaminade University of Honolulu*

Wayne Klutarits, *Jefferson College*

Shawn Knabb, *Western Washington University*

Harry Kolendrianos, *Danville Community College*

Michael J. Kuryla, *SUNY-Broome Community College*

Sungkyu Kwak, *Washburn University*

Larry LaFauci, *Johnson and Wales University*

Helen C. Lafferty, *University of Pittsburgh*

Rose LaMont, *Modesto Junior College*

Quan Vu Le, *Seattle University*

Jim Lee, *Texas A&M University, Corpus Christi*

Raymond Lee, *Benedict College*

Alan Levinsohn, *SUNY-Morrisville*

Hui Li, *Eastern Illinois University*

Stephen E. Lile, *Western Kentucky University*

Paul Lockard, *Black Hawk College*

Marty Ludlum, *Oklahoma City Community College*

Brian Lynch, *Lake Land College, Illinois*

Alyson Ma, *University of San Diego*

Y. Lal Mahajan, *Monmouth University*

Mark H. Maier, *Glendale Community College (California)*

Kelly Manley, *Gainesville State College*

Eddi Marlow, *Dyersburg State Community College (Tennessee)*

Jane Mattes, *The Community College of Baltimore City*

Koula Matzouranis, *Broward Community College, South*

Fred May, *Trident Technical College*

Steven B. McCormick, *Southeastern Illinois College*

Christopher R. McIntosh, *University of Minnesota, Duluth*

Kevin McWoodson, *Moraine Valley Community College*

Steven Medema, *University of Colorado, Denver*

Kimberly Mencken, *Baylor University*

Evelina Mengova, *California State University, Fullerton*

Lewis Metcalf, *Lake Land College, Illinois*

Arthur Meyer, *Lincoln Land Community College*

John E. Michaels, *University of Phoenix*

Green Miller, *Morehead State University*

David Mitchell, *University of South Alabama, Mobile*

Daniel Morvey, *Piedmont Technical College*

Thaddaeus Mounkurai, *Daytona Beach College*

Todd Myers, *Grossmont College*

Charles Myrick, *Dyersburg State Community College (Tennessee)*

Sung No, *Southern University A&M College*

Bill Nook, *Milwaukee Area Technical College*

Louise Nordstrom, *Nichols College*

Gerald Nyambane, *Davenport University Career Center*

Ronan O'Beirne, *American Institute of Computer Sciences (Alabama)*

Joan O'Brien, *Quincy College*

David O'Hara, *Metropolitan State University*

Albert Okunade, *University of Memphis*

Alannah Orrison, *Saddleback College*

Michael L. Palmer, *Maple Woods Community College (Missouri)*

Craig Parmley, *Ivy Tech (Indiana)*

Thomas R. Parsons, *Massachusetts Bay Path Community College*

Louis A. Patille, *University of Phoenix*

Ronald Picker, *St. Mary of the Woods College (Indiana)*

Ray Polchow, *Zane State College*

Robert Posatko, *Shippensburg University of Pennsylvania*

George Radakovic, *Indiana University of Pennsylvania*

Eric Rahimian, *Alabama A&M University*

Farhad Rassekh, *University of Hartford*

Mitchell Redlo, *Monroe Community College*

Helen Roberts, *University of Illinois, Chicago*

Judith K. Robinson, *Massachusetts Bay Path Community College*

S. Scanlon Romer, *Delta College*

Brain Rosario, *American River College*

Michael Rosen, *Milwaukee Area Technical College*

Rose M. Rubin, *University of Memphis*

Sara Saderion, *Houston Community College, SW*

David Schutte, *Mountain View College*

Mourad Sebti, *Central Texas College*

W. H. Segur, *University of Redlands*

L. Guillermo Serpa, *University of Illinois, Chicago*

Dennis Shannon, *Southwestern Illinois College*

Mehdi S. Shariati, *Kansas City Kansas Community College*

Rimma Shiptsova, *Utah State University*

Stephen Shmanske, *California State University, East Bay*

Nancy Short, *Chandler-Gilbert Community College*

Barry Simpson, *University of South Alabama, Mobile*

Garvin Smith, *Daytona Beach College*

Noel Smith, *Palm Beach Community College*

John Somers, *Portland Community College*

Don M. Soule, *University of Kentucky*

Karen Spellacy, *SUNY-Canton*

Rob Steen, *Rollins College*

Bruno Stein, *New York University*

Stephen Steller, *University of Phoenix*

Daniel Stern, *South Hills School of Business (Pennsylvania)*

Edward Stevens, *Nebraska College of Business*

Gary Stone, *Winthrop University*

Arlena Sullivan, *Jones County Junior College*

Denver O. Swaby, *Columbia Union College (Maryland)*

Max Tarpley, *Dyersburg State Community College (Tennessee)*

Henry Terrell, *University of Maryland*

Bette Lewis Tokar, *Holy Family College (Pennsylvania)*

Brian Trinque, *University of Texas, Austin*

Mark Tyrpin, *John Wood Community College*

Jose Vasquez, *University of Illinois at Urbana-Champaign*

Jim Watson, *Jefferson College, Missouri*

Jim Watson, *Jefferson College (Missouri)*

Christian Weber, *Seattle University*

Simone Wegge, *CUNY-Staten Island*

Marc Weglarski, *Macomb Community College*

Steven White, *Glendale Community College (California)*

J. Christopher Wreh, *North Central Texas College*

Elaine Gale Wrong, *Montclair State College*

Linda M. Zehr, *Chandler-Gilbert Community College*

Sandy Zingo, *Rogers State University (Oklahoma)*

Finally, to all adopters of the past nine editions, thank you. Your comments and suggestions have helped to make this the best edition yet.

—Stephen L. Slavin

Preface to the Student

What have you heard about economics? That it's dull, it's hard, it's full of undecipherable equations and incomprehensible graphs? If you were to read virtually any of the introductory economics textbooks, that's exactly what you would find.

How is this book different from all other books? Reading this book is like having a conversation with me. I'll be right there with you, illustrating various points with anecdotes and asking you to work out numerical problems as we go along.

Are you a little shaky about the math? Your worries are over. If you can add, subtract, multiply, and divide (I'll even let you use a calculator), you can do the math in this book.

How do you feel about graphs? Do you think they look like those ultramodern paintings that even the artists can't explain? You can relax. No graph in this book has more than four lines, and by the time you're through, you'll be drawing your *own* graphs.

In nearly every chapter you'll find one or two boxes labeled "Extra Help." Sometimes you can master a concept when additional examples are given. Don't be too proud to seek extra help when you need it. And when you don't need it, just skip the boxes.

Unlike virtually every other economics text, this one includes a built-in workbook. Even if your professor does not assign the questions at the end of each chapter, I urge you to answer them because they provide an excellent review.

I can't guarantee an "A" in this course, but whether you are taking it to fulfill a college requirement or planning to be an economics major, you will find that economics is neither dull nor all that hard.

—Stephen L. Slavin

Contents in *Brief*

Expanded Contents

6 The Price Elasticities of Demand and Supply 125

7 Theory of Consumer Behavior 155

8 Cost 171

9 Profit, Loss, and Perfect Competition 203

Chapter 1

A Brief Economic History of the United States

M ore than two centuries ago, some Americans believed it was "manifest destiny" that the 13 states on the eastern seaboard would one day be part of a nation that stretched from the Atlantic to the Pacific. Was it also our manifest destiny to become the greatest economy in the history of the world?

LEARNING OBJECTIVES

After reading this chapter you should be able to:

1. Summarize America's economic development in the 19th century.
2. Describe the effect of the Great Depression on our economy and evaluate the New Deal measures to bring about recovery.
3. Discuss the impact of World War II on our economy.
4. List and discuss the major recessions we have had since World War II.
5. Summarize the economic highlights of each decade since the 1950s.
6. Differentiate the "new economy" from the "old economy."
7. Assess America's place in history.

Introduction

"May you live in interesting times," reputedly an ancient Chinese curse, could well describe the economic misfortunes which overtook us in late 2007 and continued for the next couple of years.

- Our worst economic downturn since the Great Depression.
- The bursting of the housing bubble.
- A financial crisis requiring over $2.5 trillion in loans by the Federal Reserve and the U.S. Treasury.
- The mortgage crisis, threatening some 7 million American families with foreclosure.
- Over 15 million Americans officially unemployed.

Our economy is a study in contrasts. We have poverty in the midst of plenty; we have rapidly expanding industries like computer software and medical technology, and dying industries like shipbuilding, textiles, and consumer electronics; we won the cold war against communism, but we may be losing the trade war against China.

Which country has the largest economy in the world, the United States, China, or Japan? Believe it or not, our national output is much greater than that of China and Japan combined.

America is the sole superpower and has one of the highest standards of living in the world. Communism—at least the version that was practiced in the Soviet Union and Eastern Europe—to borrow a phrase from Karl Marx, has been "swept into the dustbin of history."

The baby-boom generation has earned higher incomes than any other generation in history. Indeed, Americans once considered it their birthright to do better than their parents. But that ended about 35 years ago, and a lot of young people are worrying about their futures.

In the decade of the 1990s our economy generated more than 22 million new jobs. But there were fewer Americans working in early 2010 than there were 10 years earlier.

To sum up the good and the bad: We have the world's largest economy, and one of the world's highest standard of living, and, even though our recent economic performance has been less than stellar, most Americans have decent jobs paying decent wages. But there's the downside:

The economic downside

- Our federal budget deficit is at a record high and will remain high in the foreseeable future.
- Our trade deficit has averaged nearly $650 billion over the last 5 years.
- We are borrowing nearly $2 billion a day from foreigners to finance our trade and budget deficits.
- Unless Congress acts soon, our Social Security and Medicare trust funds will run out of money well before you reach retirement age.
- When you graduate, you may not be able to get a decent job.
- Our savings rate has averaged less than 3 percent a year since the new millennium.
- The real hourly wage (after inflation) of the average worker is lower today than it was in 1973.

In these first four chapters, we'll be looking at how our economy uses its basic resources, at the workings of the law of supply and demand, and at how capitalism and other economic systems work. But first we need to ask how we got here. After all, the American economic system evolved over nearly four centuries.

Those who cannot remember the past are condemned to repeat it.

–George Santayana–

What did the great philosopher mean by this? Perhaps he meant that those who do not learn enough history the first time around will be required to repeat History 101. But whatever he meant, it is clear that to understand our economy today, we need to know how it developed over the years.

Did you see *Back to the Future?* You may have seen parts 1, 2, and 3, but let's stick with just part 1. Imagine being sent back to the 1950s. The way people lived then was very different from the way we live today—and the 1950s represented life in the fast lane compared to daily existence during the first decade of the 20th century. So before we worry about today's economy, we'll take a few steps back and look at life in this country about 200 years ago.

The American Economy in the 19th Century

Agricultural Development

America has always had a large and productive agricultural sector. At the time of the American Revolution, 9 out of every 10 Americans lived on a farm; 100 years later, however, fewer than 1 out of every 2 people worked in agriculture. Today just 1 out of every 500 Americans is a full-time farmer. But our farms not only feed America but also produce a huge surplus that is sold abroad.

Unlike Europe, 200 years ago America had an almost limitless supply of unoccupied fertile land. The federal government gave away farmland—usually 160-acre plots (one-quarter of a square mile)—to anyone willing to clear the land and farm on it. Although sometimes the government charged a token amount, it often gave away the land for free.

America had an almost limitless supply of land.

The great abundance of land was the most influential factor in our economic development during the 19th century. Not only did the availability of very cheap or free land attract millions of immigrants to our shores, but it also encouraged early marriage and large families, since every child was an additional worker to till the fields and handle the animals. Even more important, this plenitude of land, compared to amount of labor, encouraged rapid technological development.

When George Washington was inaugurated in 1789, there were about 4 million people living in the United States. By the time of the War of 1812, our population had doubled. It doubled again to 16 million in 1835 and still again by 1858. Our numbers continued to grow, but at a somewhat slower pace, reaching the 100 million mark in 1915 and the 200 million mark in 1968, and 300 million in 2006.

Although all regions of the United States remained primarily agricultural in the years following the Civil War, New England, the Middle Atlantic states, and the Midwest—with their already well-established iron, steel, textile, and apparel industries—were poised for a major industrial expansion that would last until the Great Depression. In contrast, the South, whose economy was based on the cash crops of cotton, tobacco, rice, and sugar, as well as on subsistence farming, remained primarily an agricultural region well into the 20th century. The South continued to be the poorest section of the country, a relative disadvantage that was not erased until the growth of the Sun Belt took off in the 1960s. (See the box titled "Two Economic Conflicts Leading to the Civil War.")

Southern economic development remained agricultural.

Southern agriculture developed very differently from agriculture in the other regions of the nation. We know, of course, that most of the labor was provided by slaves whose ancestors had been brought here in chains from Africa. On the average, Southern farms were

Two Economic Conflicts Leading to the Civil War

In the decades before the Civil War, the economic interests of the North and South came into sharp conflict. Northern manufacturers benefited from high protective tariffs, which kept out competing British manufacturers. The Southern states, which had only a small manufacturing sector, were forced to buy most of their manufactured goods from the North and to pay higher prices than they would have paid for British goods had there been no tariff.*

As the nation expanded westward, another conflict reached the boiling point: the expansion of slavery into the new territories. In 1860, when Abraham Lincoln had been elected president, most of the land between the Mississippi River and the Pacific Ocean had not yet been organized into states. As newly formed territories applied for membership in the Union, the big question was whether they would come in as "free states" or "slave states." Lincoln—and virtually all the other leaders of the new Republican Party—strenuously opposed the extension of slavery into the new territories of the West.

The Southern economy, especially cotton agriculture, was based on slave labor. The political leaders of the South realized that if slavery were prohibited in the new territories, it would be only a matter of time before these territories entered the Union as free states and the South was badly outvoted in Congress. And so, as Abraham Lincoln was preparing to take office in 1861, 11 Southern states seceded from the Union, touching off the Civil War, which lasted four years, cost hundreds of thousands of lives, and largely destroyed the Southern economy.

The two major consequences of the war were the freeing of 4 million black people who had been slaves and the preservation of the Union with those 11 rebel states. It would take the nation more than a century to overcome the legacies of this conflict.

---

*Tariffs are fully discussed in the chapter on international trade.

American Agricultural Technology

In the 19th century, a series of inventions vastly improved farm productivity. In the late 1840s, John Deere began to manufacture steel plows in Moline, Illinois. These were a tremendous improvement over the crude wooden plows that had previously been used.

Cyrus McCormick patented a mechanical reaper in 1834. By the time of the Civil War, McCormick's reaper had at least quadrupled the output of each farm laborer. The development of the Appleby twine binder, the Marsh brothers' harvesting machine, and the Pitts thresher, as well as Eli Whitney's cotton gin, all worked to make American agriculture the most productive in the world.

The mechanization of American agriculture, which continued into the 20th century with the introduction of the gasoline powered tractor in the 1920s, would not have been possible without a highly skilled farm workforce. Tom Brokaw described the challenge that farmers faced using this technology:

Farm boys were inventive and good with their hands. They were accustomed to finding solutions to mechanical and design problems on their own. There was no one else to ask when the tractor broke down or the threshing machine fouled, no 1-800-CALLHELP operators standing by in those days.*

---

*Tom Brokaw, *The Greatest Generation* (New York: Random House, 1999), p. 92. The "greatest generation" was the one that came of age during the Great Depression and won World War II.

---

large. By 1860, four-fifths of the farms with more than 500 acres were in the South. The plantation owners raised commercial crops such as cotton, rice, sugar, and tobacco, while the smaller farms, which were much less dependent on slave labor, produced a wider variety of crops.

In the North and the West, self-sufficient, 160-acre family farms were most common. Eventually, corn, wheat, and soybeans became important commercial crops. But in the years following the Civil War, increasing numbers of people left the farms of the North to take jobs in manufacturing.

Bad times for agriculture

Times were bad for agriculture from the end of the Civil War until the close of the century. The government's liberal land policy, combined with increased mechanization, vastly expanded farm output. The production of the nation's three basic cash crops—corn, wheat, and cotton—rose faster than did its population through most of that period. Why did production rise so rapidly? Mainly because of the rapid technological progress made during that period. (See the box titled "American Agricultural Technology.") This brings us to supply and demand, which is covered in Chapter 4 and explains why times were bad for agriculture despite expanded output. If the supply of corn increases faster than the demand for corn, what happens to the price of corn? It goes down. And this happened to wheat and cotton as well. Although other countries bought up much of the surpluses, the prices of corn, wheat, and cotton declined substantially from the end of the Civil War until the turn of the century.

Supply and demand

The National Railroad Network

The completion of the transcontinental railroads

The completion of a national railroad network in the second half of the 19th century made possible mass production, mass marketing, and mass consumption. In 1850, the United States had just 10,000 miles of track, but within 40 years the total reached 164,000 miles. The transcontinental railroads had been completed, and it was possible to get virtually anywhere in the country by train. Interestingly, however, the transcontinental lines all bypassed the South, which severely retarded its economic development well into the 20th century.

In 1836, it took travelers an entire month to get from New York to Chicago. Just 15 years later, they could make the trip by rail in less than two days. What the railroads did, in effect, was to weave the country together into a huge social and economic unit, and eventually into the world's first mass market (see the box titled "Mass Production and Mass Consumption").

Mass Production and Mass Consumption

Mass production is possible only if there is also mass consumption. In the late 19th century, once the national railway network enabled manufacturers to sell their products all over the country, and even beyond our shores, it became feasible to invest in heavy machinery and to turn out volume production, which, in turn, meant lower prices. Lower prices, of course, pushed up sales, which encouraged further investment and created more jobs. At the same time, productivity, or output per hour, was rising, which justified companies in paying higher wages, and a high-wage workforce could easily afford all the new low-priced products.

Henry Ford personified the symbiotic relationship between mass production and mass consumption. Selling millions of cars at a small unit of profit allowed Ford to keep prices low and wages high—the perfect formula for mass consumption.

So we had a mutually reinforcing relationship. Mass consumption enabled mass production, while mass production enabled mass consumption. As this process unfolded, our industrial output literally multiplied, and our standard of living soared. And nearly all of this process took place from within our own borders with only minimal help from foreign investors, suppliers, and consumers.

After World War II, the Japanese were in no position to use this method of reindustrialization. Not only had most of their plants and equipment been destroyed by American bombing, but also Japanese consumers did not have the purchasing power to buy enough manufactured goods to justify mass production of a wide range of consumer goods. And so the Japanese industrialists took the one course open to them: As they rebuilt their industrial base, they sold low-priced goods to the low end of the American market. In many cases they sold these items—textiles, black-and-white TVs, cameras, and other consumer goods—at half the prices charged in Japan.

Japanese consumers were willing to pay much higher prices for what was often relatively shoddy merchandise, simply because that was considered the socially correct thing to do. Imagine American consumers acting this way! Within a couple of decades, Japanese manufacturers, with a virtual monopoly in their home market and an expanding overseas market, were able to turn out high-volume, low-priced, high-quality products. We will look much more closely at Japanese manufacturing and trade practices in the chapter on international trade.

John Steele Gordon describes the economic impact of the railroads:

> Most East Coast rivers were navigable for only short distances inland. As a result, there really was no "American economy." Instead there was a myriad of local ones. Most food was consumed locally, and most goods were locally produced by artisans such as blacksmiths. The railroads changed all that in less than 30 years.[1]

Before railroads, shipping a ton of goods 400 miles could easily quadruple the price. But by rail, the same ton of goods could be shipped in a fraction of the time and at one-twentieth of the cost.

The Age of the Industrial Capitalist

The last quarter of the 19th century was the age of the industrial capitalist. The great empire builders—Carnegie (steel), Du Pont (chemicals), McCormick (farm equipment), Rockefeller (oil), and Swift (meat packing), among others—dominated this era. John D. Rockefeller, whose exploits will be discussed in the chapter on corporate mergers and antitrust, built the Standard Oil Trust, which controlled 90 percent of the oil business. In 1872, just before Andrew Carnegie opened the Edgar Thomson works, the United States produced less than 100,000 tons of steel. Only 25 years later, Carnegie alone was turning out 4 million tons, almost half of the total American production. Again, as supply outran demand, the price of steel dropped from $65 to $20 a ton.

The industrial capitalists not only amassed great economic power, but abused that power as well. Their excesses led to the rise of labor unions and the passage of antitrust legislation.[2]

Andrew Carnegie, American industrial capitalist

---

[1]John Steele Gordon, "The Golden Spike," *Forbes ASAP*, February 21, 2000, p. 118.

[2]See the chapters on labor unions and antitrust in *Economics* and *Microeconomics*.

The Development of the Automobile Industry

Nothing is particularly hard if you divide
it into small jobs.

–Henry Ford–

Who was the first automobile manufacturer to use a division of labor and an assembly line? Was it Henry Ford? Close, but no cigar. It was Ransom E. Olds,* in 1901, when he started turning out Oldsmobiles on a mass basis. Still another American auto pioneer, Henry Leland, believed it was possible and practical to manufacture a standardized engine with interchangeable parts. By 1908, he did just that with his Cadillac.

Henry Ford was able to carry mass production to its logical conclusion. His great contribution was the emphasis he placed on an expert combination of accuracy, continuity, the moving assembly line, and speed, through the careful timing of manufacturing, materials handling, and assembly. The assembly line speeded up work by breaking down the automaking process into a series of simple, repetitive operations.

When Ford introduced a moving assembly line—the first ever used for large-scale manufacturing—this innovation reduced the time it took to build a car from more than 12 hours to just 30 minutes. It was inspired by the continuous-flow production methods used in breweries, flour mills, and industrial bakeries, as well as in the disassembly of animal carcasses in Chicago's meat-packing plants. By installing a moving conveyer belt in his factory, Ford enabled his employees to build cars one piece at a time, instead of one car at a time. The new technique allowed individual workers to stay in one place and perform the same task repeatedly on multiple vehicles that passed by them.

Back in 1908, only 200,000 cars were registered in the United States. Just 15 years later, Ford built 57 percent of the 4 million cars and trucks produced. But soon General Motors supplanted Ford as the country's number one automobile firm, a position it continues to hold. In 1929, motor vehicle production peaked at 5.3 million units, a number that was not reached again until 1949.

---

*In earlier editions I mistakenly attributed these feats—as well as the introduction of the moving assembly line—to Henry Olds. A student, who carefully researched these questions, found that it was Henry Ford who introduced the moving assembly line.

One of the most important changes in our industrial history took place late in the 19th century, with the transition from private electric generators to centralized, utility-based power production. Freed of the need to invest in expensive electric generators, companies could secure as much electric power as they needed through a simple power-line hookup. Now even the smallest start-up manufacturers could compete with the great industrial capitalists.

The American Economy in the 20th Century

On the world's technological
cutting edge

By the turn of the century, America had become an industrial economy. Fewer than 4 in 10 people still lived on farms. We were among the world's leaders in the production of steel, coal, steamships, textiles, apparel, chemicals, and agricultural machinery. Our trade balance with the rest of the world was positive every year. While we continued to export most of our huge agricultural surpluses to Europe, increasingly we began to send the countries of that continent our manufactured goods as well.

We were also well on our way to becoming the world's first mass-consumption society. The stage had been set by the late-19th-century industrialists. At the turn of the 20th century, we were on the threshold of the automobile age (see the box titled "The Development of the Automobile Industry"). The Wright brothers would soon be flying their plane at Kitty Hawk, but commercial aviation was still a few decades away.

American technological progress—or, if the South can forgive me, Yankee ingenuity—runs the gamut from the agricultural implements previously mentioned to the telegraph, the telephone, the radio, the TV, and the computer. It includes the mass-production system perfected by Henry Ford, which made possible the era of mass consumption and the high living standards that the people of all industrialized nations enjoy today. America has long been on the world's technological cutting edge, as well as being the world's leader in manufacturing.

This technological talent, a large agricultural surplus, the world's first universal public education system, and the entrepreneurial abilities of our great industrialists combined

Henry Ford, American automobile
manufacturer

to enable the United States to emerge as the world's leading industrial power by the time of World War I. Then, too, fortune smiled on this continent by keeping it out of harm's way during the war. This same good fortune recurred during World War II; so, once again, unlike the rest of the industrial world, we emerged from the war with our industrial plant intact.

America's large and growing population has been extremely important as a market for our farmers and manufacturers. After World War II, Japanese manufacturers targeted the American market, while the much smaller Japanese market remained largely closed to American manufactured goods. Japan—with less than half our population and, until very recently, much less purchasing power than the United States—has largely financed its industrial development with American dollars. (See again the box titled "Mass Production and Mass Consumption.")

The Roaring Twenties

World War I ended on November 11, 1918. Although we had a brief depression in the early 1920s, the decade was one of almost unparalleled expansion, driven largely by the automobile industry. Another important development in the 1920s was the spreading use of electricity. During this decade, electric power production doubled. Not only was industrial use growing, but by 1929 about two out of every three homes in America had been wired and were now using electrical appliances. The telephone, the radio, the toaster, the refrigerator, and other conveniences became commonplace during the 1920s.

Between 1921 and 1929, national output rose by 50 percent and most Americans thought the prosperity would last forever. The stock market was soaring, and instant millionaires were created every day, at least on paper. It was possible, in the late 1920s, to put down just 10 percent of a stock purchase and borrow the rest on margin from a stockbroker, who, in turn, borrowed that money from a bank. If you put down $1,000, you could buy $10,000 worth of stock. If that stock doubled (that is, if it was now worth $20,000), you just made $10,000 on a $1,000 investment. Better yet, your $10,000 stake entitled you to borrow $90,000 from your broker, so you could now own $100,000 worth of stock.

This was not a bad deal—as long as the market kept going up. But, as they say, what goes up must come down. And, as you well know, the stock market came crashing down in October 1929. Although it wasn't immediately apparent, the economy had already begun its descent into a recession a couple of months before the crash. And, that recession was the beginning of the Great Depression.

Curiously, within days after the crash, several leading government and business officials—including President Hoover and John D. Rockefeller—each described economic conditions as "fundamentally sound." The next time you hear our economy described in those terms, you'll know we're in big trouble.

The postwar boom

The spreading use of electricity

How to become a millionaire in the stock market

...the chief business of the American people is business.
—President Calvin Coolidge

The 1930s: The Great Depression

> Once upon a time my opponents honored me as possessing the fabulous intellectual and economic power by which I created a worldwide depression all by myself.
>
> –President Herbert Hoover–

By the summer of 1929, the country had clearly built itself up for an economic letdown. Between 1919 and 1929, the number of cars on the road more than tripled, from fewer than 8 million to nearly 27 million, almost one automobile for every household in the nation. The automobile market was saturated. Nearly three out of four cars on the road were less than six years old, and model changes were not nearly as important then as they are today. The tire industry had been overbuilt, and textiles were suffering from overcapacity. Residential construction was already in decline, and the general business investment outlook was not that rosy.

Had the stock market not crashed and had the rest of the world not gone into a depression, we might have gotten away with a moderate business downturn. Also, had the federal government acted more expeditiously, it is quite possible that the prosperity

The August 1929 recession

of the 1920s, after a fairly short recession, could have continued well into the 1930s. But that's not what happened. What did happen completely changed the lives of the people who lived through it, as well as the course of human history itself.

Prices began to decline, investment in plant and equipment collapsed, and a drought wiped out millions of farmers. In fact, conditions grew so bad in what became known as the Dust Bowl that millions of people from the Midwest just packed their cars and drove in caravans to seek a better life in California. Their flight was immortalized in John Steinbeck's great novel *The Grapes of Wrath,* which was later made into a movie. Although most of these migrants came from other states, they were collectively called Okies, because it seemed at the time as if the entire state of Oklahoma had picked up and moved west.

There had been widespread bank failures in the late 1920s and by the end of 1930, thousands of banks had failed and the generally optimistic economic outlook had given way to one of extreme pessimism. From here on, it was all downhill. By the beginning of 1933, banks were closing all over the country; by the first week in March, every single bank in the United States had shut its doors.

When the economy hit bottom in March 1933, national output was about one-third lower than it had been in August 1929. The official unemployment rate was 25 percent, but official figures tell only part of the story. Millions of additional workers had simply given up looking for work during the depths of the Great Depression, as there was no work to be had. Yet according to the way the government compiles the unemployment rate, these people were not even counted since they were not actually looking for work.[3]

The Depression was a time of soup kitchens, people selling apples on the street, large-scale homelessness, so-called hobo jungles where poor men huddled around garbage-pail fires to keep warm, and even fairly widespread starvation. "Are you working?" and "Brother, can you spare a dime?"[4] were common greetings. People who lived in collections of shacks made of cardboard, wood, and corrugated sheet metal scornfully referred to them as Hoovervilles. Although President Herbert Hoover did eventually make a few halfhearted attempts to get the economy moving again, his greatest contribution to the economy was apparently his slogans. When he ran for the presidency in 1928, he promised "two cars in every garage" and "a chicken in every pot." As the Depression grew worse, he kept telling Americans that "prosperity is just around the corner." It's too bad he didn't have Frank Perdue in those days to stick a chicken in every pot.

While most Americans to this day blame President Hoover for not preventing the Depression, and then, doing too little to end it, perhaps the single biggest cause of the Depression was that the Federal Reserve let the money supply fall by one-third, causing deflation. And to make things still worse, it did nothing to prevent an epidemic of bank failures, causing a credit crisis.

Why did the downturn of August 1929 to March 1933 finally reverse itself? Well, for one thing, we were just about due. Business inventories had been reduced to rock-bottom levels, prices had finally stopped falling, and there was a need to replace some plants and equipment. The federal budget deficits of 1931 and 1932, even if unwillingly incurred, did provide a mild stimulus to the economy.[5]

Clearly a lot of the credit must go to the new administration of Franklin D. Roosevelt, which reopened the banks, ran large budget deficits, and eventually created government job programs that put millions of Americans back to work (see the box titled "The New Deal"). Recognizing a crisis in confidence, Roosevelt said, "The only thing we have to fear is fear itself." Putting millions of people back to work was a tremendous confidence builder. A 50-month expansion began in March 1933 and lasted until May 1937. Although output did finally reach the levels of August 1929, more than 7 million people were still unemployed.

The Dust Bowl and the "Okies"

The bank failures

Hitting bottom

Herbert Hoover, thirty-first president of the United States

Herbert Hoover and the Depression

Why did the downturn reverse itself?

I see one-third of a nation ill-housed, ill-clad, ill-nourished.
—Franklin D. Roosevelt
Second Inaugural Address,
January 1937

---

[3]How the Department of Labor computes the unemployment rate is discussed in the chapter on economic fluctuations in *Economics* and *Macroeconomics*. In Chapter 2, we'll be looking at the concept of full employment, but you can grasp intuitively that when our economy enters even a minor downturn, we are operating at less than full employment.

[4]"Brother, Can You Spare a Dime?" was a depression era song written by Yip Harburg and Jay Gorney.

[5]In Chapter 12 of *Economics* and *Macroeconomics* we'll explain how budget deficits stimulate the economy.

The New Deal

When Franklin D. Roosevelt ran for president in 1932, he promised "a new deal for the American people." Action was needed, and it was needed fast. In the first 100 days Roosevelt was in office, his administration sent a flurry of bills to Congress that were promptly passed.

The New Deal is best summarized by the three Rs: relief, recovery, and reform. Relief was aimed at alleviating the suffering of a nation that was, in President Roosevelt's words, one-third "ill-fed, ill-clothed, and ill-housed." These people needed work relief, a system similar to today's workfare (work for your welfare check) programs. About 6 million people, on average, were put to work at various jobs ranging from raking leaves and repairing public buildings to maintaining national parks and building power dams. Robert R. Russell made this observation:

> The principal objects of work-relief were to help people preserve their self-respect by enabling them to stay off the dole and to maintain their work habits against the day when they could again find employment in private enterprises. It was also hoped that the programs, by putting some purchasing power into the hands of workers and suppliers of materials, would help prime the economic pump.*

The economic recovery could not begin to take off until people again began spending money. As these 6 million Americans went back to work, they spent their paychecks on food, clothing, and shelter, and managed to pay off at least some of their debts. The most lasting effect of the New Deal was reform. The Securities and Exchange Commission (SEC) was set up to regulate the stock market and avoid a repetition of the speculative excesses of the late 1920s, which had led to the great crash of 1929. After the reform, bank deposits were insured by the Federal Deposit Insurance Corporation (FDIC) to prevent future runs on the banks by depositors, like those experienced in the early 1930s. Also, an unemployment insurance benefit program was set up to provide temporarily unemployed people with some money to tide them over. The most important reform of all was the creation of Social Security. Although even today retired people need more than their Social Security benefits to get by, there is no question that this program has provided tens of millions of retired people with a substantial income and has largely removed workers' fears of being destitute and dependent in their old age.

The New Deal was a much greater success in the long run than in the short run. While New Deal spending programs did not end the Depression, the reforms it put in place laid the foundation for unprecedented economic growth and broadly shared prosperity in the years after World War II.

---

*Robert R. Russell, *A History of the American Economic System* (New York: Appleton-Century-Crofts, 1964), p. 547.

By far, the most important reason for the success of the New Deal's first four years was the massive federal government spending that returned millions of Americans to work. This huge infusion of dollars into our economy was just what the doctor ordered. In this case, the doctor was John Maynard Keynes, the great English economist, who maintained that it didn't matter *what* the money was spent on—even paying people to dig holes in the ground and then to fill them up again—as long as enough money was spent. But in May 1937, just when it had begun to look as though the Depression was finally over, we plunged right back into it again.

What went wrong? Two things: First, the Federal Reserve Board of Governors, inexplicably more concerned about inflation than about the lingering economic depression, greatly tightened credit, making it much harder to borrow money. Second, the Roosevelt administration suddenly got that old balance-the-budget-at-all-costs religion. Government spending was sharply reduced—the budget of the Works Progress Administration was cut in half—and taxes were raised. The cost of that economic orthodoxy—which would have made sense during an economic boom—was the very sharp and deep recession of 1937–38. Tight money and a balanced budget are now considered the right policies to follow when the economy is heating up and prices are rising too quickly, but they are prescriptions for disaster when the unemployment rate is 12 percent.[6]

The ensuing downturn pushed up the official unemployment count by another 5 million, industrial production fell by 30 percent, and people began to wonder when this depression would ever end. But there really *was* some light at the end of the tunnel.

The recession of 1937–38

---

[6]These policies will be discussed in Chapters 12 and 14 of *Economics* and *Macroeconomics*.

Franklin D. Roosevelt, thirty-second
president of the United States

In April 1938, both the Roosevelt administration and the Federal Reserve Board reversed course and began to stimulate the economy. By June, the economy had turned around again, and this time the expansion would continue for seven years. The outbreak of war in Europe, the American mobilization in 1940 and 1941, and our eventual entry into the war on December 7, 1941, all propelled us toward full recovery.

When we ask what finally brought the United States out of the Great Depression, there is one clear answer: the massive federal government spending that was needed to prepare for and to fight World War II.

For most Americans the end of the Depression did not bring much relief, because the nation was now fighting an all-out war. For those who didn't get the message in those days, there was the popular reminder, "Hey, bub, don't yuh know there's a *war* goin' on?"

The country that emerged from the war was very different from the one that had entered it less than four years earlier. Prosperity had replaced depression. Now inflation had become the number one economic worry.

The 1940s: World War II and Peacetime Prosperity

Just as the Great Depression dominated the 1930s, World War II was the main event of the 1940s, especially from the day the Japanese bombed Pearl Harbor until they surrendered in August 1945. For the first time in our history, we fought a war that required a total national effort. Although the Civil War had caused tremendous casualties and had set the South back economically for generations, we had never before fought a war that consumed over one-third of our nation's total output.

At the peak of the war, more than 12 million men and women were mobilized and, not coincidentally, the unemployment rate was below 2 percent. Women, whose place was supposedly in the home, flocked to the workplace to replace the men who had gone off to war. Blacks, too, who had experienced great difficulty finding factory jobs, were hired to work in the steel mills and the defense plants in the East, the Midwest, and the West.

America's industrial might

No more than 2 or 3 percent of the defense plant workers had any experience in this area, but thanks to mass production techniques developed largely by General Motors and Ford, these workers would turn out nearly 300,000 airplanes, over 100,000 tanks, and 88,000 warships. America clearly earned its title, "Arsenal of Democracy."

Between 1939 and 1944, national output of goods and services nearly doubled, while federal government spending—mainly for defense—rose by more than 400 percent. By the middle of 1942, our economy reached full employment for the first time since 1929. To hold inflation in check, the government not only instituted price and wage controls but also issued ration coupons for meat, butter, gasoline, and other staples.

During the war, 17 million new jobs were created, while the economy grew 10 or 11 percent a year. Doris Kearns Goodwin attributed "a remarkable entrepreneurial spirit" not only to the opportunity to make huge wartime profits but to a competitiveness "developed within each business enterprise to produce better than its competitors to serve the country." A sign hanging in many defense plants read: "PLEDGE TO VICTORY: The war may be won or lost in this plant."[7]

It was American industrial might that proved the decisive factor in winning World War II. Essentially our production of ships, tanks, planes, artillery pieces, and other war matériel overwhelmed the production of the Germans and the Japanese.

Globally, we were certainly at the top of our game. With just 7 percent of the world's population, we accounted for half the world's manufacturing output, as well as 80 percent of its cars and 62 percent of its oil. Our potential rivals, Japan, Germany, France, and the United Kingdom, would need at least 15 years to repair their war-damaged industrial plant and begin competing again in world markets.

The United States and the Soviet Union were the only superpowers left standing in 1945. When the cold war quickly developed, we spent tens of billions of dollars to prop up

---

[7]Doris Kearns Goodwin, "The Way We Won: America's Economic Breakthrough during World War II," *The American Prospect,* Fall 1992, p. 68.

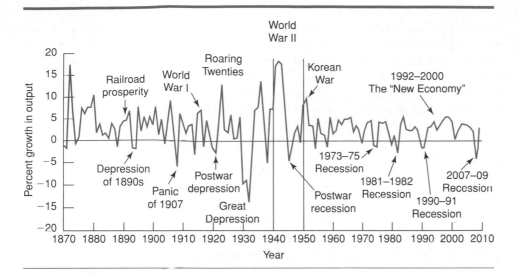

F*igure* 1

Annual Percentage Growth of U.S. Output of Goods and Services, 1870–2009

Although there were plenty of ups and downs, in most years, output grew at a rate of between 2 and 5 percent. What stands out are the booms during World War I, the Roaring Twenties, the abortive recovery from the Great Depression (in the mid-1930s), World War II, and the relative prosperity since the beginning of World War II. The two sharpest declines in output occurred during the Great Depression and after World War II. The drop after World War II was entirely due to a huge cut in defense spending, but our economy quickly reconverted to producing civilian goods and services, so the 1945 recession was actually very mild.

Sources: U.S. Department of Commerce, and AmeriTrust Company, Cleveland.

the sagging economies of the nations of Western Europe and Japan, and we spent hundreds of billions more to provide for their defense. In the four decades since the close of World War II we expended 6 percent of our national output on defense, while the Soviet Union probably expended at least triple that percentage. This great burden certainly contributed to the collapse of the Soviet Union in 1990–91, and our own heavy defense spending continues to divert substantial resources that might otherwise be used to spur our economic growth.

Figure 1 provides a snapshot of U.S. economic growth since 1870. You'll notice that our economy has been pretty stable since the end of World War II. The latter half of the 1940s was largely a time of catching up for the American economy. For years we had gone without, first during the Great Depression, and then, because so much of our resources had been diverted to the war effort. Wartime government posters urged us to:

> Use it up,
> Wear it out,
> Make it do,
> Or do without.

Once the war was over, there was a huge increase in the production of not just housing and cars, but refrigerators, small appliances, and every other consumer good that had been allowed to wear down or wear out.

Within a year after the war ended, some 12 million men and several hundred thousand women returned home to their civilian lives. Very little housing had been built during the war and the preceding depressed period, so most veterans lived in overcrowded houses and apartments, often with three generations under one roof. The first thing veterans wanted was new housing.

The federal government obligingly facilitated this need for new housing by providing Veterans Administration (VA) mortgages at about 1 percent interest and often nothing down to returning veterans. The Federal Housing Administration (FHA) supplemented the VA program with FHA mortgages to millions of other Americans. Where were these houses built? In the suburbs. By 1945, little land was available in the cities, so suburbanization was inevitable.

The suburbanization of America

Post–World War II Recessions

Since the closing months of World War II, the United States has had 12 recessions of varying length and severity. The longest and most severe was from December 2007 to June 2009 (although we do not yet have official word that the recession ended in that particular month).

> **February 1945–October 1945**
>
> **November 1948–October 1949**
>
> **July 1953–May 1954**
>
> **August 1957–April 1958**
>
> **April 1960–February 1961**
>
> **December 1969–November 1970**

November 1973–March 1975 This one was set off by a fourfold increase in the price of oil engineered by the OPEC nations (which we'll talk a lot more about in the chapter on economic fluctuations in *Economics* and *Macroeconomics*). Simultaneously, there was a worldwide shortage of foodstuffs, which drove up food prices. To make matters worse in this country, we struck a deal to export about one-quarter of our wheat and other grains to the Soviet Union. Output fell about 5 percent, and, to make matters still worse, the rate of inflation remained unacceptably high.

January 1980–July 1980 A doubling of oil prices by OPEC and a credit crunch set off by the Federal Reserve Board of Governors, which had been alarmed by an inflation rate that had reached double-digit levels, pushed us into a very brief, but fairly sharp, recession. When interest rates rose above 20 percent, the Federal Reserve allowed credit to expand and the recession ended.

July 1981–November 1982 This downturn was also set off by the Federal Reserve, which was now determined to wring inflation out of our economy. By the end of the recession—which now held the dubious distinction of being the worst downturn since the Great Depression—the unemployment rate had reached almost 11 percent. But the inflation rate had been brought down, and in late summer 1982, the Federal Reserve once again eased credit, setting the stage for the subsequent recovery. At the same time, the federal government had been cutting income tax rates, further helping along the business upturn.

July 1990–March 1991 After the longest uninterrupted peacetime expansion in our history, a fairly mild downturn was caused by a combination of sharply rising oil prices (due to Iraq's invasion of Kuwait in August 1990 and the ensuing Persian Gulf War), tight money, and a deficit-cutting budget agreement between President George Bush and Congress in October. President Bush himself termed the recovery "anemic," and its slow pace was largely responsible for his loss of the 1992 election to Bill Clinton.

March 2001–November 2001 By mid-2000, it had become apparent that many high-tech stocks in telecommunication, Internet, and computer software companies were over-valued, and consequently, investment in these industries began to sink very rapidly. Excess capacity needed to be worked off before investment would revive. What was very unusual for a recession was that consumer spending, buoyed by low interest rates, mortgage refinancing, and massive federal tax cuts, actually continued to rise throughout the recession. Then, just when recovery seemed likely, the terrorist attacks of 9/11 provided an additional economic shock, depressing the demand for air travel and hotel rooms. To counter the effects of the recession as well as to aid in the recovery from the attacks, the Bush administration pushed through Congress not only a major tax cut and tax refunds, but increased government spending. The recession was one of the mildest on record, and output began to rise in the fourth quarter of 2001.

December 2007–June 2009* Throughout the book I refer to the recession of 2007–2009 as the Great Recession. The worst economic downturn since the 1930s, its effects were expected to linger well into 2011. To avert a financial meltdown and to stimulate the economy, the Federal Reserve and the Treasury poured trillions of dollars into the economy.

Tens of millions of Americans had been using their homes like ATMs, taking out hundreds of billions of dollars every year in home equity loans to finance spending on new cars, vacation trips, shopping sprees, paying their children's college expenses, or just filling up their gas tanks. When the housing bubble burst in early 2007, it became increasingly difficult for them to keep borrowing. And the less they could borrow, the less they could spend.

The decline in housing prices had an even more direct economic effect. Hundreds of thousands of construction workers, real estate agents, mortgage brokers, financial service workers, and others with jobs in these economic sectors were thrown out of work.

During 2008 and 2009 employment fell by 8.4 million. In fact, even though our economy began growing in the second half of 2009, employment continued falling through the end of the year. In mid-2010, most economists expected a weak recovery with continued high unemployment through 2011.

---

*In early June 2010, it appeared to many economists, including myself, that the recession had ended exactly one year earlier. The Business Cycle Dating Committee of the National Bureau of Economic Research, however, had not yet decided on an official date.

Levittown, U.S.A.

No man who owns his own house and lot can be a communist.

–William Levitt–

Levittown, Long Island, a tract development of 17,000 nearly identical homes, was built right after World War II, largely for returning veterans and their families. These 800-square-foot, prefabricated homes sold for $8,000 with no down payment for veterans. William Levitt described the production process as the reverse of the Detroit assembly line:

There, the car moved while the workers stayed at their stations. In the case of our houses, it was the workers who moved, doing the same jobs at different locations. To the best of my knowledge, no one had ever done that before.*

Levittown became the prototype of suburban tract development, and the Levitts themselves built similar developments in New Jersey, Pennsylvania, and Maryland. In 1963, civil rights demonstrations targeted William Levitt's housing development in Bowie, Maryland.

Levitt admitted he had refused to sell houses to black families, because, he said, integrating his developments would put him at a competitive disadvantage. Levitt's discriminatory sales policy was no different from most other developers, who did not relent until well into the 1960s, when government pressure forced them to do so.

Of course racism was hardly confined to developers like Levitt. James T. Patterson, a historian, wrote that the Federal Housing Administration "openly screened out applicants according to its assessment of people who were 'risks.'"[†] These were mainly blacks, Hispanics, Asians, Jews, and other "unharmonious racial or nationality groups." In so doing, FHA enshrined residential segregation as a public policy of the United States government.

In New York and northern New Jersey, fewer than 100 of the 67,000 mortgages insured by the GI Bill supported home purchases by nonwhites.

*Eric Pace, "William J. Levitt, 86, Pioneer of Suburbs, Dies," *New York Times,* January 29, 1994, p. A1.

†James T. Patterson, *Grand Expectations* (New York: Oxford University Press, 1997), p. 27.

And how would these new suburbanites get to work? By car. So more highways were needed. Once again, the federal government stepped in. Before long a federally subsidized interstate highway network was being built, along with thousands of state and local highways, parkways, and freeways, as well as local streets and roads.

Hence the late 1940s and the 1950s were one big construction boom. Highway building and home construction provided millions of jobs. The automobile industry, too, was prospering after a total shutdown during the war. In the postwar era, we not only supplied all the new suburbanites with cars, but we also became the world's leading auto exporter.

The returning veterans had a lot of catching up to do. Couples had been forced to put off having children, but after the war the birthrate shot up and stayed high until the mid-1960s. This baby boom and low gasoline prices added impetus to the nation's suburbanization. Why continue to live in cramped urban quarters when a house in the suburbs was easily affordable, as it was to most middle-class and working-class Americans (see the box titled "Levittown, U.S.A.")?

In 1944 Congress passed the GI Bill of Rights, which not only offered veterans mortgage loans, as well as loans to start businesses, but also provided monthly stipends for those who wanted help with educational costs. By 1956, when the programs ended, 7.8 million veterans, about half of all who had served, had participated. A total of 2.2 million went to college, 3.5 million to technical schools below the college level, and 700,000 to agricultural schools. The GI Bill made college affordable to men from working-class and lower-middle-class backgrounds and was almost entirely responsible for enrollments more than doubling between 1940 and 1949.

The GI Bill of Rights

The 1950s: The Eisenhower Years

The economy was further stimulated by the advent of television in the early 1950s, as well as by the Korean War. It didn't really matter what individual consumers or the government spent their money on, as long as they spent it on something.

The Consequences of Suburbanization

Suburbanization was the migration of tens of millions of middle-class Americans—nearly all of them white—from our nation's large central cities to newly developed suburban towns and villages. Instead of getting to work by public transportation, these commuters now went by car. Truck transport replaced railroads as the primary way to haul freight. Millions of poor people—the large majority of whom were black or Hispanic—moved into the apartments vacated by the whites who had fled to the suburbs.

Suburbanization left our cities high and dry. As middle-class taxpayers and millions of factory jobs left the cities, their tax bases shrank. There were fewer and fewer entry-level jobs for the millions of new arrivals, largely from the rural South. Throughout the 1950s, 1960s, and 1970s, a huge concentration of poor people was left in the cities as the middle-class workers—both

black and white—continued to flee to the suburbs. By the mid-1970s, the inner cities were rife with poverty, drugs, and crime, and had become socially isolated from the rest of the country.

Still other consequences of suburbanization were our dependence on oil as our main source of energy and eventually, our dependence on foreign sources for more than half our oil. Indeed, America's love affair with the automobile has not only depleted our resources, polluted our air, destroyed our landscape, and clogged our highways but also has been a major factor in our imbalance of trade.*

---

*The damage we are doing to our nation's environment and to that of our planet is alarming, but discussing it goes beyond the scope of this book. However, in the chapter on international trade, we do have a lengthy discussion of our trade imbalance and how our growing oil imports have contributed to it.

Eisenhower would end the war and end the inflation.

General Dwight D. Eisenhower, one of the great heroes of World War II, made two key promises in his 1952 campaign for the presidency: He would end the war in Korea, and he would end the inflation we had had since the close of World War II. Eisenhower made good on both promises. Although three recessions occurred during his eight years in office, economic growth, although not as fast as it had been in the 1940s, was certainly satisfactory (see the box titled "The Consequences of Suburbanization").

What may be most significant about the Eisenhower years is what *didn't* happen rather than what did. Eisenhower made no attempt to undo the legacies of the New Deal such as Social Security, unemployment insurance, or the regulatory reforms that had been instituted. The role of the federal government as a major economic player had become a permanent one. By the end of the decade America was well on its way to becoming a suburban nation. In a sense we had attained President Herbert Hoover's 1928 campaign promise of a car in every garage and a chicken in every pot. But we did him one better. In 1950 just 10 percent of all homes had a TV; by 1960 87 percent of all American homes had at least one set.

The Soaring Sixties: The Years of Kennedy and Johnson

When John F. Kennedy ran for president in 1960, the country was mired in the third Eisenhower recession. Kennedy pledged to "get the country moving again." The economy *did* quickly rebound from the recession and the country embarked on an uninterrupted eight-year expansion. An assassin shot Kennedy before he could complete his first term; he was succeeded by Lyndon Johnson, who in his first speech as president stated simply, "Let us continue." A major tax cut, which Kennedy had been planning, was enacted in 1964 to stimulate the economy. That and our growing involvement in the Vietnam War helped bring the unemployment rate down below 4 percent by 1966. But three major spending programs, all initiated by Johnson in 1965, have had the most profound long-term effect on the economy: Medicare, Medicaid, and food stamps.

Our rapid economic growth from the mid-1940s through the late 1960s was caused largely by suburbanization. But the great changes during this period came at a substantial price (see the box titled "The Consequences of Suburbanization"). Whatever the costs and benefits, we can agree that in just two and a half decades, this process made America a very different place from what it was at the close of World War II.

The Sagging Seventies: The Stagflation Decade

The 1970s brought Americans crashing back to economic reality. In 1973, we were hit by the worst recession since the 1930s. This came on the heels of an oil price shock: The Organization of Petroleum Exporting Countries (OPEC) had quadrupled oil prices in the fall of 1973, and by then, too, we were mired in double-digit inflation, an annual rate of increase in prices of at least 10 percent. About the only good thing during this period was that we were able to add a new word to our vocabularies—*stagflation*. The first part of this word is derived from stagnation. Our economic growth, which had been fairly rapid for 25 years after World War II, had slowed to a crawl. Usually when this happened, prices would stop rising or at least would slow their rate of increase. But now the opposite had happened: We had a bad case of inflation, which gave us the second part of the word *stagflation*.

The president who seemed to have the worst economic luck of all was Jimmy Carter. He presided over mounting budget deficits that, coupled with a rapid growth of the money supply, pushed up the inflation rate to nearly double-digit levels. And then suddenly, in 1979, the Iranian revolution set off our second oil shock. Gasoline prices went through the ceiling, rising from about 70 cents a gallon to $1.25.

Alarmed at the inflation rate, which had nearly doubled in just three years, the Federal Reserve literally stopped the growth of the money supply in October 1979. By the following January we were in another recession, while the annual rate of inflation reached 18 percent. Talk about stagflation!

The 1980s: The Age of Reagan

Ronald Reagan, who overwhelmingly defeated incumbent Jimmy Carter in the 1980 presidential election, offered the answers to our most pressing economic problems. For too long, he declared, we had allowed the federal government to "tax, tax, tax, spend, spend, spend." Big government was not the answer to our problems. Only private enterprise could provide meaningful jobs and spur economic growth. If we cut tax rates, said Reagan, people would have more incentive to work, output would rise, and inflation would subside. After all, if inflation meant that too many dollars were chasing too few goods, why not produce more goods?

This brand of economics, supply-side economics, was really the flip side of Keynesian economics. Both had the same objective: to stimulate output, or supply. The Keynesians thought the way to do this was to have the government spend more money, which, in turn, would give business firms the incentive to produce more. The supply-siders said that if tax rates were cut, people would have more of an incentive to work and would increase output.

Personal income taxes were cut by a whopping 23 percent in 1981 (stretched over a three-year period), and business taxes were also slashed. This was the heart of the supply-side program. As it happened, most of the tax cuts went to the wealthy.

In January 1981, it was Ronald Reagan's ball game to win or lose. At first he seemed to be losing. He presided over still another recession, which, by the time it ended, was the new postwar record holder, at least in terms of length and depth. The second-worst recession since World War II had been that of 1973–75. But the 1981–82 recession was a little longer and somewhat worse.

By the end of 1982, the unemployment rate reached nearly 11 percent, a rate the country had not seen since the end of the Depression. But on the upside, inflation was finally brought under control. In fact, both the inflation and unemployment rates fell during the next four years, and stagflation became just a bad memory.

Still, some very troubling economic problems surfaced during the period. The unemployment rate, which had come down substantially since the end of the 1981–82 recession, seemed stuck at around 6 percent, a rate that most economists consider to be unacceptably high. A second cause for concern were the megadeficits being run by the federal government year after year. Finally, there were the foreign trade deficits, which were getting progressively larger throughout most of the 1980s.

"Read my lips."

In 1988, George H. W. Bush, who had served as Reagan's vice president for eight years and claimed to be a convert to supply-side economics, made this famous campaign promise: "Read my lips: No new taxes." Of course, the rest is history. Bush won the election, and a couple of years later, in an effort to reduce the federal budget deficit, he agreed to a major tax increase. Not only did his words come back to haunt him when he ran for reelection in 1992, but the deficit continued to rise. And to completely ruin his party, we suffered a lingering recession that began in the summer of 1990 and from which we did not completely recover until the end of 1992, with the unemployment rate still hovering above 7 percent.

The State of American Agriculture

Fewer farmers feeding more people

The story of American agriculture is the story of vastly expanding productivity. The output of farm labor doubled between 1850 and 1900, doubled again between 1900 and 1947, and doubled a third time between 1947 and 1960. In 1800 it took 370 hours to produce 100 bushels of wheat. By 1960 it took just 15 hours. In 1820 one farmer could feed 4.5 people. Today that farmer could feed over 100 people.

One of the most dramatic agricultural advances was the mechanical cotton picker, which was introduced in 1944. In an hour, a laborer could pick 20 pounds of cotton. The mechanical picker could pick one thousand pounds of cotton in the same length of time. Within just four years, millions of the Southern rural poor—both black and white—were forced off the farms and into the cities of the South, the North, and the Midwest.

While agriculture is one of the most productive sectors of our economy, only about 4.5 million people live on farms today, and less than half of them farm full time. Of 2.2 million working farms, just half produce more than $5,000 worth of agricultural products. Despite hundreds of billions of dollars in price-support payments to farmers for crops in the years since World War II, the family farm is rapidly vanishing. This is certainly ironic, since the primary purpose of these payments has been to save the family farm. During the more than seven decades that this program has been in operation, 7 out of every 10 family farms have disappeared, while three-quarters of the payments go to large corporate farms. One by one, the dairy farmers, the poultry farmers, the grain growers, and the feedlot operators are being squeezed out by the huge agricultural combines.

While we have lingering images of family farms, large farms—those with more than $250,000 in sales—now account for more than three-quarters of all agricultural sales. In the mid-1980s, their share was less than half. To keep costs down, especially when growing corn, wheat, and soybeans, a farmer needs a lot of expensive equipment and, consequently, must plant on a huge acreage.[8] In other words, you've got to become big just to survive.

Senator Dick Lugar, who owns a farm in Indiana that grows corn and soybeans, has long been a critic of huge agricultural subsidies. In a *New York Times* op-ed piece,[9] he blamed the federal government for creating and perpetuating the huge and growing mess in agriculture:

> Ineffective agricultural policy has, over the years, led to a ritual of overproduction in many crops and most certainly in the heavily supported crops of corn, wheat, cotton, rice, and soybeans and the protected speciality products like milk, sugar, and peanuts. The government has provided essentially a guaranteed income to producers of these crops. So those farmers keep producing more crops than the market wants, which keeps the price low—so low that these farmers continually ask the government for more subsidies, which they get.

The farm bill of 2002

President George W. Bush signed a 10-year $190 billion farm bill in 2002 providing the nation's largest farmers with annual subsidies of $19 billion. In 2009 the producers of corn, soybeans, wheat, rice, and cotton received almost $15 billion in subsidies. The law's defenders point out that the European Union gives its farmers $60 billion in annual subsidies, and that to compete in world markets, we need to keep our prices down. So

---

[8]The average farm has gone from 139 acres in 1910 to 435 acres today.

[9]Dick Lugar, "The Farm Bill Charade," *The New York Times,* January 21, 2002, p. A15.

what we and the Europeans are doing is subsidizing the overproduction of agricultural commodities so that we can compete against each other.

American farms are so productive that we often export more than one-third of our corn, wheat, and other crops. And yet millions of Americans go to bed hungry every night. Back in the depths of the Great Depression, hungry Americans resorted to soup kitchens for their only meals. Today some 37 million Americans make use of food pantries, soup kitchens, and other emergency food distribution programs.

on the web

The Environmental Working Group lists the subsidies paid to grain farmers by name and by zip code on its website. If you're interested in how much individual farmers are collecting, go to www.ewg.org, and click on Farming, select Farm Subsidies, and then on Farm Subsidy Database.

The "New Economy" of the Nineties

What exactly *is* the "new economy"? And is it really all that new? It is a period marked by major technological change, low inflation, low unemployment, and rapidly growing productivity. Certainly that is a fair description of the 1990s, but one may ask if other decades—the 1920s and the 1960s—might be similarly described. Perhaps judging the appropriateness of the term "new economy" might best be left to the economic historians of the future. But new or not new, the 1990s will surely go down in history as one of the most prosperous decades since the founding of the republic.

We've never been better off, but can America keep the party going?
—Jonathan Alter, *Newsweek,* February 7, 2000

The new economy could trace its beginnings back to the late 1970s when the federal government began an era of deregulation, giving the market forces of supply and demand much freer reign. In the 1980s federal income tax rates were slashed, allowing Americans to keep much more of their earnings, thereby providing greater work incentives.

As the decade of the 1990s wore on, the economic picture grew steadily brighter. The federal deficit was reduced each year from 1993 through the end of the decade, by which time we were actually running budget surpluses. Inflation was completely under control, and an economic expansion that began in the spring of 1991 reached boom proportions toward the end of the decade. Optimism spread as the stock market soared, and by February 2000, the length of our economic expansion reached 107 consecutive months—an all-time record. This record would be extended to 120 months—exactly 10 years—before the expansion finally ended in March 2001.

The 1990s was the decade of computerization. In 1990 only a handful of households were on the Internet; by the end of 2000, about 40 percent were connected. Much more significant was the spread of computerization in the business world. Indeed, by the millennium there was a terminal on almost every desk. Planes, cars, factories, and stores were completely computerized. All this clearly has made the American labor force a lot more efficient. Economists, as well as ordinary civilians, believe that our rapid economic growth has been largely the result of computerization of the workplace.

California's Silicon Valley became a hotbed of entrepreneurial innovation. New companies, financed by local venture capitalists, sprang up to perform new economic roles—eBay, Amazon.com, Netscape, Google, Yahoo, and Excite! to name just a few. As these companies went public, their founders became not just millionaires, but often instant billionaires.

Back in 1941, Henry Luce, the founder of *Life Magazine,* wrote an editorial titled "The American Century." History has certainly proven Luce right. Not only had American soldiers and economic power won World Wars I and II, but we also contained communism from the mid-1940s through the 1980s. With the collapse of the Soviet Union, we were the only military and economic superpower left standing.

The American Century

Just as no man is an island, there are no longer any purely national economies. As we've seen, the United States, which began as 13 English colonies, expanded across the continent, attracted tens of millions of immigrants, and eventually became an economic superpower, importing and exporting hundreds of billions of dollars of goods and services. Over the last three decades, our economy has become increasingly integrated with the global economy.

First there was an exodus of jobs making shoes, cheap electronics, toys, and clothing to developing countries. Next to go were jobs in steel, cars, TV manufacturing, and furniture-making. Then simple service work like writing software code and processing credit card receipts was shifted from high-wage to low-wage countries.

Now white-collar jobs are being moved offshore. The driving forces are digitization, the Internet, and high-speed data networks that span the globe. In the 1990s, hundreds of thousands of immigrants helped ease our shortage of engineers, but now, we are sending routine service and engineering tasks to nations like India, China, and Russia where a surplus of educated workers are paid a fraction of what their American counterparts earn.

The Ominous 00s

From good times to bad

A decade that began with a recession and ended with the worst economic downturn since the Great Depression cannot be called the best of times. Over 15 million people entered our labor force during the decade, but we ended that period with virtually the same number of jobs as we had in 2000.

The new economy of the 1990s gave way to the bursting of the dot-com bubble in 2000 and a mild recession in 2001. The subsequent recovery was slow, taking two and a half years for total employment to reach the level it had been at before the recession. But inflation was low and economic growth fairly brisk for the next few years. From the fall of 2005 through the end of 2007 the unemployment rate was at or below 5 percent.

The American consumer had been largely responsible for keeping our economy growing during the 2001–2007 economic expansion. Much of that spending was financed by hundreds of billions of dollars a year in home equity loans. Real estate prices were rising rapidly, home construction was booming, and mortgage brokers had relaxed their standards to the degree that they were not even checking the incomes of half the people to whom they granted mortgages. The federal government, which had been running budget surpluses began running budget deficits. Two large tax cuts and the financing of wars in Iraq and Afghanistan were largely responsible for moving us from surplus to deficit. These deficits, like consumer spending, helped spur economic growth.

As long as housing prices were rising, banks and other lenders were willing to extend larger and larger home equity loans. But when the housing bubble burst in mid-2006 and home prices began to decline, lenders were less willing to extend these loans. In addition, foreclosures began to rise very rapidly, and millions of homeowners discovered that their homes' market value had sunk below what they owed on their mortgages. Hundreds of thousands just walked away from their homes, mailing their keys to their mortgage brokers.

In December 2007 we entered the twelfth recession since the Great Depression. Largely because of the bursting of the housing bubble, our economy had begun to slow during the second half of the previous year. The ranks of the unemployed increased steadily and over 8 million people lost their jobs in 2008 and 2009. In April of 2009, the recession, then 17 months old, was the longest economic downturn since the 1930s. And when all the analysis was finally completed, the Great Recession[10] would almost surely be considered the worst recession in seven decades.

In mid-2010, when our economy was a full year into recovery, there was still a lingering concern that we could slip back again into recession. The housing market was still in the doldrums, unemployment remained very high, and the nation's output of goods and services had not yet gotten back up to the level it had been at the end of 2007 when the recession began.

In late July of 2010 it become increasingly apparent that the the economic recovery had begun to falter. More than three-quarters of the economic stimulus money had been spent, and Congressional Republicans, spurred on by millions of Tea Party members, were blocking any further major spending programs. Work on the 2010 Census was ending, and hundreds of thousands of census workers were being let go. To make matters still worse,

---

[10]Perhaps the first person to call this "the Great Recession" was Diana Furchtgott-Roth, a former chief economist at the U.S. Department of Labor, in an article, "The Great Recession of 2008?" in *The American*, December 21, 2007, www.american.com/archive/2007/december-12-07/the-great-recession-of-2008.

state and local governments, facing combined budget deficits of some $200 billion, were planning to lay off tens of thousands of teachers, police officers, and other civil servants.

There was a growing fear that the recession was not yet over. Indeed, some economists were suggesting that we were in the midst of a *double dip recession*. Although it had been widely believed that the Great Recession ended in the summer of 2009, our level of economic activity had not re-attained its pre-recession peak. In other words, we had not yet made a full recovery. So what if, say in the third and fourth quarters of 2010, out output of goods and services once again began to decline? Very likely, then we would be in the second downward phase of a double dip recession.

I've already gone out on a limb by stating in the box on page 12—and in later chapters—that the recession ended in June 2009. That's my estimate, for what it's worth. If we sink back into recession, then I'll have some egg on *my* face. Still, in late July 2010, a double dip recession was still not that likely. But only you will know for sure whether I was right or wrong.

Current Issue: America's Place in History

America, America
God shed his grace on thee

–From the song, "America the Beautiful," by
Katherine Lee Bates–

In the early years of the 20th century, the United States emerged as the world's leading industrial power, with the largest economy and the largest consumer market. By the end of World War I, we had become the greatest military power as well.

Our economic and military roles grew during the next two decades, and by the close of World War II, the United States and the Soviet Union were the world's only military superpowers. Although Western Europe and Japan eventually recovered from the devastation of the war, the United States continued to be the world's largest economy. Henry Luce was certainly correct in calling the 20th century "The American Century."

At the end of that century, although some economic problems had emerged—namely our huge budget and trade deficits—we were clearly at the top of our economic game. The dot-com bubble had not yet burst, the new economy was in full flower, and most Americans were confident that the party would go on forever. Just 10 years earlier the Soviet Union had dissolved, its Eastern European empire largely allied itself with the West, and even the most ardent militarists agreed that the costly arms race was finally over.

Back in the 19th century, the sun never set on the British Empire, but the drain of two world wars compelled the British to give up their empire. By the mid-20th century, American military bases dotted the globe, and today we have become, to a large extent, the world's policeman. Many observers believe we are overstretched both militarily and economically, and that, consequently, we will be compelled to cut back on these commitments.

Now, in the wake of the dot-com crash, the attacks on 9/11, the wars in Afghanistan and Iraq, the rising budget deficit, a lagging job market, and, of course, a near financial meltdown, the Great Recession, we may well wonder if the 21st, like the 20th, will be an American century. We wonder if Social Security and Medicare will even be there when we retire. And in the meanwhile, will we be able to live as well as our parents did?

I wish I could answer these questions, but as Benjamin Franklin once said, "A question is halfway to wisdom." As you continue reading, each of these questions will be raised again, and hopefully, we'll get closer to their answers.

Questions for Further Thought and Discussion

1. Describe, in as much detail as possible, the impact of the Great Depression on the lives of those who lived through it. If you know anyone who remembers the 1930s, ask him or her to describe those times.

2. What were the main agricultural developments over the last two centuries?

3. How have wars affected our economy? Use specific examples.

4. Inflation has been a persistent problem for most of the 20th century. What were some of its consequences?

5. In what ways were the 1990s like the 1920s, and in what ways were the two decades different?

6. When our country was being settled, there was an acute shortage of agricultural labor. Over the last 100 years millions of Americans have left the farms. How have we managed to feed our growing population with fewer and fewer farmers?

7. Today America has the world's largest economy as well as a very high standard of living. What factors in our economic history helped make this possible?

8. List the main ways the "new economy" (since the early 1990s) differs from the "old economy."

Workbook for Chapter 1 connect | ECONOMICS

Name _____ _____   Date _____

Multiple-Choice Questions

Circle the letter that corresponds to the best answer.

1. Which statement is true? (LO2)
   a) Twenty-five million Americans were officially unemployed in 1933.
   b) Our economy expanded steadily from 1933 to 1945.
   c) Once the Great Depression began in 1929, our economy moved almost steadily downhill until the beginning of 1940.
   d) None of the above.

2. In the early 19th century, the United States suffered from a scarcity of _____. (LO1)
   a) land and labor
   b) land—relative to labor
   c) labor—relative to land
   d) neither land nor labor

3. Which statement is false? (LO4, 5)
   a) President Eisenhower presided over three recessions.
   b) Our economy has not had an unemployment rate below 5 percent since the early 1940s.
   c) There were six straight years of economic expansion under President Reagan.
   d) None of the above. (All of the above are true.)

4. Which statement is true? (LO4, 5)
   a) There was a great deal of stagflation in the 1970s.
   b) We had full employment for most of the 1980s.
   c) We have had seven recessions since World War II.
   d) None of the above.

5. Each of the following were elements of the New Deal except _____. (LO2)
   a) relief, recovery, reform
   b) a massive employment program
   c) unemployment insurance and bank deposit insurance
   d) a balanced budget

6. Which of these best describes the post-World War II recessions in the United States? (LO4, 5)
   a) They were all very mild, except for the 1981–82 recession.
   b) They were all caused by rising interest rates.
   c) None lasted more than one year.
   d) Each was accompanied by a decline in output of goods and services and an increase in unemployment.

7. At the time of the American Revolution, about _____ of every 10 Americans lived on a farm. (LO1)
   a) one   c) five   e) nine
   b) three   d) seven

8. Between 1939 and 1944, federal government spending rose by more than _____. (LO3)
   a) 100%   c) 300%   e) 500%
   b) 200%   d) 400%

9. Each of the following was a year of high unemployment except _____. (LO4)
   a) 1933   c) 1944   e) 1982
   b) 1938   d) 1975

10. The year 2009 could be described as having had a relatively _____ unemployment rate and a relatively _____ rate of inflation. (LO6)
    a) low, low   c) high, low
    b) high, high   d) low, high

11. Between 1929 and 1933, output fell _____. (LO2)
    a) by about one-tenth   c) by about one-half
    b) by about one-third   d) by about two-thirds

12. The inflation rate declined during the presidency of _____. (LO5)
    a) both Eisenhower and Reagan
    b) neither Eisenhower nor Reagan
    c) Reagan
    d) Eisenhower

13. Which of the following would be the most accurate description of our economy since the end of 2007? (LO6)
    a) We have had virtually no economic problems.
    b) We experienced the worst economic mess since the Great Depression.
    c) Aside from the federal budget deficit, we have no major economic problems.
    d) Our unemployment and inflation rates have generally been relatively low.

14. The transcontinental railroads completed in the 1860s, 1870s, and 1880s all bypassed the _____. (LO1)
    a) Northeast
    b) Midwest
    c) South
    d) mountain states
    e) Far West

15. Compared to our economic history between 1870 and 1945, our economic history since 1945 could be considered _____. (LO4, 5)
    a) much more stable
    b) about as stable
    c) much less stable

16. The longest economic expansion in our history began in _____. (LO5)
    a) the spring of 1961
    b) the winter of 1982
    c) the spring of 1991
    d) the fall of 1993

17. The age of the great industrial capitalists like Carnegie, Rockefeller, and Swift was in the _____. (LO3)
    a) second quarter of the 19th century
    b) third quarter of the 19th century
    c) fourth quarter of the 19th century
    d) first quarter of the 20th century
    e) second quarter of the 20th century

18. _____ completely changed the face of the United States in the 25 years following World War II. (LO5)
    a) Almost constant warfare
    b) Suburbanization
    c) Welfare spending
    d) The loss of jobs to Japan, India, and China

19. Medicare and Medicaid were inaugurated under the administration of _____. (LO5)
    a) Franklin D. Roosevelt
    b) Harry S. Truman
    c) Dwight D. Eisenhower
    d) John F. Kennedy
    e) Lyndon B. Johnson

20. Most of the recessions since World War II lasted _____. (LO4)
    a) less than 6 months
    b) 6 to 12 months
    c) 12 to 18 months
    d) 18 to 24 months
    e) 24 to 36 months

21. Which statement is true? (LO5)
    a) President Eisenhower attempted to undo most of the New Deal.
    b) There was a major tax cut in 1964.
    c) The federal budget deficit was reduced during President Lyndon Johnson's administration.
    d) None of the above.

22. There was a major tax cut in _____. (LO5)
    a) both 1964 and 1981
    b) neither 1964 nor 1981
    c) 1964, but not in 1981
    d) 1981, but not 1964

23. Our economic growth began to slow markedly _____. (LO5)
    a) in the early 1940s
    b) in the early 1960s
    c) in the early 1970s
    d) between 1982 and 1985

24. During World War II most of the people who got jobs in defense plants were _____ who had _____ experience building planes, tanks, and warships. (LO3)
    a) men, substantial
    b) men, no
    c) women, substantial
    d) women, no

25. In the 1970s, our economy suffered from

    _____. (LO5)

    a) inflation but not stagnation

    b) stagnation but not inflation

    c) inflation and stagnation

    d) neither inflation nor stagnation

26. There were no recessions during the administration of

    _____. (LO4, 5)

    a) Dwight D. Eisenhower

    b) Ronald Reagan

    c) Bill Clinton

    d) George W. Bush

27. Our longest uninterrupted economic expansion took

    place mainly in the decade of the _____. (LO5)

    a) 1940s   c) 1960s   e) 1980s

    b) 1950s   d) 1970s   f) 1990s

28. In the 1990s our economy has generated more than

    _____ million additional jobs. (L05, 6)

    a) 5   b) 10   c) 15   d) 20

29. What set off the Great Recession? (LO4, 6)

    a) The bursting of the housing bubble.

    b) The sharp decline in oil prices.

    c) The escalation of the war in Iraq.

    d) A surge in imports from China.

30. Which statement is the most accurate? (LO2)

    a) The South had some very substantial economic
       grievances against the North in the years
       immediately preceding the Civil War.

    b) The South seceded from the Union when President
       Lincoln proclaimed that he was freeing the slaves.

    c) Aside from slavery, southern and northern
       agriculture were very similar.

    d) Most of the nation's industries were relocated
       from the North and Midwest to the South in the
       years immediately following the Civil War.

31. The massive shift of population and industry out of
    the large central cities from the late 1940s through
    the 1960s was caused by _____. (LO5)

    a) wars

    b) the mechanization of agriculture

    c) suburbanization

    d) immigration

    e) fear of nuclear war

32. Each of the following was a major contributing factor
    to suburbanization except _____. (LO5)

    a) low-interest federal loans

    b) a federal highway building program

    c) the pent-up demand for housing

    d) the baby boom

    e) federal subsidies for public transportation

33. Which statement is true? (LO2, 6)

    a) Although our economy was not performing well,
       college graduates from the classes of 2009 and
       2010 received more job offers than any other
       graduating class in history.

    b) The economic downturn that began in
       December 2007 is the longest since the 1930s.

    c) Until the time of the Great Depression, the United
       States was primarily an agricultural nation.

    d) There were no recessions during the presidency of
       Bill Clinton (January 1993–January 2001).

34. Who made this statement? "Once upon a time my
    opponents honored me as possessing the fabulous
    intellectual and economic power by which I created a
    worldwide depression all by myself." (LO2)

    a) Franklin D. Roosevelt

    b) Herbert Hoover

    c) John F. Kennedy

    d) Ronald Reagan

    e) Bill Clinton

35. Which statement is the most accurate? (LO6)

    a) The 21st century will almost definitely be another
       "American Century."

    b) The 21st, rather than the 20th, will be called
       "The American Century."

    c) The 21st century will definitely not be an
       "American Century."

    d) Although we got off to a rocky start, this century
       may well turn out to be another "American
       Century."

36. Our most rapid job growth was in the period from

    _____. (LO5, 6)

    a) 2000 to 2005

    b) 1995 to 2000

    c) 1978 to 1983

    d) 1953 to 1958

37. If you could blame just one person or group of people that caused the Great Depression, which one of the following would you choose? (LO1)
    a) President Herbert Hoover
    b) President Franklin Roosevelt
    c) the Federal Reserve Board
    d) the bankers

38. Each of the following happened during the Great Recession *except* _____. (LO6)
    a) a financial crisis
    b) the loss of more than 8 million jobs
    c) a sharp rise in the inflation rate
    d) a sharp decline in our output of goods and services

39. Which of the following is the most accurate statement? (LO7)
    a) Like the 20th century, the 21st century will definitely be "the American Century."
    b) Although we have had some recent problems, our economy is strong enough to continue to support our present global military commitments indefinitely.
    c) The United States is a fading economic and military power, and will soon be overtaken by its rivals.
    d) It is far too soon to say whether or not the 21st century will be another "American century."

Fill-In Questions

1. The low point of the Great Depression was reached in the year _____. (LO2)

2. In 1790, about _____ of every 10 Americans lived on farms. (LO1)

3. The worst recession we had since World War II occurred in _____. (LO4)

4. The country with the world's largest output is _____. (LO1)

5. In 1933, our official unemployment rate was _____%. (LO2)

6. Bills providing for Medicare and Medicaid were passed during the administration of President _____. (LO5)

7. Today one full-time American farmer feeds about _____ people. (LO5)

8. During President Dwight D. Eisenhower's two terms, there were _____ recessions. (LO4, 5)

9. Rapid technological change in agriculture during the first half of the 19th century was brought on mainly by _____. (LO1)

10. The main factor in finally bringing us out of the Great Depression was _____. (LO2, 3)

11. Since the end of World War II there have been _____ recessions. (LO4)

12. The quarter century that was completely dominated by the great industrialists like Andrew Carnegie and John D. Rockefeller began in the year _____. (LO1)

13. Passage of the _____ in 1944 enabled nearly 8 million veterans to go to school. (LO3)

14. The _____ century was termed "The American Century." (LO6)

Chapter 2

Resource Utilization

Economics is defined in various ways, but scarcity is always part of the definition. We bake an economic pie each year, which is composed of all the goods and services we have produced. No matter how we slice it, there never seems to be enough. Some people feel the main problem is how we slice the pie, while others say we should concentrate on baking a larger pie.

LEARNING OBJECTIVES

After reading this chapter you should be able to:

1. Define economics.
2. Identify the central fact of economics and explain how it relates to the economic problem.
3. Name the four economic resources and explain how they are used by the entrepreneur.
4. Explain and apply the concept of opportunity cost.
5. Describe and distinguish among the concepts of full employment, full production, and underemployment.
6. Describe the concept of the production possibilities curve and how it is used.
7. Identify and explain the three concepts upon which the law of increasing costs is based.
8. Define and explain productive efficiency.
9. Identify and explain the factors which enable an economy to grow.

Economics Defined

Economics is the efficient allocation of the scarce means of production toward the satisfaction of human wants. You're probably thinking, What did he say? Let's break it down into two parts. The scarce means of production are our resources, which we use to produce all the goods and services we buy. And why do we buy these goods and services? Because they provide us with satisfaction.

The only problem is that we don't have enough resources to produce all the goods and services we desire. Our resources are limited while our wants are relatively unlimited. In the next few pages, we'll take a closer look at the concepts of resources, scarcity, and the satisfaction of human wants. Keep in mind that we can't produce everything we'd like to purchase—there's scarcity. This is where economics comes in. We're attempting to make the best of a less-than-ideal situation. We're trying to use our resources so efficiently that we can maximize our satisfaction. Or, as François Quesnay put it back

Economics is the efficient allocation of the scarce means of production toward the satisfaction of human wants.

Economics is the science of greed.

—F. V. Meyer

in the 18th century, "To secure the greatest amount of pleasure with the least possible outlay should be the aim of all economic effort."[1]

The Central Fact of Economics: Scarcity

Scarcity and the Need to Economize

Most of us are used to economizing; we save up our scarce dollars and deny ourselves various tempting treasures so we will have enough money for that one big-ticket item—a new car, a sound system, a trip to Europe. Since our dollars are scarce and we can't buy everything we want, we economize by making do with some lower-priced items—a Cadillac instead of a Rolls Royce, chicken instead of steak, or an education at a state university rather than at an Ivy League college.

If there were no scarcity, we would not need to economize, and economists would have to find other work. Let's go back to our economic pie to see how scarcity works. Most people tend to see scarcity as not enough dollars, but as John Maynard Keynes[2] pointed out more than 70 years ago, this is an illusion. We could print all the money we want and still have scarcity. As Adam Smith noted in 1776, the wealth of nations consists of the goods and services they produce, or, on another level, the resources—the *land, labor, capital,* and *entrepreneurial ability*—that actually produce these goods and services.

The Economic Problem

John Kenneth Galbraith, American economist and social critic

In the 1950s, John Kenneth Galbraith coined the term *the affluent society,* which implied that we had the scarcity problem licked. Americans were the richest people in the world. Presumably, we had conquered poverty. But within a few years, Michael Harrington's *The Other America*[3] challenged that contention.

The economic problem, however, goes far beyond ending poverty. Even then, nearly all Americans would be relatively poor when they compared what they have with what they would like to have—or with what the Waltons, Gateses, Buffetts, Allens, and Ellisons have.

Human wants are relatively limitless. Make a list of all the things you'd like to have. Now add up their entire cost. Chances are you couldn't earn enough in a lifetime to even begin to pay for half the things on your list.

The Four Economic Resources

We need four resources, often referred to as "the means of production," to produce an output of goods and services. Every society, from a tiny island nation in the Pacific to the most complex industrial giant, needs these resources: *land, labor, capital,* and *entrepreneurial ability*. Let's consider each in turn.

Land

As a resource, land has a much broader meaning than our normal understanding of the word. It includes natural resources (such as timber, oil, coal, iron ore, soil, and water) as well as the ground in which these resources are found. Land is used not only for the extraction of minerals but for farming as well. And, of course, we build factories, office buildings, shopping centers, and homes on land. The basic payment made to the owners of land is rent.

Labor

Labor is the work and time for which employees are paid. The police officer, the computer programmer, the store manager, and the assembly-line worker all supply labor. About two-thirds of the total resource costs are paid to labor in the form of wages and salaries.

Capital

Capital is "man"-made goods used to produce other goods or services. It consists mainly of plant, equipment, and software. The United States has more capital than any other country

---

[1]François Quesnay, *Dialogues sur les Artisans,* quoted in Gide and Rist, *A History of Economic Doctrines,* 1913, pp. 10–11.

[2]Keynes, whose work we'll discuss in later chapters of *Economics* and *Macroeconomics,* was perhaps the greatest economist of the 20th century.

[3]Michael Harrington, *The Other America* (New York: Macmillan, 1962).

in the world. This capital consists of factories, office buildings, and stores. Our shopping malls, the Empire State Building, and automobile plants and steel mills (and all the equipment in them) are examples of capital. The return paid to the owners of capital is interest.

Entrepreneurial ability is the least familiar of our four basic resources. The entrepreneur sets up a business, assembles the needed resources, risks his or her own money, and reaps the profits or absorbs the losses of this enterprise. Often the entrepreneur is an innovator, such as Andrew Carnegie (U.S. Steel), John D. Rockefeller (Standard Oil), Henry Ford (Ford Motor Company), Steven Jobs (Apple Computer), Bill Gates (Microsoft), and Sam Walton (Walmart).

Entrepreneurial ability

We may consider land, labor, and capital passive resources, which are combined by the entrepreneur to produce goods and services. A successful undertaking is rewarded by profit; an unsuccessful one is penalized by loss.

In the American economy, the entrepreneur is the central figure, and our long record of economic success is an eloquent testimonial to the abundance of our entrepreneurial talents. The owners of the over 30 million businesses in this country are virtually all entrepreneurs. The vast majority either work for themselves or have just one or two employees. But they have two things in common: Each runs a business, and each risks his or her own money.

Sometimes entrepreneurs cash in on inventions—their own or someone else's. Alexander Graham Bell and Thomas Edison were two of the more famous inventors who *did* parlay their inventions into great commercial enterprises. As you know, tens of billions of dollars were earned by the founders of America Online, Amazon, eBay, Yahoo!, Google, and the thousands of other so-called dot-coms when they went public. These folks were all entrepreneurs. But have you ever heard of Tim Berners-Lee, the creator of the World Wide Web? Berners-Lee worked long and hard to ensure that the Web remained a public mass medium in cyberspace, an information thoroughfare open to all. He came up with the software standards for addressing, linking, and transferring multimedia documents over the Internet. And most amazing, Tim Berners-Lee did not try to cash in on his years of work.

Is this man an entrepreneur? Clearly he is not. He is an inventor of the first rank—like Bell and Edison—but the act of invention is not synonymous with being an entrepreneur.

Perhaps nothing more typifies American entrepreneurial talent than the Internet, which *The New York Times* termed the "Net Americana." Steve Lohr observed that "all ingredients that contribute to the entrepreneurial climate in the United States—venture capital financing, close ties between business and universities, flexible labor markets, a deregulated business environment, and a culture that celebrates risk-taking, ambition, and getting very, very rich"—fostered the formation of the Internet.[4]

What factors explain why so many of the world's greatest innovations have originated in the United States? Thomas Friedman produces a summation:

America is the greatest engine of innovation that has ever existed, and it can't be duplicated anytime soon, because it is the product of a multitude of factors: extreme freedom of thought, an emphasis on independent thinking, a steady immigration of new minds, a risk-taking culture with no stigma attached to trying and failing, a noncorrupt bureaucracy, and financial markets and a venture capital system that are unrivaled at taking new ideas and turning them into global products.[5]

Resources are scarce because they are limited in quantity. There's a finite amount of land on this planet, and at any given time a limited amount of labor, capital, and entrepreneurial ability is available. Over time, of course, the last three resources can be increased.

Our economic problem, then, is that we have limited resources available to satisfy relatively unlimited wants. The reason why you, and everyone else, can't have three cars, a town house and a country estate with servants, designer clothing, jewelry, big screen TVs in each room, and a $50,000 sound system is that we just don't have enough resources to produce everything that everyone wants. Therefore, we have to make choices, an option we call opportunity cost.

---

[4]Steve Lohr, "Welcome to the Internet, the First Global Colony," *The New York Times,* January 9, 2000, Section 4, p. 1.

[5]Thomas Friedman, "The Secret of Our Sauce," *The New York Times,* March 7, 2004, Section 4, p. 13.

Opportunity Cost

There was an accounting professor nicknamed "the phantom," who used to dash from his last class to his car, and speed off to his office. During tax season, he was almost never seen on campus, and certainly not during his office hours. One day a student managed to catch him in the parking lot. Big mistake. As he climbed into his car, the professor asked scornfully, "Do you realize how much money you're costing me?"

Unknowingly, the phantom was illustrating the concept of opportunity cost. "Every minute I waste answering your questions could be spent in my office earning money. So if I spend five minutes with you, that just cost me $10." Perhaps if the student had handed him a ten dollar bill, he could have bought a few minutes of his professor's time.

The opportunity cost of any choice is the forgone value of the next best alternative.

Because we can't have everything we want, we must make choices. The thing we give up (that is, our second choice) is called the opportunity cost of our choice. Therefore, *the opportunity cost of any choice is the forgone value of the next best alternative.*

Suppose a little boy goes into a toy store with $15. Many different toys tempt him, but he finally narrows his choice to a Monopoly game and a magic set, each costing $15. If he decides to buy the Monopoly game, the opportunity cost is foregoing the magic set. And if he buys the magic set, the opportunity cost is foregoing the Monopoly game.

Even children learn in growing up that "both" is not an admissible answer to a choice of "which one?"
—President Warren G. Harding

In some cases the next best alternative—the Monopoly game or the magic set—is virtually equal no matter what choice is made. In other cases, there's no contest. If someone were to offer you, at the same price, your favorite eight-course meal or a Big Mac, you'd have no trouble deciding (unless, of course, your favorite meal *is* a Big Mac).

If a town hires an extra police officer instead of repaving several streets, the opportunity cost of hiring the officer is not repaving the streets. To obtain more of one thing, society foregoes the opportunity of getting the next best thing.

Today, as we all know, people are living longer. This has set the stage for an ongoing generational conflict over how much of our resources should be devoted to Medicare, Social Security, nursing homes, and old age homes, and how much to child care, Head Start, and, in general, education. If we are to be a humane society, we must take care of our aging population. But if our economy is to be competitive in the global economy, we need to devote more dollars to education.

What are some of the opportunity costs *you* have incurred? What is the opportunity cost of attending college? Owning a car? Or even buying this economics text? There's even an opportunity cost of studying for an exam. How would you have otherwise spent those precious hours?

What is the opportunity cost of the wars in Iraq and Afghanistan? Because the conduct of the wars costs taxpayers about $150 billion a year, the opportunity cost of the wars is how that money might have otherwise been spent. Possibilities include reducing the federal budget deficit, a tax cut, more students loans, research for a cure for breast cancer, and a high speed rail system between pairs of major cities.

I'm sure you can think of at least a few other examples of the opportunity cost of the wars in Iraq and Afghanistan. My *own* preference would be to spend some of these resources on the reconstruction of New Orleans. It seems inconceivable that it is somehow more important to rebuild Baghdad than to rebuild that great American city.

on the web

If you'd like to read what I *really* think about our neglect in helping New Orleans to rebuild, go to www.tucsoncitizen.com/ss/opinion/41952.php.

Full Employment and Full Production

Everyone agrees that full employment is a good thing, even if we don't all agree on exactly what full employment means. Does it mean that every single person in the United States who is ready, willing, and able to work has a job? Is *that* full employment?

The answer is no. There will always be some people between jobs. On any given day thousands of Americans quit, get fired, or decide that they will enter the labor force by finding a job. Since it may take several weeks, or even several months, until they find the "right" job, there will always be some people unemployed.

If an unemployment rate of zero does not represent full employment, then what rate does? Economists cannot agree on what constitutes full employment. Some liberals insist that an unemployment rate of 4 percent constitutes full employment, while there are conservatives who feel that an unemployment rate of 6 percent would be more realistic.

Similarly, we cannot expect to fully use all our plant and equipment. A capacity utilization rate of 85 or 90 percent would surely employ virtually all of our usable plant and equipment. At any given moment there is always some factory being renovated or some machinery under repair. During wartime we might be able to use our capacity more fully, but in normal times 85 to 90 percent is the peak.

In a global economy, not only has it become increasingly difficult to define which goods and services are made in America and which originate abroad, but one may even question the relevance of a plant's location. If our steel industry were operating at full capacity, we could get still more steel from Germany, Japan, South Korea, Brazil, and other steel-producing nations. In the context of the global economy, our capacity utilization ratio is clearly much less important than it was just a few decades ago.

As long as all available resources are fully used—given the constraints we have just cited—we are at our production possibilities frontier. A few additional constraints should also be considered because they too restrict the quantity of resources available. These are institutional constraints, the laws and customs under which we live.

The so-called blue laws restrict the economic activities that may be carried out in various cities and states, mainly on Sundays. Bars and liquor stores must be closed certain hours. In some places, even retail stores must be closed on Sundays.

State and federal law carefully restricts child labor. Very young children may not be employed at all, and those below a certain age may work only a limited number of hours.

Traditionally, Americans dislike working at night or on weekends, particularly on Sundays. Consequently, we must leave most of our expensive plant and equipment idle except during daylight weekday hours. We don't consider that plant and equipment unemployed, nor do we consider those whose labor is restricted by law or custom unemployed. All of this is already allowed for in our placement of the location of the production possibilities frontier (shown in Figure 1 in the next section).

By full production, we mean that our nation's resources are being allocated in the most efficient manner possible. Not only are we using our most up-to-date technology, but we are using our land, labor, capital, and entrepreneurial ability in the most productive way.

We would not want to use the intersection of Fifth Avenue and 57th Street in Manhattan for dairy farming, nor would we want our M.D.s doing clerical work. But sometimes we do just that.

Until very recently in our history blacks, Hispanics, and women were virtually excluded from nearly all high-paying professions. Of course, this entailed personal hurt and lost income; this discrimination also cost our nation in lost output. In the sports world, until 1947, when Brooklyn Dodger owner Branch Rickey defied baseball's "color line" and signed Jackie Robinson for the team, major league baseball was played by whites only (see the box titled, "The Jackie Robinson Story"). At that time, only a tiny handful of Hispanic players were tolerated. Today there are several black and Hispanic players on every team. Today, professional basketball would hardly be described as a "white man's sport." Nor, for that matter, would the National Football League be accused of discrimination, at least at the level of player personnel. But until the late 1940s, blacks were almost entirely banned from those professional sports.

As late as the 1950s, only a few stereotypical roles were available to blacks in the movies and on TV. And, except for Desi Arnaz (Ricky Ricardo of "I Love Lucy"), there were virtually no Hispanic Americans in these entertainment media. That was America not all that long ago, when employment discrimination was the rule, not the exception.

Until recently only a tiny minority of women employed in the offices of American business were not typists or secretaries. In the 1950s and even into the 1960s, virtually every article in *Fortune* was written by a man and researched by a woman. What a waste of labor potential!

If economists were laid end to end, they would not reach a conclusion.
—George Bernard Shaw

Full production: Our nation's resources are being allocated in the most efficient manner possible.

Employment discrimination

The Jackie Robinson Story

Blacks had always been banned from professional sports, but most notoriously by the "American sport"—major league baseball. For decades there was a parallel association for blacks called the Negro leagues. Finally, the color barrier was broken in 1947 when Jackie Robinson began playing for the Brooklyn Dodgers.

Looking back, then, to all those years when black ballplayers were not permitted to play major league baseball (and basketball and football), we see that hundreds of athletes were underemployed. Not only did they suffer economically and psychologically, but the American public was deprived of watching innumerable talented athletes perform.

Jackie Robinson

In 1991 I met a few of the men who played in the Negro leagues when I was visiting Kansas City, where the Negro League Baseball Museum is located. They all knew Satchel Paige, a legendary pitcher whose fastball was so fast, the batters often couldn't even see it, let alone hit it. Sometimes Paige would wind up and pretend to throw a pitch. The catcher pounded his glove and the umpire called a strike. Then the catcher, who had the ball all along, threw it back to Paige. As great as he was, Satchel Paige didn't play in the major leagues until the twilight of his career, when he was in his late forties.

I can still picture one ad that appeared in several business magazines back in the 1950s. Four or five young women were on their knees on an office carpet sorting through piles of papers. This was an advertisement for a collator. The caption read, "When your office collator breaks down, do the girls have to stay late for a collating party?"

This ad said a great deal about those times. Forget about political correctness! Every woman (but almost no men) applying for office jobs was asked, "How fast can you type?" because those were virtually the only jobs open to women in corporate America—even to college graduates. Typing, filing, and other clerical positions were considered "women's work." The high-paying and high-status executive positions were reserved for men. So when the collator broke down, it seemed perfectly logical to ask the "girls" to stay late for a "collating party."

These are just a few of the most blatant examples of employment discrimination, a phenomenon that has diminished but has not yet been wiped out. Employment discrimination automatically means that we will have less than full production because we are not efficiently allocating our labor. In other words, there are millions of Americans who really should be doctors, engineers, corporate executives, or whatever but have been condemned to less exalted occupations solely because they happen not to be white Protestant males.

But, in the words of Bob Dylan, "the times, they are a' changin'." The civil rights revolution of the 1960s and the women's liberation movement a decade later did bring millions of blacks and women into the economic mainstream. Elite business schools began admitting large numbers of women in the mid-1970s, and today there are hundreds of women occupying the executive suites of our major corporations.[6]

We have certainly come a long way since President Franklin Roosevelt appointed Labor Secretary Frances Perkins as the first woman cabinet member in history, and, some three decades later, when President Lyndon Johnson made Housing Secretary Warren Weaver the first black cabinet member. It would be a fair description to say that the presidential administrations of George W. Bush and Barack Obama represent the face of America a whole lot better than those of presidential administrations just one generation ago.

Finally, there is the question of using the best available technology. Historically, the American economy has been on the cutting edge of technological development for almost

Using the best technology

---

[6]There is an additional discussion of employment discrimination near the end of the chapter on Labor Markets and Wages in *Economics* and *Microeconomics*.

200 years; the sewing machine, mechanical reaper, telephone, airplane, automobile, assembly line, and computer are all American inventions.

Now it's the computer software industry. Not only are we on the forefront in this rapidly expanding industry, but we produce and export more software than the rest of the world combined. Microsoft, Cisco, Oracle, and a host of other American companies are household names not just in the United States but all across the globe.

Let's tie up one more loose end before moving on to the main focus of this chapter, the production possibilities frontier. We need to be clear about distinguishing between less than full employment and underemployment of resources.

Full employment and underemployment

If we are using only 70 percent of our capacity of plant and equipment, as we do during some recessions, this would be a case of our economy operating at less than full employment of its resources. Anything less than, say, an 85 percent utilization rate would be considered below full employment.

More familiarly, when the unemployment rate is, say, 10 percent, there is clearly a substantial amount of labor unemployed. But how much *is* full employment? We never really answered that one.

As a working definition, we'll say that an unemployment rate of 5 percent represents full employment. Why not use 4 percent, as the liberal economists suggest, or the 6 percent figure favored by the conservatives? Because 5 percent represents a reasonable compromise. So we'll be working with that figure from here on, but keep in mind that not everyone agrees that a 5 percent unemployment rate represents full employment.

Unemployment means that not all our resources are being used. Less than 95 percent of our labor force is working, and less than 85 percent of our plant and equipment is being used. It also means that our land and entrepreneurial ability are not all being used.

Was our economy at full employment in 2009? Hardly. For most of that year our unemployment rate was over 9 percent while our capacity utilization rate was below 70 percent and that is exactly what you would expect during a very severe recession.

What is underemployment of resources? To be at full production, not only would we be fully employing our resources, we would also be using them in the most efficient way possible. To make all women become schoolteachers, social workers, or secretaries would grossly underuse their talents. Equally absurd—and inefficient—would be to make all white males become doctors or lawyers and all black and Hispanic males become accountants or computer programmers.

Similarly, we would not want to use that good Iowa farmland for office parks, nor would we want to locate dairy farms in the middle of our cities' central business districts. And finally, we would certainly not want to use our multimillion-dollar computer mainframes to do simple word processing.

During 2009 and 2010 perhaps the hardest hit were those Americans under 25, one quarter of whom were unemployed. But among recent college graduates who *were* employed, half were in positions not requiring college degrees. So your immediate prospects in the job market may well be either unemployment or underemployment.

These are all examples of underemployment of resources. Unfortunately, a certain amount of underemployment is built into our economy, but we need to reduce it if we are going to succeed in baking a larger economic pie.[7]

The production possibilities frontier represents our economy at full employment and full production.

This brings us, at long last, to the production possibilities curve. As we've already casually mentioned, the production possibilities frontier represents our economy at full employment and full production. However, a certain amount of underemployment of resources is built into our model. How much? Although the exact amount is not quantifiable, it is fairly large. But to the degree that employment discrimination has declined since the early 1960s, underemployment of resources may still be holding our output to 10 or 15 percent below what it would be if there were a truly efficient allocation of resources.

---

[7]Sometimes the news media refers to the underemployment rate, which is found by adding the unemployment rate to the percentage of people in the labor force who are working part-time, but would prefer to work full-time. But in this text we'll consider underemployment the less than efficient use of our resources.

The Production Possibilities Curve

Since scarcity is a fact of economic life, we need to use our resources as efficiently as possible. If we succeed, we are operating at full economic capacity. Usually there's some economic slack, but every so often we *do* manage to operate at peak efficiency. When this happens, we are on our production possibilities frontier (or production possibilities curve).

Often economics texts cast the production possibilities curve in terms of guns and butter. A country is confronted with two choices: It can produce only military goods or only civilian goods. The more guns it produces, the less butter and, of course, vice versa.

If we were to use all our resources—our land, labor, capital, and entrepreneurial ability—to make guns, we would obviously not be able to make butter at all. Similarly, if we made only butter, there would be no resources to make any guns. Virtually every country makes *some* guns and *some* butter. Japan makes relatively few military goods, while the United States devotes a much higher proportion of its resources to making guns.

You are about to encounter the second graph in this book. This graph, and each one that follows, will have a vertical axis and a horizontal axis. Both axes start at the origin of the graph, which is located in the lower left-hand corner and is usually marked with the number 0.

In Figure 1 we measure units of butter on the vertical axis. On the horizontal axis we measure units of guns. As we move to the right, the number of guns increases—1, 2, 3, 4, 5.

Guns and butter

The curve shown in the graph is drawn by connecting points A, B, C, D, E, and F. Where do these points come from? They come from Table 1. Where did we get the numbers in Table 1? They're hypothetical. In other words, I made them up.

Table 1 shows six production possibilities ranging from point A, where we produce 15 units of butter and no guns, to point F, where we produce 5 units of guns but no butter. This same information is presented in Figure 1, a graph of the production possibilities curve. We'll begin at point A, where a country's entire resources are devoted to producing butter. If the country were to produce at full capacity (using all its resources) but wanted to make some guns, they could do it by shifting some resources away from butter. This would move them from point A to point B. Instead of producing 15 units of butter, they're making only 14.

Figure 1

Production Possibilities Curve
This curve shows the range of possible combinations of outputs of guns and butter extending from 15 units of butter and no guns at point A to 5 units of guns and no butter at point F.

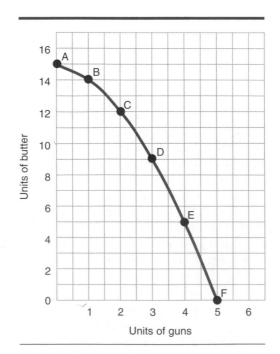

TABLE 1	Hypothetical Production Schedule for Two-Product Economy	
Point	Units of Butter	Units of Guns
A	15	0
B	14	1
C	12	2
D	9	3
E	5	4
F	0	5

Before we go any further on the curve, let's go over the numbers at points A and B. We're figuring out how many guns and how much butter are produced at each of these points. Starting at the origin, or zero, let's check out point A. It's directly above the origin, so no guns are produced. Point A is at 15 on the vertical scale, so 15 units of butter are produced.

Now we'll move on to point B, which is directly above 1 unit on the guns axis. At B we produce 1 unit of guns and 14 units of butter (shown vertically). Incidentally, to locate any point on a graph, first go across, or horizontally, then up, or vertically. Point B is 1 unit to the right, then 14 units up.

Now locate point C: 2 units across and 12 up. At C we have 2 guns and 12 butters. Next is D: 3 across and 9 up (3 guns and 9 butters). At E: 4 across and 5 up (4 guns and 5 butters). And finally F: 5 across and 0 up (5 guns and no butter).

The production possibilities curve is a hypothetical model of an economy that produces only two products—in this case, guns and butter (or military goods and civilian goods). The curve represents the various possible combinations of guns and butter that could be produced if the economy were operating at capacity, or full employment.

The production possibilities curve represents a two-product economy at full employment.

Since we usually do not operate at full employment, we are seldom on the production possibilities frontier. So let's move on to Figure 2, which shows, at point X, where we generally are. Sometimes we are in a recession, with unemployment rising beyond 8 or 9 percent, represented on the graph by point Y. A depression would be closer to the origin, perhaps shown by point Z. (Remember that the origin is located in the lower left-hand corner of the graph.)

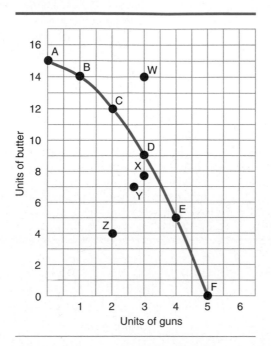

Figure 2

Points Inside and Outside the Production Possibilities Curve Since the curve represents output of guns and butter at full employment, points X, Y, and Z, which lie inside or below the curve, represent output at less than full employment. Similarly, point W represents output at more than full employment and is currently unattainable.

The Law of Increasing Costs

The production possibilities curve below reproduces Table 1. You may notice that, as we shift production from guns to butter, we have to give up increasing units of guns for each additional unit of butter. Or, shifting the other way, we would have to give up increasing units of butter for each additional unit of guns we produce.

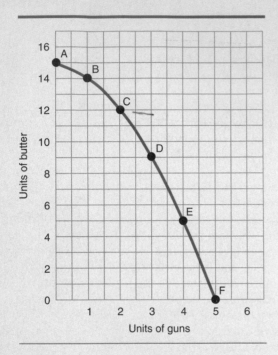

Note that as you move from A to B you produce an extra gun at the expense of 1 unit of butter, but when you move from E to F, you produce an extra gun at the expense of 5 units of butter.

We will be calling this "the law of increasing costs." Stated formally, this law says that *as the output of one good expands, the opportunity cost of producing additional units of this good increases*. In other words, as more and more of a good is produced, the production of additional units of this good will entail larger and larger opportunity costs.

The law of increasing costs is based on three concepts: (1) the law of diminishing returns, (2) diseconomies of scale, and (3) factor suitability. We've already alluded to factor suitability when we talked about using our resources in the most efficient way possible. One example was to use our computer mainframe for sophisticated data analysis rather than for simple word processing.

The law of diminishing returns, which we'll take up more formally in a later chapter, is defined this way: *If units of a resource are added to a fixed proportion of other resources, eventually marginal output will decline.* Suppose one farmer working with one tractor can produce 100 bushels of wheat on one acre of land. Two farmers, working together, can produce 220 bushels. And three, working together, can produce 350.

The marginal output of the first farmer is 100. (In other words, the first farmer added 100 bushels to output.) The marginal output of the second farmer is 120. And the marginal output of the third farmer is 130. So far, so good. We call this increasing returns.

If we keep adding farmers, do you think we'll continue to enjoy increasing returns? Won't that single acre of land start getting a little crowded? Will that one tractor be sufficient for four, five, and six farmers? Suppose we did add a fourth farmer and suppose output rose from 350 to 450. By how much did marginal output rise?

It rose by only 100. So marginal output, which had been rising by 120 and 130, has now fallen to 100. We call this diminishing returns.

Diseconomies of scale is a new term. As a business firm grows larger, it can usually cut its costs by taking advantage of quantity discounts, the use of expensive but highly productive equipment, and the development of a highly specialized and highly skilled workforce. We call these *economies of scale*. But as the firm continues to grow, these economies of scale are eventually outweighed by the inefficiencies of managing a bloated bureaucracy, which might sometimes work at cross-purposes. Most of the day could be spent writing memos, answering memos, and attending meetings. Labor and other resources become increasingly expensive, and not only are quantity discounts no longer available, but now suppliers charge premium prices for such huge orders. As costs begin to rise, diseconomies of scale have now overcome economies of scale.*

Let's look at some increasing costs. We have already seen how we have had to give up the production of some guns to produce more butter and vice versa. We'll now take this a step further. To produce additional units of guns— one gun, two guns, three guns—we will have to give up

Table A   Production Shifts from Butter to Guns

Shift from Point to Point	Change in Gun Production	Change in Butter Production
A to B	+1	−1
B to C	+1	−2
C to D	+1	−3
D to E	+1	−4
E to F	+1	−5

increasing amounts of butter. Similarly, to produce additional units of butter, we will have to give up increasing numbers of guns.

How many units of butter would we have to give up to produce each additional gun? This is shown in the table above, which is derived from the figure in this box, or, if you prefer, from Table 1 earlier in this chapter.

In the table above, as we begin to switch from butter to guns, we move from point A to point B. We give up just one unit of butter in exchange for one unit of guns. But the move from B to C isn't as good. Here we give up two butters for one gun. C to D is still worse: We give up three butters for one gun. D to E is even worse: We give up four units of butter for one gun. And the worst trade-off of all is from E to F: We lose five butters for just one gun.

This is why we call it the law of increasing relative costs. To produce more and more of one good, we have to give up increasing amounts of another good. To produce each additional gun, we have to give up increasing amounts of butter.

There are three explanations for the law of increasing relative costs. First, there's diminishing returns. If we're increasing gun production, we will need more and more resources—more land, more labor, more capital, and more entrepreneurial ability. But one or more of these resources may be relatively limited. Perhaps we will begin to run out of capital—plant and equipment—or perhaps entrepreneurial ability will run out first.

Go back to our definition of the law of diminishing returns. *If units of a resource are added to a fixed proportion of other resources, eventually marginal output will decline.* Had we been talking about farming rather than producing guns, the law of diminishing returns might have

set in as increasing amounts of capital were applied to the limited supply of rich farmland.

A second explanation for the law of increasing costs is diseconomies of scale. By shifting from butter to guns, the firm or firms making guns will grow so large that diseconomies of scale will eventually set in.

The third explanation, factor suitability, requires more extensive treatment here. We'll start at point A of Table A where we produce 15 units of butter and no guns. As we move to point B, gun production goes up by one, while butter production goes down by only one. In other words, the opportunity cost of producing one unit of guns is the loss of only one unit of butter.

Why is the opportunity cost so low? The answer lies mainly with factor suitability. We'll digress for a moment with the analogy of a pickup game of basketball. The best players are picked first, then the not-so-good ones, and finally the worst. If a couple of players from one side have to go home, the game goes on. The other side gives them their worst player.

If we're shifting from butter to guns, the butter makers will give the gun makers their worst workers. But people who are bad at producing butter are not necessarily bad at making—or shooting—guns.

When all we did was make butter, people worked at that no matter what their other skills. Even if a person were a skilled gun maker, or a gun user, what choice did he have? Presumably, then, when given the choice to make guns, those best suited for that occupation (and also poorly suited for butter making) would switch to guns.

As resources are shifted from butter to guns, the labor, land, capital, and entrepreneurial ability best suited to guns and least suited to butter will be the first to switch. But as more resources are shifted, we will be taking resources that were more and more suited to butter making and less and less suited to gun making.

Take land, for example. The first land given over to gun making might be terrible for raising cows (and hence milk and butter) but great for making guns. Eventually, however, as nearly all land was devoted to gun making, we'd be giving over fertile farmland that might not be well suited to gun production.

---

*Economies and diseconomies of scale are more fully discussed in the chapter on Cost in *Economics* and *Microeconomics*.

HELP

Figure A shows us how many apples and oranges we can produce. The more apples we produce, the fewer oranges we can produce. Similarly, the more oranges we produce, the fewer apples we can produce.

Opportunity cost tells us what we must give up. So if we increase our production of oranges by moving from point B to point C, how many apples are we giving up?

We are giving up 1 apple. Next question: If we move from point F to point D, how many oranges are we giving up?

Finding the Opportunity Cost

We are giving up 2 oranges. Now, let's take it up a notch. What is the opportunity cost of moving from A to D?

It's 3 apples, because at point A we produced 5 apples, but at point D we're producing only 2. One more question: What is the opportunity cost of moving from E to B?

It's 6 oranges, because at E we produced 10 oranges and at B, only 4.

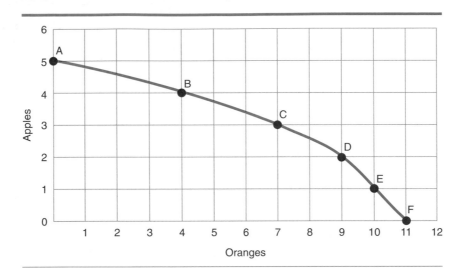

Figure A

What if we were at the origin? What would that represent? Think about it. What would be the production of guns? How about the production of butter? They would both be zero. Is that possible? During the Great Depression in the 1930s, the U.S. economy sank to point Z, but no economy has ever sunk to the origin.

Move back to the production possibilities curve, say, at point C, where we are producing 2 units of guns and 12 units of butter. Is it possible to produce more guns? Certainly. Just move down the curve to point D. Notice, however, that we now produce fewer units of butter.

At D we have 3 units of guns and 9 units of butter. When we go from C, where we have 2 guns, to D, where we have 3, gun production goes up by 1. But at the same time, butter production declines from 12 at C to only 9 at D (a decline of 3).

If we're at point C, then, we can produce more guns, but only by sacrificing some butter production. The opportunity cost of moving from C to D (that is, of producing 1 more gun) is giving up 3 units of butter.

Let's try another one, this time moving from C to B. Butter goes up from 12 to 14—a gain of 2. Meanwhile, guns go down from 2 to 1, a loss of 1. Going from C to B, a gain of 2 butters is obtained by sacrificing 1 gun. The opportunity cost of producing 2 more butters is 1 gun. If you need a little more practice, please work your way through the accompanying Extra Help box.

Except at point A, we can go somewhere else on the production possibilities curve and increase our output of butter. Similarly, anywhere but at point F, we can go somewhere else on the curve and raise our output of guns. It is possible to increase our output of *either* guns *or* butter by moving somewhere else on the curve, but there is an opportunity cost involved. The more we produce of one (by moving along the curve), the less we produce of the other. It is not possible, then, if we are anywhere on the curve, to raise our production of both guns *and* butter. Of course, over time it is possible to produce beyond our current production possibilities curve as our economy grows. We'll get to economic growth in a few minutes.

What if we're somewhere inside the production possibilities curve? Would it be possible to produce more guns *and* more butter? The answer is yes. At point Z we have an output of 2 guns and 4 butters. By moving to point D we would have 3 guns and 9 butters. Or, by going to point E, output would rise to 4 guns and 5 butters.

We are able to increase our output of both guns and butter when we move from Z to D or E because we are now making use of previously unused resources. We are moving from depression conditions to those of full employment. But when we go from C to D, we stay at full employment. The only way we can produce more guns is to produce less butter, because resources will have to be diverted from butter to gun production. As we divert increasing amounts of resources to gun production, we will be able to understand the law of increasing costs (see the box titled "The Law of Increasing Costs").

Productive Efficiency

So far we've seen that our economy generally falls short of full production. Now we'll tie that failure in to our definition of economics.

At the beginning of this chapter, we defined economics as *the efficient allocation of the scarce means of production toward the satisfaction of human wants.* The scarce means of production are our resources, land, labor, capital, and entrepreneurial ability. So how efficiently do we use our resources?

An economy is efficient whenever it is producing the maximum output allowed by a given level of technology and resources. *Productive efficiency is attained when the maximum possible output of any one good is produced, given the output of other goods.* This state of grace occurs only when we are operating on our production possibilities curve. Attainment of productive efficiency means that we can't increase the output of one good without reducing the output of some other good.

Productive efficiency is attained when the maximum possible output of any one good is produced, given the output of other goods.

As we've seen, our economy rarely attains productive efficiency, or full production. We have managed this state of grace from mid-1997 through mid-2001, when the unemployment rate dipped below 5 percent. And then, from October 2005 through February 2008, it never rose above 5 percent. The previous time our economy actually operated on its production possibilities frontier was during the Vietnam War, in 1968 and 1969.

Economic Growth

If the production possibilities curve represents the economy operating at full employment, then it would be impossible to produce at point W (of Figure 2). To go from C to W would mean producing more guns *and* more butter, something that would be beyond our economic capabilities, given the current state of technology and the amount of resources available.

Every economy will use the best available technology. At times, because a country cannot afford the most up-to-date equipment, it will use older machinery and tools. That country really has a capital problem rather than a technological one.

The best available technology

As the level of available technology improves, the production possibilities curve moves outward, as it does in Figure 3. A faster paper copier, a more smoothly operating assembly line, or a new-generation computer system are examples of technological

The Production Possibilities Frontier during World War II

World War II was a classic case of guns and butter, or, more accurately, guns *or* butter. Almost two years before we became actively involved in the war, we began increasing our arms production and drafting millions of young men into the armed services. Did this increase in military goods production mean a decrease in the production of consumer goods?

Gee, that's a very good question. And the answer is found when you go from point A to point B on the first figure shown here.

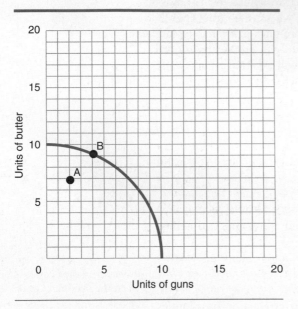

How were we able to increase the production of both guns and butter in 1940 and 1941? Because there was still a great deal of economic slack in those years. It was the tail end of the Great Depression described in Chapter 1, and there were still millions of people out of work and a great deal of idle plant and equipment that could be pressed into use.

Now we're in the war, and we're at point B in the first figure. Is it possible to further expand our output of both guns and butter? Think about it.

Is there any way we could do it? How about if there's economic growth? In the second figure shown here, we went from point B to point C by moving to a higher production possibilities curve. Is this *possible?* Over a considerable period of time, yes. But in just a couple of years? Well, remember what they used to say: There's a *war* going on. So a move from point B to point C in just a couple of years is possible during a war.

Now we're really going to push it. How about a move from point C to point D in the second figure? Is *this* move

possible? Can we raise our production of both guns *and* butter to a point beyond our production possibilities frontier without jumping to a still higher production possibilities curve?

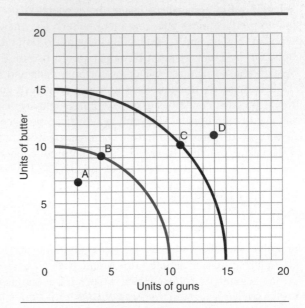

Well, what do *you* think? Remember, there's a war going on. The answer is yes. In 1942, 1943, and 1944 we did push our official unemployment rate under 3 percent, well below the 5 percent rate we would consider full employment today. Employers were so desperate for workers that they would hire practically anybody, and people who wouldn't ordinarily be in the labor market—housewives, retired people, and teenagers—were flocking to the workplace.

Meanwhile, business firms were pressing older machinery and equipment into use, because it was almost impossible to get new machinery and equipment built during the war. And so we were operating not only at full capacity but well beyond that point.

How long were we able to stay at point D? Only as long as there was a war going on. Point D represents an output of guns and butter that our economy can produce temporarily if it operates beyond its production possibilities curve. It's almost like bowling 300. You can't expect to go out and do it every night.*

---

*One can argue that we were temporarily operating on a higher production possibilities curve, and, at the end of the war, we returned to the lower production possibilities curve.

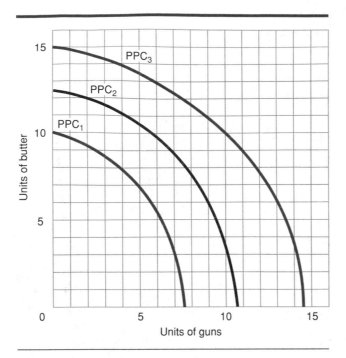

Figure 3
Production Possibilities Curves
A move from PPC₁ to PPC₂ and from PPC₂ to PPC₃ represents economic growth.

advances. And increasingly, industrial robots and bank money machines are replacing human beings at relatively routine jobs.

As you know, recent advances in information technology (or, IT, as it's often called) has boosted output per worker and cut costs. It costs FedEx $2.40 to track a package for a customer who calls by phone, but only four cents for one who visits its website. FedEx now gets about 3 million online tracking requests a day, compared with only 30,000 or 40,000 by phone.

Our economic capacity also grows when there is an expansion of labor or capital. More (or better trained) labor and more (or improved) plant and equipment would also push the production possibilities curve outward. This is illustrated in Figure 3, as we go from PPC₁ to PPC₂, and from PPC₂ to PPC₃.

Imagine that in 1991 a hypothetical nation had two choices. It could either produce a preponderance of consumer goods or a preponderance of capital goods. Which choice would lead to a faster rate of growth?

On the left side of Figure 4 we see what would have happened to the nation if it had chosen to concentrate on producing consumer goods; on the right side we see what would have happened if it had concentrated on producing capital goods. Obviously by concentrating on capital goods production, that nation would have had a much faster rate of economic growth.

The main factors spurring growth are an improving technology, more and better capital, and more and better labor. Using our resources more efficiently and reducing the unemployment of labor and capital can also raise our rate of growth. This topic is discussed more extensively in Chapter 16 of *Economics* and *Macroeconomics*.

Current Issue: Will You Be Underemployed When You Graduate?

Every spring newspaper reporters ask college placement officials about the job prospects of that year's graduating class. During good years corporate recruiters are lining up to interview the new grads. But in bad years, it's the other way around. The years 2006 and 2007 were pretty *good* and, 2008, 2009, and 2010, quite bad.

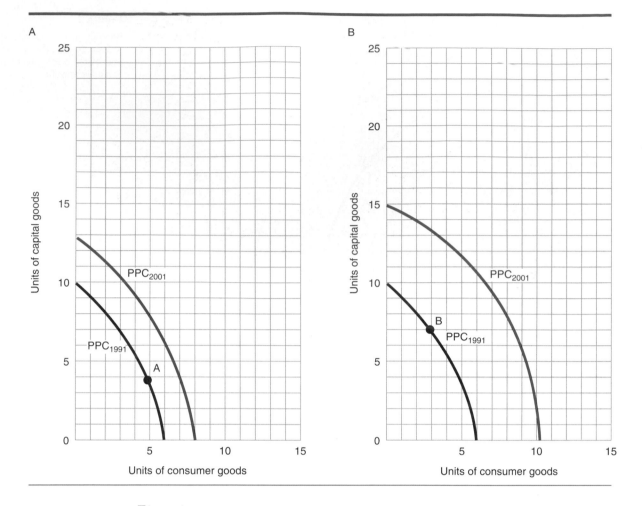

F*igure* **4**

Recent college graduates, when they can find work at all, are settling for jobs at places like Starbucks, Gap, and the post office (where 12 percent of the employees have college degrees). Half of college graduates under 25 are in positions that do not require college degrees. Which may leave a lot of parents wondering why they shelled out all that money for their children's education.

I happened to graduate during a *bad* year. My only job offer was from the recruiter from Continental Baking Company to drive a bakery truck. "But how will I use my economics?" He told me I could economize on the gasoline.

Had I taken the truck-driving job, I would have been underemployed. When you graduate, you may face the same problem. It turns out that one in five college graduates ends up in a job that does not require a college degree. In addition, many employers require a degree just as a credential. So when you start interviewing, ask yourself, "I need a degree to do *this*?"

There are millions of college grads who are asking themselves this very question. Some 37 percent of all flight attendants hold bachelor's degrees, as do 19 percent of the theater ushers, lobby attendants, and ticket takers. In addition, 13 percent of all bank tellers and 14 percent of all typists and word processors are college graduates.[8]

From time to time you'll hear reports of PhD's driving cabs, lawyers typing their own briefs, and doctors bogged down in paperwork. Perhaps there's some degree of

---

[8]Louis Uchitelle, "College Still Counts, Though Not as Much," *The New York Times,* October 2, 2005, Section 10, p. 4.

underemployment in almost everyone's future. All you can really do is avoid taking a job in which you are clearly underemployed. So when you're interviewing with prospective employers at your college placement office and that guy with the bakery truck shows up, just say no.

Questions for Further Thought and Discussion

1. If you were in a position to run our economy, what steps would you take to raise our rate of economic growth?

2. Under what circumstances can we operate outside our production possibilities curve?

3. Give an example of an opportunity cost for an individual and a nation.

4. Would it be harder for a nation to attain full employment or full production? Explain.

5. Could a nation's production possibilities curve ever shift inward? What might cause such a shift to occur?

6. What is the opportunity cost you incurred by going to college?

7. Although the U.S. is one of the world's wealthiest nations, some of the federal government's budget decisions are severely constrained by scarcity. Can you think of one such decision that was in the recent economic news?

8. Why is scarcity central to economics?

9. Can you think of any decisions you have recently made that incurred opportunity costs?

10. Do you know any entrepreneurs? What do they do?

11. Why is entrepreneurship central to every business firm?

12. Explain the law of increasing costs, using a numerical example.

13. Discuss the three concepts on which the law of increasing costs is based.

14. *Practical Application:* Underemployment of college graduates is a growing problem. If you were appointed to the board of trustees of your college, what measures would you suggest to alleviate this problem for the graduates of your school?

Workbook for Chapter 2 connect | ECONOMICS

Name _____   Date _____

Multiple-Choice Questions

Circle the letter that corresponds to the best answer.

1. The word that is central to the definition of economics is _____. (LO1)
   a) resource   c) scarcity
   b) wants   d) capital

2. We would not need to economize if _____. (LO2)
   a) the government printed more money
   b) there was no scarcity
   c) there was less output of goods and services
   d) everyone received a big pay increase

3. Human wants are _____. (LO1)
   a) relatively limited
   b) relatively unlimited
   c) easily satisfied
   d) about equal to our productive capacity

4. Which of the following is an economic resource? (LO3)
   a) gold   c) labor
   b) scarcity   d) rent

5. Each of the following is an example of capital except _____. (LO3)
   a) land   c) a computer system
   b) an office building   d) a factory

6. The opportunity cost of spending four hours studying a review book the night before a final exam would be _____. (LO4)
   a) the cost of the review book
   b) missing four hours of TV
   c) a higher grade on the exam
   d) the knowledge gained from studying

7. An economy operating its plant and equipment at full capacity implies a capacity utilization rate of _____. (LO5)
   a) 40 percent   c) 85 percent
   b) 70 percent   d) 100 percent

8. The full-production level of our economy implies _____. (LO5, 8)
   a) an efficient allocation of our resources
   b) zero unemployment
   c) our plant and equipment being operated at 100 percent capacity
   d) a high unemployment rate

9. Underemployment means _____. (LO5)
   a) the same thing as unemployment
   b) underutilization of resources
   c) a recession
   d) slow economic growth

10. The production possibilities curve represents _____. (LO6, 8)
    a) our economy at full employment but not full production
    b) our economy at full production but not full employment
    c) our economy at full production and full employment

11. If we are operating inside our production possibilities curve _____. (LO6)
    a) there is definitely a recession going on
    b) there is definitely not a recession going on
    c) there is definitely less than full employment
    d) there is definitely inflation

12. The closer we are to the origin and the farther away we are from the production possibilities curve _____. (LO6)
    a) the more unemployment there is
    b) the less unemployment there is
    c) the more guns we are producing
    d) the more butter we are producing

13. Economic growth will occur if any of the following occur except _____. (LO9)
    a) a better technology becomes available
    b) the level of consumption rises and the savings rate falls
    c) more capital becomes available
    d) more labor becomes available

14. To attain a higher rate of economic growth, we need to devote _____. (LO9)
    a) a higher proportion of our production to capital goods and a lower proportion to consumer goods
    b) a higher proportion of our production to consumer goods and a lower proportion to capital goods
    c) a higher proportion of our production to both consumer goods and capital goods
    d) a lower proportion of our production to both consumer goods and capital goods

15. Which is the most accurate statement? (LO3)
    a) Nearly every major economic innovation originated abroad and was then applied in the United States.
    b) The United States provides a poor environment for innovation.
    c) Freedom of thought, a risk-taking culture, and a noncorrupt bureaucracy have made the United States very hospitable to innovation.
    d) Although the United States was once the world's leading innovator, since we lost most of our manufacturing base, we are no longer a major innovator.

16. Which is the most accurate statement? (LO5)
    a) Most Americans are underemployed.
    b) Employment discrimination causes underemployment of labor.
    c) It is impossible for an economy to operate outside its production possibilities curve.
    d) There is no longer employment discrimination.

17. Statement 1: The old Negro leagues provide an example of underemployment.
    Statement 2: Underemployment means basically the same thing as unemployment. (LO5)
    a) Statement 1 is true and statement 2 is false.
    b) Statement 2 is true and statement 1 is false.
    c) Both statements are true.
    d) Both statements are false.

18. Employment discrimination is most closely related to _____. (LO5)
    a) specialization
    b) technology
    c) unemployment
    d) underemployment

19. Miranda Bowman, a Harvard MBA, is almost definitely _____ if she is working as a secretary. (LO5)
    a) unemployed
    b) underemployed
    c) both unemployed and underemployed
    d) neither unemployed nor underemployed

20. On the following list, the most serious problem facing today's college graduate is _____. (LO5)
    a) outsourcing of jobs to foreign countries
    b) employment discrimination
    c) unemployment
    d) underemployment

21. Which statement is true? (LO2, 3)
    a) America has always had a shortage of entrepreneurs.
    b) Our economic problem is that we have limited resources available to satisfy relatively unlimited wants.
    c) America has less economic resources today than we had 40 years ago.
    d) Aside from a few million poor people, we have very little scarcity in the United States.

22. Suppose you had $1,000 to spend. If you spent it on a vacation trip rather than on new clothes, your second choice, or 1,000 lottery tickets, your third choice, what was your opportunity cost of going on a vacation trip? (LO4)
    a) $1,000
    b) the vacation trip itself
    c) not buying the new clothes
    d) not buying the lottery tickets
    e) missing out on the $10 million lottery prize

23. Which of the following best describes the role of an entrepreneur? (LO3)
    a) the inventor of something with great commercial possibilities
    b) anyone who made a fortune by purchasing stock in a dot-com before its price shot up
    c) inventors who parlay inventions into commercial enterprises
    d) any employee earning at least $200,000 at a Fortune 500 company

24. As we produce increasing amounts of a particular good, the resources used in its production _____. (LO7)

a) become more suitable

b) become less suitable

c) continue to have the same suitability

25. The law of increasing costs is explained by each of the following except _____. (LO7)

a) the law of diminishing returns

b) diseconomies of scale

c) factor suitability

d) overspecialization

26. As a firm grows larger, _____. (LO7)

a) economies of scale set in, then diseconomies of scale

b) diseconomies of scale set in, then economies of scale

c) economies of scale and diseconomies of scale set in at the same time

d) neither economies of scale nor diseconomies of scale set in

27. The law of increasing costs states that, as _____. (LO7)

a) output rises, cost per unit rises as well

b) the output of one good expands, the opportunity cost of producing additional units of this good increases

c) economies of scale set in, costs increase

d) output rises, diminishing returns set in

28. If Figure 1 shows our production possibilities frontier during World War II, at which point were we operating? (LO6)

a) point A

b) point B

c) point C

d) point D

29. If Figure 1 shows our production possibilities frontier during the Great Depression, at which point were we operating? (LO6)

a) point A

b) point B

c) point C

d) point D

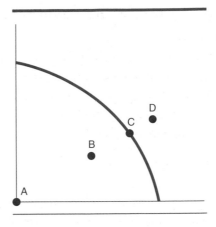

F*igure* 1

30. Which one of the following is the most accurate statement? (LO6, 9)

a) Our economy was at full employment in 2008 and 2009.

b) Our economy operated outside of its production possibilities curve in 2009 and 2010.

c) Our economy is currently operating on its production possibilities curve.

d) Our economy is currently operating inside its production possibilities curve.

31. Which statement is true? (LO6)

a) As our economy recovers from a recession, it moves closer to its production possibilities curve.

b) When an economy moves into a recession, it slides along its production possibilities curve.

c) We have never operated outside our production possibilities curve.

d) There is no way to represent a bad recession or a depression on a graph of the production possibilities curve.

32. Which one of the following statements is the most accurate? (LO6)

a) Half of all college graduates under 25 are unemployed.

b) Half of all college graduates under 25 are underemployed.

c) Half of all high school dropouts are underemployed.

d) Despite the recession, nearly all college graduates of the class of 2010 found jobs commensurate with their training and educational backgrounds.

Fill-In Questions

1. A PhD driving a cab would be considered _____. (LO5)

2. The central fact of economics is (in one word) _____. (LO2)

3. Human wants are relatively _____, while economic resources are relatively _____. (LO2, 3)

4. The law of increasing costs states that, as the output of one good expands, _____. (LO7)

5. The law of diminishing returns, diseconomies of scale, and factor suitability each provide an explanation for the law of _____. (LO7)

6. If you went into a store with $25 and couldn't decide whether to buy a pair of jeans or a jacket, and you finally decided to buy the jeans, what would be the opportunity cost of this purchase? _____. (LO4)

7. Full employment implies an unemployment rate of about _____ percent. (LO5)

8. List some constraints on our labor force that prevent our fully using our plant and equipment 24 hours a day, seven days a week. (LO5)

   (1) _____;

   (2) _____;

   and (3) _____.

9. Employment discrimination results in the _____ of our labor force. (LO5)

10. When we are efficiently allocating our resources and using the best available technology, we are operating on our _____. (LO6, 8)

11. Most of the time our economy is operating _____ its production possibilities frontier. (LO6)

12. Economic growth can be attained by: (LO9)

    (1) _____ and

    (2) _____.

Problems

1. If we were at point C of Figure 2 below, could we quickly produce substantially more houses *and* more cars? (LO6, 9)

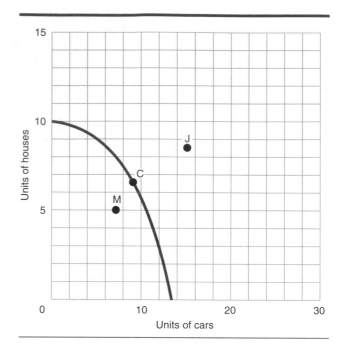

F*igure* 2

2. If we were at point M of Figure 2, could we quickly produce substantially more houses *and* more cars? (LO6, 9)

3. If we were at point C on Figure 2, could we quickly go to point J? (LO6, 9)

4. Fill in the following points on Figure 3. (LO6)

   Point X: where our economy generally operates

   Point Y: a serious recession

   Point Z: a catastrophic depression

   Point W: economic growth

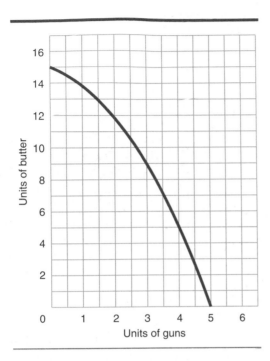

Figure 3

5. In Figure 4, fill in a new production possibilities frontier representing substantial economic growth. (LO6, 9)

6. In Figure 4, place point M where there is 100 percent unemployment. (LO6)

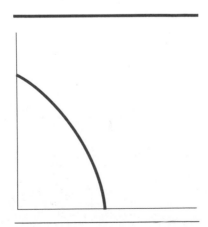

Figure 4

7. Fill in the following points on Figure 5. (LO6)

   Point A: an unemployment rate of 100 percent

   Point B: an unemployment rate of 20 percent

   Point C: an unemployment rate of 2 percent

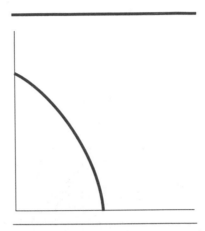

Figure 5

8. Given the information in Table 1, below, what is the opportunity cost of going from point B to point C? And of going from point D to point C? (LO4)

TABLE 1	Hypothetical Production Schedule for Two-Product Economy	
Point	Units of Butter	Units of Guns
A	15	0
B	14	1
C	12	2
D	9	3
E	5	4
F	0	5

9. Use Figure 6 to answer these questions: (LO6, 4)

    a) What is the opportunity cost of going from point B to point C?

    b) What is the opportunity cost of going from point D to point C?

    c) What is the opportunity cost of going from point B to point A?

    d) What is the opportunity cost of going from point C to point D?

10. Use the data in Figure 6 to illustrate the law of increasing costs numerically. (Hint: Start at point E and move toward point A.) (LO6, 7)

11. Put an X on Figure 7 to represent where our economy operated in 2010. (LO6)

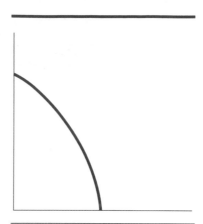

Figure 7

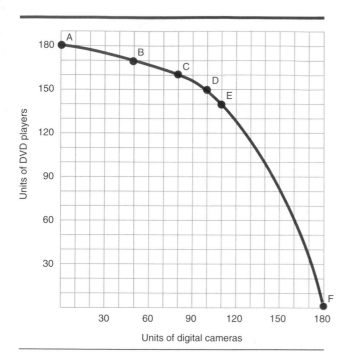

Figure 6

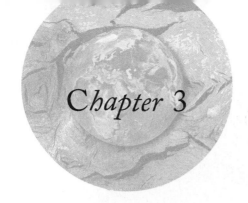

Chapter 3

The Mixed Economy

Ours is a mixed economy because there is a private sector and a public sector. Close to 90 percent of our goods and services originate in the private sector, although the government co-opts some of this production for its own use. China also has a mixed economy; the public sector produces about one-third the goods and services. Every economic system needs to put bread on the table, clothes on people's backs, and a roof over their heads. The question is how resources are used to attain these goods and services.

LEARNING OBJECTIVES

After reading this chapter you should be able to:

1. List and explain the three questions of economics.
2. Explain the concepts of the profit motive, the price mechanism, competition, and capital.
3. Analyze the circular flow model.
4. Describe and illustrate market failure and externalities.
5. Describe and explain government failure.
6. Discuss the economic role of capital and its importance.
7. Define and describe the "isms": capitalism, fascism, communism, and socialism.
8. Summarize and explain the decline and fall of the communist system.
9. Discuss the economic transformation of China.

The Three Questions of Economics

Because every country in the world is faced with scarce (limited) resources, every country must answer three questions: (1) What shall we produce? (2) How shall these goods and services be produced? (3) For whom shall the goods and services be produced? We'll take up each in turn.

What Shall We Produce?

In the United States, most of our production is geared toward consumer goods and services. About 5 percent goes toward defense. In the former Soviet Union, a much higher proportion was devoted to armaments, with a proportionately smaller percentage devoted to consumer goods and services. Japan has concentrated on building up its plant and equipment but devotes just 1 percent of its production to defense.

Who makes these decisions? In the United States and Japan there is no central planning authority, but rather a hodgepodge of corporate and government officials, as well as individual consumers and taxpayers. The Soviets *did* have a central planning authority. In

Military, consumption, or capital goods?

49

Figure 1

Sector Employment as
Percentage of Total
Employment, 1940–2010
The service sector, which accounted
for less than half the jobs in our
economy in 1940, now accounts for
82 percent.

Source: U.S. Census Bureau, *Statistical
Abstract of the United States,* 2010.

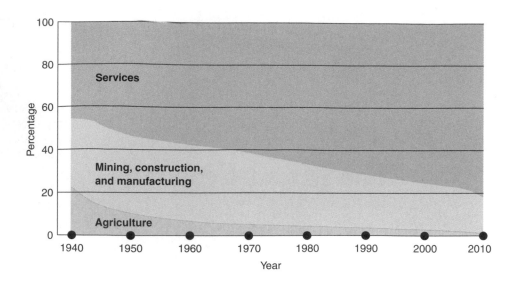

fact, every five years the Soviet government used to come up with a new plan that set goals for its economy in numbers of cars, TVs, factories, and bushels of wheat and corn to be produced.

As a nation matures, its economy shifts from agricultural to manufacturing, and then to services. This shift is reflected in employment (see Figure 1). Until about 150 years ago, most Americans worked on farms. But today, only 1 in 500 still farms full time. Today, four out of every five workers produce services.

How Shall These Goods and Services Be Produced?

In our country—and in most others as well—nearly everything is produced by private businesses. Not only are all the goods and services that consumers purchase produced by businesses, but so are most of what the government purchases. For example, when our astronauts landed on the moon, a long list of contractors and subcontractors was released. It read like a who's who in American corporations.

In socialist countries, of course, the government is the main producer of goods and services. But even in a communist country, China, there is still a substantial role for private enterprise.

For Whom Shall the Goods and Services Be Produced?

For whom shall the goods be produced?

Economics may be divided into two parts: production, which we dealt with in the first two questions, and distribution. In the first question, we asked what the economic pie should be made of; in the second, we talked about how the pie would be made. Now we are ready to divide up the pie.

Our distribution system is a modified version of one dollar, one vote. In general, the more money you have, the more you can buy. But the government also has a claim to part of the pie. Theoretically, the government takes from those who can afford to give up part of their share (taxes), spends some of those tax dollars to produce various government goods and services, and gives the rest to the old, the sick, and the poor. (Nevertheless, the rich reap a major share of the subsidies to airlines, shipping companies, defense contractors, and agriculture.)

Henry Fairlie has come up with a capitalist credo: From each according to his gullibility. To each according to his greed.

In theory, the Soviets' distributive system was diametrically opposed to ours. The communist credo "From each according to his ability, to each according to his needs" was something the Soviet leaders claimed to follow, and it does have a nice ring to it. But in actuality, their income distribution system, with its jerry-built structure of wage incentives, bonus payments, and special privileges, was probably no more equitable than our own.

To Sum Up

In a mixed economy, both the government and the market have roles in answering: (1) What shall we produce? (2) How shall these goods and services be produced? (3) For whom shall these goods and services be produced? In nearly all mixed economies the government plays a relatively minor role in production, but may play a relatively strong role in distribution.

The Invisible Hand, the Price Mechanism, and Perfect Competition

We have just set the stage for a comparison between our economic system and those of several other countries. We'll start with the competitive economic model, and then talk about the economic roles of government and of capital. These concepts, common to all economies, need to be understood before we can make comparisons among the economies of different nations.

The Invisible Hand

Adam Smith, Scottish professor of philosophy

When Adam Smith coined this term in 1776, he was thinking about an economic guidance system that always made everything come out all right. He believed that if people set out to promote the public interest, they will not do nearly as much good as they would if they pursued their own selfish interests. That's right! If all people are out for themselves, everyone will work harder, produce more, and we'll all be the richer for it. And that premise underlies the free-enterprise system.

Smith said that the entrepreneur is motivated by self-interest:

> He generally, indeed, neither intends to promote the public interest, nor knows how much he is promoting it. By preferring the support of domestic to that of foreign industry, he intends only his own gain, and he is in this, as in many other cases, led by an invisible hand to promote an end which was no part of his intention. . . . By pursuing his own interest he frequently promotes that of the society more effectually than when he really intends to promote it.[1]

Whenever a businessperson runs for public office, he or she invariably brings up the fact that his or her opponent never met a payroll. This businessperson, motivated solely by a quest for profits, provided jobs for perhaps hundreds, or even thousands, of people. His or her firm produced some good or service so desirable that buyers were willing to pay for it. And so, this aspiring politician, who went into business solely to make money, now claims credit for creating jobs and promoting the public interest. And not a word of thanks to the invisible hand.

Greed makes the world go round.

Some 20 years ago, about one-third of the food in the Soviet Union was produced on just 2 percent of the land under cultivation. That 2 percent was made up of small, privately owned plots; the other 98 percent was in the form of large collective farms. Obviously, the same farmers worked much harder on their own land than on the land whose produce was owned by the entire society. As Adam Smith said, a person pursuing his own interest "frequently promotes that of society more effectively than when he really intends to promote it."

The invisible hand is really the profit motive.

---

[1]Adam Smith, *The Wealth of Nations,* Book IV (London: Methuen, 1950), chap. II, pp. 477–78.

The Chinese communists, too, forced hundreds of millions of peasants to work on huge collective farms, and like the Soviet agricultural experiment, it had disastrous results. Robert Shiller wrote about the first American experiment in collective ownership:

> When they arrived in the New World, in 1620, the Pilgrims of Plymouth Colony tried communal ownership of the land. It didn't work: crops were not well cared for and the result was a severe food shortage. So in 1623 each family was given a private plot of land along with responsibility for maintaining it. This worked much better. As William Bradford, the second governor of Plymouth Colony, recounted in *Of Plymouth Plantation,* people worked harder when they had private plots, and the crop yield was much higher. The moral of this story—at least according to the proponents of private ownership who like to quote from it—is simple: people take better care of things they own individually than of things they hold in common.[2]

The Price Mechanism

It is often said that everyone has a price, which means that nearly all of us, for a certain sum of money, would do some pretty nasty things. The key variable here is *price*. Some of us would do these nasty things for $100, others for $1,000, others perhaps only for $1 million.

Not only does every*one* have a price, but every*thing* has a price as well. The price of a slice of pizza or a gallon of gasoline is known to all consumers. Although they vary somewhat, gas prices rarely fall below $2.00 and hardly anyone would pay $10 for a slice of pizza.

Prices send signals to producers and consumers.

Just as prices send signals to consumers, they also signal producers or sellers. If pizza goes up to $10 a slice, I'll put an oven in my living room and open for business the next day.

When consumers want more of a certain good or service, they drive the price up, which, in turn, signals producers to produce more. If the price rise is substantial and appears permanent, new firms will be attracted to the industry, thereby raising output still further.

During the 1970s, when we experienced some of the worst inflation in our history, many people called for price controls. These were very briefly and halfheartedly instituted by President Nixon, and their results in controlling inflation were decidedly mixed. Critics of controls believe they interfere with our price mechanism and the signals that mechanism sends to producers and consumers. Others, most notably John Kenneth Galbraith, have argued that the prices of our major products are administered or set by the nation's largest corporations rather than in the marketplace. What this disagreement boils down to is whether our economic system is basically competitive, with millions of buyers and sellers interacting in the marketplace, or whether our economy is dominated by a handful of corporate giants who have subverted the price system by setting prices themselves.

Competition

Competition makes the price system work.

What is competition? Is it the rivalry between Burger King and McDonald's? GM and Ford? Walmart and Target? Most economists will tell you that to have real competition, you need many firms in an industry. How many? So many that no firm is large enough to have any influence over price. So, by definition, an industry with many firms is competitive.

When Philip Morris or R. J. Reynolds announces its new prices, *those* are the prices for cigarettes. Of course, when Microsoft talks about the price of its latest version of Windows, everyone listens. No ifs, ands, or buts. No give-and-take in the marketplace. And the price mechanism? It just doesn't apply here.

To allow the price mechanism to work, we need many competing firms in each industry. There are entire industries—autos, computer software, oil refining, pharmaceuticals, retail bookstores, breakfast cereals, and long distance phone calls—which are dominated by no more than three or four firms.

---

[2]Robert J. Shiller, "American Casino," *The Atlantic Monthly,* March 2005, p. 33.

If large sectors of American industry are not very competitive, then the price system doesn't work all that well, and the invisible hand becomes even more invisible. However, even without a perfectly competitive economic system, we can't just toss the price mechanism out the window. The forces of supply and demand, however distorted, are still operating. With all their price manipulation, even the largest corporations must guide themselves by the wishes of their consumers. In conclusion, then, let's just say that we have an imperfectly functioning price system in a less than competitive economy that is guided by a not too vigorous invisible hand.

Trust

You'll find the saying, "IN GOD WE TRUST," printed on the back of our currency. Some cynic made up another saying, "In God we trust; all others pay cash"—which means, we suspect that your check might bounce, so we insist on being paid right now in cash.

But despite our cynicism, capitalism is based on trust. Lenders expect borrowers to pay them on time and in full. Sellers ship goods or provide services in advance of payment. And although all businesses guard against theft, the presumption is that the people you deal with are not out to steal from you. Indeed, we build up business relationships over time, and those relationships are based largely on trust.

Capitalism is based on trust.

Because of that underlying trust, business flows smoothly in virtually all capitalist societies. Although the parties to major transactions are bound by formal legal contracts, day-to-day business is usually conducted in person, by phone, by fax, or by e-mail.

Imagine doing business in a socialist or communist economy. You need to order a pencil. So you make out a purchase order, hand it to your supervisor, the purchase order goes up through five more levels of authority, and is then sent to a government purchasing agency where it might sit for several months before some bureaucrat gets around to taking the necessary action. If you're lucky, you'll have your pencil by the end of the year.

Of course government agencies are not all so inefficient, but the reason they are often so bound by rules and regulations is the presumption that bureaucrats can't be trusted to make any business decisions on their own. Under capitalism, we assume that individuals will do the right thing, and because most people are quite trustworthy, the system works very efficiently.

Equity and Efficiency

Under our economic system, most of the important decisions are made in the marketplace. The forces of supply and demand (that is, the price system) determine the answers to the three basic questions we raised at the beginning of the chapter: What? How? And for whom? Most economists would agree that this system leads to a very efficient allocation of resources, which, incidentally, happens to conform to our definition of economics: *Economics is the efficient allocation of the scarce means of production toward the satisfaction of human wants.*

So far, so good. But does our system lead to a fair, or equitable, distribution of income? Just look around you. You don't have to look far to see homeless people, street beggars, shopping-bag ladies, and derelicts. Indeed, there are about 37 million Americans whom the federal government has officially classified as "poor." Later in this chapter, we'll see that one of the basic functions of our government is to transfer some income from the rich and the middle class to the poor. Under the capitalist system, there are huge differences in income, with some people living in mansions and others in the streets. One of the most controversial political issues of our time is how far the government should go in redistributing some of society's income to the poor.

Is our income distributed fairly?

Very briefly, the case for efficiency is to have the government stand back and allow everyone to work hard, earn a lot of money, and keep nearly all of it. But what about the people who don't or can't work hard, and what about their children? Do we let them starve to death? The case for equity is to tax away some of the money earned by the relatively well-to-do and redistribute it to the poor. But doing so raises two questions:

✗ (1) How much money should we redistribute? and (2) Won't this "handout" just discourage the poor from working? We'll discuss this further in the chapter on income distribution and poverty toward the end of the book.

The Circular Flow Model

In Chapter 2 we talked about the four basic resources—land, labor, capital, and entrepreneurial ability. Who owns these resources? We all do. Nearly all of us sell our labor, for which we earn wages or salaries. In addition, many people own land or buildings for which they receive rent. A landlord may have just one tenant paying a few hundred dollars a month, or she may own an office building whose rent is reckoned by the square foot.

We also may receive interest payments for the use of our funds. Since much of the money we put into the bank is borrowed by businesses to invest in plant and equipment, we say that interest is a return on capital.

Finally, there are profits. Those who perform an entrepreneurial function (that is, own and run a business) receive profits for income.

What do people do with their incomes?

The question we are asking here is: What do people *do* with their incomes? What happens to the tremendous accumulation of rent, wages and salaries, interest, and profit? Mostly, it is spent on consumer goods and services, which are produced by private businesses.

This is the essence of what economists call the *circular flow model*. A model is usually a smaller, simplified version of the real thing. (Think of a model plane, a model ship, a map, or a globe.) An economic model shows us how our economy functions, tracing the flow of money, resources, and goods and services. Let's take the circular flow model step by step.

First we have some 117 million households receiving their incomes mainly from the business sector. A household may be a conventional family—a father, mother, and a couple of children—it may be a person living alone, or it may be two cohabiting adults. Any combination of people under one roof—you name it—is defined as a household.

Who owns our resources? It is not the employer who pays wages—he only handles the money. It is the product that pays wages.

—Henry Ford

We diagram the household income stream in Figure 2. Businesses send money income (rent, wages and salaries, interest, and profits) to households. We've ignored the government sector (that is, Social Security checks, welfare benefits, food stamps) and the foreign trade sector.

In Figure 3 we show where this money goes. It goes right back to the businesses as payment for all the goods and services that households buy. In sum, the households provide business with resources—land, labor, capital, and entrepreneurial ability—and use the income these resources earn to buy the goods and services produced by these same resources.

In effect, then, we have a circular flow of resources, income, goods and services, and payments for these goods and services. By combining Figures 2 and 3, we show this circular flow in Figure 4.

There are two circular flows.

We can distinguish two circular flows in Figure 4. In the inner circle, we have resources (land, labor, capital, and entrepreneurial ability) flowing from households to business firms. The business firms transform these resources into goods and services, which then flow to the households.

The outer circular flow is composed of money. Households receive wages and salaries, rent, interest, and profits from business firms. This money is spent on goods and services, so it is sent back to business firms in the form of consumer expenditures.

Thus we have two circular flows: (1) money and (2) resources, and goods and services. These two flows represent the economic activities of the private sector. Whenever any transaction takes place, someone pays for it, which is exactly what *does* happen whenever we do business.

Although the circular flow model may appear fairly complex, it actually oversimplifies the exchanges in our economy by excluding imports, exports, and the government sector. I leave it to your imagination to picture the additional flow of taxes, government purchases, and transfer payments such as unemployment and Social Security benefits. We shall now look at the government's economic role, but our analysis will be separate from our analysis of the private sector.

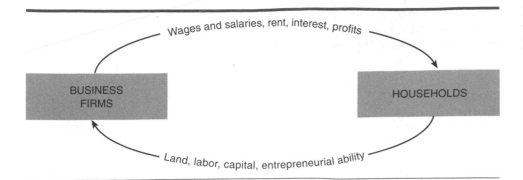

Figure 2

The Flow of Resources and Payments for Them

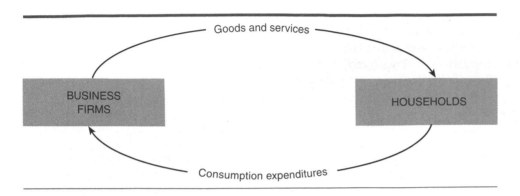

Figure 3

The Flow of Goods and Services, and Payments for Them

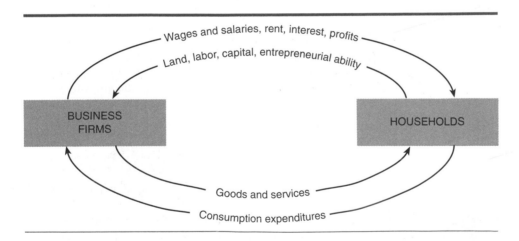

Figure 4

The Circular Flow

The Economic Role of Government

The government under our federal system has three distinct tiers. At the top is the federal, or national, government, which we generally refer to as "the government." There are also 50 state governments and tens of thousands of local governments.

Each of these units of government collects taxes, provides services, and issues regulations that have a profound effect on our economy. By taxing, spending, and regulating, the government is able somewhat to alter the outcome of the three questions: What? How? and For whom?

The government provides the legal system under which our free enterprise [e]
can operate. It enforces business contracts and defines the rights of private [ ]
Our legal system works so well that bribery is the very rare exception, [ ]
rule, as it is in so many other countries, especially in Asia and Africa.

56   CHAPTER 3

Everyone wants to live at the expense of the state. They forget that the state lives at the expense of everyone.

—Frederic Bastiat

The government also maintains our competitive system and ensures the relatively unfettered operation of the law of supply and demand. Barriers to competition are sometimes broken down by the government, particularly when a few large firms attempt to squeeze their smaller competitors out of a market. We'll discuss those efforts more fully in the chapter on corporate mergers and antitrust in *Economics* and in *Microeconomics*.

Some of what we produce is done in response to government demand for roads, schools, courthouses, stamp pads, and missile systems. Government regulations have prevented business firms from producing heroin, cyclamates (from the mid-1960s to the late 1970s), and alcoholic beverages (from 1920 to 1933), as well as prostitutes' services (except in part of the state of Nevada, where they are legal).

How things are produced is also influenced by child labor laws, health and safety regulations, and pollution control. And finally, the government, by taking over $3 trillion away from wage earners in taxes, redistributes some of these funds to the old, the disabled, and the poor, thus strongly altering the outcome of the question "For whom?"

The government must provide the infrastructure for a market system to function efficiently. In addition to ensuring that competition flourishes, the government must see that information flows freely, that property rights are protected, and that unpleasant side effects such as pollution are minimized.

Market Failure

Markets don't always provide the most desirable economic outcomes. For example, we assume a great deal of competition among firms, but what happens when some firms grow larger and larger, driving out their smaller competitors? What if one giant firm like Microsoft corners almost the entire market? In the chapter on corporate mergers and antitrust in *Economics* and *Microeconomics*, we'll see how the government has intervened to preserve competition.

When our resources are not allocated efficiently, we have market failure. So while we might prefer to leave as much as we can to the forces of demand and supply, it is sometimes necessary for the government to take action.

We'll examine three basic classes of market failure: externalities, environmental pollution, and the lack of public goods and services. Each provides the government with the opportunity to improve on the work of Adam Smith's invisible hand.

Externalities

Your own property is at stake when your neighbor's house is on fire.

—Horace (Roman poet)

When you drive to school, how much does your ride cost you? Once you figure in the cost of gas, oil, insurance, and the depreciation on your car, you might come up with a figure of, say, 35 cents a mile. We call this the cost the *private cost* of driving to school.

But there's also an *external cost.* You emit a certain amount of pollution and congestion, and we could even factor in the cost of highway construction and maintenance. It would be hard to actually come up with a monetary figure, but there is no question that your drive to school imposes a definite social, or external, cost on everyone else.

You probably never thought that driving to school was such a terrible thing, especially if there is no convenient public transportation. But you will be happy to know you are capable of doing many socially beneficial things as well. If you paint your house or plant a beautiful garden in your front yard, you will not only add to the beauty of the neighborhood, but you will also enhance its property values. So now you are providing an *external benefit.*

Let's define external cost and external benefit. *An external cost occurs when the production or consumption of some good or service inflicts costs on a third party without compensation. An external benefit occurs when some of the benefits of the production or consumption of some good or service are enjoyed by a*

External cost

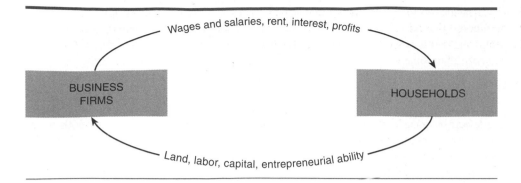

Figure 2

The Flow of Resources and Payments for Them

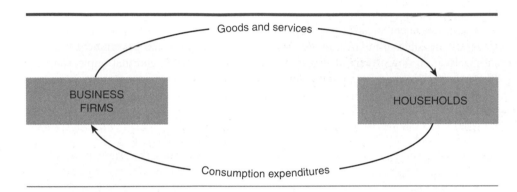

Figure 3

The Flow of Goods and Services, and Payments for Them

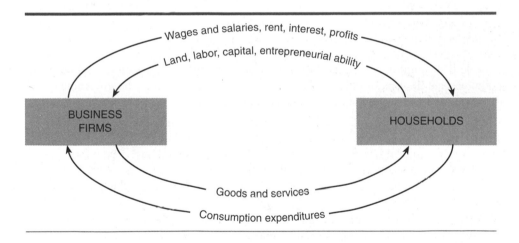

Figure 4

The Circular Flow

The Economic Role of Government

The government under our federal system has three distinct tiers. At the top is the federal, or national, government, which we generally refer to as "the government." There are also 50 state governments and tens of thousands of local governments.

Each of these units of government collects taxes, provides services, and issues regulations that have a profound effect on our economy. By taxing, spending, and regulating, the government is able somewhat to alter the outcome of the three questions: What? How? and For whom?

The government provides the legal system under which our free enterprise economy can operate. It enforces business contracts and defines the rights of private ownership. Our legal system works so well that bribery is the very rare exception, rather than the rule, as it is in so many other countries, especially in Asia and Africa.

The government also maintains our competitive system and ensures the relatively unfettered operation of the law of supply and demand. Barriers to competition are sometimes broken down by the government, particularly when a few large firms attempt to squeeze their smaller competitors out of a market. We'll discuss those efforts more fully in the chapter on corporate mergers and antitrust in *Economics* and in *Microeconomics.*

Some of what we produce is done in response to government demand for roads, schools, courthouses, stamp pads, and missile systems. Government regulations have prevented business firms from producing heroin, cyclamates (from the mid-1960s to the late 1970s), and alcoholic beverages (from 1920 to 1933), as well as prostitutes' services (except in part of the state of Nevada, where they are legal).

How things are produced is also influenced by child labor laws, health and safety regulations, and pollution control. And finally, the government, by taking over $3 trillion away from wage earners in taxes, redistributes some of these funds to the old, the disabled, and the poor, thus strongly altering the outcome of the question "For whom?"

The government must provide the infrastructure for a market system to function efficiently. In addition to ensuring that competition flourishes, the government must see that information flows freely, that property rights are protected, and that unpleasant side effects such as pollution are minimized.

Market Failure

Markets don't always provide the most desirable economic outcomes. For example, we assume a great deal of competition among firms, but what happens when some firms grow larger and larger, driving out their smaller competitors? What if one giant firm like Microsoft corners almost the entire market? In the chapter on corporate mergers and antitrust in *Economics* and *Microeconomics,* we'll see how the government has intervened to preserve competition.

When our resources are not allocated efficiently, we have market failure. So while we might prefer to leave as much as we can to the forces of demand and supply, it is sometimes necessary for the government to take action.

We'll examine three basic classes of market failure: externalities, environmental pollution, and the lack of public goods and services. Each provides the government with the opportunity to improve on the work of Adam Smith's invisible hand.

Externalities

Your own property is at stake when your neighbor's house is on fire.

–Horace (Roman poet)–

When you drive to school, how much does your ride cost you? Once you figure in the cost of gas, oil, insurance, and the depreciation on your car, you might come up with a figure of, say, 35 cents a mile. We call that 35 cents the *private cost* of driving to school.

External cost

But there's also an *external cost.* You cause a certain amount of pollution and congestion, and we could even factor in the cost of highway construction and maintenance. It would be hard to actually come up with a monetary figure, but there is no question that your drive to school imposes a definite social, or external, cost on society.

You probably never thought that driving to school was such a terrible thing, especially if there is no convenient public transportation. But you will be happy to know that you are capable of doing many socially beneficial things as well. If you paint your house and plant a beautiful garden in your front yard, you will not only add to the beauty of your neighborhood, but you will also enhance its property values. So now you are providing an *external benefit.*

External benefit

Let's define *external cost* and *external benefit. An external cost occurs when the production or consumption of some good or service inflicts costs on a third party without compensation. An external benefit occurs when some of the benefits derived from the production or consumption of some good or service are enjoyed by a third party.*

Definition of external cost and benefit

Shipbreaking

When ships grow too old and expensive to run—usually after about 25 or 30 years—their owners sell them on the international scrap market, where the typical freighter may bring a million dollars for the weight of its steel. Are the ship owners behaving in an environmentally correct manner, like those of us who return our soda cans to the grocery or deposit them in recycling bins? It turns out that they are not.

About 90 percent of the world's annual crop of 700 condemned ships are sailed right up on the beaches of China, Pakistan, India, and Bangladesh, where they are dismantled. Predictably, these once pristine beaches have become an environmental wasteland. In an *Atlantic Monthly* article, William Langewiesche describes the risks to which the workers are exposed: "falls, fires, explosions, and exposure to a variety of poisons from fuel oil, lubricants, paints, wiring, insulation, and cargo slop. Many workers are killed every year."[*]

What the United States and other industrial nations have done is exported our environmental problems to the less developed countries of the world. Langewiesche explains how this came about:

Shipbreaking was performed with cranes and heavy equipment at salvage docks by the big shipyards of the United States and Europe until the 1970s, when labor costs and environmental regulations drove most of the business to the docksides of Korea and Taiwan. Eventually, however, even these entrepreneurial countries started losing interest in the business and gradually decided they had better uses for their shipyards. This meant that the world's shipbreaking business was again up for grabs. In the 1980s enterprising businessmen in India, Bangladesh, and Pakistan seized the initiative with a simple, transforming idea: to break a ship they did not need expensive docks and tools; they could just wreck the thing—drive the ship up onto a beach as they might a fishing boat, and tear it apart by hand.[†]

---

[*]William Langewiesche, "The Shipbreakers," *The Atlantic Monthly,* August 2000, p. 34.
[†]Ibid., p. 33.

The private market, governed solely by the forces of supply and demand, does not take into account external costs and external benefits. This is market failure. When the market failure imposes a high cost on society, we demand that the government do something about it.

Basically, the government can take three types of action. If you are doing something that provides an external benefit, such as running a family farm, the government may provide you with a subsidy to encourage you to continue farming. As we saw back in Chapter 1, although the federal government has paid out hundreds of billions of dollars in farm subsidies since the 1930s, not only have most family farms disappeared, but huge corporate farms have gotten most of the subsidies.

If you are incurring external costs, the government can discourage these activities in two ways. It can tax you, or it can impose stringent regulations.

Let's consider what the government can do about air and water pollution. It could tax these activities highly enough to discourage them. A hefty tax on air pollution will force the biggest offenders to install pollution-abatement equipment. What about the disposal of nuclear waste? Do we let nuclear power plants dump it into nearby rivers but make them pay high taxes for the privilege? Hardly. The federal government heavily regulates nuclear plants.

Basically, we want to encourage activities that provide external benefits and discourage those that incur external costs. One method now used in many states is the five-cent deposit on cans and bottles. Millions of people have a monetary incentive to do the right thing by returning these bottles and cans for recycling.

A major part of the external costs of manufacturing and commerce affect our environment. Obvious examples include strips of tires along the highways, abandoned cars, acid rain, and toxic waste. The accompanying box discusses an international example of external costs—shipbreaking.

Air pollution and water pollution are perhaps the two greatest external costs of industrial economies. Let's see how the government can curb pollution.

Curbing Environmental Pollution

The incentive to pollute is much stronger than the incentive to curb pollution.

Left to its own devices, private enterprise creates a great deal of pollution. After all, it's a whole lot easier—and cheaper—to dump waste products into nearby rivers and streams, or send them up a smokestack. The government, most notably the federal Environmental Protection Agency, has taken two types of measures to lower pollution levels—command-and-control regulations and incentive-based regulations.

Command-and-Control Regulations   Automobile fuel-burning emissions are a major cause of air pollution. The federal government has imposed three regulations which have substantially reduced these emissions—mandating the use of catalytic converters on all new vehicles, fuel economy standards for all new cars, and a ban on leaded gasoline. Overall, these regulations have greatly reduced air pollution from motor vehicles. However, fuel economy standards were supposed to be raised periodically (more miles per gallon), but these increases have been periodically postponed. Furthermore, these standards are applied just to new cars, exempting minivans and sports utility vehicles (SUVs), which are classified as light trucks, and not subject to the fuel standards. Today cars are just half of all new passenger vehicles.

Since the passage of the Clean Air Act in 1972, which requires companies to reduce air pollution, there has been a marked improvement in air quality throughout much of the United States. During the decade of the 1990s alone, concentrations of sulfur dioxide and carbon monoxide decreased by 36 percent, and lead by 60 percent.

Do command-and-control regulations work? Clearly they do. But can we do better? Nearly all economists would agree we can do better using incentive-based regulations.

Incentive-Based Regulations   How can we give people an incentive to cause less air pollution? Why don't we raise gasoline taxes to the same levels as in Western Europe? Can you guess why we don't? Imagine that you are a member of Congress getting ready to vote on raising the federal tax on gasoline to $4 a gallon. Your constituents back home would not be very happy campers, and, if you were planning any kind of political future, you would not vote for this tax increase.

Emissions rights trading

Perhaps the most promising approach to incentive-based regulations is emissions rights trading, which originated as a result of the 1990 Amendments to the Clean Air Act. The government determines the permissible level of pollution and issues permits to each polluting firm. These permits allow up to a certain level of pollution, and the firms are allowed to buy or sell the permits.

What level of pollution is acceptable to you? Would you be willing to give up driving to reduce auto emissions to zero? Would you be willing to use a lot less electricity to curb emissions of electrical power plants? In general, would you be willing to accept a substantially lower standard of living if that would result in substantially less pollution? I think it's a pretty safe bet that your answer is "No!" to all three questions.

on the web

You can check out the pollution problems in your own neighborhood at www.epa.gov/epahome/commsearch.htm.

Lack of Public Goods and Services

A wide range of goods and services is supplied by our federal, state, and local governments. These include national defense; a court system; police protection; the construction and maintenance of streets, highways, bridges, plus water and sewer mains; environmental protection; public parks; and public schools. Few of these would be supplied by private enterprise because entrepreneurs would not be able to make a profit.

Interestingly, many of these goods and services *were* once supplied by private enterprise. The nation's first toll road, Pennsylvania's Lancaster Turnpike, was built two centuries ago. Private toll bridges were constructed all over the country. Even today, there are more than twice as many people who work in private security ("rent-a-cops," store and hotel detectives, building security, campus security, and private investigators, for example) than there are city and state police. Our national rail lines were once privately owned, with such fabled names as the Pennsylvania (or Pennsy) Railroad; the Baltimore and Ohio (you'll still find the B&O on the Monopoly board); the Seaboard; the Southern; the Great Northern; the New York Central; the New York, New Haven, and Hartford; the Boston and Maine; the Southern Pacific; and the storied Atchison, Topeka, and the Santa Fe.

Difference between public and private goods

Let's talk about the difference between *public* goods and *private* goods. Private goods are easy. You buy a car. It's your car. But a public good is something whose consumption by one person does not prevent its consumption by other people. Take our national defense. If you want to pay to have your home defended from nuclear attack, then everyone on your block is defended as well, even though they don't chip in a cent. Or, if your block association hires a private security firm to patrol your neighborhood, even your neighbors who were too cheap to pay their dues are protected.

Not everything produced by the public sector is a public good. We mentioned defense as a public good—something whose consumption by one person does not prevent its consumption by other people. What about a ride on a public bus? Or driving on the Jersey Turnpike? These are not public goods because only those who pay get to ride.

Public goods and services have two defining characteristics. First, they are *nonexcludable,* which means that once it exists, everyone can freely benefit from it. You can benefit from unpolluted air whether or not you helped pay for it. Second, public goods and services are *nonrivalrous,* which means that one person's benefiting from it does not reduce the amount of it available for others. Police protection for you does not prevent others from also enjoying that protection.

The two defining characteristics of public goods and services

Public goods tend to be indivisible; they usually come in large units that cannot be broken into pieces for purchase or sale in private markets. Often there is no way they can be produced by private enterprise because there is no way to exclude anyone from consuming the goods even if she or he did not pay for them. National defense is a classic example. Could you imagine putting *that* service on a pay-as-you-go basis? "I think this year I'll just skip being defended." We can't exactly move the nuclear umbrella away from my house while continuing to shield those of all my neighbors.

Not everyone favors an expansion of public goods. Aristotle observed that "What is common to many is taken least care of, for all men have a greater regard for what is their own than for what they possess in common with others." Public property is often not as well maintained as private property, because, as Aristotle noted, people will take better care of their own property than of property held in common.

Government Failure

Just as the market sometimes fails us, so does the government. Below is a short list of some of the more blatant forms of government failure. Keep in mind, however, that in most cases the government performs its functions reasonably well, so these failures should be considered exceptions and not the norm.

The United States is the only country where it takes more brains to figure your tax than to earn the money to pay it.
—Edward J. Gurney

Let's start with an obvious failure—our complex and confusing federal tax code. It costs taxpayers (in accounting fees as well as in the value of their own time) about $150 billion a year to complete their tax returns.[3] According to the Internal Revenue Service it takes 28 and a half hours to complete an average tax return with itemized deductions. The present system is so complicated that about 60 percent of all taxpayers rely on professionals to do their taxes. Even the simplest form, 1040EZ, takes on average 3 hours and 43 minutes to fill out.

The hardest thing in the world to understand is the income tax.
—Albert Einstein

Closely related are the forms the government sends all large and most medium-sized companies. It takes hundreds of hours a year to fill out these monthly, quarterly, and

---

[3]It costs business firms an additional $125 billion to comply with our tax code.

annual forms. The government compiles copious statistics on the economy, which it then publishes in thousands of monthly, quarterly, and annual reports. I enjoyed dropping in to my local federal bookstore to peruse these publications and would usually buy a few. But the stores were closed in 2003 to save money. Question: Wouldn't it then have made sense to cut down on the number of these publications? And maybe not collect so much data, thereby freeing up tens of thousands of corporate employees?

Another abject government failure is its agricultural price support program, which currently costs the taxpayers $19 billion a year, and, since its inception more than seven decades ago, has cost hundreds of billions of dollars. What is the main purpose of this program? Ostensibly the purpose is to save the family farm. But since the 1930s millions of family farms have gone out of business; most of the payments now go to huge corporate farms.

A society should be judged largely by how it treats its children. Of the 39 million Americans living in poverty, more than half are children. In the 1960s President Lyndon Johnson declared a massive war on poverty, and some 30 years later came the Welfare Reform Act of 1996. And yet, today, one of every six American children is growing up poor.

Our public education system, once the envy of the world, is now the laughingstock. While we still have some of the finest schools of higher education, our elementary, middle, and high schools have been deteriorating for decades. The fact that we need to teach the three r's—reading, writing, and arithmetic—to millions of college students pretty much says it all. While all the blame for our failing educational system cannot be placed on the government's doorstep, the fact remains that getting a decent education has become a difficult challenge for most children. I am old enough to remember when high school graduates could actually read, write, and do some algebra and geometry.

Hurricane Katrina is still fresh enough in our memory that if I asked you to grade the government's response, I'm sure you would have a pretty strong opinion. You might give a failing grade to the state and local authorities, to the federal government, or to all three. But regardless of how the blame is apportioned, Hurricane Katrina provides a very clear example of government failure.

Millions of Americans helped the hurricane victims, directly or indirectly. But these private efforts were directed at ameliorating the suffering, rather than preventing it. In hindsight, New Orleans and its suburbs should have been fully evacuated, and once the flooding took place, those left behind should have been quickly rescued. Those were not jobs for individuals, voluntary organizations, or business firms, but mainly for the federal government.

Local and state officials, as well as the Army Corps of Engineers, knew only too well that New Orleans' levees would not be able to hold back the floodwaters produced by a major hurricane. Once the city began to flood, only federal agencies such as FEMA (Federal Emergency Management Agency) had the resources to deal with a catastrophe of this magnitude. While there are plenty of places to spread the blame of the slow and halting rescue and recovery effort, maybe someone should have sent President Bush a copy of the placard President Harry Truman kept on his desk. It read: "The buck stops here."

Like you, I have a pretty strong opinion of which government officials should be blamed. Dealing with hurricanes, other natural disasters, as well as terrorist attacks is very clearly a government function. In late August and early September of 2005 our government very badly failed the people on the Gulf Coast. Will our government be better prepared when the next disaster strikes?

In contrast to government failure, large companies such as Walmart, Home Depot, and FedEx were the first responders in the wake of Hurricane Katrina. The October 3, 2005 issue of *Fortune* sings the praises of these companies, which had, as our army generals like to say, boots on the ground. While the government took precious days to act, these and other large companies made plans days in advance, and put them into effect hours after the hurricane made landfall.

Just by staying open for business, these and other companies provided a lifeline to hurricane victims. Jessica Lewis, the co-manager of the Waveland, Mississippi Walmart, had to deal with two feet of water and tons of damaged stock. Here is an account of what she saw and how she reacted:

> As the sun set on Waveland, a nightmarish scene unfolded on Highway 90. She saw neighbors wandering around with bloody feet because they had fled their homes with no shoes. Some wore only underwear. "It broke my heart to see them like this," Lewis recalls. "These were my kid's teachers. Some of them were *my* teachers. They were the parents of the kids on my kid's sports teams. They were my neighbors. They were my customers."
>
> Lewis felt there was only one thing to do. She had her stepbrother clear a path through the mess in the store with a bulldozer. Then she salvaged everything she could and handed it out in the parking lot. She gave socks and underwear to shivering Waveland police officers who had climbed into trees to escape the rising water. She handed out shoes to her barefoot neighbors and diapers for their babies. She gave people bottled water to drink and sausages, stored high in the warehouse, that hadn't been touched by the flood. She even broke into the pharmacy and got insulin and drugs for AIDS patients. "This is the right thing to do," she recalls thinking. "I hope my bosses aren't going to have a problem with that."[4]

While all Walmart managers might not have acted as altruistically as Jessica Lewis, the company made a major difference simply by staying open, keeping their stores stocked with food and water, and, in keeping with their slogan, charging low, everyday prices. Unlike price gougers who drove into the disaster area to sell portable generators for $1,500, Walmart sold theirs at their regular $300 price.

Finally, let's talk about the Medicare drug prescription plan, which was rammed through Congress in 2005 by President George W. Bush and Republican Congressional leaders and has caused mass confusion among senior citizens, pharmacists, doctors, nursing home administrators, and the dozens of participating insurance companies. When the new plan went into effect in January 2006, hundreds of thousands of senior citizens were turned away by their pharmacies when they came in to have their prescriptions filled. It would be charitable to say that the system had some glitches that needed to be worked out. Writing in *The New York Times,* Jane Gross described some of the complexities of the drug prescription plan, and the problems they have caused:

> Even those who received their new prescription drug cards on time are not home free. Each person has an ID number, an Issuer number, an Rx Bin number, an Rx PCN number and an Rx Group number. Type one digit wrong when ordering medications and the computer flashes an error message.
>
> ...
>
> Each plan also has tiered subplans, labeled bronze, silver or gold. And each of those has its own formulary, the list of drugs that are covered, and its own appeals process for those that are not. But search the plans' websites looking for instructions for appeals. "Sorry, the document you request doesn't exist," comes the mannerly reply.[5]

Capital

Capital is the crucial element in every economic system. Karl Marx's classic *Das Kapital* examined the role of capital in the mid-19th-century industrializing economy of England. According to Marx, the central figure of capitalism is the capitalist, or business owner, who makes huge profits by exploiting his workers. Capital consists mainly of plant, equipment, and software. Marx said that whoever controlled a society's capital controlled that society.

Furthermore, Marx observed that one's social consciousness was determined by one's relationship to the means of production. Inevitably, he believed, there would be a clash between the capitalists and the workers, leading to an overthrow of capitalism and the establishment of a communist society. Then the workers would own the means of

Karl Marx, German economist, historian, and philosopher

---

[4]Devin Leonard, "The Only Lifeline Was the Wal-Mart," *Fortune,* October 3, 2005, p. 75.

[5]Jane Gross, "Nursing Homes Confront New Drug Plan's Hurdles," *The New York Times,* January 15, 2006, p. 16.

Where Capital Comes From

The following hypothetical situation will illustrate the value of capital. Suppose it takes a man 10 hours to make an optical lens, while someone working with a machine can make one in just 5 hours. Let's assume that it would take 1,000 hours to build such a machine.

Assume, however, that a person working 10 hours a day is barely able to support himself and his family. (Karl Marx observed that, in most working-class families, not only did wives work, but they didn't have to worry about day care centers or baby-sitters for the children because factories employed six- and seven-year-olds.) If he could not afford to spend 100 days (1,000 hours) building the machine, he still had two choices. He could cut back on his consumption—that is, lower his family's standard of living—by working nine hours a day on the lenses and one hour a day on building the machine. Or he could work, say, an extra hour a day on the machine.

In either case, it would take 1,000 days to build the machine. If he cut back on his consumption *and* worked

an extra hour a day, it would take him 500 days to build the machine.

Once he had the machine, he'd *really* be in business. He could double his daily output from one lens a day to two a day (remember that a person working with a machine can turn out a lens in just 5 hours).

Each day, if he held his consumption to the same level, he would produce two lenses and sell one for food, rent, and other necessities. The other lens he'd save. At the end of just 100 days, he'd have saved 100 lenses. Those 100 lenses represent 1,000 hours of labor, which is exactly the same amount of labor that went into building a machine. He would probably be able to buy another machine with those 100 lenses.

Now he's *really* a capitalist! He'll hire someone to run the second machine and pay him a lens a day. And in another 100 days, he'll have a surplus of 200 lenses, and he'll be able to buy two more machines, hire a foreman to run his shop, retire to a condominium in Miami Beach at the age of 36, and be the richest kid on the block.

Capital consists of plant and equipment.

The central economic role of capital

Where did capital come from?

production. In the Soviet Union, incidentally, the means of production *were* owned by the workers, but the ruling elite, the top Communist Party officials, had real economic and political control.

The role of capital in the production process is central to why our country is rich and most of the rest of the world is poor. The reason an American farmer can produce 10 or 20 times as much as a Nigerian farmer is that the American has much more capital with which to work—combines, tractors, harvesters, and reapers. And the reason the American factory worker is more productive than the Brazilian factory worker is that our factories are much better equipped. We have a tremendous stock of computers, assembly lines, warehouses, machine tools, and so on.

Take the example of the word processor and its successor, the personal computer. In the past, a lot of business letters had to be personally or individually typed, although they were really only form letters. Today we have a PC that can be programmed to print identical texts with different addresses at the rate of one letter every couple of seconds.

Our stock of capital enables us to turn out many more goods per hour of labor than we could produce without it. Much backbreaking as well as tedious labor has been eliminated by machines. Without our capital, we would have the same living standard as that of people living in the poorer countries of Asia, Africa, and Latin America.

Where did capital come from? Essentially from savings. Some people would set aside part of their savings, go into business, and purchase plant and equipment (see the box, "Where Capital Comes From"). But we're really skipping a step.

Initially there was no capital, except for some crude plows and other farm tools. People worked from sunrise to sunset just to produce enough food to put on the table. But a few farmers, a little more prosperous than their neighbors, were able to spare some time to build better farm tools. Or they might have had enough food stored away to employ someone to build these tools. Either way, some productive resources were diverted from producing consumer goods to producing capital goods.

The factory conditions of the 19th-century England that Marx described in *Das Kapital* were barbaric, but the end result was that a surplus of consumer goods was produced. The factory owner, by paying his workers meager wages, was able to use this surplus to buy more capital goods. These enabled his factory to be more productive, creating still greater surpluses that were used to purchase still more plant and equipment.

Under Joseph Stalin, the Russians devoted a large part of their production to capital goods, literally starving the Russian population of consumer goods. To this day there is a great shortage of consumer goods in the former Soviet Union. But this shortage is no longer due to diversion of resources from production of consumer goods to the production of capital goods. It is due to the inefficiencies of the economic system itself—something we'll be looking at more closely in the closing pages of this chapter.

In the years following World War II, Japan and the countries of Western Europe, struggling to rebuild their shattered economies, held down their consumption as they concentrated on building new plant and equipment. The South Koreans and Taiwanese later followed this model of building capital.

The world's developing nations face nearly insurmountable obstacles—rapidly growing populations and very little plant and equipment. The experience of the industrializing nations in the 19th century was that, as people moved into cities from the countryside and as living standards rose, the birthrate invariably declined. But for industrialization to take place, capital must be built up. There are two ways to do this: Cut consumption or raise production. Unfortunately, most developing nations are already at subsistence levels, so no further cuts in consumption are possible without causing even greater misery. And production cannot easily be raised without at least some plant and equipment.

With the exception of the OPEC nations, which have been able to sell their oil in exchange for plant and equipment, the poorer nations of Africa, Asia, and Latin America have little hope of rising from extreme poverty. A supposed exchange of letters that took place between Mao Tse-tung and Nikita Khrushchev when China and the Soviet Union were allies in the early 1960s illustrates the futility of a third way out—foreign aid.

> Mao: Send us machinery and equipment.
> Khrushchev: Tighten your belts.
> Mao: Send us some belts.

Capital is past savings accumulated for future production.

    —Jackson Martindell

Capital is the key to our standard of living.

The "Isms": Capitalism, Communism, Fascism, and Socialism

> Q: What is the difference between capitalism and socialism?
> A: Under capitalism, man exploits man. Under socialism, it's just the opposite.
>
>   –Overheard in Warsaw–[6]

> Property is the exploitation of the weak by the strong.
> Communism is the exploitation of the strong by the weak.
>
>   –Pierre-Joseph Proudhon–[7]

During the 20th century, perhaps no three opprobriums have been hurled more often at political opponents than those of Communist! Capitalist! and Fascist! Let's compare the four great economic systems. Capitalism, as we've already seen, is characterized by private ownership of most of the means of production—that is, land, labor, capital, and entrepreneurial ability. Individuals are moved to produce by the profit motive. Production is also guided by the price system. Thus, we have millions of people competing for the consumer's dollar. The government's role in all of this is kept to a minimum; basically, it ensures that everyone sticks to the rules.

Since the early 1980s there has been a huge swing throughout much of the world towards capitalism. First capitalism took root in China, and a decade later in the former Soviet Union and in what had been its satellite empire in Eastern Europe as well. Today the great preponderance of the world's output of goods and services is produced under capitalism.

Capitalism

---

[6]Lloyd G. Reynolds, *Microeconomic Analysis and Policy,* 6th ed. (Burr Ridge, IL: Richard D. Irwin, 1988), p. 435.
[7]Pierre-Joseph Proudhon, *What Is Property?* chap. V, Part II.

Capitalism is often confused with democracy. A democracy has periodic elections in which the voters freely choose their rulers. Most capitalistic nations—for example, the United States, Japan, and the members of the European Union—are democracies.

On the opposite end of the political spectrum is the dictatorship, under which the rulers perpetuate themselves in power. Their elections do not have secret ballots, so predictably the rulers always win overwhelmingly. Indeed, Saddam Hussein received 100 percent of the vote in Iraq's 2002 presidential election.

Sometimes capitalistic dictatorships evolve into capitalistic democracies. Taiwan, South Korea, Indonesia, the Philippines, and Chile are recent examples. The Soviet Union, which has been going through a painful conversion from communism to capitalism, now holds relatively free elections, and could be considered a democracy. There are hopes that China will also evolve into a democracy. But the leaders of the Communist Party, who have handed power down from one generation to the next, show no signs of allowing free elections.

"The theory of the Communists may be summed up in the single sentence: Abolition of private property," declared Karl Marx and Friedrich Engels in *The Communist Manifesto*. Who would own everything? The state. And eventually the state would wither away and we would be left with a workers' paradise.

In the Soviet version of communism, under which the state had evidently not yet withered away, most of the capitalist roles were reversed. Instead of a guidance system of prices to direct production, a government planning committee dictated exactly *what* was produced, *how* it was produced, and *for whom* the goods and services were produced. After all, the state owned and operated nearly all of the means of production and distribution.

All of the resources used had to conform to the current five-year plan. If the goal was 2 million tractors, 100 million tons of steel, 15 million bushels of wheat, and so on, Soviet workers might have expected to be putting in a lot of overtime.

The big difference between the old Soviet economy and our own is what consumer goods and services are produced. In our economy, the market forces of supply and demand dictate what gets produced and how much of it gets produced. But a government planning agency in the Soviet Union dictated what and how much was made. In effect, central planning attempted to direct a production and distribution process that works automatically in a market economy.

How well did the Soviet communist system work? Remember the chronic shortages of consumer goods we mentioned earlier in the chapter? Although Soviet president Mikhail Gorbachev went to great lengths to shake up the bureaucracy and get the economy moving again, his efforts were futile. To raise output, he found he needed to somehow remove the heavy hand of bureaucracy from the economic controls. But as he stripped away more and more of the Communist Party's power, he found that his own power had been stripped away as well.

If the Soviet Union did not exemplify pure communism, then what country did? In the box, "Real Communism," you'll read that we have had pure communism right under our noses for many years.

One of the fundamental economic problems with *any* economy that attempts to substitute government planning for the price system (or to replace the law of demand and supply with government decrees) is that changes in price no longer help producers decide what and how much to produce. In a capitalist country, higher microwave oven prices would signal producers to produce more microwave ovens. But in the Soviet Union, there was very little inflation even though there were widespread shortages of consumer goods. In fact, the Soviets came up with a great cure for inflation. Just let everyone wait in line.

The entire Soviet economy was a Rube Goldberg contraption[8] of subsidies, fixed prices, bureaucratic rules and regulations, special privileges, and outright corruption. Had Gorbachev not acted, the entire Soviet system might well have come apart by itself over another couple of generations.

A joke that circulated in the late 1980s went like this: Under communism your pockets are full of money, but there isn't anything in the stores you can buy with it. Under capitalism, the stores are full, but you have no money in your pockets.

Communism

Communism doesn't work because people like to own stuff.
—Frank Zappa, Musician

Communist: A fellow who has given up all hope of becoming a capitalist.
—Orville Reed

They pretend to pay us, and we pretend to work.
—Polish folk definition of communism

Communism was a great system for making people equally poor.
—Thomas Friedman

---

[8]Such a device is designed to accomplish by complex means what seemingly could be done simply.

Real Communism

Several years ago, I knew a history professor at St. Francis College in Brooklyn who loved to shock his students by telling them that he had been a communist. As a young man, he had joined a Catholic religious order, lived in a commune, and shared all his possessions with his fellow seminarians. "What could be more communist than living in a commune with no private property?" he asked his students.

And so we may ask whether what they had in the Soviet Union and in Eastern Europe was really communism. How would Karl Marx have reacted to those huge bureaucratic dictatorships? Marx had foreseen "the withering away of the state," until all that was left was a society of workers who followed his credo "From each according to his ability; to each according to his needs." This sounds a lot more like that history professor's seminary than what was passing for communism in the old Soviet empire.

The Soviet regime collapsed not just because of its bureaucratic inefficiencies but also because it supported a huge military establishment that claimed between one-fifth and one-quarter of its resources and national output.

In 1922 Benito Mussolini took power in Italy, leading the world's first fascist government. "Fascism should more appropriately be called corporatism, because it is the merger of state and corporate power," he declared. In effect, then, fascism turned large corporations into extension of government, while centralizing governmental authority in one person. Although Mussolini's Italy followed this model, it was Hitler's Germany, a decade later, that truly placed power in the hands of an absolute dictator.

Fascism hasn't been in vogue since Hitler's defeat in 1945, but it does provide another model of an extreme. In Nazi Germany the ownership of resources was in private hands, while the government dictated what was to be produced.

Fascism

The problem with describing the fascist economic model is that there really *is* no model. The means of production are left in private hands, with varying degrees of governmental interference. Generally those in power are highly nationalistic, so a high proportion of output is directed toward military goods and services.

Fascists have been virulently anticommunist but have also been completely intolerant of any political opposition. The one-party state, suppression of economic freedom, and a militaristic orientation have been hallmarks of fascism.

The early 1940s were evidently the high-water mark of fascism. Although from time to time a fascist state does pop up, it appears to be a temporary phenomenon. With the possible exception of Hitler's Germany, which did put most Germans back to work after the Great Depression, albeit largely at military production, most fascist states have been economic failures that apparently collapsed of their own weight.

Socialism has not gotten the bad press that capitalism, fascism, and communism have received, perhaps because those who dislike the socialists prefer to call them communists. In fact, even Soviet government officials used to refer to themselves as socialists and their country, the U.S.S.R., was formally called the Union of Soviet Socialist Republics, although President Ronald Reagan referred to the Soviet Union as the evil empire. And the countries with socialist economies were our military allies.

Socialism

It is a socialist idea that making profits is a vice; I consider the real vice is making losses.
—Winston Churchill

The economies of such countries as Sweden, Canada, Great Britain, and, recently, France and Greece have been described as socialist, not only by government officials in those countries but by outside observers as well. In general, these economies have three characteristics: (1) government ownership of some of the means of production; (2) a substantial degree of government planning; and (3) a large-scale redistribution of income from the wealthy and the well-to-do to the middle class, working class, and the poor.

The vice of capitalism is that it stands for the unequal sharing of blessings; whereas the virtue of socialism is that it stands for the equal sharing of misery.
—Winston Churchill

One of the most familiar characteristics of socialist countries is cradle-to-grave security. Medical care, education, retirement benefits, and other essential needs are guaranteed to every citizen. All you need to do is be born.

Where does the money to pay for all of this come from? It comes from taxes. Very high income taxes and inheritance taxes fall disproportionately on the upper middle class and the rich. In Israel several years ago, a joke went around about a man who received an unusually large paycheck one week. He couldn't figure out what had happened until his wife looked at his check stub and discovered that he had been sent his deductions by mistake. Only the very wealthy must give the government more than half their pay in socialist countries, but the story *did* have a ring of truth to it.

Rather than allow the market forces to function freely, socialist governments sometimes resort to very elaborate planning schemes. And since the government usually owns the basic industries and provides the basic services, this planning merely has one hand directing the other.

Swedish socialism

Sweden is often considered the archetypal socialist country, although perhaps 90 percent of the country's industry is privately owned. It is the government's massive intervention in the private economy that gives Swedish society its socialist tone. Not only has the Swedish government kept the unemployment rate generally below 3 percent for several decades by offering industry and workers a series of subsidies and incentives, but it provides one of the most elaborate cradle-to-grave programs in the world. The government doles out $100 monthly allowances for each child and provides day care centers, free education from nursery school through college, free medical care, and very generous unemployment and retirement benefits. Women may take a year off work after the birth of a child while receiving 80 percent of their pay.

Norwegian socialism

But Sweden's brand of socialism pales in comparison to that of Norway, its Scandinavian neighbor. In addition to free day care, subsidized housing and vacations, and free medical care, Norwegians receive annual stipends of more than $1,600 for every child under 17, retirement pay for homemakers, and 44 weeks of fully paid maternity leave. How do they pay for all of this? Not only does Norway have the world's highest income tax rates, but it has a 23 percent sales tax and a gasoline tax of about $5 a gallon. Hallmarks of Norwegian society are a great disdain for the trappings of wealth and power and a profound sense of equality, which militate against a wide disparity in pay.

Perhaps this joke, which has made its rounds on the Internet, may best sum up the four isms:

Socialism: You have two cows. State takes one and gives it to someone else.
Communism: You have two cows. State takes both of them and gives you milk.
Fascism: You have two cows. State takes both of them and sells you milk.
Capitalism: You have two cows. You sell one and buy a bull.

The Decline and Fall of the Communist System

Under Joseph Stalin and his successors, from the late 1920s through the 1960s, Soviet economic growth was very rapid, as government planners concentrated on building the stock of capital goods, largely neglecting consumer goods. The government purposely set prices on consumer goods very low, often not changing them for decades. They wanted even the poorest people to be able to afford the basic necessities.

By the late 1970s, China began reforms, very gradually evolving into a market economy. However the Soviet Union, through the 1980s, continued to stagnate, devoting most of its talent and capital to its military establishment. Most of its armed forces served, basically, as an army of occupation in Eastern Europe. By the time that army was withdrawn, in 1989, and defense expenditures slashed, the Soviet Union was in political turmoil. Within two years the communists, along with the huge central planning apparatus, were gone, and the Soviet Union was dismembered into 15 separate nations, the largest of which was Russia.

Transformation in China

For decades before they attained power, the Chinese communists depicted themselves as agrarian reformers who would provide hundreds of millions of landless peasants with their own farms. But soon after attaining power they abolished virtually all private property and forced about 90 percent of the population to live and work on huge collective farms.

The communists came to power in 1949, taking over one of the world's poorest nations. For the first three decades, largely under Mao Tse-tung (his friends called him Chairman

Mao, and he liked the rest of the Chinese to refer to him as "the Great Helmsman"), the Chinese economy was dominated by Soviet-style central planning. Even though the economy absorbed two extremely disruptive setbacks—the Great Leap Forward (1958–60), during which perhaps 30 million people starved to death, and the Cultural Revolution (1966–75), both of which Mao used to consolidate power—economic growth may have averaged 9 or 10 percent a year. China was pulled up from a backward country plagued by periodic famine to one in which everyone had enough to eat and many could afford to buy TVs, refrigerators, cameras, and some of the other amenities we in the United States take for granted. In 1978 there were 1 million TV sets in China; by 1998 there were nearly 300 million. Today China leads the world with more than 800 million cellphone users.

In China, as in the former Soviet Union, the big boss of a province, or of the entire country, has held the modest title of First Secretary of the Communist Party. Back in 1978 a man named Zhao Ziyang was the First Secretary in Szechuan province, which was becoming world famous for its wonderful cuisine. Until 1978, the highly centralized Chinese planning system had slowed economic growth. Zhao issued an order that year freeing six state-owned enterprises from the control of the central planners, allowing the firms to determine their own prices and output, and even to keep any profits they earned. In just two years some 6,600 firms had been cut loose, Zhao had become the Chinese head of state, and China was well on its way to becoming a market, or capitalist, economy.

The shift toward capitalism

The farmers employed by the huge collective farms had little incentive to work hard. As John McMillan noted, "It made little difference whether a farmer worked himself to exhaustion or dozed all day under a tree. Either way, the amount he took home to feed his family was much the same."[9]

Beginning in 1979 many provincial leaders across China, independent of the central authorities in Beijing, shifted the responsibility of operating huge collective farms to the families that lived on the farms. Although each family was given a production quota to meet, any additional output could be sold at a profit. By 1984 more than 90 percent of China's agricultural land was farmed by individual households. In just six years food output rose by 60 percent.

In the late 1970s and early 1980s, reform began to take hold in the industrial sector as well. State firms were free to sell any surplus output, after having met their quotas. Simultaneously millions of tiny family-run enterprises were springing up all across the land, ranging from street peddlers, owners of tiny restaurants, and bicycle repair shops, to large factories and international trading companies. By the late 1980s, many of these large private factories were at least partially owned by Chinese businessmen from Hong Kong and Taiwan, as well as by investors from Japan, other Asian countries, and even some from Western Europe and the United States. China's southern provinces, and especially her coastal cities, have become veritable "export platforms," sending out a stream of toys, consumer electronics, textiles, clothing, and other low-tech products mainly to consumers in Japan, Europe, and North America. Between 1978 and 2000, Chinese exports rose from $5 billion to more than $200 billion, and by 2007 to $1.2 trillion. In 2009 its export surplus with the United States was $227 billion.

The agricultural and industrial reforms diluted the ideological purity that had marked the first 30 years of communist rule. In 1984 the Communist Party's Central Committee went so far as to depart from the traditional communist credo "From each according to his ability, to each according to his needs." The new slogan was "More pay for more work; less pay for less work." What this did, implicitly, was to say to budding entrepreneurs, "It's OK if you get rich—you worked hard for your money."

To get rich is glorious.
—Deng Xiaoping

Although average family income has at least quintupled since 1978, China remains a relatively poor agricultural nation with two-thirds of its population living in rural areas. But it has 1.3 billion people (one out of every five people on this planet lives in China), and it has become a world class industrial power. Already the world's largest exporter, China passed Japan in 2009 to become the number one automobile producer.

China today, despite its lip service to following the precepts of communism, has a basically capitalist economy. Although a couple of hundred large state enterprises

---

[9]John McMillan, *Reinventing the Bazaar* (New York: W. W. Norton, 2002), p. 94.

continue to spew out industrial goods, about three-quarters of the nation's output is produced by privately owned firms. Today more Chinese have stock brokerage accounts than are members of the communist party.

Current Issue: The Bridge to Nowhere

If the quest for profits motivates business owners, then what motivates members of Congress? They want to get reelected. And they're quite good at it: Over 98 percent of our representatives get reelected every two years.

The most effective campaign issue of every member of Congress is that they can bring home the bacon. They can point to the highways, bridges, rapid transit systems, military bases, and courthouses for which the federal government shelled out hundreds of millions of dollars. Never mind that, in the process, we have been running record federal budget deficits. The important thing is that your representative delivers.

Every member of Congress has a very strong incentive to bring home as much federal money as possible. So we have 435 Congressional districts competing for this money. It doesn't matter whether the projects are good or bad as long as the money is being spent. So what we have here is systematic government failure.

A handful of states, Alaska among them—are so sparsely populated that they have just one member of the House of Representatives. Alaska, for example, the third least populated state, is represented by Don Young, who happened to be the chairman of the House Committee on Transportation and Infrastructure. So perhaps it was no coincidence that when the Transit Act of 2005 was passed, Alaska got $941 million, the fourth largest amount received by any state. The two key projects funded were $231 million for a bridge near Anchorage called the "bridge to nowhere" and $233 million for another bridge connecting the tiny village of Ketchikan to an island with 50 inhabitants.

The "bridge to nowhere," to be formally called "Don Young's Way," would connect Anchorage with a swampy undeveloped port. The Ketchikan bridge would carry an estimated 100 cars a day, saving them a seven-minute ferry ride. So if the federal government would foot the bill, Alaska would take the money and run.

In 2006, in response to the widespread ridicule of this dubious project, Congress removed the federal earmark for the bridge, but allowed Alaska to use the money for other transportation projects. Among them was a $25 million "road to nowhere," which was built on the island—actually an access road to the nonexistent bridge. Faithful to its name, virtually no one among the island's 50 residents seems to make use of this road.

Questions for Further Thought and Discussion

1. The circular flow model is a simplified version of our economy. Describe how this model works.

2. What are the three basic economic questions that all economies must answer? Describe the differences in the ways capitalism and socialism answer these questions.

3. What was Adam Smith's invisible hand, and what economic function did it serve?

4. What are the two basic classes of market failure? What would be an example of each?

5. Can you think of any other government failures in addition to those listed in the chapter?

6. How far has China evolved into a market economy? To what degree has this evolution contributed to China's economic growth?

7. For many years Americans referred to the People's Republic of China as "Communist China." Why would that label be misleading today?

8. Explain why you would prefer to live in a socialist or a capitalist country.

9. *Practical Application:* Conduct your own investigation of government waste. Go to Google.com, type in "government waste," and compile a list of wasteful spending projects.

Workbook for Chapter 3 — connect ECONOMICS

Name _____   Date _____

Multiple-Choice Questions

Circle the letter that corresponds to the best answer.

1. We have a mixed economy because
   _____. (LO1)
   a) we produce guns and butter
   b) we consume domestically produced goods as well as imports
   c) we consume both goods and services
   d) there is a private sector and a public sector

2. Which does not fit with the others? (LO2)
   a) competition
   b) government planning and regulation
   c) the invisible hand
   d) the price mechanism

3. Adam Smith believed the best way to promote the
   public interest was to _____. (LO2)
   a) have the government produce most goods and services
   b) let people pursue their own selfish interests
   c) wait for individuals to set out to promote the public interest
   d) get rid of the price mechanism

4. Our economy does a very good job with respect to
   _____. (LO2)
   a) both equity and efficiency
   b) equity, but not efficiency
   c) efficiency, but not equity
   d) neither equity nor efficiency

5. Which is the most accurate statement? (LO1, 9)
   a) No country could be classified as having a communist economic system.
   b) It could be argued that every nation has a mixed economy.
   c) The United States is basically a socialist economy.
   d) The Chinese economy is evolving away from capitalism and toward pure communism.

6. Adam Smith believed people are guided by all of the
   following except _____. (LO2)
   a) the profit motive   c) the public good
   b) self-interest   d) the invisible hand

7. The price system is based on _____. (LO2)
   a) government regulation (i.e., the government sets most prices)
   b) the individual whim of the businessperson who sets it
   c) the feelings of the individual buyer
   d) supply and demand

8. Which one of the following would be the best public
   policy? (LO4)
   a) Zero tolerance for pollution.
   b) Allow private business firms to curb their own pollution.
   c) Provide business firms with incentives to curb their pollution.
   d) Hold economic growth to a minimum until pollution levels are reduced substantially.

9. In the United States, nearly all resources are owned
   by _____. (LO1)
   a) the government   c) individuals
   b) business firms   d) foreigners

10. The pilgrims who settled Plymouth, Massachusetts,
    concluded that _____. (LO2)
    a) only a social society of collective ownership would make economic sense
    b) a capitalist society with large industrial corporations would make economic sense
    c) private ownership worked better than collective ownership
    d) from each according to his ability to each according to his wants was the best course to follow

11. Wages, rent, interest, and profits flow from
    _____. (LO3)
    a) business firms to households
    b) households to business firms
    c) business firms to the government
    d) the government to business firms

69

12. Private ownership of most of the means of production is common to _____. (LO7)
    a) capitalism and communism
    b) capitalism and fascism
    c) capitalism and socialism
    d) fascism and communism

13. The price mechanism is least important under _____. (LO2, 7)
    a) capitalism
    b) socialism
    c) fascism
    d) communism

14. The five-year plan had been the main economic plan of _____. (LO7, 8)
    a) the United States
    b) Sweden
    c) Nazi Germany
    d) the Soviet Union

15. Fascism peaked in the _____. (LO7)
    a) 1920s
    b) 1930s
    c) 1940s
    d) 1950s

16. The strongest criticism of Sweden's economic system has been that _____. (LO7)
    a) it provides too many benefits
    b) its taxes are too high
    c) its taxes are too low
    d) it doesn't provide enough benefits

17. The strongest indictment of the capitalist system was written by _____. (LO7)
    a) Adam Smith
    b) John Maynard Keynes
    c) Rose D. Cohen
    d) Karl Marx

18. Karl Marx said that _____. (LO7, 8)
    a) whoever controlled a society's capital controlled that society
    b) in the long run, capitalism would survive
    c) the U.S.S.R.'s communist system was "state capitalism"
    d) capitalists and workers generally had the same economic interests

19. The main reason the American farmer can produce more than the farmer in China is that he _____. (LO1, 6)
    a) has more land
    b) has more capital
    c) has more labor
    d) is better trained

20. Capital comes from _____. (LO2, 6)
    a) gold
    b) savings
    c) high consumption
    d) the government

21. An individual can build up his/her capital _____. (LO2)
    a) by working longer hours only
    b) by cutting back on consumption only
    c) by both cutting back on consumption and working longer hours
    d) only by borrowing

22. Which is the most accurate statement about shipbreaking? (LO4)
    a) It is generally done in a manner that is environmentally sound and that minimizes dangers to workers.
    b) It is an extremely profitable activity that is sought after by the world's largest shipbuilders.
    c) Ship owners whose boats have grown too old and expensive to run usually abandon them at sea or sink them.
    d) The United States and other industrial nations have exported their environmental problems like shipbreaking to less developed countries such as India, Bangladesh, and Pakistan.

Fill-In Questions

1. The invisible hand is generally associated with (a) the _____ and (b) _____. (LO2)

2. Adam Smith believed that if people set out to promote the public interest, they will not do nearly as much good as they will if they _____. (LO2)

3. Defense spending and police protection are examples of _____. (LO4, 5)

4. Painting the outside of your house and planting a garden in your front yard are _____ to your neighbors. (LO4)

5. When you drive, rather than walk or take public transportation, you incur social costs such as _____. (LO4)

6. _____ could be described as a merger of state and corporate power. (LO6)

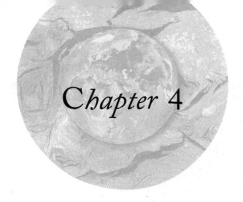

Chapter 4

Supply and Demand

A number 10
and 10B

Should your college charge you for parking, or should parking be free? Should the federal government put a ceiling of, say, $2 a gallon on gas prices? And should drug companies be forced to make prescription drug prices affordable to senior citizens? Our price system is constantly sending buyers and sellers thousands of signals. Running an economy without that system would be like flying a jumbo jet plane without an instrument panel.

Our economy has a built-in guidance system that allocates resources efficiently. This guidance system, which includes the interaction of the forces of supply and demand in the marketplace, is known as the price system. How does it work? You're about to find out.

How are you at reading graphs? Economists love to draw them, so if you're going to get through this course, you'll need to be able to read them. The main graph we like to draw has just two curves: the demand curve and the supply curve. By observing where they cross, we can easily find not only the price of a good or service, but the quantity sold.

LEARNING OBJECTIVES

After reading this chapter you should be able to:

1. Define and explain *demand* in a product or service market.
2. Define and explain *supply*.
3. Determine the equilibrium point in the market for a specific good, given data on supply and demand at different price levels.
4. Explain what causes shifts in demand and supply.

5. Explain how price ceilings cause shortages.
6. Explain how price floors cause surpluses.
7. Apply supply and demand analysis to real-world problems.

Demand

We define *demand as the schedule of quantities of a good or service that people are willing and able to buy at different prices.* And as you would suspect, the lower the price, the more people will buy.

How much would people living in Denver or in Chicago be willing and able to pay for a round-trip plane ticket for weekday travel between the two cities? Suppose we conducted a survey and were able to draw up a demand schedule like the one shown in Table 1.

Definition of demand: the schedule of quantities of a good or service that people are willing and able to buy at different prices.

71

TABLE 1	Hypothetical Daily Demand for Coach Seats on Round-Trip Weekday Flights between Denver and Chicago
Price	**Quantity Demanded**
$500	1,000
450	3,000
400	7,000
350	12,000
300	19,000
250	30,000
200	45,000
150	57,000
100	67,000

Figure 1

Hypothetical Daily Demand for Coach Seats on Round-Trip Weekday Flights between Denver and Chicago

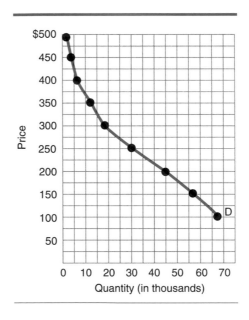

Note that, as the price declines, increasing quantities of tickets are demanded. Now look at Figure 1 to see how a graph of this demand schedule actually looks.

The demand curve slopes downward and to the right. That's because of the way we've set up our graph. Prices are on the vertical axis, with the highest price, $500, at the top. From here on, the vertical axis of every graph in this book will be measured in terms of money. The horizontal axis of Figure 1 measures the quantity sold, beginning with zero, at the origin of the graph, and getting to progressively higher quantities as we move to the right. In all the demand and supply graphs that follow, price will be on the vertical axis, and quantity on the horizontal.

Supply

Definition of supply: the schedule of quantities of a good or service that people are willing and able to sell at different prices.

Supply is defined as *the schedule of quantities of a good or service that people are willing and able to sell at different prices.* If you compare the definition of supply with that of demand, you'll find that only one word is changed. Can you find that word?

If you are a supplier, then you are willing and able to *sell* a schedule of quantities at different prices; if you are a buyer, then you are willing and able to *buy* a schedule of quantities at different prices. What's the difference, then, between supply and demand? At higher prices the suppliers are willing and able to sell larger and larger quantities, while the buyers are willing to buy smaller and smaller quantities. Similarly, as price declines, buyers are willing to buy more and sellers are willing to sell less. But we're getting a little ahead of ourselves, since you haven't yet been formally introduced to a supply schedule. So first check out Table 2, and then Figure 2, which is a graph drawn from the numbers in the table.

What happens, then, to quantity supplied as the price is lowered? It declines. It's as simple as that.

In our definitions of demand and supply, we talked about a schedule of quantities of a good or service that people are willing and able to buy or sell at different prices. But what if some buyers just don't have the money? Then those buyers are simply not counted. We say that they are not in the market. Similarly, we would exclude from the market any sellers who just don't have the goods or services to sell. I'd *love* to sell my services as a $600-an-hour corporate lawyer, but quite frankly, I just don't have those services to sell.

That brings us to a second factor not included in our definitions of supply and demand. The supply and demand for any good or service operates within a specific market. That market may be very local, as it is for food shopping; regional, as it is for used cars; national, as it is for news magazines; or even international, as it is for petroleum.

TABLE 2	Hypothetical Daily Supply for Coach Seats on Round-Trip Weekday Flights between Denver and Chicago
Price	Quantity Supplied
$500	62,000
450	59,000
400	54,000
350	48,000
300	40,000
250	30,000
200	16,000
150	7,000
100	2,000

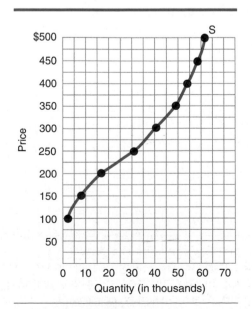

F*igure* 2

Hypothetical Daily Supply for Coach Seats on Round-Trip Weekday Flights between Denver and Chicago

Equilibrium

You've heard a lot about supply and demand—or is it demand and supply? It doesn't matter whether you put demand or supply first. What *does* matter is placing them together on the same graph. Look at Figure 3.

Can you find the equilibrium price? Did you say $250? Good! And how much is equilibrium quantity? Right again! It is 30,000.

Let's step back for a minute and analyze what we've just done. We've figured out the equilibrium price and quantity by looking at the demand and supply curves in Figure 3. So we can find equilibrium price and quantity by seeing where the supply and demand curves cross.

What is equilibrium price? It's the price at which quantity demanded equals quantity supplied. What is equilibrium quantity? It's the quantity sold when the quantity demanded is equal to the quantity supplied.

Equilibrium price is the price at which quantity demanded equals quantity supplied.

Surpluses and Shortages

Is the actual price, or market price, always equal to the equilibrium price? The answer is no. It could be higher and it could be lower. Suppose the airlines were selling tickets for $400. How many tickets would be demanded? Look back at Table 1 or, if you prefer, Figure 1 or Figure 3.

A total of 7,000 tickets would be demanded. And at a price of $400, how many tickets would be supplied?

Figure 3
Hypothetical Demand and Supply Curves

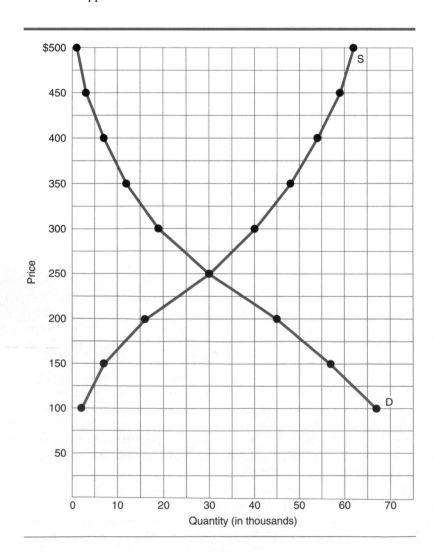

The quantity supplied would be 54,000. What we've got here is a surplus. This occurs when the actual price, or the market price, is greater than the equilibrium price. How much is that surplus? You can measure it by finding the horizontal distance between quantity demanded and quantity supplied in Figure 3. Or, you can subtract the quantity demanded that you found in Table 1 (at a price of $400) from the quantity supplied in Table 2 (also at a price of $400). Either way, the surplus comes to 47,000.

A surplus occurs when the market price is above the equilibrium price.

The quantity that sellers are willing and able to sell (54,000) is much greater than the quantity buyers are willing and able to buy (7,000). This difference (54,000 − 7,000) is the surplus (47,000). The amount that sellers can sell is restricted by how much buyers will buy.

What happens when there's a surplus? The forces of demand and supply automatically work to eliminate it. In this case, some of the airlines, which would be very unhappy about all those empty seats, would cut their prices. If the market price fell to $300, would there still be a surplus?

A glance at Figure 3 tells us that there would be. And how much would that surplus be?

It would be 21,000 seats. So *then* what would happen?

Some of the airlines would cut their prices to $250, and the buyers would flock to them. The other airlines would have no choice but to cut their price—or stop flying the Denver–Chicago route altogether. At $250, we would be at the equilibrium point. There would be no tendency for the price to change.

What if the market price were below equilibrium price? Then we'd have a shortage. How much would that shortage be if the market price in Figure 3 were $200?

A shortage occurs when the market price is below the equilibrium price.

At a price of $200, quantity demanded would be 45,000, while quantity supplied would be just 16,000. So the shortage would be 29,000.

This time the buyers would be disappointed, because they would be quite happy to pay $200 for a round-trip ticket, but most would be unable to get one without waiting for months. Many of the buyers would be willing to pay more. So what do you think would happen?

You guessed it! The market price would rise to $250. At that price—the equilibrium price—quantity demanded would equal quantity supplied, and the shortage would be eliminated.

Thus we can see that the forces of demand and supply work together to establish an equilibrium price at which there are no shortages or surpluses. At the equilibrium price, all the sellers can sell as much as they want and all the buyers can buy as much as they want. So if we were to shout, "Is everybody happy?" the buyers and sellers would all shout back "yes!"

Shifts in Demand and Supply

So far we've seen how the forces of demand and supply, or the price mechanism, send signals to buyers and sellers. For example, the surplus that resulted from a price of $400 sent a clear signal to sellers to cut their prices. Similarly, a price of $200 was accompanied by a shortage, which made many buyers unhappy. And sellers quickly realized that they could raise their price to $250 and *still* sell all the tickets they wanted to sell.

Now we'll see how shifts in supply curves and shifts in demand curves change equilibrium price and quantity, thereby sending new sets of signals to buyers and sellers. Figure 4 has a new demand curve, D_2. This represents an increase in demand because it lies entirely to the right of D_1, the original demand curve. There has been an increase in demand if the quantity demanded is larger at every price that can be compared.

Why did the demand for airline tickets increase? Let's say that newer planes were introduced that cut travel time by 30 percent.

I'd like you to find the new equilibrium price and the new equilibrium quantity. When you do, please write down your answers.

The new equilibrium price is $300, and the new equilibrium quantity is 40,000. So an increase in demand leads to an increase in both equilibrium price and quantity.

EXTRA HELP

How Changes in Demand Affect Equilibrium

If demand falls and supply stays the same, what happens to equilibrium price and equilibrium quantity? To answer those questions, sketch a graph of a supply curve, S, and a demand curve, D_1. Then draw a second demand curve, D_2, representing a decrease in demand. I've done that in this figure.

The original equilibrium price was $50, and the original equilibrium quantity was 10. Equilibrium price fell to $35, and equilibrium quantity fell to 8. So a decrease in demand leads to a decrease in equilibrium price and quantity.

What would happen to equilibrium price and equilibrium quantity if demand rose and supply stayed the same? Equilibrium price and quantity would rise.

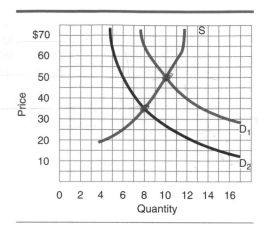

Figure 4
Increase in Demand

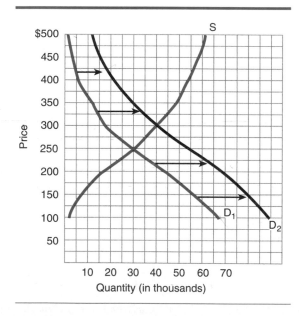

Next question: What would happen to equilibrium price and quantity if there were a decrease in demand?

There would be a decrease in both equilibrium price and quantity. Need a little extra help? Then see the box, "How Changes in Demand Affect Equilibrium."

OK, one more set of shifts and we're out of here.

Figure 5 shows an increase in supply. You'll notice that the new supply curve, S_2, is entirely to the right of S_1. There has been an increase in supply if the quantity supplied is larger at every price that can be compared.

Why did supply increase? Let's assume that the cost of jet fuel fell by 50 percent. In response, the airlines scheduled more flights. Please find the new equilibrium price and quantity, and write down your answers.

The new equilibrium price is $200, and the new equilibrium quantity is 45,000. So an increase in supply lowers equilibrium price and raises equilibrium quantity. One last question: If supply declines, what happens to equilibrium price and equilibrium quantity?

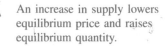

An increase in supply lowers equilibrium price and raises equilibrium quantity.

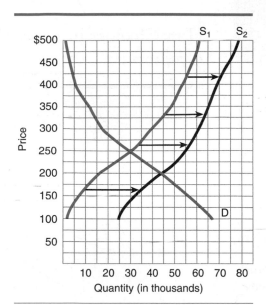

Figure 5
Increase in Supply

Now let's work out a couple of problems. First, look at Figure 6 and write down your answers to this set of questions: (*a*) If the supply curve is S$_1$, how much are the equilibrium price and quantity? (*b*) If supply changes from S$_1$ to S$_2$, does that represent an increase or decrease in supply? (*c*) How much are the new equilibrium price and quantity?

Here are the answers: (*a*) $13; 275; (*b*) decrease; and (*c*) $14; 225.

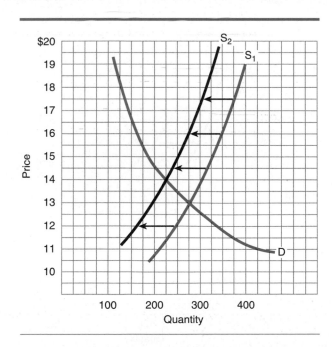

Figure 6

When supply declines, equilibrium price rises and equilibrium quantity declines. As you make your way through this text, supply and demand graphs will pop up from time to time. In every case you'll be able to find equilibrium price and quantity by locating the point of intersection of the demand and supply curves. If you need extra help, see the box, "How Changes in Supply Affect Equilibrium."

Next problem: Use Figure 7 to answer these questions: (*a*) If the demand curve is D$_1$, how much are the equilibrium price and quantity? (*b*) If demand changes from D$_1$ to D$_2$, does that represent an increase or decrease in demand? (*c*) How much are the new equilibrium price and quantity?

How Changes in Supply Affect Equilibrium

If supply rises and demand stays the same, what happens to equilibrium price and equilibrium quantity? Again, to answer those questions, sketch a graph of a demand curve, D_1, and a supply curve, S_1. Then draw a second supply curve, S_2, representing an increase in supply. I've done that in this figure.

The original equilibrium price was $12, and the original equilibrium quantity was 20. Equilibrium price fell to $9, and equilibrium quantity rose to 26. So an increase in supply leads to a decrease in equilibrium price and an increase in equilibrium quantity.

What happens to equilibrium price and equilibrium quantity if supply falls and demand stays the same? Equilibrium price rises and equilibrium quantity falls.

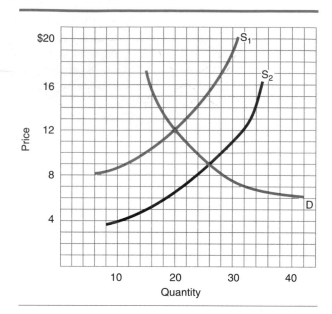

Figure 7

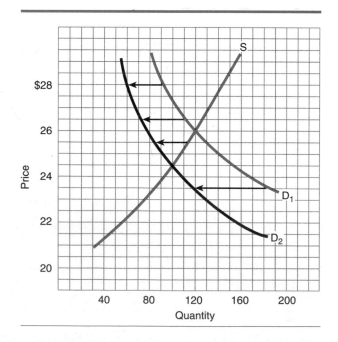

Here are the answers: (*a*) $26; 120; (*b*) decrease; and (*c*) $24.50; 100.

OK, you're taking an exam, and here's the first question: Demand rises and supply stays the same. What happens to equilibrium price and quantity? Just sketch a graph (like the one in Figure 4). Then you'll see that an increase in demand raises equilibrium price and quantity.

What happens to equilibrium price and quantity when there's a decrease in demand? Again, just sketch a graph, and you'll see that a decrease in demand lowers equilibrium price and quantity.

Next question: What happens to equilibrium price and quantity when there's an increase in supply? If your sketch looks like the one in Figure 5, you'll see that an increase in supply leads to a lower equilibrium price and a higher equilibrium quantity.

And finally, how does a decrease in supply affect equilibrium price and quantity? A decrease in supply leads to a higher equilibrium price and a lower equilibrium quantity.

Now let's return to that exam. When you're asked: How does an increase or decrease in demand affect equilibrium price and quantity, what do you do?

You just sketch a graph of a demand curve and a supply curve, and then another demand curve representing an increase or decrease in demand. Similarly, if you're asked how an increase or decrease in supply affects equilibrium price and quantity, just draw a sketch. It leads you to the right answers.

Price Ceilings and Price Floors

One of the most popular sayings of all time is "You can't repeal the law of supply and demand." Maybe not, but our government sure has a lot of fun trying. Price floors and price ceilings, which Washington has imposed from time to time, have played havoc with our price system. And taxes on selected goods and services have also altered supply and demand.

What's the difference between a floor and a ceiling? If you're standing in a room, where's the floor and where's the ceiling? As you might expect, economists turn this logic upside down. To find floors, we need to look up. How high? Somewhere above equilibrium price. And where are ceilings? Just where you'd expect economists to place them. We need to look down, somewhere below equilibrium price. A *price floor* is so named because that is the lowest the price is allowed to go in that market. Similarly, a *price ceiling* is the highest price that is allowed in that market.

Figure 8 illustrates a price floor. Equilibrium price would normally be $10, but a price floor of $15 has been established. At $15 businesses are not normally able to sell everything they offer for sale. Quantity supplied is much larger than quantity demanded. Why? At the equilibrium price of $10, sellers are willing to sell less while buyers are willing to buy more.

At a price of $15, there is a surplus of 30 units (quantity demanded is 20 and quantity supplied is 50). The government has created this price floor and surplus to keep the price at a predetermined level. This has been the case for certain agricultural commodities, most notably wheat and corn. It was hoped that these relatively high prices would encourage family farms to stay in business. That the bulk of farm price support payments has gone to huge corporate farms has not discouraged Congress from allocating billions of dollars a year toward this end.

The way the government keeps price floors in effect is by buying up the surpluses. In the case of Figure 8, the Department of Agriculture would have to buy 30 units.

You can't repeal the law of supply and demand.

Floors and surpluses

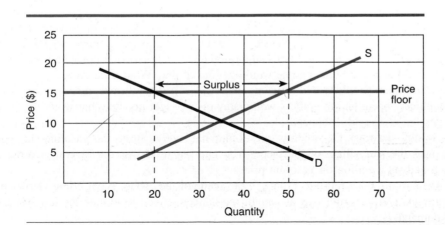

Figure 8

Price Floor and Surplus

The price can go no lower than the floor. The surplus is the amount by which the quantity supplied is greater than the quantity demanded.

Another important price floor is the minimum wage. As of July 24, 2009 the vast majority of Americans are guaranteed a minimum of $7.25 an hour. On that date the minimum hour wage is scheduled to increase from $6.55. Unless your job is not covered under the Fair Labor Standards Act, you are legally entitled to at least this wage rate.

Price ceilings are the mirror image of price floors. An example appears in Figure 9. Price ceilings are set by the government as a form of price control. "No matter what," the government tells business firms, "don't charge more than this amount."

Ceilings and shortages

A ceiling prevents prices from rising. The last time we had widespread price ceilings was during World War II. Because ceilings cause shortages, a rations system was worked out to enable everyone to obtain their "fair share" of such commodities as butter, meat, and sugar.

I remember World War II. I remember the ration books and the coupons you'd tear out when you went to the store. But chances are, even your parents don't remember the war, with its attendant shortages and rationing.

Ceilings and gas lines

Those over 35 may remember the gas lines we had in 1979, and real old-timers even recall the ones we had back in 1973. If not, imagine waiting a couple of hours in a line of cars six blocks long just to fill up your tank. What was the problem? In 1973 it was the Arab oil embargo, while the crisis in 1979 was set off by the Iranian Revolution.

How shortages are eliminated

In both cases, there was ostensibly an oil shortage. But according to the law of supply and demand, there can't really *be* any shortages. Why not? Because prices will rise. For example, in Figure 9, at a price of $25, there's a shortage. But we know the price will rise to $30 and eliminate that shortage. Why? Who drives it up? The dissatisfied buyers (the people who would rather pay more now than wait) drive it up because they are willing to pay more than $25. Note that as the price rises, the quantity demanded declines, while the quantity supplied rises. When we reach equilibrium price, quantity demanded equals quantity supplied, and the shortage is eliminated.

Figure 9

Price Ceiling and Shortage
The price can go no higher than the price ceiling. The shortage is the amount by which quantity demanded is greater than quantity supplied.

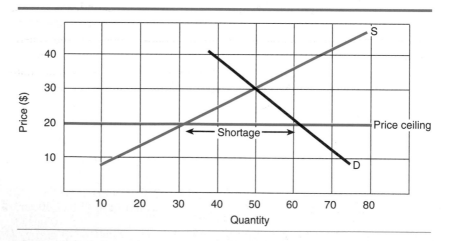

Now, I left you back in that gas line, and I know you don't want to wait two hours until it's your turn at the pump. Wouldn't you be willing to pay a few cents more if that meant you didn't have to wait? Let's suppose the gas station owner posted a higher price. What would happen? Some people would get out of line. What if he posted a still higher price? Still more people would leave the line. And as gas prices rose, more stations would miraculously open, and the others would stay open longer hours. What would happen to the gas lines? They'd disappear.

Who actually caused the shortages?

So now, let's ask the obvious question: What *really* caused the gasoline shortages? Who was the *real* villain of the piece? You guessed it! It was the federal government, which had set a ceiling on gasoline prices.

Let's return once more to Figure 9, the scene of the crime. What crime? How could you forget? Our government was caught red-handed, trying to violate the law of supply and demand.

In Figure 9, when a ceiling of $20 is established, there is a shortage of about 30 units. Had price been allowed to stay at the equilibrium level of $30, there would have been no shortage. However, at this lower price, business firms would be willing to sell about 18 units fewer than they'll sell at equilibrium, and consumers would demand about 12 units more than they would at equilibrium. This explains the shortage.

One way the market deals with a government-imposed shortage is to create what is known as a black market. Products subject to the price ceiling are sold illegally to those willing to pay considerably more. During World War II there was an extensive black market.

Two important price ceilings are rent control laws (see the box, "Rent Control: The Institution People Love to Hate") and usury laws, which put a ceiling on interest rates. Usury laws go back to biblical times when the prophets debated what, if anything, was a "fair" rate of interest. This same debate was carried on more than two millennia later by Christian scholars. And to this day we ask whether it is "moral" to charge high interest rates.

Usury laws put a ceiling on interest rates.

Rent Control: The Institution People Love to Hate

I grew up in a rent-controlled apartment and still believe that rent control worked very well at the time it was instituted. Very little new housing had been built during the 1930s because of the Great Depression and during the first half of the 1940s because of World War II. If rents had been allowed to rise to their market value in the late 1940s, my family, and hundreds of thousands—if not millions—of other families would have been forced out of their apartments.

Rent control is an institution that landlords, economists, libertarians, and nearly all good conservatives just love to hate. In fact, about the only folks who still seem to support rent control are the tenants whose rents are below what the market would have set and the politicians who voted for these laws in the first place.

Rent controls establish ceilings for how much rent may be charged for particular apartments and how much, if at all, these rents may be raised each year. The case for rent control is that it keeps down housing costs for the poor and the elderly. Actually, it keeps down housing costs for a lot of middle-class and rich people as well. Because the rent ceiling is established for each apartment regardless of who is living there, many people are paying a lot less than they could afford.

One of the perverse effects of rent control is to reduce vacancy rates. First, those paying low rents don't want to move. Second, real estate developers are reluctant to build apartment houses if their rents will be subject to controls. Still another perverse effect has been the large-scale abandonment of apartment buildings, especially in the inner cities, when landlords find that it makes more sense to walk away from their buildings than to continue losing money. These landlords had been squeezed for years by rising maintenance costs and stagnant rent rolls.

Richard Arnott has noted that "Economists have been virtually unanimous in their opposition to rent control." Why? Arnott provides a full list of reasons:

There has been widespread agreement that rent controls discourage new construction, cause abandonment, retard maintenance, reduce mobility, generate mismatch between housing units and tenants, exacerbate discrimination in rental housing, create black markets, encourage the conversion of rental to owner-occupied housing, and generally short-circuit the market mechanism for housing.*

After rent control was imposed in New York City in 1943, many landlords stopped taking care of their buildings and eventually walked away from 500,000 apartments.

Today nearly 200 cities, mostly in New York, New Jersey, and California, have some form of rent control. It is clear that this price ceiling has kept rents well below their equilibrium levels and consequently has resulted in housing shortages.

From a policy standpoint, do we want to eliminate rent controls? Would skyrocketing rents drive even more families into the ranks of the homeless? Perhaps a gradual easing of rent controls and their eventual elimination in, say, 10 or 15 years would send the right message to builders. But because these are local laws, only local governments can repeal them. And because the name of the political game is getting reelected, it is unlikely that many local politicians will find it expedient to repeal these popular laws.

---

*Richard Arnott, "Time for Revisionism on Rent Control?" *Journal of Economic Perspectives,* Winter 1995, p. 99.

EXTRA
HELP

Price Ceilings, Price Floors, Shortages, and Surpluses

Let's look at Figure 1. See if you can answer these three questions: (1) Is $10 a price ceiling or a price floor? (2) Is there a shortage or a surplus? (3) How much is it?

Let's look at Figure 2. We see that the quantity demanded is 75 and the quantity supplied is 45. The shortage is equal to quantity demanded less quantity supplied (75 − 45 = 30).

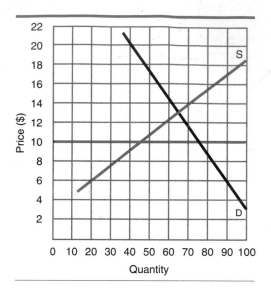

Figure 1

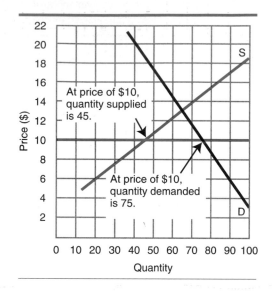

Figure 2

Solution: (1) $10 is a price ceiling because it is below equilibrium price: The ceiling is holding the market price *below* equilibrium price. (2) There is a shortage because quantity demanded is greater than quantity supplied. (3) The shortage is 30.

One dictionary definition of usury is "an unconscionable or exorbitant rate or amount of interest."[1] Many states have usury laws that prohibit banks, savings and loan associations, and certain other financial institutions from charging above specified rates of interest. What effect, if any, do these laws have?

Until the late 1970s interest rates were well below their legal ceilings. But then came double-digit inflation rates, sharply rising interest rates, and, as these interest rates reached their legal ceilings, a full-fledged credit crunch. In other words, these interest rate ceilings created a shortage of loanable funds—which is exactly what one would expect to happen when a price ceiling is set below the market's equilibrium price. In this case we're talking about the market for loanable funds and their price, the interest rate.

The confusion over the location of price floors and ceilings on the graph may be overcome by considering what the government is doing by establishing them. Normally, price would fall to the equilibrium level, but a price floor keeps price artificially high.

---

[1]*Webster's Collegiate Dictionary,* 10th ed., p. 1302.

Moving right along, answer these three questions with respect to Figure 3. (1) Is $40 a price ceiling or a price floor? (2) Is there a shortage or a surplus? (3) How much is it?

Let's look at Figure 4. We see the quantity supplied is 130 and quantity demanded is 80. The surplus is equal to quantity supplied less quantity demanded (130 − 80 = 50).

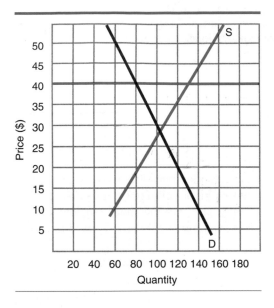

Figure 3

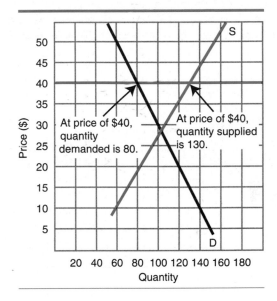

Figure 4

Solution: (1) $40 is a price floor because it is above equilibrium price: The floor is holding market price *above* equilibrium price. (2) There is a surplus because quantity supplied is greater than quantity demanded. (3) The surplus is 50.

Think of a floor holding price above equilibrium; therefore, a price floor would be located above equilibrium price.

By the same logic, a price ceiling is intended to keep price *below* equilibrium. If not for that ceiling, price would rise. Therefore, an effective price ceiling must be located below equilibrium to keep price from rising to that level.

Keep in mind, then, that the normal tendency of prices is to move toward their equilibrium levels. A price ceiling will prevent prices from rising to equilibrium, while a price floor will prevent prices from falling to equilibrium. If you need more information about ceilings, floors, shortages, and surpluses, see the box, "Price Ceilings, Price Floors, Shortages, and Surpluses."

Let's summarize: When the government sets a price floor above equilibrium price, it creates a surplus. That surplus is the amount by which the quantity supplied exceeds the quantity demanded. When the government sets a price ceiling below equilibrium price, it creates a shortage. That shortage is the amount by which the quantity demanded exceeds the quantity supplied.

83

Applications of Supply and Demand

Throughout this book we encounter many applications of supply and demand—so many, in fact, that I'm going to give you a quiz. But it will be an extremely easy quiz. There's just one answer to all these questions. Are you ready?

1. Interest rates are set by _____.
   Did you answer "supply and demand"? Good.

2. Wage rates are set by _____.

3. Rents are determined by _____.

4. The prices of nearly all goods are determined by _____.

5. The prices of nearly all services are determined by _____.

We may conclude, then, that the prices of nearly everything are determined by demand and supply.

Occasionally, however, government intervention interferes with the price mechanism and imposes price floors (or minimums) or price ceilings (or maximums). This gets economists very upset because it not only prevents the most efficient allocation of resources. It also makes it much harder to read our supply and demand graphs.

Interest Rate Determination

Let's take a closer look at the determination of the interest rate. I want to state right up front that there is no "interest rate" but rather scores of interest rates, such as mortgage rates, commercial loan rates, and short-term and long-term federal borrowing rates, as well as the interest rates paid by banks, credit unions, and other financial intermediaries. Figure 10 shows a hypothetical demand schedule for loanable funds and a corresponding hypothetical supply schedule.

We can see that $600 billion is lent (or borrowed) at an interest rate of 6 percent. In other words, the market sets the price of borrowed money at an interest rate of 6 percent. What would happen to the interest rate and to the amount of money borrowed if the supply of loanable funds increased?

Figure 10

Hypothetical Demand for and Supply of Loanable Funds

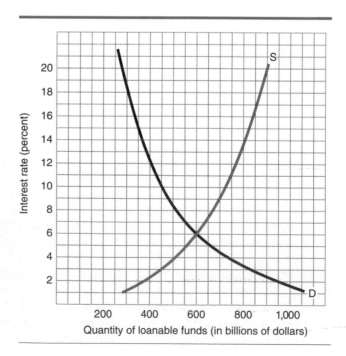

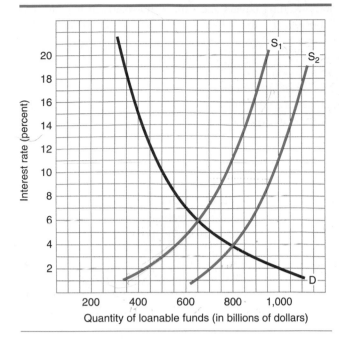

Quantity of loanable funds (in billions of dollars)

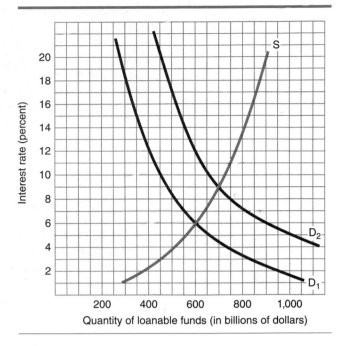

Quantity of loanable funds (in billions of dollars)

Figure 11

Hypothetical Demand for and Supply of Loanable Funds

Figure 12

Hypothetical Demand for and Supply of Loanable Funds

Did you figure it out? If you did, then you can confirm your answers by glancing at Figure 11. A rise in the supply of loanable funds leads to a decrease in the interest rate to 4 percent and an increase in the amount of money borrowed to $800 billion.

One more question: What happens to the interest rate and to the amount of money borrowed if the demand for loanable funds rises?

Did you say that the interest rate would rise and the amount of money borrowed would also rise? Good. Then what you must have done was to have sketched a graph like the one shown in Figure 12. The interest rate rose to 9 percent, and the amount of money borrowed rose to $700 billion.

College Parking

One of the big complaints on college campuses is the scarcity of parking spots for students—which means that, if you get to school after 9 o'clock, you may have to walk a half mile or even more to get to class.

Should parking be free at your school?

Is parking free at your school? Although you may well believe it should be, let's look at the consequences of free parking. The school has set the price of parking at zero. That's a price ceiling of zero. We may conclude that this price ceiling has caused a shortage of available parking spots.

Suppose that the college administration decided to charge $25 a semester to students, faculty members, administrators, and other employees (and eliminated reserved parking as well). Would this fee eliminate the parking shortage? Surely it would cut down on the quantity of parking spots demanded. But if the shortage were not completely eliminated, perhaps a fee of $50 might do the trick. Or even $100. In short, if the price of parking were set high enough, the parking shortage would disappear.

The Rationing Function of the Price System

If gasoline went up to $8 a gallon, would you cut back on your driving? Maybe you would try to do all your shopping in one trip instead of in two or three. And if gasoline went still higher, maybe you would even agree to join a car pool.

The price system is constantly sending buyers and sellers thousands of signals. The price of *this* service has gone through the roof. *That* product is on sale. *This* good is over-priced and *that* one is a bargain. When something becomes very expensive, we generally cut back. We do this not because the government ordered us to do so or because it issued ration coupons entitling everyone to only three gallons a week, but because the price system itself performed this rationing function.

Think of how most people behave at all-you-can-eat buffets. They certainly eat a lot more than they would in a regular restaurant. *Why?* The price system signals to them: This appetizer will cost them another $4.50, or that slice of pie will cost them another $3.75. At the buffet there's nothing to get them to ration how much they eat—except possibly a very full stomach. But in a regular restaurant the price system performs its rationing function so well that they end up eating less.

At the beginning of Chapter 2, economics was defined as *the efficient allocation of the scarce means of production toward the satisfaction of human wants.* In a free-market, private-enterprise economy such as ours, we depend on the price mechanism, or the forces of supply and demand, to perform that job.

The advent of the Internet has made the workings of supply and demand even more efficient. Before the Internet, we bought nearly all of our books in bookstores. Now we buy them online from a variety of sellers. If you want to buy a bestseller, your local bookstore will charge you full price. But chances are, you could find a seller online offering that same book at a steep discount. See for yourself by going to the websites that follow.

on the web

Check the price charged at your local bookstore for a couple of bestsellers and then go to these sites to see how much money you could save: www.amazon.com; www.barnesand-noble.com; www.halfprice.com; and www.ebay.com.

Last Word

We talked earlier of how the government sometimes interferes with the free operation of markets by imposing price floors and price ceilings. But the government may also ensure the smooth operation of markets by protecting property rights, guaranteeing enforcement of legal contracts, and issuing a supply of money that buyers and sellers will readily accept. Economist John McMillan has emphasized the historic importance of property rights:

Mohammed on supply and demand and property rights

> The prophet Mohammed was an early proponent of property rights. When a famine in Medina brought sharp price increases, people implored him to lessen the hardship by fixing prices. He refused because, having once been a merchant himself, he believed the buyers' and sellers' free choices should not be overridden. "Allah is the only one who sets the prices and gives prosperity and poverty," he said. "I would not want to be complained about before Allah by someone whose property or livelihood has been violated."[2]

So while governmental interference with the market system can have adverse effects, the government does have a substantial supportive role to play in a market economy. In the previous chapter we considered the role of government under economic systems ranging from capitalism to communism.

Current Issue: High Gas Prices: Something Only an Economist Could Love

On the Labor Day weekend of 2005, gas prices reached nearly $6 in some parts of the South. Customers groused about "price gouging," and many even limited their purchases to "just" $30 or $40, rather than filling their tanks.

---

[2]John McMillan, *Reinventing the Bazaar* (New York: W. W. Norton, 2002), p. 90.

What drove prices so high—*besides* the greed of the sellers? As you may remember, Hurricane Katrina, in addition to devastating New Orleans and its neighboring Gulf Coast communities, also temporarily shut down offshore oil wells which accounted for 25 percent of our domestic oil production. The storm also briefly put about 10 percent of our refineries out of commission.

What we had was a sudden drop in supply. When that happens, of course, price will go up sharply. Which is exactly what happened.

So what is there to love about high gas prices? Consider the alternative. Back in 1973 and 1979 we had similar supply problems, when shipments from the Middle East were curtailed. Although prices rose sharply, there were gas lines, sometimes six or eight blocks long. In 1979, various states imposed odd and even days to buy gas. If your license plate ended with an even number, you could buy gas on Monday, Wednesday, and Friday. If it ended with an odd number, then you were a Tuesday, Thursday, Saturday buyer.

The government's solution to the gasoline shortage in the 1970s was to restrict purchases and to hold down price increases. One unintended consequence was two- and three-hour waits on gas lines. But in 2005, the government basically took a hands-off attitude to the gasoline shortage. Prices certainly *did* go up, but there were few gas lines. Everyone was able to buy as much gas as they wanted, albeit at perhaps $3.50 or $3.75 a gallon. So the price system performed its rationing function very, very well. Although there were widespread complaints about prices, nearly everyone was much happier to pay, say, a dollar a gallon more, and not have to wait in line for an hour or two to buy gas.

Most economists believe price ceilings do more harm than good. In the short run, at least we don't have to wait in gas lines. Furthermore, because of high prices since the summer of 2005, some people cut back on their driving. In the long run, if gas prices stay high, some of them will trade in their SUVs for more gas efficient cars. Also, higher prices encourage greater exploration for oil, as well as the development of alternative energy sources. To sum up, rather than impose price controls, we should let the market forces of supply and demand reduce the shortage of gasoline.

Questions for Further Thought and Discussion

1. a. If market price is above equilibrium price, explain what happens and why.
    b. If market price is below equilibrium price, explain what happens and why.

2. a. As the price of theater tickets rises, what happens to the quantity of tickets that people are willing to buy? Explain your answer.
    b. As the price of theater tickets rises, explain what happens to the quantity of tickets that people are willing to sell. Explain your answer.

3. Where is a price ceiling with respect to equilibrium price? What will be the relative size of quantity demanded and quantity supplied?

4. How is equilibrium price affected by changes in (*a*) demand and (*b*) supply?

5. What are the two ways to depict a demand schedule? Make up a demand schedule for some good or service you often buy.

6. What is equilibrium? Why is it advantageous for the market price to be at equilibrium?

7. If you were a landlord, why would you be against rent control? A shortage occurs when the market price is below the equilibrium price.

8. *Practical Application:* How would the abolition of rent control reduce the housing shortage in some cities? Explain in terms of supply and demand.

9. *Practical Application:* Urban highways are usually very congested during morning and evening commuting times. Using supply and demand analysis, what simple step could be taken to greatly reduce congestion?

Workbook for Chapter 4 Mc Graw Hill connect |ECONOMICS

Name _____   Date _____

Multiple-Choice Questions

Circle the letter that corresponds to the best answer.

1. When demand rises and supply stays the same, _____. (LO3)
   a) equilibrium quantity rises
   b) equilibrium quantity declines
   c) equilibrium quantity stays the same

2. When supply rises and demand stays the same, _____. (LO3)
   a) equilibrium quantity rises
   b) equilibrium quantity falls
   c) equilibrium quantity stays the same

3. At equilibrium price, quantity demanded is _____. (LO3)
   a) greater than quantity supplied
   b) equal to quantity supplied
   c) smaller than quantity supplied

4. When quantity demanded is greater than quantity supplied, _____. (LO3)
   a) market price will rise
   b) market price will fall
   c) market price will stay the same

5. What happens to quantity supplied when price is lowered? (LO3)
   a) It rises.
   b) It falls.
   c) It stays the same.
   d) It cannot be determined if it rises, falls, or stays the same.

6. What happens to quantity demanded when price is raised? (LO3)
   a) It rises.
   b) It falls.
   c) It stays the same.
   d) It cannot be determined if it rises, falls, or stays the same.

7. When market price is above equilibrium price, _____. (LO3)
   a) market price will rise
   b) equilibrium price will rise
   c) market price will fall
   d) equilibrium price will fall

8. At equilibrium, quantity demanded is _____ equal to quantity supplied. (LO3)
   a) sometimes
   b) always
   c) never

9. Market price _____ equilibrium price. (LO3)
   a) must always be equal to
   b) must always be above
   c) must always be below
   d) may be equal to

10. A demand schedule is determined by the wishes and abilities of _____. (LO1)
    a) sellers
    b) buyers
    c) buyers and sellers
    d) neither sellers nor buyers

11. In Figure 1, if market price were $110, there would be _____. (LO5, 6)
    a) a shortage
    b) a surplus
    c) neither a shortage nor a surplus

12. In Figure 1, if market price were $140, there would be _____. (LO5, 6)
    a) a shortage
    b) a surplus
    c) neither a shortage nor a surplus

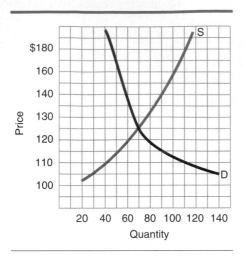

Figure 1

13. Market price may not reach equilibrium if there are _____. (LO5, 6)
    a) both price ceilings and price floors
    b) neither price ceilings nor price floors
    c) only price ceilings
    d) only price floors

14. Gas lines in the 1970s were caused by _____. (LO5, 6)
    a) price floors
    b) price ceilings
    c) both price floors and price ceilings
    d) neither price floors nor price ceilings

15. Statement 1: Price ceilings cause shortages. (LO5, 6)
    Statement 2: Interest rates are set by supply and demand, but wage rates are not.
    a) Statement 1 is true and statement 2 is false.
    b) Statement 2 is true and statement 1 is false.
    c) Both statements are true.
    d) Both statements are false.

16. If the equilibrium price of corn is $3 a bushel, and the government imposes a floor of $4 a bushel, the price of corn will _____. (LO5, 6, 7)
    a) increase to $4
    b) remain at $3
    c) rise to about $3.50
    d) be impossible to determine

17. Usury laws tend to _____. (LO5, 6)
    a) create a shortage of loanable funds
    b) create a surplus of loanable funds
    c) make it easier to obtain credit
    d) have no effect on the amount of loanable funds available

18. If the price system is allowed to function without interference and a shortage occurs, quantity demanded will _____ and quantity supplied will _____ as the price rises to its equilibrium level. (LO5, 6)
    a) rise, rise
    b) fall, fall
    c) rise, fall
    d) fall, rise

19. Which statement is true? (LO5, 6)
    a) A price floor is above equilibrium price and causes surpluses.
    b) A price floor is above equilibrium price and causes shortages.
    c) A price floor is below equilibrium price and causes surpluses.
    d) A price floor is below equilibrium price and causes shortages.

20. An increase in supply while demand remains unchanged will lead to _____. (LO3)
    a) an increase in equilibrium price and a decrease in equilibrium quantity
    b) a decrease in equilibrium price and a decrease in equilibrium quantity
    c) an increase in equilibrium price and an increase in equilibrium quantity
    d) a decrease in equilibrium price and an increase in equilibrium quantity

21. A decrease in demand while supply remains unchanged will lead to _____. (LO3)
    a) an increase in equilibrium price and quantity
    b) a decrease in equilibrium price and quantity
    c) an increase in equilibrium price and a decrease in equilibrium quantity
    d) a decrease in equilibrium price and an increase in equilibrium quantity

22. As price rises, _____. (LO1, 2)
    a) quantity demanded and quantity supplied both rise
    b) quantity demanded and quantity supplied both fall
    c) quantity demanded rises and quantity supplied falls
    d) quantity demanded falls and quantity supplied rises

23. When quantity demanded is greater than quantity supplied, there _____. (LO5, 6)
    a) is a shortage
    b) is a surplus
    c) may be either a shortage or a surplus
    d) may be neither a shortage nor a surplus

24. When quantity supplied is greater than quantity demanded, _____. (LO3)
    a) price will fall to its equilibrium level
    b) price will rise to its equilibrium level
    c) price may rise, fall, or stay the same, depending on a variety of factors

Use Figure 2 to answer questions 25 and 26.

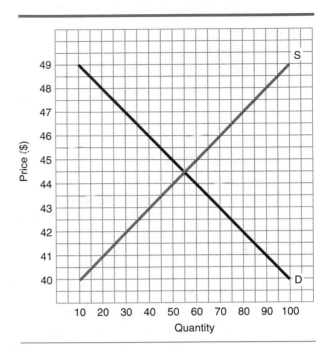

Figure 2

25. At a market price of $47, there is _____. (LO5, 6)
    a) a shortage
    b) a surplus
    c) both a shortage and a surplus
    d) neither a shortage nor a surplus

26. At a market price of $42, there is _____. (LO5, 6)
    a) a shortage
    b) a surplus
    c) both a shortage and a surplus
    d) neither a shortage nor a surplus

27. If the government set a price ceiling of 25 cents for a loaf of bread, the most likely consequence would be _____. (LO5, 6, 7)
    a) a surplus of bread
    b) no one would go hungry
    c) most Americans would put on weight
    d) a shortage of bread

91

28. Usury laws and rent control are examples of
_____. (LO5, 6)

a) price floors
b) price ceilings
c) rationing
d) the law of supply and demand

29. The best way to eliminate gas lines would be to
_____. (LO7)

a) impose government price ceilings
b) impose government price floors
c) allow the forces of supply and demand to function
d) put price gougers into jail

Fill-In Questions

1. If demand falls and supply stays the same, equilibrium price will _____, and equilibrium quantity will _____. (LO3)

2. If supply rises and demand stays the same, equilibrium price will _____, and equilibrium quantity will _____. (LO3)

3. If quantity supplied were greater than quantity demanded, market price would _____. (LO3)

4. Equilibrium price is always determined by _____ and _____. (LO3)

5. As price is lowered, quantity supplied _____. (LO3)

6. Shortages are associated with price _____; surpluses are associated with price _____. (LO5, 6)

7. If supply falls and demand remains the same, equilibrium price will _____, and equilibrium quantity will _____. (LO3)

8. Price floors and price ceilings are set by _____. (LO5, 6)

9. Interest rates are set by _____ and _____. (LO3, 7)

10. What happens to interest rates when the demand for money rises? _____. (LO3, 7)

11. When the supply of money falls, interest rates _____. (LO7)

Use Figure 3 to answer questions 12 through 15.

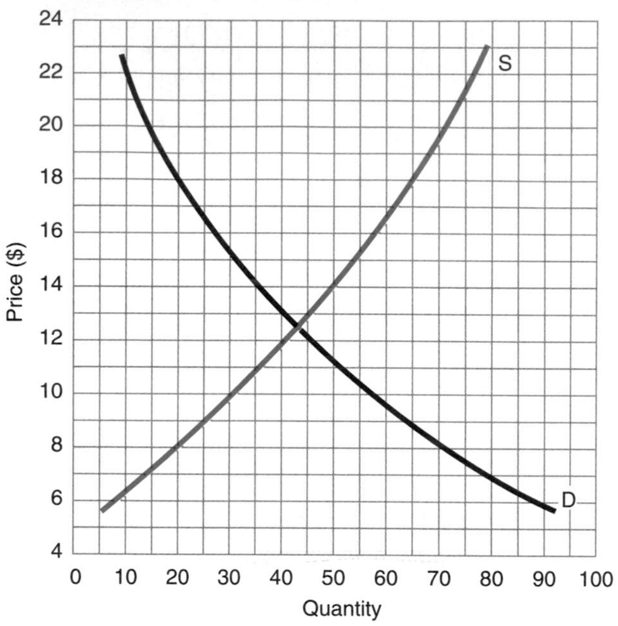

Figure 3

12. Equilibrium price is about $ _____. (LO3)

13. Equilibrium quantity is about _____. (LO3)

14. If price were $20, there would be a (shortage or surplus) _____ of _____ units of quantity. (LO5, 6)

15. If price were $8, there would be a (shortage or surplus) _____ of _____ units of quantity. (LO5, 6)

16. Price floors keep prices _____ equilibrium price; price ceilings keep prices _____ equilibrium price. (LO5, 6)

Problems

1. In Figure 4, find equilibrium price and quantity (in dollars and units, respectively). (LO3)

2. Draw in a new demand curve, D_1, on Figure 4, showing an increase in demand. What happens to equilibrium price and quantity? (LO4)

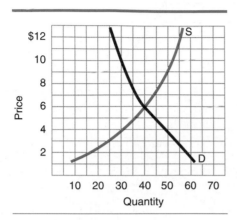

Figure 4

3. In Figure 5, find equilibrium price and quantity (in dollars and units, respectively). (LO3)

4. Draw in a new supply curve, S_1, on Figure 5, showing a decrease in supply. What happens to equilibrium price and quantity? (LO4)

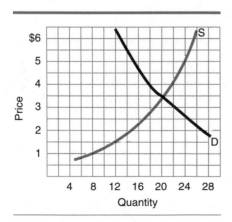

Figure 5

5. a) In Figure 6, if the demand curve is D_1, how much are equilibrium price and quantity? b) If demand changes from D_1 to D_2, does that represent an increase or decrease in demand? c) How much are the new equilibrium price and quantity? (LO3, 4)

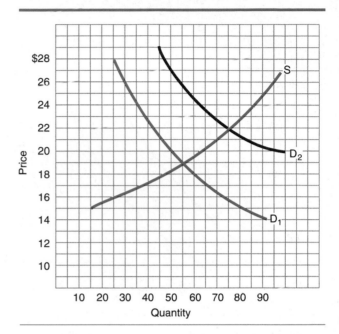

Figure 6

93

6. a) In Figure 7, if the supply curve is S_1, how much are equilibrium price and quantity? b) If the supply changes from S_1 to S_2, does that represent an increase or decrease in supply? c) How much are the new equilibrium price and quantity? (LO3, 4)

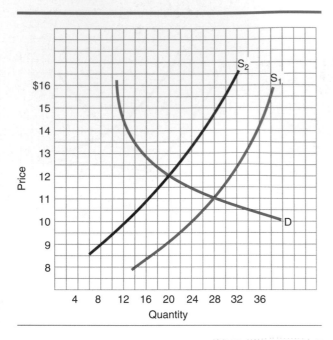

Figure 7

7. Given the information in Figure 8: a) Is $12 a price ceiling or a price floor? b) Is there a shortage or a surplus? c) How much is it (in units of quantity)? (LO5, 6)

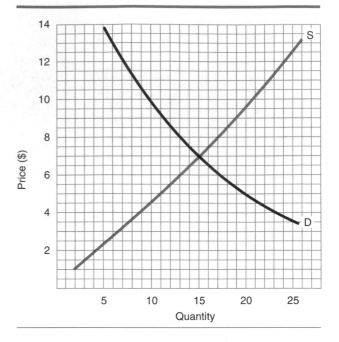

Figure 8

8. Given the information in Figure 9: a) Is $16 a price ceiling or a price floor? b) Is there a shortage or a surplus? c) How much is it (in units of quantity)? (LO5, 6)

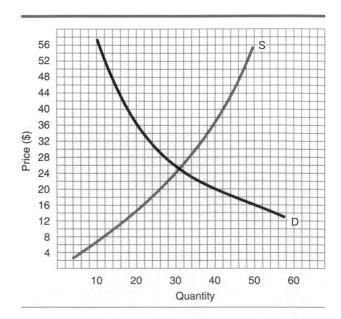

Figure 9

Chapter 5

Demand, Supply, and Equilibrium

Why do people like Oprah Winfrey, Alex Rodriguez, Derek Jeter, Jay Leno, Shaquille O'Neal, Angelina Jolie, Eddie Murphy, and Julia Roberts earn so much more than other athletes, actors, and entertainers, let alone the rest of us? What makes the price of gasoline go up and down? Why have PCs, palm pilots, and DVD players come down so much in price? The answer is that each is subject to the workings of supply and demand.

In the last chapter we showed how the interaction of supply and demand resulted in an equilibrium price and quantity. Now let's examine the workings of supply and demand much more closely and look at the factors that influence them.

Supply and demand change over time, causing changes in equilibrium price and quantity. We'll examine what causes these changes, and by the end of the chapter you'll be drawing supply and demand graphs. Before we begin, you'll need to buy at least one package of graph paper.

LEARNING OBJECTIVES

After reading this chapter you should be able to:

1. Define and differentiate between individual demand and market demand.
2. Distinguish between changes in demand and changes in quantity demanded.
3. List and discuss the causes of changes in demand.
4. Define and differentiate between individual supply and market supply.
5. Distinguish between changes in supply and changes in quantity supplied.
6. List and discuss the causes of changes in supply.
7. Draw graphs of supply and demand curves.
8. Identify equilibrium price and quantity by observing graphs.
9. Explain in terms of supply of demand why many people have trouble selling their houses.

Demand Defined

Demand is *the schedule of quantities of a good or service that people are willing and able to buy at different prices*. Let's look at the demand for sirloin steak. At $1 a pound, it would create traffic jams as people rushed to the supermarket; but at $3 a pound, sirloin steak would be somewhat less of a bargain. At $4 a pound, it would lose many of its previous buyers to chicken, chuck steak, and other substitutes.

Definition of demand

The Work of Alfred Marshall

Much of the analysis in this chapter is based on the work of Alfred Marshall, the great English economist, whose work dates back about a century. When you read some of his observations, you'll probably think that all

Alfred Marshall

he's saying is just common sense and that you might have come up with the same observations yourself. And that may well be true. The only thing is that Alfred Marshall came up with them first.

Here, for example, is Marshall's one general law of demand: "The greater the amount to be sold, the smaller must be the price at which it is offered in order that it may find purchasers; or, in other words, the amount demanded increases with a fall in price, and diminishes with a rise in price."*

To this day there are people who believe that demand is more important than supply in setting price, while others argue the opposite. But Marshall aptly compared the forces of supply and demand to the cutting done by the two blades of a pair of scissors. Just as you need two blades to cut a sheet of paper, he noted that demand and supply were equally important in setting price.

*Alfred Marshall, *Principles of Economics,* 8th ed., 1920, p. 99.

The law of demand: When the price of a good is lowered, more of it is demanded; when it is raised, less is demanded.

As the price of an item goes up, the quantity demanded falls, and as the price comes down, the quantity demanded rises. This inverse relationship may be stated as the law of demand: *When the price of a good is lowered, more of it is demanded; when it is raised, less is demanded.* There is an implicit assumption that there is no change in any other factors. The law of demand holds an honored place in the history of economic thought. (See box, "The Work of Alfred Marshall.")

There are many factors besides price that influence demand, including income, the prices of related goods and services, tastes and preferences, and price expectations. We'll discuss each of these factors a little later in the chapter.

Individual Demand and Market Demand

The law of demand holds for both individuals and markets. Individual demand is the schedule of quantities that a person would purchase at different prices. Market demand is the schedule of quantities that everyone in the market would buy at different prices.

Table 1 shows four examples of individual demand for cans of tennis balls and then adds them up to total market demand. We add straight across. For example, at a price of $30, the quantity demanded on an individual basis is 0, 1, 2, and 1. Adding them together, we get total or market demand of 4. In the same way, by adding the individual quantities demanded at a price of $25, we get 9 (2 plus 1 plus 3 plus 3). And so forth.

What is the market?

There is one interesting question about market demand: What is the market? The market is where people buy and sell. Generally there is a prevailing price in a particular market. Take gasoline. In New York City the price of regular unleaded gas at most gas stations varied between $2.95 and $3.25 in April 2010. But just across the bay in New Jersey most stations charged between $2.65 and $2.75.

New York City and New Jersey are two separate markets for gasoline. People in New York would not go to New Jersey to save 35 or 40 cents a gallon because the trip would not only be inconvenient, it would cost them an $8 toll.

The market for gasoline is very local because the money you'd save by driving to the next market would be more than offset by the money it would cost you to go there.

TABLE 1 Hypothetical Individual Demand and Market Demand Schedules for Cans of Tennis Balls

Price	Dinara	+	Svetlana	+	Serena	+	Caroline	=	Total
$30	0		1		2		1		4
25	2		1		3		3		9
20	3		2		5		4		14
15	3		3		6		6		18
10	4		5		7		7		23
5	5		6		7		8		26

Another local market is for groceries. Again, you wouldn't drive to the other side of your city or perhaps three towns down the highway just to save a dollar or two.

The market for automobiles is regional. If you live in Boston and can save a couple of hundred dollars by going to a dealer in Providence, you might make the trip, but if you live in Chicago you won't go to San Francisco to save $200 on a car.

On a very local basis, then, prices for most goods will not vary much, but as the area covered grows larger, so do price variations. If people are willing to travel to get a bargain, the market will be much larger.

The market for some goods and services may be national or even international. A company shopping for a sophisticated computer system will look all over the world for the right system at the right price. And a man who needs brain surgery or a heart transplant will not go to his local doctor and ask her to operate in her office.

I have strongly implied that a market is at a specific location. But does it *have* to be? What about business conducted over the phone or over the Internet? A market for a good or service might be local, regional, national, or global, but business in that market may well be conducted just about anywhere—even in cyberspace.

In the year 2000 two major markets *were* created in cyberspace. Fourteen of the world's largest mining and metals companies created a single procurement marketplace on the Internet, which has cut the industry's $200 billion-a-year supply bill. And 14 leading oil and gas companies joined forces in a similar project designed to put $125 billion a year of procurement spending on a common website. Other exchanges have been introduced for industries as diverse as retail and autos.

eBay has created a global market for goods that previously had mainly local markets. Its popularity induced others to start offering Internet auctions. Now, at thousands of different auction sites, people bid for computer equipment, antiques, fine art, coins, stamps, toys, comic books, jewelry, travel services, and even real estate.

Let's return again to the law of demand to see if it always applies when college tuition is raised. One would expect that if a college raised its tuition faster than that of comparable schools, the number of applicants would decline. But when Ursinus College, a small Pennsylvania school, raised its tuition in 2000 by 17.6 percent, the unexpected happened: applications rose by nearly 200. Why? Many applicants apparently concluded that if the college cost more, it must be better. Notre Dame, Bryn Mawr, Rice, and the University of Richmond had similar experiences when they raised their tuitions. While the law of demand still holds true, there *are* some exceptions.

Changes in Demand

The definition of demand is our point of departure, so to speak, when we take up changes in demand. Once again, demand is the schedule of *quantities* that people are willing and able to buy at different prices. A change in demand is a change in, or a departure from, this schedule.

TABLE 2	Hypothetical Market Demand Schedule Illustrating an Increase in Demand	
Price	(1) Quantity Demanded	(2) Quantity Demanded
$30	4	5
25	9	11
20	14	18
15	18	28
10	23	38
5	26	50

Figure 1

Increase in Demand
Note that D₂ lies to the right of D₁.
At each price people buy a larger
quantity.

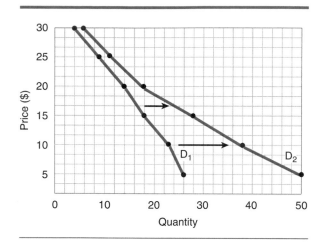

Increases in Demand

An increase in demand is an increase in the quantity people are willing and able to buy at different prices.

Using the market demand schedule in Table 1, let's say the product in question becomes much more desirable, perhaps because it is suddenly discovered that it slows the aging process. The people listed in Table 1 might well decide they are willing to pay even more for each unit.

This takes us from Table 1 to Table 2, and it involves an increase in market demand. At each price, buyers are willing to buy more. Thus, by definition, there is an increase in demand. It is important to emphasize that *an increase in demand is an increase in the quantity people are willing and able to buy at different prices.*

It will be helpful to illustrate this increase by means of a graph. This is done in Figure 1, which is drawn from the data in Table 2. Note that the second demand curve, D₂, representing the increase in demand, is to the right of D₁. You should also note that at each price, the quantity demanded in D₂ is greater than the quantity demanded in D₁.

Decreases in Demand

A decrease in demand means people are willing to buy less at each price.

Now we're ready for a decrease in demand, also illustrated in Figure 1. You should be able to guess what the decrease would be. After all, there are only two curves on the graph, and if going from D₁ to D₂ is an increase—that's right!—going from D₂ to D₁ is a decrease.

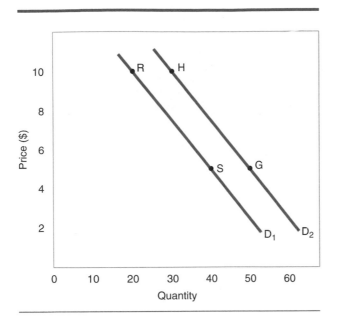

Figure 2
Demand Schedules for Chicago
Cubs Baseball Caps

A decrease in demand means people are willing and able to buy less at different prices. In Figure 1, D_1 lies entirely to the left of D_2.

Changes in Quantity Demanded and Changes in Demand

The law of demand, which we covered at the beginning of this chapter, tells us that price and quantity demanded are inversely related. When the price rises, the quantity demanded falls; when the price falls, the quantity demanded rises. Suppose we were at point R of the demand curve, D_1 in Figure 2. At that point the price is $10 and the quantity demanded is 20. If the price fell from $10 to $5, the quantity demanded would rise from 20 to 40, which would place us at point S.

So in response to a decline in price, the quantity demanded rises. Therefore a move from point R to point S represents a change in quantity demanded. Why isn't it an increase in demand? Literally millions of economics students have asked this question.

To answer it, we need to go back to our definition of demand. *Demand is a schedule of quantities of a good or service that people are willing and able to buy at different prices.* D_1 is an example of a demand schedule. If we go from point R to point S on D_1, then we are buying a larger quantity because the price was reduced. There was no increase in demand because we're still on D_1. So a move from R to S represents a change in quantity demanded.

Now we're ready to differentiate between a *change in demand* and a *change in the quantity demanded.* Graphically, if we go from one point, R, on a demand curve, to another point, S, on that same demand curve, that's a change in the quantity demanded. We are still on the same demand curve, D_1. But if we leave that demand curve to go to another one, then that's a change in demand. For example, if we go from G to R, that's a *change in demand.* OK, what *kind* of a change in demand is it? Is it an increase in demand or a decrease in demand?

Going from G to R is a *decrease in demand* because we're going from a higher demand schedule to a lower demand schedule. At each price, people will buy fewer baseball caps on D_1 than on D_2.

Now let's use Figure 2 to answer *this* question: If we move from point H to point G, does that represent an increase in demand, a decrease in demand, or a change in quantity demanded?

I hope you said that this represents a change in quantity demanded.

Figure 3

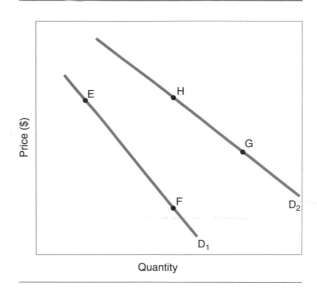

Practice Problems

Here are some problems for you to work out. Please answer with one of these three choices: (*a*) increase in demand, (*b*) decrease in demand, (*c*) change in the quantity demanded.

Use Figure 3 to answer questions 1–5:

1. A move from E to F is a(n) —————.
2. A move from D_1 to D_2 is a(n) —————.
3. A move from F to G is a(n) —————.
4. A move from G to H is a(n) —————.
5. A move from D_2 to D_1 is a(n) —————.

Let's go over each of the answers.

1. (c) Moving from E to F is a change in the quantity demanded. As long as we remain on the demand curve D_1, there's no change in demand.

2. (a) A move from D_1 to D_2 is an increase in demand because D_2 is a higher demand curve than D_1.

3. (a) From F to G is an increase in demand because the demand curve on which G is situated is higher than the demand curve on which F is situated.

4. (c) Moving from G to H is a change in the quantity demanded. As long as we remain on the demand curve D_2, there's no change in demand.

5. (b) A move from D_2 to D_1 is a decrease in demand because D_1 is a lower demand curve than D_2.

If you got each of these right, then go on to the next section. If you didn't, then you could probably use a little more practice. Please work your way through the box, "Differentiating between Changes in Demand and Changes in the Quantity Demanded."

What Causes Changes in Demand?

Changes in Income   When your income goes up, you can afford to buy more goods and services. Suppose the incomes of most Americans rise. That means a greater demand for cars, new homes, furniture, steaks, and motel rooms. Similarly, if incomes

Differentiating between Changes in Demand and Changes in the Quantity Demanded

We'll start with the definition of demand: *Demand is the schedule of quantities of a good or service that people are willing and able to buy at different prices.* So a change in demand is a departure from that schedule. A move from G to H in Figure 3 is *not* a change in demand. Why *isn't* it a change in demand? Because we stay on the same demand curve. A move from G to H is a *change in quantity demanded.* When we leave the demand curve, as we do when we go from point G to point F, there's been a change in demand. What *kind* of change? It's a decrease in demand because we went from D_2 to D_1. D_1 is a lower demand curve than D_2.

The demand curve is a graphic representation of the demand schedule. Any departure from that schedule is a change in demand. But if we just slide along the demand curve in response to a change in price, that is a change in the quantity demanded.

Using Figure A, answer each of these problems with one of these three choices: (*a*) increase in demand, (*b*) decrease in demand, (*c*) change in the quantity demanded.

1. _____ A move from V to W

2. _____ A move from W to X

3. _____ A move from D_1 to D_2.

4. _____ A move from X to Y

Here are the answers.

1. (a) A move from V to W is an increase in demand. We went from a lower demand curve, D_1, to a higher demand curve, D_2.

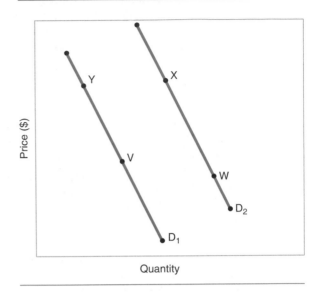

Figure A

2. (c) A move from W to X is a change in the quantity demanded, since we remained on the same demand curve.

3. (a) A move from D_1 to D_2 is an increase in demand since we went from a lower demand curve to a higher demand curve.

4. (b) A move from X to Y is a decrease in demand since we went from a higher demand curve, D_2, to a lower demand curve, D_1.

decline, as they do during recessions, there will be a smaller demand for most goods and services.

Most goods are *normal goods.* The demand for these goods varies directly with income: When income goes up, the demand for these goods goes up. When incomes decline, the demand for these goods declines as well.

However, certain goods are *inferior goods* because the demand for them varies inversely with income. For example, as income declines, the demand for potatoes, spaghetti, rice, and intercity bus rides increases. Why? Because these are the types of goods and services purchased by poorer people, and if income declines, people are poorer. As incomes rise, the demand for these inferior goods declines because people can now afford more meat, cheese, and other relatively expensive foods, and they'll take planes rather than ride in buses.

The demand for normal goods varies directly with income.

The demand for inferior goods varies inversely with income.

Changes in the Prices of Related Goods and Services Suppose tunas suddenly discovered a way to evade tuna fishermen, the supply of tuna fish drastically declined, and the price of tuna fish shot up to $5 a can. What do you think would soon happen to the price of salmon, chicken, and other close substitute goods? They would be driven up.

Let's see why this happens. First, the supply of tuna fish goes down and its price goes up. Most shoppers would say to themselves, "Five dollars a can! I've had tuna fish sandwiches for lunch every day of my life, but I'm not going to pay five dollars!" And so the former tuna fish buyers end up buying salmon and chicken. What has happened to the demand for salmon and chicken? They have gone up. And when the demand for something goes up, what happens to its price? It too goes up.

Many power plants can burn either natural gas or oil, so the prices tend to be linked. When there is a shortage of one, the price of both tends to rise.

> **The prices of substitute goods are directly related.**

Now we can generalize. The prices of substitute goods are directly related. If the price of one good goes up, people will increase their purchases of close substitutes, driving their prices up. If the price of one good comes down, people will decrease their purchases of close substitutes, driving *their* prices down.

> **The prices of complementary goods are inversely related.**

The prices of another set of goods and services, those with complementary relationships, are inversely related. That is, when the price of one goes down, the price of the other goes up, or vice versa.

Suppose airfares dropped by 50 percent. Many more people will fly, pushing up the price of hotel rooms. But what will happen if gasoline goes up to $6 a gallon? People will drive a lot less. This will lower the demand for tires, pushing down their prices.

Changes in Tastes and Preferences   Suppose the American Cancer Society and the surgeon general mounted a heavy TV campaign with rock stars, professional athletes, movie actors and actresses, and other celebrities. The message: Stop smoking. Imagine what a successful campaign would do to cigarette sales.

Sometimes tastes and preferences change by themselves over time. Over the last two decades Americans have opted for smaller cars and less-fattening foods, and growing numbers of people have become more fashion conscious, buying only designer clothing and accessories. No member of *my* generation would have guessed that children would one day demand "fashionable" sneakers at more than $150 a pair.

Patterns of food consumption have changed over time. Beginning in the 1950s, Americans became increasingly conscious of being overweight, and very soon the supermarket shelves began filling with dietary products. As each new dietary fad took hold, our preferences shifted from low calories to low carbohydrates, to low fat, to whatever the next fad dictates. And there was even a papal decree which had a major effect on eating patterns. (See box, "The Pope and the Price of Fish.")

Changes in Price Expectations   If people expect the price of a product to rise, they rush out to stock up before the price goes up. However, if the price is expected to fall, they will tend to hold off on their purchases.

The Pope and the Price of Fish

In 1966 Pope Paul VI issued a decree allowing American Catholic bishops to end year-round meatless Fridays, except during Lent. So what did this decree have to do with the price of fish?

A lot, as it turns out. Until 1966 Catholics across the nation generally ate fish every Friday. Since one of every four Americans was Catholic, that was a whole lot of fish. In an article published in the December 1968 *American Economic Review,* Frederick Bell showed that the papal/bishop action caused the average price of seven kinds of fish to fall by 12.5 percent.* The

declines ranged from 21 percent for large haddock to 2 percent for scrod.

What this all came down to was a substantial decline in the demand for fish. And when demand falls, while supply remains the same, price will fall. If a future pope were to nullify this decree, it would be interesting to see how high the price of fish would rise.

---

*F.W. Bell, "The Pope and the Price of Fish," *The American Economic Review* (1968), vol. 58, no. 5, pp. 1346–50.

Did the Cash for Clunkers Tax Credit Raise Demand for New Cars?

As part of the $787 billion economic stimulus package passed by Congress in February 2009, to encourage people to buy new, fuel-efficient cars, a tax credit of up to $4,500 was provided to those who turned in older, much less fuel-efficient vehicles. This sum was deducted from what you owed in federal income tax for the year. So if you received a $4,500 tax credit for buying a $20,000 car, that car really cost you just $15,500.

Now here's the big question: How much did this incentive actually increase demand for new cars? A total of 690,000 new vehicles were sold under the Cash for Clunkers program, but according to an analysis posted on the automotive website Edmunds.com on October 28, 2009, just 125,000 of those were vehicles that would not have been sold anyway.

Most of these sales were probably shifted forward. Because the tax credit was available for just two months, July and August of 2009, some people who had been planning to buy new cars later in the year, or even sometime in 2010, decided to take advantage of the tax credit and buy before it expired on August 24th. But we don't know how many.

There *is,* however, some data available that provides at least indirect answers to these questions. Table A lists monthly new motor vehicle sales for seven months of 2009. Let's look at these numbers.

Clearly sales for July and August got a large boost from the tax credit. It looks as though during the spring, some buyers, in anticipation of the introduction of the tax credit in July, may have held off their purchases, while

Table A Monthly New Motor Vehicle Sales, April–October 2009 (in thousands)

April	777
May	809
June	808
July	933
August	1,170
September	769
October	872

some people planning to buy new cars in the fall pushed up their purchases to take advantage of the tax credit.

From April through June, sales averaged just under 800,000 vehicles a month. Then, in July they shot up to 933,000, and in August, all the way up to 1,170,000. So sales in July were 133,000 higher than the April through June average, while August sales were 270,000 higher.

We know that 690,000 car buyers participated in the program, but July through August sales rose by just 400,000. So Cash for Clunkers raised sales by no more than 400,000. We also know that some of these buyers would otherwise have bought cars either before July or after August, but wanted to take advantage of the tax credit. The tax credit actually brought in substantially fewer than 400,000 new car buyers.

So *did* the Cash for Clunkers program raise demand for new cars? Yes. But, by how much? *That's* the big question.

When it appears that a major war will break out, people will stock up on canned food, appliances, and anything else they think may be hard to buy in the coming months. On the other hand, when prices seem inordinately high, as the Manhattan co-op and condominium market did in early 1985, potential buyers will hold out for lower prices. Incidentally, the prices of co-ops and condominiums *did* come down considerably in 1985 and 1986, partly because buyers expected a decline and waited for it to happen.

Very closely related to changes in price expectations are the introduction of a tax credit and the expiration of that credit. During the summer of 2009, the federal government provided a tax credit of up to $4,500 for people who traded in their older gas guzzlers for new fuel efficient models. Did the so-called "Cash for Clunkers" program stimulate the sale of new cars? Read all about it in the accompanying box.

Changes in Population As the nation's population increases, the demand for a particular good or service tends to increase. Mainly because of immigration—both legal and illegal—our population has been growing by more than 3 million each year, adding to the demand for food, housing, automobiles, medical care, and tens of thousands of other goods and services. Contrary to common opinion among many native-born Americans, immigration creates jobs and profit opportunities.

Supply and Demand: Opposite Sides of the Same Coin

Economists are very fond of pointing out that the prospect of making a lot of money will motivate people to work very hard. So the higher the price of a good or service, the more that will be supplied. Similarly, everybody loves a bargain, so when there's a half-price sale, eager shoppers will line up outside the store hours before it opens. So the lower the price, the greater will be the quantity demanded.

It can even be demonstrated that people who would buy a good or service at a very low price might themselves be willing to produce and sell that good or service at a very high price. Let's use typing as an example.

Can you type? I mean, can you type at all? Even using the two-finger method with four mistakes on each line? Most people can type at least *that* well.

What happens when your professor wants a term paper typed? "I don't own a PC." "My PC is down." "My printer ran out of ink." "I don't know how to type." "I have a broken hand—tomorrow I'll bring in the cast."

But if the professor insists on a typed term paper, somehow everyone eventually comes up with one. Some students pay people to type the papers. Some students even pay people to *write* them. If the going rate were $2 a page and you were a terrible typist, you will probably hire a typist, assuming you have enough money. At very low prices, then, the quantity demanded will be very high.

What if suddenly millions of term papers were assigned and, because of the unprecedented demand for typists, the price was bid up to $20 a page. Would *you* pay someone $20 a page to do what you could do yourself? Why stop there? Twenty dollars a page! Why not set yourself up in business as a typist?

Let's analyze what has happened. At very low prices, many students are willing to hire typists; but at very high prices, they'd not only do their own typing, but they'd hire themselves out as typists. This helps explain why, at very high prices, the quantity supplied will be high.

So demand and supply are really opposite sides of the same coin. At very low prices, most of us would be in the market to *buy*, while at very high prices, we would be sellers. To sum up, almost everyone has a price.

The changing age distribution of our population also affects demand. During the baby boom, 1946 to 1964, there was a tremendous rise in the demand for housing, and later, as these babies became teenagers, there was more demand for rock concert tickets, stereo systems, and designer jeans. In the second, third, and fourth decades of the 21st century, there will be a higher demand for retirement homes, nursing homes, wheelchairs, and bifocal glasses.

Supply Defined

Definition of supply

Supply is *a schedule of quantities of a good or service that people are willing and able to sell at various prices.* As prices rise, they are willing to sell more.[1] Thus we have a positive or direct relationship between price and quantity: As price rises, quantity supplied rises; as price falls, quantity supplied falls.

You may ask *why* the quantity supplied rises as price rises. There are two reasons why this happens. First, many business owners quickly realize how much more profits they could make by increasing their output. Suppose you owned an ice cream parlor and the going price of ice cream cones tripled. What would *you* do? Hire more workers? Rent extra space? Open a second store? All of the above?

So as price rises, firms already in the industry expand their output. And new firms, attracted by higher prices and the prospect of earning large profits, will enter the industry. Imagine what would happen if the price of ice cream cones shot up to $10. Not only would we have an ice cream parlor on every corner, but then America would *really* have an obesity problem.

---

[1]We're assuming there is no change in any of the factors that influence supply. These factors are listed later in the chapter in the section, "What Causes Changes in Supply?"

When you have trouble finding a plumber, an electrician, or even a doctor who will come to your house, here's a way to solve your problem. Just make that trip worth their while. Pay them well and they will come.

Over the last 20 or 30 years doctors have become very reluctant to make house calls. "You broke your leg, have a 108-degree fever, and you're hallucinating? You must be hallucinating if you think I make house calls. Why don't you hop right over to the office and we'll have a look at you?" How do you get this joker to make a house call? Do what you do when you want a ringside table at a club; grease the guy's palm. Tell your doctor there's an extra $100 in it for him if he can make it over to your place before your mortician. If $100 doesn't do it, try $200. Almost everyone can be bought for a price. The only question is: How much?

As you shall see, our analysis of supply is very similar to our analysis of demand. I would go further, however, and say that supply and demand are actually opposite sides of the same coin (see accompanying box). See if you agree that the same people who would buy something at a very low price would become sellers at a very high price.

Individual Supply and Market Supply

Individual supply is *the supply schedule of a single firm.* As we've seen, the higher the price, the greater the quantity of output supplied by an individual firm.

There are many influences on supply, including the cost of production, technological advance, the number of suppliers, the expectation of future price changes, and taxes on the good or service being sold. Each of these factors will be discussed a little later in the chapter.

Market supply is the sum of the supply schedules of all the individual firms in the industry. Table 3 presents a simplified supply schedule for the American automobile industry (excluding imports).

There are two main simplifications in this supply schedule. Obviously, all these cars and light trucks vary greatly in price, so we'll assume each of these car manufacturers produces an identical vehicle. A second simplification is that these companies would actually be willing to sell *any* car at relatively low prices. You'll also notice that by 2025 there will have been a few changes among the firms producing motor vehicles in the United States.

The right-hand column of Table 3 gave us the market supply. It is, of course, the sum of the individual supplies of the car companies; and, as we see in Figure 4, the market supply curve, like each individual supply curve, moves upward to the right. At higher and higher prices the market will supply an increasing number of cars.

on the web

What is the market supply of roundtrip plane trips from your local airport to Miami leaving on December 23 and returning on December 27? You can compile your own supply schedule by going to priceline.com, orbitz.com, expedia.com or travelocity.com

TABLE 3 Hypothetical Supply of American Cars and Light Trucks, 2025 (in thousands)

Price	Toyota	+	GM–Chrysler	+	Honda–Nissan	+	Ford	+	Hyundai–Kia	+	All Others	=	Total
$35,000	7.4		6.0		4.3		3.8		2.0		2.5		26
30,000	7.0		5.6		3.9		3.4		1.7		2.0		23
25,000	5.7		4.5		2.9		2.5		1.2		1.2		18
20,000	3.2		2.4		1.5		1.3		0.7		0.9		10
15,000	1.5		0.9		0.4		0.3		0.2		0.7		4

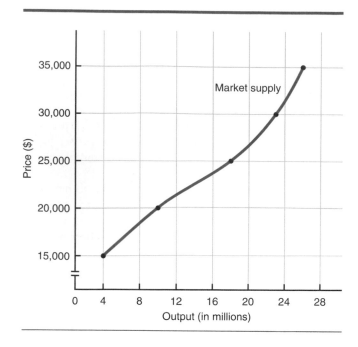

Figure 4

Hypothetical Supply of
American Cars, 2025
Note: We don't go down to 0 on
the price scale; we don't go down
to 0 on the output scale. We don't
need those figures, so why put them
in the graph?

Changes in Supply

Earlier in the chapter we went into considerable detail about changes in demand and changes in the quantity demanded. Because exactly the same reasoning applies to changes in supply and changes in the quantity supplied, we can skip that discussion and go directly to the practice problems.

Practice Problems

Here are some problems for you to work out. Please answer with one of these three choices: (*a*) increase in supply, (*b*) decrease in supply, (*c*) change in the quantity supplied.

Use Figure 5 to answer questions 1–5:

1. A move from E to F is a(n) _____.

2. A move from S_2 to S_1 is a(n) _____.

3. A move from F to G is a(n) _____.

4. A move from G to H is a(n) _____.

5. A move from S_1 to S_2 is a(n) _____.

Let's go over each of the answers.

1. (b) Going from E to F is a decrease in supply because we moved from a higher supply curve to a lower supply curve. Notice that at each price the quantity supplied is greater on S_1 than on S_2.

2. (a) A move from S_2 to S_1 is an increase in supply because we've gone from a lower supply curve to a higher supply curve. Again, at each price, the quantity supplied is greater on S_1 than on S_2.

3. (c) Moving from F to G is a change in the quantity supplied. As long as we remain on the supply curve S_2, there's no change in supply.

Figure 5

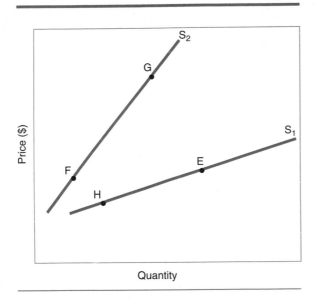

4. (a) A move from G to H is an increase in supply because we've moved from a lower to a higher supply curve. Keep in mind that at each price the quantity supplied is greater on S_1 than on S_2.

5. (b) A move from S_1 to S_2 is a decrease in supply because we've gone from a higher supply curve to a lower supply curve.

If you got all of these right, then you're ready to move on to the next section. If not, then please read the box, "Differentiating between Changes in Supply and Changes in the Quantity Supplied."

It's easy to confuse a change in supply with a change in the quantity supplied. If the price of gold rises from $450 an ounce to $500 an ounce, sellers will put more gold on the market. Is that an increase in supply or an increase in the quantity supplied?

It's an increase in the *quantity* supplied. If you'd like a little more practice differentiating between changes in supply and changes in the quantity supplied, please see the accompanying box.

What Causes Changes in Supply?

Changes in the Cost of Production   The main reason for changes in supply is changes in the cost of production. If the cost of raw materials, labor, capital, insurance, or anything else goes up, then supply goes down. For example, consider what happened when oil prices rose to record levels in mid-2005. Within months electricity bills went up sharply. Why?

Oil is the most important energy source for generating electricity. So, when the price of oil went up, so did the cost of producing electricity. Electric utilities were no longer willing to supply as much electricity at any given price as they had been before the oil price hike. In effect, then, the rise in the price of oil lowered the supply of electricity, resulting in higher electric bills.

The same analysis applies to changes in other costs of doing business—for example, interest, rent, and wages. An increase in these costs tends to reduce supply, while a decrease in costs pushes up the supply of that good or service.

Technological Advance   A technological improvement will increase supply. For example, look at the improvements in personal computers over the last 15 years. In addition, we are able to build PCs at much lower cost.

EXTRA
HELP

Differentiating between Changes in Supply and Changes in Quantity Supplied

Let's go back to the definition of supply, which is *the schedule of quantities of a good or service that people are willing and able to sell at various prices.* So a change in supply is a departure from that schedule. A move from F to G on the higher supply curve in Figure 5 is *not* a change in supply. Why not? Because we stay on that supply curve. A move from F to G is a change in quantity supplied. When we leave that supply curve, as we do when we go from point F to point H, a change in supply has taken place.

The supply curve is the graphic representation of the supply schedule. Any departure from that schedule is a change in supply. But if we just slide along the supply curve, in response to a change in price, then what we have is a change in the quantity supplied.

When we go from S_2 to S_1, we say that there has been an *increase* in supply. But doesn't S_1 *look* lower than S_2? It may *look* lower, but what's important here is that S_1 lies entirely *to the right of* S_2. And so, at every price, sellers on S_1 are willing to sell larger quantities than sellers on S_2 will sell.

Now we'll do another set of problems, using Figure B and these choices: (*a*) an increase in supply, (*b*) a decrease in supply, (*c*) a change in the quantity supplied.

1. _____ A move from J to K
2. _____ A move from K to L
3. _____ A move from L to M

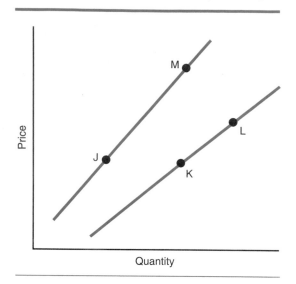

Figure B

1. (a) The move from J to K is an increase in supply because we have moved to a higher supply curve (at *every* price, more is offered for sale).

2. (c) When we go from K to L we stay on the same supply curve, so it is just a change in the quantity supplied.

3. (b) The move from L to M is the opposite of that from J to K, so it is a decrease in supply.

Prices of Other Goods   Changes in the prices of other goods can shift the supply curve for a product. If the price of corn rises, a farmer may cut back on the production of wheat. Or if the price of hair transplants declines, some dermatologists may do more face-lifts.

Change in the Number of Suppliers   When more sellers enter an industry, supply rises. Consider, for example, the proliferation of video rental stores over the last 25 years, as the VCR, and, more recently, the DVD player became increasingly popular. Personal trainers, tanning salons, cell phone stores, health clubs, stores that do nails, and the newly minted dot-coms have seemingly materialized out of thin air. When new firms enter an industry, supply rises; when firms leave, supply falls.

Changes in Taxes   Still another factor that affects supply is taxes. The basic effect of a tax increase is to raise production costs and reduce supply. The effect of taxes on supply will be taken up in the next chapter.

Expectation of Future Price Changes   We'll consider one more influence on supply: the expectation of future price changes. If prices are expected to rise sharply, suppliers will try to hold current production off the market in anticipation of these higher prices. Suppose you make hula hoops and you have inside information that their price will triple in a few weeks. What do you do? You hold your hoops off the market, thereby reducing supply and driving up price. On the other hand, if you expect a steep drop in prices, what will you do? You'll try to offer your entire inventory at lower prices, which thereby increases supply.

Random Causes   When Hurricane Katrina hit the Gulf Coast in 2005, it knocked out about one-quarter of our oil refinery capacity. This, of course, reduced our oil supply. During the Arab oil embargo of 1973, about one-tenth of our oil supply was temporarily cut off. Bad weather, wars, and other unpredictable occurrences can affect our supply of various goods. Our vulnerability has been magnified in recent years by our growing dependence on imports of oil, consumer electronics, and vital components of goods that are manufactured here.

Graphing the Demand and Supply Curves

From here on we're going to be drawing a lot of graphs. Once we set up a graph, we plot demand and supply curves by connecting the dots. You will find it a lot easier to draw your graphs on graph paper, and your answers will be much more accurate. So if you have not yet purchased a package of graph paper, please go out right now and buy one. In fact, buy two, because you'll run through a couple of packages over the next few weeks.

Graphing the Demand Curve

This is a hands-on approach to economics. What we're going to do now is graph the demand schedule shown in Table 4. I'm going to talk you through this step-by-step. The first step is to set up the axes of the graph. The vertical axis measures price, and the horizontal axis measures quantity. This is a convention that we follow consistently in economics—price (or some other variable measured in money) goes on the vertical axis, and quantity (often output) is measured on the horizontal axis.

Graphing step by step

Step 2 is to figure out our scales of measurement. On the vertical axis we measure price from $13 down to $8. There's a temptation to go all the way down to a price of zero, but that just wastes your time. Ideally a graph should take up about two-thirds of a sheet of graph paper.

Setting up the vertical axis

Step 3 is to set up the horizontal axis, or quantity scale.

Setting up the horizontal axis

Ready for the third step? All right, then, here it comes. Put numbers on your quantity scale. Here you can start with 0 directly under the price scale and work your way across to the right. Go ahead and put in the numbers on your horizontal axis. Did you number the quantities consecutively from 0 to 26? That is not a good idea because consecutive numbering—one number to each line (or box) on your graph—makes it hard to read.

You'd be much better off numbering by fours or fives. It's easier to read a scale that has numbers that are an inch apart, rather than just $\frac{1}{4}$-inch apart.

Remember, you have to be able to read your graph and to reach accurate conclusions on the basis of your observations.

TABLE 4	Hypothetical Demand Schedule
Price	Quantity Demanded
$13	1
12	2
11	4
10	8
9	15
8	20

Figure 6
Demand Curve

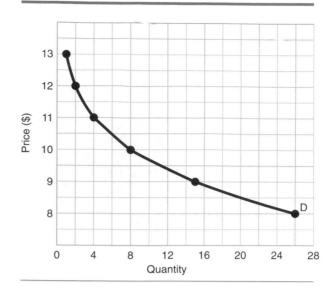

Plotting the demand curve

Step 4: Place dots for each of the points (or coordinates) of your demand curve on the graph. Use the data from Table 4.

Step 5: Connect the dots freehand. Let your eyes guide you into drawing a smooth curve. Use a pencil to draw your curve. Always draw your graphs in pencil. Can you guess why? You guessed it! If you mess up, you can erase your mistake and not have to start all over again. Before exams I warn my students about never drawing their graphs in ink. But about midway through the exam I hear paper being crumpled and students muttering under their breath. And *they're* the ones who tell me at the end of the test that I didn't give them enough time.

Now connect your dots and then see if your graph looks like the one I drew in Figure 6. If it does, great! If it doesn't, then check each of your dots with each of mine and see where you went astray. Throughout the next 8 chapters, I'll be asking you to do calculations and to draw graphs, and then to check your work. You'll be getting most things right, but remember that you can learn a lot from your mistakes.

The law of demand: The lower the price of a good or service, the greater the quantity that people are willing and able to buy.

Notice that the demand curve slopes downward and to the right as quantity rises. At high prices people buy little, but as price declines they buy more. We have an inverse relationship: As price comes down, quantity purchased goes up. This is the law of demand. More formally stated, *the law of demand tells us that the lower the price of a good or service, the greater the quantity that people will buy.* So the demand curve's downward slope reflects the law of demand.

So much for demand. Now we're ready for supply. We'll follow exactly the same procedure we followed for demand: We'll use data from a table to draw a graph of a supply curve. Then we'll put our two curves together in one graph to see one of the longest-playing acts in the entire history of economic thought: the law of demand and supply. Or is it the law of supply and demand? Actually, either one is fine.

Graphing the Supply Curve

Now use the data in Table 5 to draw the graph of a supply curve. Use a separate piece of graph paper, set up your axes, plot out each of the five points, and connect them to obtain your supply curve. Remember to do it in pencil and to draw a smooth freehand curve. Then see whether it came out like mine in Figure 7.

The law of supply: The higher the price of a good or service, the greater the quantity that people are willing and able to sell.

You'll observe that the supply curve slopes upward and to the right as quantity rises. As price rises, then, quantity supplied rises as well. This is a direct relationship: Price and quantity supplied move in the same direction—which happens to be the law of supply. In more formal terms, *the higher the price of a good or service, the greater the quantity that people are willing and able to sell.* So the upward slope of the supply curve reflects the law of supply.

TABLE 5	Hypothetical Supply Schedule
Price	Quantity Supplied
$13	23
12	20
11	15
10	8
9	3
8	1

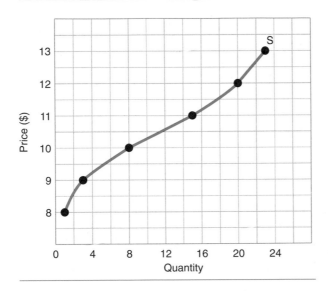

Figure 7
Supply Curve

The Equilibrium Point

At equilibrium, quantity demanded and quantity supplied are equal. At a certain price, all buyers who are willing to buy will be able to. And all sellers who are willing to sell will also be able to. That price is the equilibrium price.

Let's use the data from Table 6 to draw demand and supply curves on a graph. Draw your own graph, and then see if it looks like the one I drew in Figure 8.

Now we're ready to find our equilibrium price and quantity. At the equilibrium point, quantity demanded is equal to quantity supplied. It's the point at which the demand and supply curves cross. Please jot down your equilibrium price and quantity.

Did you get an equilibrium price of $10 and an equilibrium quantity of 8? Excellent! We can always find these at the equilibrium point, where the supply and demand curves cross.

An alternate way of finding equilibrium price and quantity is by looking at the supply and demand table, when it is available. If you take a look at the quantities demanded and supplied in Table 6, you'll see very quickly that the equilibrium price is $10 and the equilibrium quantity is 8. At that point quantity demand equals quantity supplied.

If price is determined by supply and demand, we may ask whether one or the other is more important. More than a century ago the great classical economist Alfred Marshall wrote, "We might as reasonably dispute whether it is the upper or the under blade of a pair of scissors that cuts a piece of paper as whether price is set by demand or supply."[2] In short, supply and demand are equally important in setting price.

Price always tends toward its equilibrium level. If it should happen to be set higher, say at $12, it will fall to its equilibrium level of $10. And if it is set lower than $10, it will rise to that level. Let's see why this happens.

The equilibrium point is where the demand and supply curves cross.

It's easy to train economists. Just teach a parrot to say "supply and demand."
—Thomas Carlyle

[2]See Alfred Marshall, *The Principles of Economics*, 8th ed., 1920, p. 348. The first edition came out in 1890.

TABLE 6	Hypothetical Demand and Supply Schedules	
Price	Quantity Demanded	Quantity Supplied
$13	1	23
12	2	20
11	4	15
10	8	8
9	15	3
8	26	1

Figure 8

Demand, Supply, and Equilibrium

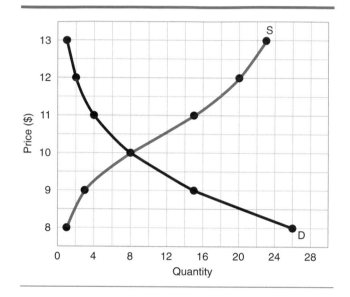

At a market price of $12 the quantity supplied is 20, but the quantity demanded is just 2. Some unhappy sellers will say, "Here I go without a sale when I would have been willing to settle for a lower price." What will they do? They will lower their price. And when they do—let's say to $11—most of the other sellers will also lower theirs. *Why?* Because otherwise they would sell nothing. Why would any buyers pay any sellers $12 when others are selling for $11?

Will market price fall any further? At $11 quantity supplied is 11, but quantity demanded is just 4. Market price is not yet low enough, because there are still some unhappy sellers who are willing to lower their price. When price falls to $10, are we at equilibrium?

We certainly are, because at a price of $10 quantity demanded equals quantity supplied. What if the market price happened to be below equilibrium price—say at $9? What will happen—and why?

At $9 the quantity demanded is 15, but quantity supplied is just 3. Some unhappy buyers, willing to pay more, will bid up the price to $10.

You might have noticed that when the market price is above equilibrium price, two things happen as it falls to the equilibrium level. Quantity demanded rises and quantity supplied falls. Similarly, when market price is below equilibrium price, as price rises to the equilibrium level, quantity demanded falls and quantity supplied rises.

Above equilibrium price there are surpluses.

An alternative way to look at prices above and below equilibrium is in terms of surpluses and shortages. When the price is above $10, there is a surplus. Quantity supplied is greater than quantity demanded, and this difference is the surplus. For example, at a price of $11, the surplus is 11. How is the surplus eliminated? As we've just seen, by letting the price fall. The surplus, then, eliminates itself through the price mechanism.

Finding Equilibrium Price and Quantity

If we draw our graphs accurately, we can usually find equilibrium price and quantity in a couple of seconds, especially if we've used graph paper. But sometimes we need to do further analysis to find really accurate equilibrium prices and quantities.

First, please draw a graph of the demand and supply curves for the information shown in Table C.

If you did a good job, your graph probably looks a lot like mine in Figure C. Now comes the analysis. How much is equilibrium price? Go ahead and write down your best guess. What did you get? Maybe $12.50? I hate to tell you, but $12.50 is not the right answer. The way to find the right answer is to go back to Table C and do a little analysis. We want to find the price that is closest to equilibrium price. Is it $12 or $13? Take your time. Don't let me rush you. OK, time's up. Equilibrium price is a little closer to $13 than to $12.

How do I *know* this? Easy. At a price of $13, quantity demanded is 7 and quantity supplied is 12. So they're 5 units apart. Now check out the quantity demanded and the quantity supplied at a price of $12. Quantity demanded is 12 and quantity supplied is 6; they're 6 units apart. In other words, we are a little closer to equilibrium at a price of $13 than at a price of $12.

So what *is* the equilibrium price? Would $12.60 be correct? Sure. How about $12.58? Yes! $12.56? $12.61? $12.62? Any one of these is a fine answer, because each is a little closer to $13 than to $12. Anything between $12.55 and $12.65 is fine. We're not talking about economics being an exact science here, but more of an art.

TABLE C	Hypothetical Demand and Supply Schedules	
Price	Quantity Demanded	Quantity Supplied
$15	2	19
14	4	17
13	7	12
12	12	6
11	20	3

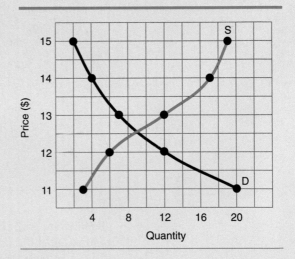

Figure C

When the price is too low, there is a shortage. A shortage of 12 units occurs when the price is $9. But the shortage disappears when the price rises automatically to its equilibrium level of $10.[3]

Below equilibrium price there are shortages.

Equilibrium price is the result of the forces of supply and demand. Together they determine equilibrium price. There will be no tendency for a price to change once it has reached its equilibrium. However, if either demand or supply (or both) changes, there will be a new equilibrium price.

A price is pushed toward equilibrium by the market forces of supply and demand. In other words, the price of any good or service is set by the law of supply and demand. That makes things easy for economists. Why are Rolls Royces so expensive? Supply and demand. Why is rice so cheap? Supply and demand. As long as the government does not interfere with the private market, the forces of supply and demand set the prices of everything. Or, as the popular saying goes, you can't repeal the law of supply and demand.

At equilibrium everyone is happy. Buyers can buy as much as they are willing and able to at that price. And sellers can sell as much as they are willing and able to at that price. Quantity demanded equals quantity supplied, and the market is said to *clear*.

Nine times out of 10, we can make an accurate reading of the equilibrium price and quantity by just glancing at a supply and demand graph. But if you'd *really* like to have an accurate reading, then see the box, "Finding Equilibrium Price and Quantity."

---

[3]Shortages and surpluses were discussed much more extensively in Chapter 4.

Shifts in Demand and Supply

What happens to equilibrium price and quantity when there are shifts in demand and supply? Let's begin with the equilibrium point in Figure 9, when the demand schedule is D_1 and the supply schedule is S. How much is equilibrium price and equilibrium quantity?

Figure 9

The Effect of Shifts in
Demand on Equilibrium Price
and Quantity

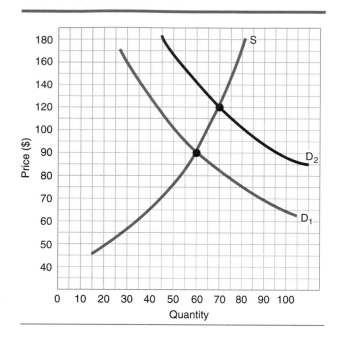

Figure 9

The Effect of Shifts in
Demand on Equilibrium Price
and Quantity

Equilibrium price is $90 and equilibrium quantity is 60. Suppose the demand schedule shifts from D_1 to D_2. Does this represent and *increase* or a *decrease* in demand?

This is an *increase* in demand. How much is the new equilibrium price and quantity?

The new equilibrium price is $120 and the new equilibrium quantity is 70. So an increase in demand—with no change in supply—leads to an increase in equilibrium price and quantity.

Next question: How does a *decrease* in demand affect equilibrium price and quantity?

If the demand schedule shifts from D_2 to D_1, equilibrium price falls from $120 to $90, while equilibrium quantity falls from 70 to 60.

Now let's look at the effect of shifts in supply on equilibrium price and quantity, which are shown in Figure 10. Does a shift from S_1 to S_2 represent an *increase* or a *decrease* in supply?

It represents a *decrease* in supply. When the equilibrium point is S_1 and D, how much is equilibrium price and quantity?

Equilibrium price is $20 and equilibrium quantity is 32. Next question: If supply falls from S_1 to S_2, how much is the new equilibrium price and quantity?

The new equilibrium price is $30 and the new equilibrium quantity is 16. So a fall in supply leads to a higher equilibrium price and a lower equilibrium quantity.

Finally, if there is an *increase* in supply, what happens to equilibrium price and quantity?

If we go from S_2 to S_1, equilibrium price falls from $30 to $20, while equilibrium quantity rises from 16 to 32.

Let's summarize how shifts in demand and supply affect equilibrium price and quantity:

(1) An increase in demand leads to an increase in equilibrium price and quantity.

(2) A decrease in demand leads to a decrease in equilibrium price and quantity.

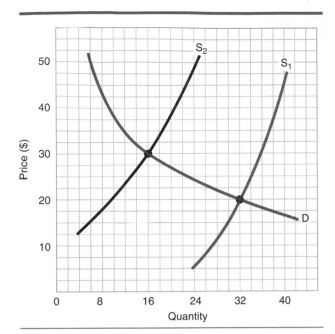

(3) An increase in supply leads to a decrease in equilibrium price and an increase in equilibrium quantity.

(4) A decrease in supply leads to an increase in equilibrium price and a decrease in equilibrium quantity.

On the next exam you might be asked at least one question about how a shift in demand or supply will affect equilibrium price or quantity. If you memorized the preceding four statements, you'll probably get the right answer. But there's a much easier way.

Suppose the question involves an increase in demand. Just sketch a graph of a demand curve and a supply curve, and add a second demand curve. You'll see immediately that equilibrium price and quantity went up. Or, if you're asked what happens to equilibrium price if demand *decreases,* you can easily see that equilibrium price and quantity went down. Similarly, you can draw a graph to help you answer questions dealing with the effect of supply shifts on equilibrium price and quantity.

If you would like further practice working with shifts in demand and supply, just turn back to the corresponding section of Chapter 4.

So far we've seen what happens to equilibrium price and quantity when there is a shift in either the demand curve or the supply curve. What if both curves shift at the same time? You find out what happens by reading the accompanying box.

Current Issue: Why Can't I Sell My House?

My neighbors, the Fergusons, had lived on our block for over 30 years. The Fergusons' children had grown up, gotten married, and had started their own families. So Mr. and Mrs. Ferguson decided to sell their house and move to a smaller house about 50 miles away.

Most of the houses in our neighborhood were sold over the last 10 years for two main reasons. Like the Fergusons, the owners didn't need such large houses any more. And because real estate prices had risen very rapidly, they could sell their homes for eight or ten times what they had paid for them.

The Fergusons had not sold their house by the time they moved. No problem, their broker said, indicating there were plenty of interested buyers. Yeah, the house needed a little work, but so did most of the other houses in our neighborhood. Mr. Ferguson would come by every couple of weeks to mow the lawn and spruce things up.

Simultaneous Shifts in Demand and Supply

What happens to equilibrium price and quantity when there are changes in demand *and* supply? First, let's look at a problem where demand and supply both increase.

We'll begin with Figure A. What happens to equilibrium price and equilibrium quantity when demand and supply both rise?

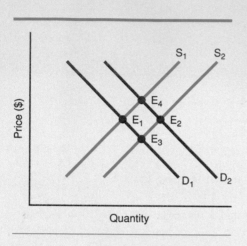

Figure A

Demand goes from D_1 to D_2, and supply rises from S_1 to S_2. We've gone from E_1 to E_2. Equilibrium price stays the same, while equilibrium quantity rises. May we conclude, then, that when demand and supply both increase, equilibrium price will stay the same and equilibrium quantity will rise?

Not necessarily. Look at Figure B. What happens to equilibrium price and quantity when demand rises from D_1 to D_2 and supply rises from S_1 to S_2?

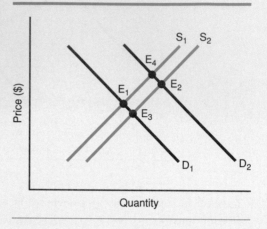

Figure B

Both equilibrium price and quantity rise. Why? Because there was a bigger increase in demand than in supply. The increase in demand pushed *up* equilibrium price more than the increase in supply pushed *down* equilibrium price. If demand and supply increase, but the increase in demand is bigger than the increase in supply, both equilibrium price and quantity will rise.

In the meanwhile, real estate prices stopped climbing. Still, each month a few more houses were sold, as old families moved out and new ones moved in. But the Ferguson house stood empty.

Question: Why couldn't they sell their house? Think about this question for a minute and then, even if you're not sure, just guess at the answer.

OK, time's up. Did you say that maybe their price was too high? Then you're right!

The Fergusons could have sold their house two years ago if they would have been willing to accept about $20,000 less than they were asking. In fact, when they finally *did* sell, that's about what they took. The Fergusons' mistake, of course, was thinking that real estate prices would keep going up. But they guessed wrong.

As sellers, we can learn a valuable lesson from the Fergusons' experience. If someone were to ask them today, "What would you have done differently?" they'd answer, "We would have accepted a lower price."

So now we can make a general observation. You can sell virtually any good or service for which there is a demand. As long as people are willing and able to pay you for that good or service, you can sell it. If you want to sell something pretty quickly and get no bites, what do you do?

Moving right along to Figure C, what happens to equilibrium price and quantity when demand and supply both increase?

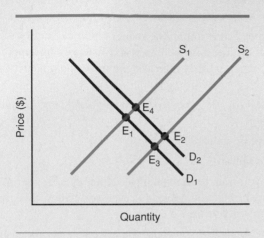

Figure C

Going from E_1 to E_2, we find that equilibrium price fell and equilibrium demand rose. Why? Because the increase in supply pushed *down* equilibrium price more than the increase in supply pushed it *up*.

Now let's shift gears and talk about the effects of simultaneous *decreases* in demand and supply. In Figure A, when demand and supply both decrease, what happens to equilibrium price and quantity?

Equilibrium price falls and equilibrium quantity stays the same. This happens when the fall in demand and supply is equal.

In Figure B, what happens to equilibrium price and quantity in response to a decrease in demand and supply?

Equilibrium price falls and equilibrium quantity falls.

And finally, in Figure C, what happens to equilibrium price and quantity in response to a decrease in demand and supply?

Equilibrium price rises and equilibrium quantity falls.

We've been working our way up to a set of still more challenging questions: What happens to equilibrium price and quantity when (a) demand increases and supply decreases; (b) supply increases and demand decreases? We'll go back to Figure A, and this time we'll ask: If demand rises from D_1 to D_2 and supply falls from S_2 to S_1, what happens to equilibrium price and quantity? Our starting point is E_3.

We end up at E_4, where price has risen and equilibrium quantity has stayed the same. This is what happens when demand rises and supply falls by the same amount.

Next question: In Figure B, what happens to equilibrium price and quantity when demand rises from D_1 and supply falls from S_2 to S_1? Our starting point is E_3.

Equilibrium price and quantity both rise. One last question: What happens to equilibrium price and quantity in Figure C when demand rises from D_1 to D_2 and supply falls from S_2 to S_1? Our starting point is E_3.

Going from E_3 to E_4, we find that equilibrium price rises and equilibrium quantity falls.

Do you need to memorize all this stuff? No! To help you answer questions like these, just sketch a supply and demand graph, and, chances are, the answers will not be that hard to find.

You lower your price. And if there are *still* no buyers willing to pay your price? You keep lowering it until you make a sale.

So the next time you hear someone say, "I can't sell my house," or better yet, "No one wants to buy my house," you know just what to tell him.

on the web

www.zillow.com How much is *your* house worth? Go to this website, type in your street address and zip code and you'll find out in about three seconds.

Questions for Further Thought and Discussion

1. Suppose a nearby concert hall booked a different one of your favorite performers every night for the next month. Make up a table showing your demand schedule for tickets.

2. What inferior goods do you buy? Would you continue to buy them if your income doubled?

3. Explain how the price of a good you buy is affected by changes in the prices of (a) substitute goods; (b) complementary goods.

4. Use examples from your own experience to illustrate (a) a change in demand; (b) a change in the quantity demanded. Draw a graph for each example showing what happened to prices.

5. Give one example from actual firms or industries for each of the factors that cause changes in supply. Draw a graph for each example showing what happens to price and quantity supplied.

6. It has just been reported that Happy Smile toothpaste reduces your cavities by 70 percent, while whitening your teeth and freshening your breath. Using supply and demand curves, demonstrate the report's likely effect on the price and quantity of this toothpaste's sales.

7. Do you agree with this statement: "As price goes up, demand goes down"? Explain your answer.

8. Why does the demand curve slope downward?

9. Why does the supply curve slope upward?

10. If you were a seller, why would you want to limit supply—either by keeping out new market entrants or by establishing production quotas for everyone? Show this graphically. And why would you hate that if you were a consumer?

11. How could an economic crisis in Southeast Asia cause the price you pay for gasoline to fall? Show this graphically.

12. If marijuana were legalized, what do you think would happen to the supply and demand curves and the price? Show this graphically.

13. *Practical Application:* You're moving into a new house one week from today. Checking the local newspaper and the phone book, you find 10 movers. Each one of them gives you a quote at least $1,000 more than you think you should pay. Explain what you will do in terms of demand and supply.

14. *Practical Application:* During recessions Walmart's low prices attract more customers. Explain why this means that Walmart is selling inferior goods.

15. *Practical Application:* The American Medical Association announces that eating three apples a day will promote good health. How would this affect the demand for apples and the equilibrium price and the quantity sold?

16. *Web Activity:* Find the cheapest possible round-trip New York–Los Angeles flight that leaves New York on December 1st and returns from Los Angeles on December 8th. Try priceline.com and Travelocity.com

17. *Web Activity:* Go on eBay.com to find the highest and lowest current auction prices for "Seinfeld complete set seasons 1 through 9."

Workbook for Chapter 5

Name _____ Date _____

Multiple-Choice Questions

Circle the letter that corresponds to the best answer.

1. As price rises _____. (LO4)
   a) supply rises
   b) supply falls
   c) quantity supplied rises
   d) quantity supplied falls

2. Goods for which demand is directly (positively) related to income are called _____. (LO1)
   a) substitute goods
   b) complementary goods
   c) inferior goods
   d) normal goods

3. Change in which of the following would not quickly cause a shift in demand? (LO2, 3)
   a) Number of buyers
   b) Tastes
   c) Buyers' perception of quality of product
   d) Income
   e) Price

4. A shift in the supply curve for gasoline in the United States would result if _____. (LO5)
   a) people decided to travel more by automobile
   b) the OPEC nations decided to stop sales of crude oil to the United States
   c) the price of gasoline increased
   d) the price of gasoline decreased
   e) the price of mass transit increased

5. If the price of a product rises and as a result businesses increase their production, then _____. (LO5)
   a) supply has increased
   b) supply has decreased
   c) quantity supplied has increased
   d) quantity supplied has decreased
   e) both supply and quantity supplied have increased

6. Changes in supply may be caused by changes in _____. (LO5)
   a) the cost of factors of production
   b) the level of technology
   c) the number of suppliers
   d) all of the above
   e) none of the above

7. Each of the following may lead to a change in the demand for product A except _____. (LO2)
   a) a change in the price of product A
   b) a change in people's taste for product A
   c) a change in people's incomes
   d) a change in the price of product B (a substitute for product A)

8. The retail market for gasoline is _____. (LO1)
   a) local   c) national
   b) regional   d) international

9. Suppose the price of a service falls and people buy more of that service. What has happened? (LO 2)
   a) Quantity demanded changed.
   b) Demand increased.
   c) Demand decreased.

10. An increase in the wage rate paid to construction workers will tend to _____. (LO5)
    a) decrease the demand for homes
    b) cause a movement along the supply curve for new homes
    c) decrease the supply of new homes
    d) increase the supply of new homes

11. If the rise in the price of service A leads to a fall in the price of service B, we may conclude that, _____. (LO2)
    a) services A and B are substitutes
    b) services A and B are complements
    c) services A and B are neither substitutes nor complements

12. An increase in the demand for steak could be caused quickly by a(n) _____. (LO2)
    a) fall in the price of steak
    b) increase in the supply of steak
    c) expectation of a future cutback in the supply of steak
    d) a decline in the price of chicken

13. The demand for an inferior good is _____. (LO1, 2)
    a) positively related to its own price
    b) negatively related to income
    c) unaffected by consumer tastes and preferences
    d) insensitive to changes in prices of its complements

14. A decrease in supply can be brought about by _____. (LO5)
    a) a price increase
    b) a price decrease
    c) a random event like a hurricane or an earthquake
    d) a change in consumers' tastes or preferences

15. Which statement is true? (LO1, 2, 4)
    a) A change in demand is the same thing as a change in the quantity demanded.
    b) The supply curve moves upward to the left.
    c) The law of demand is no longer valid.
    d) A rise in income will increase the demand for normal goods.

16. When market price is above equilibrium price, the market price will be driven _____. (LO6)
    a) up by unhappy buyers
    b) up by unhappy sellers
    c) down by unhappy buyers
    d) down by unhappy sellers

For questions 17 and 18, use the information in Figure 1.

17. Equilibrium price is _____. (LO8)
    a) below $8   c) between $8 and $10
    b) $8   d) above $10

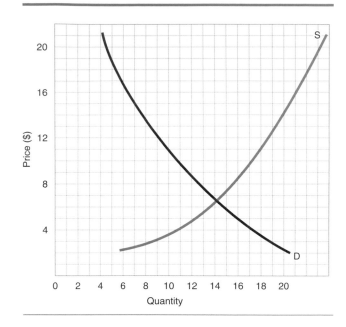

Figure 1

18. Equilibrium quantity is _____. (LO8)
    a) below 13   c) between 13 and 15
    b) 13   d) above 15

For questions 19–22, use the information in Figure 2 and use choices a, b, and c. (LO2)

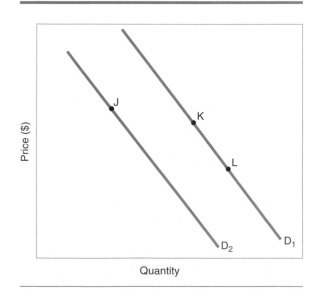

Figure 2

a) an increase in demand

b) a decrease in demand

c) a change in quantity demanded

_____ 19. A move from J to K

_____ 20. A move from K to L

_____ 21. A move from D1 to D2

_____ 22. A move from L to J

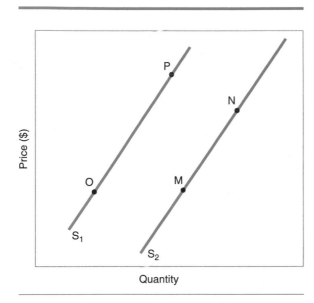

Figure 3

For questions 23–26, use the information in Figure 3 and use choices a, b, and c. (LO5)

a) an increase in supply

b) a decrease in supply

c) a change in the quantity supplied

_____ 23. A move from M to N

_____ 24. A move from S1 to S2

_____ 25. A move from N to 0

_____ 26. A move from O to P

27. If the price of cameras falls, there will be a(n)

_____. (LO2, 3, 5)

a) decrease in the demand for film

b) decrease in the quantity of cameras demanded

c) decrease in the supply of cameras

d) increase in the demand for cameras

e) increase in the quantity of cameras demanded

28. The market demand for a good will decrease

_____. (LO1, 2, 3)

a) as income decreases if the good is an inferior good

b) if the market price of a substitute good increases

c) as income decreases if the good is a normal good

d) if the market price of a complementary good decreases

e) as the number of consumers in the market increases

29. A decrease in demand means that the quantity

demanded _____. (LO2)

a) does not fall at any price

b) falls only at the equilibrium price

c) falls at a few prices

d) falls at most prices

e) falls at all prices

30. An increase in the supply of running shoes will—assuming demand is unchanged—lead to

_____. (LO7)

a) an increase in equilibrium price and an increase in equilibrium quantity

b) a decrease in equilibrium price and a decrease in equilibrium quantity

c) an increase in equilibrium price and a decrease in equilibrium quantity

d) a decrease in equilibrium price and an increase in equilibrium quantity

For questions 31–34, use choices a, b, c, d, e, and f. (LO8)

a) may rise, fall or remain the same

b) may rise or remain the same

c) may fall or remain the same

d) will rise

e) will fall

f) will remain the same

31. If demand and supply both rise, then equilibrium price _____.

32. If demand and supply both fall, then equilibrium quantity _____.

33. If demand rises and supply falls, then equilibrium price _____.

34. If demand falls and supply rises, then equilibrium quantity _____.

35. The American Cancer Society announces the results of a study of 10,000 smokers and nonsmokers. A 21-year-old smoker who continues smoking two packs a day has a life-time expectancy that is 20 years shorter than a 21-year-old nonsmoker. As a result of this announcement, the cigarette equilibrium _____. (LO3)

a) price will rise and quantity sold will rise

b) price will rise and quantity sold will fall

c) price will fall and quantity sold will fall

d) price will fall and quantity sold will rise

36. The reason many homeowners cannot sell their homes when housing prices are falling is because _____. (LO9)

a) there are no buyers in the market

b) there are too many houses on the market

c) no one can get a mortgage

d) the homeowners are not willing to lower their prices enough

Fill-In Questions

1. As price rises, quantity supplied _____. (LO4)

2. At _____, quantity demanded equals quantity supplied. (LO8)

3. As price falls, quantity demanded _____. (LO4)

4. An increase in supply is shown graphically by a shift of the supply curve to the _____. (LO5)

5. The main reason for changes in supply is changes in the _____. (LO5)

6. If business owners expected a steep drop in prices, they would take action which would tend to _____ supply. (LO5)

Problems

1. Given the information in Table 1, draw a graph of the demand and supply curves on a piece of graph paper. (LO7)

TABLE 1

Price	Quantity Demanded	Quantity Supplied
$10	1	35
9	10	33
8	18	29
7	24	24
6	28	17
5	30	10
4	31	2

2. Equilibrium price is $_____; equilibrium quantity is _____. (LO7, 8)

3. Given the information in Table 2, draw a graph of the demand and supply curves on a piece of graph paper. (LO7)

TABLE 2

Price	Quantity Demanded	Quantity Supplied
$15	1	27
14	4	25
13	9	21
12	16	12
11	22	6
10	26	2

4. Equilibrium price is $ _____; equilibrium quantity is _____. (LO7, 8)

5. Draw a demand curve, D_1, in Figure 4. Then draw a second demand curve, D_2, that illustrates a decrease in demand. (LO7)

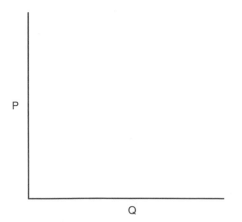

Figure 4

122

6. Draw a supply curve, S_1, in Figure 5, and a second supply curve, S_2, that represents an increase in supply. (LO7)

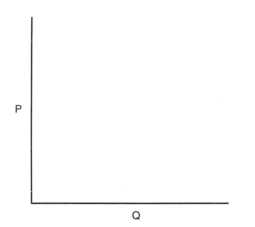

P

Q

Figure 5

7. A major technological improvement leads to a large decrease in the cost of production. Using Figure 6 draw a new supply curve, S_2, to reflect this change. Then state the new equilibrium price and quantity. (LO7, 8)

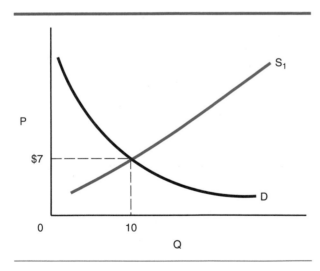

P

$7

S_1

D

0

10

Q

Figure 6

8. Draw a graph in Figure 7 illustrating a simultaneous increase in supply and demand. Label all four curves and both equilibrium points. (LO7)

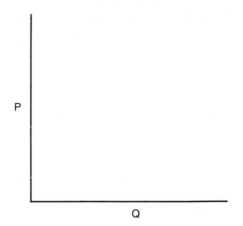

P

Q

Figure 7

9. Draw a graph in Figure 8 illustrating a simultaneous increase in supply and decrease in demand. Label all four curves and both equilibrium points. (LO7)

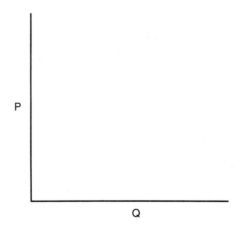

P

Q

Figure 8

123

Chapter 6

The Price Elasticities of Demand and Supply

If the government wants to discourage teen smoking by raising the price of cigarettes with a <u>hefty</u> tax, will it work? How big would the price increase need to be to induce, say, a 50 percent drop in teen smoking? Would such a price increase affect teens and adults equally? Lawmakers rely on economists to answer such questions by estimating elasticities.

In this chapter we'll continue our analysis of supply and demand to include *how much* of the quantity demanded responds to a change in price—what economists call *elasticity of demand*. Similarly, *elasticity of supply* measures responsiveness of the quantity supplied to change in price. These concepts are useful economic tools because they allow us to make predictions about what will happen in markets when prices or quantities change.

LEARNING OBJECTIVES

After reading this chapter you should be able to:

1. Interpret and calculate the elasticity of demand.
2. List and discuss the determinants of elasticity.
3. Examine the relationship between elasticity and total revenue.
4. Define and examine income elasticity of demand and cross elasticity of demand.
5. Discuss the elasticity of supply.
6. Name and discuss the three phases of the elasticity of supply over time.
7. Analyze and measure tax incidence.

The Elasticity of Demand

How much we buy of any good or service is determined by three main factors—its price, our income, and the prices of related goods. Did you cut back your driving when the price of gasoline went through the roof during the last few years? If your income doubled, how would your consumption patterns change? And if airfares come way down, would you consider flying rather than driving on those 250-mile trips you take?

Unless you are either a billionaire or a living saint, chances are you're pretty price conscious. You know from the law of demand, which we introduced near the beginning of the last chapter, that quantity demanded varies inversely with price. For nearly all goods and services, the higher the price, the lower the quantity demanded. In this section we're going to look at the responsiveness of the quantity demanded to changes in three different variables—the price of that good, the price of a related good, and the income of the buyer. But for most of the time, we'll be looking at the responsiveness of the quantity demanded to price changes of that good. We call that the price elasticity of demand.

The Price Elasticity of Demand

The elasticity of demand for a good or service measures the change in quantity demanded in response to change in price. In other words, elasticity measures the sensitivity (measured in percentage change) of quantity demanded because of a change (percentage) in price. When price goes up, we know that quantity demanded declines. But by how much? Elasticity provides us with a way of measuring this response. And we measure the responsiveness of quantity demanded to a change in price by calculating the coefficient of price elasticity of demand (E_p) as follows.

Measuring Elasticity

$$E_p = \frac{\text{Percentage change in quantity demanded}}{\text{Percentage change in price}}$$

We'll start with this problem. A business firm has been selling 100 kitchen chairs a week. It runs a sale, charging $8 instead of the usual $10. People recognize this great bargain, and sales go up to 140 chairs. If P_1 is the initial price charged and P_2 is the sale price, Q_1 the initial quantity sold and Q_2 the quantity sold during the sale, we can calculate the coefficient of price elasticity of demand as follows:

Elasticity formula

$$E_p = \frac{\text{Percentage change in quantity demanded}}{\text{Percentage change in price}} = \frac{Q_2 - Q_1}{Q_2 + Q_1} \cdot \frac{P_2 + P_1}{P_2 - P_1}$$

This formula looks a lot more complicated than it is (see the box, "Why We Don't Use a Simpler Elasticity Formula"). It simply calls for finding the percentage change in quantity and the percentage change in price, and then dividing the former by the latter. Go ahead and substitute into the formula in the space below and then solve.

Solution: $P_1 = 10$; $P_2 = 8$; $Q_1 = 100$; and $Q_2 = 140$.

$$\frac{140 - 100}{140 + 100} \cdot \frac{8 + 10}{8 - 10} = \frac{40}{240} \cdot \frac{18}{-2} = \frac{1}{6} \cdot \frac{9}{-1} = \frac{9}{-6} = \frac{3}{-2} = -1.5$$

Because the demand curve is downward sloping, price and quantity are inversely related. As price declines, the quantity demanded increases, and vice versa. So the price elasticity of demand will always be a negative number. But by convention, economists ignore the minus sign and use the absolute value. So instead of our answer being -1.5, we'll state it as 1.5. A coefficient of 1.5 for price elasticity of demand means that for every 1 percent change in price, there will be a corresponding 1.5 percent change in quantity demanded in the opposite direction of the price change.

Why We Don't Use a Simpler Elasticity Formula

Considering that elasticity is the percentage that quantity sold changes in response to a 1 percent change in price, wouldn't it be a lot easier to use the formula *percentage change in quantity divided by percentage change in price?* The answer is yes. For very small percentage changes in price and quantity demanded, dividing percentage change in quantity by percentage change in price is fine. But this formula is much less accurate when we're dealing with larger percentage changes. Let's try it for this problem. Price drops from $10 to $9, and quantity demanded rises from 100 to 120.

Using the formula:

$$\frac{\text{Percentage change in quantity}}{\text{Percentage change in price}}$$

we get:

$$\frac{20\%}{10\%} = 2$$

So far, so good. Now let's look at the same price range but reverse the direction so that price rises from $9 to $10 and quantity demanded falls from 120 to 100. Here our percentage change in quantity divided by percentage change in price would be:

$$\frac{16\frac{2}{3}\%}{11\frac{1}{9}\%} = 1.5$$

That's quite a discrepancy for the range of the demand schedule between $9 and $10. When price is lowered from $10 to $9, elasticity is 2, but when it is raised from $9 to $10, elasticity is only 1.5. Therefore, the same formula measuring elasticity over the same range of the demand curve yields two very different answers.

Let's try the more complex formula on the same data. Go ahead and do it in the space provided below, first trying the price decrease and then the price increase.

Solution: $P_1 = \$10$; $P_2 = \$9$; $Q_1 = 100$; and $Q_2 = 120$.

$$\frac{120 - 100}{120 + 100} \cdot \frac{9 + 10}{9 - 10} = \frac{\overset{1}{\cancel{20}}}{\underset{11}{\cancel{220}}} \cdot \frac{19}{-1} = \frac{19}{-11} = -1.72727^*$$

(when price rises from $9 to $10)

$P_1 = \$9$; $P_2 = \$10$; $Q_1 = 120$; and $Q_2 = 100$.

$$\frac{100 - 120}{100 + 120} \cdot \frac{10 + 9}{10 - 9} = \frac{-20}{220} \cdot \frac{19}{1} = -1.72727^*$$

*You may round off at one decimal place for elasticity problems ($-1.72727 = -1.7$) or at two places (-1.73).

Most students initially have some difficulty calculating elasticity, so we'll work out a few more problems in the accompanying Extra Help box.

The Meaning of Elasticity

What does all this mean? First, we say that when elasticity is greater than 1, demand is elastic. Remember, elasticity is the percentage change in quantity demanded brought about by a price change. It is percentage change in quantity divided by percentage change in price. For elasticity to be greater than 1, percentage change in quantity must be greater than percentage change in price. A price change of a certain percentage causes quantity to change by a larger percentage. When this happens, we say demand is elastic. For example, if the coefficient of price elasticity of demand is 10, that means for every 1 percent change in price, there will be a corresponding 10 percent change in quantity demanded. In this example, we would say demand is very elastic. We mean that the quantity demanded is responsive to price changes.

When demand is elastic, it stretches as price changes. And when demand is not very elastic, it does not stretch much.

Elasticity is a simple number—2, 3.5, or 0.5, for example. It's a number that represents the percentage change in quantity demanded of a good resulting from each 1 percent change in that good's price. So an elasticity of 2 means that a 1 percent price change leads to a 2 percent change in quantity. What about elasticities of 3.5 and 0.5?

When demand is elastic, the quantity demanded is very responsive to price changes.

Practice Problems Finding Price Elasticity of Demand

Problem: Price is raised from $40 to $41, and quantity sold declines from 15 to 12. Solve in the space below.

Problem: Price is raised from $30 to $33, and quantity demanded falls from 100 to 90.

Solution: $P_1 = \$40$; $P_2 = \$41$; $Q_1 = 15$; and $Q_2 = 12$.

$$\frac{12 - 15}{12 + 15} \cdot \frac{41 + 40}{41 - 40} = \frac{-3}{\underset{1}{27}} \cdot \frac{\overset{3}{81}}{1} = \frac{-9}{1} = -9$$

Solution: $P_1 = \$30$; $P_2 = \$33$; $Q_1 = 100$; and $Q_2 = 90$.

$$\frac{90 - 100}{90 + 100} \cdot \frac{33 + 30}{33 - 30} = \frac{-10}{190} \cdot \frac{63}{3} = \frac{-1}{19} \cdot \frac{21}{1} = -1.11$$

Problem: Price is lowered from $5 to $4, and quantity demanded rises from 80 to 82.

Solution: $P_1 = \$5$; $P_2 = \$4$; $Q_1 = 80$; and $Q_2 = 82$.

$$\frac{82 - 80}{82 + 80} \cdot \frac{4 + 5}{4 - 5} = \frac{-2}{\underset{18}{162}} \cdot \frac{\overset{1}{9}}{1} = \frac{-2}{18} = \frac{-1}{9} = -0.11$$

When elasticity is 3.5, a 1 percent change in price results in a 3.5 percent change in quantity demanded. And when elasticity is 0.5, a 1 percent change in price leads to an 0.5 percent change in quantity demanded.

Inelastic demand is defined as an elasticity of less than 1; anything from 0 to 0.99 is inelastic. We can also make somewhat finer distinctions. An elasticity of 0.1 or 0.2 would be very inelastic, while one of 0.8 or 0.9 would be slightly inelastic. Similarly, an elasticity of 1.5 or 2 would be slightly elastic. And one of 8 or 10 would be very elastic.

The border between elastic and inelastic is 1. We call this *unit elastic*. Thus, if elasticity is less than 1, it is inelastic. If it is exactly 1, it is unit elastic. If elasticity is more than 1, it is elastic.

Now we'll deal with perfect elasticity and perfect inelasticity. Figure 1 shows a perfectly elastic demand curve. It is horizontal. Go ahead and calculate its elasticity from a quantity of 10 to a quantity of 20. Note that price remains fixed at $8.

Solution: $P_1 = \$8$; $P_2 = \$8$; $Q_1 = 10$; and $Q_2 = 20$.

$$\frac{20 - 10}{20 + 10} \cdot \frac{8 + 8}{8 - 8} = \frac{-10}{30} \cdot \frac{16}{0} = \frac{-1}{3} \cdot \frac{16}{0} = \infty$$

Figure 1
Perfectly Elastic Demand Curve

How big is infinity? Big. Very, very big. How elastic is the demand curve in Figure 1? Very, very elastic. Infinitely elastic, or as we say here, perfectly elastic.

Now we'll move on to perfect inelasticity. If perfect elasticity is ∞, how large is perfect inelasticity? −∞? Nope. Go back to what I said about the range of inelasticity—anything from 0 to 0.99. The lowest it can go is 0. That's perfect inelasticity.

Using the data in Figure 2, calculate the elasticity of the vertical demand curve. Quantity stays put at 15, but price varies. Let's say the price has fallen from 20 to 10. Calculate the elasticity. Again, use the formula, substitute, and solve below.

Solution: $P_1 = 20$; $P_2 = 10$; $Q_1 = 15$; $Q_2 = 15$.

$$\frac{15 - 15}{15 + 15} \cdot \frac{10 + 20}{10 - 20} = \frac{0}{\cancel{30}} \cdot \frac{\overset{1}{\cancel{30}}}{-10} = \frac{0}{-10} = 0$$

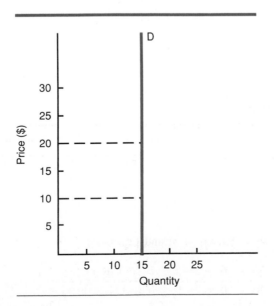

Figure 2
Perfectly Inelastic Demand Curve

Figure 3
Relative Elasticity of Demand
Curves

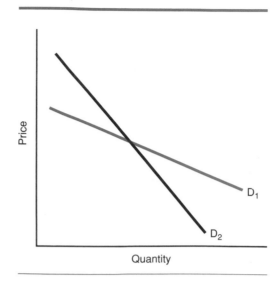

How many times does 10 go into 0? None. You can't divide *any* number into 0. Therefore, elasticity is 0. The elasticity of a perfectly inelastic line is 0.

Next we'll consider relative elasticity. If a vertical line is perfectly inelastic and a horizontal line is perfectly elastic, what about lines that are somewhere in between? Figure 3 has two such lines. The question here is, which of the two is more elastic, D_1 or D_2?

D_1 is more elastic because it is closer to being flat. Remember, the more flat the demand curve is, the more elastic it is; and the steeper the curve, the more inelastic it is.

Finally, we'll calculate the elasticity of a straight line. Surprisingly, it is not constant. Using Figure 4, let's calculate the elasticity at three points. First, do the calculations when price falls from $10 to $9 and quantity rises from 1 to 2.

Solution: $P_1 = \$10$; $P_2 = \$9$; $Q_1 = 1$; and $Q_2 = 2$.

$$\frac{2-1}{2+1} \cdot \frac{9+10}{9-10} = \frac{1}{3} \cdot \frac{19}{-1} = \frac{19}{-3} = -6.33$$

An elasticity of 6.33 is fairly high.

Moving right along, let's calculate the elasticity when price falls from $6 to $5 and the quantity demanded rises from 5 to 6.

Solution: $P_1 = \$6$; $P_2 = \$5$; $Q_1 = 5$; and $Q_2 = 6$.

$$\frac{6-5}{6+5} \cdot \frac{5+6}{5-6} = \frac{1}{11} \cdot \frac{11}{-1} = -1$$

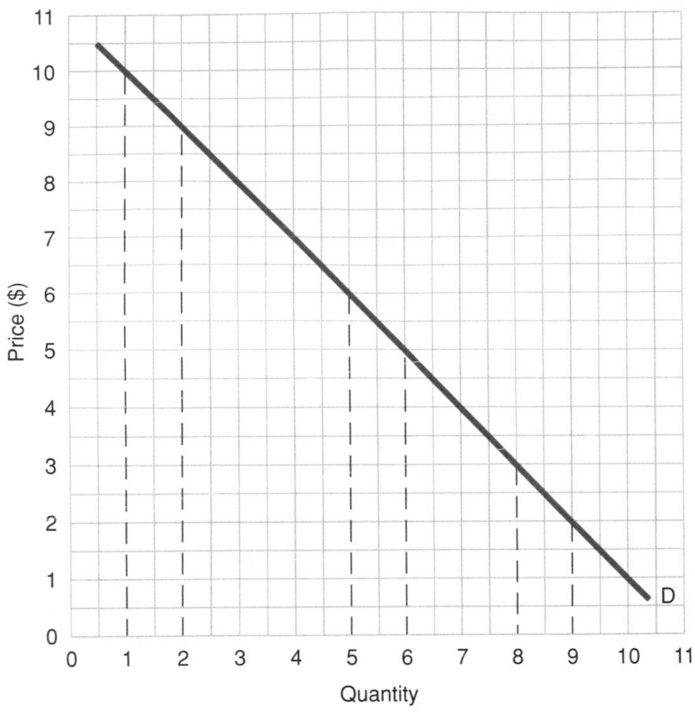

Figure 4
Straight-Line Demand Curve

What we have here is unit elasticity, when a price change causes quantity demanded to change by the same percentage. Note that in Figure 4 this occurs at the middle of the demand curve.

Now let's calculate the elasticity when price falls from $3 to $2 and quantity demanded rises from 8 to 9.

Solution: $P_1 = \$3$; $P_2 = \$2$; $Q_1 = 8$; and $Q_2 = 9$.

$$\frac{9-8}{9+8} \cdot \frac{2+3}{2-3} = \frac{1}{17} \cdot \frac{5}{-1} = \frac{5}{-17} = -0.29$$

The answer, 0.29, is rather inelastic. When we compare the three elasticities we calculated, this time moving to Figure 5, we reach this conclusion: A straight-line demand curve that moves downward to the right is very elastic at the top and progressively less elastic as we move down the curve. As we approach the lower right end of the curve, demand becomes more and more inelastic.

Do you smoke? Well, whether you do or you don't, do you think the demand for cigarettes is elastic or inelastic? Are cigarettes a necessity? I'll let the smokers answer that one. Are there any close substitutes? Lollipops? Chewing gum? Hey, if these were such wonderful substitutes, you wouldn't have nearly so many smokers.

In general, it would be safe to say that the demand for cigarettes is inelastic. How inelastic? If you're really curious, then check out the box, "Do Higher Cigarette Prices Stop Smoking?"

Figure 5
Elasticity of Straight-Line
Demand Curve

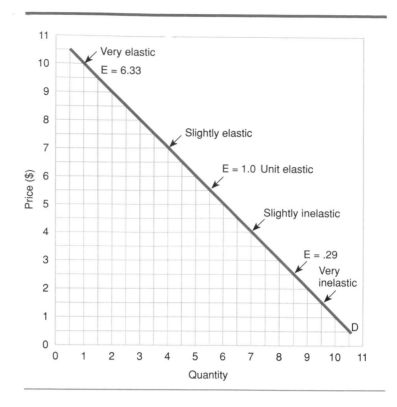

Do Higher Cigarette Prices Stop Smoking?

Let's face it: smokers have less fun. Everywhere they go there are No Smoking signs and they're usually forced to stand outside even in the rain and snow. To add insult to injury, the price of a pack of cigarettes has doubled in just a few years.

Now you would think that an awful lot of people must have given up smoking. A study by Michael Grossman, Gary Becker, and Kevin Murphy found that a 10 percent increase in cigarette prices reduced current consumption among adults by 4 percent, and over a five-year period cigarette consumption fell by 7.5 percent.

Another study by the U.S. General Accounting Office revealed that the elasticity of demand for cigarettes among teenagers was somewhat higher—between 0.76 and 1.2. In a survey tracking 25,000 eighth-graders since 1988, Donna B. Gilleskie and Koleman S. Strumpf of the University of North Carolina found that raising taxes by $1 per pack would reduce the likelihood of smoking by half.

This raises an interesting public policy issue. The surgeon general keeps reminding us on every pack of cigarettes about all the terrible things smoking will do to us. But even more effective would be a hefty tax of two or three dollars on every pack, as there is in Canada, Great Britain, Ireland, Denmark, Norway, and a few other countries. Canada's tax of $3 per pack has helped cut per capita consumption by more than 50 percent since 1980.

How responsive would you be to price changes in music downloads? Since 2003, when Apple CEO Steve Jobs negotiated with the major record labels, they struck a deal of 99 cents a song and $10 for a whole CD, those prices became the industry standard. *Newsweek* columnist, Steven Levy, raised *this* question:

> Yet is 99 cents the magic number? No way. A couple of years ago, the music service Rhapsody funded a test: for a few weeks it subsidized a price cut of songs to 49 cents, and cut album prices from 10 bucks to five. Sales went up *sixfold*.[1]

---

[1]See Steven Levy, "How Much Is Music Worth?" *Newsweek*, October 29, 2007, p. 20.

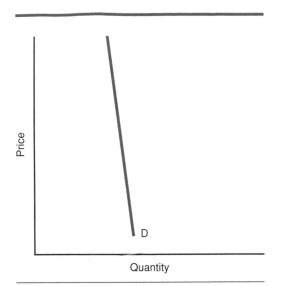

Figure 6
Relatively Inelastic Demand
Curve

Determinants of the Degree of Elasticity of Demand

The demand for certain goods and services is relatively elastic, while that for others is relatively inelastic. Consider heart medicine, for example. Suppose this medicine keeps you alive, and suppose its price doubles. Would you cut back on your purchases? Your demand curve would probably look like the one in Figure 6.

Do you think that a person who needs heart medicine would cut back on the quantity she buys because its price doubles? A few people might do this. Why? Because they might not be able to afford it. Maybe one or two poor souls would say it's just not worth what they're being charged.

When AZT was first sold to people who are HIV-positive, plenty of people simply couldn't afford to pay $800 to $1,000 a month. As its price came down, the quantity purchased rose somewhat. And so, Figure 6 might well represent the demand for a life-extending drug. It's not perfectly inelastic because at extremely high prices some people just can't afford the drug.

Can you think of any other examples of goods or services for which there are nearly perfectly inelastic demands? What about a diabetic's demand for insulin? A heroin or crack addict's demand? Or a thirsty man's demand for water, especially if he happens to be out in the desert?

How elastic is the demand for gasoline? In the mid-1970s, when the price of oil more than tripled, American consumption of gasoline fell sharply. But when gasoline prices again tripled in 1999 and 2000, there was no appreciable cutback in gasoline sales. Instead, some people switched from using expensive premium gasoline to regular. And sales of the very largest sports utility vehicles (SUVs) fell somewhat.

One might reason that the demand for gasoline has become more inelastic since the mid-1970s. But there are two major differences between now and the mid-1970s. First, gasoline is much cheaper today, after you adjust its price for inflation. So why cut back, when you can still afford a full tank? And second, there are no gas shortages or long gas station lines as there were back in the 1970s. Back then plenty of drivers refused to spend hours waiting on a gas line, and there were others who couldn't find a nearby station that was open.

Our experience was similar when the average retail gasoline price jumped from $1.87 a gallon in September 2004 to $2.90 a year later—a 55 percent increase. Yet gasoline consumption dropped only 3.5 percent. But there were a couple of extenuating circumstances. First, many consumers probably viewed recent price increases as

TABLE 1 Elasticity of Demand of Selected Goods and Services

Household electricity	0.13	Gasoline	0.60
Bread	0.15	Milk	0.63
Telephone service	0.26	Beer	0.90
Medical care	0.31	Motor vehicles	1.14
Legal services	0.37	Restaurant meals	2.27
Clothing	0.49		

Source: Compiled from numerous sources.

temporary, so why trade in that SUV for a more fuel-efficient vehicle? And then, too, most people's incomes are much higher than they were back in the 1970s, so gasoline—even at $3 a gallon—is still a relative small expense relative to buyers' incomes.

We can conclude that the demand for gasoline today is indeed inelastic (see Table 1). But, in the long run, more and more Americans may be shopping for fuel-efficient vehicles.

Can you think of any good or service for which demand is exactly unit elastic? OK, that's really an unfair question. You'll find the answer in the box, "The Cookie Monster's Unit Elasticity of Demand."

What about relatively elastic demand? Take steak, for example. When its price goes too high, we substitute chicken, fish, and other meats for our steak dinners.

The most important influence on the elasticity of demand is availability of substitutes.

What makes demand elastic or inelastic? By far the most important influence is the availability of substitutes. Steak has a number of reasonably close substitutes. If its price gets too high, people will buy other cuts of beef or fish and fowl instead. A relatively small percentage increase in price leads to a large percentage decline in quantity demanded.

In the case of heart medicine, demand is quite inelastic; there are no close substitutes. If price rises, quantity sold will not fall much.

Is the product a necessity rather than a luxury?

There are other influences on the degree of elasticity in addition to the availability of substitutes. If the product is a necessity rather than a luxury, its demand will tend to be more inelastic. When the price of a movie ticket goes up by a dollar, you might stay home and watch television; but if the price of gasoline goes up by, say, 50 percent, you'll still buy it because you need to drive places.

When you can purchase a good or service for just a tiny percent of your income, your demand will tend to be relatively inelastic. But if you're buying a big ticket item, then your demand will tend to be relatively elastic.

The Cookie Monster's Unit Elasticity of Demand

The easiest example to use to understand elasticity is the behavior of the Cookie Monster on *Sesame Street*. As nearly every American under the age of thirty-five knows, the Cookie Monster (CM) eats only cookies. Assume that his income is $100 per week and that the price of a cookie is $1. If the price doubles, he cuts his consumption in half; the amount that he spends on cookies stays constant at $100. This means that CM's **price elasticity of demand** for cookies is exactly −1. His demand is **unit-elastic.***

*Excerpted from Daniel S. Hamermesh, *Economics Is Everywhere* (New York: McGraw-Hill, 2004), p. 49.

Suppose you make $20,000 a year and you're interested in a used car selling for $5,000. If the seller were willing to drop the price by 5 percent to $4,750, that small percentage price cut might be enough to induce you to buy that car.

Over time the demand for a particular good often becomes more elastic. Take gasoline. If its price doubles, will people stop driving to work? To school? To the store? For the first year or two, there may be little you can do except cut back on your less essential driving. But when it comes time to buy a new car, you're likely to look for one that gives really good gas mileage. You may look for a job that's closer to home. Also, over time, the high price of gas may lead to the development of substitute fuels.

The passage of time

Finally, the number of uses a product has affects the elasticity of its demand. The more uses, the higher the elasticity. Salt, for example, has two main uses: to season food and to make your sidewalk less slippery when it snows. At $30 a pound, salt will still be purchased by most people to season food, but only when the price gets down to around 30 cents a pound will salt be used on the sidewalks.

Number of uses

Water has a great number of uses. The price of water happens to be very, very low, so we use it not just to drink, to bathe in, but to wash our car and water our lawn. If all our water cost, say, what bottled water cost, then our demand for water would be very inelastic. Few of us would water our lawns if doing so cost us a dollar a pint.

Does a food that's kosher (i.e., something that observant Jews are allowed to eat) have a higher elasticity of demand than one that isn't (for example, ham, pork, shellfish)? Does being kosher help sales? As you'll see in the accompanying box, it doesn't hurt.

<u>What makes demand elastic?</u>

- <u>Close substitutes are available.</u>
- <u>The product is a luxury rather than a necessity.</u>
- <u>The price of the product is high relative to buyers' incomes.</u>
- <u>Over time, the demand for a product becomes more elastic.</u>
- <u>The more uses for a product, the greater its elasticity.</u>

Advertising

What is the purpose of advertising? Everyone knows it's supposed to get the consumer to buy more of a good or service. Some industries (such as tobacco, automobiles, airlines, toothpaste, breakfast cereals, and liquor) spend very heavily on advertising. In terms of what we've already discussed, we'll talk about how advertising affects demand.

In a nutshell, advertisers try to make demand for their products greater but, at the same time, less elastic. They want to push their firm's demand curve over to the right; but they also want to make it steeper or more vertical.

Yes, I sell people things they don't need. I can't, however, sell them something they don't want. Even with advertising. Even if I were of a mind to.
—John O'Toole, Chairman, Foote Cone & Belding (advertising agency)

You Don't Have to Be Jewish to Eat Kosher

Only a small fraction of those buying kosher food do so for religious reasons—Jews, Muslims, and Seventh Day Adventists have similar dietary laws. Most of the rest buy it for health-related reasons—they are vegans, vegetarians, lactose-intolerant, or have other food allergies.

Sales of kosher food has more than quintupled since 1996. Albertsons, Pathmark, ShopRite, Kmart, Walmart, and other chains all have aggressively retooled their kosher offerings.

Question: What has this tremendous expansion of the kosher food market done to the elasticity of demand for kosher food? Clearly the more uses a product has, the higher its elasticity of demand.*

*Sherri Day, "Forget Rye Bread, You Don't Have to Be Jewish to Eat Kosher," *The New York Times,* June 28, 2003, p. B1.

Advertising is legalized lying.
        —H. G. Wells

*Advertising may be described
as the science of arresting the
human intelligence long enough
to get money from it.*

        —Stephen Leacock,
                economist

First, advertising seeks an increase in demand. A second way in which advertising can influence a product's demand curve is by making it more inelastic. This is often done by means of brand identification.

Two similar products, Bayer aspirin and St. Joseph's aspirin, have been extremely well advertised. The fact that both are familiar product names alone attests to their popularity. If you go into the drugstore and see Squibb, Johnson & Johnson, and Bayer aspirin, which do you buy? Do you buy Bayer even if it's more expensive?

Aspirin is aspirin. What's in the Squibb and Johnson & Johnson bottles is identical to what Bayer puts in its bottles. But Bayer has convinced large numbers of people that somehow its aspirin is better, so people are willing to pay more for it. Right on the bottle it says "Genuine Bayer Aspirin," which may raise doubts about the genuineness of the aspirin sold by the competition. Bayer's advertising has been able to make its demand curve more inelastic. This company could raise its price, yet not lose many sales. That is the essence of inelastic demand.

McDonald's has been especially successful in advertising its brand name. Here is a report from the *New York Daily News* on a study of the effect of advertising on preschoolers:

> Stanford University researcher Tom Robinson, who conducted the study, said kids' perceptions of taste were "physically altered by the branding."
>
> And it's not just burgers and fries. Carrots, milk and apple juice tasted better to the kids when they were wrapped in the Golden Arches.
>
> The study had youngsters sample identical McDonald's foods in name-brand and unmarked wrappers. The unmarked foods always lost the taste test. Robinson said it was remarkable how children so young were already so influenced by advertising.
>
> The study involved 63 low-income children ages 3 to 5 from Head Start centers in San Mateo County, Calif.[2]

Advertising attempts to change the way we *think* about a product. It tries to make us think a product is more useful, more desirable, or more of a necessity. Ideally, an ad will make us feel we *must* have that product. To the degree that advertising is successful, the demand curve is made steeper and is pushed farther to the right, as in Figure 7.

An advertising campaign may attempt to convince consumers that a certain good or service is not only unique but actually a necessity. If you were running the advertising

Figure 7
An Increased and Less Elastic Demand

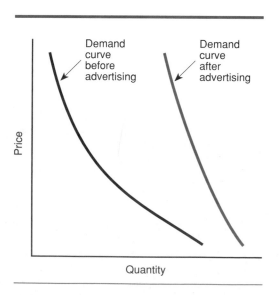

2http://www.nydailynews.com/lifestyle/health/2007/08/07/2007-08-07_for_kids_it_tastes_be...

campaign for a medical group doing hair transplants, you would try to convince millions of middle-aged men that a transplant would not only change their lives, but that only *your* doctors could do it right. If your ads were completely successful, the demand curve for hair transplants from your firm would be very inelastic.

Price elasticity of demand is closely related to the total revenue earned by a firm. We'll examine that relationship in the next section.

Elasticity and Total Revenue

Elastic Demand and Total Revenue

If you owned a haircutting salon and gave 20 haircuts at a price of $10, how much would your total revenue be? It would be $200 ($10 × 20). *Total revenue is price times output sold.*

Suppose price were raised from $10 to $12 and quantity demanded fell from 20 to 12. Let's try a three-part question:

1. Calculate elasticity.
2. State whether demand is elastic, unit elastic, or inelastic.
3. Calculate total revenue where price is $10 and $12. (See Table 2.)

TABLE 2	Hypothetical Revenue Schedule	
Price	Quantity Demanded	Total Revenue
$10	20	$200
12	12	144

Solution: $P_1 = \$10$; $P_2 = \$12$; $Q_1 = 20$; and $Q_2 = 12$.

$$\frac{12 - 20}{12 + 20} \cdot \frac{12 + 10}{12 - 10} = \frac{\overset{1}{\cancel{-8}}}{\underset{4}{\cancel{32}}} \cdot \frac{\overset{11}{\cancel{22}}}{\underset{1}{\cancel{2}}} = \frac{-11}{4} = -2.75$$

The coefficient of elasticity being greater than 1, demand is elastic. What happened to total revenue when price is raised from $10 to $12? It fell from $200 to $144.

We see, then, that *when demand is elastic, if we were to raise price, total revenue would fall.* This would make another good exam question: "If price rises and demand is elastic, total revenue will (*a*) rise, (*b*) fall, or (*c*) remain the same."

> If demand is elastic, a price increase will lead to a fall in total revenue.

What do most students do when their instructor goes over this problem and tells them it might make a good exam question? They write down what appears in italic type in the previous paragraph. Then, on the exam, if they happen to remember that rule—there will be about 20 such rules to memorize—they'll get it right. After the test, the rule is forgotten along with 99 percent of the other material that was memorized.

In this course you can figure out a lot of the answers to exam questions right on the spot. Take the exam question I quoted: "If price rises and demand is elastic, total revenue will (*a*) rise, (*b*) fall, or (*c*) remain the same." To figure this out, make up a problem like the one we just did. The key here is that you want demand to be elastic. That means percentage change in quantity is greater than percentage change in price.

To derive our next rule, we'll use the same problem we've just solved (when elasticity was found to be 2.75). Try this question: "If price declines and demand is elastic, total revenue will (*a*) rise, (*b*) fall, or (*c*) remain the same." In that problem, when price dropped from $12 to $10, what happened to total revenue?

Seeing that total revenue rose from $144 to $200, we can state our second rule. *When demand is elastic, if we were to lower price, total revenue would rise.*

Inelastic Demand and Total Revenue

Now we're ready for the third and fourth rules. What happens to total revenue when demand is inelastic and price is raised? You can make up your own problem, or if you like, use the data from our straight-line graph in Figure 5. When price was raised from $2 to $3, quantity demanded declined from 9 to 8. How much, then, is total revenue at a price of $2 and at a price of $3?

At a price of $2, it is $18 ($2 × 9); at a price of $3, it is $24 ($3 × 8). We now have our third rule. *When demand is inelastic, if we were to raise price, total revenue would rise.*

> If demand is elastic, a price increase will lead to an increase in total revenue.

Can you guess the fourth rule? Using the same data but reversing the process (that is, lowering price), we find: *When demand is inelastic and price is lowered, total revenue will fall.* (Price goes from $3 to $2, and total revenue falls from $24 to $18.)

As a businessperson facing an inelastic demand curve, you would never lower your price, because your total revenue would decline. You would be selling *more* units and getting *less* revenue. If someone offered to buy 8 units from you for $24, would you agree to sell 9 units for $18? *Think* about it. What would happen to your total revenue? What would happen to your total cost? Obviously, your total revenue would decline from $24 to $18. And your total cost? Surely it would cost you more to produce 9 units than 8 units. If your total revenue goes down and your total cost goes up when you lower your price, it would hardly make sense to do so (see Table 3).

TABLE 3 Elasticity of Demand and Total Revenue
If demand is elastic:
when price is raised, total revenue falls.
when price is lowered, total revenue rises.
If demand is inelastic:
when price is raised, total revenue rises.
when price is lowered, total revenue falls.

All of this is summed up in the accompanying box, "How Total Revenue Varies with Elasticity." As you'll see, when price elasticity of demand is 1, a firm maximizes its total revenue.

Income Elasticity of Demand

In the last chapter we talked about normal goods and inferior goods. You may remember that as a person's income rises, her demand for a normal good rises, while her demand for an inferior good falls.

Income elasticity of demand measures how the consumption of various goods and services respond to change in income. Income elasticity of demand is defined as the quantity demanded divided by the percentage change in income:

$$E_I = \frac{\text{Percentage change in quantity demanded}}{\text{Percentage change in income}}$$

How Total Revenue Varies with Elasticity

Earlier in this chapter we calculated the elasticity of a straight-line demand curve. Now let's see how total revenue varies with elasticity. We've reproduced the same graph (Figure 4) that we worked with before. Please go ahead and calculate the total revenue when the price is $9, $8, and $7.

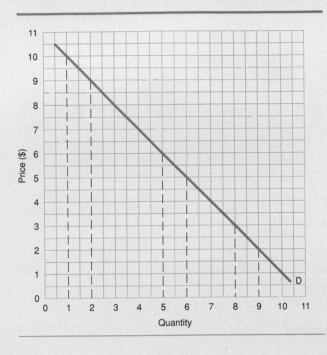

Figure A
Straight-Line Demand Curve

Solution:

$$Total\ Revenue = price \times output$$
$$\$18 = \$9 \times 2$$
$$24 = 8 \times 3$$
$$28 = 7 \times 4$$

We see so far that when price is lowered, total revenue is increasing. Since we are moving down this straight-line demand curve, elasticity is decreasing. Now let's calculate the total revenue for prices of $6, $5, $4, and $3.

Solution:

$$Total\ Revenue = price \times output$$
$$\$30 = \$6 \times 5$$
$$30 = 5 \times 6$$
$$28 = 4 \times 7$$
$$24 = 3 \times 8$$

Once we get past the point of unitary elasticity between prices of $6 and $5, total revenue declines as price is lowered.

Let's go over what's been happening. According to the law of demand, when a seller lowers her price, she will sell more of her output. In this problem, for each dollar she lowers her price, she sells one more unit of output. That's the good news. The *bad* news is that when she lowers her price, she lowers it for each unit of output. For example, when she lowers her price from $8 to $7, she increases her sales from 3 units to 4 units. But instead of getting $8 for each of those first 3 units, now she gets just $7.

Let's summarize our findings. As we move down the demand curve, elasticity declines while total revenue increases. Total revenue reaches a maximum at unit elasticity. As we continue lowering price, demand becomes increasingly inelastic, while total revenue continues falling.

Let's consider the income elasticity for concert tickets. Suppose your income rises by 10 percent and you decide to increase your purchases of concert tickets by 30 percent. Find your income elasticity for concert tickets.

Solution:

$$E_I = \frac{Percentage\ change\ in\ quantity\ demanded}{Percentage\ change\ in\ income} = \frac{30\%}{10\%} = 3.0$$

So your income elasticity for concert tickets is 3.0. Just like price elasticity of demand, any income elasticity greater than 1 is considered elastic. So concert tickets have a demand that is income elastic.

If you buy 10 percent more compact discs in response to a 20 percent increase in income, find your income elasticity for compact discs.

Solution:

$$E_I = \frac{\text{Percentage change in quantity demanded}}{\text{Percentage change in income}} = \frac{10\%}{20\%} = 0.5$$

Your income elasticity of demand for compact discs is 0.5. Any income elasticity less than 1 is considered inelastic. So compact discs have a demand that is income inelastic.

These two examples—concert tickets and compact discs—illustrate positive income elasticity. If income elasticity for a good or service is positive, then we can say that the good or service is *normal*. But if the income elasticity is negative, then that good or service is *inferior*. Examples of inferior goods are potatoes, rice, and spaghetti. Intercity bus rides and courses in cosmetology are inferior services.

If *your* income went all the way down, what would *you* do? You might eat a lot more rice, potatoes, and spaghetti. During a couple of my bouts with extreme poverty, I bought huge jars of peanut butter and of marmalade, which I would spread on white bread. In addition to always having something to eat, I never needed to plan meals.

Cross Elasticity of Demand

The demand for one good is sometimes affected by prices changes in other goods. For example, when the price of steak goes up, some people will buy less steak and more fish. So a rise in the price of steak will increase the demand for fish. We say, then, that steak and fish are substitute goods. Suppose that the price of gasoline doubles. What happens to the demand for motor oil?

If the price of gasoline doubles, then people will drive less, and, consequently, the demand for motor oil will fall. Gasoline and motor oil are complementary goods.

How can we tell if two goods are substitutes or complements? All we need to do is calculate the *cross elasticity of demand*. This measures the responsiveness of the demand for good A to a change in the price of good B, indicating how much more or less of good A is purchased as the price of good B changes. Cross elasticity is defined as the percentage change in quantity demanded of one good (A), divided by the percentage change in the price of a related good (B).

$$E_{AB} = \frac{\text{Percentage change in quantity of A demanded}}{\text{Percentage change in price of B}}$$

If the price of steak increases by 20 percent and the quantity of fish demanded increases by 10 percent, find the cross elasticity of demand for these two goods.

$$E_{AB} = \frac{\text{Percentage change in quantity of A demanded}}{\text{Percentage change in price of B}} = \frac{10\%}{20\%} = 0.5$$

The cross elasticity of demand is 0.5. When it's positive, then the goods are substitutes. Now let's calculate the cross elasticity of demand for motor oil and gasoline. Suppose that the price of gasoline rises by 100 percent and the quantity of motor oil demanded falls by 50 percent. Do your work right here and then see if it matches mine.

Solution:

$$E_{AB} = \frac{\text{Percentage change in quantity of A demanded}}{\text{Percentage change in price of B}} = \frac{-50\%}{100\%} = -0.5$$

We know that when the cross elasticity of demand is positive, the goods are substitutes. Since the cross elasticity of demand between gasoline and motor oil is negative, these are complementary goods. <u>When the price of one goes up, the quantity demanded of the other goes down.</u>

Price Elasticity of Supply

Our analysis of the price elasticity of supply parallels our analysis of the price elasticity of demand. This time around, however, we'll take a few shortcuts. Let us begin with the simplified formula:

<u>Elasticity of supply is the responsiveness of quantity to changes in price.</u>

$$\frac{\text{Percentage change in quantity supplied}}{\text{Percentage change in price}}$$

You'll remember that the demand curve slopes downward to the right, so that price and quantity are inversely related, and the price elasticity of demand is negative (although, by convention, we take its absolute value). The supply curve slopes upward to the right, so price and quantity are directly related. According to the law of supply, which we covered in the last chapter, as price changes, quantity supply changes in the same direction. Consequently, when we calculate the price elasticity of supply, it will be positive.

Next, let's discuss the meaning of the elasticity of supply. Not surprisingly, it has pretty much the same meaning as the elasticity of demand. It measures the responsiveness of the quantity supplied to changes in price. A high elasticity of, say, 10 means a 1 percent change in price brings about a 10 percent change in quantity supplied. And, similarly, an elasticity of 0.2 means a 10 percent change in price gives rise to just a 2 percent change in quantity supplied.

Now we'll look at a few graphs illustrating elasticity of supply. We'll start with perfect elasticity, then look at perfect inelasticity, and close with relative elasticity.

Figure 8 shows a perfectly elastic supply curve, which is exactly the same as a perfectly elastic demand curve. Figure 9 shows a perfectly inelastic supply curve, which would be identical to a perfectly inelastic demand curve.

Supply tends to be inelastic during very short periods of time. In the United States right after World War II, it was nearly impossible to get a car at *any* price. It took time to convert from tank, jeep, and plane production back to turning out those shiny new Hudsons, Studebakers, Kaiser-Fraisers, Nashes, and Packards. Even if you were willing to part with a big one—that's right, a thousand bucks—you still had to put your name on a year-long waiting list. Supply became more elastic after a few years, as more firms entered the industry and existing firms increased their output.

As you might even know from personal experience, Americans don't like to wait. Why didn't we just import the cars we needed from Japan, Korea, Germany, and other automobile-producing nations? After all, today, barely half of all the cars we buy are made by American firms. Back in 1945, though, the United States was the only large industrial nation with its factories still intact. Those of Japan, France, Germany, Italy,

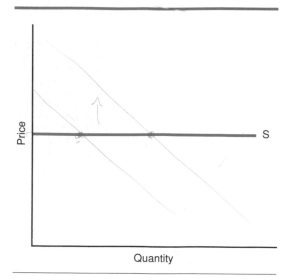

Figure 8
Perfectly Elastic Supply Curve

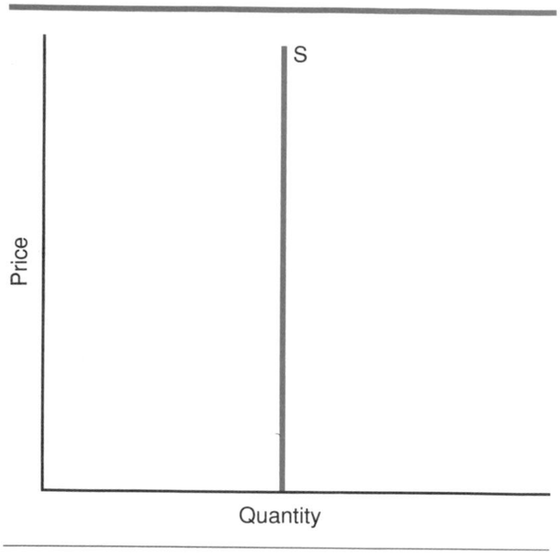

Figure 9
Perfectly Inelastic Supply Curve

the United Kingdom, and most other advanced economies had been largely destroyed by wartime bombing. So in the late 1940s if you wanted to buy a car, you bought one made in Detroit.

Finally, take a look at relative elasticities of supply in Figure 10. Which curve is more elastic? You should recognize S_2 as the more elastic because it's flatter and quantity supplied would be fairly responsive to price changes.

Elasticity over Time

We've mentioned that supply grows more elastic over time, especially when enough time has passed for new firms to enter the industry and for existing firms to increase their output. Economists have identified three distinct time periods, which we'll look at now.

(1) The Market Period   The *market period* is the time immediately after a change in market price during which sellers can't respond by changing the quantity supplied. The classic example is the strawberry farmer who arrives at a farmers' market with

Figure 10
Relative Elasticities of Supply

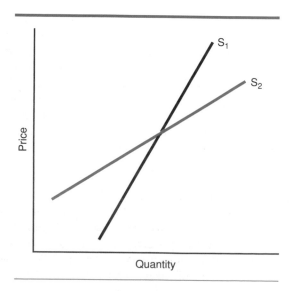

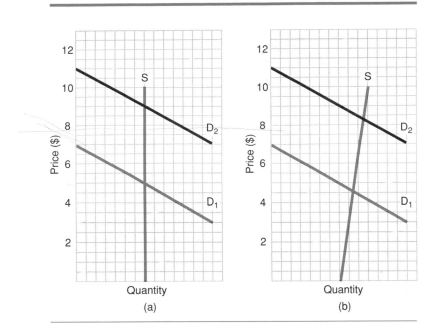

Figure 11
The Market Period
(a) Initially the price is $5 (where S and D_1 cross). Demand increases to D_2, raising price to $9. Supply is perfectly inelastic, so suppliers cannot sell more even though they want to.
(b) When demand rises from D_1 to D_2, price increases from $5 to $8.40. Sellers are able to raise their output just slightly, as indicated by the very inelastic supply curve.

100 buckets of strawberries. This is her entire inventory of ripe strawberries. What does her supply curve look like?

It looks like the one in Figure 11(a). So, even though the price rose from $5 a bucket to $9 a bucket, she cannot add to her supply of 100 buckets. The farmer's supply curve is perfectly inelastic. She has no time to respond to this increase in demand and its resulting price increase.

We know that ripe strawberries are perishable: They need to be sold before they go bad. So let's say that, instead of rising, demand fell in Figure 11(a) from D_2 to D_1. The seller would be forced to accept the lower price of $5. She would not be in a position to withhold any of her supply of strawberries because they will spoil in another few days. Under such circumstances, at the end of the day, sellers of perishable goods often discount their prices by 50 percent or even more.

Does this mean that in the market period, all supply curves are perfectly inelastic? While they may well be for those selling perishables as well as products that will soon be obsolete (like today's newspapers and this week's news magazines), other producers might be able to carry an inventory of goods that they could sell if the price went up unexpectedly. The supply curve for those producers in the immediate market period might look like the one in Figure 11(b). This supply curve has some positive slope, indicating that a higher price *does* induce a somewhat higher quantity supplied. Because of this, the price in Figure 11(b) rises to just $8.40, rather than $9 as it did in Figure 11(a).

(2) The Short Run   In the *short run* a business firm has a fixed productive capacity. A firm that manufactures cars, for example, has a fixed number of assembly lines, but those assembly lines, which are regularly run in two eight-hour shifts, can be extended to three. A store that is open from 8 A.M. to 6 P.M. can stay open another couple of hours each evening. And so, an increase in demand will result in considerably more output [see Figure 12(a)].

(3) The Long Run   In the *long run* there is sufficient time for a firm to alter its productive capacity, it can leave the industry, and new firms can enter the industry. When demand rises—and when that rise is considered to be long lasting—then at least some existing firms will add to their plant and equipment, and new firms, attracted by the higher price, will enter the industry. Alternatively, if demand falls, some or all firms will cut back on their plant and equipment, while others may leave the industry.

Figure 12

The Short Run and the Long Run

(a) Initially price is at $5 (where D_1 and S intersect). When demand rises to D_2, price rises to $7.50 in the short run. Suppliers are able to expand output in the short run, perhaps by hiring more workers and expanding business hours.
So the price rose from $5.00 to $7.50, and, in response, quantity supplied rose. You'll notice, then, that *there was no change in supply—only a change in quantity supplied.*
(b) When demand rises from D_1 to D_2, price rises from $5 to $6.50. Sellers are able to expand output quite a lot in the long run, perhaps by adding workers, plant, and equipment. And new firms are attracted to the industry by the higher price.

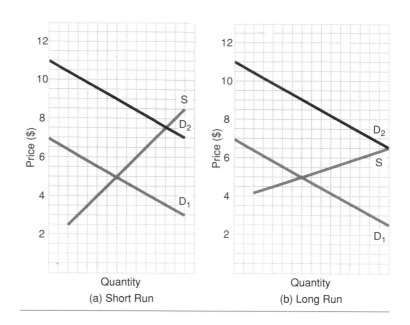

The long-run response to an increase in demand is shown in Figure 12(b). Note that the supply curve in Figure 12(b) is more elastic than that in Figure 12(a). And so, in the long run, industry supply will be more elastic than in the short run. And in the market period, industry supply is either perfectly inelastic or very inelastic. The longer the time horizon, the more elastic is supply.

Think of the transition from the market period of the short run to the long run as a continuous process. When demand rises, the price will shoot up from $5 to $9, Figure 11(a), or $8.40, Figure 11(b). Over time it will decline to $7.50 in the short run and to $6.50 in the long run. But, since this price decline is part of a continuous process, it may fall by a few cents a week—or maybe at a somewhat different speed—until it finally settles at $6.50. How long this process will take depends on the industry; we'll consider this in more detail in another couple of chapters.

In the next section we'll be using supply and demand analysis to see how taxes affect equilibrium price and quantity. And we'll see how the elasticities of supply and demand determine the relative tax burden imposed on buyers and sellers.

Tax Incidence

Tax incidence tells us who really pays a tax, or who bears the burden. In cases like the personal income tax and the payroll tax, which are both direct taxes, the burden clearly falls on the taxpayer. But when we're dealing with indirect taxes such as excise and sales taxes, the incidence is less clear.

A tax lowers supply and raises price.

A tax on a good or service will raise its price. In terms of supply, such a tax, in effect, lowers supply. This is so because at every price sellers will be offering less for sale. Supply is defined as the quantities people are willing and able to sell at different prices, so this tax will shift the supply curve to the left. As a result of the tax, people are willing and able to sell less at every price. That is a decrease in supply.

Who bears the burden of a tax? Most people would say the consumer does. After all, doesn't the seller merely act as the agent for the government and collect the tax? Or, put slightly differently, doesn't the seller just pass the tax on to the consumer?

There's only one way to find out, and that's to do a few measurements. We'll begin with price and output. Assume supply is S_1 in Figure 13; how much are price and output? Price is $8, and output is 8.

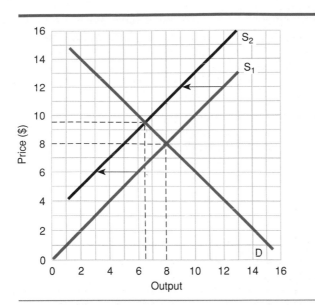

Figure 13
Decrease in Supply
When supply falls from S_1 to S_2, price rises from $8 to $9.50; output falls from 8 to 6.5. Who bears the burden of this $3 tax? It is borne equally by the buyer and the seller.

Ready for a curveball? Here it comes. How much do you think the tax is if it lowers supply from S_1 to S_2? Hint: Measure it vertically. Did you get $3 (the vertical distance from S_1 to S_2 at an output of 8)? Good! We're about halfway to figuring out who bears the burden of this tax.

We've represented a tax increase as a decrease in supply, from S_1 to S_2. So we need to find the new price and quantity. What are they? Price climbs to $9.50, while quantity falls to 6.5. OK, who bears the burden of this tax? Ask yourself, Was the consumer any worse off after the tax increase? She *was?* Why? Because she had to pay a higher price. How *much* higher? One dollar and 50 cents higher. She had to absorb half of the $3 tax.

In this case, then, the tax burden is shared by the buyer and the seller. Can you guess what factor determines where the burden falls? It's the relative elasticities of supply and demand. This is illustrated in the three panels of Figure 14. In Figure 14(a) (the

A tax increase leads to a decrease in supply.

What factor determines the tax burden?

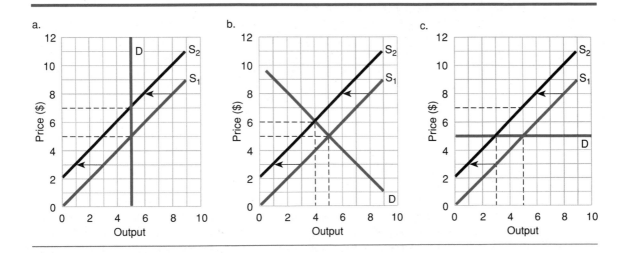

Figure 14
Decreases in Supply Due to Tax
(a) When demand is perfectly inelastic, a decrease in supply from S_1 to S_2 represents a tax of $2, which is borne entirely by the buyer. We see that because the price rises from $5 to $7.
(b) When the elasticities of demand and supply are equal, the burden of the $2 tax is borne equally by the buyer and the seller; each pays $1. We can see that because the price rises from $5 to $6.
(c) When demand is perfectly elastic, a tax increase of $2 is borne entirely by the seller. Note that price remained at $5.

left panel) we have a perfectly inelastic demand curve. When a $2 tax is imposed, who pays it? Obviously, the buyer does. In Figure 14(b) (the middle panel), where the elasticities of demand and supply are equal, the tax burden is shared equally. And when demand is perfectly elastic, as in Figure 14(c) (the right panel), the burden falls entirely on the seller, because price stays at $5 and the seller must absorb the entire $2 tax.

Let's step back a bit and generalize. When demand is perfectly inelastic [Figure 14(a)], the buyer bears the entire tax burden. And when demand is perfectly elastic [Figure 14(c)], the tax burden falls entirely on the seller. In other words, as elasticity of demand rises, the tax burden is shifted from the buyer to the seller.

We can also do a parallel analysis on the elasticity of supply. But we're not going to. We'll just summarize the results. When supply is perfectly inelastic, the seller bears the entire tax burden. And when supply is perfectly elastic? You guessed it: The buyer bears the entire burden. To conclude, as the elasticity of supply rises, the tax burden shifts from the seller to the buyer.

We are left with two conclusions: (1) As elasticity of demand rises, the tax burden is shifted from the buyer to the seller. (2) As the elasticity of supply rises, the tax burden is shifted from the seller to the buyer.

Who bears the burden of a tax? It all comes down to the relative elasticities of demand and supply. We need to make one more set of comparisons. We need to compare the relative elasticities of demand and supply. This is shown in Figure 15, where a tax of $2 has been imposed. In Figure 15(a) (the left panel), where supply is relatively inelastic (to demand), the tax is borne largely by the seller (because price rises just 50 cents, from $5 to $5.50). But when supply is relatively elastic [in Figure 15(b), the right panel], price rises from $5 to $6.50. This means the buyer must pay $1.50 of the $2 tax.

Once you're really good with tax burdens, all you'll need to do is glance at a graph and you'll know the relative tax burdens of the buyer and the seller. Then, if you find yourself in a juice bar and the guy next to you starts complaining about taxes, you can whip out some graph paper and show him all about the relative elasticities of supply and demand. And, who knows, he might even buy you a glass of carrot juice.

> When demand is perfectly inelastic, the burden falls entirely on the buyer.

> When supply is perfectly inelastic, the burden falls entirely on the seller.

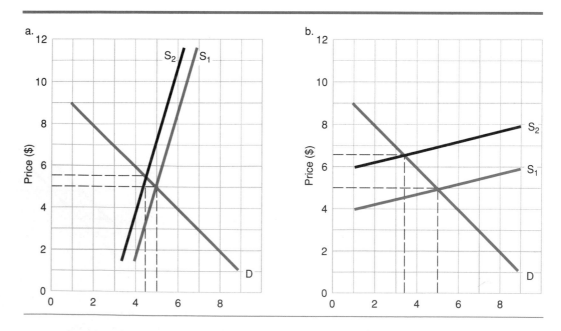

Figure 15

Decreases in Supply Due to Tax

In the left graph (panel a), a $2 tax increase pushes up price from $5 to $5.50. How much of this tax is borne by the buyer and how much by the seller?

The buyer pays $0.50 and the seller pays $1.50. In the right graph (panel b), a $2 tax pushes up price from $5 to $6.50. How much of this tax is borne by the buyer and how much by the seller? The buyer pays $1.50 and the seller pays $0.50.

Death and Taxes

In 2001, at President George W. Bush's behest, Congress voted to phase out the federal estate tax, which falls on estates valued at more than $1.5 million. All estates will be tax-free in 2010.* Question: Would some of those who were dying hang on for a few more days or weeks, so that their heirs would reap a substantial tax savings?

The answer is "Yes!" according to a study by University of Michigan economists Wojciech Kopczuk and Joel Slemrod. Their findings were reported by *BusinessWeek:*

> ... they examined death rates of those affected by 13 estate-tax changes from 1917 to 1984. Somewhat to their surprise, they found that in cases where tax rates were raised, death rates tended to be higher in the weeks before the rise went into effect. And in

cases where tax rates were cut, death rates were higher in the weeks following the cut.

> The researchers estimate that a $10,000 tax saving seems to boost the probability of someone dying just before a tax increase by 1 percent, while the same saving increases the probability of dying just after a tax cut by almost 2.5 percent. "Evidently," says Slemrod, "some people are able to will themselves to survive a bit longer if it will enrich their heirs."

---

*Unless a new law is passed, in 2011 the estate tax will be reinstated.
Source: *BusinessWeek,* April 9, 2001, p. 24.

You have probably heard the aphorism that the only sure things in life are death and taxes. In the accompanying box, we reveal an actual relationship between these two great inevitabilities.

Current Issue: The Price Elasticity of Demand for Oil

The two main consumer uses for oil are gasoline for cars and home heating oil. In the very short run, the demand for these products is almost perfectly inelastic. In the long run, however, when people are buying new cars, many more will opt for more fuel-efficient vehicles, just as they did after the two oil crises in 1973 and 1979. From the mid-1970s through the mid-1980s American car buyers traded in their American-made gas guzzlers for Japanese-made compacts and subcompacts.

Between early 2002 and summer of 2008 the price of oil shot up from $20 to $145 a barrel. As gasoline topped $4 a gallon, did Americans switch to more fuel-efficient vehicles? Not exactly. Instead of trading in their SUVs, they often opted to just add a Honda Civic, a Toyota Corolla, a Nissan Versa, or a Mini Cooper. Still, between April 2007 and April 2008 the sale of SUVs did fall by 25 percent.

A study by Christopher Knittel, a University of California, Davis, economics professor, found that between 1975 and 1980, whenever gasoline went up by 20 percent, drivers cut their gas consumption by 6 percent. But from March 2001 to March 2006, drivers reduced consumption just 1 percent for every 20 percent price increase.[3] How do we explain this sharp decline in the elasticity of demand for gasoline over the last three decades?

Experts note that commuters are driving longer distances to work because of suburban sprawl, that improvements in mass transit have fallen behind over the years and that driving to malls and ferrying children around has become part of the American lifestyle.[4]

---

[3]See Clifford Kraus, "Drivers Offer a Collective Ho-Hum as Gasoline Prices Soar," *The New York Times,* March 30th, 2007, p. C1.

[4]Op. cit., p. C5

Some suggest high gas prices mean less to many families than they once did, and credit cards have eased the immediate pain at the pump.

There were similar results in the heating oil market. Although home heating oil prices went through the roof, so to speak, in the spring of 2000, few people sold their homes or switched from oil to gas heat. But in the long run, we can expect fewer oil furnaces to be installed in new homes and gas heat to become considerably more popular. Indeed, you may even notice a few more solar panels on the roofs of your neighborhood houses.

Questions for Further Thought and Discussion

1. As you move down a straight-line demand curve, what happens to its elasticity? Can you prove this with a numerical example?

2. If demand is elastic and price is raised, what happens to total revenue? Can you prove this?

3. Estimate your elasticity of demand for (a) gasoline; (b) cigarettes; (c) video rentals.

4. Why is industry supply more elastic in the long run than in the short run, and more elastic in the short run than in the market period?

5. How do the relative elasticities of demand and supply affect the relative tax burdens of the buyer and the seller?

6. What are the major determinants of the elasticity of demand?

7. When would you want to own a business that sells price-elastic products? Why?

8. Draw a demand curve with unitary elasticity everywhere. (Hint: Think about total revenue.)

9. *Practical Application:* You live in a drafty old house that was once owned by your great grandparents. When the price of home heating oil triples, it now costs you over $2,000 a month to heat your house, which is a lot more than you can afford. What would you do in the market period, the short run, and the long run?

10. *Practical Application:* If the elasticity of demand for cigarettes among teenagers is 0.5, how much would the price of a pack of cigarettes have to be raised from $10 to cut teenage smoking by 20 percent?

Workbook for Chapter 6

Name _____   Date _____

Multiple-Choice Questions

Circle the letter that corresponds to the best answer.

1. If demand is inelastic and price is raised, total revenue will _____. (LO3)
   a) rise
   b) fall
   c) stay the same
   d) possibly rise or possibly fall

2. If demand is elastic and price is lowered, total revenue will _____. (LO3)
   a) rise
   b) fall
   c) stay the same
   d) possibly rise or possibly fall

3. Over time the supply of a particular good or service tends to _____. (LO5)
   a) become more elastic
   b) become less elastic
   c) stay about the same

4. Demand is elastic when _____. (LO1)
   a) percentage change in price is greater than percentage change in quantity
   b) percentage change in quantity is greater than percentage change in price
   c) the demand curve is vertical
   d) price increases raise total revenue

5. A perfectly elastic supply curve is _____. (LO1)
   a) a horizontal line
   b) a vertical line
   c) neither a horizontal nor a vertical line

6. A 5 percent increase in the price of sugar causes the quantity demanded to fall by 15 percent. The demand for sugar is _____. (LO1)
   a) perfectly elastic
   b) elastic
   c) unit elastic
   d) inelastic
   e) perfectly inelastic

7. Which statement is true about the graph in Figure 1? (LO1)
   a) Demand is perfectly elastic.
   b) Demand is perfectly inelastic.
   c) Demand is more elastic at point X than at point Y.
   d) Demand is more elastic at point Y than at point X.

Figure 1

8. The advertiser wants to push her product's demand curve _____. (LO2)
   a) to the right and make it more elastic
   b) to the right and make it less elastic
   c) to the left and make it more elastic
   d) to the left and make it less elastic

9. Demand is elastic if _____. (LO1)
    a) percentage change in quantity is greater than percentage change in price
    b) percentage change in price is greater than percentage change in quantity
    c) percentage change in quantity demand is zero
    d) percentage change in price is zero
    e) percentage change in quantity is equal to percentage change in price

10. The most important determinant of the degree of elasticity of demand is _____. (LO2)
    a) whether the item is a big-ticket item
    b) whether the item is a luxury
    c) how many uses the product has
    d) the availability of substitutes

11. Statement I. A perfectly elastic demand curve has an elasticity of zero.
    Statement II. When demand is elastic and price is raised, total revenue will fall. (LO1)
    a) Statement I is true, and statement II is false.
    b) Statement II is true, and statement I is false.
    c) Both statements are true.
    d) Both statements are false.

12. Statement I. When demand is inelastic and price is lowered, total revenue will rise.
    Statement II. Demand is unit elastic when elasticity is one. (LO3)
    a) Statement I is true, and statement II is false.
    b) Statement II is true, and statement I is false.
    c) Both statements are true.
    d) Both statements are false.

13. When demand is perfectly elastic, a tax increase is borne _____. (LO7)
    a) only by the buyer   c) mostly by the buyer
    b) only by the seller   d) mostly by the seller

14. If supply is perfectly inelastic, a tax increase is borne _____. (LO7)
    a) only by the buyer
    b) only by the seller
    c) mostly by the buyer
    d) mostly by the seller

15. A tax will _____. (LO7)
    a) lower price and raise supply
    b) lower price and lower supply

c) raise price and lower supply
d) raise price and raise supply

16. When demand is relatively inelastic and supply is relatively elastic, the burden of a tax will be borne _____. (LO7)
    a) mainly by sellers
    b) mainly by buyers
    c) equally between sellers and buyers
    d) it is impossible to determine the relative burdens of the tax

Use Figure 2 to answer questions 17 through 20.

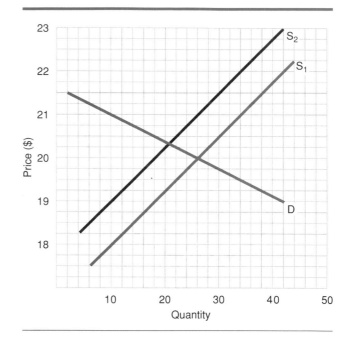

Figure 2

17. How much is the tax? (LO7)
    a) $.35   d) $1.00
    b) $.50   e) $1.50
    c) $.65

18. About how much of the tax is paid by consumers in the form of higher prices? (LO7)
    a) 10 cents   d) 50 cents
    b) 20 cents   e) 65 cents
    c) 35 cents

19. About how much of the tax is paid by the sellers? (LO7)
    a) 80 cents   d) 35 cents
    b) 65 cents   e) 10 cents
    c) 50 cents

20. As a result of the tax, the consumption of this good falls by about _____. (LO7)
    a) 4   d) 7
    b) 5   e) 8
    c) 6

21. The imposition of a tax _____. (LO7)
    a) raises both supply and demand
    b) lowers neither supply nor demand
    c) lowers only supply
    d) lowers only demand

22. Supply is most elastic in _____. (LO6)
    a) the market period
    b) the short run
    c) the long run

23. Which is the most accurate statement? (LO7, 5)
    a) The demand for gasoline is very elastic.
    b) The demand for home heating oil is very inelastic.
    c) The seller of a perishable commodity has a relatively elastic supply.
    d) Most firms can double their output in the short run.

24. Figure 3 shows _____. (LO1, 5)
    a) a perfectly inelastic supply curve
    b) a perfectly inelastic demand curve
    c) a perfectly inelastic demand curve or a perfectly inelastic supply curve
    d) none of the above

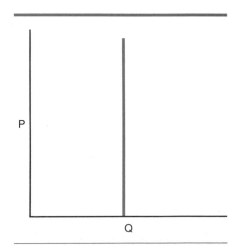

Figure 3

25. If your income goes down by 15 percent and you cut back on your manicures by 25 percent, then your demand for manicures is _____. (LO4)
    a) income elastic
    b) income inelastic
    c) income elastic and income inelastic
    d) neither income elastic nor income inelastic

26. If our income elasticity for vacation trips is 2.8, we may conclude that vacation trips are _____. (LO1)
    a) a normal service
    b) an inferior service
    c) both a normal service and an inferior service
    d) neither a normal service nor an inferior service

27. When the cross elasticity of demand for two services is negative, then these services are _____. (LO4)
    a) complements
    b) substitutes
    c) both complements and substitutes
    d) neither complements nor substitutes

28. A firm seeking to maximize its total revenue would lower its price until price elasticity of demand was _____. (LO3)
    a) a maximum
    b) a minimum
    c) one

29. If the price of iPods is reduced by 50 percent and the quantity of songs demanded on iTunes rises by 25 percent, then the cross elasticity of demand for iPods and iTune songs is _____. (LO4)
    a) 5.0
    b) 1.0
    c) 0.5
    d) 0.25

30. During a very bad recession the nation's disposable income fell by 10 percent, while its consumption of a certain good rose by 5 percent. That good was _____ good. (LO4)
    a) a complementary
    b) a substitute
    c) a normal good
    d) an inferior good

31. Movie tickets and DVD rentals are _____ services. (LO4)
   a) inferior
   b) complementary
   c) substitute
   d) highly inelastic

32. Total revenue would be maximized when elasticity is _____. (LO3)
   a) above 10
   b) rising
   c) falling
   d) 1
   e) 0

33. The firm with this demand curve shown in Figure 4 would receive the highest total revenue at point _____. (LO3)
   a) A
   b) B
   c) C
   d) D
   e) E

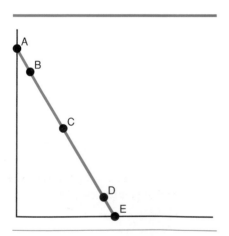

Figure 4

Fill-In Questions

1. Elasticity of demand is a measure of the responsiveness of _____ to changes in price. (LO1)

2. Over time the elasticity of supply for a particular good or service tends to become _____. (LO5)

3. A tax on a service that has a relatively elastic demand and a relatively inelastic supply will be borne mainly by the _____. (LO7)

4. A perfectly elastic supply curve can be shown graphically as _____. (LO5)

5. A tax cut _____ supply. (LO7)

Problems

1. Draw a perfectly elastic supply curve. (LO5)

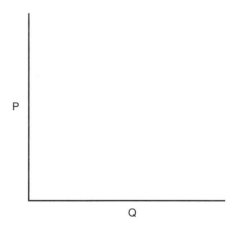

2. Draw a perfectly inelastic supply curve. (LO5)

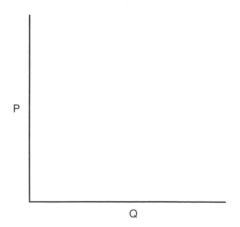

3. Draw a supply curve, S_1. Then draw a more elastic supply curve, S_2. (LO5)

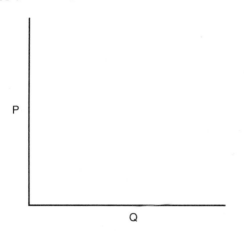

4. If price were increased from $40 to $42 and quantity demanded fell from 50 to 45, calculate elasticity; state whether demand is elastic, unit elastic, or inelastic; and find how much total revenue was when price was $40 and $42. (LO1, 3)

5. If price were lowered from $50 to $43 and quantity demanded rose from 15 to 16, calculate elasticity; state whether demand is elastic, unit elastic, or inelastic; and find how much total revenue was when price was $50 and $43. (LO1, 3)

6. Draw a demand curve, D_1. Then draw a second demand curve, D_2, that is less elastic. (LO1)

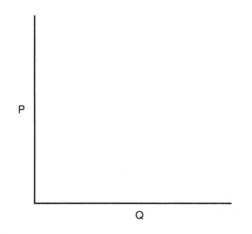

7. Draw a perfectly elastic demand curve and state its elasticity. (LO1)

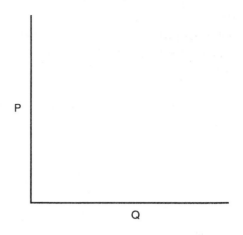

8. On the demand curve shown in Figure 5, label the curve where it is very elastic, unit elastic, and very inelastic. (LO1)

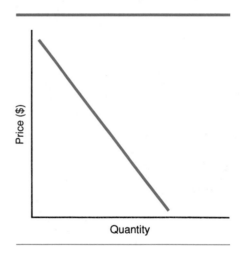

Figure 5

9. If elasticity of demand is 2 and price is raised from $10 to $11, by what percentage will quantity demanded fall? (LO1)

10. If elasticity of demand is 0.5 and price is lowered from $20 to $19, by what percentage will quantity demanded rise? (LO1)

11. In Figure 6: (a) How much is the tax? (b) How much of this tax is borne by the buyer and how much is borne by the seller? (LO7)

12. If the price of laser eye surgery falls by 50 percent and the quantity of contact lenses demanded falls by 25 percent, find the cross elasticity of demand for these two goods. (LO4)

13. If your income rises by 20 percent and you decide to increase your purchases of clothing by 10 percent, find your income elasticity for clothing. (LO4)

14. If the elasticity of demand is 5, and the price of a cup of coffee is $2, how much would the seller need to reduce her price in order to increase the quantity sold by 50 percent? (LO1)

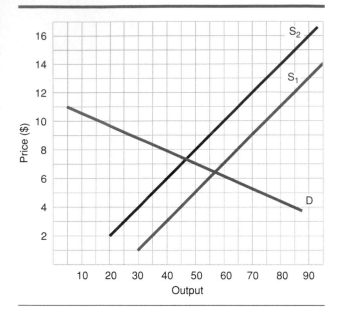

Figure 6

Chapter 7

Theory of Consumer Behavior

A ren't you tired of getting ripped off by unscrupulous merchants who overcharge their customers? Don't you agree that the prices of so-called designer jeans, designer sun glasses, and even designer bottled water are ridiculous? Aren't you so fed up that you're just not going to *take* it anymore? Well, I've got some good news and some bad news. The bad news is that sellers will keep charging whatever outrageous prices they feel like charging. And the good news? You don't have to pay those prices. Because if you look around, none of these sellers is exactly putting a gun to your head.

There's a rest stop on the Belt Parkway at Plum Beach, which, of course, is in Brooklyn. The water fountains are usually not working, but there's a guy in a truck selling cans of soda for $1.75. If you were really thirsty, would you pay $1.75? If you did, would you feel that you were being ripped off? By the time you have finished this chapter, you may have changed your mind. In the strange and wonderful world of utility, no buyer is ever ripped off.

Why do people buy goods and services? Because they derive some utility or value from them. We measure that utility by how much consumers are willing to pay.

LEARNING OBJECTIVES

After reading this chapter you should be able to:

1. Define and explain marginal utility.
2. Apply the law of diminishing marginal utility.
3. Measure total utility.
4. Discuss and analyze maximizing utility.
5. Define and solve the water–diamond paradox.
6. Measure consumer surplus.

You may recall from earlier chapters that Adam Smith established that individuals act in their own self-interest. The 19th-century British economist, Jeremy Bentham, applied this observation to human behavior: Individuals make choices in order to promote pleasure and to avoid pain. In sum, we make our choices in a way that *maximizes* the degree of satisfaction we gain from our activities. So what are we waiting for? Let's maximize our pleasure and minimize our pain.

Utility

What Is Utility?

Everything is worth what its purchaser will pay for it.

–Publilius Syrus (1st century B.C.E.)–

Utility is measured by how much you are willing to pay for something.

People often confuse utility and usefulness. "Why did he buy that thing? It has no utility." In economics that would be a self-contradicting statement. Utility means only that you think enough of something to buy it.

Suppose you were ravenously hungry and came upon a hamburger stand. If the attendant told you that he had just one hamburger left—you're hungry enough to put away four—and that you'd have to pay $3 for it, would you buy it?

If you did, that hamburger would have given you at least $3 worth of utility. What if you had refused to pay $3, but when he lowered the price to $2.75 you bought it? Then that hamburger's utility would have been $2.75.

You were still hungry and soon came upon a second hamburger stand. You said to yourself as you approached, "I'd be willing to spend $2 on a second hamburger." Why not $2.75? Because you're not as hungry as you were before you wolfed down that $2.75 hamburger.

Suppose you spent $2 on a second hamburger and would be willing to pay just $1 for a third. Notice how the utility derived from consuming that third hamburger is much less than what the second one was worth.

If you managed to find someone who would let you have that third hamburger for no more than a dollar, what then? You'd try to get a fourth hamburger for a quarter. Why only a quarter? Because you're feeling a little piggy, and besides, I need you to be a little hungry still so I can illustrate a couple of things.

Table 1 sums things up. That's your demand schedule for hamburgers when you're ravenously hungry.

Marginal Utility

Marginal utility

The law of diminishing marginal utility

You've seen that the first hamburger you consumed had a utility of $2.75, the second had a utility of $2, the third, $1, and the fourth, 25 cents. Thus you just derived your marginal utility schedule. It appears in Table 2.

Marginal utility is the additional utility derived from consuming one more unit of some good or service. What happens to your marginal utility as you consume more and more hamburgers? It declines from $2.75 to $2 to $1 to 25 cents.

We've come to the law of diminishing marginal utility. As we consume more and more of a good or service, we like it less and less. That might be OK for an exam answer, but I have to be a bit more elegant here, so let's restate the law as follows. As we consume increasing amounts of a good or service, we derive diminishing utility, or satisfaction, from each additional unit consumed.

Think about it. How many movies would you want to go to in a day? In a week? How many plane trips to Europe would you want to take in a month? How many times do you want to take this economics course?

| TABLE 1 | Hypothetical Demand Schedule for Hamburgers |

Price	Quantity Demanded
$2.75	1
2.00	2
1.00	3
.25	4

TABLE 2	Hypothetical Marginal Utility Schedule
Units Purchased	Marginal Utility
1	$2.75
2	2.00
3	1.00
4	.25

Total Utility

Are you ready to put all of this together? Let's hope everything *will* come together when we look at total utility. *Total utility is the utility you derive from consuming a certain number of units of a good or service.* To get total utility, just add up the marginal utilities of all the units purchased. Table 3 does this for your hamburgers.

Total utility

Let's go over Table 3 column-by-column. The first two columns come from Table 1, which is your hypothetical demand schedule for hamburgers. The third column, "Marginal Utility," shows how much utility you derive from the first, second, third, and fourth hamburgers.

Can you figure out how we got the fourth column, "Total Utility"? Start with a total utility of $2.75. That's the marginal utility of the first hamburger. How much is the second hamburger worth to you? It's worth $2; so what's the total utility of two hamburgers? It's $4.75—$2.75 for the first hamburger plus $2 for the second.

How much is the total utility of three hamburgers? It's $5.75—$2.75 for the first plus $2 for the second plus $1 for the third. And finally, how much is the total utility of four hamburgers? It comes to $6 ($2.75 + $2 + $1 + $.25).

There are two ways to find total utility. First, we can add up the marginal utilities of the items purchased, in this case hamburgers. A shortcut would be to add the marginal utility of the last hamburger purchased to the total utility of the previous hamburgers purchased. For example, the total utility of three hamburgers is $5.75. The marginal utility of the fourth hamburger is $.25; just add that to the $5.75 to get a total utility of $6 for four hamburgers.

Are you comfortable calculating marginal utility and total utility? If you are, please go directly to the next section, on maximizing utility. But if you need more practice, then you'll find help in the box "Calculating Marginal Utility and Total Utility."

Maximizing Utility

How much we buy of any good or service depends on its price and on our marginal utility schedule. Go back to the hamburger example. We can see in Table 3 how many hamburgers we'd buy at each price. Unlike that example, however, in real life there's usually only one price. No one will offer us that first hamburger at $2.75, the second at $2, the third at $1, and the fourth at a quarter. For every good or service at any given time, there's just one price.

What we do, then, with our limited incomes is try to spend our money on what will give us the most satisfaction or utility. Keep in mind that as we consume more and more of any good or service, according to the law of diminishing marginal utility, its marginal utility declines. How much do we buy? We keep buying more and more until our marginal utility declines to the level of the price.

TABLE 3	Hypothetical Utility Schedules		
Price	Units Purchased	Marginal Utility	Total Utility
$2.75	1	$2.75	$2.75
2.00	2	2.00	4.75
1.00	3	1.00	5.75
.25	4	.25	6.00

Calculating Marginal Utility and Total Utility

We'll start with a demand schedule for College of Staten Island sweatshirts, shown in Table A. We can use this demand schedule to derive a marginal utility schedule and a total utility schedule for Karen Jones. How much utility does she derive from that first sweatshirt? Obviously, she gets $15 worth. So now you have her marginal utility and total utility from one sweatshirt. Put those numbers in Table A below and then complete the table.

The second table shows Karen Jones's marginal utility and total utility schedules. Make sure that your figures in Table A match mine in Table B.

Did you get everything right? If you did, you may skip the rest of this box. But stay with it if you need more help.

Look at the marginal utility column. Now look at the price column (to the far left on Table B). You'll notice

that they're identical. Check back to Table 3. You see that the price column and the marginal utility column are also identical. So when you're filling in the marginal utility column, just copy the price column.

Now let's tackle total utility. Marginal utility and total utility are identical at a quantity of one. At a quantity of two, total utility is found by adding the marginal utility at quantity one plus the marginal utility at quantity two. So total utility ($27) = $15 + $12. How do we find total utility at a quantity of three? We add the first three marginal utilities: $15 + $12 + $10 = $37.

At a quantity of four, total utility ($44) = $15 + $12 + $10 + $7. At a quantity of five, total utility ($49) = $15 + $12 + $10 + $7 + $5. And at a quantity of six, total utility ($53) = $15 + $12 + $10 + $7 + $5 + $4.

Table A

Price	Quantity Demanded	Marginal Utility	Total Utility
$15	1	15	15
12	2	12	27
10	3	10	37
7	4	7	44
5	5	5	49
4	6	4	53

Table B

Price	Quantity Demanded	Marginal Utility	Total Utility
$15	1	$15	$15
12	2	12	27
10	3	10	37
7	4	7	44
5	5	5	49
4	6	4	53

$$\frac{\text{Marginal utility}}{\text{Price}} = 1$$

Because we buy a good or service up to the point at which its marginal utility is equal to its price, we could form this simple equation:

$$\frac{\text{Marginal utility}}{\text{Price}} = 1$$

For example, if the price of hamburgers were 25 cents, we'd buy four hamburgers. The marginal utility of the fourth hamburger would be 25 cents. So

$$\frac{\text{Marginal utility}}{\text{Price}} = \frac{25¢}{25¢} = 1$$

A person distributes his income in such a way as to equalize the utility of the final increments of all commodities consumed.

—W. Stanley Jevons,
Theory of Political Economy

If we buy hamburgers up to the point where $\frac{\text{MU of hamburgers}}{\text{P of hamburgers}} = 1$, we will do the same with everything else we buy. How many CDs do we buy? We keep buying them until their MU falls to the level of their price. If there are 93 different CDs we like equally, do we buy them all, even if we have the money? Maybe we buy two or three. The first one we buy is worth more to us than the price if we go ahead and buy a second one; and that second one is worth more than the price if we buy a third CD. If we stop at three, the third CD is worth the price, but a fourth would not be.

We keep buying CDs until their MU declines to the price level. In fact, the same thing can be said about everything we buy. To generalize,

$$\frac{MU_1}{P_1} = \frac{MU_2}{P_2} = \frac{MU_3}{P_3} = \frac{MU_n}{P_n}$$

General utility formula

We have been making an implicit assumption throughout our discussion of utility: We are getting bargains on each unit we purchase until the last one. The MU of that last one is just equal to price, but the MU of the earlier units purchased is greater than price. This is the assumption on which consumer surplus is based.

Suppose that a good or service were free. How many units would you consume? You would keep consuming units until the item's marginal utility fell to zero.

If movies were free, you might go to three or four a week. I once knew a guy who went to four a day. Not only did he love movies, but he didn't work, go to school, or engage in any other productive activity.

We have seen that as we consume more units, not only does marginal utility decline, but total utility keeps rising. But what happens when marginal utility falls to zero? At that point we don't consume any more of that good or service. And our total utility is at a maximum.

If, for some reason, we consumed still another unit, our marginal utility would become negative. That unit would be worth less than zero. An extra hamburger that would make us sick or a movie that we didn't have time to see or didn't really *want* to see would decrease total utility. And so, in conclusion, we maximize our total utility when our marginal utility falls to zero.

Is there ever a precise way to measure utility? Surprisingly, there is. In fact, if you're willing to go to Salt Lake City, you can measure your own utility for a restaurant meal (see the accompanying box).

The Water–Diamond Paradox

How come water, which is essential to life, is so cheap, while diamonds, which are not at all essential, are so expensive? We now have enough utility theory under our belts to resolve this apparent paradox.

First, the law of diminishing marginal utility tells us that as we consume increasing amounts of a good or service, we derive decreasing utility (or satisfaction) from each additional unit consumed. Second, we know from the general utility formula that we'll

---

The Pay-What-You-Want Restaurant

One World Everybody Eats (aka One World Café), a buffet-style restaurant serving freshly prepared dishes, was opened in 2003. In an article on more.com, Jennifer Margulis describes how things work there:

A hand-lettered sign asks customers to "donate a fair, respectable amount", similar to what they'd pay in other restaurants. Anyone too strapped to make even the most minimal payment can volunteer to wash dishes, cut vegetables, clean up or garden (one hour = one meal). . . .*

How much do customers actually pay? The average donation is usually between $8 and $10 per meal. The restaurant's main way of making ends meet is ensuring that virtually all of its food gets eaten. While other eateries often throw out as much as half their food, One World Everybody Eats wastes almost nothing. It has just one rule: Don't ask for more than you can eat.

If you'd like to measure your utility for a meal, there may now be a pay-what-you-want restaurant closer to home. SAME Café (So All May Eat) in Denver, One World Spokane, and Potager in Arlington, Texas also provide this opportunity. I am old enough to remember the penny scales that dispensed tickets with your weights and your fortune. Now we've get restaurants that provide meals and also enable you to measure your utility.

---

*Jennifer Margulis, "No Prices. No Menu. No Wastes," more.com, May 2009.

keep buying more of a good or service until its marginal utility falls to the level of its price. Therefore:

$$\frac{\text{MU of water}}{\text{P of water}} = \frac{\text{MU of diamonds}}{\text{P of diamonds}}$$

The price of water in most parts of the world is low because it is abundant. But the price of diamonds is high because they are not abundant.

We consume a great deal of water, so the marginal utility of the last gallon consumed is as low as its price. But we buy very few diamonds, so the marginal utility of the last carat purchased is very high.

Imagine what would happen if diamonds were to become plentiful and water were to become scarce. The marginal utility of water would go way up, along with its price. And the marginal utility and price of diamonds would fall. Not only that, but there would no longer be a water–diamond paradox.

on the web

Why are diamonds in such short supply? Go to www.adiamondisforever.com, then click on How to Buy (at the bottom of the page), and then on Diamond Facts.

Some Limitations of Utility Applications

What is the utility of an hour with a personal trainer? What is the utility of a ballpoint pen? What is the utility of the economics course you're taking?

The answer to each of these questions is that there *is* no answer, because utility is not inherent in a particular good or service. It is simply a measure of what the buyer is willing to pay. So an hour with a personal trainer may be worth $100 to Becky Sharp, but only $40 to Alexei Karamazov. One of your classmates might have been willing to pay $5,000 to take this economics course, but perhaps you would not pay one penny more than you had to.

So it would be meaningless to state that a certain good is worth, say, $10. Or that a certain service has a value of $50. We *may* say that a particular good is worth $10 to Margaret Thatcher. Or that a service is worth $50 to John Galt.

One of the basic functions of our federal government is to transfer money from most taxpayers to the poor in the form of welfare payments, food stamps, Medicaid, free school lunches, and housing assistance. One may draw the inference that the poor would derive more utility from the goods and services they now can afford than would the more affluent taxpayers. Is this a correct assumption?

Well, it *sounds* reasonable. But we can't make that assumption. We can't assume, for example, that if a poor person found a 10-dollar bill, he would derive more utility spending it than a rich person. It would seem *reasonable* that the poor person would derive more utility, but we can't make interpersonal utility comparisons. We *can* observe *one* person's spending behavior and determine *her* utility schedule, but we have no basis on which to compare that of two or more people.

We also need to consider that a person's utility schedule can change over time. If you decided to lose some weight, or you wanted to eat better, then surely your demand for Godiva chocolates would go down. And that would lower your utility schedule for those chocolates. Similarly, if you suddenly got a yen for travel, there would be a major upward shift in your utility schedule for airplane tickets.

Consumer Surplus

You may remember the great English economist Alfred Marshall from the last chapter. Here's his description of consumer surplus:

> The price which a person pays for a thing can never exceed, and seldom comes up to, that which he would be willing to pay rather than go without it, so that the satisfaction which he

gets from its purchase generally exceeds that which he gives up in paying away its price; and he thus derives from the purchase a surplus of satisfaction. It may be called consumer's surplus.

Today we define consumer's surplus, or consumer surplus, a little more succinctly: *Consumer surplus is the difference between what you pay for some good or service and what you would have been willing to pay.*   Definition of consumer surplus

I used to live in a very classy neighborhood. In fact, this neighborhood was so classy that none of the supermarkets bothered to stay open on Sunday. One tiny grocery store was open all the time, and I made a point of never shopping there because the place was an unbelievable rip-off.

As fate would have it, a friend who was visiting on a Sunday wanted meatballs and spaghetti. I warned her that the only place to buy it was at that store. She went there and came back with an eight-ounce can. "How much?" I asked.

"Don't ask," she replied.

Later I saw the price on the can. It was $5.99.

Was my friend ripped off? The answer, surprisingly, is no. Forget about the store being open on Sunday, the convenience, and all the rest. The bottom line is my friend bought that can of meatballs and spaghetti. If it wasn't worth at least $5.99 to her, she wouldn't have bought it.

When you're really thirsty, wouldn't you be willing to pay $3 for a bottle of water if you had to? You might be very angry, but as we like to say here in Brooklyn, no one was twisting your arm.

In the previous section, we said a person keeps buying more and more of a good or service until that person's marginal utility for that item falls to the price level. Therefore, each unit purchased except the last one was a bargain because MU was greater than price. This can be seen in Figure 1, where we once again use the hamburger example from the beginning of the chapter.

If the price of hamburgers were a quarter, you would purchase four and the consumer surplus would be the triangular area above the price line in Figure 1. The total consumer surplus would be based on the difference between what you paid for each hamburger

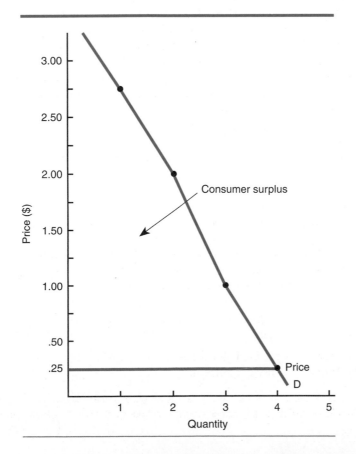

Figure 1

Consumer Surplus
Since the consumer's surplus is the difference between the price you pay and the price you would have been *willing* to pay, then the consumer surplus in this graph would be represented by the area to the left of the demand curve (what you would have been willing to pay) and above the price line.

TABLE 4 Hypothetical Demand Schedule for Sessions with a Personal Trainer

Price	Quantity Demanded	Marginal Utility	Total Utility
$50	1	——	——
40	2	——	——
30	3	——	——
25	4	——	——
20	5	——	——
15	6	——	——

TABLE 5 Hypothetical Utility Schedule for Sessions with a Personal Trainer

Price	Quantity Demanded	Marginal Utility	Total Utility
$50	1	$50	$ 50
40	2	40	90
30	3	30	120
25	4	25	145
20	5	20	165
15	6	15	180

(25 cents) and what you would have been willing to pay. You would have been willing to pay $2.75 for the first one, so your consumer surplus on the first hamburger is $2.50. You would have been willing to pay $2 for the second, so on that one your consumer surplus is $1.75. Similarly, on the third hamburger your consumer surplus is $1.00 − .25 = $.75. On the fourth hamburger, MU = Price (25 cents = 25 cents), so there is no consumer surplus. Your total consumer surplus would be $2.50 + $1.75 + $.75 = $5. Looked at another way, your total utility derived from the four hamburgers is $6, and if you pay 25 cents for each of four hamburgers, $6 minus $1 equals a consumer surplus of $5.

The next time you go shopping, don't complain about being ripped off. No one ever paid more than he or she was willing to pay; no one ever bought anything whose price exceeded its utility; and anyone who ever bought several units of the same product at a fixed price enjoyed a consumer surplus.

Let's calculate another consumer surplus. I'm getting a little tired of hamburgers, so let's do exercise sessions with a personal trainer. Enough sessions and you'll be on the next U.S. Olympic team. Use just the information in Table 4 to find the consumer surplus you'll enjoy by purchasing four sessions.

The key thing to remember in solving this problem is the definition of consumer surplus: the difference between what you pay for something and what you would have been willing to pay. How much did you pay for four sessions? If you bought four, then the price must have been $25; so you paid $100 (4 × $25). Now, how much would you have been *willing* to pay for these four sessions? In other words, how much total utility do you derive from four personal training sessions? To find that out, we need to fill in Table 5.

We see from Table 5 that four sessions have a total utility of $145. If you have to pay only $100 for these sessions, then your consumer surplus is $45 ($145 − $100).

Next question: How much would your consumer surplus be if you purchased six sessions? Work it out right here:

Use the demand schedule in Table A to find the consumer surplus if a quantity of six is purchased.

Table A

Price	Quantity Demanded	Marginal Utility	Total Utility
$100	1	------	------
80	2	------	------
65	3	------	------
55	4	------	------
50	5	------	------
45	6	------	------

How much do we have to pay for six units? The answer is $270 (6 × 45). Next, how much would we be willing to pay for these six units? Your filled-in table should look like Table B, which indicates that the total utility of six units is $395.

Table B

Price	Quantity Demanded	Marginal Utility	Total Utility
$100	1	$100	$100
80	2	80	180
65	3	65	245
55	4	55	300
50	5	50	350
45	6	45	395

Finding the Consumer Surplus

Now all we have to do is simple subtraction. We start with what we are willing to pay for six units, a total utility of $395, and subtract what we have to pay, $270. The calculation is $395 − $270 = $125. Thus $125 is our consumer surplus.

Can you find how much the consumer surplus would be if we purchased five units? Figure it out in this space.

Total utility of five units is $350. We would have to pay $250 (5 × $50). Consumer surplus is $350 − 250 = $100.

How much would the consumer surplus be if we bought three units?

Total utility of three units is $245. We would have to pay $195 (3 × $65). Consumer surplus is $245 − $195 = $50.

You would have been willing to pay $180 for the six sessions, as that's the total utility you would derive from these sessions. But you would buy six sessions only if the price were $15 per session. So you would have to pay $90 (6 × $15) for these sessions. Your consumer surplus would be $180 − $90 = $90.

Need a little more practice? You'll get it in the Extra Help box, "Finding the Consumer Surplus."

If you were a seller, is there anything you could do about cutting down on the consumer surplus of each of your customers? Not as long as you charged only one price. Now the Coca-Cola Company has begun testing a vending machine that can automatically raise prices for its drinks in hot weather. Actually in Japan, some vending machines already use wireless modems to adjust their prices based on the temperature outside.

Do Price Gougers Rip Us Off?

Let's go back to a couple of questions we asked at the beginning of the chapter: If you were really thirsty, would you pay $1.50 for a can of soda? And if you paid $1.50, were you ripped off?

If you answered "yes" to the first question, did you also answer "yes" to the second question? I hate to tell you, but if you agreed to pay $1.50 for the soda, then you were *not* ripped off. Nobody held a gun to your head, forcing you to buy that soda. You derived at least $1.50 of utility from the can of soda or you never would have spent the money. So no, you were *not* ripped off.

So we can derive this rule of thumb: *Even if you pay a very high price for a good or service, you are not getting ripped off.* But maybe there *is* an exception to this rule. Maybe during disasters, whether natural or man-made, this rule doesn't always hold.

Disasters usually bring out the best and the worst in us. The attacks of 9/11 induced an almost unprecedented outpouring of volunteers, food, protective clothing, and equipment. But disaster victims have also been subject to widespread price gouging and profiteering.

In the summer and early fall of 2004, Florida was pounded by one major hurricane after another. Here's the opening paragraph of a *New York Times* article describing price gouging in the aftermath of Hurricane Charley:[1]

> Greg Lawrence talks about the $10 bag of ice. Kenneth Kleppach says he was clipped for nearly three times the advertised price for a hotel room. And a man with a chain saw told Jerry Olmstead that he could clear the oak tree off his roof, but it would cost $10,500.

It would appear that the hotel was guilty of deceptive advertising, which is illegal. If it had openly advertised its actual room prices, then if you paid that price, you were not overpaying. If there's one thing you should remember from this chapter it's this: Nobody overpays.[2]

Do you remember the great blackout of 2003? At about 4 o'clock on an otherwise pleasant August afternoon, most of the East Coast experienced a power failure that lasted over 12 hours. There were instant entrepreneurs out on the streets of New York and other cities hawking tiny votive candles for $2, bottled water for $5, and flashlights for $10. Were these people unscrupulous price gougers or just businesspeople providing the supply of goods for which there was an increased demand? In economics, we can't make moral judgments. But we *can* ask whether their customers were being ripped off. The answer is "no."

Current Issue: All-You-Can-Eat Buffets

All-you-can-eat buffets are great places to do utility experiments because you can always identify the dividing line between positive and negative marginal utility. Let's suppose that you love pizza and there's an all-you-can-eat pizza buffet just down the block from you. So you're in there almost every night. And when you arrive, you're ravenously hungry. Question: How many slices do you eat?

---

[1] Joseph B. Treaster, "With Storm Gone, Floridians Are Hit with Price Gouging," *The New York Times,* August 18, 2004, p. Al.

[2] Some of the most outrageous price gouging took place soon after Hurricane Katrina devastated parts of the Gulf Coast in August 2005. Six-dollar-a-gallon gasoline, $300 generators selling for $1,500, and dozens of other necessities selling for three, four, or five times their normal prices were quite common. For more on this, see the end of the section, "Government Failure," in Chapter 3.

Let's say that you always have four slices. In fact, you can't quite finish that fourth slice. Next question: How much marginal utility would you have gotten from a fifth slice?

Answer: Less than zero. Your marginal utility from that fifth slice would have been negative. How much marginal utility do you get from the fourth slice?

Answer: Not a lot, since you can't finish it. But that fourth slice provided you with *some* marginal utility.

So the next time you go to an all-you-can-eat restaurant, keep in mind that you're there to carry out a marginal utility experiment. If your friends don't believe you, just bring along this book and I'll vouch for you.

Questions for Further Thought and Discussion

1. Explain the law of diminishing marginal utility, and give an example to illustrate it.

2. If you were to consume five hamburgers at Wendy's, would you enjoy a consumer surplus? Explain your answer.

3. How do we measure utility? Are interpersonal comparisons valid? Why or why not?

4. Why would Tommy Watson eventually reach the point of negative marginal utility at an all-you-can-eat restaurant?

5. Explain the water–diamond paradox.

6. *Practical Application:* What if you could walk into a music store and get as many CDs as you wanted for free, provided that you listened to 30 seconds of each song on each CD? Question: How many CDs would you listen to? Explain your answer in terms of marginal utility.

7. *Practical Application:* Miles Standish invented a 60-calorie 6-ounce milk shake, which he sold at his candy store. He noticed that each of his customers purchased at least two shakes. (a) Can you figure out how many of his customers were enjoying a consumer surplus? (b) How could Mr. Standish lower their consumer surplus?

Workbook for Chapter 7

Name _____   Date _____

Self-Review Examination

Questions 1–8: Answer true or false.

_____ 1. The water–diamond paradox has never been resolved. (LO5)

_____ 2. Total utility will rise as long as marginal utility is rising. (LO1, 3)

_____ 3. The concept of consumer surplus was formulated by Alfred Marshall. (LO6)

_____ 4. Total utility is at a maximum when marginal utility is zero. (LO1, 3)

_____ 5. We are maximizing our utility when the marginal utility of each good or service we purchase is equal to its price. (LO1, 2)

_____ 6. Utility is measured by a product's usefulness. (LO1)

_____ 7. As increasing amounts of a product are consumed, marginal utility will decline. (LO2)

_____ 8. If Matthew Avischious were to purchase five drinks at $1 each, he would enjoy a consumer surplus. (LO6)

9. State the general utility formula. (LO4)

10. Define marginal utility. (LO1)

11. Explain the law of diminishing marginal utility. (LO2)

12. What is a consumer surplus? (LO6)

Multiple-Choice Questions

Circle the letter that corresponds to the best answer.

1. If we know Olivia King's demand schedule, we can find _____. (LO1, 3)
   a) her marginal activity, but not her total utility
   b) her total utility, but not her marginal utility
   c) both her total utility and her marginal utility
   d) neither her total utility nor her marginal utility

2. If a service is free, you will consume more and more of it until _____. (LO2)
   a) your marginal utility is zero
   b) your total utility is zero
   c) both your marginal utility and your total utility are zero
   d) neither your marginal utility nor your total utility is zero

3. A product's utility to a buyer is measured by _____. (LO1)
   a) its usefulness
   b) its price
   c) how much the buyer is willing to pay for it
   d) none of the above

4. As the price of a service rises, _____. (LO6)
   a) the consumer surplus decreases
   b) the consumer surplus increases
   c) the consumer surplus may increase or decrease

5. In Figure 1 (price is OA) consumer surplus is bounded by _____. (LO6)
   a) OBD   c) ABC
   b) OACD   d) none of these

Figure 1

6. When Kelly Ziegenfuss buys five units of a particular good or service, _____. (LO6)
   a) she has no consumer surplus
   b) she has a consumer surplus
   c) there is no way of knowing whether she has a consumer surplus

7. Lauren Elise Ballard would be maximizing her total utility when _____. (LO3)
   a) she had a consumer surplus
   b) her marginal utility was zero
   c) her marginal utility was equal to her total utility
   d) she had no consumer surplus

8. Which statement is true? (LO1, 6)
   a) Most people have the same utility schedules.
   b) Most people enjoy a consumer surplus for at least some of the things they buy.
   c) We will consume additional units of a product until our consumer surplus is zero.
   d) The utility of a product is measured by its usefulness.

9. Which statement is false? (LO2, 5)
   a) The water–diamond paradox can be resolved with the help of the law of diminishing marginal utility.
   b) We will consume a service when its marginal utility is equal to its price.
   c) The law of diminishing marginal utility has little validity today.
   d) None is false.

10. As Keith Collins buys more and more of any good or service, his _____. (LO3)
    a) total utility and marginal utility both decline
    b) total utility and marginal utility both rise
    c) total utility rises and marginal utility declines
    d) total utility declines and marginal utility rises

11. Doug Horn will buy more and more of a good or service until _____. (LO4)
    a) marginal utility is greater than price
    b) price is greater than marginal utility
    c) price is equal to marginal utility

12. In Figure 2 (price is JK) consumer surplus is bounded by _____. (LO6)
    a) JKMN   c) JLN
    b) KLM   d) none of these

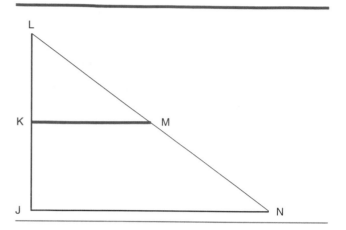

Figure 2

13. If the marginal utility you derived from the last video game you played was $1.75 and the game cost 50 cents to play, _____. (LO1, 2)
    a) you have been playing the game too long
    b) you haven't been playing the game long enough
    c) there is no way to determine whether you have played the game long enough

14. If a 10-dollar bill was found lying on the sidewalk, _____. (LO1)
    a) if a rich person found it, she would get more utility from what she could buy with it than a poor person
    b) if a poor person found it, she would get more utility from what she could buy with it than a rich person
    c) there is no way to determine whether a rich person or a poor person who found the money would get more utility from what she could buy with it

15. Which statement is the most accurate? (LO1)
    a) Your utility schedule for chewing gum can never change, since it is based on your demand schedule for chewing gum.
    b) Interpersonal utility comparisons cannot be made unless people buy that good at the same price.
    c) Everyone gets the same utility from taking a biology course.
    d) A good or service does not have any inherent utility, so we cannot say that a day at a beauty spa is worth $250.

16. You are definitely enjoying a consumer surplus when you _____. (LO6)
    a) go on an amusement park ride 10 times in a row
    b) go to the same amusement park once a summer for 10 years in a row
    c) take 10 courses a year at your college
    d) take 10 friends to the movies

17. Haley Megan Fosnough-Biersmith goes shopping for shoes and has plenty of money with her. She will keep buying shoes until _____. (LO3)
    a) her total utility equals the price
    b) her marginal utility equals the price
    c) she runs out of money
    d) the store runs out of shoes

18. Colin Kelley maximizes his utility when _____. (LO4)
    a) the marginal utility of everything he buys is equal to its price
    b) the marginal utility of everything he buys is zero
    c) he no longer enjoys a consumer surplus
    d) he buys only the lowest-priced goods and services

19. Which statement is true? (LO1)
    a) The utility of a plasma TV is greater than the utility of a 2001 Honda Accord.
    b) A $50 ticket to a Broadway show provides the ticket-holder with more utility than a $100 ticket to a different Broadway show.
    c) No one would pay for a service that provided him with no utility.
    d) A one-hour dance lesson would provide ten different people with exactly the same utility.

20. If this year's Nobel Prize winner in physics gives a free lecture at your school and just eight people attend, you may conclude that _____. (LO1)
    a) no one derived any utility from his lecture
    b) none of the people who attended would have come if there had been an admission fee
    c) the lecture must have been at an inconvenient time.
    d) at least some of the people who attended enjoyed a consumer surplus.

21. Which statement would be true about a person who goes to an all-you-can-eat restaurant? (LO2)
    a) She will never eat more food than she would at a regular restaurant.
    b) She will eat until closing time.
    c) She will eat until the marginal utility of the last portion of food is zero.
    d) She will keep eating while her marginal utility is rising.

22. Price gouging can take place only when _____. (LO1, 6)
    a) there is a natural disaster
    b) buyers are poorly informed about market conditions
    c) some buyers are willing to pay the asking price, however high
    d) the forces of supply and demand are not operating

23. Price gouging will _____. (LO6)
    a) raise consumer surplus
    b) lower consumer surplus
    c) have no effect on consumer surplus

24. If food were free in your school cafeteria, you would keep eating until _____. (LO2)
    a) your total utility was zero
    b) your marginal utility was zero
    c) your consumer surplus was zero
    d) you were sick

Problems

1. Suppose Table 1 shows your demand schedule for cans of soda. (a) What is your total utility from three cans of soda? (b) What is your marginal utility from the third can of soda? (c) If price were $1.50, how much would your consumer surplus be? (LO1, 3, 6)

169

TABLE 1

Price	Quantity Demanded
$3.00	1
2.00	2
1.50	3

2. Suppose Table 2 shows your demand schedule for CDs. (a) What is your total utility from four CDs? (b) What is your marginal utility from the fourth CD? (c) If the price is $2, how much will your consumer surplus be? (LO1, 3, 6)

TABLE 2

Price	Quantity Demanded
$10	1
8	2
6	3
4	4
2	5

3. Suppose that at three units purchased, marginal utility is $8 and total utility is $30. If the marginal utility of the fourth unit purchased is $6, how much is the total utility of four units? (LO4)

4. You're in the desert on an extremely hot day and become quite thirsty. Luckily you come upon a stand where they're selling bottled water. You would be willing to pay $10 for the first bottle, $5 for the second bottle, and $1 for the third. Luckily they're charging just a dollar. (a) How many bottles do you buy? (b) How much is your marginal utility from the third bottle? (c) How much is the total utility you will get from the three bottles? (d) How much is your consumer surplus? (LO1, 3, 6)

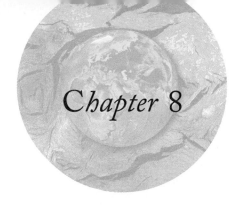

Chapter 8

Cost

There are about 30 million business firms in the United States, so it would not be a stretch to say that sometime in your life you may own or at least help run a business. The most important equation of any business firm is Total revenue − Total cost = Profit. In Chapter 17 (Chapter 5 of *Microeconomics*) we looked at total revenue, and now we'll look at total cost. In the next chapter we'll find profit.

LEARNING OBJECTIVES

After reading this chapter you should be able to:

1. Define and analyze fixed costs, variable costs, and total cost.
2. Discuss and measure marginal cost.
3. Distinguish between the short run and the long run.
4. Define and calculate average fixed, variable, and total cost.
5. Graph and analyze the AFC, AVC, ATC, and MC curves.

6. Analyze the production function and its relationship to the law of diminishing returns.
7. List the factors contributing to economies and diseconomies of scale.
8. Explain and differentiate between the shut-down and go-out-of-business decisions.

Costs

In a business firm costs are half the picture. The other half is sales or total revenue. The equation that every businessperson knows better than anything else in the world is

$$\text{Sales} - \text{Costs} = \text{Profit}$$

It can also be stated this way:

$$\text{Total Revenue} - \text{Total Costs} = \text{Profit}$$

If you write it vertically—

$$\begin{array}{r} \text{Total Revenue} \\ -\,\text{Total Cost} \\ \hline \text{Profit} \end{array}$$

—you can quickly grasp what is meant by looking at "the bottom line."

We are going to analyze costs in two ways. First we'll divide them into fixed and variable costs. A little later we'll divide them into costs in the short and long runs.

Fixed costs stay the same no matter how much output changes.

Fixed Costs

Examples of fixed costs are rent, insurance premiums, salaries of employees under guaranteed contracts, property taxes, interest payments, and most of the depreciation allowances on plant and equipment. Even when a firm's output is zero, it incurs the same fixed costs.

Fixed costs are sometimes called *sunk costs* because once you've obligated yourself to pay them, that money has been sunk into your firm. Fixed costs are your firm's overhead. The trick, as we'll see in the next chapter, is to spread your overhead over a large output.

Variable Costs

Variable costs vary with output.

When output rises, variable costs rise; when output falls, variable costs fall. What are examples of variable costs? The most important is wages, particularly the wages of production workers. If you cut back on output, you lay off some of these people. If you reduce output to zero, none of them will be paid.

Another variable cost is fuel. When you raise or lower output, you vary your fuel bill. The same is true with raw materials (for example, steel, glass, and rubber in automobile production). Electricity, telephone use, advertising, and shipping are other variable costs.

Some costs can have a component or part that is fixed and part that is variable. Take electricity. The more you use, the higher your bill—so we would generally consider electricity a variable cost. But, even if your output fell to zero and you never turned on a light, you would still have to pay a minimum bill. The same with your phone bill. It could vary substantially with your firm's output, but even if you don't make one call, you'll have to pay a minimum bill.

on the web

How much are the fixed and variable costs of renting a car for a week at Chicago's O'Hare Airport? Go to www.budget.com or www.avis.com

Total Cost

Total cost is the sum of fixed cost and variable cost.

The data in Table 1 illustrate total cost, fixed cost, and variable cost. Note that as output rises, fixed cost stays the same and variable cost rises. Note also how the increase in total cost is due to the increase in variable cost. These relationships may also be observed in Figure 1, which is based on Table 1.

Marginal Cost

Marginal cost is the cost of producing one additional unit of output.

Marginal cost is the cost of producing one additional unit of output. The concept of margin is extremely important in economic analysis, so I've listed the main examples that you'll encounter in this course in the box, "The Concept of Margin."

Using the data in Table 1, see if you can find the marginal cost of producing the first unit of output. Go ahead and write down your answer.

TABLE 1 Hypothetical Cost Schedule for a Catering Hall on Saturday Nights

Output	Fixed Cost	Variable Cost	Total Cost
1	$1,000	$ 400	$1,400
2	1,000	700	1,700
3	1,000	1,100	2,100
4	1,000	1,700	2,700
5	1,000	2,700	3,700
6	1,000	4,500	5,500
7	1,000	7,500	8,500

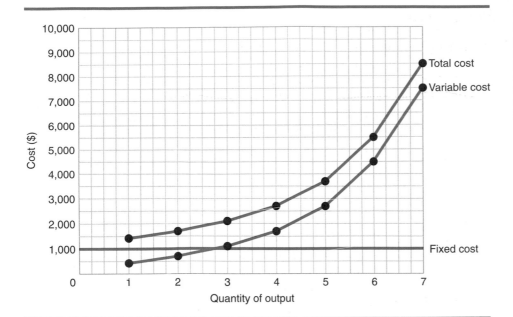

Figure 1
Fixed, Variable, and Total Cost
Since the fixed cost is $1,000, the total cost curve is $1,000 higher than the variable cost curve for each unit of output. Note, also, that total cost and variable cost rise with output, while fixed cost is constant.
Data source: Table 1.

Did you get $400? If you did, that's great. If not, then you need to read the Extra Help box, "Finding Marginal Cost When the Output is 0."

Now find the marginal costs of producing the second, third, fourth, fifth, sixth, and seventh units of output. Write down your answers here:

Solution:
Marginal cost of second unit = $1,700 − $1,400 = $300
Marginal cost of third unit   = $2,100 − $1,700 = $400
Marginal cost of fourth unit   = $2,700 − $2,100 = $600
Marginal cost of fifth unit   = $3,700 − $2,700 = $1,000
Marginal cost of sixth unit   = $5,500 − $3,700 = $1,800
Marginal cost of seventh unit = $8,500 − $5,500 = $3,000

You may have heard of the roller coaster ride in Coney Island called the Cyclone. It costs $6 for the first ride, but, if you stay on, additional rides are just $4. Does it cost the ride operator *less* money to give you the second ride than it does to give you the first ride? What do you *think?*

The Concept of Margin

In economics the word *marginal* means "additional" or "incremental." So a *marginal cost is the cost of producing one additional unit of output.* A parallel concept, which we'll be using in the next chapter, is *marginal revenue. Marginal revenue is the additional revenue derived from selling one more unit of output.*

In Chapter 5 of *Economics* and *Macroeconomics* we used the marginal propensities to consume and save.

The marginal propensity to consume tells us what percentage of each dollar of additional income we spend; the marginal propensity to save tells us what percentage of each dollar of additional income we save. And, in Chapter 7 of *Economics* and *Macroeconomics,* we worked with the marginal tax rate, which tells us what percentage of each dollar of additional income we pay in taxes.

Finding Marginal Cost When the Output is 0

Finding the marginal cost of the first unit of output is a little tricky. You need to subtract the total cost of producing 0 units of output from the total cost of producing 1 unit of output.

Reading from Table 1, we see that total cost at an output of 1 is $1,400. OK, how much is total cost when the output is 0? Remember that total cost = fixed cost + variable cost. How much is fixed cost in Table 1?

It's $1,000. And how much is variable cost when the output is 0? Variable cost is always $0 when the output

is 0. So total cost at an output of $0 is equal to the fixed cost of $1,000.

Here's one more problem to work out. Suppose that fixed cost is $500, and at an output of 1, total cost is $800. How much is marginal cost at an output of 1?

The answer is $300. Total cost at an output of 1 − total cost at an output of 0 = $800 − $500 = $300. Remember that at an output of 0, total cost = fixed cost, which in this case is $500.

It turns out that the answer is yes. First let's suppose that everyone got off after one ride and all new people got on. How long would it take to get everyone off, and then the new riders on and strapped in? Two minutes? Three minutes? As they say, time is money.

The marginal cost of giving you a second ride is less than the cost of your first ride. So the ride operator provides you with a monetary incentive to stay on. The next time a seller offers you a second item at a discount, she may be doing it because the second item cost her less to produce than the first.

TABLE 2	Hypothetical Cost Schedule for a Firm			
Output	Fixed Cost	Variable Cost	Total Cost	Marginal Cost
0	$500	$ 0	____	____
1	____	200	____	____
2	____	300	____	____
3	____	450	____	____
4	____	650	____	____
5	____	950	____	____
6	____	1,500	____	____

Here's another problem to work out. Fill in the columns for total cost and marginal cost in Table 2. Round your answers to the nearest dollar. After you've done this problem, you can check your answers against those in Table 3.

TABLE 3	Hypothetical Cost Schedule for a Firm			
Output	Fixed Cost	Variable Cost	Total Cost	Marginal Cost
0	$500	$ 0	$ 500	____
1	____	200	700	$200
2	____	300	800	100
3	____	450	950	150
4	____	650	1,150	200
5	____	950	1,450	300
6	____	1,500	2,000	550

Before we get into the short run and the long run, I'd like to go back over fixed cost, variable cost, and total cost when the output is 0. Suppose that at an output of 0 fixed cost is $200. How much are variable cost and total cost?

At an output of 0, variable cost is always $0. Therefore the total cost (fixed cost + variable cost) is $200. At an output of 0, total cost is equal to fixed cost. Let's do one more. At an output of 0, if fixed cost is $1,000, how much are variable cost and total cost?

Variable cost is 0 and total cost is $1,000.

The Short Run and the Long Run

The present time is always in the short run. The short run extends for some time into the future—sometimes a few weeks, possibly a few years. During the short run a firm has two options: It can continue operating, or it can shut down and produce no output. In the long run a firm also has two options: to stay in business or to go out of business.

The short run is the length of time it takes all fixed costs to become variable costs.

The Short Run

As long as there are any fixed costs, we are in the short run. How long is the short run? In some businesses, only a couple of minutes. One example is the ticket scalper hoping to sell some football tickets 10 minutes before kickoff.

How long are Christmas tree venders in business? Maybe for about three weeks. Their main fixed cost is their inventory. Ideally they sell out on December 24th, while any trees left over are virtually worthless. So Christmas tree vendors have a short run of about three weeks.

Most firms have considerably longer short runs. A firm with some employers under long-term contract might have a short run of 8 or 10 years. A steel firm might need a couple of years to pay off such fixed costs as interest and rent. Even a grocery store would need several months to find someone to sublet the store and to discharge its other obligations.

The Long Run

The long run is the time at which all costs become variable costs. But the long run never exists except in theory. Why not? Because you'll never have a situation in which all your costs are variable. It would mean no rent, no interest, no insurance, no depreciation, and no guaranteed salaries. That would indeed be a hard way to do business.

Toward the end of the short run, as the times for paying off various fixed costs approach, you have to decide whether you're going to stay in business. If you are, when your lease is up, you sign a new one. When a machine wears out, you replace it. And so forth.

You never really reach the long run. Like Moses, you can see the mountains of Canaan from afar, but you never get to set foot in the promised land. On any given day you can gaze out beyond your short run to your long run, but as you proceed through the short run, you have to make decisions that will push your long run farther and farther into the future. Or, as economist Abba Lerner has put it, "In the long run, we are simply in another short run."

Average Cost

Suppose you're interested in selling hot dogs at the beach. There are dozens of other hot dog venders, each of whom charges $1.50 for each hot dog. You add up all your costs, including the rent for a cart, the cost of hot dogs, buns, mustard, sauerkraut, relish, heating fuel, and napkins. Your total cost is $250 and you expect to sell 200 hot dogs a day. How much is your average cost per hot dog?

It's $1.25. So you'd make a 25 cent profit on each hot dog. What if your total cost came to $300? Find your average cost and your profit per hot dog.

Your average cost would be $1.50. Since you'd be charging $1.50 per hot dog, you'd make zero profit.

In this section we'll find average fixed cost, average variable cost, and average total cost. To get each, we do simple division, dividing by output.

Average Fixed Cost

Average fixed cost (AFC) is fixed cost divided by output.

Average fixed cost gets progressively smaller as output rises because we are dividing a larger and larger denominator into a numerator that stays the same. If fixed cost is $1,000 how much will average fixed cost be at one unit of output?

$$\text{AFC} = \frac{\text{Fixed cost}}{\text{Output}}$$

$$\text{Average fixed cost (AFC)} = \frac{\text{Fixed cost}}{\text{Output}} = \frac{1,000}{1} = 1,000$$

Now figure out AFC at two units of output. Just plug the numbers into the formula.

$$\text{AFC} = \frac{\text{Fixed cost}}{\text{Output}} = \frac{1,000}{2} = 500$$

Calculate AFC for three, four, five, and six units of output to the nearest dollar in the space below. Use your figures to fill the AFC column of Table 4.

Solutions:

$$\text{AFC} = \frac{\text{Fixed cost}}{\text{Output}}$$

$$\frac{1,000}{3} = 333; \frac{1,000}{4} = 250; \frac{1,000}{5} = 200; \frac{1,000}{6} = 167$$

Average Variable Cost

Average variable cost (AVC) is variable cost divided by output.

Unlike fixed cost, variable cost rises with output. What about AVC? Usually it declines for a while as output increases. Eventually, however, AVC will level off and begin to rise.

Table 4 shows a variable cost schedule. I've worked out the AVC for 1 and 2 units of output. I'd like you to work out the rest and fill in that column of the table.

$$\text{AVC} = \frac{\text{Variable cost}}{\text{Output}}$$

$$\text{Average variable cost (AVC)} = \frac{\text{Variable cost}}{\text{Output}} = \frac{500}{1} = 500$$

$$\frac{800}{2} = 400$$

TABLE 4 Hypothetical Cost Schedule*

Output	Variable Cost	Total Cost	Average Fixed Cost	Average Variable Cost	Average Total Cost
1	$ 500	$1,500	——	$500	$1,500
2	800	1,800	——	400	900
3	1,000	2,000	——	——	——
4	1,300	2,300	——	——	——
5	1,700	2,700	——	——	——
6	2,400	3,400	——	——	——

*The fixed-cost column is omitted to save space. You can easily derive fixed cost, since at each output variable cost is $1,000 less than total cost.

Average Total Cost

Like AVC, ATC declines with output for a while but eventually levels off and then begins to rise. We'll see that ATC lags slightly behind AVC, leveling off when AVC begins to rise and not rising until after AVC is well on the way up.

Average total cost (ATC) is total cost divided by output.

We'll use Table 4 to get in some practice. I'll work out ATC for the first two outputs, and you work out the rest.

$$\text{Average total cost (ATC)} = \frac{\text{Total cost}}{\text{Output}} = \frac{1,500}{1} = 1,500$$

$$\frac{1,800}{2} = 900$$

$$\text{ATC} = \frac{\text{Total cost}}{\text{Output}}$$

You'll find everything worked out in Table 5. I'd like you to note that AFC and AVC add up to the ATC at each output. You can use this as a check on your work. If they don't add up, you've made a mistake.[1]

TABLE 5 Hypothetical Cost Schedule

Output	Variable Cost	Total Cost	Average Fixed Cost	Average Variable Cost	Average Total Cost
1	$ 500	$1,500	$1,000	$500	$1,500
2	800	1,800	500	400	900
3	1,000	2,000	333	333	667
4	1,300	2,300	250	325	575
5	1,700	2,700	200	340	540
6	2,400	3,400	167	400	567

We'll work out one more table and then move on to graphs. Table 6 has all the numbers you'll need to calculate AFC, AVC, and ATC. Please fill in Table 6, including

TABLE 6 Hypothetical Cost Schedule

Output	Variable Cost	Total Cost	AFC	AVC	ATC	Marginal Cost
1	$ 200	———	———	———	———	———
2	300	———	———	———	———	———
3	420	———	———	———	———	———
4	580	———	———	———	———	———
5	800	———	———	———	———	———
6	1,200	———	———	———	———	———
7	1,900	———	———	———	———	———

---

[1]You may have noticed that AFC and AVC don't add up to ATC when the output is 3. This slight discrepancy is actually due to rounding: $333\frac{1}{3} + 333\frac{1}{3} = 666\frac{2}{3}$. I rounded $333\frac{1}{3}$ down to 333 and $666\frac{2}{3}$ up to 667, so when the sum of AFC and AVC doesn't exactly equal ATC, it is probably due to rounding.

TABLE 7	Hypothetical Cost Schedule					
Output	Variable Cost	Total Cost	AFC	AVC	ATC	Marginal Cost
1	$ 200	$ 700	$500	$200	$700	$200
2	300	800	250	150	400	100
3	420	920	166.67	140	306.67	120
4	580	1,080	125	145	270	160
5	800	1,300	100	160	260	220
6	1,200	1,700	83.33	200	283.33	400
7	1,900	2,400	71.43	271.43	342.86	700

the marginal cost (MC). Work out your answers this time to the nearest cent. Assume fixed cost is $500. Check your work using Table 7.

Graphing the AFC, AVC, ATC, and MC Curves

Much of microeconomic procedure involves three steps: filling in a table, drawing a graph based on that table, and doing an analysis of the graph. We're ready for the second step.

Plan your graph before you draw it.

When you draw a graph, you should plan it first. Label both axes. Figure out how high you'll need to go. Then figure out your scale. Will each box on your graph paper represent $5, $10, or $20? To draw a proper graph, you need graph paper. If you *still* haven't purchased at least one package of graph paper, you need to go out right now to get one or two packages.

Your output will be from 1 to 7. What will be the highest point on your graph? Both ATC and MC have highs of $700. So the vertical axis should go up to $700. When students begin to draw graphs, they connect all the points with straight lines, often using rulers. For starters, don't use a ruler to connect the points. You're drawing curves, not a series of straight lines that meet each other at odd little angles.

The AFC curve, which is not used very often in microeconomic analysis, is plotted in the accompanying box, "Distinguishing between Fixed Cost and Average Fixed Cost." I'd like you to draw a graph of the AVC, ATC, and MC curves. If you've drawn them correctly, they'll come out like those in Figure 2.

The most important thing is the shape of the AVC and ATC curves. Both are U-shaped, and both are intersected by the MC curve at their minimum points.

Why does the MC curve pass through the AVC and ATC curves at their minimum points?

Why does the MC curve pass through the AVC and ATC curves at their minimum points? The basic reason is that each marginal value changes the average value. If you *really* want to know why, see the box, "Computing Your Exam Average."

Incidentally, when you draw the curves, if you start with the MC curve, it will be much easier to draw in the AVC and ATC curves.

We'll try another problem. First fill in Table 8. A completed version appears in Table 9. Assume here that fixed cost is $400. Work out each answer to the nearest dollar.

I hope your table matches Table 9. Now we're ready for the graph. We'll use only three of the curves in the analysis that comes a little later in the chapter—the AVC, ATC, and MC. The AFC curve doesn't serve any analytic purpose, so from here on we won't draw it.

Now I'd like you to draw a graph of the AVC, ATC, and MC curves on a piece of graph paper. Remember, start with the MC curve because you need that curve to help you plot the minimum points of the AVC and ATC curves. Still not convinced? Then just trust me.

Distinguishing between Fixed Cost and Average Fixed Cost

Using a piece of graph paper, see whether you can draw the average fixed cost curve, using the data in Table 7. Then on the same graph, draw the fixed cost curve. If your graph looks like the one in this box, then you don't need any extra help.

If your AFC curve looks different, make sure you plotted each point correctly. If you're having trouble plotting points, you definitely need to reread the early sections of Chapter 17 (Chapter 5 in *Microeconomics*), where I went over how to plot graphs.

The AFC curve sweeps downward to the right, getting closer and closer to the output axis. When drawn correctly, it should be a very smooth curve.

The fixed cost curve is always a perfectly horizontal line. In this case, fixed cost is $500, so the fixed cost curve runs straight across the graph at a cost of $500. It stays fixed at $500 no matter what the output.

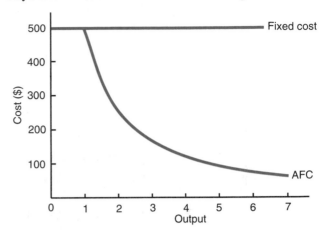

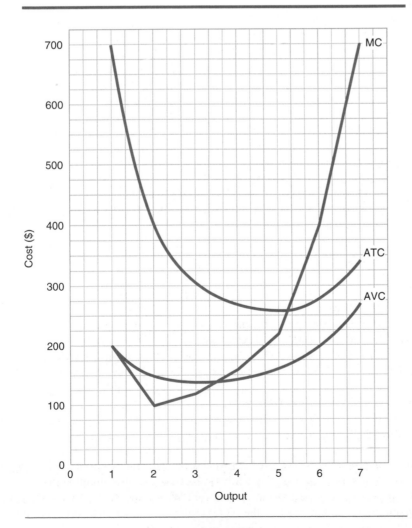

Figure 2

Average Total Cost, Average Variable Cost, and Marginal Cost
The marginal cost curve intersects the ATC and the AVC at their minimum points.

Computing Your Exam Average

We'll digress for a moment by discussing grades on exams. Suppose you took three exams and scored 80, 70, and 60. Your average would be 70. What if, on the next exam, you got a 66? What would your average be? It would be 276/4 = 69.

Suppose on the next exam you got a 67? Now what would your average be? It would be 343/5 = 68.6. If you got a 68 on the next exam, what would happen to your average? 411/6 = 68.5.

If your next exam mark was exactly 68.5? 479.5/7 = 68.5. No change.

If you scored a 69 on the next exam, what would your average be? 548.5/8 = 68.56.

All of this is meant to show you how the marginal score affects the average score. Note that as long as the marginal score is below the average score, the latter is declining, but when the marginal score is 68.5, it is equal to the average score. And the average score is neither rising nor falling; it is at its minimum point.

Similarly, when MC intersects AVC and ATC, it does so at their minimum points. As long as MC is below AVC, AVC must be falling. Once MC cuts through the AVC curve, the latter begins to rise. The same is true of the relationship between MC and ATC.

	Variable	Total				Marginal
Output	Cost	Cost	AFC	AVC	ATC	Cost
1	$100	____	____	____	____	____
2	150	____	____	____	____	____
3	210	____	____	____	____	____
4	300	____	____	____	____	____
5	430	____	____	____	____	____
6	600	____	____	____	____	____
7	819	____	____	____	____	____

TABLE 8 Hypothetical Cost Schedule*

*Fixed cost = $400.

Compare your graph with the one in Figure 3. How did your minimum points come out on the AVC and ATC curves? If you drew your curves in the order I suggested—MC first, then AVC and ATC—your MC should have intersected both the AVC and ATC curves at their minimum points.

TABLE 9 Hypothetical Cost Schedule

	Variable	Total				Marginal
Output	Cost	Cost	AFC	AVC	ATC	Cost
1	$100	$ 500	$400	$100	$500	$100
2	150	550	200	75	275	50
3	210	610	133	70	203	60
4	300	700	100	75	175	90
5	430	830	80	86	166	130
6	600	1,000	67	100	167	170
7	819	1,219	57	117	174	219

Before we move on to the even more spectacular analysis toward the end of the chapter, we'll do a bit of preliminary analysis. Read off the minimum points of the AVC and ATC curves. At what outputs do they occur? Write down these two values: the output at which the minimum point of the AVC occurs and how much AVC is at that point. Then do the same for the minimum point on the ATC curve.

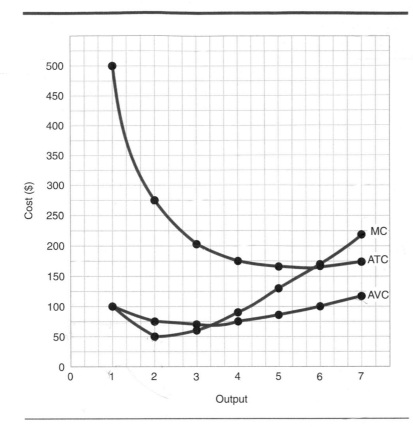

Figure 3

Average Variable, Average Total, and Marginal Cost
How much is the minimum point of this firm's ATC curve? Answer: a bit less than $166 (I'll call it $165). You can't really tell just by looking at the graph: You have to look at the ATC figures in Table 9 at outputs of 5 and 6 and then, since we're looking for a minimum point, come up with a number slightly less than $166.

    Your answers should be within these ranges: For AVC, your output should be somewhere between 3.3 and 3.4. AVC is a bit less than $70. How *much* less? Probably around $69, or $69 and change. Where do we get these numbers? If you were careful when you drew your graph—if you weren't, use mine—AVC is $70 at an output of 3. MC is still a bit below AVC at $60. As output goes beyond 3, MC continues to rise while AVC declines slightly.

    For the minimum point of the ATC curve, your output should be around 5.8. ATC is between $165 and $165.90. Notice that the MC curve intersects the ATC curve between outputs of 5 and 6, but closer to 6. Note that at an output of 5, ATC is $166, and at an output of 6, it is $167, but because the MC curve cuts the ATC curve at its minimum point, ATC must be *less* than $166.

    It might seem to you that we are reading Figure 3 with great precision, perhaps a little too *much* precision. For example, to the naked eye, is it really clear that the minimum point of the ATC curve is between $165 and $165.90? Hardly. But we use Table 9 to guide us. We want a number that is slightly less than $166. Why not $164.25? All right, all right—you're twisting my arm. I personally think $164.25 is a bit low. On an exam I'd mark it right, but I can't vouch for *your* professor.

    The most difficult part of graphing the ATC and AVC curves is making sure that they are crossed at their minimum points by the MC curve. You can get a little more help with this in the accompanying box.

Why Are the AVC and ATC Curves U-Shaped?

As output rises, initially both average variable cost and average total cost decline, reach minimum points, and then begin to rise. This makes these curves U-shaped. Before we tackle the question of *why* they are U-shaped, let's ask and answer a related question. Why does the AVC curve reach a minimum before the ATC curve?

    Average total cost is the sum of average fixed cost and average variable cost. We know that, as long as output is expanding, AFC is declining. But, as you can see

Graphing the Average Total Cost Curve

The points shown in Figure A—$50.00, $32.50, $25.00, etc.—are points on a firm's average total cost curve. Very carefully connect all these points; this will give us the firm's average total cost curve.

Now we come to one of the most crucial questions of this course. How much is the minimum point of the ATC curve you've just drawn? Please write down your answer in dollars and cents.

Let's see how you did. Does your ATC curve look like the one I drew in Figure B? Does it continue to decline from $22.50 until it touches the MC curve? And after reaching a minimum at that point, does your ATC curve begin to rise again as it moves towards $22.00?

Next question: What is the minimum point of your ATC curve in dollars and cents? *I* see it as $21.80. What did *you* get?

Your answer *must* be a little lower than $22.00, because $22.00 is *not* the minimum point of the ATC curve. That occurs when the MC and the ATC curves intersect. The ATC is declining until it crosses the MC and then it begins to rise. It rises from an output of 120 to an output of 140, where it reaches a value of $22.00.

So how much *is* the value of ATC at its minimum point? There *is* no one correct answer. I would accept anything between $21.25 and $21.99. And if you got me on a good day, I'd go as low as $21.00.

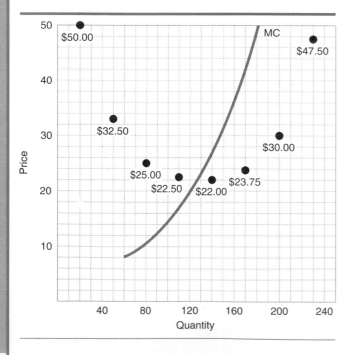

Figure A

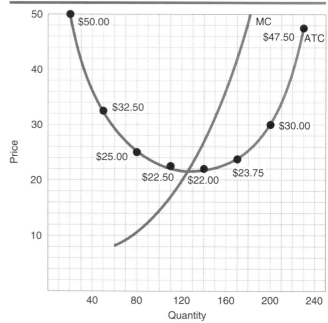

Figure B

from Figures 2 and 3, AFC declines at a declining rate (that is, more and more slowly) as output rises. Average variable cost, in contrast, declines at a declining rate, reaches a minimum, and then begins to rise at an increasing rate (faster and faster). Eventually the increase in AVC outweighs the decrease in AFC. At that point ATC begins to rise.

Now we know why AVC begins to rise before ATC begins to rise. And we also know that it is the rise in AVC that ultimately pushes up ATC. Do you follow so far? OK, then *why* does AVC begin to rise? *That* is the $1 million question. To answer that question we'll need to look at three related concepts—the law of diminishing returns, economies of scale, and diseconomies of scale.

The Production Function and the Law of Diminishing Returns

A business owner tries to keep her costs down by getting the maximum output from using the best combination of the factors of production—land, labor, and capital. To do so, she may try different production functions, which would tell her how much output she can produce with varying amounts of factor inputs. *A production function is the relationship between the maximum amounts of output a firm can produce and various quantities of inputs*.

Resources may be used in various proportions. For example, a farmer may either plant crops on 400 acres or cultivate 200 more intensively. Similarly, a bank may either install hundreds of ATMs or hire hundreds of real tellers. Using resources in different proportions will yield varying amounts of output.

Using the data in Table 10, we see that one person working alone turns out two log cabins a month, while two people working together can turn out five per month. If you've ever attempted to move a 500-pound log, you know it's easier to have someone at the other end of the log. Perhaps three people can work together even more efficiently.

The first three workers give us increasing returns (or increasing marginal returns). Working together, they can get a lot more done than if each worked alone. But note what happens when we hire a fourth worker. This person raises output, but only by 3. With the fourth worker we have the onset of diminishing returns (or diminishing marginal output).

Why is this so? Because three people may be an ideal number to move and lift 500-pound logs. The fourth worker is certainly a help, but proportionately, she doesn't add as much as the third worker.   Diminishing marginal output

A fifth worker adds still less to output (2 units) and a sixth worker even less (1 unit). In other words, five people can manage building log cabins almost as well as six. As we add the seventh worker, we find that he is superfluous. From the fourth to the seventh worker, we have *diminishing returns*.

The eighth worker is actually in the way, having a marginal output of minus one. Returns become negative when this eighth worker is added. A ninth worker gets in the way even more. The eighth and ninth workers have negative returns.   Negative returns

---

TABLE 10   The Law of Diminishing Returns: Building Log Cabins

Number of Workers	Total Output	Marginal* Output	
0	0	0	
1	2	2	Increasing returns
2	5	3	Increasing returns
3	9	4	Increasing returns
4	12	3	Diminishing returns
5	14	2	Diminishing returns
6	15	1	Diminishing returns
7	15	0	Diminishing returns
8	14	−1	Diminishing and negative returns
9	11	−3	Diminishing and negative returns

*Marginal output is the additional output produced by the last worker hired. Thus the first worker adds 2 units to output, so his marginal output is 2. The second worker hired adds 3 units of output (output has risen from 2 to 5), so his marginal output is 3. When a third worker is hired, total output jumps to 9. Marginal output has therefore risen by 4.

Figure 4
Building Log Cabins: Total
Output and Marginal Output

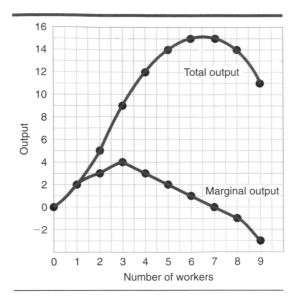

What would be the maximum number of workers you would hire? The answer is six. If the wage rate were very low, you would hire up to six. The seventh worker, however, adds nothing to output, and the eighth and ninth get in the way, thereby reducing output.

Let's see how all this looks graphically. We see in Figure 4 how total output and marginal output rise as more workers after the first three workers are added. But after the third worker, total output begins to rise more slowly. And marginal output? It begins to decline. Hence, diminishing returns.

Total output reaches a maximum with the addition of the sixth worker, then levels off, so that the seventh worker adds 0 output. And what is the marginal output of the seventh worker?

The marginal output of the seventh worker is 0. If we add an eighth and ninth worker, what happens to total output? It declines. And marginal output? It becomes negative.

The law of diminishing returns states that, *as successive units of a variable resource (say, labor) are added to a fixed set of resources (say, land and capital), beyond some point the extra, or marginal, product attributable to each additional unit of the variable resource will decline*. So if we added more and more farm workers to an acre of land, beyond some point (say, after the third worker), the extra output that that fourth worker added would be less than the extra output that the third worker added. We'll consider how this law applies to agricultural production and to office work.

Let's now apply the law of diminishing returns to an office. You're working in an office that is 15 feet long and 10 feet wide. Your job is to type, run a small switchboard, act as a receptionist, and do filing. You really could use some help because the phone keeps ringing, visitors keep arriving, you keep getting more papers to file, and you've got a whole pile of correspondence to type. So a second worker is hired, and you divide up the work. That way neither of you will have your work constantly interrupted. On the down side, you now have to share your office. But the two of you working together produce three times as much work as you did working alone.

Let's say that a third person was hired to work in your office. Would output go up? Yes. But now the office is *really* getting crowded. Suppose that a fourth, fifth, sixth, seventh, and eighth worker were hired. Imagine how crowded your office would be. Indeed, you'd end up sitting on one another's desks, maybe on one another's laps. At some point total output would begin to decline, and *negative returns* would set in.

It would be absurd for a company to have workers beyond the point of negative returns, or even to approach that point. However, we would certainly want to keep hiring workers who yielded *increasing returns*. And, if the firm found it profitable to increase output still further, it would keep hiring workers even though their returns were diminishing.

Declining ATC in Drugs

Here is an excerpt from the 1999 annual report of the Federal Reserve Bank of Dallas:

It takes roughly $350 million to bring the average new drug to market. That's just for the first pill. Making the second costs closer to a penny. Clearly, nobody's going to pay $350 million for that first pill. So to make medicine affordable, drug companies have to spread the cost of developing their products over years and years of sales. The larger the sales, the less each unit can cost the consumer. Assuming $350 million in development costs and 1¢ marginal production cost thereafter, the average cost of making a pill would fall from $350 million for producing just one to $350.01 each for making a million to 4¢ each for sales of 10 billion. Prices fall in inverse proportion to the size of the market. This example illustrates that for pharmaceuticals demand is not the enemy of price but its friend. The higher the demand, the lower the price because, after all, you can't have quantity discounts without quantity.

Average Cost of a Pill	
Quantity	Cost
1	$350,000,000.00
10	35,000,000.01
100	3,500,000.01
1,000	350,000.01
10,000	35,000.01
100,000	3,500.01
1,000,000	350.01
10,000,000	35.01
100,000,000	3.51
1,000,000,000	.36
10,000,000,000	.04

Economies of Scale

Economies of scale are the economies of mass production, which drive down average total cost. They are largely responsible for the declining part of the ATC curve. Large-scale enterprise is expected to be more efficient than small business. And in general, we expect large firms to be able to undersell small firms. One reason for this belief is that large firms can often get quantity discounts when they buy raw materials or inventory (Safeway, Target, and Walmart, for example, use a system of central buying and warehousing). A manufacturer will be able to give you a better price if she can deliver 10,000 cartons of tuna fish to one warehouse rather than 100 cartons to 100 different stores. Also, it costs less to sell your final product in quantity than to sell it piece by piece. For this reason, a wholesaler has much lower prices than a retailer. Buying and selling in large quantities, then, is one reason for economies of scale.

Quantity discounts

As a firm grows, it takes advantage of being established. Its salespeople are known, it has established outlets and delivery routes, and its brand name becomes familiar. These advantages will mount as the firm continues to grow.

Economies of being established

When a company has a very high fixed cost and a low marginal cost, its ATC curve will slope downward almost indefinitely. Software, CDs, DVDs, and drugs are some of the products in this category. In addition, economies of scale tend to dominate industries that deliver their goods or services through a network, such as telephone, television, radio, fax, e-mail, the Internet, package delivery, and pipelines. In the box, "Declining ATC in Drugs," you'll see the economies of scale realized in the pharmaceutical industry.

Spreading fixed cost

Economies of scale in computer software are almost mind-boggling. The cost of producing copies of a software program is virtually zero. Microsoft merely licenses its computer code to PC makers, who then install it. Whether Microsoft sells 100 million or 200 million copies, its costs are all in developing the code to begin with. As in the case of the drug companies, there are very high fixed costs and minimal marginal costs.

Economies of Scale in Entertainment and Communications

In entertainment and the Internet, where there are huge fixed costs, the cost of serving additional customers is generally very small. These points are illustrated in an article by Robert H. Frank, a Cornell University economics professor.

The cost of producing a movie or writing Internet access software, for example, is essentially the same whether the product attracts one million buyers or 100 million.

So the more customers a company serves, the more cheaply it can sell its product and still make money . . .

So the trick is to make a big investment that will attract millions of customers, spreading that fixed cost over millions of units of output.

If Time Warner's Home Box Office bids for star performers or spends more on elaborate special effects for its made-for-TV movies, it can attract more subscribers, yet it will not have to charge each customer a higher price to cover its increased costs. And having a better product would help HBO lure subscribers away from Showtime and Cinemax, reinforcing the initial advantage.

Similar forces govern the contest to provide Internet access. Because many of the biggest costs of delivering Internet service are fixed, the average cost per subscriber declines sharply with the number of subscribers served. *

*Robert H. Frank, "A Merger's Message: Dominate or Die," *The New York Times,* January 11, 2000, p. A25.

What does it cost online music sellers like Apple's iTunes Music Store to sell one more CD download? Maybe one or two cents. Which is about the same as it cost companies selling video on demand to rent or sell one more video download.

Adam Smith's pin factory

In 1776 in *The Wealth of Nations,* Adam Smith noted three other advantages. When a firm is large enough to provide specialized jobs for its workers, economies of scale will follow. He used a pin factory as an example.

One worker, said Smith, "could scarce, perhaps, with his utmost industry, make one pin in a day, and certainly could not make twenty." He then described how pin making has become specialized: "One man draws out the wire, another straights it, a third cuts it, a fourth points it, a fifth grinds it at the top for receiving the head."[2]

There are three distinct advantages to producing pins in this manner. First, the workers become good at their jobs—better than they would be if they went from one function to another. Second, they don't waste time going from one task to another. Third, the factory can employ specialized and expensive equipment because it will be fully used. For example, a special die to draw the wire can be purchased because it will be used continually; and a machine to cut the wire can be purchased for the same reason.

Ten pin makers, working on their own, could turn out at most a total of 200 pins. Smith estimated that 10 people working together in a factory could produce 48,000 pins a day, which is a prime example of economies of scale.

If a company gets too large, break it into smaller parts. Once people start not knowing the people in the building and it starts to become impersonal, it's time to break up a company.

—Richard Branson, founder, Virgin Group

Economies of scale enable a business firm to reduce its costs per unit of output as output expands (see the box, "Economies of Scale in Entertainment and Communications"). Often these cost reductions can be passed on to the consumer in the form of lower prices. One outgrowth of expansion is increasing specialization. People's jobs become more and more specialized, as they did in Adam Smith's pin factory. But with the growth of specialization are sown the seeds of inefficiency, rising costs, and diseconomies of scale.

Diseconomies of Scale

Diseconomies of scale are the inefficiencies that become endemic in large firms. Diseconomies of scale are evidenced by the rising part of the ATC curve.

---

[2] Adam Smith, *The Wealth of Nations* (London: Methuen, 1950), Book 1, Chapter 1, pp. 8–9.

As a business grows larger, it will create a bureaucracy. Early in the company's history, the founder hired all her employees personally. As the firm grew, she had her foreman do the hiring. Today, if you try to get a job at a large company, you have to go through the personnel (or human resources) department, then meet your prospective supervisor, then meet your prospective supervisor's supervisor, and perhaps meet several other members of "the team"—or work your way through some other variation of this process. In the early days of the company, there was no such thing as a third interview.

The growing bureaucracy

A huge hierarchy of corporate authority is established—a hierarchy that might have once made sense, but that now may either have little relevant function or actually work at cross-purposes. The American automobile industry is a good case in point. Fewer than half the employees of GM, Ford, and Chrysler actually make cars. The rest do sales, advertising, market research, litigation, accounting, personnel work, budgeting, or public relations and the like for their companies—anything but make cars.

Expansion means complexity, and complexity means decay.

You may have heard of C. Northcote Parkinson, who formulated Parkinson's Law: "Work expands so as to fill the time available for its completion." Just picture all those seemingly busy bureaucrats scurrying around, firing off memos, talking on the phone, and rushing off to meetings. But no discernible output results. Parkinson added a corollary: "Work expands to occupy the people available for its completion." If Parkinson is right, then large organizations are filled with important-looking people who appear very busy but are doing virtually no real work.

Parkinson's Law

Big business breeds bureaucracy and bureaucrats act exactly as big government does.
—Theordore K. Quinn, General Electric officer in the 1920s and 1930s

Even the quantity discounts enjoyed by large firms will eventually disappear as the firms use up so many resources that they bid up their prices. If a company rents office space, it can save money by renting several floors in a building. But if the firm needs much of the downtown office space in a city, it will end up paying more per square foot. Similarly, suppliers who gladly give quantity discounts for large orders will have to raise their prices to a customer who purchases their entire output. Furthermore, other customers will bid up prices rather than see their own supplies cut off.

Size works against excellence.
—Bill Gates, cofounder and chairman, Microsoft

Depicting the stages of growth of several large corporations, we start with the initial spurt, during which economies of scale are operative and unit costs are declining. As the companies mature and output continues to rise, unit costs stay about the same. This stage is sometimes called *proportional returns to scale*.

In the final stage, which many large corporations have reached, diseconomies of scale set in. The corporate dinosaurs, beset with rising unit costs, are now so huge that they may no longer be able to compete.

When I had a prescription filled at Rite Aid, I received a circular listing an 800 number to call about getting a flu shot. I called that day, and after the standard runaround, finally got through to a customer service representative. He informed me that they had run out of vaccine, so Rite Aid was no longer providing flu shots. So why, I asked, was the store still giving out these notices? The poor guy didn't have a clue.

It would be fair to assume that a small neighborhood pharmacy would not be making this systematic error. But when you've got a nationwide chain, the left hand does not always know what the right hand is doing.

A Summing Up

At the beginning of this section we asked why the AVC and ATC curves are U-shaped. Now that we have covered the law of diminishing returns, economies of scale, and diseconomies of scale, we can answer this question.

ATC is the sum of AFC and AVC. AFC declines by smaller and smaller increments as output rises. So, as output rises, ATC is pushed down by smaller and smaller increments.

Remember that we often have the sequence of increasing returns, diminishing returns, and negative returns. Increasing returns would initially drive down AVC. But eventually diminishing returns would drive up AVC. We won't worry about negative returns, because no firm would hire workers or engage other resources that would cause output to decline.

What's the Difference between Shutting Down and Going Out of Business?

One big difference between shutting down and going out of business is that after you've shut down you're still paying bills, but when you've gone out of business you're "free at last!"* That's right! Once you've legally left the industry, you have no more bills to pay because you have no more costs—fixed *or* variable.

When you've shut down operations, you may still owe money on your lease, insurance premiums may be due, and you may still be paying off a loan. There may be employees under contract who have been guaranteed salaries even if there is no work for them. In addition, if you have a shut-down plant, you might need employees to maintain the equipment, keep the pipes from freezing, and keep out intruders. And if there are hazardous waste materials on the premises, these may have to be disposed of before you can legally go out of business.

---

*This was the conclusion of Dr. Martin Luther King, Jr.'s stirring 1963 "I Have a Dream" speech. He was not, of course, discussing the difference between shutting down and going out of business.

 Economies of scale drive down AFC, but at smaller and smaller increments. Diseconomies of scale drive up AVC as output rises and eventually exceed economies of scale, at which point AVC begins to rise.

To sum up, the overlapping forces of increasing returns and economies of scale drive down ATC, but eventually the overlapping forces of diminishing returns and diseconomies of scale push ATC back up again.

The U-shaped ATC is very important not only in economic analysis but also in business strategy, especially in answering questions such as: What size factory or store or office should we build? How many workers should we hire? What would be the output at which our firm would operate most efficiently? We'll answer the first of these questions in the next section and answer the others in later chapters.

The Decision to Operate or Shut Down

A firm has two options in the short run.

A firm has two options in the short run: It can either operate or shut down. If it operates, it will produce the output that will yield the highest possible profits; if it is losing money, it will operate at that output at which losses are minimized.

If the firm shuts down, its output is zero. Shutting down does not mean zero total costs. The firm must still meet its fixed costs. Look at Table 1 again. At an output of zero, fixed costs—and therefore total costs—are $1,000.

Why can't the firm go out of business in the short run? Because it still has fixed costs (see the box, "What's the Difference between Shutting Down and Going Out of Business?"). These obligations must be discharged. Any plant, equipment, inventory, and raw materials must also be sold off. All of this takes time. How long? In some types of business, such as retail food, garment manufacturing, TV production, and most service industries, it would be a matter of two or three months. But in heavy industry, such as iron and steel, nonferrous metals, automobiles, timber, oil refining, and other types of manufacturing, it might take a couple of years.

We'll work out some problems involving the shut-down decision. If a firm has fixed costs of $5 million, variable costs of $6 million, and total revenue of $7 million, what does it do in the short run? It has a choice: (1) operate or (2) shut down.

If you owned this firm, what would *you* do? No matter what you do, you'll lose money. If you operate, your total cost will be $11 million ($5 million fixed cost plus $6 million variable cost). Total Revenue − Costs = Profit, so $7 million − $11 million = −$4 million. That's not too good.

How much will you lose if you shut down? You will still have to pay out $5 million in fixed costs. Your variable cost will be zero. How much will your sales be? Zero. If you shut down, you produce nothing. If you shut down, your fixed and total costs are the same—$5 million. As total revenue is zero, you lose $5 million by shutting down.

What do you do? Shut down and lose $5 million, or operate and lose $4 million? Remember, in the short run, these are your only options. What you then do is operate. It's a lot better to lose $4 million than to lose $5 million. Can you go on month after month—and possibly year after year—losing so much money? You can't. In the long run you have the added option of going out of business.

Here's another problem. What does this firm do in the short run if its fixed costs are $10 million, its variable costs are $9 million, and its total revenue is $8 million? Will the firm operate or shut down? Back up your answer with numbers after you've figured out the right choice.

If the firm shuts down, it will lose its $10 million in fixed costs. If it operates, it will have total revenue of $8 million and total costs of $19 million ($10 million fixed plus $9 million variable). If the firm operates, it will lose $11 million (total revenue of $8 million minus costs of $19 million). So the firm will shut down because it's obviously better to lose $10 million than $11 million.

We'll try one more problem. What does a firm do in the short run with total revenue of $10 million, variable costs of $12 million, and fixed costs of $8 million?

If the firm shuts down, it will lose its $8 million in fixed costs. If it operates, it will lose $10 million (total revenue of $10 million minus total costs of $20 million). Clearly, it shuts down.

We are now ready for another rule. When does a firm operate in the short run? *A firm will operate in the short run when total revenue exceeds variable costs.* Go back to the first problem. Total revenue was $7 million, and variable costs were $6 million. By operating, it added $7 million in total revenue and had to pay out only an additional $6 million in costs. By operating, it cut its losses by $1 million.

A firm will shut down when variable costs exceed total revenue. Check back to the second and third problems. In the second problem, when variable costs are $9 million and total revenue is $8 million, the firm saves $1 million by shutting down. In the third problem, variable costs are $12 million and total revenue $10 million, so $2 million is saved by shutting down.

Stop! We need to pause, catch our breath—and summarize the last three problems. Table 11 provides that summary.

In the short run a firm has two options: (1) operate or (2) shut down. It operates when total revenue exceeds variable costs. And when variable costs are greater than total revenue, it shuts down. What if variable costs equal total revenue? Flip a coin.

A firm will operate in the short run when prospective sales exceed variable costs.

A firm will shut down in the short run when variable costs exceed prospective sales.

TABLE 11	Summary Table of Last Three Problems *(All dollar figures in millions)*		
	Problem 1	Problem 2	Problem 3
Fixed costs	5	10	8
Variable costs	6	9	12
Total revenue	7	8	10
Decision	Operate	Shut down	Shut down

Case Study: The πr^2 Publishing Company

The chances are pretty good that someday you will start your own business. You'll probably start out with an idea, a specific skill, a knowledge of an industry, a few connections, and whatever money you'll need not just to start the business but to live on until you're making a profit.

Ginny Crisonino and I had written a precalculus book, which John Wiley and Sons had published in 1999. Why not write a basic mathematic book for college students? So we did. After having a compositor whip our manuscript into shape, we had 10,000 copies printed. Those two fixed costs set us back close to $70,000.

We then did a mailing to 26,000 math professors offering them a free examination copy of our book and some 1,300 replied. Our fulfillment house in New Hampshire sent out the books. Within a couple of months we started getting book orders. In our first year we had sales of $56,000, fixed costs of $73,000, and variable costs of $18,000.

So how did we do? On the one hand, we did lose $35,000. Should we have shut down? I'm sure you said no, since our sales were more than three times our variable costs. And, as it happened, we still had about 6,500 books left, so it was a no-brainer to stay in business for at least another year. In the second year, we had sales of $65,000, fixed costs of $4,000, and variable costs of $22,000. That left us with a profit of $39,000.

Neither Ginny or I have been able to quit our day jobs yet, but our book is in a second edition, and πr^2 Publishing Company is still turning a profit.

If you were to go into business, perhaps your two biggest worries would be having enough money to live on while you're launching your business, and then, in the short run, covering your variables. If you need to quit your day job to have enough time to run your company, then you better have enough money socked away to last you at least until you can begin taking some money out of the business. While you're still in the short run, your sales should be greater than your variable costs, or you should shut down operations. In the accompanying box, you can read about my own recent experience starting the πr^2 Publishing Company.

The Decision to Go Out of Business or Stay in Business

In the short run the businessowner must decide whether to operate or shut down. In the long run the owner is faced with two different options. The long-run choices are easier: (1) stay in business or (2) go out of business. If a firm has total revenue of $4 million, fixed costs of $3 million, and variable costs of $2 million, what does it do in the long run?

This firm will go out of business because in the long run it will be losing money. Total revenue of $4 million − Total costs of $5 million ($3 million fixed + $2 million variable) = −$1 million profit.

What would you do in the long run if your firm's total revenue were $8 million, fixed costs were $4 million, and variable costs were $3 million?

You would stay in business because you would make a profit of $1 million (total revenue of $8 million minus costs of $7 million).

In summary, then, we have two long-run options: (1) stay in business or (2) go out of business. If a firm's total revenue is greater than its total costs (variable cost plus fixed cost), it will stay in business. But if total costs exceed total revenue, the firm will go out of business.

We'll need to qualify this. If a firm lost one dollar, that loss would obviously be unlikely to drive it out of business. Some very large firms have lost hundreds of millions of dollars for several years running and *still* have not gone out of business. Fine. They are the exceptions that prove the rule (see the box, "Does Everybody Who's Losing Money Go Out of Business?"). The rule is that if your total costs exceed your total revenue, you'll go out of business in the long run.

Deriving the Shut-down and Break-even Points

The firm can make the same shut-down or operate decision on the basis of price and average variable cost. Let's see why. Total revenue is the product of price times output. In order words, Total revenue = Price × Output. Average variable cost is equal to variable cost divided by output. We can put it this way:

$$\text{Average variable cost} = \frac{\text{Variable cost}}{\text{Output}}$$

If we're at the shut-down point, then Total revenue = Variable cost. If we divided total revenue by output and variable cost by output, we'd get this:

$$\frac{\text{Total revenue}}{\text{Output}} = \frac{\text{Variable cost}}{\text{Output}}$$

$$\frac{\text{Price} \times \cancel{\text{Output}}}{\cancel{\text{Output}}} = \text{Average variable cost}$$

$$\text{Price} = \text{Average variable cost}$$

Now we can restate our rules: If price is greater than average variable cost, the firm will operate. If average variable cost is greater than price, the firm will shut down.

Moving right along, let's take another look at the decision to stay in business or go out of business. We know that average total cost is equal to total cost divided by output, which we can put this way:

$$\text{Average total cost} = \frac{\text{Total cost}}{\text{Output}}$$

If we're at the break-even point, then Total revenue = Total cost. If we divided total revenue by output and total cost by output, we'd get this:

$$\frac{\text{Total revenue}}{\text{Output}} = \frac{\text{Total cost}}{\text{Output}}$$

$$\frac{\text{Price} \times \cancel{\text{Output}}}{\cancel{\text{Output}}} = \text{Average total cost}$$

$$\text{Price} = \text{Average total cost}$$

Again, we can restate our rules: If price is greater than average total cost, the firm will stay in business. If average total cost is greater than price, the firm will shut down.

We can illustrate the shut-down or operate decision graphically. In the accompanying box, we derived the shut-down point and concluded that if price is greater than average variable cost, the firm will operate, but if average variable cost is greater than price, the firm will shut down.

Exactly where on a firm's average variable cost curve do you think you'd find the shut-down point? At its minimum point? Is that your final answer? Then you're right! Please turn back to Figure 2 and tell me how much the output is at the shut-down point.

It looks like 3.4. Now what would be the lowest price the firm would accept in the short run?

Does Everybody Who's Losing Money Go Out of Business?

Mom and Pop run a little grocery in a tiny town somewhere in northwestern Nebraska. You can go there anytime between 6:00 A.M. and midnight to buy some of the stuff you forgot to pick up at the supermarket. And if you forget your wallet, no problem. Your credit is good there.

If Mom and Pop ever sat down and figured out how much money was coming in each week and how much they were paying out, they'd probably close up their store and go to work for someone else. Or maybe not.

There's a lot to be said for being your own boss and making your own hours, even if they do happen to be from 6:00 A.M. to midnight.

Now according to our analysis, if sales do not cover total costs in the long run, the firm will go out of business. But maybe Mom and Pop's store is the exception that proves the rule. The rule says you go out of business if you're not at least breaking even. But if you look hard enough, you'll almost always be able to find some people who don't follow this rule.

It appears to be about $140. Well, I hate to tell you, but it's *not* $140. How can I possibly tell? Remember what we said about tables and graphs—that if a graph is drawn from the data in a table, it cannot be more accurate than the table? So let's go back to Table 7, which was used to draw Figure 2. How much is AVC at an output of 3? It's $140. OK, go back to Figure 2 and you'll see that the minimum point of the AVC is at an output of 3.4. So if AVC is $140 at an output of 3, it must be a little lower at an output of 3.4. So we'll say that it's $139 (or $139.50, or even $139.99).

What is the lowest price the firm can accept in the short run and still operate? It's $139. What would the firm do if the price were $138? It would shut down.

What is the lowest price the firm would accept in the short run and still operate if we use the information in Figure 3 (based on data from Table 9)?

The answer is $69 (or $69.50, or $69.99). If the price were $70, what would the firm do in the short run? It would operate. If the price were $68, what would the firm do in the short run? It would shut down.

So, if the price is above the shut-down point, in the short run the firm will operate. But if, in the short run, the price is below the shut-down point, the firm will shut down.

We'll use the same analysis to find out how the firm will behave in the long run with respect to the break-even point. Using the information from Figure 2 and Table 7, what is the lowest price the firm can accept in the long run and stay in business?

It would be $259 (or $259 and change, for example, $259.75). What would the firm do in the long run if the price were $265? It would stay in business. What would it do in the long run if the price were $250? It would go out of business.

Now look at Figure 3 and Table 9. What is the lowest price the firm can accept in the long run? It would be $165.90. This is a judgment call. I personally would not be comfortable going as low as $165. But I would mark $165 right on an exam. How about $164? Don't push it.

OK, what would the firm do in the long run if the price were $162? It would go out of business. And if it were $170? It would stay in business.

Just to wrap things up, in Figure 5, we've labeled the shut-down and break-even points. Inspecting them visually, what is the lowest price the firm can accept in the short run (and still operate) and in the long run (and stay in business)?

Figure 5

Average Total Cost, Average Variable Cost, and Marginal Cost

The shut-down point is at the minimum point of the AVC curve and the break-even point is at the minimum point of the ATC curve.

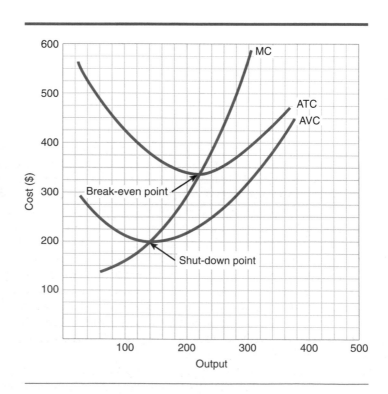

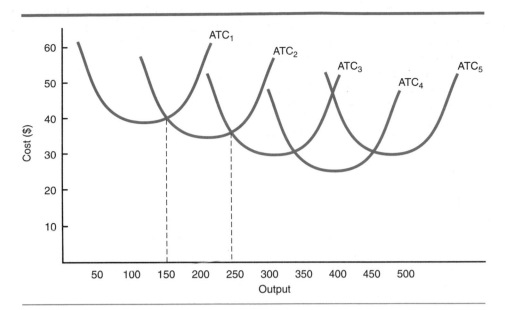

Figure 6
Varying Factory Capacities
Each of these ATCs represents a different size factory, with a different optimum level of output represented by the minimum point on the ATC curve. ATC_1 has the lowest capacity, while ATC_5 has the highest. Which size factory would a firm choose to build to produce 400 units of output? The answer is ATC_4.

The lowest price the firm will accept in the short run is $200. The lowest price it will accept in the long run is $336.

Choosing Plant Size

We have been making an implicit assumption about the business firm. We've assumed it has been operating with a plant of given size. What's wrong with assuming that? Nothing, unless the firm alters the size of its plant.

What is a plant? It's a factory, office, store, or any combination of factories, offices, or stores. The plant used by Procter & Gamble consists of hundreds of factories and offices. The plant of General Motors consists of hundreds of car lots, factories, and offices, and the plant of Kone's ice-cream parlor on Kings Highway in Brooklyn consists of that one store (and, some would say, of the Kone "boys," who must now be in their 80s).

What is a plant?

If a firm were to build a larger factory, it might be able to lower its costs. For example, looking at Figure 6, ATC_2 reflects lower costs than does ATC_1 for outputs greater than 150. And ATC_3 reflects lower costs than does ATC_2 for outputs of more than 250.

How much would it cost to produce at ATC_1's break-even point? How much would it cost to produce at the break-even points of ATC_2 and ATC_3?

Note we have declining costs: $39 at the break-even point of ATC_1, $34 at that of ATC_2, $30 at that of ATC_3, and $26 at that of ATC_4. Why are costs declining? For a variety of reasons, which could be lumped under the heading of economies of scale. These economies include quantity discounts by making massive purchases from trade suppliers and the three economies noted in Adam Smith's discussion of mass production in a pin factory. These economies are specialization at a particular job, the use of specialized machinery, and the time saved by not having workers go from job to job.

Just as a firm may realize economies of scale as output rises, a certain point is reached when ATCs begin to rise. Here the diseconomies of scale set in. Basically, the firm grows so large that management becomes inefficient. One hand does not know what the other is doing. Divisions of a corporation begin to work at cross-purposes.

Thus, as the firm grows in size and output, it increases its plant. ATC will fall through a certain range of output, but eventually it will begin to rise. This is seen in Figure 6. Costs decline from ATC_1 to ATC_2 to ATC_3 to ATC_4. After ATC_4, they begin to rise.

When a firm grows, it increases its plant.

In the short run, a firm is stuck with a certain size plant. If output were 175 and the firm were operating with ATC_1, the firm could do nothing about it in the short run. But

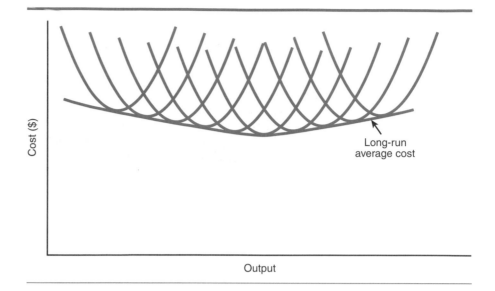

in the long run, it would expand so it could operate a plant that would be better suited to producing at 175. That plant would be signified by ATC_2. If it were producing in plant ATC_5 with an output of 500, if output should decline to 275 and that decline were perceived as a permanent decline, the firm would contract its plant size to ATC_3.

The Long-Run Average Total Cost Curve

Figure 6 shows us five different plant sizes, but in the long run, there are an infinite number of possible ATC curves, each of which corresponds to a different plant size.

These changes in the size of plant are long-run changes; they take time. New factories, offices, and stores would have to be constructed. Old ones would have to be sold or sublet. In the long run, a firm could be virtually any size, provided, of course, it had the requisite financing to expand.

Figure 7 is a graphic representation of the long-run average total cost curve, which is a compilation of all possible short-run average cost curves. While a true long-run average cost curve would include an infinite number of short-run average cost curves, we'll leave it up to your imagination to picture what a truly accurate graph would look like.

As a firm grows, it takes advantage of economies of scale, which account for the downward slope of the long-run average cost curve. But eventually, diseconomies of scale set in. When the diseconomies of scale begin to outweigh the economies of scale, the long-run average cost curve begins to slope upward.

Current Issue: Wedding Hall or City Hall?[3]

You don't need an economist to tell you that deciding to have a big wedding is, among other things, an economic decision. Because there's no way you can have a big wedding for less than, what, $20,000? Unless, of course, you get married at home, order take-out, and let your Uncle Al tend bar.

Whether your wedding is big or small, you're going to incur certain fixed costs—the flowers, the photographer, the videographer, the wedding hall, the gowns, the tux rentals, and the clergyman or clergywoman. Your variable costs will include the food and drinks. And what you have to pay for the wedding hall will vary with the number of guests.

---

[3]Bonnie Varker, a McGraw-Hill sales rep based in California, suggested this topic.

A larger, more expensive wedding, of course, will increase the value of the gifts you receive. Think of that as your revenue.

Let's suppose that a small wedding—just 100 close friends and family members—at the Elks or the American Legion Hall costs you $20,000. And you pull in $10,000 in gifts. A large wedding—300 guests at the country club—runs you $100,000. And you get gifts worth $50,000. Of course there's no way to put a monetary value on the fun you'll have. And presumably, the bigger the wedding, the more fun it will be.

OK, do you go for the small wedding or the large one? You'll lose $10,000 by having the small one and $50,000 by having the large one. Most couples would probably opt for the large one. Hey, you get married only once, or maybe twice.

Questions for Further Thought and Discussion

1. What happens to the difference between ATC and AVC as a firm's output expands? Explain.

2. How would you distinguish between the short run and the long run?

3. What are economies of scale? Please give an example. What are diseconomies of scale? Please give an example.

4. Your rich uncle died and left you $100,000, which you decided to use for your own Internet business. What business will you go into, and what will be your fixed and variable costs? Show how your business can take advantage of economies of scale.

5. Can a firm losing money go out of business in the short run? If it can't, explain why not.

6. Why are there no fixed costs in the long run?

7. Why is a business firm never in the long run?

8. On what basis does a firm decide whether or not to shut down? On what basis does it decide whether or not to go out of business?

9. What are the fixed and variable costs for a car wash? Is it likely to experience economies of scale?

10. *Practical Application:* Should you fix your old car—or buy a new one? Answer in terms of fixed and variable costs.

11. *Practical Application:* You have decided to open some movie theaters. Should you open six 200-seat theaters at six different locations, or open the six 200-seat theaters in one large building? Explain your answer in terms of economies of scale and diseconomies of scale.

12. *Web Activity:* How much are the fixed and variable costs of renting a compact car for a week at Boston's Logan Airport? Go to www.budget.com or www.avis.com

Workbook for Chapter 8

Name _____   Date _____

Multiple-Choice Questions

Circle the letter that corresponds to the best answer.

1. Al and George's used car lot has total revenue of $5 million, fixed costs of $8 million, and variable costs of $4 million. In the short run the firm will _____, and in the long run it will _____. (LO8)
   a) shut down, go out of business
   b) shut down, stay in business
   c) operate, stay in business
   ✓ d) operate, go out of business

2. The decision to shut down is made in _____. (LO8)
   a) both the short run and the long run
   b) neither the short run nor the long run
   c) the long run
   ✓ d) the short run

3. When MC is rising but still below ATC, then _____. (LO5)
   ✓ a) ATC is declining
   b) ATC is constant
   c) ATC is rising
   d) there is no way of determining what ATC is doing

4. In general a firm's _____. (LO2)
   a) total cost rises as output rises up to a certain point and then begins to decline
   b) marginal cost rises as output rises up to a certain point and then begins to decline
   ✓ c) average total cost declines as output rises up to a certain point and then begins to rise

5. If AVC is declining, then _____. (LO5)
   ✓ a) marginal cost must be less than AVC
   b) marginal cost must be greater than ATC
   c) AVC must be greater than AFC

6. Which of the following is most likely to be a variable cost? (LO1)
   a) Real estate taxes
   b) Rental payments of IBM equipment
   c) Interest on bonded indebtedness
   ✓ d) Fuel and power payments

7. When output is 0, fixed cost is _____ and variable cost is _____. (LO1)
   a) 0, 0
   b) 0, more than 0
   ✓ c) more than 0, 0
   d) more than 0, more than 0

8. Which of these statements is false? (LO8)
   a) When the firm shuts down, output is zero.
   b) When variable cost is zero, output is zero.
   ✓ c) When output is zero, total cost is zero.
   d) None of these is false.

9. Total cost is the sum of _____. (LO1)
   a) marginal cost and fixed cost
   b) marginal cost and variable cost
   ✓ c) variable cost and fixed cost

10. In the short run, _____. (LO3)
    a) all costs are fixed costs
    b) all costs are variable costs
    ✓ c) some costs are fixed costs
    d) all costs are marginal costs

11. Which statement is true? (LO8)
    a) A firm will operate in the short run when total revenue exceeds fixed costs.
    ✓ b) A firm will operate in the short run when total revenue exceeds variable costs.
    c) A firm will shut down when total cost exceeds total revenue.
    d) None of these statements is true.

12. A firm has a fixed cost of $100,000, and variable cost is $90,000 at an output of one. How much is marginal cost at an output of one? (LO2)
   a) $10,000
   b) $90,000
   c) $100,000
   d) $190,000
   e) There is insufficient information to answer the question.

13. Parkinson's Law is an example of
   _____. (LO7)
   a) economies of scale
   b) diseconomies of scale
   c) Adam Smith's pin factory
   d) the firm's search for its most profitable output

14. In the short run, a firm has two options:
   _____. (LO8)
   a) stay in business or go out of business
   b) stay in business or shut down
   c) operate or go out of business
   d) operate or shut down

15. As output expands to larger and larger numbers,
   _____ continues to decline. (LO5)
   a) AFC
   b) AVC
   c) ATC
   d) MC

16. As output increases, eventually _____. (LO7)
   a) economies of scale become larger than diseconomies of scale
   b) diseconomies of scale become larger than economies of scale
   c) economies of scale and diseconomies of scale both increase
   d) economies of scale and diseconomies of scale both decrease

17. The salaries paid to people who are in the middle of three-year guaranteed contracts are
   _____. (LO1)
   a) a fixed cost
   b) a variable cost
   c) a fixed cost or a variable cost
   d) neither a fixed cost nor a variable cost

18. The marginal cost curve intersects _____
   at its/their minimum point(s). (LO5)
   a) the ATC, but not the AVC
   b) the AVC, but not the ATC
   c) both the ATC and the AVC
   d) neither the ATC nor the AVC

19. Average variable cost is found by dividing
   _____. (LO4)
   a) variable cost by output
   b) output by variable cost
   c) marginal cost by output
   d) output by marginal cost

20. Statement 1: AVC can never be higher than ATC. Statement 2: AVC and marginal cost are equal at an output of one _____. (LO4)
   a) Statement 1 is true, and statement 2 is false.
   b) Statement 2 is true, and statement 1 is false.
   c) Both statements are true.
   d) Both statements are false.

21. In Figure 1, if you want to produce an output of 100, in the long run you will choose a plant whose size is represented by _____. (LO7)
   a) ATC$_1$
   b) ATC$_2$
   c) ATC$_3$
   d) ATC$_4$
   e) ATC$_5$

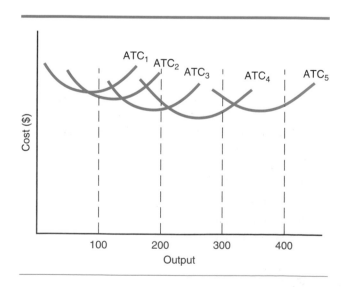

Figure 1

22. In Figure 1, if you want to produce an output of 200, in the long run you will choose a plant whose size is represented by _____. (LO7)
    a) ATC_1
    b) ATC_2
    c) ATC_3
    d) ATC_4
    e) ATC_5

23. Which statement is false? (LO4, 5)
    a) AFC plus AVC equals ATC.
    b) Marginal cost equals AVC at an output of one.
    c) AVC equals ATC at an output of one.
    d) None is false.

24. As output rises, the difference between ATC and AVC _____. (LO5)
    a) rises
    b) stays the same
    c) falls

25. Adam Smith noted each of the following economies of scale except _____. (LO7)
    a) specialization
    b) employment of expensive equipment
    c) saving of time that would otherwise be spent going from one task to another
    d) diminishing returns

26. In general, as output rises you first attain _____. (LO6)
    a) increasing returns, then diminishing returns, then negative returns
    b) diminishing returns, then negative returns, then increasing returns
    c) negative returns, then increasing returns, then diminishing returns
    d) increasing returns, then negative returns, then diminishing returns

27. The law of diminishing returns may also be called the law of _____. (LO6)
    a) diminishing marginal output
    b) diminishing positive returns
    c) negative returns
    d) increasing returns

28. Each of the following provides an example of economies of scale *except* _____. (LO7)
    a) the computer software industry
    b) the pharmaceutical industry
    c) Adam Smith's pin factory
    d) movie and TV production
    e) the services of psychiatrists, personal trainers, barbers, and beauticians

29. We find price by dividing _____. (LO8)
    a) total revenue by output
    b) output by total revenue
    c) total cost by output
    d) output by total cost

30. The marginal cost curve intersects the average variable cost curve at the _____. (LO5)
    a) shut-down point
    b) break-even point
    c) maximum profit point

31. If price is above ATC, the firm will _____. (LO6, 8)
    a) shut down in the short run and go out of business in the long run
    b) shut down in the short run and stay in business in the long run
    c) operate in the short run and go out of business in the long run
    d) operate in the short run and stay in business in the long run

32. A production function shows a firm how to _____. (LO6)
    a) maximize profit
    b) maximize output
    c) minimize losses
    d) minimize output

33. When total output is maximized, marginal output is _____. (LO6)
    a) rising
    b) falling
    c) positive
    d) negative
    e) zero

34. Which of the following is the most accurate statement? (LO1, 8)
    a) Virtually no one getting married thinks that considering whether or not to have a large wedding is mainly an economic decision.
    b) Most American families holding large weddings get by for less than $2,000.
    c) When making a wedding, it is impossible to think in terms of fixed costs and variable costs.
    d) Whether to hold a wedding in city hall or in a wedding hall is at least partially an economic decision.

Fill-In Questions

1. In the long run a business has two options: to __stay in business__ or to __go out__. (LO3, 8)

2. Variable costs change with __output__. (LO1)

3. At zero units of output, total cost is equal to __fixed cost__. (LO1)

4. The short run is the length of time it takes all fixed costs to become __variable cost__. (LO3)

5. In the short run a firm has two options: (1) __operate__ or (2) __shut down__. (LO3, 8)

6. A firm will operate in the short run as long as __TR__ are greater than __VC__; a firm will operate in the long run as long as __TR__ are greater than __TC__. (LO8)

7. When AVC is less than price, in the short run the firm will __operate__. (LO8)

8. Total revenue divided by output equals __price__. (LO8)

Problems

1. Fill in Table 1. (LO2, 4)

TABLE 1

Output	Fixed Cost	Variable Cost	Total Cost	Marginal Cost
0	$800	____	____	____
1		$100	____	____
2		150	____	____
3		200	____	____
4		270	____	____
5		360	____	____

2. If a firm's total revenue is $5 billion, its fixed costs are $3 billion, and its variable costs are $1.5 billion, what does it do: (a) in the short run? (b) in the long run? (LO8)

3. If a firm's total revenue is $20 million, its fixed costs are $12 million, and its variable costs are $22 million, what does it do: (a) in the short run? (b) in the long run? (LO8)

Answer Questions 4 through 7 using Table 2.

TABLE 2

Output	Variable Cost	Total Cost	AVC	ATC	Marginal Cost
1	$ 400	____	____	____	____
2	700	____	____	____	____
3	900	____	____	____	____
4	1,350	____	____	____	____
5	2,000	____	____	____	____
6	3,000	____	____	____	____

4. Given: Fixed cost = $500. Fill in Table 2. (LO2, 4)

5. On a piece of graph paper, draw a graph of the ATC, AVC, and MC curves. (LO5)

6. State the minimum point of the ATC curve in dollars and cents. (LO5)

7. State the minimum point of the AVC curve in dollars and cents. (LO5)

8. a) Fill in the marginal output column of Table 3. (LO6)

TABLE 3

Number of Workers	Total Output	Marginal Output
0	0	
1	1	_____
2	3	_____
3	6	_____
4	9	_____
5	11	_____
6	13	_____
7	14	_____
8	14	_____
9	13	_____
10	11	_____
11	8	_____

b) Diminishing returns set in with the _____ worker. (LO6)

c) Negative returns set in with the _____ worker. (LO6)

9. a) Fill in the marginal output column of Table 4. (LO6)

TABLE 4

Number of Workers	Total Output	Marginal Output
0	0	
1	3	_____
2	7	_____
3	10	_____
4	12	_____
5	13	_____
6	13	_____
7	12	_____
8	10	_____

b) Given the information in Table 3, diminishing returns set in with the _____ worker. (LO6)

c) Negative returns set in with the _____ worker. (LO6)

10. A Toyota plant has fixed costs of $300 million and variable costs of $540 million. If it produces 60,000 cars, how much is the average total cost of producing one car? (LO4)

11. If it cost Amazon.com $10 million to set up a database of potential customers and $100,000 each time it e-mailed them an advertising message, what would be the average total cost of sending out 10 e-mails? What would be the average total cost of sending out 100 e-mails? (LO4)

Use Figure 2 to answer problems 12 through 15.

12. If the price is below $11, what will the firm do: (a) in the short run? (b) in the long run? (LO8)

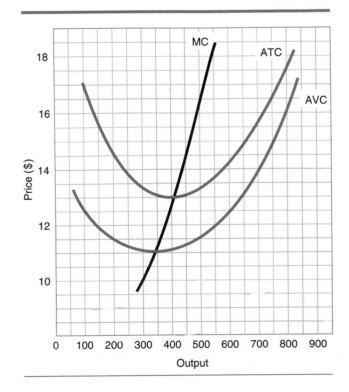

Figure 2

13. If the price is between $11 and $13, what will the firm do: (a) in the short run? (b) in the long run? (LO8)

14. If the price is above $13, what will the firm do: (a) in the short run? (b) in the long run? (LO8)

15. Please label the firm's break-even point and shut-down point in Figure 2. (LO5)

Use the information in Figure 3 to answer problems 16 through 18.

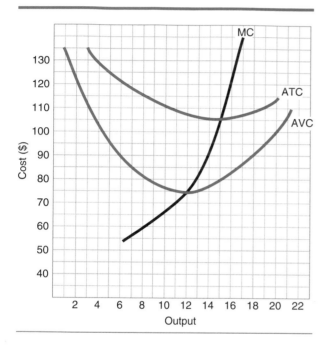

Figure 3

16. What is the lowest price the firm would accept in the short run? (LO8)

17. What is the lowest price the firm would accept in the long run? (LO8)

18. On Figure 3, label the shut-down and break-even points. (LO5)

19. You just got closed out of an economics course you need to graduate and need to persuade the department chair to open another section. She tells you that the school will have to pay a part-time instructor $3,000 to teach the course, and that there will be an additional $50 in administrative costs per student to run the course. If tuition is $600 for the course, how many students would you need to sign up for the course to run? (LO1, 8)

Chapter 9

Profit, Loss, and Perfect Competition

sk any businessowner why she went into business and the chances are she'll answer, "To make money." If she's from Brooklyn, she might add, "I didn't go into business for my health." This is not to say that every businessowner spends every waking hour chasing down every last penny of profit. But we can say that making money, or, more specifically, making a large profit, is the driving force in our economy.

We can say, then, that every businessowner tries to <u>maximize her profits</u>, and, if needed, <u>minimize her losses</u>. Later in the chapter we'll introduce the concept of perfect competition—in which many firms sell the same good or service. We'll see that this fierce competition forces the firms to produce at peak efficiency.

LEARNING OBJECTIVES

After reading this chapter you should be able to:

1. Define and measure marginal revenue and total revenue.
2. Distinguish between and calculate economic profit and accounting profit.
3. Analyze graphically profit maximization and loss minimization.
4. List and discuss the characteristics of perfect competition.
5. Distinguish between the short run and the long run for the perfect competitor.
6. Graph and analyze the short-run and long-run supply curves.
7. Explain economic efficiency.

In the first part of this chapter we'll see how a firm calculates its profit or loss, and then how it can derive its short-run and long-run supply curves. In the second part we'll see how the perfect competitor, in his quest to maximize his profit, behaves in the short run and the long run. The perfect competitor is one of many firms producing an identical product. In subsequent chapters we'll look at the other forms of competition—monopoly, monopolisitic competition, and oligopoly.

Part I: Profit and Loss

Just in case you might have forgotten, from time to time we'll remind you that the profit motive is what drives people to go into business. We'll begin by looking at total revenue and marginal revenue, which are two important variables used in calculating profit.

Total Revenue and Marginal Revenue

In the last chapter we introduced the concept of marginal cost. Marginal revenue is a parallel concept. Using both concepts, we'll be able to find the output at which a firm maximizes its profit and to calculate that profit.

Total revenue is price times output sold.

If your firm sold four workstations at $3,200 each, calculate your total revenue. The answer is $12,800. *Total revenue is price times output sold.*

Marginal revenue is the increase in total revenue when output sold goes up by one unit.

Now let's do marginal revenue. Suppose you sold five workstations instead of four. How much would your total revenue be? It would be $16,000 (5 × $3,200). Your marginal revenue from selling that fifth workstation would be $3,200. *Marginal revenue is the increase in total revenue when output sold goes up by one unit. We can also say that marginal revenue is the additional revenue derived from selling one more unit of output.*

We'll be assuming for the next two chapters that a seller can sell as much output as he or she wants at the market price. Thus, if the market price is $5, we can easily calculate the total revenue and marginal revenue. I'd like you to do that by filling in Table 1. Then you can check your work by looking at Table 2.

TABLE 1	Revenue Schedule for Jill Peterson and Kaitlyn Ziegenfuss, Fashion Consultants		
Output	Price	Total Revenue	Marginal Revenue
1	$5	_____	_____
2	5	_____	_____
3	5	_____	_____
4	5	_____	_____
5	5	_____	_____
6	5	_____	_____

Graphing Demand and Marginal Revenue

Now we're ready to draw the graph of the demand and marginal revenue curves. The demand curve for this firm is the output, which runs from 1 to 6, at a price of $5. And the marginal revenue curve is the output, from 1 to 6, at whatever the price happens to be. Go ahead and draw a graph of the firm's demand and MR curves on graph paper.

Check your work against Figure 1. You should have drawn just one line, perfectly elastic, which serves as the firm's demand and MR curves. When price is constant, so is MR, and MR and demand are identical.

TABLE 2	Revenue Schedule for Jill Peterson and Kaitlyn Ziegenfuss, Fashion Consultants		
Output	Price	Total Revenue	Marginal Revenue
1	$5	$ 5	$5
2	5	10	5
3	5	15	5
4	5	20	5
5	5	25	5
6	5	30	5

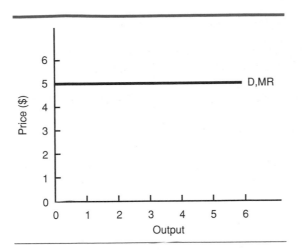

Figure 1
Demand and Marginal Revenue
Curves

Economic and Accounting Profit

To find a firm's profit, we use this simple formula:

$$\text{Total Profit} = \text{Total Revenue} - \text{Total Cost}$$

If your company had a total revenue of $4,300,000 and a total cost of $3,750,000, how much would its total profit be?

It would be $550,000 ($4,300,000 − $3,750,000). Your accountant would tell you that your total profit is $550,000. So we'll call that your accounting profit.

Accounting profit is what's left over from sales after the firm has paid all its explicit, or dollar, costs—rent, wages, cost of goods sold, insurance, advertising, fuel, taxes. What the businessowner keeps is the accounting profit. But the economist makes some additional deductions, called "implicit costs."

Implicit costs are a business firm's *opportunity costs*. What is an *opportunity cost*? Near the beginning of Chapter 2, I said: *The opportunity cost of any choice is the forgone value of the next best alternative.* If you work for yourself, the opportunity cost of that choice is the income you forgo by not doing the same work for someone else. And what is the opportunity cost of investing $1 million of your own money in your business? It's the interest you could have earned on your money by investing it in an equally risky business owned by someone else.

What, then, are the implicit (or opportunity) costs of a family business? These costs include a return on your investment, wages that you and your family members could have earned doing the same work for another firm, rent on the space used in your house, and wear and tear on your car when it is used for your business. Your accountant will probably include these last two costs but will not deal with the first two.

OK, you and your spouse start a business and your accountant says you made a profit of $85,000. Suppose you've invested $100,000 of your own money in your business. You could have earned $15,000 in interest had you lent these funds to another business of comparable risk. If you and your spouse, instead of working 12 hours a day for your business, had worked for another firm, the two of you would have earned $70,000. The economist will subtract this $85,000 in implicit costs from your $85,000 in accounting profits. And poof—your economic profit is zero.

Why, you ask, should implicit costs be subtracted from accounting profits? Because they represent alternatives that you have forgone to have your own business. You *could* have earned $15,000 interest on your $100,000 by investing it elsewhere, and you and your spouse *could* have earned $70,000 by working for someone else. The cost of forgoing these opportunities—your opportunity cost—is $85,000. Being in business for yourselves cost you $85,000.

Accounting profit

Economic profit

Accounting Profit versus Economic Profit

Let's compare the accounting profit of Bonnie's Bargain Bazaar.

Item	Accounting Profit	Economic Profit
Total revenue	$700,000	$700,000
Less explicit costs:		
Wages and salaries	200,000	200,000
Cost of goods sold	150,000	150,000
Advertising	50,000	50,000
Phone, electricity, and other office expenses	20,000	20,000
Less implicit costs:		
Foregone salaries	0	120,000
Foregone interest	0	10,000
Foregone rent	0	20,000
Equals profit	$280,000	$130,000

As you can see, when figuring accounting profit, we subtract explicit costs from total revenue. But to find economic profit, we subtract both explicit and implicit costs from total revenue.

Being in your own business is working 80 hours a week so that you can avoid working 40 hours a week for someone else.

—Ramona E. F. Arnett, President, Ramona Enterprises

Why stay in business if your economic profit is zero? Because you *are* still making accounting profit. And you wouldn't do any better if you invested your money elsewhere and worked for someone else; you'd be in exactly the same economic situation. And, of course, by having your own business, you're your own boss.

When economic profit becomes negative—particularly if these losses are substantial and appear permanent—many people will close their businesses and go to work for other companies. Going back to our example, they will then be able to earn $85,000 a year ($15,000 in interest and $70,000 in wages). If you'd like more practice finding economic and accounting profit, see the accompanying box, "Accounting Profit versus Economic Profit."

Even going to college has both implicit and explicit costs. Do you know how much going to college *really* costs you? Read the box, "What Is the Cost of a College Education?"

Profit Maximization and Loss Minimization

There are three ways to calculate profit or loss. The easiest way, if you happen to have the information in tabular form, is to just subtract total cost from total revenue. Go ahead and calculate the profit or loss for each of the outputs listed in Table 3.

You probably got the same results I got in Table 4. So it appears that the firm maximized its profit at an output of 4, when its profit was $3.

A second method of calculating profit and loss is marginal analysis, which we'll be using throughout this chapter, and also in the following three chapters. Then, toward the end of this chapter, we'll introduce a third method, which is a variant of marginal analysis, which involves reading points from a graph.

What Is the Cost of a College Education?

How much does it cost you to go to college? If you attend a public college or university, your out-of-pocket expenses might come to between $5,000 and $15,000, depending largely on whether you live on campus and are an in-state or out-of-state resident. Attending a private college might set you back over $40,000 a year.

But those are your explicit costs. What about your implicit costs? Like dozens of college athletes who forego their senior year to join the pros, what if you quit college and got a full-time job? How much could you earn? Let's suppose you're currently working part-time and summers for a software firm, earning $15,000. You're offered a full-time job at a starting salary of $40,000. What would you do?

Let's get back to our original question: What is the cost of a college education? Suppose that you live at home and pay $7,000 for tuition, fees, books, and other college expenses. You earn $15,000 working part-time

and summers, but you could earn $40,000 by working full-time. What is it costing you to go to college? Do the math and write down your answer.

Solution: Cost of going to college = explicit cost ($7,000) + implicit cost ($40,000 − $15,000 = $25,000) = $32,000. If you were to take the full-time job, you would have $32,000 more than if you stayed in college.

It should be clear that going to college involves not just an explicit cost, but an implicit cost, which would be your foregone income. The foregone income of a college athlete good enough to play pro ball is often enough to induce him to leave school before graduation. But unless you expect to be a first- or second-round draft choice, you might not want to give up college for a day job.

TABLE 3 Total Revenue and Total Cost Schedule for Jill Peterson and Kaitlyn Ziegenfuss, Fashion Consultants

Output	Price	Total Revenue	Total Cost	Profit
1	$5	$ 5	$ 8	____
2	5	10	11	____
3	5	15	13	____
4	5	20	17	____
5	5	25	23	____
6	5	30	31	____

TABLE 4 Total Revenue, and Total Cost Profit Schedule for Jill Peterson and Kaitlyn Ziegenfuss, Fashion Consultants

Output	Price	Total Revenue	Total Cost	Profit
1	$5	$ 5	$ 8	−$3
2	5	10	11	−1
3	5	15	13	2
4	5	20	17	3
5	5	25	23	2
6	5	30	31	−1

Now we're ready to do some marginal analysis, which is the basis of much of microeconomic decision making. The big decision we'll be making here is choosing the output at which the business firm should produce. If we choose correctly, profits will be maximized (or losses minimized).

TABLE 5	Cost and Revenue Schedule for Sam and Rachel Whittingham, Clothiers						
Output	Price	Total Revenue	Marginal Revenue	Total Cost	ATC	Marginal Cost	Total Profit
1	$500	____	____	$1,000	____	____	____
2	500	____	____	1,500	____	____	____
3	500	____	____	1,800	____	____	____
4	500	____	____	2,000	____	____	____
5	500	____	____	2,300	____	____	____
6	500	____	____	2,850	____	____	____
7	500	____	____	3,710	____	____	____

I'd like you to fill in the columns in Table 5 corresponding to total revenue, marginal revenue, average total cost (ATC), marginal cost, and total profit. Make sure your work matches that in Table 6. Once you've done that, see if you can figure out the output at which the firm maximizes its total profit.

TABLE 6	Cost and Revenue Schedule for Sam and Rachel Whittingham, Clothiers: Solution						
Output ×	Price =	Total Revenue	Marginal Revenue	Total Cost	ATC	Marginal Cost	Total Profit
1	$500	$ 500	$500	$1,000	$1,000	—	−$500
2	500	1,000	500	1,500	750	500	−500
3	500	1,500	500	1,800	600	300	−300
4	500	2,000	500	2,000	500	200	0
5	500	2,500	500	2,300	460	300	200
6	500	3,000	500	2,850	475	550	150
7	500	3,500	500	3,710	530	860	−210

Did you get an output of 5? At that output total profit is $200. But we can do even better. The maximum profit point in this problem is actually between two outputs. How do we know? We can find out by drawing a graph of the firm's ATC, MC, and demand curves. (The firm's demand and marginal revenue curves are identical—in this case a horizontal line drawn at a price of $500.) So go ahead and draw this on a piece of graph paper, and then see if your graph looks like Figure 2.

Are you ready for some marginal analysis? All right, then, we're going to start with a very important rule: _A firm will maximize its profit or minimize its loss at the output where MC = MR._ If you look at Figure 2, you'll see that MC = MR at two different outputs. Profit is maximized only when MC = MR and MC is rising. You'll also notice that in Figure 3, MC = MR once when MC is falling and once when it is rising. Just remember that we maximize our profit when MC = MR and MC is rising. Now let's see how this rule applies to Figure 2. At what output does MC = MR?

MC = MR at an output of 5.75. (Your estimate may be slightly different.) Let's calculate total profit at that output. We'll use this formula:

$$\text{Total profit} = \text{Output (Price} - \text{ATC)}$$

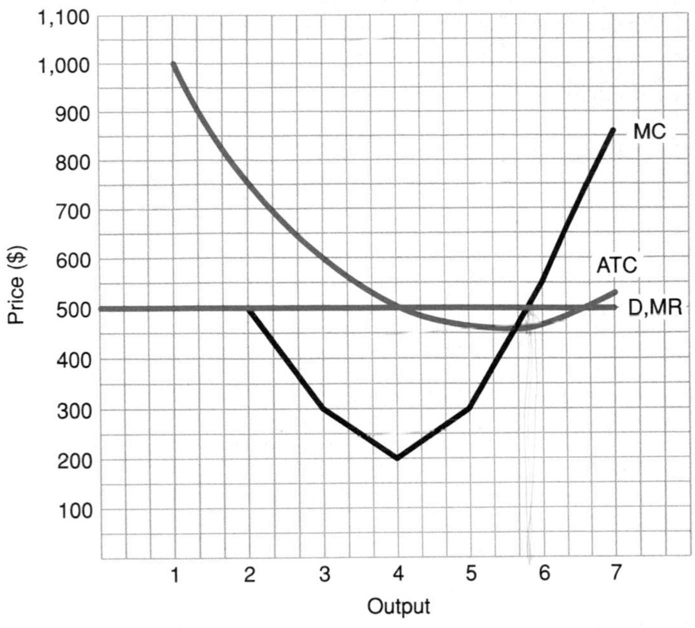

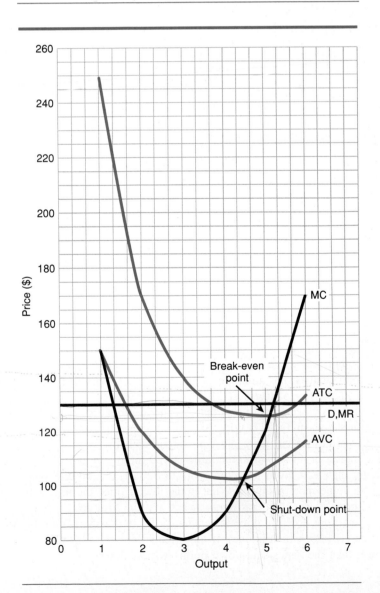

Figure 2

Hypothetical D, MR, MC, and ATC Curves

Figure 3

The Shut-Down and Break-Even Points

What is the lowest price this firm will accept in the short run and in the long run? In the short run, the firm will not accept any price below $101, the shut-down point. If the price is below $101, the firm will shut down in the short run. In the long run, the firm will not accept any price below $125.50. If price is below $125.50, the firm will go out of business in the long run.

We can substitute actual numbers for output, price, and ATC. So substitute and then solve for total profit. Do your work right here:

What did you get? I got $201.25. Here's my work:

$$\text{Total profit} = \text{Output (Price} - \text{ATC)}$$
$$= 5.75\ (\$500 - \$465)$$
$$= 5.75\ (\$35)$$
$$= \$201.25$$

The numbers I substituted for output and ATC are not written in stone. Two people with perfect vision could look at Figure 2 and see slightly different outputs and ATCs. But we *do* know that we are maximizing our profit at the output at which the MC and MR curves cross. So when we calculate total profit, we *should* get something a little higher than $200.

Using the same analysis and the same formula, we can calculate a firm's total loss. We've done that in the accompanying box, "Calculating a Firm's Total Loss."

The most important thing we've covered so far in this chapter is that the firm will always produce at the output at which MC = MR. At that output it will be maximizing its profit or minimizing its losses. Using this information, we can now derive the firm's short-run and long-run supply curves (see the box "Calculating a Firm's Total Loss").

A Summing Up

We're going to do a little more graphical analysis. I'll supply the graph (Figure 3), and you supply the analysis. Figure 3 is based on Table 7.

First, calculate total profit. Follow our usual three-step method: (1) write down the formula, (2) plug in the numbers, and (3) solve.

Solution:

$$\text{Total profit} = \text{(Price} - \text{ATC)} \times \text{Output}$$
$$= (\$130 - \$126) \times 5.2$$
$$= \$4 \times 5.2$$
$$= \$20.80$$

You'll want to watch out for a couple of things here. First, when you're picking an ATC, remember it will be the ATC at the output at which you are maximizing your total profit. That output looks like 5.2 or so. At *that* output, ATC is *more* than it is at the break-even point (that is, the minimum point of the ATC curve). I see it as $126. *You* may see it as $125.90 or $126.10.

A second thing to watch out for is that your total profit *must* come out to more than any total profit shown in Table 7. Why? We are maximizing our total profit at an output of 5.2, so the profit we calculate must be larger than the profit at any other output. Because the largest profit shown in the table is $20 (at an output of 5), *your* total profit *must* be larger than $20. Even if it comes out to $20.01, that's big enough.

Ready for some more analysis? What is the lowest price the firm will accept in the short run? If price is less than that figure, what will the firm do?

The firm will not accept a price lower than $101 in the short run (you may see this as $100.50 or $101.25, which is fine). If the price is less, the firm will shut down. So if price is lower than the firm's shut-down point, it shuts down.

ADVANCED WORK

Calculating a Firm's Total Loss

We're going to use the same analysis, the same formula, and the same data that we did when we calculated the firm's total profit. This time, however, let's assume that the price is just $400. We've shown this in Figure A. Let's calculate the firm's loss.

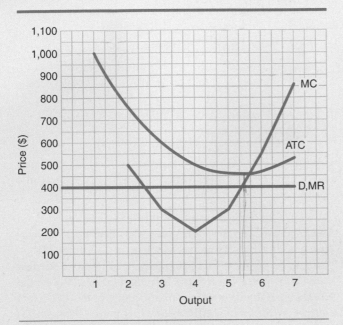

Figure A
Hypothetical D, MR, MC, and ATC Curves

Because ATC will be greater than price, total profit will be a negative number, which means the firm is losing money.

$$\text{Total profit} = \text{Output (Price} - \text{ATC)}$$
$$= 5.35\ (\$400 - \$456)$$
$$= 5.35\ (-\$56)$$
$$= -\$299.60$$

The firm has minimized its losses at an output of 5.35, because that's where the MC and MR curves cross. Any other output would result in still greater losses.

At any given time, a business firm will have a certain set of cost curves: AVC, ATC, and MC. These curves are determined mainly by the firm's capital stock—its plant and equipment. Over time the curves can change; but at any given time they're fixed. What concerns us here is the MC curve. We can assume it doesn't change.

What about MR? That changes with price. Because the firm will always operate where MC equals MR, there is an infinite number of possible prices and therefore an infinite number of MRs, but only one MC curve. It follows, then, that we could slide along the MC curve so that no matter what the MR, MC would equal MR.

Let's go over these points. MC must equal MR. MC stays the same. MR can change—to any value. Whenever price changes we have a new MR line, but the MC curve remains the same. The MC will equal MR, but at some other point on the MC curve.

This can be illustrated. In the graph in Figure B, based on the accompanying table, we'll start with MC = MR at an output of 9. MR = $43. At an output of 8, MC = MR = $28. At an output of 7, MC = MR = $19. And so forth down the MC curve.

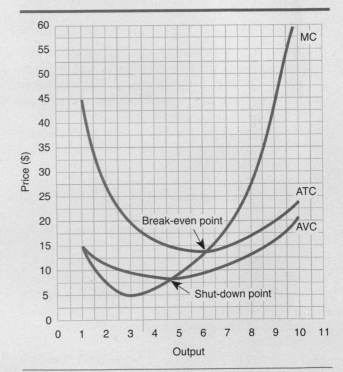

Figure B
Derivation of Firm's Short-Run and Long-Run Supply Curves

When we get below an output of about 6.1, we run into a problem. We're losing money. In the long run no firm will stay in business if it's losing money, so for every output above 6.1 we can just move along the MC curve and, in effect, we will be moving along the firm's long-run supply curve.

Hypothetical Schedule of Costs*

Output	Variable Cost	Total Cost	AVC	ATC	Marginal Cost
1	$ 15	$ 45	$15	$45	$15
2	22	52	11	26	7
3	27	57	9	19	5
4	34	64	8.50	16	7
5	44	74	8.80	14.80	10
6	58	88	9.67	14.67	14
7	77	107	11	15.29	19
8	105	135	13.33	16.88	28
9	148	178	16.23	19.78	43
10	210	240	21	24	62

*Fixed cost = $30.

Now hold it right there! *What* did I just say? I said, "We can just move along the MC curve and, in effect, we will be moving along the firm's long-run supply curve." So now I'm calling the firm's MC curve (above a certain output) its long-run supply curve. Where did *that* come from? It came from our definition of supply, which was given at the beginning of Chapter 3: *Supply is a schedule of quantities of a good or service that people are willing to sell at various prices.* This is exactly what we've derived by examining the firm's MC curve at various prices.

At outputs below 6.1, the firm is losing money because ATC is above price. Remember that price and MR are the same. Below an output of 6.1, MC is less than ATC; and because the firm will produce where MC equals MR, it should be obvious that below an output of 6.1, MR is less than ATC. In other words, the firm would be receiving less for each unit sold than the cost of producing that unit.

This is consistent with what we concluded toward the end of the last chapter—that in the long run a firm will go out of business if total cost is greater than sales. It is exactly the same thing to say that a firm will go out of business if ATC is greater than price (or MR). Why? Because if we divide total cost by output, we get ATC. If we divide total revenue by output, we get price.* In other words, since we would go out of business if total cost were greater than sales, we'd also go out of business if ATC were greater than price.

Let's go on to the firm's short-run supply curve. If we continue our way down the firm's MC curve below an output of 6.1, we find that at an output of 5, MC = MR = $10. At an output of 4, MC = MR = $7. But we see that at an output of about 4.6, the MC curve passes through the AVC curve, signifying the minimum point of the AVC. This means any price (and MR) below that point (about $8.25) will be below AVC.

In the last chapter we introduced two sets of rules for the firm in the short run and in the long run. In the short run, the firm will (a) shut down if AVC is greater than price; (b) operate if price is greater than AVC. In the long run the firm will (a) go out of business if ATC is greater than price; (b) stay in business if price is greater than ATC.

Thus the firm's short-run supply curve does not go below the point at which MC is lower than AVC. In this case, the short-run supply curve does not go below an output of 4.6. We call this the shut-down point. *The firm's short-run supply curve begins at the shut-down point and moves up the firm's MC curve as far as it goes.* It does *not* stop at the point at which the MC curve intersects the ATC curve. The short-run supply curve runs all the way up the firm's MC curve.

The firm's long-run supply curve also runs up the MC curve, beginning at the point at which the MC curve intersects the ATC curve. That is called the break-even point. In this case, it is at an output of 6.1. *A firm's long-run supply curve begins at the break-even point and runs all the way up the MC curve.*

---

*Total revenue = Price × Output. Total revenue/Output = Price.

TABLE 7

Output	Variable Cost	Total Cost	Average Variable Cost	Average Total Cost	Marginal Cost	Total Profits
1	$150	$250	$150	$250	$150	−$120
2	240	340	120	170	90	−80
3	320	420	106.67	140	80	−30
4	410	510	102.50	127.50	90	+10
5	530	630	106	126	120	+20
6	700	800	116.67	133.33	170	−20

What is the lowest price the firm will accept in the long run? If price is less than that figure, what will the firm do?

The firm will not accept a price of less than $125.50 in the long run. Why can't we use $126? Because the *minimum* point on the firm's ATC curve—the break-even point—occurs at an output of somewhat more than 5, and we know from Table 7 that ATC is $126 at an output of 5. Therefore, if price is less than $125.50 (I'll take anything from $125.90 down to $125), the firm will go out of business in the long run.

Here is one last set of questions. How much will the firm's output be in the short run and the long run if the price is $170? In both the short run and the long run, the output will be 6. At an output of 6, MC is $170, so MC equals MR, and the firm is maximizing its profit.

If the price is $115, find output in the short run and the long run. In the short run output will be about 4.75 (MC equals MR). How much will output be in the long run? This is a trick question. The answer is zero. Why? Because $115 is below the firm's break-even point, so it is less than the lowest price the firm would accept in the long run (that is, the lowest price that could induce the firm to stay in business).

And finally, if the price is $90, what will the firm's output be in the short run and the long run? The answer to both questions is zero. In the short run, because the price is lower than the shut-down point, the firm will shut down and produce nothing. And in the long run the firm will go out of business.

If all of this is not perfectly clear, then work out the problems in the box, "Finding the Firm's Short-Run and Long-Run Supply Curves, and Shut-Down and Break-Even Points."

Efficiency

So far, we've concentrated on a firm's most profitable output. But we are concerned with more than just profits in economics. We are also concerned with efficiency.

Efficiency is such an important economic concept that it is part of the definition of economics: *Economics is the efficient allocation of the scarce means of production toward the satisfaction of human wants.* It's time to explain just what the word *efficient* means.

We say that a firm is operating at peak efficiency if its average total cost is held to a minimum.[1] How much would that output be in Figure 4? The answer is 10. You'll notice that the peak efficiency output is also where the break-even point is located.

How much is the most profitable output in Figure 4? It is 11. OK, if you owned this firm, would you produce at an output of 10 or 11? I hope you said 11. Given the choice of operating at peak efficiency or most profitably, we assume that every businessowner would choose the latter.

---

[1] We are confining our definition to productive efficiency, which means producing output at the least possible cost. We are not considering allocative efficiency, which occurs when firms produce the output that is most valued by consumers. Allocative efficiency is covered in a more advanced course.

Finding the Firm's Short-Run and Long-Run Supply Curves, and Shut-Down and Break-Even Points

First I'd like you to label the firm's short-run and long-run supply curves in Figure A. Then label the shut-down and break-even points.

Once you've done that, check your work against mine in Figure B. Next I'd like you to write down the lowest price this firm would accept in the short run and the lowest price it would accept in the long run.

The lowest price the firm would accept in the short run is $28; the lowest price it would accept in the long run is $48.

Last set of questions: (1) If the price is $50, what will the firm's output be in the short run and in the long run?

(2) If the price is $40, what will the firm's output be in the short run and in the long run?

Answers: (1) If the price is $50, the firm will have an output of 10.1 (you might even call it 10) in both the short run and the long run. (2) If the price is $40, the firm will have an output of 9.1 in the short run. In the long run it will go out of business; so its output will be 0.

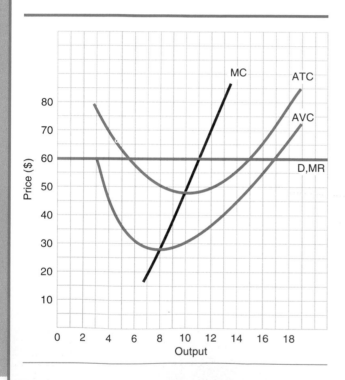

Figure A

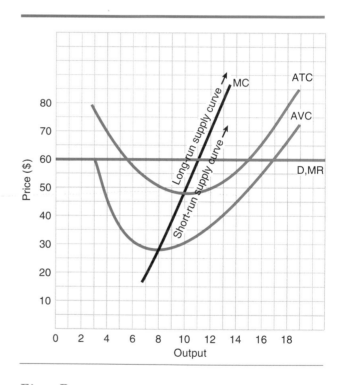

Figure B

This is not to say that a businessowner may ignore efficiency. Indeed, we shall see later in this chapter that the perfect competitor is driven to produce at peak efficiency in the long run.

Review of Efficiency and Profit Maximization

If *you* were running a business, would you try to run it at peak efficiency or would you try to maximize your profits? It is a basic assumption of microeconomics that businessowners would choose profitability over efficiency every time. Using graphic analysis, we know we're operating most efficiently when our output is at the break-even point, where

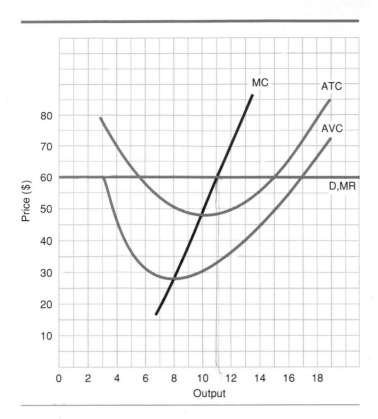

Figure 4
The Most Efficient Output
How much is this firm's most efficient output? This occurs at an output of 10, which is the minimum point (the break-even point) on the ATC.

the MC intersects the ATC curve. And we know we're operating most profitably if we're at the output at which the MC and MR curves cross. If you'd like to take a closer look at the most efficient and most profitable outputs, please see the accompanying box, "A Closer Look at the Most Efficient and Most Profitable Outputs."

Part II: Perfect Competition

Definition of Perfect Competition

Perfect competition, as economists wistfully point out, is an ideal state of affairs, which, unfortunately, does not exist in any industry. So if it doesn't exist, why do you need to read about it? Just look at Judeo-Christian tradition. We're all sinners, but we still need to know right from wrong. Perfect competition fulfills the ideal of always being right. It's a goal we should strive to approach, even if we can never hope to attain its state of grace. But who knows—maybe we'll get lucky.

How wonderful *is* the perfect competitor? In the long run, the perfectly competitive firm is forced to operate at the break-even point in order to survive. This means that it is operating at peak efficiency. In addition, the price it gets is just equal to the minimum point of its ATC (in other words, the break-even point), so it charges the lowest possible price it can, while remaining in business. When we've gotten through this chapter and the next three, we'll see that in the long run, the perfect competitor charges the lowest price and operates most efficiently.

For our purposes, perfect competition will be considered an unattainable standard by which the other forms of competition—monopoly, monopolistic competition, and oligopoly—will be judged. Thus, even though it doesn't exist, perfect competition has its uses.

A Closer Look at the Most Efficient and Most Profitable Outputs

Figure A highlights two relationships. First, we can see that the output at which the firm operates at peak efficiency, 5.67, is clearly less than the output at which it maximizes its profit (5.7). And second, the ATC at output 5.67 ($53.00) is just a drop lower than it is at an output of 5.7 ($53.20).

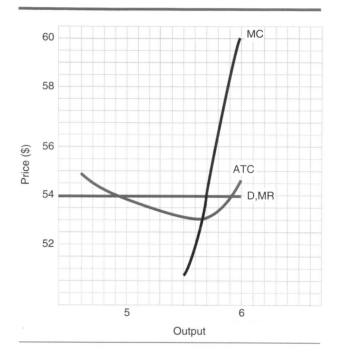

Figure A

Definition of perfect competition

Perfect competition is a market structure with many well-informed sellers and buyers of an identical product and no barriers to entering or leaving the market. Let's deal with these characteristics one at a time.

Under perfect competition, there are so many firms that no one firm is large enough to have any influence over price. What is influence? If any action taken by the firm has any effect on price, that's influence. If a firm, by withholding half of its output from the market, were able to push up price, that would be influence. If a firm doubled its output and forced down price, that too would be influence. Even if a firm made prices go up by leaving the industry, *that* would be influence on price.

The industry operating under perfect competition includes many firms. How many? So many that no single firm has any influence on price. How many would *that* be? There's no exact answer, but we can agree on some numbers. Would a million firms be many? Obviously, yes. Would 80,000? Definitely. Ten thousand? Yes. Would three be many? No! Ten? No! Seventeen? No.

There's no clear dividing line. Students don't seem very happy with "more than 17 but fewer than 10,000." If you want my guess—and it's only an arbitrary number—I'd say perhaps 200 firms would constitute many. But that's just *my* guess, and in microeconomics there's no one correct answer to this question of how many is many.

We're assuming, too, that no firm has more than, say, 1 percent of market share. Our definition of perfect competition would go right out the window if one of the many firms sold half the industry output.

The perfect competitor is a price taker rather than a price maker. Price is set by industrywide supply and demand; the perfect competitor can take it or leave it.

Another part of the definition of perfect competition has to do with the product. *For perfect competition to take place, all the firms in the industry must sell an identical, or standardized, product.* That is, those who buy the product cannot distinguish what one seller offers from what another seller offers. So, in the buyer's mind, the products are identical. The buyer has no reason to prefer one seller to another. Are all hamburgers identical? Is the Whopper identical to the Big Mac? Are Wendy's hamburgers identical to those of White Castle? Maybe *you* can differentiate among these choices, but what if every buyer in the market considered them identical? Then they *would* be identical.

This identity takes place in the minds of the buyers. If they think all cars—Toyotas, Fords, Volkswagens, Lincolns, and Cadillacs—are the same, then they are all the same. If all buyers are indifferent about whether they're offered station wagons, stretch limos, or subcompacts, all cars are identical. A car is a car. Remember: the customer is always right.

My friend's father, a man in his late 80s, provided me with one of the best examples of a identical product—food. We were talking about grocery shopping in his neighborhood, where there happen to be some great stores. But he was completely indifferent as to where he shopped, or indeed, even what he bought. After all, he said, "Food is food."

Now we can define perfect competition. A perfectly competitive industry *has many firms selling an identical product.* How many is many? So many that no one firm can influence price. What is identical? A product is identical in the minds of buyers if they have no reason to prefer one seller to another.

> A perfectly competitive industry has many firms selling an identical product.

We've already discussed the two most important characteristics—actually, requirements—of perfect competition: many firms and an identical product. Two additional characteristics are perfect mobility and perfect knowledge.

> Two additional characteristics are perfect mobility and perfect knowledge.

Firms must be free to move wherever there's an opportunity for profits. Land, labor, and capital will move where they can secure the highest possible return. An entrepreneur will give up his or her business and work for someone else if the wage offered is higher than the firm's profit.

Usually certain barriers to entry in various markets inhibit mobility. Licenses, long-term contracts, government franchises, patents, and control over vital resources are some of these barriers. Under perfect competition, there would be perfect mobility, and none of these barriers could exist. As in an open game of poker, anyone with a sufficient stake is welcome to play. In fact, hundreds of firms are entering or leaving each year. There are no significant barriers to entry, with the possible exception of money.[2]

> Perfect mobility

Perfect knowledge or information is another characteristic. Everyone knows about every possible economic opportunity. One example would be the market for audiologists in New York; everyone knows every job that exists and every opening when it occurs. In fact, if one person leaves one job for another, several other people become involved in a game of musical chairs as each fills the next vacated position. The audiologist from New York Eye and Ear who fills the position at Brooklyn Jewish Hospital leaves a position vacant at New York Eye and Ear. His or her position is taken by someone from Long Island College Hospital, which now leaves that person's position open. And so forth. See the box, "More Perfect Knowledge," for another example.

> Perfect knowledge

Agriculture, particularly wheat growing, has been held up as an example of perfect or near-perfect competition. The stock market, the foreign exchange market, and new markets springing up on the Internet (see "On the Web: The Market for Silver Dollars") come fairly close to perfectly competitive markets. But economists still have

---

[2]To go into any business these days, you not only need to lay out several thousand dollars for rent, inventory, equipment, advertising, and possibly salaries, but you also need money on which to live for at least six months.

More Perfect Knowledge

The computerization of the business world in the 1980s and 1990s, and the advent of the Internet in the second half of the 1990s, has brought wide sectors of business very close to a state of perfect knowledge. Tens of thousands of stockbrokers and millions of investors are hooked into the world's leading stock exchanges and have up-to-the-second information on stock prices, bids, and shares sold.

BusinessWeek reports that "business-to-business auction site Free Markets Inc. says that purchasers are saving anywhere from 2 percent to 25 percent by letting suppliers bid for business online."* And, of course, orbitz.com, Price.com, eBay, and a host of other online websites provide the consumer with an incredible mass of information on where to purchase everything from the cheapest airline tickets to the cheapest groceries.

---

*Jennifer Reingold and Marcia Stepanek, *BusinessWeek*, February 14, 2000, p. 114.

not been able to come up with any examples of truly perfect competition. If you can come up with a good example, then I suggest you become an economics major, go on to graduate school for your PhD, and write your doctoral dissertation on perfect competition.

on the web

The Market for Silver Dollars

How much is a silver dollar worth? That would depend on several factors including its condition, the year it was minted, and whether it's an Eisenhower, Liberty, or Morgan dollar. You could get a pretty good idea of what that coin is worth by going to www. ebay.com, click on "Coins & Paper Money" under Categories; then select "Coins: U.S." and click on "Dollars." You'll find page after page of silver dollars being auctioned. Does eBay provide a perfectly competitive market for silver dollars—or for any other product, for that matter? No, but in the coin collector's market, it does come pretty close.

The Perfect Competitor's Demand Curve

Horizontal demand curve

The perfect competitor faces a horizontal, or perfectly elastic, demand curve (see Figure 5). As we noted in the last chapter, a firm with a perfectly elastic demand curve has an identical MR curve. This is significant because the firm can sell as much as it wants to sell at the market price. It's not necessary to lower price to sell more.

What determines the market price? Supply and demand. The graph on the left side of Figure 5 has a supply curve and a demand curve. Where they cross is the point of market price.

In our graph, the market price is $6. The firm can sell all it wants to sell at that price. What would happen if it should raise its price one penny to $6.01? It would lose all its sales to its many competitors who would still be charging $6, so the firm would never raise its price above market price.

Would a firm ever lower its price below market price, say to $5.99? Why would it do that? To get sales away from its competitors? There is no need to do this because the perfect competitor can sell as much as he or she desires at the market price. There is no point in charging less.

Why is the demand curve flat instead of curving downward to the right?

If the firm's demand curve is derived from the intersection of the industry demand and supply curves, why is it flat? Why isn't it sloping downward to the right like the industry demand curve? Actually, it is. I know it doesn't look that way, but it really is.

A D V A N C E D WORK

Why the Firm's Demand Curve Is Flat

Look at the scale of industry output in Figure 5; it's in the millions. The output scale of the individual firm goes up to 30. When the industry demand curve slopes downward to the right, it does so over millions of units of output. For example, as the price falls from $6 to $5, output goes from 4 million to 5.5 million. In fact, it takes a price change of just $1 to bring about a change in the quantity demanded of 1.5 million units.

The graph on the right side of Figure 5 deals with output changes between 0 and 30 units. It would take a far greater change in output to change price, even by one cent. That's why the demand curve of the individual firm is seen as flat; and that's why the firm is too small to have any effect on price.

Theoretically, the firm's demand curve slopes ever so slightly downward to the right. But we can't see that slope, so we draw a perfectly horizontal curve and consider it perfectly elastic.

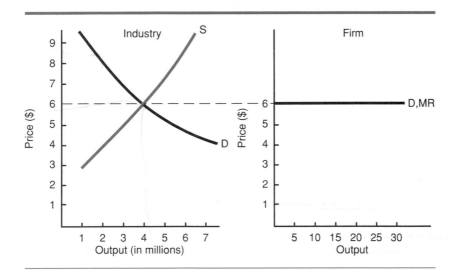

Figure 5

Perfect Competition: How Price Is Set
The intersection of the industry supply and demand curves sets the price that is taken by the individual firm, in this case, $6.

If you'd like to know more about this, please see the Advanced Work box, "Why the Firm's Demand Curve Is Flat."

The Short Run

In the short run the perfect competitor may make a profit or lose money. In the long run, as we'll see, the perfect competitor just breaks even.

Short run: profit or loss

Long run: break even

Figure 6 shows one example of a perfect competitor in the short run. Is the firm making a profit or is it losing money? How do you know?

You can always tell by looking at the demand curve and the ATC curve. If the demand curve is above the ATC curve at any point, the firm will make a profit. If the demand curve is always below the ATC curve, the firm will lose money.

In this case, the firm is losing money. How much? You should be able to figure that out for yourself. Go ahead. You'll find the solution in Figure 7.

Did you get a loss of $20? If you didn't, check your price and output. Clearly, the price is $6 and the output is 8. What about ATC? I saw it as $8.50. But suppose you saw it as $8.45. Then your total loss would have come to $19.60. Would this be wrong? It would be no more wrong than $20. When I drew this graph, I wanted ATC to be exactly $8.50, but if it looked to you like $8.45, then that's what it is.

Figure 6

The Perfect Competitor in the
Short Run

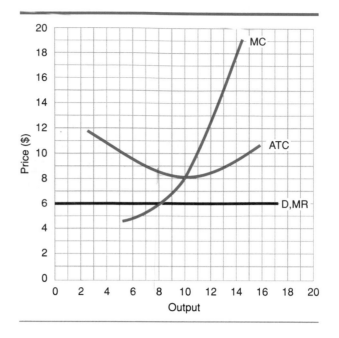

Figure 7

The Perfect Competitor in the
Short Run: Solution

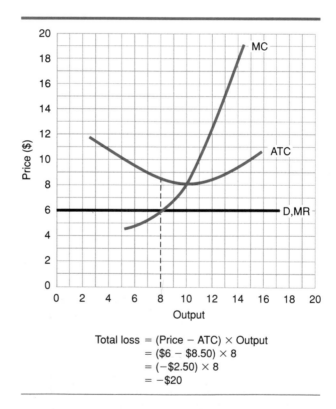

Total loss = (Price − ATC) × Output
        = ($6 − $8.50) × 8
        = (−$2.50) × 8
        = −$20

Here's another problem. In this case, is the firm losing money or is it making a profit? Check out the demand and ATC curves. How much is the profit or loss? Figure it out; you have the tools. The problem is Figure 8; the solution is Figure 9.

Is this graph beginning to look familiar? It should be. In Figures 6 and 7 the firm is losing money—$20 to be exact—but this same firm looks a lot better in Figures 8 and 9, where it is turning a profit of $20.90.

How can this same firm with the same MC and ATC be making a profit in one set of graphs and taking a loss in another set? The answer lies in the forces beyond its control. What *kind* of forces? The forces of supply and demand. Let's look at them.

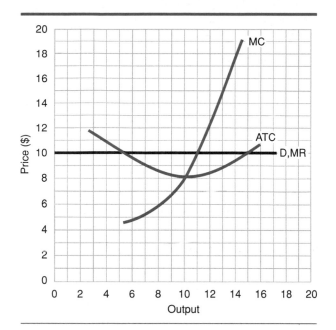

Figure 8
The Perfect Competitor in the
Short Run

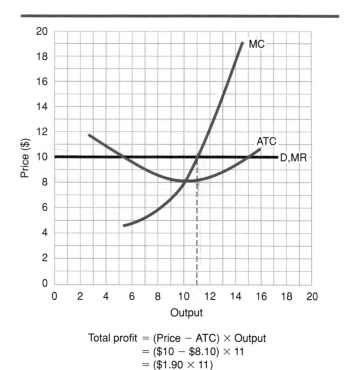

Figure 9
The Perfect Competitor in the
Short Run: Solution

Total profit = (Price − ATC) × Output
= ($10 − $8.10) × 11
= ($1.90 × 11)
= $20.90

If you read ATC as anywhere between $8.05 and $8.15 (and calculated a total profit of anything between $20.35 and $21.45), then you're right on the mark. But for analytic purposes, we'll need to show a profit of more than $20 (see the box, "Maximizing Total Profit and Maximizing Profit per Unit").

A double graph appears in Figure 10. The right side reproduces Figure 6 (or 7), which shows the firm losing money. The left side shows industry supply and demand.

The important thing to notice is that <u>price is the same for the firm and the industry.</u> <u>The price is set by industry supply and demand. It then becomes the demand/MR curve</u> <u>for the firm, which can sell as much as it wants at that price.</u> Also note that the amount

Price is the same for the firm and the industry.

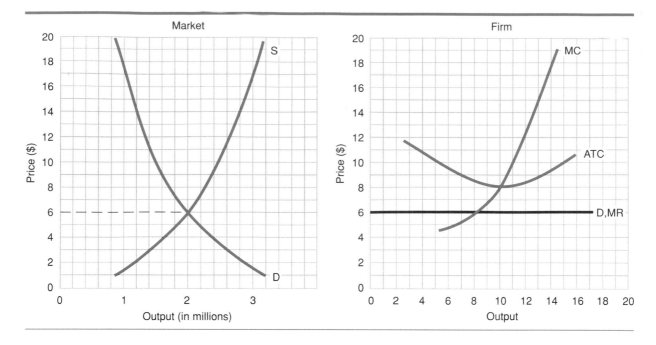

Figure 10

Taking a Loss in the Short Run: The Firm and the Industry
Since the ATC curve lies above the demand curve, the firm is losing money at a price of $6. Question: How do we get to the long run, where the firm is breaking even?

the firm does choose to sell is determined by the intersection of the firm's MC curve with its demand/MR curve. (For a further discussion of graphs, see the box, "Maximizing Total Profit and Maximizing Profit per Unit.")

The same analysis can be applied in Figure 11, the right side of which is taken from Figure 8 (or 9), where the firm is making a profit. Again, notice the price set in the industry market is identical to the price taken by the firm.

In the short run a firm will either make a profit or take a loss. There is a remote possibility that it will break even, but that possibility is about the same as the possibility of a tossed coin landing on its edge instead of on its head or tail. It's something you can count on happening about as often as white Christmases—in Hawaii.

The Long Run

In the long run, firms may enter or leave the industry.

In the long run there is time for firms to enter or leave the industry. This factor ensures that the firm will make zero profits in the long run. What was an unlikely outcome for the firm in the short run—zero profits—becomes an absolute certainty in the long run.

Remember that in the long run, no firm will accept losses. It will simply close up shop and go out of business. Given the situation in Figures 6, 7, and 10, where the individual firm is losing money, it will leave the industry. But you'll remember from the beginning of the chapter, one firm cannot influence price. So if one firm leaves the industry, market price will not be affected.

If one firm is losing money, presumably others are, too; given the extent of the short-run losses this individual firm is suffering, chances are other firms are also ready to go out of business. When enough firms go out of business, industry supply declines from S_1 to S_2, which pushes price up from $6 to $8. This price rise is reflected in a new demand curve for the firm on the right side of Figure 12. In short, a decline in industry supply from S_1 to S_2 raises industry price from $6 to $8. This price increase pushes up the firm's demand curve from D_1 to D_2 (in the right graph).

ADVANCED WORK

Maximizing Total Profit and Maximizing Profit per Unit

To find total profit we use the following formula: (Price − ATC) × Output. For instance, we calculated the total profit in Figure 5 to be $20.90 by using that formula. The formula for profit per unit of output is simple: Price − ATC.

To summarize, our total profit is the profit we make by selling our entire output. In other words, it's our profit per unit multiplied by our output. And our profit per unit is the profit we make on each unit of output sold.

When do we maximize our profit per unit? Obviously when the difference between price and ATC is at a maximum. This can be found by visually inspecting Figure 9. Price, which is read from the demand curve, is $10. At what output is ATC at a minimum? At the break-even point, where the MC curve crosses the ATC curve. The break-even point is at an output of 10.

How much is ATC at an output of 10? It's $8. How much is profit per unit at an output of 10? It's $2. Well, you may ask, why not produce at an output of 10 and maximize our profit per unit? That's a good question you're asking. Can you tell me why we are better off producing 11 units of output, even though we have a profit margin (or profit per unit) of only $1.90?

Think about it. All right, then, did you figure out that at 11 units of output we make a larger total profit ($1.90 × 11 = $20.90) than at 10 units of output ($2 × 10 = $20)? Remember, we assume that every businessowner has one main objective: to maximize profits. So if you have to choose between maximizing your total profit or maximizing your profit per unit, you'll go for total profit every time.

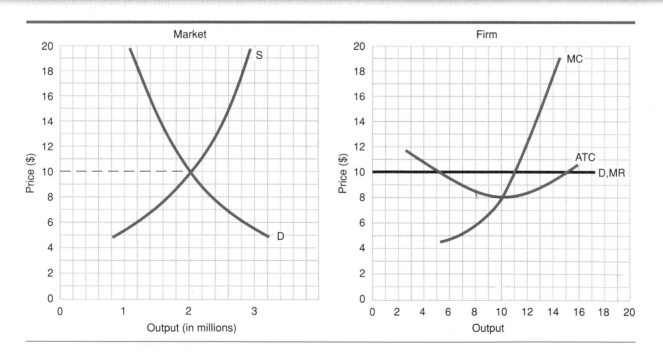

Figure 11

Making a Profit in the Short Run: The Firm and the Industry
Since the ATC curve lies below the demand curve for some outputs, this firm is making a profit. Question: How do we get to the long run, where the firm is breaking even?

There is a secondary effect on the firms that remain in the industry. Each will expand output slightly to the right. On the right side of Figure 12, we see that the firm's output rises from 8 to 10.

Figure 13 is based on Figure 11. It shows the long-run effect of a short-run profit. If one firm is making a profit, we can assume others are, too. New firms will spring up, as entrepreneurs enter the industry to get their share of the profits. As more and more firms enter the industry, market supply increases, pushing the supply curve up from S_1 to S_2 (see the left side of Figure 13). As market supply rises, market price comes down until it reaches $8.

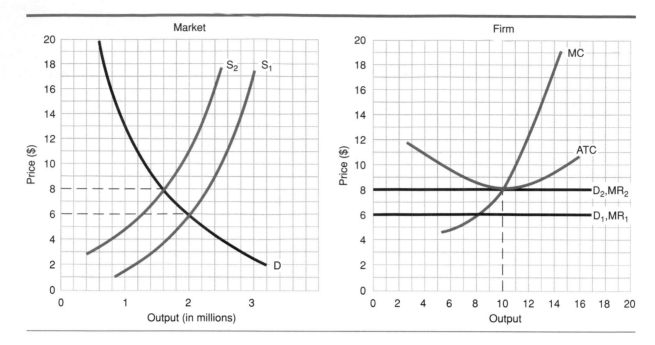

F*igure* 12

Going from Taking a Loss in the Short Run to Breaking Even in the Long Run
At a price of $6 the firm is losing money and so, too, are all the other firms in the industry. Some leave the industry in the long run, pushing the supply down from S_1 to S_2, which, in turn, pushes up the industry price to $8. At that price the firm breaks even.

Here, once again, industry price and the price taken by the individual firm are identical. The output for the individual firm has been reduced slightly; but, more significantly, the new firms that entered the industry have increased market supply. This, in turn, reduced the price to $8, and profits for the individual firm are now zero. Along with this, as we can see on the right side of Figure 13, output has fallen from 11 to 10.

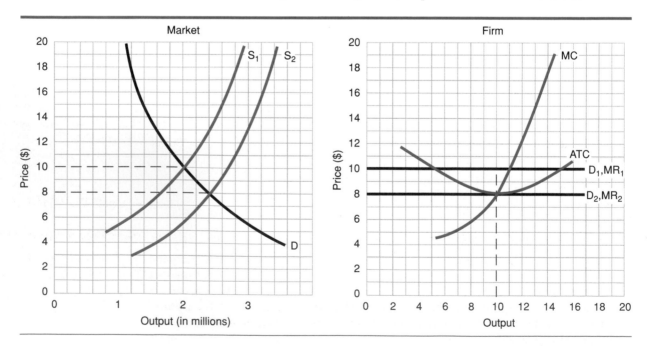

F*igure* 13

Going from Making a Profit in the Short Run to Breaking Even in the Long Run
At a price of $10 all firms in the industry are making a profit. New firms are attracted to the industry, pushing the supply drive up from S_1 to S_2. This reduces industry price to $8, at which all firms just break even.

Showing Total Profits and Losses Graphically

Face it. Economists sometimes like to show off a little, and one way we really get to shine is when we draw some truly elegant graphs. So buckle your seat belt because we are about to take off.

By drawing just a couple of dotted lines and then multiplying two numbers, you can quickly calculate a firm's total profit. In Figure A I drew a vertical dotted line down from the intersection of the MR and MC curves at 50 units of output. Then I drew a horizontal dotted line from the ATC curve at 50 units of output straight across to the price scale.

Of course, we could have used the tried-and-true method:

$$\begin{array}{ll} \text{Price} & \$10 \\ -\text{ATC} & -8 \\ \hline & \$\ 2 \times \text{output (50)} = \$100 \end{array}$$

We can also find total loss graphically by drawing just two dotted lines and multiplying. I've worked out a problem in Figure B.

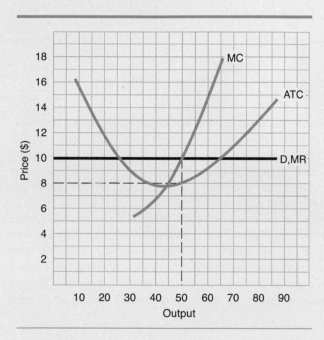

Figure A

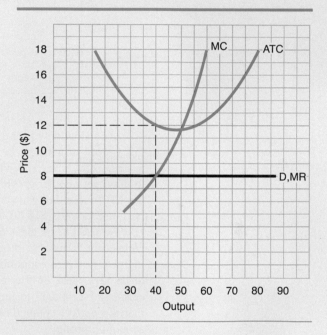

Figure B

Now it's easy to find total profit. It is the area of the box that is bounded by the two dotted lines, the demand curve, and the price scale. To find that area, simply multiply the distance of the vertical line ($2) and the horizontal line (50 units of output). How much is $2 × 50? It's $100.

Our loss box is $4 × 40, or a loss of $160. Just like our box for total profit, it is bounded by the two dotted lines, the demand curve, and the price scale. Again, we can find our loss (or negative profit) this way:

$$\begin{array}{ll} \text{Price} & \$8 \\ -\text{ATC} & -12 \\ \hline & \$\ 4 \times \text{output (40)} = \$160 \end{array}$$

The right side of Figure 12 and the right side of Figure 13 look identical. Notice that the ATC and the demand/MR curves are tangent (just touching). At the point of tangency, MC equals MR, so that is where the firm produces. ATC equals price at that point, so profit is zero.

Still another way to find total profit and total loss is to draw a couple of dashed lines on a graph to form a box. By multiplying the height and length of this box, or rectangle, you can find a firm's total profit or total loss. This method is illustrated in the box, "Showing Total Profits and Losses Graphically."

Figure 14

The Perfect Competitor in the Long Run
In the long run the firm breaks even. The ATC curve is tangent to the demand curve at an output of $10 and a price of $18.50. Note that at that output, MC = MR.

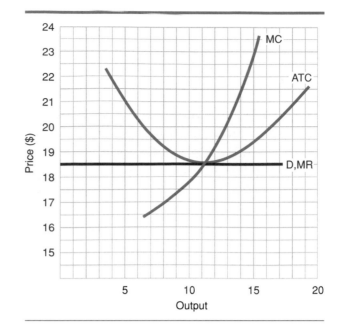

Let's slow down for a minute to catch our breath. We've talked about the firm making a profit or taking a loss in the short run and just breaking even in the long run. But to make sure that you're clear on what the firm's long-run situation looks like, I'm going to draw yet another graph. Figure 14 shows the firm's demand and MR curve tangent to the ATC curve. So, what are the firm's long-run price and output? Have you figured them out? The price is $18.50, and the output is 11.

We need to be clear on just what we mean by profit. When we say that the perfect competitor earns zero profit in the long run, are we saying that she earns zero accounting profit or zero economic profit? We are talking about zero *economic* profit. We need to be very clear on this point. A firm that has $800,000 in sales, $600,000 in explicit costs, and $200,000 in implicit costs earns zero economic profits. So whenever we say that the perfect competitor earns zero profits in the long run, we're talking about zero economic profits.

Third Method of Calculating Profit and Loss

Sometimes we can calculate profit or loss by just glancing at a graph and doing some fast multiplication. In Figure 15, total profit is bounded by the rectangle EFGH, which we call the profit box. So total profit is represented by the area of that rectangle. As you know, the area of a rectangle is found by multiplying its length times its width. The length of this rectangle is EF and its width is FG. Do the math and write down the total profit.

Use the profit box EFGH to find total profit. Profit per unit, FG, is $12.50 and quantity sold, EF, is 70.

Solution:

$$EF\ (70) \times FG\ (\$12.50) = \$875 \text{ total profit}$$

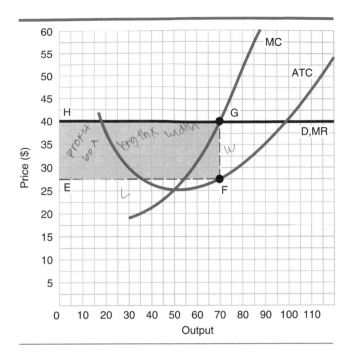

Figure 15
Alternate Calculation of Profit
Profit per unit ($12.50) × quantity sold (70) = $875.

In Figure 16 the firm is losing money. How much? Work it out by finding the area of rectangle JKLM.

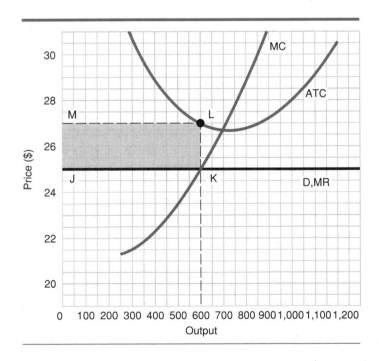

Figure 16
Alternate Calculation of Loss

Use the loss box JKLM to find total loss. Loss per unit ($2) × quantity sold (600) = total loss of $1,200.

Solution:

$$\text{JK } (600) \times \text{KL } (\$2) = \$1,200 \text{ total loss}$$

The Perfect Competitor: A Price Taker, Not a Price Maker

If you own a store, you get to decide how much to charge your customers. But if you happen to be a perfect competitor, you don't have that privilege; you're a price taker, not a price maker. What price do you take? You take the market price. In Figures 12 and 13, we showed how the market works. The industrywide supply and demand determine the market price. If you feel that price is too low, about the only thing you could do is to close up shop and leave the industry. Otherwise you have no choice but to charge what everyone else is charging.

Although you're way too young to remember the original Broadway musicals, there are lines from the songs of *South Pacific* and *Oklahoma!* that illustrate the plight of a farmer who grows corn. The lines from *South Pacific,* "I am corny as Kansas in August," and from *Oklahoma!,* "The corn is as high as an elephant's eye," attest to the abundance of our corn crop. If you were to drive through the Grain Plains in August, you'd see field after field of corn and wheat.

Grain farmers are about as close as we come to perfect competitors. And more likely than not, you'll hear them complaining about crop prices. If the price is just $3 a bushel, the farmer, as the price taker, has no choice but to sell his entire output at that price. The farmer, then, is the classic price taker.

Efficiency, Price, and Profit

Efficiency defined

You remember the concept of efficiency from earlier in the chapter. We define *efficient* as cheap. When a firm is an efficient producer, it produces its product at a relatively low cost. A firm operates at peak efficiency when it produces its product at the lowest possible cost. That would be at the minimum point of its ATC curve—the break-even point.

For the perfect competitor in the long run, the most profitable output is at the minimum point of its ATC curve. Check it out in Figure 14. At any other output, the firm would lose money; just to stay in business, it must operate at peak efficiency.

Competition is the keen cutting edge of business, always shaving away at costs.

—Henry Ford

This is the hallmark of perfect competition. The firm, not through any virtues of its owners but because of the degree of competition in the marketplace, is forced to operate at peak efficiency. As we'll see in the next three chapters, the other forms of competition do not force peak efficiency.

Perfect competition is very good for consumers; they can buy at cost. That's right, price is equal to ATC. Remember, there's no economic profit. And consumers have the firm's competitors to thank for such a low price. Competition will keep businessowners honest—that is, if there's enough competition.

In the next three chapters we'll introduce the three other forms of competition. But we can tell you in advance that in the long run the perfect competitor sells at a lower price and operates more efficiently. And, by selling at cost, the perfect competitor makes no economic profit. Under perfect competition you don't need a friend in the business to find someone who will sell to you at cost. In the long run, *every* perfect competitor sells at cost.

Current Issue: The Internet Effect: A More Perfect Knowledge and Lower Prices

You can now find almost anything on the Internet by using Google, Yahoo, or some other search engine. And, of course, like tens of millions of other buyers or sellers around the world, you can find a ready market on eBay. In sum, the Internet has moved entire markets much closer to the ideal of perfect knowledge. It's also lowered barriers to entry in many markets, bringing us much closer to perfect competition in the markets for many goods and services.

For example, I've recently started collecting silver dollars, primarily from the 1880s and 1890s. Sellers post pictures of coins on eBay, where people all over the world can place bids. Before the Internet, you might find just a couple of coin dealers nearby, and unless you were a coin expert, these dealers would know a lot more than you about how much these coins were worth.

Let's look at the strange case of the price of term life insurance, which fell dramatically in the 1990s, while the prices of other types of insurance, including medical and automobile coverage, were certainly not falling. What happened? According to the authors of *Freakonomics,*

> The Internet happened. In the spring of 1996, Quotesmith.com became the first of several websites that enabled a customer to compare, within seconds, the price of term life insurance sold by dozens of different companies. For such websites, term life insurance was a perfect product. Unlike other forms of insurance—including whole life insurance, which is a far more complicated financial instrument—term life policies are fairly homogeneous: one thirty-year, guaranteed policy for $1 million is essentially identical to the next. So what really matters is the price. Shopping around for the cheapest policy, a process that had been convoluted and time-consuming, was suddenly made simple. With customers able to instantaneously find the cheapest policy, the more expensive companies had no choice but to lower their prices. Suddenly customers were paying $1 billion less a year for term life insurance.[3]

The Net has converted what had been local, regional, or national markets into worldwide markets. By bringing together all these buyers and sellers, it has enabled many industries to move closer to the perfectly competitive model. Firms can much more easily enter and leave each industry than traditional brick-and-mortar businesses. If you were to make a list of what you and other members of your family bought or sold on the Internet over the last few weeks, you might conclude that your family has contributed toward making business more competitive.

---

on the web

Paying too much for gasoline? Just go to www.gasbuddy.com, type in your zip code, and you'll find the lowest gas prices at nearby stations.

Questions for Further Thought and Discussion

1. How do you find the most efficient output, and how do you find the most profitable output?

2. At the output at which a firm maximizes its profits, what two variables are equal? At the output at which a firm minimizes its losses, what two variables are equal?

3. Is the analysis for maximizing profits the same as that for minimizing losses? Explain why it is or why it isn't.

4. What is the difference between the firm's short-run supply curve and its long-run supply curve? Make up an example to explain your answer.

5. At the output at which MC = MR, suppose that price were higher than AVC but lower than ATC. What should the firm do in the short run and the long run? Explain your answer.

6. Does the perfect competitor always break even in the long run? Explain why or why not.

---

[3]Steven D. Levitt and Stephen J. Dubner, *Freakonomics* (New York: William Morrow, 2005), p. 66.

7. If the perfect competitor is losing money in the short run, what happens in the market to drive up price?

8. Two characteristics of perfect competition are perfect mobility and perfect knowledge. Make up an example of each.

9. Can you think of any dot-coms that may be considered perfect competitors?

10. Although perfect competition may not exist, explain why it is relevant to the study of microeconomics.

11. Explain why a perfectly competitive firm won't advertise.

12. *Practical Application:* How have you used the Internet to search for product information and lower prices?

13. *Practical Application:* Why might a firm produce at a loss in the short run rather than shut down? Make up an example to illustrate your answer.

14. *Practical Application:* Calculate the economic cost of your college education. How much more is it than the accounting cost?

15. *Practical Application:* I'm going to make you an offer you can't refuse. I'll sell you my highly profitable indoor batting and driving range for just $1,000,000. I clear $100,000 a year in profits, and the place practically runs itself. I'm the manager, but basically I just hang out all day hitting baseballs and golf balls whenever I feel like it. If you act right now, the place is yours. You'll have a 20-year lease, which you can break any time you want, and, if things don't work out over the next two years, I will buy the business back from you for the same million dollars you paid for it. So, will you take my offer or not? Explain why you would or would not.

16. *Web Activity:* Is the coin collector's market close to being perfectly competitive? Let's use the example of silver dollars auctioned on eBay. Go to www.ebay.com, click on "Coins & Paper Money" under Categories, and select "Coins: U.S." Then type in "1890s Morgan silver dollar," and click on search. After checking the prices of the coins, would you say the market is close to being perfectly competitive? Why or why not?

Workbook for Chapter 9

Name ______________________ Date ______________________

Multiple-Choice Questions

Circle the letter that corresponds to the best answer.

1. A firm with explicit costs of $2,000,000, no implicit costs, and total revenue of $3,000,000 would have __________. (LO2)
   a) zero economic profit
   b) zero accounting profit
   c) an accounting profit and an economic profit of $1,000,000
   d) a higher economic profit than an accounting profit
   e) a higher accounting profit than economic profit

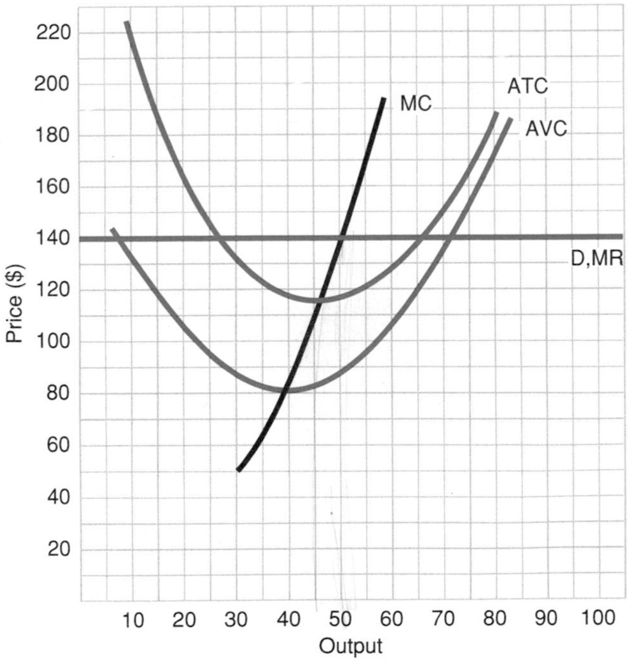

Figure 1

2. In Figure 1, at which output is the firm operating most efficiently? (LO7)
   a) 30
   b) 39
   c) 46
   d) 50

3. The marginal cost curve intersects the ATC curve at its __________. (LO5)
   a) minimum point, which is the break-even point
   b) maximum point, which is the break-even point
   c) minimum point, which is the shut-down point
   d) maximum point, which is the shut-down point

4. A profit-maximizing firm will increase production when __________. (LO3)
   a) price is less than marginal cost
   b) price equals marginal cost
   c) price exceeds marginal revenue
   d) price exceeds marginal cost

5. The lowest point on a firm's short-run supply curve is at the __________. (LO6)
   a) break-even point
   b) shut-down point
   c) most profitable output point
   d) lowest point on the marginal cost curve

6. A firm will operate at that output where MC equals MR __________. (LO3)
   a) only when it is maximizing its profits
   b) only when it is minimizing its losses
   c) both when it is maximizing its profits and when it is minimizing its losses
   d) neither when it is maximizing its profits nor minimizing its losses

7. When marginal cost is rising but is less than average total cost, we are definitely below the __________. (LO6)
   a) shut-down point
   b) break-even point
   c) maximum profit point

8. Which statement is true? (LO2)
   a) Accounting profits are greater than economic profits.
   b) Economic profits are greater than accounting profits.
   c) Accounting profits are equal to economic profits.

9. Statement 1: Price is equal to total revenue divided by output. Statement 2: A firm never maximizes profits. (LO3)

   a) Statement 1 is true, and statement 2 is false.

   b) Statement 2 is true, and statement 1 is false.

   c) Both statements are true.

   d) Both statements are false.

10. If a firm is producing a level of output at which that output's marginal cost is less than the price of the good, _____. (LO3)

    a) it is producing too much to maximize its profits

    b) it is probably maximizing its profits

    c) higher profits could be obtained with increased production

    d) none of the above

11. The firm's long-run supply curve runs along its _____ curve. (LO6)

    a) ATC   c) MC

    b) AVC   d) MR

12. A firm will operate at that output at which MC = MR _____. (LO1, 6)

    a) only in the short run

    b) only in the long run

    c) in both the short run and the long run

    d) in neither the short run nor the long run

13. At an output of 5, MC = $49 and ATC = $52. At an output of 6, MC = $59 and ATC = $53. At the break-even point, ATC is _____. (LO6)

    a) above $53

    b) $53

    c) between $52 and $53

    d) $52

    e) less than $52

14. Statement 1: The firm's short-run supply curve runs up the marginal cost curve from the shut-down point to the break-even point.
    Statement 2: The firm will not accept a price below the break-even point in the short run. (LO6)

    a) Statement 1 is true, and statement 2 is false.

    b) Statement 2 is true, and statement 1 is false.

    c) Both statements are true.

    d) Both statements are false.

15. A business firm is in the short run _____. (LO6)

    a) virtually all the time   d) rarely

    b) most of the time   e) never

    c) occasionally

16. If the price is between the shut-down point and the break-even point, the firm is in the _____. (LO6)

    a) short run making a profit

    b) short run taking a loss

    c) long run making a profit

    d) long run taking a loss

17. The most efficient output of a firm is located _____. (LO1, 7)

    a) at the shut-down point

    b) at the break-even point

    c) where MC = MR

    d) when the vertical distance between AVC and ATC is at a maximum

18. Which one of these markets would definitely *not* be perfectly competitive? (LO4)

    a) Foreign currency

    b) Wheat

    c) HDTVs

    d) The New York Stock Exchange

19. Perfect competition is _____. (LO4)

    a) the prevalent form of competition in the United States

    b) the only form of competition in the United States

    c) found occasionally

    d) probably impossible to find

20. Under perfect competition, _____. (LO4)

    a) many firms have some influence over price

    b) a few firms have influence over price

    c) no firm has any influence over price

21. Under perfect competition, there are _____. (LO4)

    a) many firms producing an identical product

    b) a few firms producing an identical product

    c) many firms producing a differentiated product

    d) a few firms producing a differentiated product

22. The perfect competitor is _____. (LO4)
    a) a price maker rather than a price taker
    b) a price taker rather than a price maker
    c) a price taker and a price maker
    d) neither a price maker or a price taker

23. The determination of whether two products are
    identical _____. (LO4)
    a) is done by market research
    b) takes place in the minds of the buyers
    c) is done by the government
    d) is done by the sellers

24. The perfect competitor's demand curve is
    _____. (LO4)
    a) always horizontal
    b) always vertical
    c) sometimes horizontal
    d) sometimes vertical

25. Which statement about the perfect competitor is
    true? (LO4)
    a) She may charge a little below market price to get
       more customers.
    b) She may charge a little above market price to
       imply that her product is superior.
    c) She will always charge the market price.
    d) None of these statements is true.

26. Each of the following is a characteristic of perfect
    competition except _____. (LO4)
    a) many firms
    b) identical products
    c) perfect mobility
    d) varying prices charged by different firms

27. In the short run the perfect competitor will probably
    _____. (LO5)
    a) make a profit or break even
    b) take a loss or break even
    c) make a profit or take a loss

28. In the long run the perfect competitor will
    _____. (LO5)
    a) make a profit
    b) break even
    c) take a loss

29. Under perfect competition _____ profits are
    always zero in the long run. (LO5)
    a) accounting
    b) economic
    c) both economic and accounting
    d) neither accounting or economic

Use the choices below to answer questions 30 and 31.
    a) in the long run making a profit
    b) in the long run breaking even
    c) in the long run taking a loss
    d) in the short run making a profit
    e) in the short run breaking even
    f) in the short run taking a loss

30. Figure 2 shows the perfect competitor
    _____. (LO5)

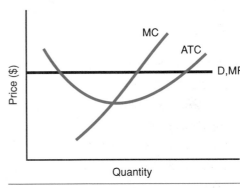

Figure 2

31. Figure 3 shows the perfect competitor
    _____. (LO5)

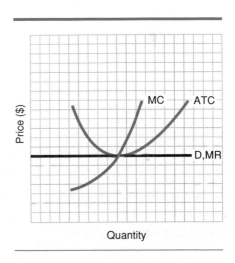

Figure 3

32. The perfect competitor's demand and marginal revenue curves are _____. (LO5)

    a) identical only in the long run

    b) identical only in the short run

    c) never identical

    d) always identical

33. The most efficient output _____. (LO7)

    a) is always equal to the most profitable output for the perfect competitor

    b) is never equal to the most profitable output for the perfect competitor

    c) is equal to the most profitable output for the perfect competitor only in the long run

    d) is equal to the most profitable output for the perfect competitor only in the short run

Use Figure 4 to answer questions 34 through 37.

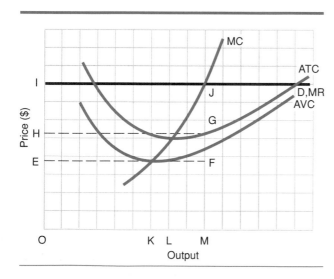

Figure 4

34. Total profit _____. (LO3)

    a) is the rectangle bounded by EFJI

    b) is the rectangle bounded by EFGH

    c) is the rectangle bounded by HGJI

    d) cannot be found on this graph

35. Output _____. (LO3)

    a) is OK

    b) is OL

    c) is OM

    d) cannot be found on this graph

36. Profit per unit is _____. (LO3)

    a) MF   d) FJ

    b) MG   e) GJ

    c) MJ

37. The firm's most efficient output _____. (LO7)

    a) is OK

    b) is OL

    c) is OM

    d) cannot be determined on this graph

38. Statement I: The advent of the Internet has brought "perfect knowledge" closer to reality.
    Statement II: The cost of businesses buying their supplies online is convenient, but they generally pay more than they would if they used customary channels. (LO3)

    a) Statement I is true, and statement II is false.

    b) Statement II is true, and statement I is false.

    c) Both statements are true.

    d) Both statements are false.

39. Statement I: No firm will stay in business more than one year if it is losing large sums of money.
    Statement II: Many dot-coms have lost money in the short run. (LO3)

    a) Statement I is true, and statement II is false.

    b) Statement II is true, and statement I is false.

    c) Both statements are true.

    d) Both statements are false.

40. When an industry is in long-run equilibrium economic profits are _____ and _____ will be entering or leaving the industry. (LO5)

    a) zero, some

    b) zero, none

    c) positive, some

    d) positive, none

41. If a perfectly competitive firm sells 10 units of output at a price of $10 per unit, its marginal revenue per unit is _____. (LO1, 5)

    a) $1   d) more than $1, but less than $10

    b) $10

    c) $100   e) more than $10, but less than $100

Fill-In Questions

1. Under perfect competition there are so many firms that no one firm has any influence over _____. (LO3)

2. The determination that a product is identical takes place in _____. (LO3)

3. The perfect competitor's demand curve is a _____; the marginal revenue curve is a _____. (LO1, 5)

4. A perfect competitor would never charge more than market price because _____; the perfect competitor would never charge less than market price because _____. (LO5)

5. In the short run the perfect competitor may make a _____ or take a _____; in the long run the perfect competitor will _____. (LO5)

6. In a perfectly competitive industry, if firms are making profits _____, which will result in zero profits in the long run; if there are losses in the short run, _____, resulting in zero profits (and losses) in the long run. (LO5)

7. The perfect competitor operates at the _____ point of her average total cost curve in the long run. (LO5)

8. If the firms in a competitive industry are earning profits, in the long run new firms will _____. But if most firms are losing money, then in the long run some of the firms will _____. (LO6)

Problems

Use Figure 5 for problems 1–6.

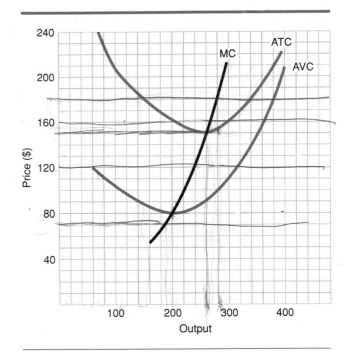

Figure 5

1. How much will output be in the short run if the price is (a) $70? (b) $120? (c) $160? (LO5, 6)

2. How much is the firm's most efficient output? (LO7)

3. If price is $180, how much is total profit? (LO3)

4. If price is $120, how much is total profit? (Hint: You might consider this a trick question.) (LO3)

5. How much is output at (a) the break-even point? (b) the shut-down point? (LO6)

6. How much is the lowest price the firm will accept in (a) the short run? (b) the long run? (LO6)

Use Figure 6 for problems 7–12.

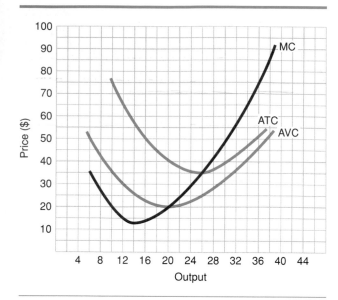

Figure 6

7. How much is the most efficient output? (LO7)

8. a) If the price is $55, how much is the most profitable output? (LO5)
   b) Calculate total profit. (LO5)

9. How much is output in the short run if price is (a) $65? (b) $30? (c) $15? (LO6)

10. If price is $30, what will the firm do in (a) the short run? (b) the long run? (LO6)

11. Label the break-even and shut-down points. (LO6)

12. Label the short-run supply curve and the long-run supply curve. (LO6)

13. At an output of 14, MC = $50 and ATC = $55. At an output of 15, MC = $65 and ATC = $56. Estimate the ATC at the break-even point. (LO5)

14. At an output of 9, MC = $20 and AVC = $25. At an output of 10, MC = $32 and AVC = $26. What is the lowest price the firm will accept in the short run? (LO6)

15. You should do this problem in four steps. First: Fill in Table 1. Assume fixed cost is $100 and price is $64. (LO3)

TABLE 1

Output	Variable Cost	Total Cost	Average Variable Cost	Average Total Cost	Marginal Cost
1	$ 30	_____	_____	_____	_____
2	50	_____	_____	_____	_____
3	80	_____	_____	_____	_____
4	125	_____	_____	_____	_____
5	190	_____	_____	_____	_____
6	280	_____	_____	_____	_____

Second: Fill in Table 2. (LO6)

TABLE 2

If Price Were	What Would the Firm Do in the:		How Much Would Output Be in the Short Run?
	Short Run?	Long Run?	
$90	_____	_____	_____
40	_____	_____	_____
20	_____	_____	_____

Third: Draw a graph of the firm's demand, marginal revenue, average variable cost, average total cost, and marginal cost curves on a piece of graph paper. Be sure to label the graph correctly. On the graph, indicate the break-even and shut-down points and the firm's short-run and long-run supply curves. (LO5)

Fourth: Calculate total profit in the space below, then answer questions (a) through (d).

(a) The minimum price the firm will accept in the short run is $ _____. (b) The minimum price the firm will accept in the long run is $ _____. (LO6)

(c) The output at which the firm will maximize profits is _____. (d) The output at which the firm will operate most efficiently is _____. (LO7)

16. (a) Find the total profit or total loss of the firm shown in Figure 7. (b) Is the firm in the short run or the long run? (c) How much is the firm's most efficient output? (d) What is the lowest price the firm would accept in the long run? (LO5, 6)

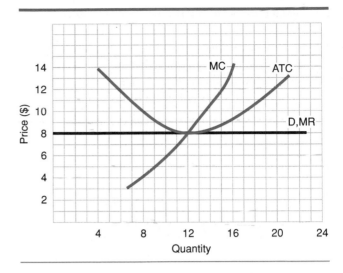

Figure 8

18. (a) Find the total profit or total loss of the firm shown in Figure 9. (b) Is the firm in the short run or the long run? (c) How much is the firm's most efficient output? (d) What is the lowest price the firm would accept in the long run? (LO5, 6, 7)

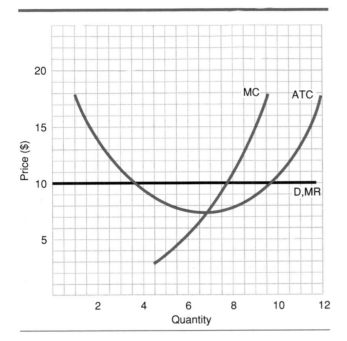

Figure 7

17. (a) Find the total profit or total loss of the firm shown in Figure 8. (b) Is the firm in the short run or the long run? (c) How much is the firm's most efficient output? (d) What is the lowest price the firm would accept in the long run? (LO5, 6)

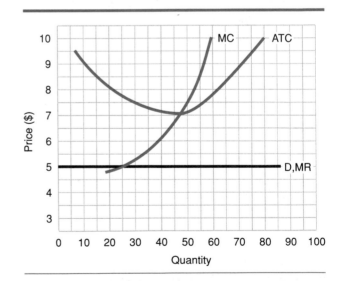

Figure 9

19. Given the industry supply and demand shown on the right side of Figure 10, use the left side of the figure to draw the perfect competitor's demand, marginal revenue, average total cost, and marginal cost curves for its long-run situation. (LO5)

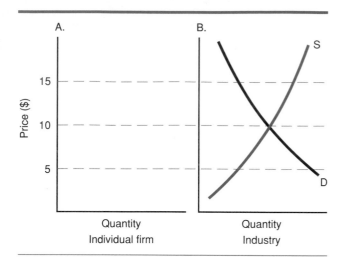

Figure 10

Chapter 10

Monopoly

We've talked enough about perfect competition, an ideal state that probably does not exist. Welcome to the real world of imperfect competition. We'll begin here with monopoly and then go on to monopolistic competition and oligopoly in the next two chapters. When we've completed our analysis of these competitive states, you will probably conclude what I concluded a long time ago: that nobody's perfect.

When you were a kid, did you ever play the game of Monopoly? The whole idea was to control strips of properties, such as Boardwalk and Park Place. Some people get to play Monopoly even after they've grown up—and they get to keep all the money. In this and the next three chapters, we'll see how this game is played by the big kids.

LEARNING OBJECTIVES

After reading this chapter you should be able to:

1. Analyze and discuss the graph of the monopolist.
2. Calculate the profit or loss of the monopolist.
3. Differentiate between the short run and the long run for the monopolist.
4. List and discuss the barriers to entry into a monopolized industry.
5. List and discuss the limits to monopoly power.
6. Explain how economies of scale and natural monopoly affect control of an industry.
7. Identify and discuss the factors that make bigness bad.
8. List the pros and cons of allowing a Walmart supercenter to open in your community.

Monopoly Defined

A monopoly is the only firm in an industry. There's nobody else selling anything like what the monopolist is producing. In other words, there are no close substitutes.

A monopoly is a firm that produces all the output in an industry.

Examples of monopoly include DeBeers diamonds, the local gas and electric companies, and your local phone company. During the years after World War II, IBM, Xerox, the International Nickel Company, and Alcoa (Aluminum Company of America) also had monopolies.

One might ask how close substitutes would need to be to disqualify firms from being monopolies. Surely a Chevrolet Silverado is a reasonably close substitute for a Toyota Camry. Further, there are many close substitutes for a Xerox photocopying machine, but there are no close substitutes for diamonds, gas, electricity, and local phone calls.

What are close substitutes?

We need to ask *why* there are no close substitutes for the monopolist's goods or services. Has the monopolist erected barriers to keep out potential competitors, or is there some other explanation as to why the monopolist is the sole producer? We'll talk about barriers to entry later in the chapter.

We should also distinguish between local and national monopolies. Someone may be the only doctor in the vicinity and have a local monopoly, but there are more than 700,000 doctors in the United States. A hardware store, grocery, drugstore, or dry cleaners may have a monopoly in its neighborhood, but each may have several competitors within a few miles.

The Graph of the Monopolist

The distinguishing characteristic of imperfect competition

The distinguishing characteristic of imperfect competition is that the firm's demand curve is no longer a perfectly elastic horizontal line; now it curves downward to the right. This means the imperfect competitor will have to lower price to sell more.

Using the data in Table 1, we'll draw our four standard curves: demand, marginal revenue, marginal cost, and average total cost. First, fill in Table 1 and check your figures against those in Table 2. Please observe that the demand and marginal revenue schedules no longer coincide.

A common mistake students make when filling out Table 1 is to use some number (in this case, 20) for MC at one unit of output. We'll review exactly what MC is; then we'll see why there's no way of finding MC at one unit of output.

Marginal cost is the additional cost of producing one more unit of output.

Do you recall the definition of marginal cost? *MC is the additional cost of producing one more unit of output.* Remember that as output rises, fixed cost stays the same and variable cost rises. So far, so good. The only problem is we don't know how much fixed cost is at one unit of output; nor do we know how much variable cost is at one unit of output. The MC of the first unit of output would be total cost at output one minus total cost at output zero. How much is total cost at output zero? It's fixed cost. But we

TABLE 1	Hypothetical Demand and Cost Schedule for a Monopoly					
Output	Price	Total Revenue	Marginal Revenue	Total Cost	ATC	MC
1	$16	——	——	$20	——	——
2	15	——	——	30	——	——
3	14	——	——	36	——	——
4	13	——	——	42	——	——
5	12	——	——	50	——	——
6	11	——	——	63	——	——
7	10	——	——	84	——	——

TABLE 2	Hypothetical Demand and Cost Schedule for a Monopoly						
Output	Price	Total Revenue	Marginal Revenue	Total Cost	ATC	MC	Total Profit
1	$16	$16	$16	$20	$20	——	−$ 4
2	15	30	14	30	15	$10	0
3	14	42	12	36	12	6	6
4	13	52	10	42	10.50	6	10
5	12	60	8	50	10	8	10
6	11	66	6	63	10.50	13	3
7	10	70	4	84	12	21	−14

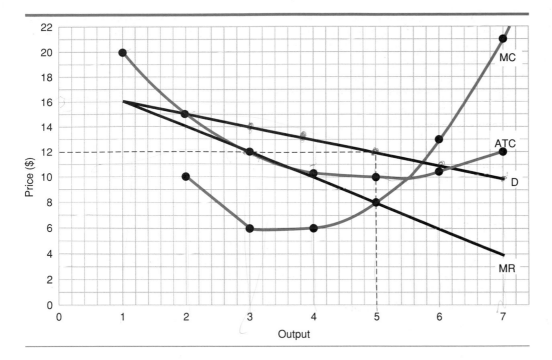

Figure 1

The Monopolist Making a Profit

The monopolist will make a profit if for some range of output her ATC lies below her demand curve. In this instance, the monopolist maximizes her profit at five units of output charging a price of $12.

don't know fixed cost, so we can't figure out MC at output one. For the remaining outputs, we *can* figure out MC because we know how much total cost rises. Now use the data you've written in Table 1 to draw a graph of the D, MR, MC, and ATC curves of the monopolist. Remember to use graph paper.

Look at the graph you drew and see whether it matches the one in Figure 1. The ATC and MC curves are the same as they were for the perfect competitor. I hope your MC intersects your ATC at its minimum point. Also note that the demand and marginal revenue curves slope downward to the right. At one unit of output, the demand and marginal revenue curves share the same point—$16—but the MR curve then slopes down much faster. In fact, when the demand curve is a straight line, the marginal revenue curve is also a straight line that falls twice as quickly. If you want to know why, take a look at the box, "Why the MR Curve Declines Faster than the Demand Curve."

Why the MR Curve Declines Faster than the Demand Curve

In Table 2, when the output is one, price is $16; but to sell two units of output, the seller must lower price to $15. Two units at $15 equals $30 (total revenue). Notice that the seller can't charge $16 for the first unit and $15 for the second. That's because the seller has to post one price. (If the seller manages to charge more than one price, we have price discrimination, which we'll talk about in the next chapter.)

When price is lowered to $15 total revenue is $30. Marginal revenue is $14 (total revenue of $30 at two units of output minus total revenue of $16 at one unit of output). At two units of output, because we charge a price of $15, the point on the demand curve is $15. So, at two units of output, we have $15 on the demand curve and $14 on the MR curve.

To sell three units, the seller must lower price to $14. That yields a total revenue of $42 and an MR of $12 ($42 − $30). So, at three units of output, we're at $14 on the demand curve and $12 on the MR curve.

Let's summarize. If the seller lowers price to sell more output, the price is lowered on all units of output, not just on the last one. This drives down MR faster than price (which is read off the demand curve). Note also that the MR curve descends twice as quickly as the D curve.

When the demand curve falls $1 to $15 at two units of output, the MR curve falls $2 to $14. At three units of output, when the demand curve falls $1 to $14, the MR curve falls $2 to $12.

Calculating the Monopolist's Profit

At what output does the monopolist produce?

Now we'll get down to business. At what output does the monopolist produce? Go ahead and perform the marginal analysis to determine the most profitable output. I'll tell you the first step. Look at Figure 1 and find the point at which your marginal cost curve crosses your marginal revenue curve. That's your output. Do your calculations right here:

According to Figure 1, MC equals MR at 5 units of output. Using the formula for total profit, we find:

$$\text{Total profit} = (\text{Price} - \text{ATC}) \times \text{Output}$$
$$= (\$12 - \$10) \times 5$$
$$= \$2 \times 5$$
$$= \$10$$

We have a conflict here that didn't exist under perfect competition. The perfect competitor produced at the most profitable output, which in the long run always happened to be the most efficient output. But we see that the monopolist does not produce where output is at its most efficient level (the minimum point of the ATC curve). Remember, *every firm will produce at its most profitable output, where MC equals MR.* If that does not happen to be the most efficient output and if, for example, that firm is a bakery—get ready for a terrible pun—then that's the way the cookie crumbles. Finding the monopolist's price and output is a little harder than finding the price and output for the perfect competition. If you need more practice, see the box, "How to Find the Monopolist's Price and Output."

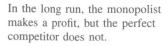

Every firm produces where MC = MR.

Looking at Figure 1, let's compare the price of the monopolist with that of the perfect competitor. In the very long run the perfect competitor would charge $9.90, the minimum point of its ATC curve, while the monopolist's price is $12. Next, let's compare output. The perfect competitor would produce at an output of 5.5, which is where ATC is at its minimum, but the monopolist's output is 5.

In the long run, the monopolist makes a profit, but the perfect competitor does not.

To summarize, the monopolist makes a profit, whereas in the long run the perfect competitor makes no profit. The monopolist operates at less than peak efficiency, while the perfect competitor operates at peak efficiency (the lowest point on the ATC curve). Finally, the perfect competitor charges a lower price and produces a larger output than the monopolist.[1]

This last point bears some explanation. The monopolist operates on a much larger scale than does the individual perfect competitor. But the sum of output under perfect competition would be larger than it would be under monopoly.

I haven't bothered to distinguish between the short run and the long run mainly because the monopolist has no rivals. With perfect competition, the fact that the firms entered the industry (attracted by profits) or left the industry (driven out of business by

---

[1]In theory, the perfect competitor produces 5.5 units and the monopolist 5. But because the perfect competitor is a tiny firm, we can't really compare its output with that of the monopolist, who produces the industry's entire output. Thus, when we say the perfect competitor would produce an output of 5.5, we must realize that the firm would no longer be a perfect competitor. Do you follow this? If you don't, don't worry. This is only a footnote.

How to Find the Monopolist's Price and Output

Let's go over how the monopolist sets price step-by-step, using Figure 1. Step 1: The monopolist chooses her output by finding where the MC and MR curves cross. Step 2: By moving down along the dashed line, we find that the output she chose is 5.

Step 3: We move up the dotted line from MC = MR to the demand curve. Step 4: We move horizontally along the dotted line to a price of $12.

Here's another one for you to work out. How much is the output and price of the monopolist represented by Figure A?

If we move down from where the MC and MR curves cross, we find that the output is 20. To find price we go up from where the MC and MR curves cross to the demand curve, and then horizontally to the price axis. This gives us a price of $9.

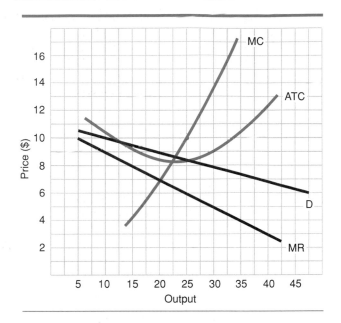

Figure A

losses) made the short run differ from the long run. Under monopoly, even larger profits wouldn't attract rival firms; otherwise, there would no longer be a monopoly. If a monopoly were losing money, in the long run it, too, would go out of business.

Review of the Monopolist's Economic Analysis

I've thrown a lot of new stuff at you, so let's step back for a few minutes and review the monopolist's table and graph. (For extra help, see the box, "How to Read a Graph.") Microeconomics is based largely on the three-step problems you've come to know and love: (1) filling in the table, (2) drawing the graph, and (3) doing the analysis.

You may begin by filling in Table 3 and then seeing whether your numbers correspond to the data in Table 4.

TABLE 3

Output	Price	Total Revenue	Marginal Revenue	Total Cost	ATC	MC
1	$21	——	——	$30	——	——
2	20	——	——	40	——	——
3	19	——	——	48	——	——
4	18	——	——	57	——	——
5	17	——	——	70	——	——
6	16	——	——	93	——	——

Next comes the graph. Draw the demand, marginal revenue, marginal cost, and average total cost curves on a piece of graph paper. Then check your work with that in Figure 2.

How to Read a Graph

Let's go over some of the points we've already covered. How much is the output of the monopolist shown in Figure B? Write down your answer. Next question. How much is price? Again, write down your answer. Finally, how much is total profit? Work it out in the space here.

Did you notice that once we find output (where MC = MR), everything else lines up? Price is located on the demand curve above the output of 4.2. ATC is on the ATC curve, also above an output of 4.2. When we find total profit, we plug price, ATC, and output into our formula.

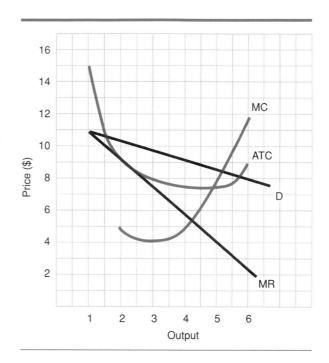

We'll go over each of these questions in turn. First, *our output is always determined by the intersection of the MC and MR curves.* That occurs at an output of about 4.2.

How much is price? *Price is read off the demand curve.* Where on the demand curve—at what output? At the maximum profit output we just found—4.2. How much is price at that output? It appears to be about $9. And how much is ATC? Go straight up from where MC crosses MR to the ATC curve. It looks like about $7.50.

Next we calculate total profit.

$$\text{Total profit} = (\text{Price} - \text{ATC}) \times \text{Output}$$
$$= (\$9 - \$7.50) \times 4.2$$
$$= \$1.50 \times 4.2$$
$$= \$6.30$$

*F*igure B

Are you ready to do some analysis? We need to find the monopolist's total profit. Do that right here. Then check your work with the calculations that follow.

$$\text{Total profit} = (\text{Price} - \text{ATC}) \times \text{Output}$$
$$= (\$17 - \$14) \times 5$$
$$= \$3 \times 5$$
$$= \$15$$

I'm not going to let you off the hook just yet. Try these three questions.

1. At what output would the firm produce most efficiently?

2. At what output would the perfect competitor produce in the long run?

3. What price would the perfect competitor charge in the long run?

Figure 2
The Monopolist Making a Profit

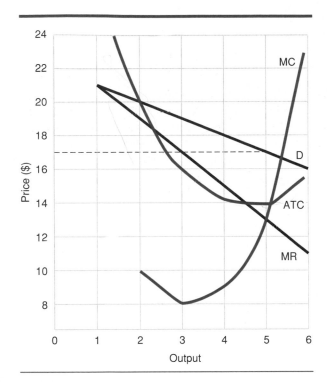

TABLE 4

Output	Price	Total Revenue	Marginal Revenue	Total Cost	ATC	MC	Total Profit
1	$21	21	21	$30	30	——	−$ 9
2	20	40	19	40	20	10	0
3	19	57	17	48	16	8	9
4	18	72	15	57	14.25	9	15
5	17	85	13	70	14	13	15
6	16	96	11	93	15.50	23	3

Here are the answers.

1. The output at which the firm would produce most efficiently would be about 5.1, which is the minimum point of the ATC curve.
2. The perfect competitor would produce at an output of 5.1 in the long run.
3. In the long run the perfect competitor would charge a price of about $13.97 (the minimum, or break-even, point of the ATC curve). I'll take anything between $13.90 and $13.99.

The Monopolist Losing Money

If a monopolist *does* lose money, what would her graph look like? It might look like the one in Figure 3. Please find the firm's price, output, and total loss. Write your answers here:

Solution: The price is $18.50 and the output is 200.

$$\text{Total profit} = (\text{Price} - \text{ATC}) \times \text{Output}$$
$$= (\$18.50 - \$20.40) \times 200$$
$$= -\$1.90 \times 200$$
$$= -\$380$$

Figure 3

Monopolist Taking a Loss

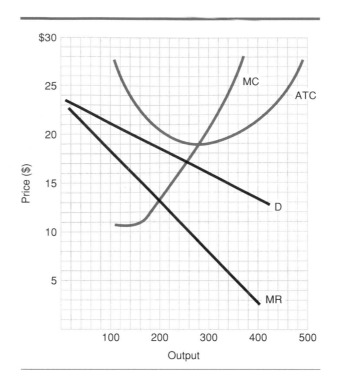

Is this firm in the short run or the long run? It's in the short run. What will the firm do in the long run? It will go out of business.

Alternative Method of Calculating Monopolist's Profit or Loss

Can you find the monopolist's profit using the information in Figure 4? It might help to shade in the profit box.

Using the profit box, QRST, you can multiply the output (350) by the difference between price and ATC ($25) to get a total profit of $8,750. In effect, then, you're multiplying TS by QT.

In Figure 5 you'll find Figure 4 redrawn showing the profit box QRST shaded in.

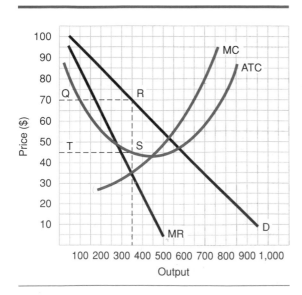

Figure 4

Monopolist Making a Profit

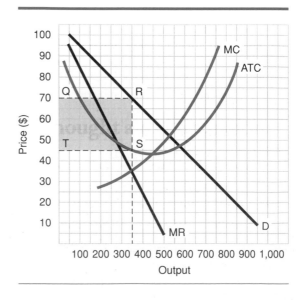

Figure 5

Monopolist Making a Profit

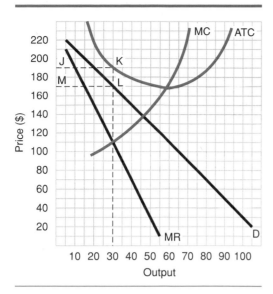

Figure 6
Monopolist Taking a Loss

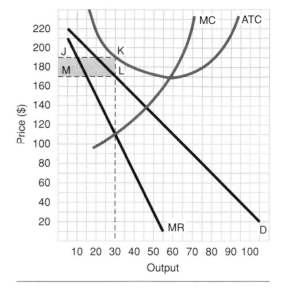

Figure 7
Monopolist Taking a Loss

Now we're ready to find the monopolist's loss in Figure 6. Again shade in the loss box and do the math.

Using the loss box, JKLM, you can multiply the output (30) by the difference between price and ATC (−$20) to get a total loss of $600. Figure 7 shows the loss box shaded in.

The Monopolist in the Short Run and in the Long Run

No distinction is made for the monopolist between the short and long runs. Why not? Because no other firms will enter or leave the industry; by definition, the monopolist is the only firm.

There is no distinction between the short run and the long run for the monopolist.

If the firm is losing money, is it in the short run or the long run? What do *you* think?

It must be in the short run because no firm will stay in business if it's losing money. If the monopolist is making a profit, is it in the long run or the short run? Can you tell? Think about it.

If the firm were in the short run, would this monopolist stay in business? Yes! And so it would continue to make a profit. In the long run, then, it would still be making a profit. Therefore, there is no way to distinguish between the long run and the short run if the firm is making a profit.

Let's sum things up. If the firm is making a profit, for analytic purposes, it doesn't matter whether it's in the short run or the long run. If the firm is losing money, it must be in the short run; in the long run it will go out of business.

Are All Monopolies Big Companies?

The answer is no. Many monopolies are tiny firms operating in very tiny markets. What matters is size relative to the market—the proverbial big fish in the small pond.

Chances are there's only one bookstore on your college campus. That store would have a monopoly even though it's not nearly as big as some of the Barnes and Noble superstores. The only video rental store in a small town would have a monopoly. There are tens of thousands of gas stations, convenience stores, restaurants, cleaners, and repair shops that have monopolies in their communities.

Barriers to Entry

Does the cafeteria at your school have a monopoly? Does it serve either Pepsi or Coke, but not both? Have you noticed that Microsoft sells more computer operating systems than all its rivals put together? How do these companies manage to maintain their monopolies? In many cases, monopolies are protected by barriers to entry into their industries.

We'll consider each of five barriers to entry in turn: (1) control over an essential resource, (2) economies of scale, (3) legal barriers, (4) required scale for innovation, and (5) economies of being established.

Basic resources are land, labor, and capital.

Control over an Essential Resource   The Metropolitan Opera has a near monopoly because it has most of the world's opera stars (labor) under contract. Until the early 1960s the National Football League (NFL) had a monopoly, but this was challenged by the American Football League. The NFL had virtually all the established star football players under contract, so the AFL went after college stars. In 1965 the New York Jets signed University of Alabama star quarterback Joe Namath for the then unheard-of sum of $427,000; that action broke the back of the NFL's monopoly.

Until the mid-1980s DeBeers Diamond Company in South Africa owned nearly 90 percent of the world's diamond mines, and the International Nickel Company of Canada controls about 90 percent of the world's nickel reserves. The Standard Oil Company controlled the oil industry in the 1880s until the early 1900s because it owned more than 90 percent of the nation's oil fields and refineries. At that same time the American Tobacco Company controlled 90 percent of U.S. tobacco production.[2]

Economies of Scale   Typically, heavy industry—iron and steel, copper, aluminum, and automobiles—has high setup costs. But once your plant and equipment are set up, you can take advantage of economies of scale by increasing your output. Thus we are really talking about two necessary conditions for realizing economies of scale: having the wherewithal to set up and having sufficient demand for your product.

Imagine how difficult it would be to set up a rival phone network or even a rival electric company in a large city. What protects monopolies from potential rivals is that they're selling enough units to have a relatively low ATC. If you were to enter the industry, how could you hope to have the capital to set yourself up to compete effectively?

Figure 8 illustrates the problem of economies of scale faced by the small producer of cars. At relatively low levels of production, say 100,000 to 200,000 cars, the firm will not be able to take advantage of the economies of mass production that are available to rival firms. According to this illustration, ATC continues to decline appreciably through an output of at least 700,000.

Legal barriers include licensing, franchises, and patents.

Licensing

Legal Barriers   These include licensing, franchises, and patents. The whole idea is for the government to allow only one firm or a group of individuals to do business.

Licensing prevents just anybody from driving a taxi, cutting hair, peddling on the street, practicing medicine, or burying bodies. Often the licensing procedure is designed to hold down the number of people going into a certain field to keep prices high. The state of Arizona requires that hairstylists take 1,600 hours of classroom instruction at a cosmetology school approved by the government. The cost? Ten thousand dollars. In Oregon hairstylists are even better trained since they are required to receive 2,500 hours of instruction.

Patents

Patents are granted to investors so that they have a chance to get rich before someone else uses their ideas (see the box, "How Do You Stop Others from Stealing Your Idea?"). The patent holders have 20 years to get their act together. In some cases, perhaps most notably U.S. Shoe Machinery Company, a firm buys up patents and uses them to

---

[2]In 1911 the Supreme Court broke up these monopolies. (See the chapter titled "Corporate Mergers and Antitrust.")

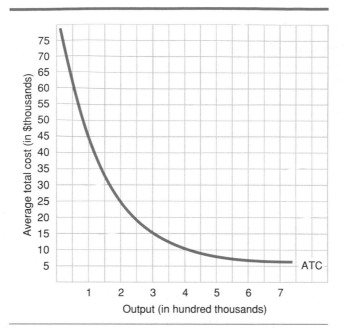

Figure 8
Hypothetical Production Costs
for Cars
This would be an example of
decreasing costs, where economies
of scale drive down ATC through
an output of at least 700,000 cars.

How Do You Stop Others from Stealing Your Idea?

Two budding entrepreneurs in Houston noticed that people who had put their drinks down at parties often forgot which glass was theirs. So they set up a business selling wineglass jewelry, which helped people identify their drink glass. In their first year, they signed up 90 stores in Texas to carry their product and racked up sales of $35,000.

But quite soon competing products selling for lower prices drove them out of business. Should they have patented their idea? While the idea could not qualify for a patent, perhaps a trademark for their company logo and a copyright for the design might have helped.

prevent competition. A common practice is to obtain a patent on a new product or process and then, before the 20 years are up, obtain a new patent on some improvement or innovation. Japanese firms have been able to dominate the consumer electronics industry by successfully obtaining patents on each innovation to the original product.

Patents are essential to pharmaceutical companies, which may spend hundreds of millions of dollars developing a drug. They would be a lot less willing to spend so much money on research if their competitors could immediately capitalize on this research and sell close substitutes. By and large, it appears that patents do speed up technological advance and the consequent flow of new products to the consumer.

The most important legal barrier is the government franchise. And the most important form of local franchise is the public utility—your gas and electric companies. There's only one to a locality. The local government grants the franchise, and, like it or not, the company's got you. Monopolies don't have to worry about giving poor service at outrageous prices. Where else can you go? (See the box, "At Rutgers Coke Is the Only Choice.")

Government franchises

Required Scale for Innovation   Do you know anyone who's invented a board game? Have they thought of taking it to Parker Brothers, the company that sells Monopoly? Or someone who wants to sell a greeting card idea to Hallmark? Or a new toy to Mattel? Most inventors don't have the wherewithal to produce and market their ideas, but they would usually be quite happy to hand them over to one of the big guys for a slice of the sales or profits.

At Rutgers Coke Is the Only Choice

Outbidding Pepsi by about $2.5 million, the Coca-Cola Company paid Rutgers, the State University of New Jersey, some $10 million in 1994 for exclusive rights to sell its products to some 48,000 students on three campuses over the next decade. On-campus food and beverage vendors may sell only Coca-Cola Company beverages, which include Nestea iced tea, Sprite, Minute Maid drinks, and, of course, every variety of diet and regular Coke. The football coach will even be doused with Powerade, rather than Gatorade.

Rutgers, of course, is not the first school to sell an exclusive franchise to a private vendor. If you happen to visit any of Penn State's 21 campuses, you might think you're at Pepsi-Cola University. The school has a ten-year, $14 million dollar deal for exclusive rights for *that* company's products. The next time you're in *your* school cafeteria or snack bar, see whether it sells both Coke and Pepsi. If it doesn't, you'll know who's got the franchise.

While individuals come up with all the great ideas, only large firms have the money and know-how to bring them to the marketplace. However, the vast proliferation of dot-coms, many of which have found venture capital to carry them until they are ready to go public (that is, sell stock to raise still more capital), certainly proves that you don't necessarily have to be big to innovate.

Economies of Being Established   Companies that have been operating for many years have recognizable brand names, and their sales representatives have established territories. Most important, the seller and buyer have a long-standing relationship. A retailer can count on her supplier for fast, reliable service.

A new company, with newly hired sales reps just learning their routes, will have a hard time prying customers from a well-established competitor. How can you convince a retailer to buy your product or service when she never saw you before and is unfamiliar with what you're selling? For these reasons, the economies of being established make it difficult to take market share from a company that may have been doing business before you were born.

But wait—there's more. Established firms selling to retailers, especially supermarkets, already have their products on the shelves. And just as possession is nine-tenths of the law, once a firm's products are on a shelf, it's very hard for newcomers to dislodge those products. In the box, "Finding Space on the Shelf," we see that the economies of being established include monopolizing shelf space.

Finding Space on the Shelf

Have you ever wondered why a bookstore places certain books in its window? Or right by the cash register? Or why certain publishers have their books piled on tables or on entire shelves? Chances are those publishers paid extra bucks for that placement. On the shelves of retail stores, just like in real estate, location is everything.

Consumer goods manufacturers pay over $100 billion a year for shelf space, of which food companies spend about $60 billion on what is termed givebacks or slotting fees. Most large supermarket chains charge slotting fees, but significantly, Walmart does not.

Until I started studying economics, I thought that the reason a refrigerated display case was filled with Carvel's ice cream was because Carvel's was nice enough to donate the display case. But Carvel's is paying for more than just the case.

Is paying for shelf space anticompetitive? After several small manufacturers complained about being shut out of stores, the Federal Trade Commission has been conducting an ongoing investigation.

Another advantage of being established is setting the industry standard, as does Microsoft in computer software and Matsushita in VCR format. Why does *your* VCR have a VHS format rather than a (Sony) Betamax format? Mainly because nearly all available tapes are VHS. Back in the late 1970s when Sony and Matsushita went head-to-head, Sony's one-hour tapes were too short for movies. Since Matsushita produced two-hour tapes, their VHS format very quickly became the industry standard (see the box, "Setting the Standard").

And talking about the advantages of being established, it's hard not to notice that virtually everyone drives a car powered by gasoline. Would you believe that the Stanley Steamer set a world speed record of 122 miles an hour way back in 1909? That's right—a steam-powered car. If the manufacturer had not priced it as a luxury vehicle and instead had striven for economies of scale as Henry Ford was doing, we might all be driving Stanley Steamers. And perhaps sometime soon, more and more of us will be driving electric cars. Which brings us to the limits of monopoly power.

Limits to Monopoly Power

First, we'll consider limits to the five barriers to entry. We saw how the National Football League lost its monopoly when it lost control over an essential resource—star football players. Similarly, Alcoa, which at one time controlled nearly all the world's known bauxite (aluminum ore) reserves, lost its monopoly when other reserves were discovered.[3]

Economies of scale and high capital requirements are a significant barrier to entry, but by 1990 Nissan, Honda, Toyota, Mazda, and Mitsubishi joined the parade of American automobile producers. Of course, each of these producers was set up by its friendly giant company back home.

Finally, even legal barriers have been overcome. Rival phone companies have gone to court to win the right to plug into local phone companies while providing a competing and generally lower-priced long-distance service. In general, however, government franchises are there for a reason: In some industries it makes economic sense to have only one firm in a given locality; so the franchise may well be a barrier we don't want to overcome.

Limits to the five barriers to entry

---

[3]The Alcoa case is discussed in the chapter "Corporate Mergers and Antitrust."

The ultimate limit to monopoly power may come from the government or from the market itself. If a firm gets too big or too bad, the federal government may decide to trim that firm's sails. We'll examine this issue in the chapter, "Corporate Mergers and Antitrust."

The market limits monopoly power through the development of substitutes.

Let's consider how the market limits monopoly power, basically through the development of substitutes. Take Kleenex, for example. To this day, some people call tissues "Kleenexes." In the late 1940s Kleenex was the only paper tissue on the market, so *tissues* and *Kleenexes* could properly be considered synonymous. But over the years scores of competitors have sprung up, and today the market share of Kleenex is very small indeed.

Another interesting case is that of Xerox. Having invented the first "dry" photocopy machine, Xerox had the market all to itself during the late 1950s and early 1960s. Shortly thereafter, IBM, Savin, Canon, Sharp, Pitney-Bowes, Multilith-Addressograph, and a multitude of other firms began marketing their own photocopiers. Nonetheless, to this day when someone needs a photocopy, chances are he or she will ask you to "xerox" it—which is a lot easier than asking you to "multilith-addressograph" it.

You certainly weren't expecting to read about male impotence in an economics textbook, but I'm sure you know the name of the drug that treats it. Viagra is a household name. Since it was introduced by Pfizer in 1998, it had the market entirely to itself. But in 2004 two new drugs were introduced—Levitra (made by GlaxoSmithKline and Bayer) and Cialis (Eli Lilly). Although Viagra rivals Coca-Cola as one of the most widely known brands in the world, there goes its monopoly.

Economies of Scale and Natural Monopoly

Two justifications for monopoly

There are really only two justifications for monopoly: economies of scale and natural monopoly. Economies of scale justify bigness because only a firm with a large output can produce near the minimum point of its long-run ATC curve. When the firm's output is so large that it is almost equal to the output of the entire industry, this state of monopoly is justified by calling it efficient. Of course, we have just seen that the firm is not operating at the minimum point of its ATC curve (see Figure 2), but that's another story.

What Is Natural Monopoly?

Natural monopoly is closely related to economies of scale. Some think a natural monopoly occurs when someone gains complete control of the wheat germ supply or of the entire crop of Florida oranges. Close, but no cigar. Cigar? No, even Cuban cigars are not a natural monopoly.

Examples of natural monopolies

Examples of natural monopolies are the local gas and electric companies, the local phone companies, and local cable TV companies. Why are these natural monopolies? Because they can provide cheaper service as monopolies than could several competing firms. Let's see why.

In Figure 9A, one electric company serves an entire suburban town. Pictured here is one street in that town, its houses lined up properly just as they might be anywhere in suburbia. Every house on the block uses the same company. After all, what choice do they have?

Figure 9B shows four competing electric companies on an identical street of an identical town somewhere else in suburbia. Notice the four power lines running along the street. In this town there's freedom of choice; you can hook up with any of these four companies.

There's only one problem with this arrangement. It's much more expensive. You see, each company, assuming customers are evenly distributed, does only one-quarter of the business that would be done by a company that had a monopoly. While it must construct

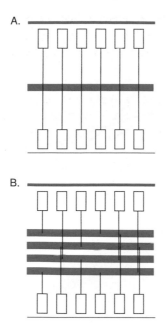

Figure 9
One Electric Company Is Better than Four
Panel A shows a single electric transmission feeder cable serving all the homes on one block. Panel B shows four cables serving that same block. It is a lot more efficient (and cheaper) to have one cable than four.

the same system of power lines, it realizes only one-quarter of the output. Its costs are much higher than those of the monopoly.[4]

From society's viewpoint, these higher costs reflect a great waste of resources. Why construct four parallel power lines when one will do as nicely? And, one might add parenthetically, why dig up the street four times rather than once to lay and repair the cables?

This is the case for natural monopoly. It's cheaper, it's more efficient, and it's more convenient. The bottom line is that our bills are much lower.

Another case for natural monopoly can be made with respect to local telephone service. Imagine if we had four, six, or eight competing phone companies. Placing a call would be like playing Russian roulette. Imagine your surprise if you actually got through!

Imagine if we had six or eight competing local phone companies.

It would not be easy to conduct business. "Let's see now, I call this client on the orange phone, my lawyer on the gray phone, and my accountant on the yellow phone." And what if the president needs to reach his opposite number in the Kremlin in a hurry and can't remember: "Was it the red phone for the Kremlin and the green phone for McDonald's—or was it the other way around?" You can imagine the puzzlement in Moscow at getting an order for two Big Macs and a large order of fries.

Speaking of fries, would you believe that the snack stand at a multiplex movie theater can be a natural monopoly? Surely the multiplex realizes great economies of scale by operating one large stand, which is busy all the time, rather than 20 separate stands in 20 scattered movie theaters. But unlike Walmart and other big box stores, these folks don't often pass on their savings to their moviegoer customers in the form of lower prices.

The 1996 Telecommunications Act allowed the local phone companies into the long-distance market but only after they could prove that their local markets were open to competition. So *are* the Bells (among them Verizon, BellSouth, Qwest, and SBC) allowing local rivals into their markets by making their lines available? Under the Telecom Act, regulators in many states are finally forcing the Bells to lower wholesale rates for local service. Competitors such as Sprint, Talk America, Trinsic, and Supra Telecom control about 15 percent of the local market.

---

[4]Technically, these are average fixed costs. They're four times as high as that of the electric company that has a monopoly. For example, if it cost $4 million to lay cable through a town, and if 40,000 families lived in the town, the monopoly would have an AFC of $100 ($4,000,000/40,000). Each of the four competing companies would have an AFC of $400 per family ($4,000,000/10,000).

The Market Situation of the
Rochester Electric Company
If free to set its own price, the
company would charge $11.10. But
the New York State Public Service
Commission could set the price
lower, say at $10.75.

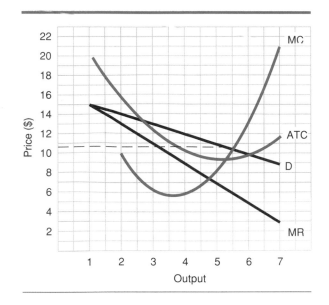

Two Policy Alternatives

Two ways to prevent public
utilities from charging
outrageous prices are:
(1) government regulation and
(2) government ownership.

We have accepted certain instances of monopoly—mainly, local public utility companies. These companies are natural monopolies and provide the public with better and more cheaply priced service than it would get from most competing firms. How can we prevent these public utilities from taking advantage of their power and charging outrageous prices? There are two ways: (1) government regulation and (2) government ownership.

Government Regulation   Suppose Figure 10 represents the market situation of the Rochester Electric Company, which is now regulated by the New York State Public Service Commission.

The commission would have two objectives: a lower price for electricity consumers and a higher output of electricity than we see in Figure 9. To accomplish both ends, the commission would set the price of electricity at about $10.75, which is lower than the current market price of $11.10. How much would output now be? How about total profit?

Using the formula for total profit, we get:

$$\text{Total profit} = (\text{Price} - \text{ATC}) \times \text{Output}$$
$$= (\$10.75 - \$9.30) \times 5.25$$
$$= \$1.45 \times 5.25$$
$$= \$7.61$$

This is illustrated in Figure 10. Consumers now pay a lower price and receive more electricity than they would have under an unregulated monopoly. But this is not a perfect solution because even the regulated natural monopoly does not necessarily produce at the minimum point of its ATC curve.

Government Ownership   The second option for a natural monopoly is government ownership. The post office, the Tennessee Valley Authority, Amtrak, the New York State Power Authority, the New Jersey Transit System, and the Metropolitan Transit Authority of Boston are all examples.

Are government-owned
enterprises inefficient?

Are these inefficient government boondoggles whose jobs could be better done by private enterprise? Consider the origins of the New Jersey public transportation system. When the private bus lines were unable to operate even with massive public subsidies, the state of New Jersey reluctantly took them over.

The case of the Tennessee Valley Authority (TVA) is even stranger. TVA uses itself as a yardstick with which to measure the costs of power provided by privately owned utilities. The latter complain about "unfair" government competition, and they do have a point because TVA sometimes provides electricity at half the cost of that incurred by privately owned companies.

This is rather interesting when one considers the origins of TVA. Much of rural Tennessee, Arkansas, and Alabama, as well as parts of other states near the Tennessee Valley, were not provided with electricity by private power companies as late as the early 1930s because they were not deemed worthy customers. They were too poor, they lived too far apart, and it was simply not economically feasible to run transmission cables into this part of the country. So TVA, without competing with private companies, went into this area and provided it with electricity at half the going rate.

The general thrust of public policy in the area of natural monopoly is to let private enterprise do the job but to regulate prices closely. Only as a last resort, when private enterprise is unwilling or unable to do the job, does the government take on the job itself.

Let private enterprise do the job—if it can.

Is Bigness Good or Bad?

It's both. If you're a big company, do you necessarily behave badly? Why do big companies—Microsoft, Walmart, General Motors, the oil, tobacco, and pharmaceutical companies, and the giant defense contractors—seem to have such bad reputations? And can a case be made that bigness is good?

When Is Bigness Bad?

From what we've seen so far, monopoly isn't *all* bad. At times only a monopolist can fully take advantage of economies of scale; and in certain instances, particularly with respect to local public utilities, there are natural monopolies. In the case of Xerox, Kleenex, and IBM, these innovative companies once had monopolies simply because each was the first to enter its field.

Why, then, do so many people dislike monopolies? For one thing, monopolies tend to be inefficient. As illustrated earlier in Figures 1 and 2, a monopoly does not produce at the minimum point of its ATC curve. Furthermore, by always restricting output to some point to the left of that minimum, the monopoly is preventing resources from being allocated in the most efficient manner. Land, labor, and capital that would have otherwise flowed into the monopolized industry are kept out and will eventually find their way into other industries where they will not be as efficiently used.

Bigness can also mean inefficiency. In the chapter before last, we talked about corporate bureaucracies and diseconomies of scale. This problem has become acute among the giant firms that are often referred to as "corporate dinosaurs." The box titled, "The Corporate Hierarchy" takes a critical look at this growing problem.

Bigness can also mean inefficiency.

When Is Bigness Good?

To be big is not necessarily to behave badly. Natural monopolies, for example, taking advantage of economies of scale, deliver services much more cheaply than could a multitude of competing firms. And in general, large firms can take advantage of economies of scale.

Sometimes a firm, such as Xerox, IBM, or Microsoft, is the first to enter an industry. Should we ask such a firm to wait until each of its competitors can catch up? Or do we allow them to grow very large? Perhaps the question we should ask is whether a firm is big because it is very bad or because it is very good.

Walmart, while technically not a monopoly, is certainly the dominant retailer in the United States. Question: Is it good or bad? Read the Current Issue at the end of this chapter and then decide for yourself.

The Corporate Hierarchy

Americans are fond of creating pecking orders, and the bureaucratic managerial structures set up to run America's large corporations are prime examples. In Japan and Germany where the corporate hierarchy is substantially flatter, chief executive officers earn 10 times what their average employees earn. But in the United States the average CEO pulls down more than 400 times the earnings of the average worker. In the chart you'll find that since 1980 the disparity between the salaries of CEOs and ordinary workers has increased almost tenfold.

incentives. But it's just the structure our own huge corporations have. The tip of the hierarchy passes orders down to the troops. The rank-and-file worker is rarely consulted and does not identify with the company or with the product it produces. Furthermore, the people who are making the decisions at the top have virtually no contact with their customers. The end result is often a high-cost, low-quality product.

The large college textbook publishers—McGraw-Hill (which publishes my book), Sage Reuters, Houghton-Mifflin, Pearson, John Wiley and Sons, and

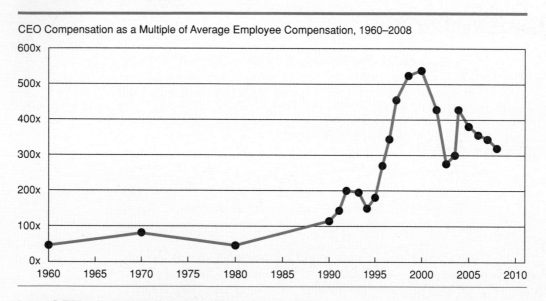

CEO Compensation as a Multiple of Average Employee Compensation, 1960–2008

Sources: G. William Domhoff, "Wealth, Income, and Power," September 2005.
http://sociology.ucsc.edu/whorulesamerica/power/wealth.html
http://www.aflcio.org/corporatewatch/paywatch/pay/index.cfm

In ancient Greece, Plato recommended that a community's highest wage should not exceed five times its lowest. So today's CEOs have gone over 50 times beyond the philosopher's suggested pay grade.

Our leading corporations have become so complex, so overmanaged, so distant from their customers, and so alienating to their rank-and-file employees that it is a wonder they have been able to function as well as they have. Perhaps the dilemma is best summed up by management consultant Ichak Adizes: "Good organizations should be structured by geniuses so that idiots can run them. Unfortunately, most American organizations are structured by idiots so that it takes a genius to run them."*

This structure is not efficient. It allows no feedback from consumers, no competition, and very few work

W. W. Norton—are major exceptions to the hierarchical rule. Their sales representatives provide daily feedback from their customers, who happen to be your professors. Their editors, regional managers, marketing managers, as well as national sales managers have had years of selling experience themselves, and often accompany the sales reps on visits to colleges. Although these companies certainly do exhibit the trappings of corporate status and privilege, the decision makers are a lot closer to the customer than the rest of Corporate America.

---

*Quoted in Steven Schlosstein, *The End of the American Century* (New York: Congdon & Weed, 1989), p. 108.

The Economic Case against Bigness

I'll start with the obvious. Does the monopolist operate at the minimum point of her ATC curve? No! Just glance back at Figures 1 and 2.

The best of all monopoly profits is a quiet life.

—John Hicks

Because the monopolist is not pressed by competition, there is no great incentive to control costs or to use resources efficiently. Indeed, there is no need to spend much money on research and development, to improve manufacturing processes, to develop new products, or to be responsive to customer needs.

A monopolist can charge her customers higher prices and provide poorer service than she would if she had competitors. I mean, where else can you go? Have you ever lost your temper dealing with your local bank (assuming it's the only one in town), the phone company, or the gas or electric company? You've heard the phrase "The customer is always right"? Not when you're dealing with a monopoly.

One of the most important effects of the growing amount of foreign competition, especially from the Japanese, is the new emphasis on product quality. American cars, specialty steel, machine tools, and a whole host of consumer products have all enjoyed tremendous quality improvement over the last 15 years. It is a virtual certainty that without the spur of foreign competition, the quality standards of American products would not have improved nearly as much.

Conclusion

Is monopoly good, bad, or indifferent? One fair conclusion is that natural monopoly would be good, if only its power were not abused. But monopolies based on other factors—I refrain from calling them "unnatural monopolies"—must be looked on with suspicion. They may be up to no good, and they also may be illegal.

In a sense, virtually all firms are monopolies. The last gas station before the turnpike entrance, the only bar on your block, and the only grocery in your neighborhood that stays open until midnight are all monopolies. The test they must pass is whether or not there are close substitutes.

Who decides this? The buyers do. If the buyers in your local area think that your store is the only game in town—that no one else even comes close—then you have a monopoly. But let's not get carried away. No one is going to drive 50 miles just to buy your gas, drink your beer, or buy a quart of milk at your store. What you've got is a very local monopoly. You may even be earning an economic profit, but you're not exactly Exxon.

From this discussion we shall make a very neat segue into monopolistic competition, which is the subject of the next chapter. By blending some elements of monopoly and some elements of perfect competition, we will obtain a mixture of firms that we encounter every day in the real world.

Last Word

As technological change accelerates in the communications field, we are increasingly asking ourselves, "Just what constitutes a monopoly?" In the early years of the new millennium, Apple's iPod emerged as the clear leader in the sale of MP3 players, garnering about three-quarters of the market—a near monopoly.[5] But then, in mid-2007, the company came out with its iPhone, a combined cell phone, MP3 player, and Web browser. Steve Jobs, the company's CEO, said then that he hoped the iPhone would capture 1 percent of the cell phone market within a couple of years.

So while the iPod had a near monopoly in the media player market, Jobs's aspiration for the iPhone was much more modest. But as the iPhone helps the cell phone, Web browser, and media player markets converge, we need to ask this question: Can *any*

---

[5]Full disclosure: I own some Apple stock.

company expect to attain monopoly status in this market? Because this market is so fragmented and its technology changing so rapidly, it seems unlikely that any company will become the dominant player, let alone a monopoly.

Current Issue: Would You Allow Walmart to Open a Supercenter in Your Community?

Let's start with two facts almost everyone agrees on:

1. Walmart lives up to the slogan printed right on every shopping bag, "Always low prices. *Always*." After all, 20 million daily shoppers can't *all* be wrong.
2. Walmart's full-time employees' average hourly wages are about $10 an hour—perhaps 30 percent lower than those paid by competitors.

These two facts create a personal conflict for many of us. After all, who can resist all those bargains? But those bargains are subsidized by low wages.

Here's another conflict to mull over. Walmart imports $20 billion a year of microwave ovens, TVs, DVD players, toys, shoes, apparel and other goods from China. It then passes along the savings in the form of low prices. But these imports not only add to our trade deficit, they put some Americans out of work.

Is Walmart anti-union? Not even one of its more than 4,000 stores is unionized. (See the chapter on labor unions in *Economics* and *Microeconomics*.) And a unionized Walmart would pay higher wages and provide better medical benefits.

As Walmart grew, so too did its bargaining power over its suppliers. By passing on these bargains to its customers, it could sell huge quantities of merchandise at amazingly low prices. This brought in more customers, which enabled Walmart to grow even larger and get even better deals from its suppliers.

Walmart relentlessly drives down its costs—not just by paying relatively low wages and squeezing its suppliers—but by running a ruthlessly efficient, lean and mean operation. Its customers have an average family income of $35,000, and save about $1,000 a year by shopping there, while more affluent families save even more. And while its wages are admittedly low, virtually each new store is flooded by job applicants. One may conclude, then, that Walmart's low everyday wages are dictated more by supply and demand than by a desire to exploit its hired help.

Does Walmart discriminate against its female employees? (See the chapter on labor markets and wage rates in *Economics* and *Microeconomics*.) A huge class-action suit has been filed on behalf of 1.6 million past and current employees. The suit notes that women make up over 72 percent of all hourly employees, but just one-third of the store managers are women. The jury may be out on this case for some time to come.

In recent years Walmart has been successfully sued by groups of its employees over pay and working conditions:

- In 2005 a California court ordered the company to pay $172 million to 116,000 hourly workers in damages for failing to provide meal breaks.
- In 2006 a Pennsylvania jury ordered Walmart to pay $78 million to 187,000 current and former employees for not paying them when they worked through rest breaks and worked off the clock. A year later a judge increased that award to $188 million to include damages, interest, and lawyers' fees. Walmart is appealing.
- In 2007 Walmart reached an agreement with the U.S. Department of Labor to pay $34 million in back wages plus interest to settle a federal lawsuit that accused the company of violating overtime laws involving 86,680 workers.
- In 2008 Walmart settled a suit for $54 million filed by employees in its Minnesota stores accusing the company of wage violations.

- In all, Walmart has faced over 70 lawsuits across the country in which workers have accused the company of making them miss required breaks or work off the clock. In late 2008 Walmart announced that it had agreed to settle 63 of these cases, and paying out between $352 million and $640 million, depending on how many claims affected workers submit.

According to one recent academic study, when Walmart enters a market, prices decrease by 8 percent in rural areas and 5 percent in urban areas. When you factor in the price cuts other retailers must make to compete, Walmart has saved consumers well over $100 billion a year. Far more than any other business firm, it has been responsible for holding down our rate of inflation.

In 2005, the company announced a new health plan with premiums as low as $11 a month, but still leaving many employees paying thousands of dollars in out-of-pocket medical expenses. By 2008 just over half of Walmart's workers had company health insurance and 46 percent of their children were uninsured or on Medicaid.

Has Walmart driven smaller retailers out of business? Clearly it has. Often, soon after a Walmart supercenter opened, local supermarkets as well as smaller groceries were forced to close. Indeed, big box retailers as well as giant suburban shopping malls are responsible for the demise of downtown shopping areas, not just in cities, but in small towns as well.

Perhaps Walmart attained its finest hour simply by remaining open for business in the wake of Hurricane Katrina. By keeping their stores stocked with food and water, it provided a lifeline to hurricane victims. Significantly, while some other sellers were price gouging, Walmart lived by its motto, *"Always low prices. Always."* This is more fully discussed in Chapter 3.

More and more communities have opposed the opening of new Walmarts. Other communities welcomed Walmart, not just because of its low prices, but for the new jobs it provided. Would *you* allow Walmart to open a supercenter in your community?

on the web

To learn more about the good and the bad about Walmart, you can go to these sites: pro: http://walmartstores.com/pressroom and con: http://walmartwatch.com

Questions for Further Thought and Discussion

1. Are very large firms economically justifiable? What are the pros and cons of bigness?

2. A monopolist can control her price or the quantity she sells, but she can't control both. Explain this statement.

3. Make the case for natural monopolies.

4. Are all monopolies large firms? Make up an example of a monopoly that is a small firm.

5. How does the demand curve faced by the monopolist differ from that confronting the perfect competitor? Why do they differ?

6. What are the main barriers to entry? Explain how each barrier can foster monopoly.

7. Pharmaceutical companies can turn out pills for pennies and sell them for dollars. Many people who need these drugs can't afford them. How can these companies justify charging so much?

8. *Practical Application:* Walmart wants to open a superstore near you. List the reasons why you think they (a) should be allowed to do so; (b) should not be allowed to do so.

9. *Practical Application:* Does your college bookstore have a monopoly? In what ways is that a good thing? In what ways does the store abuse its monopoly power?

Workbook for Chapter 10

Name _____   Date _____

Multiple-Choice Questions

Circle the letter that corresponds to the best answer.

1. Which statement is true? (LO1)
   a) All monopolists' products have close substitutes.
   b) Most firms in the United States are monopolies.
   c) There are no monopolies in the United States.
   d) A monopoly is a firm that produces all the output in an industry.
   e) None of these statements is true.

2. The monopolist is _____. (LO1)
   a) an imperfect competitor and has a horizontal demand curve
   b) an imperfect competitor and has a downward sloping demand curve
   c) a perfect competitor and has a horizontal demand curve
   d) a perfect competitor and has a downward sloping demand curve

3. A downward sloping demand curve means _____. (LO1)
   a) you have to lower your price to sell more
   b) demand falls as output rises
   c) demand rises as output rises
   d) total revenue declines as price is lowered

4. The monopolist's demand and marginal revenue curves _____. (LO1)
   a) are exactly the same
   b) are completely different
   c) coincide only at one unit of output
   d) cross

5. The monopolist produces _____. (LO1, 2)
   a) where MC equals MR
   b) at the minimum point of ATC
   c) at maximum output
   d) when price is highest

6. If a monopolist has a straight-line demand curve, its marginal revenue curve _____. (LO1)
   a) will be the same as the demand curve
   b) will fall twice as quickly as the demand curve
   c) will lie below the demand curve at all points
   d) will cross the demand curve

7. Which statement is true? (LO2)
   a) The monopolist and the perfect competitor both produce where MC equals MR.
   b) Neither the monopolist nor the perfect competitor produce where MC equals MR.
   c) The monopolist, but not the perfect competitor, produces where MC equals MR.
   d) The perfect competitor, but not the monopolist, produces where MC equals MR.

8. Which statement is true about economic profit in the long run? (LO2, 3)
   a) Both the monopolist and the perfect competitor make one.
   b) Neither the monopolist nor the perfect competitor makes one.
   c) Only the perfect competitor makes one.
   d) Only the monopolist makes one.

9. Which statement is true? (LO3)
   a) The monopolist cannot lose money.
   b) The monopolist always operates a large firm.
   c) The monopolist will not lose money in the short run.
   d) The monopolist will not lose money in the long run.

10. Price is always read off the _____ curve. (LO1, 2)
    a) MC   c) ATC
    b) MR   d) demand

11. The most efficient output is found _____. (LO3)
    a) where MC and MR cross
    b) at the bottom of the ATC curve
    c) when the demand and MR curves are equal
    d) where the ATC and demand curves cross

12. When the monopolist is losing money, _____. (LO3)
    a) we are in the short run
    b) we are in the long run
    c) it is impossible to tell if we are in the short run or the long run
    d) we have to go back and check our work because monopolists don't lose money

13. The basis for monopoly in the automobile industry would most likely be _____. (LO4)
    a) control over an essential resource
    b) economies of scale
    c) legal barriers

14. Which statement is true? (LO4, 5)
    a) It is impossible for monopolies to exist in the United States.
    b) Once a monopoly is set up, it is impossible to dislodge it.
    c) Monopolies can be overcome only by market forces.
    d) Monopolies can be overcome only by the government.
    e) None of these statements is true.

15. Which of the following is a natural monopoly? (LO6)
    a) The National Football League
    b) A local phone company
    c) DeBeers Diamond Company
    d) IBM

16. Each of the following is true about Walmart EXCEPT that _____. (LO8)
    a) it is the largest employer in the United States
    b) it is the largest company in the world
    c) it pays its employees, on average, about the same as its competitors
    d) it drives hard bargains with suppliers and passes along the savings to its customers

17. An example of government ownership of a monopoly is _____. (LO6)
    a) the Tennessee Valley Authority
    b) the New York State Public Service Commission
    c) AT&T
    d) General Motors

18. Who said, "Good organizations should be structured by geniuses so that idiots can run them. Unfortunately, most American organizations are structured by idiots so that it takes a genius to run them"? (LO7)
    a) Ichak Adizes
    b) Robert Frost
    c) John Hicks
    d) General Douglas MacArthur
    e) President Dwight D. Eisenhower

19. The average American CEO earns _____ times the earnings of the average worker. (LO7)
    a) 10 to 15
    b) 25 to 40
    c) 100 to 150
    d) 300 to 600
    e) 1,000 to 1,200

20. Which statement is true? (LO7)
    a) The monopolist is just as driven as the competitive firm to control costs and use resources efficiently.
    b) The monopolist often charges his customers higher prices and provides poorer service than he would if he had competitors.
    c) Growing foreign competition has had no effect on the quality of American products.
    d) None of these statements is true.

21. The monopolist produces at the minimum point of her ATC curve _____. (LO2)
    a) all the time
    b) most of the time
    c) some of the time
    d) none of the time

22. Each of the following is an example of successfully setting a standard except _____. (LO5)
    a) Microsoft Windows
    b) QWERTY
    c) the VHS format
    d) the electric car

23. Which is the most accurate statement? (LO6)
    a) The rationale for natural monopoly has been strengthened by deregulation.
    b) Your local phone and electric companies will probably continue to be monopolies for at least another 50 years.
    c) Deregulation and competition tend to lower costs.
    d) Natural monopoly never had any economic basis.

Use the graph in Figure 1 to answer questions 24 and 25.

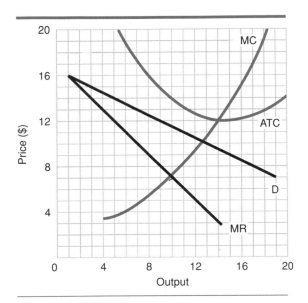

Figure 1

24. If this firm produced at optimum efficiency, it would have an output of _____. (LO2)
    a) less than 10
    b) 10
    c) more than 10, but less than 14
    d) 14
    e) more than 14

25. This firm is _____. (LO2)
    a) making a profit of $25
    b) making a profit of 0
    c) taking a loss of $25
    d) taking a loss of $30
    e) taking a loss of $50

Fill-In Questions

1. A monopoly is a firm that produces _____ _____. (LO1)

2. A monopoly is a firm that has _____ _____ substitutes. (LO1)

3. The demand curve of an imperfect competitor slopes _____ _____. (LO1)

4. The monopolist always produces at that output at which _____ is equal to _____. (LO2)

5. If a firm's demand curve is a straight line sloping downward to the right, its marginal revenue curve will be a _____ _____. (LO1)

6. In the long run the perfect competitor makes _____ profit; in the long run the monopolist makes _____ profit. (LO3)

7. The five barriers to entering a monopolized industry are
    (1) _____;
    (2) _____;
    (3) _____;
    (4) _____;
    and (5) _____. (LO4)

8. There are really only two justifications for monopoly:
    (1) _____
    and (2) _____. (LO6)

9. Local gas and electric companies, the phone company, and local cable TV companies are all examples of _____ monopolies. (LO6)

10. The main economic criticism of monopolies and big business in general is that they are _____. (LO7)

11. There are two ways to prevent public utilities from taking advantage of their power: (1) _____ and (2) _____ . (LO6)

Problems

1. (a) Fill in Table 1. (b) Using your own piece of graph paper, draw a graph of the firm's demand, marginal revenue, marginal cost, and average total cost curves. (c) Calculate the firm's total profit. (d) If the firm operates at optimum efficiency, how much will its output be? (e) If the firm were a perfect competitor, how much would its price be in the long run? (LO1, 2, 3)

TABLE 1

Output	Price	Total Revenue	Marginal Revenue	Total Cost	ATC	MC
1	$19	——	——	$25	——	——
2	18	——	——	40	——	——
3	17	——	——	50	——	——
4	16	——	——	58	——	——
5	15	——	——	65	——	——
6	14	——	——	74	——	——
7	13	——	——	87	——	——

2. (a) Fill in Table 2. (b) Using your own piece of graph paper, draw a graph of the firm's demand, marginal revenue, marginal cost, and average total cost curves. (c) Calculate the firm's total profit. (d) If the firm operates at optimum efficiency, how much will its output be? (e) If the firm were a perfect competitor, how much would its price be in the long run? (LO1, 2, 3)

TABLE 2

Output	Price	Total Revenue	Marginal Revenue	Total Cost	ATC	MC
1	$22	——	——	$30	——	——
2	21	——	——	42	——	——
3	20	——	——	51	——	——
4	19	——	——	60	——	——
5	18	——	——	70	——	——
6	17	——	——	82	——	——
7	16	——	——	98	——	——

3. (a) Using the data from Figure 2, calculate the firm's total profit. (b) If the firm operates at optimum efficiency, how much will its output be? (c) If the firm were a perfect competitor, how much would its price be in the long run? (LO1, 2, 3)

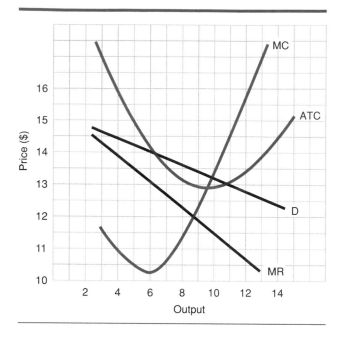

Figure 2

4. (a) Using the data from Figure 3, calculate the firm's total profit. (b) If the firm operates at optimum efficiency, how much will its output be? (c) If the firm were a perfect competitor, how much would its price be in the long run? (LO1, 2, 3)

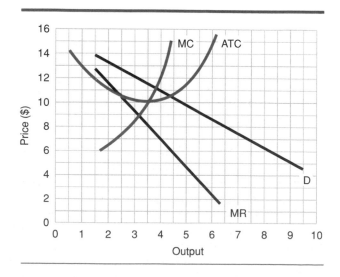

Figure 3

Chapter 11

Monopolistic Competition

W hy do you shop at one drugstore rather than another? Why do you frequent particular restaurants, beauty parlors, video stores, and coffee shops? Do you always shop at the stores that charge the lowest prices? Let's examine these questions and see if we can come up with some answers.

More than 99 percent of the 30 million business firms in the United States are monopolistic competitors. So the least we can do is give them a chapter all to themselves.

LEARNING OBJECTIVES

After reading this chapter you should be able to:

1. Differentiate between the monopolistic competitor in the short run and the long run.
2. Define and examine product differentiation.
3. List and discuss the characteristics of monopolistic competition.

4. Define and illustrate price discrimination.
5. Assess the efficiency of the monopolistic competitor.

Monopolistic Competition Defined

A monopolistically competitive industry has many firms selling a differentiated product. How many is many? So many that no one firm has any significant influence over price. Although this is our working definition, monopolistic competitors do have some influence over price because their products are differentiated. But it's a very *small* influence.

Definition of monopolistic competition

We now encounter a differentiated product for the first time. Note that the definition of monopolistic competition differs from that of perfect competition only in the element of a differentiated product. You'll remember that under perfect competition, all the sellers sold an identical product.

Why did we say the product was identical? Because none of the buyers differentiated among the products for sale. Each was considered the same: Number 2 wheat is number 2 wheat; a large grade A egg is a large grade A egg.

If the buyer doesn't differentiate among the versions of the product sold, the products are identical. If he does differentiate, the product is then differentiated. Who determines whether the product is differentiated or identical? The buyer—that's who.

The difference between identical and differentiated

Like the perfect competitor, the monopolistic competitor operates with perfect information. And as under perfect competition, firms can easily enter or leave the industry.

The Monopolistic Competitor in the Short Run

The monopolistic competitor can make a profit or take a loss in the short run.

Like the perfect competitor, the monopolistic competitor can make a profit or take a loss in the short run; but in the long run the firm will break even. The reason the monopolistic competitor makes zero economic profits in the long run is the same as that under perfect competition.

In the long run, if firms are losing money, many will leave the industry, lowering industry supply and raising market price. And if, in the long run, firms are realizing substantial profits, new firms will be attracted to the industry, thus raising supply and lowering market price. But we're getting ahead of ourselves.

Figure 1 shows a monopolistic competitor in the short run. Notice how its demand and MR curves slope downward, like those of the monopolist. Theoretically, we may opt for a somewhat more elastic demand curve for the monopolistic competitor than for the monopolist because the latter faces the demand curve for the entire industry. The monopolistic competitor, as only one firm in a crowded industry, must have a very elastic demand curve because there are many close substitutes for the firm's product. In fact, no one can get too far out of line with respect to price because buyers are always ready to purchase substitutes from a rival firm.

Very elastic demand curve

Getting back to Figure 1, how much is the firm's output? How much is its price? How much profit does it make? Work it out right here:

First the output. When MC equals MR, output is 60. We find that at an output of 60, the price, which we read off the demand curve, is $15, and the ATC is $12.10 or so. Now we can write down our standard equation, substitute, and solve:

$$\text{Total profit} = (\text{Price} - \text{ATC}) \times \text{Output}$$
$$= (\$15 - \$12.10) \times 60$$
$$= \$2.90 \times 60$$
$$= \$174$$

Now we're ready for Figure 2, which also shows the monopolistic competitor in the short run. How much is output? Is the firm making a profit or taking a loss? How much is it?

$$\text{Total profit} = (\text{Price} - \text{ATC}) \times \text{Output}$$
$$= (\$11 - \$12.80) \times 42$$
$$= -\$1.80 \times 42$$
$$= -\$75.60$$

I'm not above admitting that even *I* cannot read my *own* graphs with any greater precision than the average reader. So, if your price, output, ATC, and, consequently, loss are a little different from mine—no problem. I'll accept any loss that's within the range of $70 to $80.

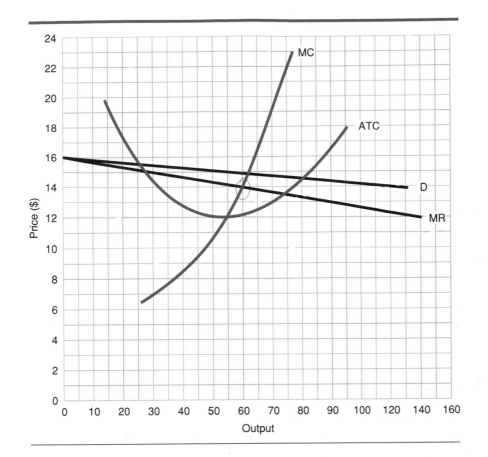

Figure 1

Monopolistic Competitor Making a Profit in the Short Run
The monopolistic competitor makes a profit only in the short run. How much is this firm's price and output? The price is $15 and the output is 60.

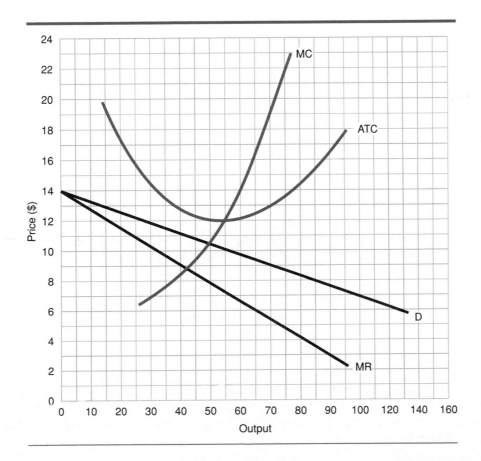

Figure 2

Monopolistic Competitor Taking a Loss in the Short Run
The monopolistic competitor will take a loss only in the short run. How much is this monopolistic competitor's price and output? Price is $11 and output is 42.

The Monopolistic Competitor in the Long Run

The monopolistic competitor makes zero economic profits in the long run.

As I said earlier, in the long run the monopolistic competitor makes zero economic profits. If there are short-run profits, more firms will enter the industry, driving down market price and profits. If there are losses, some firms will leave the industry, pushing up market price and reducing losses.

Figure 3 is a model of the monopolistic competitor in the long run. Note how the point at which the MC and MR curves cross is directly below the price. Output is 40, and price is $12.25. Note also that price is equal to ATC at that output.

Were the firm to produce at any other output, what would happen to its profits? I'm sure you figured out that they would be losses. At any other output, the demand curve lies below the ATC curve, so price is less than ATC.

Note that the price in Figure 3 is higher than the minimum point of the ATC curve. This means that in the long run price is higher under monopolistic competition than it is under perfect competition.

What about output? Again, because the monopolistic competitor produces to the left of the minimum point of its ATC curve, output is lower than it is under perfect competition.

Who is more efficient: the perfect competitor or the monopolistic competitor?

Finally, we have efficiency. Who is more efficient: the monopolistic competitor or the perfect competitor? There is one test for efficiency: What is your ATC? Because the perfect competitor produces at the minimum point of its ATC curve and the monopolistic competitor does not, clearly the perfect competitor is more efficient.

To sum up, both the monopolistic competitor and the perfect competitor make zero economic profits in the long run. The monopolistic competitor charges a higher price and has a lower output than the perfect competitor. And the perfect competitor is a more efficient producer than is the monopolistic competitor.

Figure 4 provides a comparison of a monopolistic competitor and a perfect competitor in the long run. As you'll notice, the monopolistic competitor charges a higher

Figure 3

Monopolistic Competitor Breaking Even in the Long Run
In the long run, the monopolistic competitor must break even. Note that the ATC curve is tangent to the demand curve and that at that same output, MC = MR. How much is price and output for this firm? Price is $12.25 and output is 40.

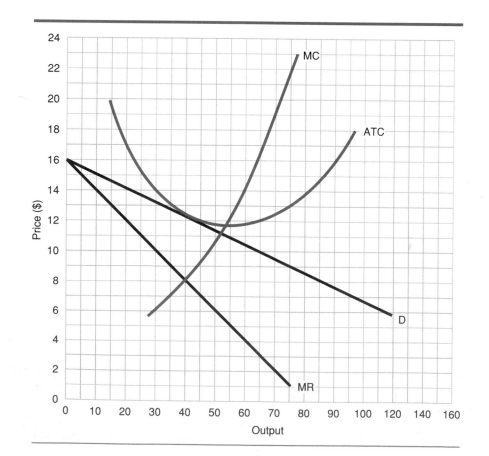

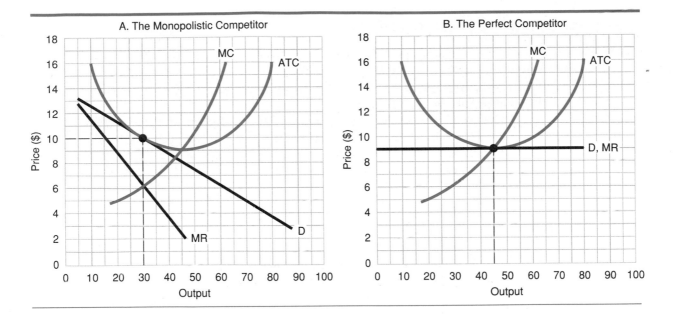

F*igure* 4
The Monopolistic Competitor and the Perfect Competitor in the Long Run

price ($10) than the perfect competitor ($9). The monopolistic competitor has a lower output (30) than the perfect competitor (45). Also, since the perfect competitor produces at the minimum point of her ATC curve, she is a more efficient producer than the monopolistic competitor, who has a higher ATC—$10 vs. $9.

Product Differentiation

Product differentiation is crucial to monopolistic competition. In fact, the product differentiation is really what stands between perfect competition and the real world. People differentiate among many similar products.

The crucial factor is product differentiation.

What makes one good or service differ from another? We need only for the buyer to believe there's a difference, because product differentiation takes place in the buyer's mind. What's the difference between a Toyota Camry and a Corvette? There is absolutely no difference between these two cars *if* the buyer sees no difference. Suppose someone is given the choice and says, "I don't care. They're both the same to me." To this buyer, the cars are identical. One is longer, maybe; one has nicer upholstery.

Americans are provided with a wide array of shampoos, breakfast cereals, candy bars, facial and bath soaps, soft drinks, ballpoint pens, and thousands of other consumer goods. Similarly, we can choose from among huge numbers of lawyers, accountants, physical therapists, chiropractors, advertising agencies, public relations firms, service stations, and restaurants. People living in most other countries don't have all the consumer choices that Americans do, so they don't engage in nearly as much product differentiation as Americans.

We're always differentiating, and our basis doesn't have to be taste, smell, size, or even any physical differences among the products. Two music shops might carry the same CDs; both shops charge exactly the same prices. Both shops are conveniently located. But one is usually crowded and the other is always empty.

We're always differentiating.

Why? Ambience. Perhaps one place lets you listen to a CD before you buy it. Perhaps one store will take special orders for you. Perhaps the salesclerks and owners are nice, helpful people, while in the other store they're all grouches.

Now we're dealing with a differentiated product. The CDs are the same. The prices are the same. But one store's got ambience up to here, and the other has to send out for it.

Customization: Taking Product Differentiation One Step Further

The trend toward customization is taking product differentiation one step further. When you're buying a new car, you can pick something from the lot, or, if you don't mind waiting a few weeks, you can order a car customized to your specifications. Now, however, you can configure your vehicle to your specifications on the Internet and climb behind the wheel within just a few days. More and more, manufacturers like SONY, Dell, and Apple are allowing customers to bypass retailers and buy direct. Toyota and other carmakers have equipped their showrooms in Japan with Internet terminals.

Publishers are at the forefront of product customization. Some publish books on demand. In other words, if there's some out-of-print book that you'd like to buy, they can just print it up for you. Very soon you'll be able to walk into a bookstore, ask them for virtually any book, and it will be waiting for you when you return from the coffee bar. College textbook publishers accommodate professors by custom publishing book-long collections of articles to be read by their students. And, finally, here's some news you may be able to use. If you, or anyone you know, should happen to have a novel you would like to have published—with an audience presumably limited to friends and family—there are new digital publishing houses (for example, iUniverse and Replica Books) that will get your book into print.

The buyer prefers Mr. Nice Guy's store over the grouch's store, so we have a differentiated product.

When sellers try to get buyers to differentiate between their products and those of competitors, the sellers do so based on more than physical differences between their product and other versions of it. Also used are convenience, ambience, reputations of the sellers, and appeals to your vanity, unconscious fears, and desires, as well as snob appeal. To all that we can now add customizing products to suit individual tastes (see the box on customization).

Is McDonald's a monopolistic competitor? *Think* about it. First, does McDonald's produce a differentiated product? To answer one question with another, do customers differentiate between a Big Mac and Burger King's Whopper? To judge from their advertising, both companies seem to think so.

Next question: Is McDonald's one of many firms in the industry? Well, what's the industry? Ready-to-eat burgers and fries? Or fast food? What do *you* think? Fast food? I agree. So McDonald's 13,000 U.S. outlets compete with almost a quarter million other fast-food outlets. What percentage of fast-food outlets within five miles of your home are McDonald's? So McDonald's, although a huge chain, is basically a monopolistic competitor.

on the web

Booksellers try to get you to differentiate between the books they sell and the books sold by other booksellers, even though each may be selling the same books at the same prices. See how differently www.barnesandnoble.com and www.amazon.com present *Ragtime*, by E. L. Doctorow; *Time and Again*, by Jack Finney; and *The Age of Turbulence*, by Alan Greenspan.

Advertising and Monopolistic Competition

One of the most important ways that the monopolistic competitor can differentiate his good or service from those of his competitors is by advertising. "Best food in town," "Reliable Service," "No Waiting," and "Free Delivery," are all ways of letting potential customers know why his firm is better than the competition.

In recent decades law firms that specialize in personal injury claims have aggressively advertised their expertise. Here is a sampling of ads taken from the Brooklyn Verizon Yellow Pages:

- Serious Injury? We come to you—home or hospital. No fee unless successful.
- Get Money for Your Injuries. No Fee Unless You Collect.
- Get the cash that you deserve.
- Accident with a truck? Make them pay!

While these ads may seem a little undignified for attorneys, they *do* get results. The ads inform potential customers of the availability of their services, and that customers won't have to pay anything unless they win their lawsuits. Of course the attorneys get to keep a large slice of any settlement they might win, but that's another story.

Advertising not only provides information about a good or service and stimulates sales, but it helps a new firm break into the business. A drugstore might paper the neighborhood with circulars and advertise in the local paper. A gas station might place an oil change discount coupon on the windshield of every parked car in the vicinity. So in general, advertising can level the playing field, enabling the new kid on the block to compete head-to-head with his more established rivals.

But advertising, of course, does have a downside. It can be quite bothersome finding circulars on your windshield or strewn on your front walk, and being bombarded by commercials on the radio and TV. But perhaps worse still, advertising can substantially boost the cost—and, consequently, the price—of a good or service. In a worst case scenario, we might have dozens of monopolistic competitors whose ubiquitous ads end up canceling each other without boosting sales. And the consumers end up getting stuck with the bill in the form of higher prices.

The Typical Monopolistic Competitor

Nearly all business firms in the United States are monopolistic competitors. They are monopolistic rather than perfect competitors because, in the mind of the buyer, their products are differentiated from one another. The monopolistic element is the uniqueness of each seller.

You walk into your neighborhood tavern. By the time you have bellied up to the bar, your drink is waiting for you. OK, so it's only a Diet Coke with a twist of lemon. It's the thought that counts. The bartender, by silently placing your usual in front of your spot at the bar has announced, "This woman is one of my regulars. She doesn't even have to say anything. I know what she drinks, and I know where she likes to sit."

The bartender has accorded you a certain status, a sense of belonging. It's something the perfect competitor can't provide, unless, of course, *all* bars happen to do this. Walk into a strange bar and see whether the bartender puts a drink down in front of you before you've ordered. If this happens—*and* if it's what you always order—then that drink's on me.

Each monopolistic competitor attempts to set his firm apart from the competition. The main way of doing this is through advertising. As we saw in the "Demand" chapter, when this is done successfully, the demand curve faced by the monopolistic competitor becomes more vertical or inelastic. Buyers are willing to pay more for this product because they believe it's wonderful. Or they'll undergo acts of great physical endurance: "I'd walk a mile for a Camel."

The monopolistic competitor tries to set his or her product apart from the competition.

Typical monopolistic competitors are grocery stores, drugstores, restaurants and fast-food emporiums, gas stations, hardware stores, 99-cent stores, dry cleaners and laundries, (small) accounting and law firms, doctors, dentists, electricians, plumbers, and all the other small businesses you'd see along any Main Street, USA. Each has many competitors, and each produces a differentiated product.

Think of all the 7-Elevens, diners, coffee shops, greasy spoons, beauty parlors and barbershops, mom-and-pop groceries and general stores, bars, hamburger joints, and millions of other tiny retail stores where people spend time eating, drinking, getting

---

Why Service Stinks*

How many times have you called a company's service number and gotten a prerecorded message when you needed to talk to a live person? How many times have you been put on hold for 20 minutes because "all our representatives are currently assisting other customers"?[†] Why *does* service stink? It's simple, explains *Business-Week:* Providing a live person costs a lot more than playing a recording.

And it's a question of who is calling. "The top 20 percent of customers at a typical commercial bank generate up to six times as much revenue as they cost, while the bottom fifth costs three to four times more than they make for the company."[‡] So you want to keep your best customers happy while sometimes doing everything you can to lose your least desirable customers. To do this, many large compa-

nies have set up two-tier, three-tier, or even four-tier customer service departments. For example, one New England electric utility provides its top 350 business clients with six customer-service representatives. The next tier of 700 is handled by six more, and the next 30,000 have just two reps to service their needs. And the remaining 300,000 residential customers at the lowest end? They get an 800 number with a recorded message.

---

*BusinessWeek, October 23, 2000, cover story.

[†]There's a great website which shows you how to cut through all those automated menus and talk directly with a fellow human. Go to www.gethuman.com and click on FAQ for a listing of the phone numbers of prompts of hundreds of large companies.

[‡]*BusinessWeek,* op. cit., p. 126.

---

groomed, or picking up a couple of everyday household items. Most of them dispense one thing, and you won't find it on the menu. It's local gossip. People stop by in the morning with last night's news, and later that afternoon they come to pick up that day's latest scoop. If you lived in a small town, where would *you* rather do business?

You eat in one luncheonette rather than any of the others because the counterman talks to you while you're having lunch or the waitress keeps your coffee cup filled. You prefer one grocery because they'll take your order over the phone. You'd rather shop in a particular drugstore because it has a much more cheerful atmosphere than all the other drugstores in town.

Small businesses often provide better service than larger businesses, mainly because they can provide personal contact (see the box, "Why Service Stinks"). When you have a problem, you can go right to the top and talk directly with the boss (which is especially easy when it's a one-person business). You are dealing with a live human being rather than a computer-based mailing, a recorded message, or an unnavigable website.

Why do business at one store rather than at its competitors?

Ambience, cleanliness, personal attention, convenience of location, easy credit, free delivery service, and good service in general are all reasons why buyers might shop at one store rather than at its competitors. Thus product differentiation does not necessarily mean there are any physical differences among the products. They might all be the same, but how they're sold may make all the difference.

On the other hand, there are, of course, some very real physical product differences. Different brands of orange juice, beer, cigars, ice cream, and hamburgers *do* taste different and *are* different in physical composition. Buyers often differentiate based on real physical differences among products. But differentiation takes place only in the buyer's mind, and it may or may not be based on real physical differences.

Price Discrimination

Price discrimination[1] sounds like a terrible thing, something that violates our basic constitutional rights. Sometimes it's bad, and other times it's not bad at all. In fact, price discrimination is often a disguised subsidy to the poor.

Definition of price discrimination

Price discrimination occurs when a seller charges two or more prices for the same good or service. Doctors often charge rich patients 10 times what they charge poor

---

[1]Although price discrimination is generally associated with monopolists, you don't have to be a monopolist—or even a very large firm—to engage in price discrimination.

patients for the same service. Airlines sometimes allow riders under 16 years of age to fly for half the regular fair ("youthfare").

Like elsewhere, restaurants near the retirement communities of South Florida are busier during mealtimes. To create more business during slack time, many offer their "blue plate specials," which are low-priced meals served before 5 P.M., or, in some cases, before 6 P.M. So now the restaurants are filled with senior citizens, many of whom would have been unwilling and/or unable to pay the prices on the regular dinner menu. This arrangement works out well for buyers and sellers. The buyers get to dine out for less money, while the sellers get more business during slack time.

The most notorious example of price discrimination was probably that of A&P markets during the 1940s. A&P had three grades of canned goods: A, B, and C. Grade A was presumably of the highest quality, B was fairly good, and C was—well, C was edible. My mother told me that she always bought grade A, even though it was the most expensive. Nothing but the best for our family.

My parents were friendly with another family in the neighborhood. The husband, a man in his early 50s, found out he had stomach cancer. "Aha!" exclaimed my mother, "Mrs. S. always bought grade C!"

A few years later the Federal Trade Commission (FTC) prohibited A&P from selling grades A, B, and C. The FTC didn't do this because of Mr. S.'s stomach cancer, but because there was absolutely no difference among the grades.

Why did A&P go to all this trouble to concoct such an elaborate subterfuge? Because by creating separate grades of canned peas, corn, beans, and other foods, it was able to reap tens of millions of dollars in profits.

The firm that practices price discrimination needs to be able to distinguish between two or more separate groups of buyers. The doctor clearly does this when she sizes up the patient's ability to pay, so when you go to the doctor, wear your most raggedy clothes, ask whether food stamps are accepted, and be sure to say you're a college student.

To practice price discrimination, you need to be able to
(1) distinguish between at least two sets of buyers and
(2) prevent one set of buyers from reselling the product to another set.

In addition to distinguishing among separate groups of buyers, the price discriminator must be able to prevent buyers from reselling the product (i.e., stop those who buy at a low price from selling to those who would otherwise buy at a higher price).[2] If the 15-and-a-half-year-old buys an airline ticket at half fare and resells it to someone who is 35 years old, the airline loses money. Most 15-and-a-half-year-olds don't have lots of money, so the special fare is a way of filling an otherwise empty seat; but when the 35-year-old flies half-fare and would have been willing to pay full fare, the airline loses money. In the case of A&P, there was no problem preventing the grade C customers from reselling their food to the grade A customers because shoppers voluntarily separated themselves into these markets.

We've been talking about how the monopolistic competitor can increase his profits by practicing price discrimination. Let's work out an example to show how he actually manages to do this. To keep things simple we're assuming he has constant returns to scale. So he can increase his output from 1 to 200 at the same average total cost of $4. Consequently his marginal cost between each of those outputs is also $4.

In Figure 5, we see that he maximizes his profit at an output 45. Go ahead and calculate his profit.

Solution:

$$\text{Profit} = (\text{Price} - \text{ATC}) \times \text{Output}$$
$$= (\$7 - \$4) \times 45$$
$$= \$3 \times 45$$
$$= \$135$$

Figure 6 shows what happens when this monopolistic competitor practices price discrimination by charging $8 to one group of buyers (panel a) and $6.50 to a second group

---

[2]Remember when you passed your 12th birthday and could no longer get into the movies at the children's price? Did you ever get a younger-looking kid to buy your ticket for you and try to pass yourself off as under 12 to the ticket taker? What? You *still* do it?

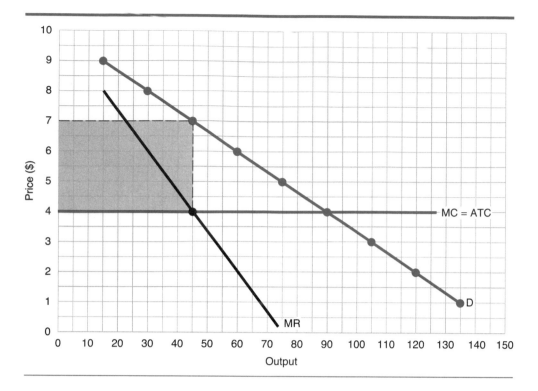

Figure 5
Monopolistic Competitor Charging One Price

of buyers (panel b). You'll notice that the buyers paying the higher price have a less elastic demand curve than the buyers paying the lower price.

First calculate the profit the monopolistic competitor earns by charging $8 to the buyers in panel a.

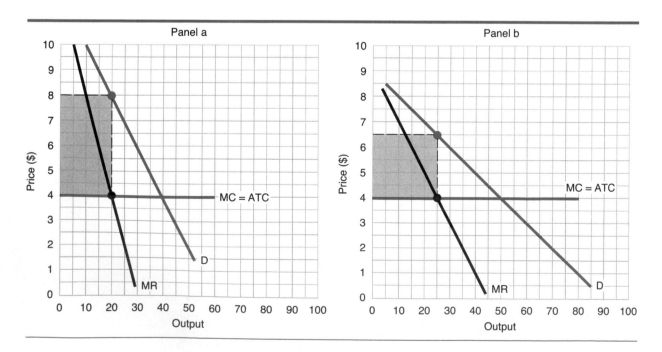

Figure 6
Monopolistic Competitor Practicing Price Discrimination

Solution:

$$\begin{aligned}
\text{Profit} &= (\text{Price} - \text{ATC}) \times \text{Output} \\
&= (\$8 - \$4) \times 20 \\
&= \$4 \times 20 \\
&= \$80
\end{aligned}$$

Now calculate the profit he earns by charging $6.50 to the buyers in panel b.

Solution:

$$\begin{aligned}
\text{Profit} &= (\text{Price} - \text{ATC}) \times \text{Output} \\
&= (\$6.50 - \$4) \times 25 \\
&= \$2.50 \times 25 \\
&= \$62.50
\end{aligned}$$

If this monopolistic competitor made a profit of $80 from the first group of buyers and $62.50 from the second group of buyers, his total profit comes to $142.50. Had he not practiced price discrimination (see Figure 5), he would have charged all buyers the same price, $7, and earned a total profit of just $135. By separating his markets and charging two different prices, he increased his profit by $7.50.

Let's return again to those airlines. How come a flight from New York to Houston costs three times as much if you don't stay over on Saturday night? You probably figured out that, since business travelers want to get home on weekends, the airlines can charge them more. This is clear-cut price discrimination. But the airlines know they can get away with this because business travel and leisure travel are two separate markets. Imagine if the airlines and other practitioners of price discrimination knew their markets so well that each customer's demand schedule became a separate market. This would make possible *perfect price discrimination* (see the box, "Perfect Price Discrimination").

Before the advent of Medicare, Medicaid, HMOs, and private health insurance, doctors customarily practiced price discrimination. But they did so in a very good way. They usually charged their relatively rich patients as much as ten times more than they did their poorer patients. In essence, the rich were subsidizing the poor. Was their medical treatment the same? Pretty much, although maybe the doctors didn't always order expensive lab work for the poorer patients. And, of course, doctors may have spent a bit more time schmoozing with the wealthier patients.

To a lesser degree storeowners also practiced price discrimination—again in a good way. The poor were often extended credit, lower prices, and even freebies. This type of price discrimination is much less in evidence today. But you can get a pretty good idea of how it worked 60, 70, and 80 years ago by watching old movies like *The Last Angry Man* (in which Paul Muni played an aging doctor who continued practicing in a neighborhood that had grown increasingly poor) and *To Kill a Mockingbird* (in which Gregory Peck plays a depression-era Georgia lawyer who accepted farm produce for legal fees).

The next time you see or hear the words, new introductory offer, the chances are good that these are the words of a price discriminator. The company is offering new customers a special deal that is not available to old customers (see the box, "New Customers Get Better Deals than Old Customers").

There are vending machines that now charge more for a can of soda on a hot day than on other days. Would *you* be willing to pay a higher price on a hot day? Because of consumer protests, the Coca-Cola Company put off installing these machines in the United States.

Price discrimination is woven into our economic fabric, and in most cases it is basically a mechanism for rationing scarce goods and services. For example, because nearly everyone seems to want to go to the movies at eight on Saturday night, the theaters

ADVANCED WORK

Perfect Price Discrimination

If price discrimination were carried to its logical conclusion, we would have perfect price discrimination. Every buyer in the market would lose his or her entire consumer surplus in the process.

Let's review the definition of consumer surplus, which was discussed in the "Theory of Consumer Behavior" chapter: *Consumer surplus is the difference between what you pay for some good or service and what you would have been willing to pay.* We'll start with a very simple situation. Amanda is willing to pay $30 for a pair of jeans, and Kristin is willing to pay $25. If the seller were to charge $20, then Amanda would enjoy a consumer surplus of $10 and Kristin would enjoy one of $5. But if the seller *knew* how much each woman was willing to pay for a pair of jeans, and if the seller were able to tell Amanda that the price was $30 and tell Kristin separately that the price was $25, he would completely eliminate their consumer surpluses.

Now we'll add another wrinkle. Suppose Amanda is willing to pay $30 for the first pair of jeans and $20 for the second. And suppose Kristin is willing to pay $25 for the first pair and $15 for the second. If the seller knew this and was able to take advantage of this information, he would charge Amanda $30 for the first pair and $20 for the second. And Kristin would be charged $25 for the first pair and $15 for the second.

Now we'll wind things up. Imagine there are 20 buyers in the market for jeans. The seller has somehow found out exactly how much each pair of jeans is worth to each of the buyers. By charging them *exactly* those prices, he will have managed to carry out perfect price discrimination. Of course, it would be virtually impossible to carry out price discrimination on such a large scale. But when you think about all those ridiculous sets of rules the airlines set up—tickets must be purchased 7 or 14 or 21 days in advance, no refunds, no changes, and you've got to stay over for at least one Saturday night—what they're really trying to do is squeeze out as much of their customers' consumer surpluses as they can.

encourage moviegoers to see films at other times by charging considerably less. But the main motivation for price discrimination is, of course, to raise profits. If price discrimination were carried to its logical conclusion, we would have perfect price discrimination.

New Customers Get Better Deals than Old Customers

There are many cases where new customers get a better deal than old customers do. This is true for sales from the Victoria's Secret catalog: The company's computerized records tell it when you last bought. The catalog offers lower prices if your last purchase was a long time ago. Similarly, this week Roadrunner cable modems are offering a $19.95 monthly price for three months (instead of the usual $44.95) if you sign on now. Both represent good examples of pure demand-based **price discrimination:** The good or service offered is identical, and the only difference between customers is how wedded to the good or service they appear to be. The companies assume that frequent buyers or long-term users will buy anyway and thus they have an **inelastic demand.** Another precondition for price discrimination is met too: The companies are sure beforehand that the low-priced good or service—the lingerie or the high-speed Internet connection—will not be resold.*

*Excerpted from Daniel Hamermesh, *Economics Is Everywhere* (New York: McGraw-Hill, 2004), pp. 150–51.

Is the Monopolistic Competitor Inefficient?

It appears from our analysis of the long-run position of the monopolistic competitor in Figure 3 that the firm does not produce at the minimum point of its ATC curve. Economists criticize monopolistic competition as wasteful on two counts: too many firms in the industry and overdifferentiation.

Are there too many firms in monopolistically competitive industries?

Are there too many beauty parlors? Not if you want to get your hair done on Friday or Saturday afternoon. Too many gas stations? Not when there are gas lines. Too many Chinese restaurants? Not on Sundays. Are there too many grocery stores and too many real estate offices? Only when they're not busy. But most business firms, which apparently carry excess capacity during certain times of the day or the week, are set up to handle peak loads, so there aren't necessarily too many monopolistic competitors.

With respect to the second criticism, is there really overdifferentiation? Perhaps there don't seem to be substantial differences among grocery stores, drugstores, luncheonettes, dry cleaners, and ice-cream parlors, but consider the alternative. Consider the drab monotony of the stores in much of Eastern Europe, including the old Soviet Union. Maybe this lack of differentiation, this standardization, enables the sellers to cut costs somewhat. But is it worth it?

What are you *really* buying when you go to a fancy restaurant? Surely not just a meal. Undoubtedly you'll order something on a somewhat higher culinary plane than a Big Mac, large fries, and a Coke, but is that meal worth $80? It is when it is served by a waiter with a phony French accent, there are flowers on your table, a nice linen tablecloth, candlelight, soft music, and a solicitous maitre d', plus the restaurant is a restored 18th-century carriage house. (See Current Issue, "Selling Status," on the next page.)

Monopolistic competition, with its attendant product differentiation, may be viewed as wasteful and inefficient, and a case can easily be made that it is. Think of all the money spent on advertising, packaging, marketing, and sales promotion, as well as interiors, facades, and window displays. These expenses add perhaps 10 or 20 percent to the prices of most things we buy; so we may well ask, Is it worth it? *You* decide.

I'll bet you're saying to yourself, "There he goes again, copping out and passing the buck." And you're right. You see, the buck stops with you because it's *your* buck and it's *your* decision about how to spend it.

Do you want to spend it on advertising, ambience, service, and convenience, or are you basically a no-frills person? Do you usually buy no-frills brands in the supermarket, fly coach rather than first-class, drive an economy car, and consider dinner in a fast-food emporium "eating out"? If you have answered yes to each of these questions, you are indeed a no-frills person who knows the value of a dollar.

However, if you answered no to all the above, you are clearly a person of refined taste and high style—a very *au courant* person (that's French for "up-to-date"). Whether we like it or not, product differentiation is the way monopolistic competitors compete. And whether we're aware of it or not, our entire environment is flavored by product differentiation. Imagine that next December every commercial Christmas display is done in black and white. Imagine what our supermarkets would look like with all black-and-white boxes, jars, and cans. And imagine what people would look like if they all wore the same styles and colors. In a word, product differentiation adds flavor, texture, and variety to our lives. Whether we want to pay the price is a matter of individual taste.

The product differentiation engendered by monopolistic competition is a strong counterforce to the McDonaldization of America. In the opening paragraph of a book review, Karal Ann Marling paints a vivid picture of our country.

> One source of a pervasive millennial malaise is the perception that American life has come down to a couple of monster corporations selling the same Gap chinos and Egg McMuffins on every corner, from sea to shining sea—that the rich pageantry of the national folklife, in all its pungent variety, has played itself out in a roadside litter of discarded clamshell burger boxes and chicken buckets. Every city looks just the same, its presence marked upon the landscape not by impressive civic monuments but by a garishly lighted corridor of brand-name drive-ins, pointing the way from the Interstate to an all but abandoned urban center: McDonald's, Arby's, Wendy's, Taco Bell, Pizza Hut. Topeka or Syracuse, Cheyenne or Memphis—only the order of the pseudo-haciendas and the golden arches changes.[3]

Finally, let's consider the nature of competition. Monopolistic competitors *do* compete with respect to price, but they compete still more vigorously with respect to ambience, service, and the rest of the intangibles that attract customers. In this arena American

A hamburger by any other name costs twice as much.

—Evan Esar

Is monopolistic competition wasteful and inefficient?

Can you imagine a no-frills world?

---

[3]Karal Ann Marling, "Sameness Is Glorious," *New York Times Book Review,* December 26, 1999, p. 34.

business does engage in lively, innovative competition. The next time you're walking along a shopping street, take note of how the storekeepers try to entice you with their window displays. To the degree that they're successful, they have induced you to differentiate their products from all the others. That is what monopolistic competition is all about.

Current Issue: Selling Status

Starbucks does a great job selling status, along with its coffee and hot chocolate. You can pay $2.20 for a hot chocolate or $3.20 for a white chocolate mocha. Why the dollar price differential? After all, how much more does it cost to make the white chocolate mocha than to make the plain hot chocolate? Maybe a few cents. Tim Harford observes that "By charging wildly different prices for products that have largely the same cost, Starbucks is able to smoke out customers who are less sensitive about the price."[4]

Harford also asks why airport departure areas across the world are so shoddy. Or why the stewardesses stand ready to physically restrain coach passengers who attempt to leave a plane before the last first-class passenger has left the aircraft. The first-class passengers paid for first-class treatment. If everyone is treated first class, there'd be no point in paying a premium price.

You can buy a perfectly good wrist watch in Walgreen's or Rite Aid for less than $15, one that will tell time just as accurately as one of those fancy watches for which people pay over $10,000. If you took a blind taste, you could probably find a bunch of chocolates that you liked as well as Godivas—but cost much less than $45 a pound. And if you're a clever shopper, maybe you do your Christmas shopping at discount stores and use wrapping paper from Tiffany's.

Have you ever thought about opening a restaurant? Restaurants are getting to be pretty complicated places considering that local laws usually dictate that you segregate your diners by smoking preference (pro or con). Why not segregate *your* diners by *status*?

That's *right*! We've got a table for two in our low-status section. What's that? Oh, there's a 15-minute wait for a high-status table. What's the difference? Well, if you need to ask, then you probably *belong* in the low-status section.

Do the high-status diners get better food? No, the food's the same. And the service? The same. Then what *is* the difference? Price. That's right—we charge twice as much for the same food and service in the high-status section as in the low-status section.

How can we get away with that? It's easy. Everyone knows who's in which section. We know the cheapos and the big spenders, the tightwads and the sports.

Why are people willing to pay twice as much for the same food and the same service? They're paying for status. And by selling status, you can really boost your profits. So go ahead and open your restaurant. And save a nice table for me. In which section? I'll give you three guesses.

Questions for Further Thought and Discussion

1. In what respects does a monopolistic competitor differ from a perfect competitor?
2. Explain why the monopolistic competitor breaks even in the long run.
3. Is the monopolistic competitor inefficient? Try to argue the question from both sides.
4. What are the two necessary conditions under which price discrimination can take place? Give an example of price discrimination.
5. Do monopolistically competitive industries have too many firms, each of which produces too little?

[4]Tim Harford, *The Undercover Economist* (New York: Oxford University Press, 2006), p. 35.

6. Are you in favor of price discrimination or against it? Try to argue pro and con.

7. What are the ways in which a firm can differentiate its product from those of its competitors?

8. *Practical Application:* Make a list of five firms with whom you or your family members have done business this week. Which are monopolistic competitors?

9. *Practical Application:* Suppose you just purchased a men's clothing store in a huge shopping mall. How would you differentiate your store's wares from those of your competitors?

10. *Practical Application:* If you ran a restaurant located very near several retirement communities, how would you practice price discrimination? Hint: Did someone just say "Early Bird Special," or was that "Blue Plate Dinner"?

Name _____   Date _____

Multiple-Choice Questions

Circle the letter that corresponds to the best answer.

1. Monopolistic competition differs from perfect competition only with respect

   to _____. (LO2)
   a) the number of firms in the industry
   b) product differentiation
   c) barriers to entry
   d) economies of scale

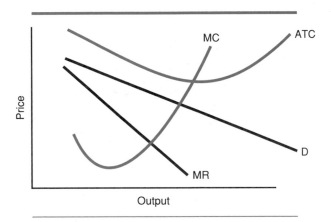

Figure 1

2. In the long run the monopolistic competitor in

   Figure 1 is _____. (LO1, 5)
   a) more efficient than the perfect competitor
   b) less efficient than the perfect competitor
   c) as efficient as the perfect competitor

3. In the short run the monopolistic competitor will be

   _____. (LO1)
   a) definitely making a profit
   b) definitely taking a loss
   c) definitely breaking even
   d) either taking a loss or making a profit

4. In the long run the monopolistic competitor will be

   _____. (LO1)
   a) making a profit   c) breaking even
   b) taking a loss

5. Each of the following would be a form of price

   discrimination *except* _____. (LO4)
   a) providing low-priced meals to senior citizens who dine before 6 P.M.
   b) charging higher airfares to business travelers than to vacationers
   c) charging one high price to all customers
   d) charging adults more than children for movie admissions

6. Product differentiation can take place

   _____. (LO2)
   a) only if there are physical differences among the products
   b) only if there are no physical differences among the products
   c) whether or not there are physical differences among the products

7. Which statement is true? (LO3)
   a) When you decide which doctor to go to, your only concern is the quality of the medical service you will receive.
   b) People differentiate among goods and services based not only on physical differences but also on ambience, convenience, and service.
   c) Monopolistic competitors are usually large firms.
   d) None of these statements is true.

8. Which of the following would not be a monopolistic competitor? (LO3)
   a) Thursa Sotak's hair salon
   b) Keith and Cathi Collins' mom-and-pop grocery store
   c) Adam Avischious, a storefront lawyer
   d) Kelley's family restaurant owned by Robin Kelley, Caroline Kelley, and Claire Kelley
   e) All are monopolistic competitors.

9. Which statement about price discrimination is true? (LO4)
   a) It generally hurts the poor.
   b) It is inherently evil.
   c) It involves charging at least two separate prices for the same good or service.
   d) It generally involves deceiving the consumer.

10. Each of the following is an example of price discrimination except _____. (LO4)
    a) airline "youthfares"
    b) higher-price movie tickets after 5:00 P.M. and on weekends
    c) doctors charging more to patients who need lab tests
    d) A&P's old grades A, B, and C

11. In the long run in monopolistic competition _____. (LO1)
    a) most firms make a profit
    b) the absence of entry barriers ensures that there are no profits
    c) economies of scale ensure that there are no profits
    d) most firms lose money

12. Which statement is true? (LO1, 3)
    a) Most firms in the United States are monopolistic competitors.
    b) Most firms in the United States are perfect competitors.
    c) Most consumers would prefer lower prices and less product differentiation.
    d) None of these statements is true.

13. Perfect price discrimination eliminates _____ of the customer's consumer surplus. (LO4)
    a) all   b) most   c) some   d) none

14. Which statement is true about perfect price discrimination? (LO4)
    a) It is very common.
    b) It is illegal.
    c) The larger the market, the more likely one is to find it.
    d) None of these statements is true.

15. Price discrimination _____. (LO4)
    a) often works to the advantage of the poor
    b) generally helps rich customers
    c) is very hard to find in the United States
    d) is illegal in the United States

16. Under perfect price discrimination _____. (LO4)
    a) consumer surplus is zero
    b) consumer surplus is maximized
    c) consumer surplus is a constant no matter what price is charged
    d) consumer surplus rises as price is lowered

Fill-In Questions

1. The most crucial feature of monopolistic competition is _____. (LO3)

2. A monopolistic competitor makes a profit only in the _____. (LO1)

3. The monopolistic competitor's demand curve slopes _____. (LO1)

4. Price discrimination occurs when a seller charges _____ for the same good or service. (LO4)

5. The monopolistic competitor _____ produces at the minimum point of his or her ATC curve. (LO5)

Problems

1. Given the information in Figure 2, how much profit does this monopolistic competitor make? (LO1)

2. Is the firm in Figure 2 operating in the short run or the long run? How do you know? (LO1)

3. Draw a graph of a monopolistic competitor in the long run on a piece of graph paper. (LO1)

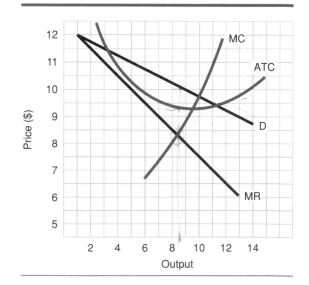

Figure 2

Chapter 12

Oligopoly

The prefix *oli* means "few." An oligarchy is a government controlled by only a few rulers. An oligopoly is an industry controlled by only a few firms.

In the previous chapter I mentioned that over 99 percent of our business firms are monopolistic competitors. In this chapter, we'll be talking about oligopolies, which are industries dominated by just a few firms. How do you explain how oligopolists, that constitute less than 1 percent of all business firms, produce most of our output of goods and services?

The answer is some oligopolists are very large firms—like Dell, IBM, Walt Disney, McDonald's, United Parcel Service, and ExxonMobil. So it would be accurate to say that our economy is dominated by large oligopolists. In this chapter we'll see how they compete among themselves.

LEARNING OBJECTIVES

After reading this chapter you should be able to:

1. Define and measure concentration ratios and the Herfindahl-Hirschman index.
2. Describe and discuss the competitive spectrum.
3. Analyze the kinked demand curve.
4. Explain and discuss administered prices.
5. Experiment with game theory.
6. Discuss the effects of cutthroat competition in the college textbook market.

Oligopoly Defined

An oligopoly is an industry with just a few sellers. How few? So few that at least one firm is large enough to influence price.

Oligopoly is the prevalent type of industrial competition in the United States as well as in most of Europe, Japan, and southeast Asia. Table 1 lists some of the more important American industries that are oligopolies. Perhaps two-thirds of our GDP is accounted for by firms in oligopolistic industries.

Is the product identical or differentiated? It doesn't matter. In the case of the steel, copper, and aluminum industries, the product happens to be identical; but in most other industries, the product is differentiated.

The crucial factor under oligopoly is the small number of firms in the industry. Because there are so few firms, every competitor must think continually about the actions of its rivals. What each does could make or break the others. Thus there is a kind of interdependence among oligopolists.

> An oligopoly is an industry with just a few sellers.

> Is product identical or differentiated?

TABLE 1 Concentration Ratios in Selected Industries, 2010

Industry	Largest Firms	Concentration Ratio
Airlines*	Continental/United, Delta, American, Southwest	63
Beverages	Coca-Cola, Pepsi, Anheuser-Busch, Coors	90
College Textbooks	Cengage, McGraw-Hill, Pearson	72
Computer Software	Microsoft, Oracle, Computer Assoc. Int., Compuware	60
Energy	Duke, Reliant, Utilicorp, Avista	45
Entertainment	Walt Disney, Viacom, Clear Channel, USA Networks	55
Food Production	IBP, Archer Daniels Midland, Farmland Industries, Tyson Foods	55
Food Services	McDonald's, Tricon, Darden, Wendy's	43
Forest and Paper Products	International Paper, Georgia-Pacific, Weyerhaeuser, Kimberly-Clark	58
Mail, Package, and Freight Delivery	United Parcel Service, FedEx, Pittston, Airborne Freight	85
Motor Vehicles	General Motors, Ford, Toyota, Honda	63
Personal Computers	Dell, Hewlett-Packard, Acer, Apple	72
Petroleum Refining	ExxonMobil, Texaco, Chevron, USX	67
Pipelines	Enron, Dynegy, El Paso, Williams	82
Railroads	Union Pacific, Burlington No. Santa Fe, CSX, Norfolk Southwestern	80
Telecommunications	AT&T, Verizon, SBC, Worldcom	56
Tobacco	Philip Morris, R.J. Reynolds, Universal	95
Wholesalers: Food and Grocery	Supervalue, Sysco, Fleming, Genex	68
Wholesalers: Health Care	McKesson HBOC, Cardinal Health, Berger Brunswig, Amerisource Health	84

*Delta and Northwest merged in 2008 to form the world's largest airline. The merged company is called Delta. In May 2010, Continental and United merged—subject to the approval of the Justice Department—to replace Delta as the world's largest airline.

Sources: www.census.gov/epcd/www/concentration.html; scattered sources used by author.

Because the graph of the oligopolist is similar to that of the monopolist, we will analyze it in exactly the same manner with respect to price, output, profit, and efficiency. Price is higher than the minimum point of the ATC curve, and output is somewhat to the left of this point. And so, just like the monopolist, the oligopolist has a higher price and a lower output than does the perfect competitor.

The oligopolist, like the monopolist and unlike the perfect competitor and monopolistic competitor, makes a profit. Because the oligopolist does not produce at the minimum point of its ATC curve, it is not as efficient as the perfect competitor.

We're going to consider a whole range of oligopolistic models, from close collusion to cutthroat competition. But first, let's look at concentration ratios and the Herfindahl-Hirschman index, two measures of the degree of oligopoly in various industries.

Two Measures of the Degree of Oligopolization

Looking at the percentage share of sales of the leading firms is one way of measuring how concentrated an industry is. This is called the industry's concentration ratio. A second way to measure this is to calculate the Herfindahl-Hirschman index, which, it turns out, is a lot easier to do than to say.

Concentration Ratios

Economists use concentration ratios as a quantitative measure of oligopoly. *The total percentage share of industry sales of the four leading firms is the industry concentration ratio.* Industries with high ratios are very oligopolistic.

How much is the concentration ratio for an industry whose four largest firms produce, respectively, 10, 8, 7, and 5 percent of the industry's output? Work it out right here:

The total percentage share of industry sales of the four leading firms is the industry concentration ratio.

Just add them together to get 30.

The concentration ratios in Table 1 range from 43 in food services to 95 in tobacco. Railroads, pipelines, health care wholesalers, and mail, package, and freight delivery are all in the 80s. Remember that the concentration ratio is the total percentage share of industry sales of the four leading firms.

Two key shortcomings of concentration ratios should be noted. First, they don't include imports. For example, in the motor vehicle industry, with a concentration ratio of 63, imported cars and light trucks account for about one-third of the American market. Although Toyota and Honda are listed among the top four American automakers, the concentration ratio does not take into account over 1 million Japanese imports, not to mention the hundreds of thousands of Volkswagens, Saabs, BMWs, Audis, Jaguars, Porsches, and Rolls Royces the United States also imports.

Two key shortcomings

Concentration ratios have become less meaningful as foreign imports have increased. For instance, we get 80 percent of our consumer electronics and two thirds of our oil from abroad, so concentration ratios in these industries are meaningless. Perhaps in a world with unrestricted international trade, which would make our world a veritable global village, we could replace national concentration ratios with international concentration ratios. In the meantime we'll go with what we have in Table 1.

The second shortcoming is that the concentration ratios tell us nothing about the competitive structure of the rest of the industry. Are the remaining firms all relatively large, as in the cigarette industry, which has a total of just 13 firms, or are they small, as in the aircraft and engine parts industry, which totals about 190 firms? This distinction *perbedaan* is important because when the remaining firms are large, they are not as easily dominated by the top four as are dozens of relatively small firms.

The American automobile industry, which was long a classic example of oligopoly, has been changing drastically in recent years (see the box, "Oligopoly in the Automobile Industry"). Not only have imports made a substantial impact, but foreign-owned companies now make over half the cars made in the United States. The imports have made the automobile industry's concentration ratio much less relevant, while the transplants have been reducing that ratio. But these developments have been an unmitigated boon to the car buyer, who is reaping the benefits of lower prices and much higher quality.

As globalization proceeds, we also need to look at the degree of concentration in the world market for various goods. Almost 75 percent of the global market in iron ore is controlled by just three firms. Owens Illinois alone has rolled up roughly half the global capacity to supply glass containers. General Electric builds 60 percent of large gas turbines as well as 60 percent of large wind turbines. Even in sneakers, Nike and Adidas split a 60 percent share of the global market.

The Herfindahl-Hirschman Index (HHI)

The Herfindahl-Hirschman index (HHI) is *the sum of the squares of the market shares of each firm in the industry.* We'll start with a monopoly. One firm has all the sales, or 100 percent of the market share. So its HHI would be 100^2, or $100 \times 100 = 10,000$.

The Herfindahl-Hirschman index is the sum of the squares of the market shares of each firm in the industry.

Now that's some big Herfindahl-Hirschman index! In fact, they just don't come any bigger than that. What is the HHI of *every* monopoly? That's right—it's 10,000.

Oligopoly in the Automobile Industry

The automobile industry has long been considered the archetypal American oligopoly. Until the arrival of Volkswagen in Pennsylvania (which closed up shop in 1988), followed by the six Japanese "transplants," the entire industry consisted of just four firms. More than 95 percent of our cars were made by the Big Three—General Motors, Ford, and Chrysler—and the rest by American Motors, which has since merged with Chrysler. So until very recently the American automobile industry had a concentration ratio of 100.

But there were two major changes during the last three decades. The first was set off by the gasoline shortages we had in 1973 (the Arab oil embargo) and in 1979 (the Iranian Revolution). The higher gas prices that followed made fuel-efficient cars—particularly Japanese cars—much more attractive to the American buyer. Imports, which had been limited to just 10 percent of the market, shot up to about 30 percent by the mid-1980s.

Of equal long-run significance to the industry has been the advent of the Japanese transplants, which began setting up assembly lines during the 1980s. Today foreign owned firms assemble 54.6 percent of the motor vehicles produced in the U.S. And once again, we're back to the Big Four—General Motors, Toyota, Ford, and Honda.

Table A   Market Share of Top Six U.S. Makers of Cars and Light Trucks, April 2010

Company	Market Share
General Motors	18.7%
Ford	17.0
Toyota	16.0
Honda	11.6
Chrysler	9.7
Nissan	6.5
Other Companies*	21.5

*Each of these other companies is a foreign company.
Source: The New York Times, May 4, 2010, p. B3.

Now *you'll* get a chance to compute a few HHIs. Find the HHI of an industry with just two firms, both of which have 50 percent market shares. Work it out right here:

Solution: $50^2 + 50^2 = 2,500 + 2,500 = 5,000$.

Now let's add another wrinkle. Find the HHI of an industry that has four firms, each with a 25 percent market share:

Solution: $25^2 + 25^2 + 25^2 + 25^2 = 625 + 625 + 625 + 625 = 2,500$.

Can you see where all this is going? The less concentrated an industry, the lower its HHI. And here's one last question. Imagine an industry with 100 firms, each with an equal market share. Without going through all the work, see if you can figure out the HHI.

It would come to 100: $1^2 + 1^2 + 1^2 \ldots + 1^2 = 100$.

The Justice Department uses the HHI to decide whether an industry is highly concentrated and considers an industry with an HHI of under 1,800 to be competitive. This measure is preferred to four-firm concentration ratios because the index is based on the shares of *all* firms in an industry.

The Competitive Spectrum

We shall now consider the possible degrees of competition, from cartels and open collusion down through cutthroat competition. These possibilities are shown in Figure 7, toward the end of this section.

Cartels

With so few firms in our basic industries, there is a strong temptation for the leading firms to band together to restrict output and, consequently, increase prices and profits. An extreme case is a cartel, where the firms behave as a monopoly in a manner similar to that of the Organization of Petroleum Exporting Countries (OPEC) in the world oil market. More formally, *a cartel is a combination of firms that acts as if it were a single firm.*

Given a certain market demand for a good or service over which an oligopoly exercises little control, firms that openly collude can control industry supply and, to a large degree, market price. For example, by withholding part or most of supply, the colluding firms can bid the market price way up. This was done by OPEC in 1973 when the price of oil quadrupled (see Figure 1).

If the cartel is able to operate successfully, securing the full support of all its members (who don't try to undercut the cartel price by selling some extra output under the table), its situation will approximate that of a monopoly. Just like a monopoly, which faces the entire market demand curve, the cartel will control the entire industry supply. OPEC, which controlled most of the world's oil exports, was able to take advantage of a relatively inelastic demand for oil by withholding supply in late 1973 and early 1974, thereby quadrupling world oil prices.

When the price of oil rises, there is a growing temptation for OPEC members to cheat by producing and selling more than their quotas. Remember that these are all sovereign nations, so unless their cheating is blatant, it will most likely go undetected. But OPEC members also have a strong incentive to *not* cheat. After all, the main purpose of their organization is to keep up the price of oil by withholding some of it from the world market. Widespread cheating would defeat that purpose. Still, in 2009 Iran, Angola, and Venezuela all far exceeded their quotas.

OPEC has a great deal of market power, but it is responsible for less than half the world's oil exports and less than one-third of all oil production. Who are its members? They are listed in Figure 2 and are mainly situated on the Persian Gulf, the world's largest known oil field. In addition to these 12 OPEC members, in recent years two other major oil exporters, Mexico and Norway, have raised and lowered production in step with the OPEC nations.

In 1999, when oil was selling at just $10 a barrel, OPEC members agreed to cut production. By March of 2000, the price of oil topped $34 a barrel.

In the summer of 2008, when the price of oil reached $147, economists grew increasingly concerned that the high cost of oil might set off a worldwide economic slowdown. Some observers thought that the oil ministers of the members of OPEC might consider

A cartel is an extreme case of oligopoly.

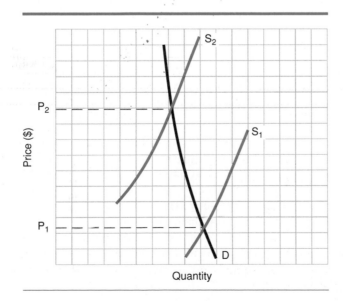

Figure 1

Withholding Supply to Raise Price

When supply is lowered from S_1 to S_2, price rises from P_1 to P_2.

F*igure* 2

Daily Output and Capacity of
12 Members of OPEC,
March 2010

Saudi Arabia is, by far, the largest
producer.

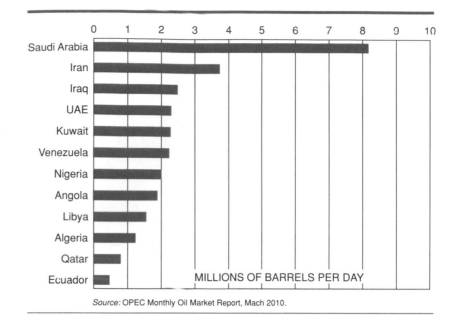

Source: OPEC Monthly Oil Market Report, Mach 2010.

increasing production to at least prevent further increases in the price of oil. But they decided against any immediate action. Their thinking was that even if most of the world went into recession, the demand for oil would not fall substantially. As it turned out, demand did fall during the severe worldwide recession, forcing the price of oil below $35 by early 2009.

Cartels have also operated locally; perhaps the most notorious example is the mob-run New York trash cartel. After a 10-year investigation of the Mafia's longtime control of the garbage-hauling industry in New York City and its northern suburbs, three men, reputedly mobsters, and 14 hauling company owners, pleaded guilty to setting up a property rights system in which they claimed the permanent right to the locations where they picked up garbage, shared profits from their contracts, and disguised their profit sharing through sham transactions and false tax returns. Two years later, the cost of garbage removal tumbled 30 to 40 percent for most of the city's 200,000 commercial buildings, restaurants, stores, private hospitals, and private schools, which have to hire commercial haulers.

on the web

To find the latest OPEC output figures, go to www.opec.org, find Publications/Reports and click on Monthly Oil Market Report. The output figures are near the end of the report.

Open Collusion

Open collusion operates like the Mafia.

Slightly less extreme than a cartel would be a territorial division of the market among the firms in the industry. This would be a division similar to that of the Mafia, if indeed there really is such an organization. An oligopolistic division of the market might go something like this. All prostitution, dope, loan-sharking, and gambling in New England is run by Steve (The Fence); New York is run by Frankie (Big Frank); Philly and Atlantic City are run by Max (Tiny); the Midwest is run by Mike (The Banker); Florida by Joey (Three Fingers); the Gulf Coast by Paddy (The Professor); the mountain states by Benny (Dog Ears); and the West Coast by Anthony (Fat Tony).

Nobody messes with anyone else's territory. The arrangement will continue until there is a new power alignment within the family or a new firm tries to enter the industry.

This cozy arrangement would give each operation a regional monopoly. On a national basis, each operation's market situation is depicted by Figure 3.

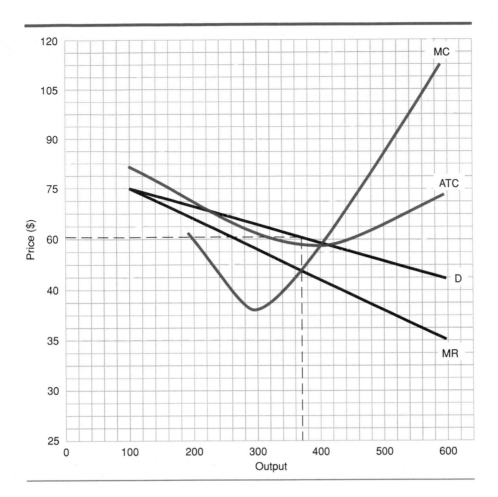

Figure 3
The Colluding Oligopolist
This graph could also belong to the monopolist or the monopolistic competitor in the short run.

You may have noticed that this graph is identical to that of a monopoly. Although the firm may have only 15 or 20 percent of the market, its pricing behavior is that of the monopolist, and the results are similar. Compared to the perfect competitor, the colluding oligopolist charges a higher price (not one equal to the minimum point of the ATC curve); has a higher ATC (and is therefore less efficient); restricts output (that is, operates to the left of the minimum point of the ATC); and finally, unlike the perfect competitor, makes a profit.

These are extreme cases, but they would be illegal, even during the last few years of less-than-stringent enforcement of the antitrust laws. Now, as we move to somewhat less extreme cases of collusion, we begin to enter the realm of reality. This brings us to the celebrated electric machinery conspiracy case.

Covert Collusion

In the late 1950s officials of General Electric, Westinghouse, Allis-Chalmers, and other leading electrical firms met periodically at various hotels and motels around the country. These secret meetings were set up to fix the prices of electric transformers, turbines, and other electrical equipment. Although government contracts were awarded based on the lowest sealed bid, the conspirators rigged the bidding so that even the lowest bid would be extremely profitable. In fact, the firms took turns making low bids. The public, too, was bilked of hundreds of millions of dollars in higher prices.

Finally, in 1961, the U.S. Supreme Court found seven high-ranking company officials guilty of illegal price-fixing and market-sharing agreements. They were given fines, which their companies took care of, and short jail sentences, during which time their salaries were paid. On release from jail each was given back his old job. Talk about tying yellow ribbons round the old oak tree!

A case of price-fixing

The Penalty Box

When a hockey player commits a flagrant foul, he's asked to sit in the penalty box. As we'll see in the next chapter, a bunch of corporate executives have received substantial prison sentences for their crimes. But not everyone found guilty of serious corporate crime goes to prison. Sometimes their companies are merely fined and they promise to mend their ways.

 That's how our system of justice generally deals with covert collusion, price fixing, and related crimes. In 1996 the Archer Daniels Midland Company pleaded guilty and paid a $100 million criminal fine for its role in two international conspiracies to fix prices to eliminate competition and allocate sales in the lysine and citric acid markets. Three former executives were sentenced to prison terms ranging from two to two-and-a-half years, and two of the three former executives were also fined $350,000 each.

In 1999 an arrangement was uncovered that fixed worldwide vitamin prices as much as 25 percent above the market level. Hoffmann-La Roche, a Swiss pharmaceutical conglomerate that controls about 40 percent of the worldwide vitamin market, settled with the U.S. Justice Department, paying a $500 million penalty. A second company, BASF AG of Germany, agreed to pay a $225 million fine for its role in the conspiracy. In 2001 the European Commission fined Hoffmann-La Roche an additional $752 million and BASF an additional $260 million.

In 2004 Schering-Plough agreed to pay $350 million in fines and plead guilty to criminal charges for selling its products to private health care providers for far less than it sold them to Medicaid. Indeed, we can probably look forward to a stream of cases involving overbilling of both Medicaid and Medicare.

As a footnote to this story, some 11 years later two of the companies involved in the 1961 case, General Electric and Westinghouse, were charged with fixing prices on turbine generators. Oh well, nobody's perfect.

In 2008, in the mother of all price-fixing cases, the European Commission (which we'll cover in more detail in the next chapter) fined the four companies controlling the European continent's auto glass market a record $1.77 billion. The French glass maker, Saint-Gobain, which paid a fine of $1.1 billion, and Pikington, a British unit of Nippon Sheet Glass of Japan fined $470 million, were found guilty of fixing prices, restricting supplies, and dividing markets in Europe. These repeat offenders had been fined the year before for fixing the prices of flat glass for buildings and homes.

Executives from the companies had met at airports and hotels in Brussels, Frankfort, and Paris to divide up the market and discuss their contracts with automakers. What happened to those employees found responsible for this illegal behavior? They did not go to jail, nor were they even fired. But they *were* demoted.

Other cases of collusion

Covert collusion, while frowned upon in the United States (see "The Penalty Box"), is often the way business is done in Asia. In Japan, the *dango* (see accompanying box) is a formal negotiating process, under which firms take turns making low bids on government construction projects. In contrast, in the United States, usually construction firms, without consulting among themselves, submit bids, and the lowest bidder will win.

Price Leadership

Playing follow-the-leader

Short of meeting in hotel rooms to set prices secretly, do oligopolists conspire in more overt fashion? Until the 1930s U.S. Steel exercised open price leadership in the steel industry. On one day U.S. Steel would post a price for a particular type of steel, and the next day Bethlehem, Republic, Armco, Inland, and the rest of the industry would post an identical price, down to the last hundredth of a cent.

At the turn of the 20th century the leaders of the major steel firms actually collectively agreed on prices at dinners held periodically by Judge Gary, president of U.S. Steel. Since those days, not only has it become much more difficult to get away with collusion, but the companies could no longer take the full cost of these dinners as tax write-offs because only 80 percent of business "entertainment" expenses are deductible.

The Dango

Covert collusion is the way much business is done in the Japanese construction industry. When the government asks for bids on a construction project, one firm will bid lower than its competitors. But they're not really competing. The firms negotiate among themselves to decide which firm will make the lowest bid and get the job. That negotiating process is *dango*.

Usually the firms take turns making the low bid. That way every company gets some of the business. But just to keep everyone happy, the low bidder actually pays each of its competitors thousands of dollars in compensation. In addition, government bureaucrats are paid off as well.

Here's how *dango* works. The government announces that it is accepting bids on a project and sets a ceiling price. After the so-called competitors confer among themselves, they make bids on the project. But the firm that has been designated to win the contract makes a bid just below the ceiling price.

What if a new firm enters the industry and bids lower? The government bureaucrats will say that this firm cannot be given the contract because it had not been awarded any previous contracts. How does the firm break in? It must pay its dues by joining the *dango*.*

---

*See John McMillan, *Reinventing the Bazaar* (New York: W. W. Norton, 2002), pp. 141–47.

Another form of price leadership that has sprung up in recent years is the setting of the prime rate of interest by the nation's leading banks. That rate might stay the same for several months until suddenly 2 of the top 10 banks raise their prime by a quarter of a percent, and within 24 hours, the rest of the nation's 7,000 banks raise theirs a quarter of a percent. What is interesting here is that rarely do the same banks change the rate two times in a row, but in virtually every instance the other banks all play follow-the-leader. Bankers and other oligopolists engaging in price leadership would have us believe that they are "locked in competition" and that the forces of supply and demand dictate the same price to everyone. But this explanation strains credulity because no two firms—and certainly not 7,000—face exactly the same demand schedules or have the same cost schedules.

The prime rate set by big banks is a form of price leadership.

When is collusion most likely to succeed? Mainly when there are few firms in the industry and when there are high barriers to entry. Basically, it's much easier to keep secrets—when you're violating the antitrust laws, you have to keep secrets—when there aren't too many people to deal with. In a far-fetched example, in the 1950s the American Communist Party was considered a group of people conspiring to advocate the violent overthrow of the American government. It turned out that several thousand of their somewhat fewer than 20,000 card-carrying members were actually FBI agents or paid informers. Some conspiracy!

Collusion is most likely to succeed when there are few firms and high barriers to entry.

Conspiracies need to be kept very small. When entry barriers, particularly capital requirements, are high enough, conspirators don't have to worry about new firms entering the industry and, presumably, being taken into the conspiracy.

Cutthroat Competition

> It is ridiculous to call this an industry. This is rat eat rat; dog eat dog. I'll kill 'em, and I'm going to kill 'em before they kill me. You're talking about the American way of survival of the fittest.
>
> –Ray Kroc (founder of McDonald's)–

Welcome to the world of cutthroat competition, the world in which oligopolistic firms take no prisoners. Although we won't be getting into industrial espionage, you can be sure that industrial spies are lurking everywhere. Each firm wants to know exactly what its competitors are doing and how they will react to any changes in price that it might initiate. The dynamics of oligopoly under cutthroat competition are very different from those of oligopoly with collusion.

Figure 4
The Kinked Demand Curve

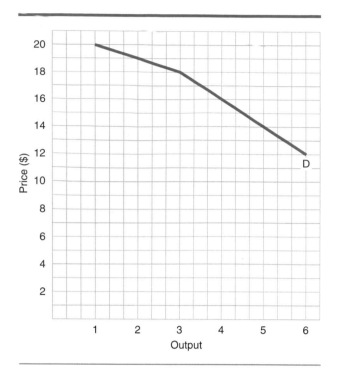

Now we deal with the extreme case of oligopolists who are cutthroat competitors, firms that do not exchange so much as a knowing wink. Each is out to maximize its profits. These oligopolists are ready to cut the throats of their competitors, figuratively speaking, of course.

The uniqueness of this situation leads us to the phenomenon of the kinked demand curve, pictured in Figure 4. For the first time in this textbook, we have a firm's demand curve that is not a straight line.

Why does the demand curve of the fiercely competing oligopolist have a kink? The answer is that it is based on the oligopolist's assumption about his rivals' behavior in response to his own actions. The oligopolist can make three possible pricing decisions: raise price, lower price, or not change price.

Suppose the price has been the same for a fairly long period of time. The oligopolist thinks about raising price. If I raise my price, what will my competitors do? Who knows? What would *I* do if one of my rivals raised her price? If I did nothing, I would get some of my rival's customers, so I wouldn't change my price.

Even though I hate to admit it, my competitors are as smart as I am, so if *my* response to a rival's price increase is to keep my price the same and get some of my rival's customers, surely my rivals would respond in the same way to my price increase. Therefore, I don't raise my price.

What about lowering my price and stealing some of my competitors' customers? Now I ask myself, how would *I* react? I'd immediately lower my price in response to a price cut by one of my competitors. And my competitors would lower their prices in response to my lowering mine. So I won't lower my price.

If I don't lower my price (because my competitors would follow) and if I don't raise my price (because my competitors won't follow), what *do* I do? Nothing. I leave my price where it is.

What makes sense for me also makes sense for my competitors. None of them will raise or lower price. We all keep price where it is, and that happens to be at the kink in the demand curve.

This explains why price does not change often under extremely competitive oligopoly. A firm is afraid to make a move for fear of what its rivals might or might not do. Underlying that fear is the memory of price wars touched off by one firm lowering its price. Hence it's better to leave well enough alone.

Fast food chains like McDonald's and Burger King are definitely cutthroat competitors. Daniel Hamermesh shows how their behavior is virtually predicted by the kinked demand curve.

> The major fast-food chains seem to be unable to break the ninety-nine-cent barrier for burger prices. The standard burger price goes above $1 occasionally, and then one of the major companies begins selling "Value Meals" or the equivalent, and the others have to cut back prices to attract customers. This is classic "kinked demand curve" behavior: If you raise your price in an oligopoly and the others don't, you lose lots of sales. (If the market were competitive, you couldn't raise price at all without losing all your sales.)[1]

Are Costco and Sam's Club cutthroat competitors? Definitely. Perhaps the classic case would be two or three gas stations located at the same intersection engaged in a price war. First one would cut its prices, and then, five minutes later, the others would go even lower. This might go on for just a few hours, or maybe even several days. Eventually the gas station owners would come to their senses and prices would go back up to their old levels.

Now you're going to catch a break. We're not going to make you fill in any more tables or draw any more graphs, at least in *this* chapter. Just glance at Figure 5, which is based on Table 2, and see if you can find the output at which the competitive oligopolist produces.

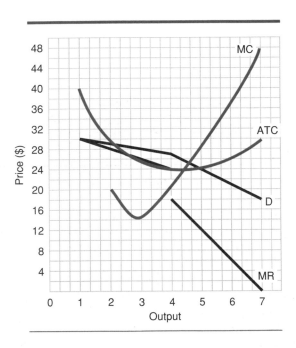

Figure 5
The Cutthroat Oligopolist
How much is the price and output of this firm? The price is $27 (at the kink of the demand curve), and the output is 4 (note that MC = MR at this output).

TABLE 2 Hypothetical Demand and Cost Schedules for a Competitive Oligopolist

Output	Price	Total Revenue	Marginal Revenue	Total Cost	ATC	Marginal Cost	Total Profit
1	$30	$ 30	$30	$ 40	$40	—	−$10
2	29	58	28	60	30	$20	−2
3	28	84	26	75	25	15	9
4	27	108	24	96	24	21	12
5	24	120	12	125	25	29	−5
6	21	126	6	162	27	37	−36
7	18	126	0	210	13	48	−84

---

[1]Daniel Hamermesh, *Economics Is Everywhere* (New York: McGraw-Hill, 2002), pp. 161–62.

Administered Prices

Administered prices are set by large corporations for relatively long periods of time, without responding to the normal market forces, mainly, changes in demand. For example, although demand fell substantially during the Great Depression, many firms, most notably the railroads, did not lower their prices.

We already saw how, under the constraints of fierce competition, the oligopolist is reluctant to raise or lower price. Prices are said to be sticky.

If we take the firm's MC curve as its supply curve, we will see that the oligopolist operates within a fairly wide range of possible MRs before it is necessary to change price. Look back at Figure 4. Because of the discontinuity of the MR curve (the vertical broken line), the firm will charge the same price at the same output no matter how much MC varies within the range of $18 to $24 and still equals MR.

Administered prices are peculiar to oligopoly. Perfect competitors and monopolistic competitors are too small to dictate price. Monopolists will change their output and price in response to changes in demand in order to maximize their profits. But under competitive oligopoly, the firms will rarely shift output on price because they will continue to maximize profit as long as MC is within the range of MR.

Clearly, she produces at an output of 4, because at that output the MC and MR curves cross. Next, calculate the firm's profit.

Solution: Output, which is directly under the kink, is 4. Price, which is at the kink, is $27. Remember that price is *always* read off the demand curve. And now, total profit:

$$\text{Total profit} = (\text{Price} - \text{ATC}) \times \text{Output}$$
$$= (\$27 - \$24) \times 4$$
$$= \$3 \times 4$$
$$= \$12$$

Can you come up with an easier way of finding the firm's total profit? Look at Table 2 again. Did you figure it out yet? Just subtract total cost from total revenue at an output of 4 ($108 − $96 = $12). Once you know the output, all you need to do is subtract TC from TR.

In passing, let us note that the oligopolistic firm does not produce at the minimum point of its ATC curve, so we do not have peak efficiency even though there is considerable competition. Price tends to stay at $27. This is the main reason why, under competition, oligopolists' prices tend to be "sticky." We call such sticky prices *administered prices,* which is the topic of the box by that name.

Game Theory

One of the major themes of this chapter is that before oligopolists make any major decisions, they must take into account the anticipated reactions of their competitors. Like chess players, they need to think several moves ahead. *Game theory is the study of how people behave in strategic situations.* It can be applied to chess, bridge, poker, and, as you have probably surmised, the behavior of oligopolists.

The Maine Water Company and the Michigan Water Company produce identical bottles of water. Because they are the nation's only two bottled water companies, they constitute a duopoly. *A duopoly is an industry with just two firms.*

Would these firms be better off colluding or competing? If they *were* to compete, their competition would be based entirely on price. To keep things simple, let's limit them to two prices—a *high* price and a *low* price.

	Profit		Profit
(1) Maine: low price	$8	(2) Maine: low price	$15
Michigan: low price	8	Michigan: high price	5
	Profit		Profit
(3) Maine: high price	$ 5	(4) Maine: high price	$12
Michigan: low price	15	Michigan: high price	12

Figure 6
Four Profit Outcomes for the Bottled Water Duopoly

That would give us four possible combinations: (1) Maine charges a low price and Michigan charges a low price; (2) Maine charges a low price and Michigan charges a high price; (3) Maine charges a high price and Michigan charges a low price; and (4) Maine charges a high price and Michigan charges a high price. These four combinations, along with the companies' corresponding profits, are shown in Figure 6.

In combinations (1) and (3), one firm charges a low price and the other charges a high price. In both cases, the firm charging the low price makes a profit of $15, while the firm charging a high price makes a profit of just $5. The reason for this disparity, of course, is that the firm charging the low price is getting most of the sales.

Now let's see what happens to profits when both firms charge the same low price. In combination (1), they each make a profit of $8. When the firms both charge the same high price [combination (4)], they each make a profit of $12.

Looking at these four possible profit outcomes, can you figure out what these two firms will do? Will they compete or will they collude? What would *you* do?

Let's say that you own the Maine Water Company. If you compete with the Michigan Water Company, you face three possible outcomes—(1) profit of $8; (2) profit of $15; and (3) profit of $5. If you collude, then your company and your rival would agree to charge a high price, and each of you would make $12 profit.

From your knowledge of cutthroat competition, you know that if you lower your price, your competitor will lower hers. That's outcome (1), which leaves you with a profit of just $8. Cutthroat competition also excludes outcome (2). Now if you raise your price, your cutthroat competitor will keep hers low, which is outcome (3). So what outcome makes the most sense for your firm and hers? It's outcome (4), where you both collude to charge high prices. Then you each make a $12 profit.

Applying game theory to duopoly, we find a great incentive to collude. In fact, this incentive exists even when there are, say 5, 10, or even 15 competitors in an industry. But as we'll see in the next chapter, the courts have often found that collusion to restrain competition is illegal.

Conclusion

Let's take a look at the chart in Figure 7. At one end we have the cartel, which no longer operates within the American economy although it may be found in world markets (most notably in the oil market). At the opposite end of the spectrum we have the cutthroat competitor, the firm that will stop at nothing to beat out its rivals. Industrial espionage and sabotage, underselling, disparaging of rival products, and other unfair competitive practices are the trademarks of such firms.

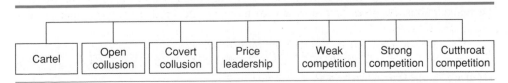

Figure 7
The Competitive Spectrum

Near the middle are the mildly competing oligopolists and the occasionally cooperating oligopolists. Sometimes their leaders are called corporate statesmen.

Where on this spectrum is American industry?

Where on this spectrum is American industry? Where do we place the industries listed back in Table 1? Near the middle? Toward the cutthroat end of the spectrum? Or toward the cartel end?

The answer is that there *is* no answer. You won't pin me down on this one. There are two reasons why there is no answer to this question.

First, there is no one place where American industry is located because different industries have different competitive situations. In short, some oligopolistic industries are more competitive than others, so to say that *all* industries are located at a certain point on the spectrum—regardless of where—has got to be wrong.

Second, there is widespread disagreement about the degree of competition in any given industry. Take banking, for example. If one were to judge the degree of competitiveness among banks by all the newspaper advertising they do to attract depositors and to get people to take out car loans and mortgages, it would appear that this is a very competitive industry. But one would reach quite a different conclusion by observing that when one or two major banks change their prime rate of interest, within a day or so all the other major banks, not to mention the rest of the banks around the country, play follow-the-leader.

Current Issue: Cutthroat Competition in the College Textbook Market

Do you buy your books new or used? Textbook prices have been going up much faster than the rate of inflation. In fact, the typical college text now costs over $100. At many community colleges, students pay more for their books than they do for their tuition. And so, not surprisingly, they often try to buy used books.

Publishers get to play the role of bad guys. They're the ones charging those outrageous prices, and, on top of that, they seem to change editions every other year. While economics texts do need to be periodically updated, do math and chemistry books?

Chances are, your college bookstore has a contract with your school to buy back your books at half price if they are being used the next semester. These texts are then resold at three-fourths the original price.[2]

Let's consider a $100 textbook. In theory, your college bookstore is supposed to buy it back from you for half price, or $50, and then resell it as a $75 used book. But as you know, college bookstores often give you less than half price for the books they buy back.

Students will have the choice of buying a new book for $100 or a used book for $75. Bookstore managers usually prefer selling used books because they'll make a larger profit than on new books. Generally they'll have to pay the publisher over $75 for that new $100 book.

Why do publishers charge so much for their books? The main reason is that they are also providing several costly ancillary products—test banks, instructor's manuals, videos, computerized tutorials, PowerPoint lecture notes, overhead transparencies, and FastFax testing. Indeed, it cost publishers well over $1 million to launch a new major textbook.

Do professors use all of these ancillaries? Some professors use some of them, while others use none of them. Then why not publish some no-frills texts and charge no-frills prices? A few decades ago, there were over 20 major textbook publishers, but today just five publish 80 percent of all college texts. Now, besides having much less competition, the major publishers seem to follow a herd mentality. If some professors want a video

---

[2]If the book is *not* going to be used the next semester at your school, the bookstore manager, out of the kindness of his heart, may give you two or three bucks for your book—and then ship it to another college bookstore owned by the same chain where the book *is* being used.

or a 10,000-question test bank, then we better provide these, because our competitors certainly will.

Let's suppose that one publisher actually *did* put out a textbook without ancillaries and cut the price by, say, 50 percent. Wouldn't a lot of professors order that book to save their students all that money? Well, the sad truth is that most professors have gotten quite used to all the ancillaries that come with their textbooks, so if one publisher stopped supplying them, the professors would just switch to another publisher who did.

In addition, the Big Three—McGraw-Hill (which publishes my book), Pearson, and Cengage (formerly Thompson)—have hundreds of sales reps who call upon your professors to drum up sales. It costs well over $100,000 a year to keep each sales rep out in the field. If one of the Big Three fired its sales reps, it could save a bundle of money, and maybe cut textbook prices by one-third. But what would happen to its sales?

Let's look at one more factor in the textbook business. Unlike nearly any other market, you, as the consumer, have only one choice to make: Do I buy my books new or used? Your professors decide which texts you'll buy, and even *they* generally get to pick that text from one of just three publishers. But if students could choose their own texts, you could bet that the publishers would start producing no-frills texts at much lower prices.

Questions for Further Thought and Discussion

1. The American automobile industry is an archetypical oligopoly. Show why this statement is true.

2. Where is American industry on the competitive spectrum? Instead of answering this question, you may criticize it.

3. What are the two measures of the degree of oligopolization? Work out a numerical problem using each of them.

4. Explain the cutthroat competitor's reasons for not raising or lowering his price, thereby accounting for the kink in his demand curve.

5. What are administered prices, and how are they set?

6. Should covert collusion be illegal?

7. *Practical Application:* Suppose an organization of college professors decided to bring down textbook prices. What measures could be taken to persuade publishers to lower their prices?

8. *Practical Application:* Your school has eight megadorms, each housing 2,000 students. Four different student-owned and -operated pizza delivery services operate on campus. Each delivers to all eight dorms. How would you go about organizing a cartel that could increase everyone's profit?

Name _____   Date _____

Multiple-Choice Questions

Circle the letter that corresponds to the best answer.

1. Which statement is true? (LO1)

   a) All oligopolies have only a few firms.

   b) Most oligopolies have only a few firms.

   c) Some oligopolies have only a few firms.

2. The motor vehicle industry has a concentration ratio
   of almost _____ percent. (LO1)

   a) 5   d) 65

   b) 25   e) 85

   c) 45

3. Administered prices are most likely to occur under
   _____. (LO4, 6)

   a) perfect competition   c) monopoly

   b) monopolistic competition   d) oligopoly

4. Price is _____. (LO3)

   a) always read off the demand curve

   b) sometimes read off the demand curve

   c) always read off the marginal revenue curve

   d) sometimes read off the marginal revenue curve

5. In the U.S. today collusion is _____. (LO2)

   a) illegal and does not exist

   b) illegal and does exist

   c) legal and does not exist

   d) legal and does exist

6. Which statement is true? (LO4)

   a) All firms in oligopolistic industries are large.

   b) Most firms in the United States are oligopolies.

   c) The crucial factor in oligopolistic industries is
      product differentiation.

   d) Most of our GDP is produced by oligopolies.

7. Which of the following is not an oligopolist? (LO4)

   a) ExxonMobil

   b) General Motors

   c) Your local phone company

   d) Xerox

8. Which statement about oligopolies is false? (LO3)

   a) They operate at the minimum points of their ATC
      curves.

   b) They charge higher prices than perfect
      competitors.

   c) They make profits in the long run.

   d) They cannot legally form cartels in the United
      States.

9. Which statement is false? (LO1)

   a) The cigarette and auto industries have high
      concentration ratios.

   b) OPEC is a cartel.

   c) Most oligopolies engage in outright collusion.

   d) None of these statements is false.

10. The electric machinery case involved
    _____. (LO2)

    a) a cartel   c) cutthroat competition

    b) covert collusion   d) none of the above

11. The least competitive industry is one that has
    _____. (LO2)

    a) price leadership   c) overt collusion

    b) covert collusion   d) a cartel

12. Which one of these could not be considered cutthroat
    competitors? (LO2)

    a) Members of Japanese dangos

    b) McDonald's and Burger King

    c) Costco and Sam's Club

    d) Gas stations on the same intersection

13. Which statement is true? (LO2)
   a) Most of American industry is engaged in cutthroat competition.
   b) Most of American industry does not compete.
   c) Some oligopolistic industries are more competitive than others.
   d) None of these statements is true.

14. An industry that is highly concentrated might have a Herfindahl-Hirschman index of ________. (LO1)
   a) 20,000
   b) 2,000
   c) 800
   d) 100
   e) 1

15. An industry that has 100 firms, each with a 1 percent market share, would have a Herfindahl-Hirschman index of ________. (LO1)
   a) 1
   b) 10
   c) 100
   d) 1,000
   e) 10,000

Use Table 1 to answer questions 16 through 19.

TABLE 1

Industry X		Industry Y		Industry Z	
Firm	Market Share (%)	Firm	Market Share (%)	Firm	Market Share (%)
1	25	1	35	1	30
2	25	2	20	2	30
3	15	3	15	3	20
4	10	4	15	4	10
5	10	5	10	5	5
6	10	6	5	6	5
7	5				

16. The highest concentration ratio ________. (LO1)
   a) is in Industry X
   b) is in Industry Y
   c) is in Industry Z
   d) cannot be determined

17. The highest Herfindahl-Hirschman index ________. (LO1)
   a) is in Industry X
   b) is in Industry Y
   c) is in Industry Z
   d) cannot be determined

18. Which statement is true? (LO1)
   a) Industry X is more concentrated than Industry Y.
   b) Industry Y is more concentrated than Industry Z.
   c) Industry Z is more concentrated than Industry X.
   d) Industries X, Y, and Z have the same concentration ratio.

19. Which statement is true? (LO1)
   a) Industry X has a higher Herfindahl-Hirschman index than Industry Y.
   b) Industry Y has a higher Herfindahl-Hirschman index than Industry Z.
   c) Industry Z has a higher Herfindahl-Hirschman index than Industry X.
   d) Industries X, Y, and Z have the same Herfindahl-Hirschman index.

20. Which statement is true? (LO2)
   a) Two-thirds of all cars and light trucks sold in the United States are either imported or made by Japanese firms in this country.
   b) Toyota and Honda are the largest makers of cars and light trucks in the United States.
   c) Japanese companies make about 10 percent of all cars and light trucks in the United States.
   d) None of these statements is true.

21. Imports have made the automobile industry's concentration ratio much ________ relevant, while the Japanese transplants have been ________ that ratio. (LO1)
   a) more, reducing
   b) more, increasing
   c) less, reducing
   d) less, increasing

22. A monopoly would have a concentration ratio of ________ and a Herfindahl-Hirschman index of ________. (LO1)
   a) 100, 100
   b) 10,000, 10,000
   c) 10,000, 100
   d) 100, 10,000

23. Which statement is true? (LO1)
   a) The higher the Herfindahl-Hirschman index, the higher the degree of concentration.
   b) The lower the Herfindahl-Hirschman index, the higher the degree of concentration.
   c) The Herfindahl-Hirschman index remains constant as the degree of concentration rises.
   d) There is no relationship between the Herfindahl-Hirschman index and the degree of concentration.

24. Compared to the perfect competitor in the long run, the cutthroat oligopolist has a _____. (LO3)
    a) lower price and lower profits
    b) higher price and higher profits
    c) higher price and lower profits
    d) lower price and higher profits

25. According to the theory of the kinked demand curve, if a firm were to raise its price, its competitors would _____. (LO3)
    a) lower theirs
    b) raise theirs
    c) keep theirs the same

26. According to the theory of the kinked demand curve, if a firm were to lower its price, its competitors would _____. (LO3)
    a) lower theirs
    b) raise theirs
    c) keep theirs the same

27. The kinked demand curve depicts _____. (LO3)
    a) cutthroat competition
    c) collusive oligopoly
    b) cartels
    d) price leadership

28. The kinked demand curve is associated with _____. (LO3)
    a) sticky prices
    c) covert collusion
    b) OPEC
    d) none of the above

29. The discontinuity in the oligopolist's marginal revenue curve occurs _____. (LO3)
    a) to the right of the kink
    b) to the left of the kink
    c) directly below the kink
    d) at different places at different times

30. The Japanese *dango* is _____. (LO2)
    a) a way to ensure that government construction contracts will always go to the low bidder
    b) a negotiating process under which construction firms take turns receiving government contracts
    c) a cartel whose sole purpose is to keep construction prices high
    d) an organization that helps new firms enter the construction industry

31. Which one of the following statements is true? (LO6)
    a) Competition among college textbook publishers has kept prices from rising even further.

    b) The college textbook publishing industry is highly oligopolized.
    c) If it were not for the sale of used books, college textbook publishers would make much smaller profits.
    d) Because college textbooks are often accompanied by supplements, this has tended to keep their prices down.

32. Game theory can be applied to each of the following concepts *except* _____. (LO5)
    a) a monopoly
    b) a cutthroat competition
    c) the kinked demand curve
    d) duopoly

33. College textbook publishing is most accurately described as _____. (LO2, 6)
    a) a duopoly
    c) open collusion
    b) a cutthroat oligopoly
    d) a cartel

34. Game theory predicts that in a market controlled by four firms producing an identical service, each will ultimately charge _____ price. (LO5)
    a) a high
    c) a low
    b) an intermediate

Fill-In Questions

1. An oligopoly is an industry with _____ _____. (LO1)

2. One measure of the degree of competitiveness (or of oligopoly) is called a _____. (LO1)

3. The oligopolist _____ at the minimum point of her ATC curve. (LO3)

4. The total _____ of industry sales by the four leading firms is the industry concentration ratio. (LO1)

5. The most important cartel in the world today is _____ _____. (LO2)

6. An important Supreme Court case involving covert collusion was the _____ case. (LO2)

7. U.S. Steel and a few cigarette companies were all engaged in _____ to attain their economic ends. (LO2)

8. The sign of cutthroat competition on a graph would be the _____. (LO3)

9. One of the outcomes of the kinked demand curve is _____ prices. (LO3, 6)

10. Administered prices are set by _____ for _____ without responding to _____. (LO4, 6)

11. Administered prices are peculiar to _____ _____. (LO4)

Problems

1. Given the information in Table 2, calculate the concentration ratio of this industry. *Show your work.* (LO1)

TABLE 2

Firm	Percent of Sales
A	14%
B	4
C	23
D	5
E	2
F	8
G	17
H	10
I	2
J	15
Total	100%

2. (a) How much is the concentration ratio in the industry shown in Table 3? (b) Calculate the Herfindahl-Hirschman index in this industry. (LO1)

TABLE 3

Firm	Market Share
1	30%
2	20
3	20
4	10
5	10
6	5
7	5

3. (a) How much is the concentration ratio in the industry shown in Table 4? (b) Calculate the Herfindahl-Hirschman index in this industry. (LO1)

TABLE 4

Firm	Market Share
1	40%
2	15
3	10
4	10
5	10
6	5
7	5
8	5

4. Given the information in Figure 1, calculate the firm's profit. (LO3)

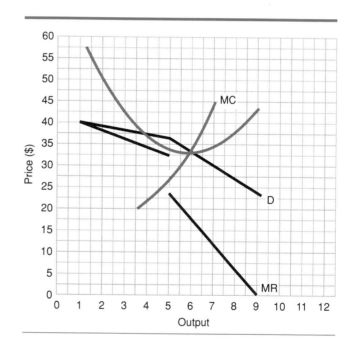

Figure 1

5. Given the information in Figure 2, answer these questions: (LO3)

a) How much is the firm's output?

b) How much is the firm's profit?

c) What type of oligopolist is this?

d) If the firm were a perfect competitor, how much would its output be in the long run?

e) If the firm were a perfect competitor, how much would its price be in the long run?

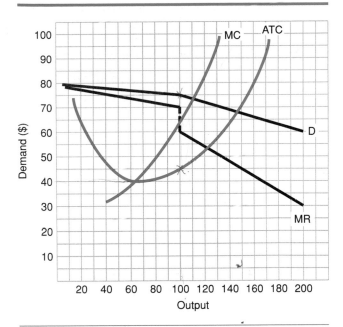

Figure 2

Appendix

The Four Types of Competition:
A Review

This appendix will summarize some of the high points of the last four chapters, especially the graphs. No new material will be introduced.

LEARNING OBJECTIVES

After reading this appendix you should be able to:

1. Define and analyze perfect competition.
2. Define and analyze monopoly.
3. Define and analyze monopolistic competition.
4. Define and analyze oligopoly.

Perfect Competition

A perfectly competitive industry has many firms selling an identical product. How many is many? So many that no one firm can influence price. What is identical? A product is identical in the minds of buyers when they have no reason to prefer one seller to another.

Definition of perfect competition

In the long run, if the firm has been losing money, it may well leave the industry. Enough firms will leave to reduce market supply and raise price enough to eliminate the economic losses of the firms that remain in the industry. Thus, in the long run, the perfect competitor will make zero economic profit.

The long run

In the long run, if the firm has been making a profit, additional firms will have been attracted to the industry, raising industry supply and reducing market price. Thus, in the long run, profit is reduced to zero.

In the long run the perfect competitor's price is equal to the low point on the firm's ATC curve. Because the firm produces at that output, it operates at peak efficiency. That is, it operates at the minimum point of its ATC curve, which means it produces at the lowest possible cost.

Here's a nice exam question: Draw the demand curve for the perfect competitor and state its elasticity.

You would draw a horizontal line. Its elasticity would be infinity or undefined. In other words, it would be perfectly elastic.

Are there any perfectly competitive industries? Perhaps not, but wheat, soybeans, and corn may come pretty close.

Monopoly

A monopoly is a firm that produces all the output in an industry. There's nobody else selling anything like what the monopolist is producing. In other words, there are no close substitutes.

There is no distinction between the short run and the long run under monopoly because the monopolist is the only firm in the industry. No firms enter or leave, as they do with perfect competition. The market demand curve *is* the monopolist's demand curve.

What does the monopolist's demand curve look like? It's a line that slopes downward to the right. So to sell additional output, the monopolist must lower her price.

What are examples of monopolies? Microsoft's near monopoly of computer operating systems comes to mind. Patented drugs for which there are no close substitutes. Viagra had a monopoly at least until 2004, when other male impotence drugs came on the market. Local phone, gas, electric, and cable TV service are also monopolies. Major league baseball, football, basketball, and hockey are certainly monopolies as well.

Monopolistic Competition

A monopolistically competitive industry has many firms selling a differentiated product. How many is many? So many that no one firm has any significant influence over price.

If the buyer doesn't differentiate among the various products sold, the product is identical. If the buyer does differentiate, the product is differentiated. Who determines whether the product is differentiated or identical? The buyer does.

Like the perfect competitor, the monopolistic competitor can make a profit or take a loss in the short run, but in the long run, the firm will break even. The reason the monopolistic competitor makes zero economic profits in the long run is the same as that under perfect competition.

In the long run, if firms are losing money, then many will leave the industry, thus lowering industry supply and raising market price. If firms are realizing substantial profits in the long run, then new firms will be attracted to the industry, thus raising supply and lowering market price.

Like the perfect competitor, the monopolistic competitor is a small firm, one of many in its industry. But what's the main difference between the monopolistic competitor and the perfect competitor? Here's a hint: Go back to the definitions of perfect competition and monopolistic competition.

The main difference between them is that perfect competitors produce *identical* products while monopolistic competitors produce *differentiated* products.

Examples of monopolistic competitors are restaurants, convenience stores, haircutting salons, clothing stores, real estate brokers, law firms, medical offices, bars, and nearly all retail stores.

Oligopoly

An oligopoly is an industry with just a few sellers. How few? So few that at least one firm is large enough to influence price.

Examples of oligopolies are the automobile, breakfast cereal, airline, beverage, entertainment, aircraft, petroleum refining, and tobacco industries.

Perfect Competition versus Imperfect Competition

The perfectly competitive model is an ideal, rarely if ever attained in a world of imperfect competition. Indeed, more than 99 percent of the business firms in the United States are monopolistic competitors. Virtually all of the rest are oligopolies and monopolies.

TABLE A–1 The Four Types of Competition: Number of Sellers and Type of Product

Type of Competition	Number of Sellers	Type of Product
Perfect competition	Many	Identical
Monopoly	One	Unique
Monopolistic competition	Many	Differentiated
Oligopoly	Few	Either identical or differentiated

TABLE A–2 The Four Types of Competition: Price and Output in Long Run

Type of Competition	Price	Output
Perfect competition	At minimum ATC	At minimum ATC
Monopoly	Higher than minimum ATC	Restricted (to left of minimum ATC)
Monopolistic competition	Higher than minimum ATC	Restricted (to left of minimum ATC)
Oligopoly	Higher than minimum ATC	Restricted (to left of minimum ATC)

TABLE A–3 The Four Types of Competition: Profit and Efficiency in Long Run

Type of Competition	Profit	Efficiency
Perfect competition	Zero economic profit	Peak efficiency
Monopoly	Makes an economic profit	Less than peak efficiency
Monopolistic competition	Zero economic profit	Less than peak efficiency
Oligopoly	Makes an economic profit	Less than peak efficiency

Now let's look at some tables listing the characteristics of perfect competition and imperfect competition, which includes monopoly, oligopoly, and monopolistic competition.

Summary Tables

Tables A–1, A–2, and A–3 summarize what we've covered here with respect to number of sellers, type of product, price, output, profit, and efficiency.

Questions for Further Thought and Discussion

1. How does perfect competition compare to monopolistic competition with respect to price, profit in the long run, average total cost, and output?

2. How does perfect competition compare to monopoly with respect to price, profit in the long run, average total cost, and output?

3. How does perfect competition compare to oligopoly with respect to price, profit in the long run, average total cost, and output?

Workbook for Appendix to ![McGraw Hill] connect | ECONOMICS
Chapter 12

Name _____   Date _____

Multiple-Choice Questions

Write in the letter that corresponds to the best answer for questions 1 through 28, using choice a), b), c), or d). (LO1, 2, 3, 4)

    a) perfect competitor/competition

    b) monopolist/monopoly

    c) monopolistic competitor/competition

    d) oligopolist/oligopoly

1. A firm in an industry with many sellers selling a differentiated product would be a(n) _____.

2. A firm that faces the entire demand curve of an industry would be a(n) _____.

3. In the long run only a(n) _____ operates at the minimum point of its ATC curve.

4. The crucial factor in _____ is the low number of sellers.

5. The crucial factor in _____ is product differentiation.

6. Under _____ and _____, there are no profits in the long run.

7. A firm with many sellers and an identical product is a(n) _____.

8. The kinked demand curve takes place under competitive _____.

9. With respect to computer operating systems, Microsoft is a(n) _____.

10. A mom-and-pop grocery in Harlem is a(n) _____.

11. Most firms in the United States are _____.

12. Imperfect competition includes _____, _____, and _____.

13. A company making a profit in the long run would be a(n) _____ or a(n) _____.

14. If there are many firms in the industry, we are talking about either _____ or _____.

15. The most efficient producer is the _____.

16. Jennifer Ziegenfuss owns a firm that manufactures cell phones that double as garage door openers. Another firm, owned by Jared Collins, produces the same product. A third firm, owned by Daniel Quinn, also makes this product. The only other firm manufacturing cell phone–garage door openers is owned by Robert Roan. This industry is a(n) _____.

17. The airline industry is a(n) _____.

18. Ford Motor Company is a(n) _____.

19. Wheat growing is an example of _____.

20. A camera store in downtown Chicago is a(n) _____.

21. An industry with seven firms is a(n) _____.

22. A firm that faces a downward sloping demand curve is *not* a(n) _____.

23. An industry with 100,000 firms is either a(n) _____ or a(n) _____.

24. Most college bookstores are _____.

25. Major league baseball is a(n) _____.

26. A firm that operates at peak efficiency in the long run must be a(n) _____.

27. A firm that makes a profit in the long run must be either a(n) _____ or a(n) _____.

28. A firm producing a differentiated product must be either a(n) _____ or a(n) _____.

Fill-In Questions

1. How many firms is many? So many that _____ _____. (LO4)

2. A product is identical in the _____. (LO1, 3)

3. Under any type of competition, if firms are losing money in the long run, _____ _____. If firms are making a profit in the long run, _____ _____. (LO1, 2, 3, 4)

4. In the long run the perfect competitor's price is equal to the _____ on the firm's ATC curve. Therefore, the firm is operating at _____ efficiency. (LO1)

5. A monopolist's product has no _____. (LO2)

6. The monopolist's price is _____ than the perfect competitor's; in the long run the monopolist's profit is _____ than the perfect competitor's. (LO1, 2)

7. A monopolistically competitive industry has _____ firms selling a _____ product. (LO1, 3)

8. Product differentiation takes place in the _____ _____. (LO3)

9. In the long run the monopolistic competitor's price is _____ the minimum point on its ATC curve. (LO3)

10. An oligopoly is an industry with _____ _____. (LO4)

11. Only the _____ in the _____ produces at the minimum point of its ATC. (LO1)

12. The perfect competitor has a _____ demand curve. (LO1)

Chapter 13

Corporate Mergers and Antitrust

There has been an unmistakable trend toward bigness in business since the mid-1980s. Corporate mergers and takeovers have become so common that anything less than a $10 billion deal is not even considered financial news. Let's see how this trend developed and how the government has attempted to regulate it.

LEARNING OBJECTIVES

After reading this chapter you should be able to:

1. Define and explain antitrust.
2. List and discuss the major antitrust laws.
3. Discuss the origins and practice of modern antitrust.
4. Name and analyze the types of mergers.
5. List and discuss the main industries that were deregulated since the late 1970s.
6. Discuss and assess corporate corruption.
7. Summarize the trend toward bigness.
8. Explain how pharmaceutical fraud is a type of corporate fraud.

A Historical Perspective on Corporate Concentration

The history of the American economy since the Civil War has been one of growing corporate concentration. Like the tides, this concentration has had its ebbs and flows.

A high-water mark was reached in the early years of this century when J. P. Morgan put together a couple of huge deals with his fellow captains of industry, Andrew Carnegie, Edward Harriman, and John D. Rockefeller. Then, in the years before World War I, came the first trustbusters, Presidents Teddy Roosevelt and William Howard Taft. A new wave of corporate mergers took place in the 1920s, only to be succeeded by the antitrust enforcement policies of Presidents Franklin Roosevelt and Harry Truman in the 1930s and 1940s. After that, a new wave of mergers continued for the next five decades.

During the last century and a quarter, a few hundred huge companies came to dominate our economy. There have been a few reverses—the 1911 breakup of the Standard Oil and American Tobacco trusts, and the antitrust enforcement of the 30s and 40s, and the more recent breakup of AT&T—but the trend has been unmistakable.

> The nature of a market society is to push toward a higher degree of concentration, and the nature of antitrust is to push back toward a more deconcentrated, competitive environment.
>
> –Louis Galambos, business historian, Johns Hopkins University–

Antitrust

The Political Background

John D. Rockefeller, American oil magnate

What is a trust?

The common view is that during the 19th century the federal government rarely intervened in the economy, allowing businesses to go their own ways. There were, however, two major forms of intervention, both of which were key issues in the events leading up to the Civil War.

First, at various times the government passed a high protective tariff that generally made certain imports more expensive and greatly aided northern manufacturers. Second, the transcontinental railroad, which completely bypassed the South, was built with a tremendous amount of federal aid. This aid took the form of 10-mile strips of land on alternating sides of the track, so that for every mile of track built, the railroad received 10 square miles of land.

Both policies were benevolent with respect to big business, so few protests were raised about government intervention in that arena. Furthermore, with the election of Abraham Lincoln in 1860, the Republican Party would dominate the federal government for the next 70 years. This was the political backdrop in which the first antitrust legislation was passed in 1890. The Sherman Antitrust Act was passed by a Republican Congress and signed by a Republican president. For "the party of big business" to have passed a law such as this, the economic situation had to have been pretty desperate.

The late 19th century was the era of the "trust." Trusts were cartels that set prices and allocated sales among their member firms. In some cases, most blatantly oil, a single company was formed that controlled most or all production in the industry. The Standard Oil trust, which was carved out of 39 independent oil companies by John D. Rockefeller, controlled 90 percent of all U.S. oil production, refining, and marketing. In 1892, 40 independent sugar companies formed the American Sugar Refining Company. Still other trusts were formed in meat packing, cottonseed and linseed oil, lead, leather, whiskey, tobacco, electrical goods, coal, steel, and the railroads.

The Standard Oil trust was so powerful that it forced the railroads not only to grant it discounts, and not grant them to their competitors, but even to give it "drawbacks"—that is, payments on every shipment of oil refined by *rival* firms. This was such a blatant restraint of trade that it angered even the staunchest probusiness congressional Republicans.

In his landmark work on those times, Matthew Josephson pictured

> an America in which the citizen was born to drink the milk furnished by the milk Trust, eat the beef of the beef Trust, illuminate his home by grace of the oil Trust, and die and be carried off by the coffin Trust.[1]

Even more grating were the insults hurled at the public by those who ran these huge industrial empires. The great financier J. P. Morgan proclaimed, "I owe the public nothing." Probably the most famous was the remark by railroad tycoon Billy Vanderbilt: "The public be damned. I am working for my stockholders."[2]

The Sherman Antitrust Act

Sherman had mixed feelings about the growing concentration of corporate power and its abuses. After all, he was a leader of the Republicans, the party of big business. He hoped his law would slow the powerful trend toward monopolization of American industry, but the language of the law was left rather vague. In 1890 Congress passed the Sherman Antitrust Act to curb the trust movement. Named after Senator John

---

[1]Matthew Josephson, *The Robber Barons* (New York: Harcourt Brace Jovanovich, 1962), p. 358.
[2]Ibid., p. 187.

The Breakup of Standard Oil

In 1911 the Supreme Court ordered the breakup of the Standard Oil Company for violating the Sherman Act. The five largest pieces were Standard Oil of New York, New Jersey, Ohio, Indiana, and California.

Standard Oil of New York evolved into Standard Oil Company of New York, into SOCONY-Mobil-Vacuum, and finally, into Mobil Oil, the nation's second-largest oil company.

Standard Oil of New Jersey became ESSO, and nearly 20 years ago it became Exxon, the largest oil company in the world.

Standard Oil of Ohio (Sohio), is still known by its original name, while Standard Oil of California, SoCal, became Chevron and is now ChevronTexaco.

Additional derivative firms include Continental Oil (now part of Du Pont), Marathon Oil (which merged with U.S. Steel), and Atlantic Richfield.

Exxon and Mobil, the world's two largest oil companies, both part of the original Standard Oil trust, merged in 1999, becoming ExxonMobil. And Atlantic Richfield (later known as ARCO) and Amoco (formerly Standard Oil of Indiana) are now both part of British Petroleum. So apparently the old Standard Oil trust is not dead after all.

Sherman, this law remains the most important piece of antitrust legislation in our nation's history.

The key passage stated that "every contract, combination in the form of trust or otherwise, in restraint of commerce among the several states, or with foreign nations, is hereby declared illegal." It went on to state, "Every person who shall monopolize, or conspire with any other person or persons to monopolize any part of the trade or commerce of the several states, or with foreign nations, shall be guilty of a misdemeanor." *The key passage*

Finally, after years of preparation by the Roosevelt and Taft administrations, suits were brought against two of the biggest trusts of the day, the Standard Oil and American Tobacco trusts. In the first case the Standard Oil Trust was split into 34 separately owned companies, the five largest of which were later known as Exxon, Mobil, Sohio (Standard Oil of Ohio), Amoco, and Chevron (see the box, "The Breakup of Standard Oil"). The American Tobacco Company was broken up into three companies: the American Tobacco Company, Liggett & Myers, and P. Lorillard. *Standard Oil and American Tobacco cases*

Were these trusts broken up because they were big? No! Bigness per se did not offend the Court. The trusts were broken up because they had behaved badly.

What had the Standard Oil trust done that was bad? It had forced the railroads, which were then the basic means of shipping oil, to give it rebates or discounts not just on the oil it shipped but even on the oil shipped by its competitors. You can justify asking for a rebate on your *own* freight charges, but imagine forcing the railroads to pay you a rebate on your competitors' freight charges. Basically, it was using its tremendous market power to force its rivals out of business.[3]

The problem with the Supreme Court's interpretation of Sherman was that it did not prohibit monopoly per se, but prohibited only certain illegal tactics that had been practiced by Standard Oil and American Tobacco. Clearly the Court was even more conservative than other Republican branches of government—the president and Congress. Nevertheless, the breakup of these companies was a radical measure that indicated how serious the problem of monopolization had become to the rest of the business establishment. In a sense, then, their breakup was deemed necessary to preserve the status quo.

From this decision the Supreme Court formulated its "rule of reason," which set the tone for antitrust enforcement for the next two decades. Bigness itself was no offense as long as that bigness was not used against rival firms. *The rule of reason*

---

[3]The Interstate Commerce Act of 1887 prohibited granting rebates to large shippers.

Mere size is no offense.

The rule of reason was applied in the *U.S. Steel* case of 1920 when President Woodrow Wilson's administration sought the same legal remedy against the steel trust that had been applied nine years earlier against the oil and tobacco trusts. The Court concluded that the U.S. Steel Corporation, which produced more than half of the nation's steel, did not violate the Sherman Act just because it was big. The Court pronounced: "The corporation is undoubtedly of impressive size. . . . But we must adhere to the law, and the law does not make mere size an offense, or the existence of unexerted power an offense." And the very existence of competitors disproved the contention that U.S. Steel had misused its power.

So not *all* trusts were illegal, but only *unreasonable* restraints of trade. Remember the fairy tale of the three little pigs accosted by the big bad wolf, who told them, "I'll huff and I'll puff and I'll blow your house down"? Well the Supreme Court's rule of reason said that the wolf not only had to be big and bad, but he actually had to blow that house down. Bigness and bad intentions alone were not illegal per se. So even though the folks running U.S. Steel had intended to drive out their competitors, the fact that they had not succeeded was proof enough that they had done nothing illegal.

The Clayton Antitrust Act

For the first time since before the Civil War, the Democrats finally sat in the driver's seat, with Woodrow Wilson occupying the White House and a Democratic majority in both houses of Congress. In 1914 they passed two laws aimed at bolstering the Sherman Act by specifically outlawing all the bad business practices that continued to go unpunished.

The Clayton Act prohibited practices that lessened competition or tended to create a monopoly.

The Clayton Antitrust Act prohibited five business practices when their effect was to "substantially lessen competition or tend to create a monopoly."

1. *Price discrimination.* This was introduced in the chapter, "Monopolistic Competition," using the examples of airlines charging half fare to teenagers, doctors charging widely varying rates based on patients' incomes, and the grades A, B, and C set up by A&P. Generally, the courts have not held price discrimination to be illegal.

2. *Interlocking stockholding.* This occurs when one firm buys the stock of another. Although this goes on every day, on occasion the courts will find it illegal. In the 1950s, Du Pont, together with Christiana Securities, both controlled by the Du Pont family, were forced to sell the huge block of General Motors stock they had accumulated.[4] The question is whether a stock acquisition is deemed to lessen competition.

3. *Interlocking directorates.* It is expressly forbidden for a person who is a director of one corporation to sit on the board of another corporation that is in the same industry. This obvious conflict of interest could easily be detected as corporate boards are widely published.

4. *Tying contracts.* It is illegal to sell one product on the condition that another product or products be purchased from the same seller. For example, the law prohibits General Electric from telling a buyer it can purchase GE toasters only if it also purchases GE lightbulbs.

5. *Exclusive dealings.* It is illegal to tell a retailer that he or she must not carry some rival firm's product line. For example, Panasonic cannot tell an appliance dealer that if he wants to carry Panasonic televisions and VCRs, he can't also carry Sony and Sharp competing products.

The Federal Trade Commission Act (1914)

FTC as a watchdog

The Federal Trade Commission (FTC) was set up as a watchdog against the anticompetitive practices outlawed by the Sherman and Clayton acts. Although empowered to investigate anticompetitive business practices and issue cease-and-desist orders, the courts

---

[4]Du Pont bought about 25 percent of General Motors' stock in 1919. Over the next four decades GM bought most of its seat-cover fabrics, paints, and glues from Du Pont. In 1957 the Supreme Court found that other firms had been unfairly excluded from selling paint, glues, and fabrics to GM and forced Du Pont to sell its GM stock.

stripped most of its powers by the 1920s. In 1938 the Wheeler-Lea Amendment gave the Federal Trade Commission what has become its most important job: preventing false and deceptive advertising.

In recent years the FTC has been playing a much more active role in approving or disapproving mergers. In 1995 it blocked the proposed merger of the Rite Aid and Revco drugstore chains, contending that the combination would leave millions of consumers with no low-cost outlet for prescription drugs. That same year, it did allow the merger of two pharmaceutical giants, Ciba-Geigy and Sandoz, but only after forcing them to divest themselves of $1 billion in assets to prevent the combined company from dominating several market segments.

When Staples and Office Depot proposed merging in 1997, they agreed to sell hundreds of their stores. Nevertheless the FTC did not approve the deal, arguing that the office supply superstores were a market in themselves, distinct from the much larger market for office goods sold through catalogues, discount chains, and stationery stores.

Another merger that never happened was Barnes & Noble's (the nation's largest bookstore chain) acquisition of the Ingram Book Group, the nation's biggest book wholesaler. The Federal Trade Commission chairman, Robert Pitofsky, voiced concern about the effect on the smaller, independent bookstores, who depended on Ingram for just-in-time delivery. Another concern was whether a new company, as Amazon.com had been in the mid-1990s, could now get started on the Internet if it depended on Ingram, whose new parent, Barnes & Noble, also sold books on the Internet. Barnes & Noble decided to back out of the deal to avoid a protracted legal battle.

Modern Antitrust

> We understand that companies have to be of sufficient size and scope to play in the global marketplace.
>
> –Joel Klein,
> Chief, U.S. Justice Department
> Antitrust Division during Clinton Administration–

Antitrust enforcement evolved over the last century, growing more stringent or lax, depending on the presidential administration as well as the political leanings of the Supreme Court justices and the judges sitting in the lower federal courts. In Europe, enforcement varied from country to country, but with the formation and consolidation of the European Union, a unified approach to antitrust has evolved, especially since 1997.

Partial Breakdown of the Rule of Reason

Keep in mind that the Supreme Court continued to be dominated, right into the 1940s, by a conservative majority who had been appointed by the almost unbroken string of Republican presidents who served from the Civil War to the Great Depression. To ensure that the Sherman Act was not applied too vigorously, the justices developed the "rule of reason" doctrine. First applied in the 1911 *Standard Oil* case and then refined in the 1920 *U.S. Steel* case, the rule prevailed until the Alcoa case of 1945. Until then, you had to be big *and* bad before the Court would find you guilty under Sherman.

The membership of the Supreme Court changed radically during the Roosevelt and Truman administrations, which extended from 1933 to 1953. In a landmark 1945 decision, the Court found that the Aluminum Company of America (Alcoa), which held 90   Alcoa case
percent of the aluminum market, was an illegal monopoly.

The two arguments that Alcoa presented in its defense were rejected. The first, based directly on the rule of reason, was that although it did have a nominal monopoly on aluminum production, it had not intended to exclude competitors and had not, in fact, behaved badly. This argument was rejected by the Court, which noted that the absence of competitors was itself proof of monopolizing.

The second argument advanced by Alcoa was to define the relevant market more broadly than just aluminum. Steel, copper, and even recycled aluminum should be included as well, which would reduce Alcoa's market share from 90 percent to about one-third. This argument, too, was rejected by the Court.

Judge Learned Hand said, "Congress did not condone 'good trusts' and condemn 'bad' ones; it forbade all." A 90 percent share of the market "is enough to constitute a monopoly; it is doubtful whether 60 or 64 percent would be enough, and certainly 33 percent is not."

The Alcoa decision eclipsed the rule of reason.

The *Alcoa* decision appeared to sweep away the last vestiges of the rule of reason, making monopoly itself, and not merely monopolization, illegal. This change was underscored by the fact that Alcoa had been big but hadn't been bad.

The *Alcoa* case represented the high-water mark of antitrust enforcement. Eight years later, in the *Du Pont* case, the defendant was able to use the relevant market argument that Alcoa had unsuccessfully raised. Du Pont and a licensee had 100 percent of the nation's cellophane market (and 75 percent of the market for transparent wrapping material). But the Court accepted the argument that the relevant market included all "flexible packaging materials," such as aluminum foil and waxed paper. Du Pont had only 18 percent of the flexible packaging materials market, which would hardly constitute a monopoly.

The 60 Percent Rule

A firm must be big and bad.

What has apparently evolved from these antitrust decisions is what might be called "the 60 percent rule." Should a firm have a share of at least 60 percent of the relevant market *and* should that firm have behaved badly toward its competitors, it would then be subject to prosecution. However, whether it would be prosecuted would depend on the political and economic outlook of the current administration, and whether it would be found guilty would depend on the outlook of the nine Supreme Court justices.

Two Landmark Cases

AT&T   AT&T was accused of having a monopoly on local phone service (which it could hardly contest) and of making it hard for its long-distance competitors (such as MCI and Sprint) to use its local phone network. In 1984 in exchange for giving up its 22 local phone companies, AT&T was not only allowed to keep its long-distance service, Bell Labs, and Western Electric, but it was allowed to enter the telecommunications–computer field.

Microsoft   Windows, the Microsoft operating system, runs on more than 90 percent of the 100 million PCs sold in the world each year. The Justice Department was concerned that the company would use this virtual monopoly to force computer makers to use software products it might create in the future, further extending that monopoly.

For two decades Microsoft has made computers more powerful and easier to use for millions of consumers by adding more to its program, from point-and-click icons to fax software. But its growing market power has enabled the company to crush competitors, thus eliminating competition and innovation and probably harming consumers. What were once separate products, such as Microsoft's Web browser, Internet Explorer, were pulled in to become features of Microsoft's Windows operating program.

By bundling Internet Explorer with Windows, PC manufacturers were given no choice but to use the Microsoft browser. Netscape's browser, Navigator, which at one time had had 80 percent of the market, saw its market share reduced to just 7 percent by 2002, and that company is now part of AOL Time Warner.

In 1995 Microsoft signed a consent decree with the government that prohibits the company from tying the purchase of one product to another but that does allow it to develop "integrated" products. In 1997 the Justice Department brought suit, contending that Microsoft was violating its consent decree by forcing PC makers to take Internet

Explorer as a condition of licensing Windows. The company contends that Explorer and Windows are not separate products but a single integrated product.

The case bounced back and forth between the Federal District Court and the Federal Court of Appeals, finally resulting in a 2002 settlement between the federal government and Microsoft. Here are the main terms of this settlement:

- Microsoft cannot restrict the freedom of PC makers to install non-Microsoft software, and is prohibited from retaliating against PC makers for shipping machines with competing software.

- Microsoft must sell Windows under the same terms to all PC makers.

- Microsoft must disclose technical information of software to rivals so that their products run smoothly on Windows.

- Microsoft cannot retaliate against any software or hardware company for developing software that competes with Microsoft.

European Antitrust

Antitrust enforcement in the European Union is conducted by the European Commission, which not only approves or prohibits mergers between Europe-based corporations, but also plays an increasingly important antitrust role with respect to other corporations doing substantial business in Europe.

In recent years the European Commission has shifted the emphasis in antitrust policy from the fulfillment of legal requirements to an examination of the consequences on competition. In rejecting a combination of Volvo (which produces trucks in addition to its better-known cars) and Scania (another large Swedish truck-maker) announced in 1999, the Commission declared such a merger would dominate the Scandanavian market and hold a virtual monopoly for heavy trucks in Sweden.

In 1997 the Federal Trade Commission approved the merger of Boeing, which builds 60 percent of the world's commercial aircraft, and McDonnell Douglas, whose market share had shrunk to just under 10 percent (the remaining 30 percent is built by Airbus Industrie, the European consortium). One reservation the FTC had concerning the merger was Boeing's 20-year contracts to be sole supplier of new jets to American, Delta, and Continental airlines. The European Commission, which is the executive arm of the 25-nation European Union, considered these supply arrangements a threat to the survival of Airbus, and was set to reject the merger.

How, you may ask, can these European guys reject a merger between two American firms? Although the Commission could not technically block the deal, it could make it difficult for Boeing-McDonnell to do business in Europe by imposing fines of up to 10 percent of the company's worldwide revenues. One day before the Commission was to vote, Boeing-McDonnell blinked. It agreed to alter its use of the exclusive aircraft supply contracts.

In 1998 the European Commission, along with antitrust regulators in Australia and Canada, apparently forced the cancellation of an announced merger between two Big Six accounting firms, Ernst & Young and KPMG Peat Marwick. One of the concerns was that the merger would lead to the layoff of thousands of employees, this at a time of high unemployment in Europe.

Another deal that was blocked by the European Commission in 2000 was between Time Warner and EMI Group of Britain. This was to be a joint venture that would have created a giant in the music business—one with more than 2,500 musicians, including superstars like David Bowie and the Rolling Stones and accounting for more than 2,000 new albums a year. The commission thought that the Warner-EMI monolith could strangle Internet access by leveraging its media assets, especially in music. The more AOL Time Warner makes its music available online, the more Europeans become dependent on the Americans for their Net-delivered entertainment. Also, other music companies may be forced to offer their wares on AOL's network to reach customers.

In 2004 the European Commission ruled that Microsoft had broken European Union law by using its "near monopoly" to squeeze out software rivals. In early 2008, after being fined a total of over $2 billion in fines, the company finally agreed to comply with the European Commission's order to share details of its Windows operating system with rival software competitors, allowing them to build programs that could work with Windows. Bloomberg.com summarized this agreement:

> Microsoft will publish the so-called protocols used to connect its most popular software to other programs, eliminating an advantage its products had over rivals. It will license some patents at low royalty rates and put out 30,000 pages of Windows documentation that had only been under a license.[5]

on the web

You will find everything you could ever want to know about antitrust at www.antitrust institute.org. Click on Antitrust Resources in the top column.

Types of Mergers

Horizontal mergers

Horizontal Mergers

A horizontal merger is the conventional merger. Two firms in the same industry form one larger company. Usually a larger firm swallows a smaller one. When John D. Rockefeller was running Standard Oil, he swallowed 39 competing firms.

Horizontal integration has become particularly prevalent among the airlines, oil companies, banks, and companies in the communications field. The legal problem with horizontal mergers is that they appear to violate the Sherman Act. Two competing firms that merge may well lessen competition. The question is, Where do the Justice Department and the courts draw the line? If the number-two firm merges with the number-three firm, does this lessen competition? The answer depends on the makeup of the administration at the time, which may vary from the relatively restrictive Roosevelt and Truman administrations to the relatively permissive Reagan administration, as well as on the makeup of the courts, which see personnel shifts as justices retire and presidents appoint new ones. In 1999, when the number-one and number-two oil companies, Exxon and Mobil, announced their plans to merge, there was scarcely a peep out of the Antitrust Division of the Clinton administration's Justice Department.

Vertical mergers

Vertical Mergers

When firms that have been engaged in different parts of an industrial process or in manufacturing and selling join together, we have a vertical merger. A maker of TVs and stereos that bought out a retail chain and marketed its TVs and stereos through this new outlet would be an example. If an auto company merged with a steel mill, a tire company, or a glass manufacturer, we would have a vertically integrated company.

Janet Lowe described this process in the entertainment field:

> The purchase of the entertainment giant MCA by Matsushita and Columbia Pictures by Sony represented an effort to complete a vertical structure by these two companies. They already produce much of the high-technology equipment used in the entertainment industry; the companies wanted to add to that the technology of programming that was transmitted by their own equipment.[6]

---

[5]www.bloomberg.com

[6]Janet Lowe, *The Secret Empire: How 25 Multinationals Rule the World* (Burr Ridge, IL: Business One Irwin, 1992), p. 65.

Walt Disney's 1995 acquisition of the ABC network provided Disney with a ready market in which to show its made-for-TV films. Similarly, the 1989 purchase of Time Inc. by Warner Communications (originally known as Warner Brothers, the filmmaker) gave it Time's book list, from which it has been making movies.

Despite some spectacularly large vertical mergers in recent years, including the largest in American corporate history—AOL and Time Warner—vertical mergers have generally not worked out too well, and appear to be losing their popularity. The AOL Time Warner vision of combining editorial content and Internet services under the same corporate roof has turned out to be an expensive folly. Nor have other media mergers based on the same theory, such as Disney's acquisition of ABC, done all that well.

Back in the great industrial age of the last quarter of the 19th century, manufacturers needed to control every aspect of their businesses—the acquisition of raw materials, shipping, manufacturing, and marketing—in order to assure reliability. But today that's no longer necessary. It's more flexible and efficient to specialize in one activity and then buy from or sell to a number of outside companies. So what we can look forward to is fewer and fewer vertical mergers.

Conglomerate Mergers

Two companies in unrelated fields

A conglomerate merger occurs between two companies in unrelated industries—telephones and hotels, real estate and auto parts, oil and steel. A conglomerate, the product of such mergers, is a group of unrelated companies under one corporate umbrella. The term comes from the Latin *conglomerare,* meaning "to roll together."

The huge wave of conglomerate mergers in the 1960s was the cutting edge of the long-term trend toward corporate concentration. About 80 percent of the mergers during that decade were of the conglomerate variety. Firms that were minuscule in the 1950s became corporate giants over the course of 10 or 15 years.

Conglomerating has several advantages. In addition to providing ready-made markets for the goods and services produced by various divisions, the very diversity of the company is insurance against economic adversity. A downturn in one industry will not hurt too much because the firm is diversified into many industries. A strike in one component firm or division will shut down only a small part of the entire conglomerate because virtually all unions are organized along industry or craft lines. For example, if the Screen Actors Guild (Ronald Reagan was its first president) went on strike, Viacom, which owns Paramount, would hardly notice.

The king of conglomerates today is General Electric, a mix of manufacturing, finance, and broadcasting, including NBC. Although General Electric is considered one of the nation's best-run corporations, conglomeration sometimes does not work out well. The companies do not mesh, and inefficiencies often result. Despite the advantages of conglomeration, by the 1980s there were very few conglomerate mergers. It had been found that highly diversified companies were hard to manage, and there was a strong trend toward de-diversification through the 1980s and 1990s, as conglomerates spun off divisions and concentrated on their core businesses.

Deregulation

In the late 1970s a consensus had formed among government and corporate officials that regulations were holding down economic growth. Under Presidents Jimmy Carter and Ronald Reagan, regulations were cut back and government fiat was largely supplanted by the market forces of demand and supply.

Ronald Reagan spoke to the frustrations of millions of people who ran businesses of all sizes when he said back in 1980 that he would "get the government off the backs of the American people." Reagan estimated that American businesses spent upwards of

Deregulation: The Record Since the Late 1970s

Under the administrations of Jimmy Carter and Ronald Reagan, a great deal of deregulation took place in banking, the airlines, long-distance trucking, and long-distance phone calling. In banking, the country ended up with the savings and loan debacle (discussed in Chapter 13 of *Economics* and *Macroeconomics*), costing American taxpayers almost $300 billion. But the effects of deregulation in the other industries have been much more salutary.

Until the passage of the Airline Deregulation Act in 1978, the Civil Aeronautics Board controlled fares, assigned routes, and controlled industry entry. Indeed, no new carriers had been permitted to enter major interstate routes since the board's creation in 1938. But by the early 1980s, the airlines were free to set their own prices and select their own routes. Perhaps a victim of its own success, deregulation accelerated the increasing volume of air traffic, resulting in greater delays and the possibility of more midair collisions. Although the industry is still in flux after a series of bankruptcies and mergers*, labor productivity is up sharply, costs have been cut, and airfares have dropped by about a third, on an inflation-adjusted basis. However, they have risen substantially on routes of less than 750 miles.

Before deregulation, the Interstate Commerce Commission sometimes forced truckers to take roundabout routes and to return with empty trucks from long hauls. According to *The Economist,* "America's trucking industry was a cosy, regulated semi-cartel, with a few big companies dominating most regions." But after deregulation in the early 1980s, hundreds of thousands of small firms went into business, as the number of trucking firms shot up from 10,000 to 45,000. Most important for consumers, shipping prices dropped.[†]

You're probably not old enough to remember when, in the early 1980s, AT&T still had a monopoly on all phone calls—local *and* long distance. The 1984 breakup of AT&T left it with its long-distance business, but the regional Baby Bells spun off into independent companies that handle local and intrastate (within a state) calls. Competition—as well as rapid technological advances—have driven down the cost of long-distance phone calls to just a fraction of what they cost 25 years ago.

*Such familiar airlines as T.W.A., Pan Am, Eastern, National, People Express, and, in 2008, Northwest have either shut down or been acquired by other airlines.
[†]*The Economist,* June 3, 2000, p. 66.

$100 billion a year just to follow all the federal rules and regulations and to employ people to fill out all the required forms. Did he succeed in cutting the red tape? Not really, inasmuch as the pile of paperwork imposed by the federal government is now higher than ever. The box, "Deregulation: The Record Since the Late 1970s" discusses the effects of the deregulation of three major industries—the airlines, long-distance trucking, and long-distance phone calling.[7]

At this juncture the results of deregulation have been quite good. Clearly prices have been held down by competition among the long-haul trucking firms, the long-distance phone companies, and the airlines. But fierce competition has driven several major airline carriers out of business and in the four years after 9/11 the airlines lost a total of $32 billion. In 2006 the industry finally began turning a profit.

Corporate Misconduct

Beware of false profits.

Corporate stockholders, employees, creditors, and customers have long assumed that our corporate leaders run their companies efficiently and honestly. They expected audited corporate financial statements to provide an accurate picture of each firm's sales, costs, profits, and financial viability. But when dishonest officials at firms like Enron (at the time, the nation's seventh largest company), WorldCom, Global Crossing, and Arthur Andersen (recently one the world's largest CPA firms) knowingly cheat and lie, the public begins to lose its confidence in the integrity of *all* corporations.

---

[7]The railroads (1976–80) and the natural gas industry (1978) were also deregulated. In Chapter 13 (of *Economics* and *Macroeconomics*) we talked about the disastrous effects of deregulation on the savings and loan industry.

The Scorecard for Scandal

As in baseball, it's sometimes hard to identify all the corporate crooks without a scorecard. Here's a very brief summary of whose been accused of doing what.

As of April 1, 2006, here's the lineup of the corporate criminals drawing the longest sentences:

The Corporate Cheat Sheet

Company	Primary Allegations
Enron	Fraudently inflated financial results; conspiracy; money laundering
WorldCom	Fraud; improper profiting from IPOs; inappropriate company loans; conspiracy
Xerox	Fraudulently inflated financial results to profit from bonuses and stock sales
Adelphia	Fraud; misuse of corporate funds by founding family
Tyco	Tax evasion; misuse of company funds to inflate stock value; inappropriate company loans
ImClone	Insider trading; tax evasion; obstructing justice
Qwest	Improperly profited from IPOs; fraudulently inflated financial results; insider trading
Global Crossing	Fraudulently inflated financial results; cashed in stock just before bankruptcy
HealthSouth	Fraudulently inflated financial results; conspiracy
Investment banks	Abuse of conflicts of interest
AIG	Used misleading accounting techniques to artificially bolster profits

Source: The Economist, June 28, 2003, p. 7; www.marketwatch.com

What's the common thread running through all these charges? It's that the people running these companies used their insider knowledge for ill-gained profits. Saul Waksal, who headed ImClone, sold a huge block of his stock (and possibly alerted his friend, Martha Stewart, to sell her much smaller holdings), when he learned that an experimental drug his company produced to fight cancer would not be approved by the Federal Drug Administration. Sentencing Waksal to seven years in prison, Judge William H. Pauley III told him: "You abused your position of trust as chief executive officer of a major corporation and undermined the public's confidence in the integrity of the financial markets. Then you tried to lie your way out of it, showing a complete disregard for the firm administration of justice."

Several officers of Enron conspired to artificially inflate profits, pushing up the stock price, and then selling their shares before the price plunged to virtually zero. As of November 2003, 14 executives of HealthSouth agreed to plead guilty of conspiring to overstate earnings by about $2.5 billion to keep its stock price from collapsing. On the other side of the ledger, WorldCom officials managed to hide $3.8 billion in expenses.

- Bernard Ebbers, former CEO of WorldCom, received a 25-year jail sentence for his role in an $11 billion accounting fraud.

- Jamie Olis, a Dynergy executive, got a 24-year jail sentence for devising a scheme to falsify his company's books.

- John Rigas got 15 years in prison, and his son, Timothy Rigas, got 15 years for looting hundreds of millions of dollars from Adelphia.

- Fifteen former Enron officials received jail sentences, largely for concealing the sinking financial condition of the company while unloading their personal holdings of Enron stock. They included Jeffrey Skilling (24 years), Andrew Fastow (6 years), and Ben F. Gilsan Jr. (5 years). Former CEO, Kenneth Lay, who faced a long jail term, died before he could begin serving.

- CEO Dennis Kozlowski stole $150 million from Tyco and received an 8-year jail term.

- Quest Communications CEO Joseph Nacchio received a 6-year sentence for insider trading.

We have seen executives make hundreds of millions of dollars selling stock before their companies collapsed, as did Enron's chief executive officer, Kenneth Lay and Jeffrey Skilling, his second-in-command. They were not selling shares on which they had risked their *own* money. Most got shares from stock options, and some were given shares by their companies only weeks before they dumped them on public investors. Compounding the injustice at Enron, the company invested virtually all of its employees' pension funds in Enron stock, which became worthless in just a few months. Meanwhile Arthur Andersen, which was responsible for auditing the books, gave Enron repeated clean bills of financial health. Like Enron, it was forced into bankruptcy (see the box, "The Scorecard for Scandal").

In an editorial *BusinessWeek* explained why corporate corruption hurts not just employees and stockholders, but our entire economy.

> The truth is economists don't usually compute the tax that is imposed on economic growth by corruption. They should. In the past few years, we have witnessed conflicts of interest and manipulation within the initial public offering, mutual-fund, investment banking, and insurance markets. These rigged markets stifle innovation, erode discipline in the markets, channel money into less productive activities, add expense, and undermine national competitiveness.[8]

How Effective Is Antitrust?

What do we want antitrust to do?

What do we want antitrust to do? If we want to create something approximating perfect competition, antitrust has failed miserably. If we would like to prevent further oligopolization of American industry, it has been a qualified success. *How* qualified?

Things could have been a lot worse without antitrust.

Well, things could have been a lot worse. Without antitrust, there would have been no legal means for the government to curb even those mergers that most blatantly stifled competition. Furthermore, many firms hesitate to merge because they are fairly certain the Justice Department *would* take legal action.

The Trend toward Bigness

One of the refreshing things about economists is that we can all look at exactly the same data and come to widely varying conclusions. One view is that economic competition has grown in recent years for three reasons. First, there's much more foreign competition. However, as huge foreign firms buy up American firms (we'll talk about this in the final chapter, "International Finance") or squeeze them out of business, we may end up with *less* competition than we had before the foreign firms began competing. The second reason is the declining importance of manufacturing (which is dominated by relatively large firms) relative to the service industries (where smaller firms prevail); this makes for a lot more competition. And third, the rise of new industries, such as production of microcomputers and computer software, has created many small, highly competitive firms.

All that said, as you can see in Table 1, 7 of the 10 largest mergers in U.S. history took place in 1998, 1999, and 2000. Six of these were in communications. All these mergers are part of a worldwide trend which shows no sign of slowing. Table 2 lists the world's largest mergers, including those involving American corporations.

Since every one of the companies listed in Tables 1 and 2 does business in many different countries, the distinction between American and foreign companies is becoming blurred. For example, we think of Honda and Toyota as Japanese firms, but they make a lot of their cars here—and in other countries as well. Two of the largest corporations in Canada are General Motors and Ford. The term for a firm that does business in many different countries is *multinational*. Perhaps in the not-too-distant future virtually all large corporations will be considered multinationals, and no one will bother mentioning their national origin.

---

[8]"The High Cost of Corruption," *BusinessWeek*, November 29, 2004, p. 156.

TABLE 1	The Largest U.S. Corporate Mergers and Acquisitions		
Acquirer	Acquisition	Year	Value of Transaction in $ Billions
AOL (America Online)	Time Warner	2000	$183
Pfizer	Warner-Lambert	2000	90
Exxon	Mobil	1999	86
Travelers Group	Citicorp	1998	73
SBC	Ameritech	1998	72
Comcast	AT&T Broadband	2001	72
Bell Atlantic	GTE	1998	71
AT&T	Tele-Communications	1999	70
AT&T	BellSouth	2006	67
Pfizer	Wyeth	2009	67
NationsBank	Bank America	1998	62
Pfizer	Pharmacia	2001	61
British Petroleum	Amoco	1998	59
JP Morgan Chase	Bank One Corp	2004	59
Qwest Communications	U.S. West	1999	56
Procter & Gamble	Gillette	2005	55
AT&T	MediaOne Group	2000	52

Source: Securities Data Corp.; *The World Almanac,* 2003; *The Wall Street Journal,* March 6, 2006, p. C1; www.wikipedia.com

Within this context one may begin to question the relevance of monopoly and antitrust enforcement. Because the markets are global, few companies are reaching the size and scale that should cause concern about monopolies. And how does one nation—even one with the economic clout of the United States—enforce its antitrust laws in the global marketplace?

TABLE 2	The Largest Worldwide Corporate Mergers and Acquisitions		
Acquirer	Acquisition	Date Announced	Value ($ Billions)
Vodafone AirTouch	Mannesmann	2000	$203
America Online (AOL)	Time Warner	2000	183
Pfizer	Warner-Lambert	2000	90
Exxon	Mobil	1999	86
Glaxco Wellcome	SmithKline Beecham	2000	76
Royal Dutch Petroleum	Shell Transport & Trading	2004	74
Travelers Group	Citicorp	1998	73
SBC	Ameritech	1998	72
Comcast	AT&T Broadband	2001	72
Bell Atlantic	GTE	1998	71
AT&T	Tele-Communications	1999	70

Source: Thompson Financial Securities Data; www.wikipedia.com

Current Issue: Pharmaceutical Fraud

Corporate fraud is not limited to just insider trading, inflated financial results, misuse of company funds, and outright stealing. Perhaps even more alarming has been the practice of some large pharmaceutical companies—most notably Pfizer—to aggressively market drugs for uses which had not been approved by the Federal Drug Administration. This practice was not just illegal, but was hazardous to the health of millions of Americans whose doctors prescribed these drugs.

In 2009 Pfizer agreed to pay $2.3 billion to settle civil and criminal allegations that it had illegally marketed its painkiller, Bextra. This was the largest criminal fine of any kind. The government had charged that executives and sales representatives throughout Pfizer planned and executed schemes to illegally market not only Bextra, but also Geodon, an antipsychotic; Zyvox, an antibiotic; and Lyrica, which treats nerve pain.

While Bextra had been approved by the Federal Drug Administration for the treatment of arthritis and menstrual cramps, it had not been approved for the treatment of acute pain, nor was it shown to be more effective than ibuprofen. But Pfizer instructed its sales representatives to tell doctors that the drug could be used to treat acute pain—and at doses well above those approved, even though the drug's dangers, which included kidney, skin, and heart risks, increased with the dosage. Indeed, the drug was withdrawn from the market for *all* uses in 2008 because of its risks to the heart and skin.

This was not just an isolated case, either for this company or for the industry. It was Pfizer's fourth settlement over illegal marketing activities since 2002. In 2004, it paid a $430 million fine for illegally marketing Neurontin, an epilepsy drug, and signed a corporate integrity agreement—a companywide promise to behave.

Also in 2009, Eli Lilly agreed to pay $1.4 billion to settle charges it illegally promoted its antipsychotic drug, Zyprexa, for unapproved uses. And AstraZeneca reached a $520 million agreement to settle investigations into illegal marketing of its psychiatric drug, Seroquel.

Questions for Further Thought and Discussion

1. How effective is antitrust?

2. Trace the strength of the corporate merger movement since the early 1980s.

3. What was the historical and political background against which the Sherman Antitrust Act was passed?

4. Trace the use of the rule of reason since it was first applied in the *U.S. Steel* case.

5. Should the antitrust authorities stop more corporate mergers than they currently do? What are some of the pros and cons?

6. Suppose a proposed merger will simultaneously lessen competition and reduce unit costs through economies of scale. Do you think such a merger should be allowed?

7. Do you think the size of a firm's market share or its conduct is the more reasonable basis for antitrust regulation? Explain your answer.

8. Use the example of any industry to support the argument that the global economy is making monopoly and antitrust enforcement irrelevant.

9. Has deregulation been successful? Use examples of two industries to support your answer.

10. *Practical Application:* Do you think Microsoft should be broken up into two or even three separate corporations? Give at least two reasons to support your conclusion.

Workbook for Chapter 13 connect | ECONOMICS

Name _____   Date _____

Multiple-Choice Questions

Circle the letter that corresponds to the best answer.

1. The Microsoft case ended with _____. (LO3)
   a) a clear-cut win for the federal government
   b) a compromise settlement between Microsoft and the federal government
   c) a guilty plea by Microsoft, but no breakup of the company
   d) an abandonment of the case by the federal government

2. The first trustbusters were Presidents _____. (LO2)
   a) Teddy Roosevelt and William Howard Taft
   b) Franklin Roosevelt and Harry Truman
   c) Dwight D. Eisenhower and John Kennedy
   d) Jimmy Carter and Ronald Reagan

3. A key passage of the _____ Act stated that "every contract, combination in the form of trust or otherwise, in restraint of commerce among the several states, or with foreign nations, is hereby declared illegal." (LO2)
   a) Clayton
   b) FTC
   c) U.S. Communications
   d) Sherman

4. The trusts won only the _____ case. (LO2)
   a) AT&T
   b) U.S. Steel
   c) American Tobacco
   d) Standard Oil

5. In 1911 the Supreme Court decided to _____. (LO2)
   a) allow the trusts to keep functioning as they had in the past
   b) break up the trusts
   c) let the trusts off with small fines
   d) put the leaders of the trusts in jail

6. Until the *Alcoa* case, the Supreme Court generally held that _____. (LO3)
   a) bigness was all right as long as the company wasn't bad
   b) bigness was all right under any circumstances
   c) a company could do as it pleased as long as it wasn't big

7. The Supreme Court's rule of reason was applied _____. (LO3)
   a) from the time of the Civil War
   b) from 1911 to 1945
   c) after 1945
   d) after 1970

8. The high-water mark of antitrust enforcement was marked by the _____ case. (LO3)
   a) *Alcoa*
   b) *U.S. Steel*
   c) *Du Pont*
   d) *Microsoft*

9. The Clayton Antitrust Act prohibited each of the following except _____. (LO2)
   a) price discrimination
   b) interlocking stockholding
   c) interlocking directorates
   d) trusts

10. The most important job of the Federal Trade Commission today is to _____. (LO3)
    a) prevent false and deceptive advertising
    b) break up unlawful trusts
    c) issue cease-and-desist orders when anticompetitive business practices occur
    d) promote commerce with foreign nations

11. The rule of reason today is _____. (LO3)
    a) outlawed
    b) partially in force
    c) completely irrelevant

12. Antitrust today could best be summed up by the

_____. (LO3)

   a) 90 percent rule   c) rule of reason

   b) 60 percent rule   d) one-year rule

13. Which would be the most accurate statement? (LO6)

   a) The honesty of our corporate leaders is beyond question.

   b) Most corporate leaders are dishonest.

   c) Even if a corporation "cooks" its books, the CPA firm it hires to audit its books will quickly find out and blow the whistle.

   d) Enron was not the only American corporation in recent years to be guilty of corporate misconduct.

14. The merger between Exxon and Mobil was subject to

antitrust regulation by _____. (LO4)

   a) the Justice Department only

   b) the European Commission only

   c) both the Justice Department and the European Commission

   d) neither the Justice Department nor the European Commission

15. In the 1950s and 1960s the predominant form of

merger was the _____ merger. (LO4)

   a) horizontal   c) conglomerate

   b) vertical   d) diversifying

16. Which is the most accurate statement? (LO6)

   a) Virtually no chief executive officers of large corporations have gone to prison in recent years.

   b) About one-quarter of the chief executive officers of the 500 largest American corporations have either gone to prison, paid large fines, or both.

   c) Although some chief executive officers of large corporations have received prison sentences, none has been longer than three years.

   d) Martha Stewart was the only person to do actual time in prison for corporate crime.

   e) In recent years some corporate executives have received prison sentences of over 5 years.

17. When two firms in the same industry form one larger

company, this is a _____ merger. (LO4)

   a) horizontal   c) conglomerate

   b) vertical   d) diversifying

18. Which statement is true? (LO4, 7)

   a) Conglomerate mergers are all vertical mergers.

   b) General Electric is the largest conglomerate in the United States.

   c) There is no discernable trend toward corporate bigness.

   d) Most of the largest corporate mergers in the world are between firms located outside the United States.

19. Which statement is true? (LO3)

   a) Microsoft is subject to American antitrust laws, but not those of Europe, Asia, or elsewhere.

   b) Microsoft has never been involved in an antitrust suit.

   c) The European Commission fined Microsoft over $600 billion for its anticompetitive behavior.

   d) Microsoft has always gone out of its way to be helpful to its competitors.

20. Since the early 1980s the size of companies acquired

in mergers has been _____. (LO7)

   a) getting smaller

   b) staying about the same

   c) getting larger

21. In general, the deregulation of the airlines and

interstate trucking led to _____. (LO5)

   a) lower costs and lower prices

   b) higher costs and higher prices

   c) higher costs and lower prices

   d) lower costs and higher prices

22. The acquisitions of Time by Warner and ABC by

Walt Disney were examples of _____

mergers. (LO4)

   a) horizontal

   b) vertical

   c) conglomerate

23. Deregulation of the trucking industry resulted in

_____. (LO5)

   a) many more firms and lower prices

   b) many more firms and higher prices

   c) fewer firms and lower prices

   d) fewer firms and higher prices

24. Which one of the industries listed below has had the largest mergers during the last five years? (LO7)

    a) Steel manufacturing

    b) Automobile production

    c) Communications

    d) Trucking

25. Which one of these statements is false? (LO7)

    a) Most of the largest U.S. corporate mergers and acquisitions have occurred since 1995.

    b) The U.S. government has stopped only a few mergers from occurring.

    c) There have been several large banking mergers in recent years.

    d) Virtually all large mergers have transaction values of more than $100 billion.

26. Which statement is true? (LO4)

    a) Most of the largest corporate mergers in our history took place during the period 1998–2000.

    b) There have been virtually no large mergers in banking or communications.

    c) Nearly all large corporations are conglomerates.

    d) Enron continues to be one of our largest corporations.

27. Which is the most accurate statement about the recent corporate scandals? (LO6)

    a) Although the companies involved got some bad publicity, none of the executives had to do jail time.

    b) There were only two or three corporations that engaged in illegal behavior.

    c) One of the main charges was fraudulently inflated financial results.

    d) Virtually all large American corporations were caught in illegal insider dealings.

28. The most common corporate crime is _____. (LO6)

    a) taking advantage of insider knowledge for ill-gained profits

    b) embezzlement

    c) overstating costs

    d) overcharging customers

29. The greatest damage caused by the corporate scandals of the last few years was to _____. (LO6)

    a) the employees of those companies

    b) the U.S. Treasury, which was bilked out of billions of tax dollars

    c) the customers of those companies

    d) the public trust in financial markets

30. Which would be the most accurate statement about the recent wave of corporate corruption? (LO6)

    a) It has hurt employees, stockholders, and, in general, the entire economy.

    b) It has actually been very healthy for our economy.

    c) It has very little bearing on employees, stockholders, or the economy.

    d) None of these statements is accurate.

31. Which of the following statements is the most accurate? (LO8)

    a) Corporate fraud invariably involves some form of illegal financial manipulation.

    b) Corporate fraud is confined almost entirely to the financial services industry.

    c) Pfizer, which paid a $2.3 billion fine for selling a drug for a use that had not been approved by the Federal Drug Administration, was guilty of corporate fraud.

    d) Because of the threat of heavy fines and long prison sentences, corporate fraud is no longer a serious problem.

Fill-In Questions

1. The first trustbuster presidents were _____ and _____. (LO1, 2)

2. In 1911 the Supreme Court broke up the _____ _____ and the _____. (LO2)

3. In the late 19th century trusts were formed. They were _____; the largest trust was the _____ _____ trust. (LO1, 2)

4. "Every person who shall monopolize, or conspire with any other person or persons to monopolize, any part of the trade or commerce of the several states, or with foreign nations, shall be guilty of a misdemeanor" was a key passage of the _____ Act. (LO2)

5. The first case to be tried under the Sherman Act was the _____ case; the companies were found guilty of _____. (LO2)

6. In 1911 the Supreme Court broke up the _____ _____ trust into three component parts:
   (1) _____;
   (2) _____;
   and (3) _____. (LO2)

7. The Supreme Court broke up the trusts in 1911 because they _____. (LO2)

8. "Bigness was no offense" was the underpinning of the _____. (LO3)

9. A _____ makes the sale of one product conditional on the purchase of another product or products from the same seller; _____ stipulate that a retailer must not carry some rival firm's product line. (LO2, 3)

10. Expressly forbidding a person who is a director of one corporation to sit on the board of another corporation in the same industry is a provision of the _____ Act. (LO2)

11. _____ used the relevant market argument successfully in its case, just eight years after the *Alcoa* case. (LO3)

12. By the 1950s and 1960s, the most prevalent type of merger was the _____ merger. (LO4)

13. A vertical merger takes place when two firms that _____ join together, while a horizontal merger takes place when two firms that _____ _____ join together. (LO4)

14. Had there been no antitrust, there probably would have been _____. (LO7)

Chapter 14

Demand in the Factor Market

Every few chapters you can hear the gears grinding as we head off in another direction. So buckle up because here we go again. This time we're moving away from how businesses compete to how they manage their resources. In the preceding six chapters we analyzed the behavior of firms as sellers in the market for final goods and services; now we'll analyze how they behave in the market for factors of production.

Chapter 2 was about the factors of production, or resources. In this chapter we'll see how their prices are determined. We'll use the concept of marginal revenue product to determine how many units of a factor will be hired by perfect and imperfect competitors. As we shall see, the law of demand and supply plays a central role.

LEARNING OBJECTIVES

After reading this chapter you should be able to:

1. Define and analyze derived demand.
2. Define and measure productivity.
3. Discuss and measure marginal revenue product.
4. Discuss changes in resource demand and list the four reasons for these changes.

5. Differentiate between the substitution effect and the output effect.
6. Explain and analyze the optimum resource mix for the firm.

Derived Demand

Demand for goods and services is sometimes called *final demand*. Examples of final demand are the demand for cars, TVs, haircuts, medical services, or gasoline.

Now we'll look at *derived demand*, which is the demand for the resources which are used to produce goods and services. There are four resources: land, labor, capital, and entrepreneurial ability. The demand for these resources is derived from the demand for the final products. For example, the demand for land on which to grow corn is derived from the demand for corn, and the demand for labor with which to produce cars is derived from the demand for cars.

What is derived demand derived from?

A change in final demand brings about a change in derived demand. A sharp rise in the price of oil from the fall of 2007 to the summer of 2008 led to a decline in the demand for large cars. This caused massive layoffs in Detroit. Thus a decline in the demand for the final product, cars, led to a decline in the derived demand for the resource of autoworkers. In 1973 the Russian wheat crop failed and the Soviet Union made massive

It is not the employer who pays wages—he only handles the money. It is the customer who pays the wages.
—Henry Ford

purchases of American wheat. This, in turn, drove up the demand for farm labor and farmland in the United States.

Productivity

In addition to the demand for the final product, two other factors influence the demand for the productive resources (land, labor, capital, and entrepreneurial ability). First we'll consider the productivity of the resource and then the relative prices of substitutable resources.

Productivity is *output per unit of input*. What exactly is meant by *productivity* and *unit of input?* Productivity itself is really measured by how much is produced.

What about units of input? Inputs measure the quantities of the four resources—land, labor, capital, and entrepreneurial ability. Thus, a unit of input might be an hour of labor, an acre of land, or an automobile assembly line. We haven't yet figured a way of quantifying entrepreneurial ability.

Let's put these concepts together. Productivity is output per unit of input. If John produces 8 microchips per hour and Sally produces 16, Sally is twice as productive as John. If 30 bushels of wheat are harvested from acre one and 10 bushels from acre two, acre one is three times as productive as acre two.

The more productive a resource is, the more it will be in demand. Obviously, acre one is in much greater demand than is acre two. This would be reflected in both their prices and their rents. Similarly, Sally can obtain much higher wages than John because she is so much more productive.

Productivity is output per unit of input.

Prices of Substitute Resources

A given good or service can usually be produced in many different ways. The producer can use various combinations of resources. The Chinese, for example, didn't have many capital goods available six decades ago, so when they built a factory they used a very labor-intensive method of construction. Thousands of workers dug the hole for the foundation, carting off the dirt in wicker baskets. In the United States, where we have a great deal of capital equipment, we use a capital-intensive method of production. Bulldozers and other earth-moving equipment get the job done with much less labor.

In each country the cheapest production method available is used. Ethiopia happens to be a labor-intensive country because capital is relatively expensive. In the United States we use a capital-intensive method because labor is relatively expensive.

Photocopy machines are so expensive in Ethiopia that you won't find them in many neighborhood stores, and they certainly aren't standard equipment in home offices. Suppose you need to send out 50 copies of your résumé. Will you type out each copy or type one and photocopy the rest? Figure it out. Do you type individual résumés when you're looking for a job, or do you get a hundred photocopied or offset for 5 cents apiece? If the wage rate were just 10 or 15 cents an hour—as it still is in some of the poorer countries of the world—you'd be typing your résumés.

When wages rise, many companies seek to substitute machinery for relatively expensive labor. By automating, they will be able to lower their costs of production. If land became more expensive, farmers would work each acre much more intensively, substituting labor and capital for relatively more expensive land.

The demand for a resource is its marginal revenue product schedule. After we see how this schedule is derived, we'll return to our discussion of the determinants of the demand for a resource and how changes in those determinants change that demand.

Every country uses the cheapest production method.

ADVANCED WORK

The Concept of Margin in Economic Analysis

We discussed diminishing returns in Chapter 16 of *Economics* and *Macroeconomics*. If you were to glance back at that section, you'd see that the marginal physical product we're computing here is identical to the marginal output we computed there.

Indeed, all of our marginal concepts—marginal physical product, marginal output, marginal cost, marginal revenue, and the soon-to-be-introduced marginal revenue product—are cut from the same cloth, so to speak. Let's define each.

- Marginal output, or marginal physical product, is the additional output produced by one more unit of a resource.

- Marginal cost is the cost of producing one additional unit of output.

- Marginal revenue is the additional revenue for selling one more unit of output.

- Marginal revenue product is the additional revenue obtained by selling the output produced by one more unit of a resource.

The concept of margin is central to economic analysis. These marginal concepts enable us to figure out exactly what mix of resources we should use, what output we should produce, and what price we should charge in order to maximize our profits—which remains, of course, our bottom line.

Marginal Revenue Product (MRP)

The demand for resources is derived mainly from the demand for the final product. Resource productivity and the relative prices of substitutable resources also help determine price. Now we're ready to see how a firm decides how much of a resource to purchase.

How much of a resource a firm will purchase depends on three things: (1) the price of that resource, (2) the productivity of that resource, and (3) the selling price of the final product that the resource helps to produce. We'll go through a few numerical examples to find out how much land, labor, and capital will be purchased by a firm. Along the way, we'll introduce three new terms: *marginal physical product, marginal revenue product,* and *marginal revenue product schedule.* The last is the firm's demand schedule for a given resource. (See the Advanced Work box, "The Concept of Margin in Economic Analysis.")

How much of a resource is purchased depends on three things.

Table 1 has an output schedule for a firm that is using up to 10 units of labor. Fill in the column for marginal physical product. Do it in ink so we can sell a lot of new books. Just treat marginal physical product as you've treated marginal cost and marginal

TABLE 1 Hypothetical Output of Labor Hired by a Firm

Units of Labor	Output	Marginal Physical Product
1	15	——
2	29	——
3	41	——
4	51	——
5	58	——
6	62	——
7	63	——
8	63	——
9	62	——
10	60	——

Productivity and Marginal Physical Product

The relationship between productivity and marginal physical product, or marginal output, could stand some clarification. Suppose a machine operator produces 100 units per hour. That's her productivity. A second machine operator is hired. If their combined output is 198, then their average productivity is 99 (198/2 = 99).

We can also say that the marginal output, or marginal physical product, of the second worker is 98. However, we're not saying that the second worker is not as productive as the first worker, but just that if a second worker were added, output would rise by 98.

TABLE 2	Hypothetical Output of Labor Hired by a Firm	
Units of Labor	Output	Marginal Physical Product
1	15	15
2	29	14
3	41	12
4	51	10
5	58	7
6	62	4
7	63	·1
8	63	0
9	62	−1
10	60	−2

revenue. Marginal physical product is simply the additional output produced by one more unit of input (in this case, one more unit of labor).[1]

I hope your marginal physical product schedule checks out with mine in Table 2. Notice that the marginal physical product is zero with the 8th worker and negative with the 9th and 10th workers. The 8th worker adds nothing to output, while the 9th and 10th workers are in the way. No business firm would hire more than seven workers under these circumstances, even if the wage rate were a penny an hour. (For extra help, see the box, "Productivity and Marginal Physical Product.")

Table 3 has a column for price. Why is it always the same no matter how large output is? Because in this case we're dealing with a perfect competitor. In a few pages we'll work with imperfect competitors.

Go ahead and fill in the third column of Table 3. That should be a cinch for you by this time. Now for the fifth column, total revenue product. Try your luck on this one.

Let's check your methodology. Did you multiply output (column 2) by price (column 4)? If you did, you definitely got total revenue product (column 5) right because it's pretty hard to multiply a number by 10 and get the wrong answer.

Oh yes, I almost forgot! How do we find marginal revenue product? First, we'll define it. **MRP** is *the additional revenue obtained by selling the output produced by one more unit of a resource*. To find MRP, just take the difference in total revenue product

MRP is the additional revenue obtained by selling the output produced by one more unit of a resource.

---

[1]You'll notice that the second worker adds less to output than the first worker, and that the third adds less to output than the second. Why? Diminishing returns is why. If you're really interested in the whys and wherefores of diminishing returns, this topic was discussed toward the end of Chapter 16 of *Economics* and *Macroeconomics*.

TABLE 3	Hypothetical Marginal Revenue Product Schedule				
(1) Units of Land	(2) Output	(3) Marginal Physical Product	(4) Price	(5) Total Revenue Product	(6) Marginal Revenue Product
1	20	——	$10	——	——
2	38	——	10	——	——
3	53	——	10	——	——
4	65	——	10	——	——
5	73	——	10	——	——
6	78	——	10	——	——
7	80	——	10	——	——
8	80	——	10	——	——
9	79	——	10	——	——

between units of land. We'll start with the first unit of land; it produces a total revenue product of $200. Because zero units of land produce no revenue, the MRP of the first unit of land is $200. How about the second unit of land? Just take the total revenue produced by two units of land and subtract the total revenue produced by one unit of land. And so forth. After you've done that for all nine units, check your results with those in Table 4.

TABLE 4	Hypothetical Marginal Revenue Product Schedule				
(1) Units of Land	(2) Output	(3) Marginal Physical Product	(4) Price × output = Product	(5) Total Revenue Product	(6) Marginal Revenue Product
1	20	20	$10	$200	$200
2	38 {38 − 20	18	10	380 {380 − 200	180
3	53	15	10	530	150
4	65	12	10	650	120
5	73	8	10	730	80
6	78	5	10	780	50
7	80	2	10	800	20
8	80	0	10	800	0
9	79	−1	10	790	−10

You may have noticed that you can also find MRP by multiplying marginal physical product by price. In Table 4, one unit of land has MRP of 20 and a price of $10 (20 × $10 = MRP of $200). The second unit of land has MRP of 18 and a price of $10 (18 × $10 = $180). Can you use this shortcut to find MRP? You can when you're finding the MRP of the perfect competitor. But in another couple of pages we'll be finding the MRP of the imperfect competitor. To do that you'll have to use our original method—taking differences in total revenue product produced by additional units of a resource.

Now we're ready to do some marginal analysis using Table 4. How many units of land would you hire if you needed to pay $200 rent per unit? Think about it. How much is that land worth to you? The answer lies in the MRP schedule, which is the firm's demand schedule for land.

Let's do some marginal analysis.

OK, time's up. You'd hire just one unit of land because only that first unit is worth $200. Sorry if you missed that one, but don't despair. I'll give you another chance.

How many units of land would you hire if the rent were $150? Go back to the MRP schedule. What do you say? Three units? Did you say three units? If you did, then you may proceed to the next plateau.

Careful now. How many units of land would you hire if its price were $90? Assume the land is indivisible. That means you can't subdivide it. OK, what's your answer? Four units? Five units? Sorry, only one guess to a customer. The answer is: four units. Why not five? Because the fifth unit of land is worth only $80 according to your own MRP schedule. Would you shell out $90 for something worth only $80 to you? I hope you wouldn't.

TABLE 5	Hypothetical MRP Schedule				
(1) Units of Labor	(2) Output	(3) Marginal Physical Product	(4) Price	(5) Total Revenue Product	(6) Marginal Revenue Product
1	18	———	$12	———	———
2	34	———	12	———	———
3	48	———	12	———	———
4	59	———	12	———	———
5	68	———	12	———	———
6	74	———	12	———	———
7	77	———	12	———	———
8	78	———	12	———	———

Let's work out one more MRP schedule. Fill in Table 5, and then check your work with the figures in Table 6.

TABLE 6	Hypothetical MRP Schedule of the Perfect Competitor				
(1) Units of Labor	(2) Output	(3) Marginal Physical Product	(4) Price	(5) Total Revenue Product	(6) Marginal Revenue Product
1	18	18	$12	$216	$216
2	34	16	12	408	192
3	48	14	12	576	168
4	59	11	12	708	132
5	68	9	12	816	108
6	74	6	12	888	72
7	77	3	12	924	36
8	78	1	12	936	12

One last question: Is the firm whose MRP schedule is shown in Table 6 a perfect competitor or an imperfect competitor? The envelope, please. The answer is: The firm is a perfect competitor. How do we know? We know because the firm can sell its entire output at the same price—$12.

How many workers would you hire if the wage rate were $72? And how much would your firm's wage bill be? You would hire six workers and your firm's wage bill would be $432. Next set of questions: How many workers would you hire if the wage rate were $144 and what would your firm's wage bill come to? You would hire three workers and your wage bill would be $432.

The MRP of the Imperfect Competitor

How do we distinguish between the perfect competitor and the imperfect competitor? Suppose we compare the demand curve of the perfect competitor with those of the monopolist, the monopolistic competitor, and the oligopolist. While the perfect competitor has a horizontal demand curve, the demand curves of the others slope downward to the right. A horizontal demand curve reflects the fact that the firm can sell its entire output at a constant price. A downwardly sloping demand curve means the firm must continually lower its price to sell more and more output.

How do we distinguish between the perfect competitor and the imperfect competitor?

TABLE 7	Hypothetical MRP Schedule				
(1) Units of Labor	(2) Output	(3) Marginal Physical Product	(4) Price	(5) Total Revenue Product	(6) Marginal Revenue Product
1	18	18	$12	——	——
2	34	16	11	——	——
3	48	14	10	——	——
4	59	11	9	——	——
5	68	9	8	——	——
6	74	6	7	——	——
7	77	3	6	——	——
8	78	1	5	——	——

We're concerned here with how a downwardly sloping demand curve for the final product affects the demand for resources. In Table 7 we have the same outputs and marginal physical products as in Table 6, but instead of a constant price, it lowers as output increases. This reflects the downwardly sloping demand curve of the imperfect competitor.

TABLE 8	Hypothetical MRP Schedule of the Imperfect Competitor				
(1) Units of Labor	(2) Output	(3) Marginal Physical Product	(4) Price × output	(5) Total Revenue Product	(6) Marginal Revenue Product
1	18	18	$12 × 18	$216	$216
2	34	16	11	374	158
3	48	14	10	480	106
4	59	11	9	531	51
5	68	9	8	544	13
6	74	6	7	518	−26
7	77	3	6	462	−56
8	78	1	5	390	−72

Fill in the columns for total revenue product and MRP in Table 7, and then check your work with the data in Table 8.

Does your Table 7 match my Table 8? If it does, go on to the next paragraph. If it doesn't, then please read the box, "Finding the Imperfect Competitor's MRP."

How many workers would the firm hire if the wage rate were $150? How much would the wage bill come to? At a wage rate of $150, two workers would be hired, so the firm's wage bill would be $300.

EXTRA
HELP

Finding the Imperfect Competitor's MRP

How much was your MRP for two units of labor in Table 7? Was it $176? And for the third unit of labor, was your MRP $140? What you did, then, was try to find MRP by multiplying marginal physical product by price, and that simply does not work for the imperfect competitor.

What *does* work in finding the MRP of the second unit of labor is subtracting the total revenue product of the first unit of labor from the total revenue product of the second unit of labor. Go back to Table 7 and do that. Did you get $158? Good. Now find the MRP of the third unit of labor. Subtract the total revenue product of the second unit of labor from the total revenue product of the third unit of labor. I'll bet you got $106.

For practice, fill in Table A.

Table A

Units of Labor	Output	Marginal Physical Product	Price	Total Revenue Product	Marginal Revenue Product
1	10		8		
2	19		7		
3	27		6		

How did you do? I hope your Table A is identical to Table B.

Table B

Units of Labor	Output	Marginal Physical Product	Price	Total Revenue Product	Marginal Revenue Product
1	10	10	8	80	80
2	19	9	7	133	53
3	27	8	6	162	29

If the wage rate were $51, how many workers would be hired? How much would the firm's wage bill be? At a $51 wage rate, four workers would be hired, and the firm would pay $204 in wages.

If we take a numerical example from Tables 6 and 8, this will become clear. Using Table 6 of the perfect competitor, one unit of labor produces 18 units of output, which is sold at $12, yielding total revenue product of $216. Two workers produce 34 units of output sold at $12 each for a total revenue product of $408.

The imperfect competitor (Table 8) has somewhat different data. The first worker produces 18 units sold at $12 each for a total revenue product of $216; but two workers producing 34 units sold at just $11 produce a total revenue product of only $374.

Why do two workers under perfect competition produce a product sold for $408 while the same two workers under imperfect competition produce a product sold for only $374? The answer is that the perfect competitor can sell as much as she wants to sell at a constant price, while the imperfect competitor must lower her price to sell additional units of output.

The MRP schedule is derived from the total revenue product schedule. It follows that because the total revenue product of the imperfect competitor rises more slowly than that of the perfect competitor, the imperfect competitor's MRP schedule will decline more rapidly.

Changes in Resource Demand

Changes in Resource Demand versus Changes in Quantity of Resource Demanded

Our analysis of MRP parallels our earlier analysis of demand for a final product. Now, however, we're talking about a firm's demand for a resource. In other words, *the MRP*

schedule is a firm's demand schedule for a resource. As the price of that resource
declines, the firm demands larger quantities.

The Four Reasons for Changes in Resource Demand

Four things cause shifts in the MRP schedule: (1) changes in the demand for the final
product, (2) productivity changes, (3) changes in the prices of other resources, and
(4) changes in the quantities of other resources.

Changes in the Demand for the Final Product   This is by far the most important
influence on the demand for a factor of production. A firm that had no sales would have
no demand for land, labor, capital, or entrepreneurial ability. Looking at things more
optimistically, let's suppose the demand for the final product shown in Table 4 were to
rise so much that its price was driven from $10 to $20. What would happen to the firm's
MRP schedule?

    Would the MRP schedule in Table 4 be raised or lowered (i.e., will the firm's demand
for land be raised or lowered)? There's only one way to find out. Turn back to Table 4,
change price from $10 to $20, and recalculate the MRP schedule. Once you've done
the necessary calculations, check your work with that in Table 9. Obviously, MRP
doubled.

> The most important influence on resource demand is a change in the demand for the final product.

Productivity Changes   Productivity is output per unit of input. If output per unit of
input is doubled, what will happen to productivity? Check it out, using the data in
Table 6. Double the marginal physical product and multiply each figure by price.

    What happened to your MRP? It doubled at each price, right?

    Now we'll ask what raises productivity. Nearly all of any increase comes from two
sources: better capital and better trained and educated labor. The computerization of the
American industrial and service sectors has been the main factor responsible for the
growth of productivity increases of the last decade. Not only have we introduced more
and better computer systems, but many members of our labor force, particularly workers
in office jobs, have acquired the skills to use them.

> What raises productivity?

Changes in the Prices of Other Resources   There are four factors of production.
Sometimes one factor may be used as a substitute for another. When land is scarce, as
it is in Bangladesh, labor is substituted for land. Each acre of land is cultivated much
more intensively than it would be in the United States. When a new machine replaces
several workers, we are substituting capital for labor.

TABLE 9   Hypothetical MRP Schedule

(1) Units of Land	(2) Output	(3) Marginal Physical Product	(4) Price	(5) Total Revenue Product	(6) Marginal Revenue Product
1	20	20	$20	$ 400	$400
2	38	18	20	760	360
3	53	15	20	1,060	300
4	65	12	20	1,300	240
5	73	8	20	1,460	160
6	78	5	20	1,560	100
7	80	2	20	1,600	40
8	80	0	20	1,600	0
9	79	−1	20	1,580	−20

Substitute Factors If the price of a factor of production, say labor, goes up, business firms tend to substitute capital or land for some of their now more expensive workers. This is the substitution effect. Similarly, a decline in the wage rate will lead to a substitution of labor for capital or land. We're assuming, of course, that the price of capital or land hasn't changed (or if it has, it hasn't fallen as much as the wage rate).

The substitution effect

There's also an output effect, which works in the opposite direction. When the price of any resource rises, this raises the cost of production, which in turn lowers the supply of the final product. When supply falls, price rises, consequently reducing output. In other words, according to the output effect, if the cost of a factor of production rises, output will decline, thereby reducing the employment of all factors of production. Conversely, a decline in the cost of a factor will raise output, thereby raising the use of all factors of production.

The output effect

In sum:

1. *The substitution effect: If the price of a resource rises, other resources will be substituted for it.* If the price of a resource is lowered, it will be substituted for other resources.

2. *The output effect: If the price of a resource rises, output of the final product will decline,* thereby lowering the employment of all resources. If the price of a resource falls, output of the final product will rise, thereby increasing the employment of all resources.

The two effects are contradictory.

What we have, then, are contradictory effects. When the price of a resource rises, for example, the substitution effect dictates that more of the other resources will be used, thus increasing their employment. But the output effect pushes their employment down.

Which effect is stronger?

Which effect is stronger? Take the case of the introduction of computers in offices. The substitution effect pushed down the employment of labor, but the output effect pushed it way up. White-collar employment has risen sharply since the introduction of computers, so the output effect has clearly outweighed the substitution effect.

Now you *know* I'm going to present a case where the substitution effect outweighs the output effect. Output rose with the mechanization of agriculture in the South during the late 1940s, but more than three-quarters of the agricultural labor force in the deep South was forced off the land. Here the substitution effect (of capital for labor) swamped the output effect.

Sometimes, then, the substitution effect is stronger than the output effect, while at other times the opposite holds true. Thus, if you are asked whether automation raises or lowers the employment of labor, you will sound well informed when you explain that it will raise employment if the output effect is stronger and lower it if the substitution effect dominates.

Complementary Factors Although resources are usually substitutable at least to some degree, they also usually work well together. In fact, you need at least some labor to produce virtually every good or service, and labor productivity may be greatly enhanced by land, capital, and entrepreneurial ability.

Complementary factors of production

We say that two factors are complements in production if an increase in the use of one requires an increase in the use of the other. If a bicycle messenger service purchased 100 new bicycles, it would need to hire 100 messengers to ride them; or if 100 new messengers were hired, the firm would need to purchase 100 bicycles.

To carry our example still further, suppose the price of bicycles rose substantially. What would happen to the firm's demand for bicycles? (Hint: This is a trick question.)

If you said that nothing happens to the firm's demand for bicycles, you'd be right. Next question: If the price of bicycles rose substantially, what would happen to the quantity of bicycles demanded by the firm?

It would fall. Next question: If the price of bicycles rose substantially, what would happen to the firm's demand for bike riders? (This is not a trick question.)

The firm's demand for bike riders would decline.

What if the wage rate for bicycle riders rose substantially? What would happen for the firm's demand for riders?

I hope you were not tricked by that question and answered that a change in price does not lead to a change in demand. OK, then, if the wage rate for bike riders rose substantially, what happened to the quantity of bike riders demanded by the firm?

The quantity of riders demanded by the firm went down. Last question: If the wage rate of bike riders went up substantially, what happened to the firm's demand for bicycles?

The firm's demand for bicycles went down.

Now we can generalize. When the price of a resource rises, the demand for a complementary resource will fall; when the price of a resource falls, the demand for a complementary resource rises.

Changes in the Quantities of Other Resources

If we go back to one of the eternal questions of economics—Why are workers in one country more productive than those in another country?—the answer is that they have more land, capital, and entrepreneurial ability with which to work.

As already noted, the farmer in Bangladesh has a lot less land with which to work than the American farmer has, and the Chinese construction worker has a lot less capital backing him than his American counterpart does. It would follow that an increase in land would greatly raise the productivity of the farmer in Bangladesh, while the Chinese construction worker's productivity would soar if he were given heavy construction equipment.

We can conclude, then, that an addition of complementary resources would raise the MRP of any given resource, while a decrease in complementary resources would have the opposite effect.

Why are workers in one country more productive than those in another country?

Optimum Resource Mix for the Firm

So far, we have been deciding how much of a resource should be hired by a firm. We hire more and more labor until the MRP of the last worker hired is equal to the going wage rate. Similarly, we hire land until the MRP of the last unit of land hired is equal to the going rent. Finally, more and more capital is hired until the last unit of capital hired is equal to the interest rate.

We can generalize by saying that the firm will use increasing amounts of a resource until the MRP of that resource is equal to its price. We'd hire workers until the MRP of labor equals the price of labor (or the wage rate). Suppose we divide both sides of the equation by the price of labor.

$$(1)\quad \text{MRP of labor} = \text{Price of labor}$$

$$(2)\quad \frac{\text{MRP of labor}}{\text{Price of labor}} = \frac{\text{Price of labor}}{\text{Price of labor}}$$

This may be simplified to:

$$(3)\quad \frac{\text{MRP of labor}}{\text{Price of labor}} = 1$$

$\dfrac{\text{MRP of labor}}{\text{Price of labor}} = 1$

Remember, anything divided by itself equals one.
Now let's do the same thing with land.

$$(1)\quad \text{MRP of land} = \text{Price of land}$$

$$(2)\quad \frac{\text{MRP of land}}{\text{Price of land}} = \frac{\text{Price of land}}{\text{Price of land}}$$

$$(3)\quad \frac{\text{MRP of land}}{\text{Price of land}} = 1$$

$\dfrac{\text{MRP of land}}{\text{Price of land}} = 1$

And with capital:

$$(1)\ \text{MRP of capital} = \text{Price of capital}$$

$$(2)\ \frac{\text{MRP of capital}}{\text{Price of capital}} = \frac{\text{Price of capital}}{\text{Price of capital}}$$

$$(3)\ \frac{\text{MRP of capital}}{\text{Price of capital}} = 1$$

$$\frac{\text{MRP of capital}}{\text{Price of capital}} = 1$$

$$\frac{\text{MRP of labor}}{\text{Price of labor}} = 1$$

$$\frac{\text{MRP of land}}{\text{Price of land}} = 1$$

$$\frac{\text{MRP of capital}}{\text{Price of capital}} = 1$$

A firm will keep hiring more and more of a resource up to the point at which the MRP is equal to its price.

Next, we may combine the three equations into one.

$$\frac{\text{MRP of labor}}{\text{Price of labor}} = \frac{\text{MRP of land}}{\text{Price of land}} = \frac{\text{MRP of capital}}{\text{Price of capital}} = 1$$

After all, things equal to the same thing (in this case, 1) are equal to each other.

The reason I dragged you through all of this (besides showing off my algebra) is to reinforce the conclusion we reached a few minutes ago: *A firm will keep hiring more and more of a resource up to the point at which its MRP is equal to its price*. This great truth enables us to do another set of problems. You could have slept through everything up to this point and still get this problem set right.

TABLE 10	Hypothetical MRP Schedules for a Firm				
Units of Land	MRP of Land	Units of Capital	MRP of Capital	Units of Labor	MRP of Labor
1	$12	1	$15	1	$30
2	10	2	13	2	26
3	8	3	10	3	21
4	6	4	7	4	15
5	4	5	3	5	8
6	2	6	0	6	1
Rent = $8		Interest = $3		Wage rate = $15	

Given the data in Table 10, how many units of land, capital, and labor would you hire? It's easy. Reread the italicized statement in the previous paragraph.

The answers? Do we have the envelope? Ah yes. We would hire three units of land, five units of capital, and four units of labor.

Next we're going to take up each of the four resources in turn, beginning with labor in the next two chapters. The questions we will answer are why the wage rates are what they are, and why rent, interest, and profit are what *they* are.

Current Issue: Washing Machines and Women's Liberation

I can remember my mother scrubbing clothes on a washboard and hanging them on a clothesline which stretched from our living room window to a telephone pole about 20 feet away. It was a really big deal when our landlord installed a washing machine in our basement. On the downside, we lived in an apartment house with 47 other families.

Washing machines had come down enough in price during the 1950s that almost every home had one. At the same time, Laundromats sprang up, it seemed, on every other block.

Perhaps the washing machine played as much of a role in liberating housewives from housework as the women's liberation movement did in the 1970s.

Vacuum cleaners, dishwashers, microwave ovens, blenders, toasters, and other household appliances also made housework much easier. And, in the wake of the women's liberation movement, husbands began to pitch in with housework and child care.

Of course we know what came next—most of these women eventually went out and got jobs. Instead of spending long hours washing clothes by hand and hanging them outside to dry, women now had more free time. Most of them went out to work.

From an economic prospective, as the price of a capital good (the washer/dryer) was significantly reduced, tens of millions of housewives substituted capital for labor. Now let's look at the substitution and output effects. The lower price of capital lowered the number of hours women spent doing housework. So the substitution of capital for labor lowered the employment of housewives. But as women left their homes to take paying jobs, their employment rose. So the output effect of the declining price of capital was an increase in the employment of former housewives.

Which was greater—the substitution effect or the output effect? I would say that the output effect outweighed the substitution effect. In other words, the decline in the employment of housewives was smaller than the increase in the paid employment of the former housewives.

Questions for Further Thought and Discussion

1. As output rises, which MRP curve declines more quickly—the MRP of the perfect competitor or the MRP of the imperfect competitor? Explain your answer.

2. How is the demand for a resource affected by (a) changes in the demand for the final product and (b) productivity changes?

3. Using the substitution and output effects, explain how a decline in the price of resource A might cause an increase in the demand for substitute resource B.

4. *Practical Application:* If automatic dishwashers and human dishwashers can be substituted for one another, and if the wage rate for dishwashers rises, what happens to the demand for automatic dishwashers according to (a) the substitution effect and (b) the output effect?

Workbook for Chapter 14 connect | ECONOMICS

Name _____   Date _____

Multiple-Choice Questions

Circle the letter that corresponds to the best answer.

1. Derived demand is the demand for
   _____. (LO1)
   a) final goods and services
   b) resources ✓
   c) final goods as well as services and resources
   d) neither final goods and services nor resources

2. When the demand for wheat rises, the demand for
   farm labor _____. (LO1)
   a) rises ✓
   b) falls
   c) may rise or fall

3. The demand for resources is based on
   _____. (LO1, 2)
   a) only the demand for the final product
   b) only the productivity of the resource
   c) both the demand for the final product and the
      productivity of the resource ✓
   d) neither the demand for the final product nor the
      productivity of the resource

4. Which statement is true? (LO1)
   a) Resources and final products are both measured
      by units of input.
   b) Resources and final products are both measured
      by units of output.
   c) Resources are measured by units of input, and
      final demand is measured by units of output. ✓
   d) Resources are measured by units of output, and
      final products are measured by units of input.

5. Which statement is true? (LO2)
   a) Productivity is output per unit of input. ✓
   b) Productivity is input per unit of output.
   c) Productivity is neither of the above.

6. Relative to the Chinese economy, the U.S. economy
   is _____. (LO2)
   a) more capital intensive ✓
   b) more labor intensive
   c) more labor intensive and more capital intensive
   d) less labor intensive and less capital intensive

7. The added output for which one additional input of
   labor is responsible is its _____. (LO3)
   a) marginal revenue product
   b) marginal physical product ✓
   c) average revenue product
   d) average physical product

8. The firm's demand schedule for a resource is its
   _____ schedule. (LO3)
   a) MPP   c) total revenue
   b) MRP ✓   d) output

9. The firm will hire workers until the wage rate and the
   _____ of the last worker hired are equal. (LO3)
   a) marginal physical product
   b) MRP ✓
   c) output

10. A firm will operate at that point where _____ is
    equal to one. (LO3, 6)
    a) the marginal physical product of capital/price of
       capital
    b) the MRP of capital/price of capital ✓
    c) the price of capital/marginal physical product of
       capital
    d) the price of capital/MRP of capital

11. A firm will keep hiring more and more of a resource
    up to the point at which its MRP is equal to
    _____. (LO6)
    a) one
    b) its marginal physical product
    c) its price ✓
    d) its output

12. If the MRP of the last worker hired is lower than the wage rate, the firm has _____. (LO3)
    a) hired too many workers
    b) hired too few workers
    c) hired the right number of workers

13. If the wage rate is higher than the MRP of the last worker hired, _____. (LO3)
    a) the firm might be able to profitably hire at least one more worker
    b) the firm has already hired too many workers
    c) there is no way of knowing whether the firm has too few or too many workers

14. The most important influence on a firm's demand for a factor of production is _____. (LO4)
    a) the quantities of other resources
    b) the prices of other resources
    c) its productivity
    d) the demand for the final product

15. If the price that a perfect competitor receives for her final product doubles, the firm's MRP schedule will _____. (LO3)
    a) rise
    b) fall
    c) double at each price
    d) stay about the same

16. The most effective way to increase the productivity of labor would be to _____. (LO2)
    a) increase capital
    b) increase labor
    c) lower capital
    d) shift workers from white-collar work to blue-collar work

17. Capital and labor are _____ factors of production. (LO5)
    a) substitute
    b) complementary
    c) both complementary and substitute
    d) neither complementary nor substitute

18. Automation will raise the level of employment if the _____. (LO5)
    a) output effect is equal to the substitution effect
    b) output effect is greater than the substitution effect
    c) substitution effect is greater than the output effect

19. A firm will try to be in each of these situations except _____. (LO6)
    a) MRP of capital = Price of capital
    b) MRP of land/Price of land = 1
    c) 1 − Price of labor = MRP of labor
    d) MRP of land/Price of land = MRP of labor/Price of labor

20. The decline in washing machine prices in the 1950s led to an increase in the employment of women because the _____. (LO5)
    a) output effect outweighed the substitution effect
    b) substitution effect outweighed the output effect
    c) substitution and output effects offset each other

Fill-In Questions

1. A firm will use increasing amounts of a resource until the ___MRP___ of that resource is equal to its ___price___. (LO3)

2. If Melissa produces twice as much per hour as Adam, we would say that she is ___twice___ as productive as he is. (LO2)

3. Our economy is relatively ___capital___ intensive, while the Chinese economy is relatively ___labor___ intensive. (LO2)

4. If farmland became five times as expensive, farmers would use much more ___capital___ and ___labor___ per acre. (LO5)

5. When the productivity of a resource rises, its ___MPP___ and its ___MRP___ also rise. (LO2)

6. When the price of a substitute resource declines, the price of a resource will ___decline___. (LO4, 5)

7. The MRP of the fourth unit of output = the ___total revenue product of the 4th unit___ less the ___total revenue product of the 3rd unit___. (LO3)

344

8. The producer's surplus of rented land is the difference between how much this land is

___worth to the firm___ and how much ___it actually had to pay in rent___. (LO5)

9. A firm will keep hiring more and more of a resource up to the point at which its ___MRP___ is equal to ___the price of the resource___. (LO3)

10. A firm will keep leasing additional units of land until the MRP of that land is equal to the ___rent___. (LO3)

11. An increase in the productivity of labor will ___raise___ the MRP of labor. (LO2, 3)

12. If the price of labor goes up and a firm replaces some workers with machines, this is the ___substitution___ effect; when the price of a resource declines and the level of production consequently rises, this is the ___output___ effect. (LO5)

13. If labor and capital are complementary resources and the price of labor goes up, then the employment of capital ___declines___. (LO4, 5)

Problems

1. (a) Fill in Table 1. (b) Is the firm a perfect or an imperfect competitor? (c) If the wage rate were $60, how many workers would be hired? How much would the total wage bill come to? (d) If the wage rate were $35, how many workers would be hired? How much would the total wage bill come to? (LO3)

TABLE 1

(1) Units of Labor	(2) Output	(3) Marginal Physical Product	(4) Price	(5) Total Revenue Product	(6) Marginal Revenue Product
1	15	___	$6	___	___
2	28	___	6	___	___
3	40	___	6	___	___
4	50	___	6	___	___
5	57	___	6	___	___
6	62	___	6	___	___
7	64	___	6	___	___
8	65	___	6	___	___

2. (a) Fill in Table 2. (b) Is the firm a perfect or an imperfect competitor? (c) If the wage rate were $250, how many workers would be hired? How much would the total wage bill come to? (d) If the wage rate were $99, how many workers would be hired? How much would the total wage bill come to? (LO3)

TABLE 2

(1) Units of Labor	(2) Output	(3) Marginal Physical Product	(4) Price	(5) Total Revenue Product	(6) Marginal Revenue Product
1	22	___	$20	___	___
2	43	___	19	___	___
3	63	___	18	___	___
4	81	___	17	___	___
5	96	___	16	___	___
6	109	___	15	___	___
7	119	___	14	___	___
8	127	___	13	___	___

3. Given the data in Table 3, how many units of land, labor, and capital would you hire? (LO6)

TABLE 3

Units of Land	MRP of Land	Units of Capital	MRP of Capital	Units of Labor	MRP of Labor
1	$20	1	$35	1	$31
2	17	2	33	2	24
3	13	3	27	3	16
4	8	4	20	4	9
5	2	5	12	5	5
6	1	6	4	6	2
Rent = $8		Interest = $27		Wage rate = $24	

4. A perfect competitor charges a price of $5. The first worker he would hire would have a marginal physical product of 20, the second worker he would hire would have a marginal physical product of 18, the third worker would have a marginal physical product of 16, and the fourth worker would have a marginal physical product of 14. (a) How many workers would he hire if the wage rate were $90? How much would his wage bill be? (b) How many workers would he hire if the wage rate were $70? How much would his wage bill come to? (LO3)

Chapter 15

Labor Unions

Until the late 1930s the standard workweek was six days. As in the Book of Genesis, the Sabbath was the one day of rest. When labor unions secured a 40-hour, 5-day workweek, it quickly became the new standard not just for the unionized workforce, but for nearly everyone else as well. In 1938 the Fair Labor Standards Act required that employers pay time and a half for nearly everyone who put in more than 40 hours. Rather than pay this premium, many employers held the workweek to 40 hours and hired more employees to take up the slack. Today just one in eight American workers is a union member, but without labor unions, we might all still be working a six-day week.

America needs a raise.
—John Sweeney,
President, AFL–CIO

LEARNING OBJECTIVES

After reading this chapter you should be able to:

1. Summarize the early history of the labor movement.
2. List and explain the major labor legislation.
3. Define and differentiate between craft and industrial unions.
4. Summarize union organizing since the 1950s.
5. Discuss and distinguish between the economic power of unions and employers.
6. Assess the process of collective bargaining.
7. Discuss the pros and cons of the card check law.

A Short History of the American Labor Movement

The Early Years

Labor unions are a traditional American institution, with their own national holiday, replete with parades, speeches, and picnics. This, of course, was not always so. Until the 1940s most Americans had unfavorable opinions of unions. In the popular mind, they were subversive organizations set up to obtain exorbitant wage increases and possibly overthrow the American economic system. Union leaders were regarded as racketeers, communists, or political bosses. And some were guilty as charged.

Labor unions were considered subversive until the 1940s.

Although the trade union movement in the United States is some two centuries old, most labor historians consider the modern era to have begun with the founding of the original American Federation of Labor in 1886 or with its predecessor, the Knights of Labor, which rose to prominence in the mid-1880s. Within the ranks of these organizations

The AF of L rang in the modern era of unions in 1886.

there was an almost continual struggle between those who sought specific gains—better wages, hours, and working conditions—and those who advocated more far-reaching reforms—a universal eight-hour day, elimination of the wage system, and the establishment of producers' cooperatives to replace private enterprise.

By the late 1880s the American Federation of Labor, or the AF of L (AFL) as it became known, had become the predominant labor organization. Samuel Gompers, who served as its president until his death in 1924, stressed the importance of "bread-and-butter unionism." Why the AF of L succeeded where the Knights had failed is explained largely by their opposing philosophies as well as by the changing conditions of the American economy.

The emergence of the large corporation, which replaced the small workshop, meant the wage relationship was here to stay. Forget about small producers' cooperatives and start worrying about securing enough bargaining strength to obtain better wages, hours, and working conditions. An individual worker has little bargaining power against a huge corporation, but thousands of workers, banded together in craft unions—the ironworkers, cigar makers, carpenters—did have a certain amount of leverage. They could, if they didn't get what they wanted, withhold their labor. In other words, they could go out on strike.

This might not sound all that radical, but during the first three decades of the 20th century most Americans saw unions as subversive, foreign, and, in some cases, downright evil. Employers fought them tooth and nail. Union members were blacklisted, those suspected of having union sympathies were fired, court orders were obtained to prohibit strikes as well as milder forms of union activity, and sometimes private detectives, labor goons, and sympathetic local police were used to put down strikes violently.

Key Labor Legislation

National Labor Relations Act (Wagner Act, 1935)   The Wagner Act and the Taft-Hartley Act are by far the two most important pieces of labor legislation. The Wagner Act, named for New York Senator Robert Wagner, committed the federal government to promote collective bargaining and to support union organizing.

The Wagner Act prohibited employers from engaging in such "unfair labor practices" as (1) coercion or interference with employees who are organizing or bargaining; (2) refusal to bargain in good faith with a union legally representing employees; and (3) in general, penalizing employees for union activity.

The act set up a three-member (now a five-member) board to protect workers in organizing unions and to administer representation elections (that is, to determine which union will represent the workers of a company). If 30 percent of the employees in an entire company, or just one unit of that company, decide to be represented by a union, these people petition the National Labor Relations Board to conduct an election. If the union gets a majority of votes, it then represents *all* the employees of that company or unit, even those who are not members of the union.

This law put the force of the federal government behind collective bargaining, at the same time lending unions a certain legitimacy. It established unions as an American institution. In addition, the Wagner Act provided the necessary machinery to ensure that large corporations would allow unions to organize and would bargain in good faith.

During World War II strikes were considered unpatriotic; but 1946 set a record for strikes—a record that still stands. The late 1940s were a time of inflation and prosperity, and labor used the strike weapon to get what it considered its fair share of the economic pie. Partially in response to these disturbances, the Republicans captured control of Congress in 1946 for the first time in 14 years. They felt they had a mandate not only to redress the imbalance between the power of labor and the power of management, but as many observers noted, "to put labor in its place."

Taft-Hartley Act (1947)   Just as the Wagner Act protected employee rights, the Taft-Hartley Act protected employer rights. Here are its three main provisions: (1) it allows the president to call an 80-day "cooling-off" period; (2) it allows the states to ban the union shop; and (3) it severely limits the closed shop.

Bread-and-butter unionism

The wage relationship was here to stay.

Wagner Act

Prohibition of unfair labor practices

The Wagner Act put the force of the government behind collective bargaining.

Taft-Hartley Act

The Closed Shop, Union Shop, Open Shop, and "Right-to-Work" Laws

(1) Closed shop An employer may hire only union members. The Taft-Hartley Act outlawed this arrangement, but sometimes union hiring halls operate as de facto closed shops. If an employer, generally a construction firm, hires only those sent by the union, we have a closed shop, even though it is nominally a union shop.

(2) Union shop Under a union shop contract, all employees must join the union, usually within 30 days after they are hired. This arrangement effectively increases union membership because many workers would not have joined unless they were forced to. A variation of the union shop is the agency shop, in which you don't have to join the union, but you must pay dues.

(3) Open shop No one is forced to join the union, although it does represent all the workers in contract negotiations. Union members often resent nonmembers who are "getting a free ride," because they don't have to pay dues.

(4) Right-to-work laws Section 14b of the Taft-Hartley Act permitted the states to pass laws prohibiting the union shop. Some 20 states have done this, which means in those states you can work in a shop that is organized without having to join the union. Organized labor has struggled in vain since 1947 to get this controversial section repealed because these right-to-work laws have been responsible for lower union membership in the states that passed them.

Strikes that "imperil the national health or safety" may be halted by court order at the request of the president, who determines which strikes imperil Americans' health and safety. If a settlement is not reached during the 80 days allowed, the union may resume the strike.

The 80-day cooling-off period puts the union at a strategic disadvantage. For 80 days the company can stockpile inventory, making it easier for it to weather a strike and perhaps less likely to make concessions. However, by committing itself to ensuring labor peace, not to mention to protecting the nation's health and safety, the administration is more likely to put pressure on both parties to settle their dispute.

80-day cooling-off period

The most controversial part of the law is Section 14b. This section allows the states to enact "right-to-work" laws, which prohibit union shop contracts. (About 20 states—mainly in the South—have laws prohibiting contracts that require union membership as a condition of employment.)

Section 14b: right-to-work laws

The act severely limits the extent of the closed shop (closed to nonunion members). However, unions have sometimes gotten around this prohibition by calling a closed shop a union shop (see the nearby box).

Closed shop

Taft-Hartley also prohibits jurisdictional disputes and secondary boycotts. A jurisdictional dispute occurs when two unions, each vying to organize a company, picket that company, which has no dispute with either union. A secondary boycott is directed against a company that isn't party to a strike, such as a trade supplier or a customer or a retail outlet.

Jurisdictional disputes and secondary boycotts are prohibited.

Craft Unions versus Industrial Unions

As you can see from Figure 1, union membership rose spectacularly from the mid-1930s to the mid-1940s. The major impetus was the Wagner Act, which legitimized unions and facilitated their organizing workers in the nation's basic industries of auto, steel, and rubber. During this time a split developed within the AFL, leading to the formation of the Congress of Industrial Organizations (CIO) in 1935. The split was caused by a dispute over whether to organize along craft lines, as the AFL had been doing for 50 years, or along industry lines, as advocated by the leaders of the CIO.

Union membership rose spectacularly in the mid-1930s.

Craft unions are organized along the lines of particular occupations, such as air traffic controllers, plumbers, operating engineers, airline pilots, or teachers. In general these are relatively well-paid jobs requiring years of training.

Craft unions

Industrial unions, such as the United Steel Workers, the United Auto Workers, and the United Mine Workers, are organized along industry lines, without regard to craft.

Industrial unions

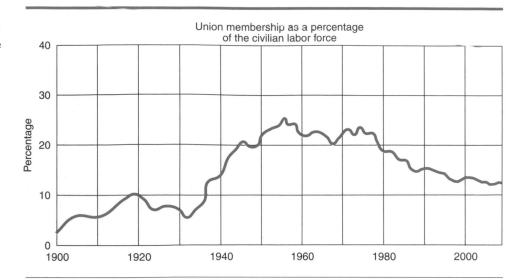

Lumped together in one union are skilled and unskilled workers doing varied types of work. What bonds them is that they all work in the same industry.

In some industries, particularly those with unskilled or semiskilled mass-production workers, it makes more sense to organize along industrial rather than craft lines. Unlike plumbers or airline pilots, the people who put together cars can be trained in a couple of hours—and replaced just as quickly. They simply don't have a craft that sets them apart from their co-workers.

The conflict within the AFL over whether to organize along craft or industrial lines led to the great schism of the organization in 1935. Most of the AFL leadership, who headed the craft and building trades unions, believed that machinists, for example, whether employed in autos, steel, or any other industry, should be organized into a machinists' union. But the leaders of the breakaway Congress of Industrial Organizations believed all the workers in an industry should be organized into an industrywide union regardless of craft.

In the mid- to late 1930s there was a tremendous spurt of labor organizing by the CIO in steel, autos, rubber, oil, and other areas of heavy industry. The AFL also began organizing along industrial lines during this period. As we can see in Figure 1, these were the golden days of union organizing.

AFL–CIO merger

The Taft-Hartley Act unintentionally sparked efforts to reunite the AFL and the CIO. The main obstacle to the merger was no longer the philosophical one of whether organization should be carried out along craft or industrial lines. That issue had been settled by the late 1930s when the AFL began to organize its own industrial unions. In 1955 the two groups merged to form the AFL–CIO.

The 5 states with the lowest percentage of union members were in the South—North Carolina (3.1), Arkansas (4.2), South Carolina (4.5), Georgia (4.6), and Virginia (4.7). No surprise there. The most highly unionized states were New York (25.2), Hawaii (23.5), Alaska (22.3), and Washington (20.2). Two factors were largely responsible for this vast differential in the unionization rates of these two groups of states. The states with very low unionization rates are all "right-to-work" states, which makes union organizing very difficult. And the states with very high unionization rates all have heavy concentrations of manufacturing industries, which have generally been relatively easy for unions to organize.[1]

Union Organizing since the 1950s

By the 1940s unions had become a well-established and widely-accepted American institution. Indeed, we can thank them not just for the eight-hour workday and the five-day

---

[1]If you're interested in politics, it is striking that the 10 most heavily unionized states are all so-called "blue states," which tend to vote Democratic, while the 10 least unionized states are all so-called "red states," which tend to vote Republican.

workweek, but for paid vacations, health-care benefits and pensions, safety regulations, bans on sweatshops and child labor, and other workplace advances we now take for granted.[2]

The South continues to be the least unionized section of the country. Long the target of AFL–CIO organizers, this region has remained a tough nut to crack. Right-to-work laws, strong local conservatism, and antiunion feeling, as well as the economic power of the local firms, have kept labor organizing at a low ebb.

Union membership peaked decades ago (see Figure 1). Today just 12.3 percent of the labor force is unionized. Millions of workers have shifted from manufacturing to service industries, and it is much harder to organize computer programmers, insurance adjusters, and financial analysts than it is to organize factory workers.

Walmart has 1.4 million employees in the United States, but not one is a member of a union. In 2000 the United Food and Commercial Workers did manage to organize butchers in a Texas Walmart, but two weeks later the company closed down its meat-cutting departments nationwide. In 2005 a store in Quebec, Canada, where employees voted to unionize, was also closed.[3]

The only Walmart workers in North America covered by a union contract are the eight employees of the automotive department of a store in Gatineau, Quebec. A contract, imposed by a Quebec government arbitrator in 2008, is a three-year agreement which provides the eight employees with an improved wage scale, annual raises, and a grievance process for settling disputes.

Why has Walmart been such a tough nut for unions to crack? Aside from management's fierce opposition, there are two other important factors: Walmart has a large part-time, transient workforce and many Walmart employees work in Southern states where unionism isn't welcome.

In 2005 the United Food and Commercial Workers suspended its strategy of seeking to unionize Walmart store by store. "When you're dealing with a company that's so big and ruthless, you can't even get enough leverage going store by store," said Paul Blank, the union's Walmart campaign director. "Even when you win an organizing drive, you lose because the company will simply shut down a store."[4]

While Walmart is fiercely antiunion at home, it sometimes sings a different tune overseas. In 1999 it purchased Asda, a unionized chain of stores which now accounts for one-tenth of Walmart's sales in Britain. Until 2006, the company *did* negotiate separate collective bargaining agreements with the union in each workplace. But in that year, threatened with a costly strike, Walmart reached an agreement that established nationwide collective bargaining for distribution center employees. The union, which is now free to recruit new members on the job, is hoping to establish a national collective bargaining agreement for Asda's retail store employees as well.

Is Walmart the nation's only large retail chain that's non-union? Hardly. Target, Walgreens, Best Buy, Home Depot, and Lowe's are also non-union.

The United Auto Workers, whose hourly workforce at the Big Three (General Motors, Ford, and Chrysler) has shrunk to just 139,000 from a peak of 1.5 million in the mid-1970s, is caught in a bind. It has been unable to organize in any of the foreign-owned plants (owned by Honda, Toyota, Nissan, and other companies), located mainly in the South. Until now, to make unionization less attractive, the foreign-owned factories have boosted wages very close to the UAW's $25 an hour. But as they gain market share, the pressure to match Big Three wages will lessen. Former UAW president Douglas Fraser, now a labor studies professor at Wayne State University in Detroit, has observed, "Sooner or later . . . the Big Three are going to say, 'We're becoming noncompetitive, and unless you organize the transplants, we're going to have to modify the proposals we make to you.'"[5]

---

[2]See Philip M. Dine, *State of the Unions* (New York: McGraw-Hill, 2008), p. xix.

[3]Was the store closed because Walmart wanted to keep out the union? Quebec's provincial labor commission found that Walmart had good and sufficient cause to close the store. The United Food and Commercial Workers Union took the case to court, and it finally reached Canada's highest court. In 2009, that court upheld the decision of the Quebec provincial labor commission.

[4]Steven Greenhouse, "Opponents of Walmart to Coordinate Efforts," *The New York Times*, April 3, 2005, p. 20.

[5]See *BusinessWeek*, June 10, 2002, p. 78.

| TABLE 1 | Membership of Largest Labor Unions, 2009 |

Union	Membership
National Education Association	3,100,000
Service Employees International Union	2,200,000
International Brotherhood of Teamsters	1,400,000
American Federation of State, County and Municipal Employees	1,400,000
American Federation of Teachers	1,400,000
United Food and Commercial Workers	1,300,000
United Steel Workers	700,000
International Brotherhood of Electrical Workers	700,000
Communications Workers of America	550,000
United Auto Workers	500,000
Laborers' International Union	500,000

Had the employers of the past generation dealt fairly with men, there would have been no trade unions.

—Stanley Baldwin,
former Prime Minister,
Great Britain

Which is the biggest labor union today? As you can see in Table 1, it's the National Education Association, with 3.1 million members.

There has been a precipitous decline in private sector union membership over the last five decades. Back in 1955 more than a third of American workers in the private sector belonged to a union. As late as 1973 24.2 percent of all workers in the private sector were union members, but just 6.9 percent were members in 2009 (see Figure 2). These losses were partially offset by the unionization of the public sector. In 2009, 37.4 percent of the public sector was unionized. In fact, the 7.9 million unionized public sector workers now outnumber the 7.4 million workers employed in the private sector. Union membership as a percentage of the labor force has been falling since the mid-1950s (see Figure 1), but the decline in big craft and industrial unions has been even faster. Which unions in Table 1 have large numbers of government employees? They are the National Education Association (number 1); the Service Employees International Union (number 2) (a substantial minority of members are government employees); the American Federation of State, County, and Municipal Employees; and the American Federation of Teachers (tied for third place).

Figure 2

Private Sector Union Membership as a Percentage of Total Private Sector Employment, 1973–2009
In 1973 nearly one of every four people working in the private sector was a union member. By 2009 fewer than one in thirteen was a union member.
Source: Bureau of Labor Statistics.

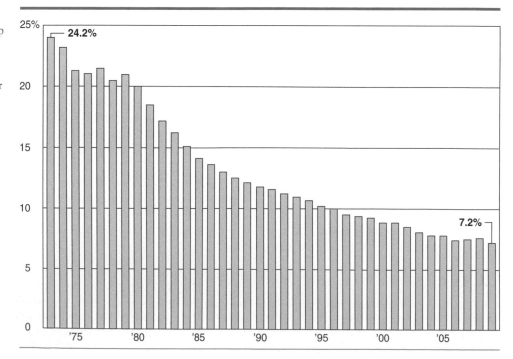

on the web

To get the most current figures on union membership, go to www.stats.bls.gov. Use A-Z Index in the upper right corner. Click on U and then Union membership.

The Formation of Change to Win

Upset with declining union membership, five large unions withdrew from the AFL–CIO in 2005, taking with them 40 percent of the federation's members. The Teamsters, the Service Employees' International Union, the United Food and Commercial Workers, the Laborers' International Union, and Unite Here! (which represents hotel, restaurant, textile, and apparel workers)—formed the Change to Win coalition. They were joined by the United Farm Workers, which left the AFL–CIO a few months later, and the Carpenters and Joiners, which had pulled out of the AFL–CIO in 2001.

The new 5.4 million-member group hopes to stanch labor's decline by mounting a national recruiting drive involving entire industries. It has targeted the 50 million workers whose jobs cannot be sent overseas or be replaced by machines. Many of these jobs pay poverty-level wages and include janitors, dishwashers, hotel maids, cashiers, nursing home aides, and security guards. Possible targets for unionization drives include Home Depot, Federal Express, Walmart, as well as the large hotel chains. Change to Win chairwoman Anna Burger declared that "Organizing is our core principle. It is our North Star."

America is one of the *least* unionized industrial nations in the world. Among the nations shown in Figure 3, which has data for the year 2006, the United States and France had, by far, the lowest unionization rates.

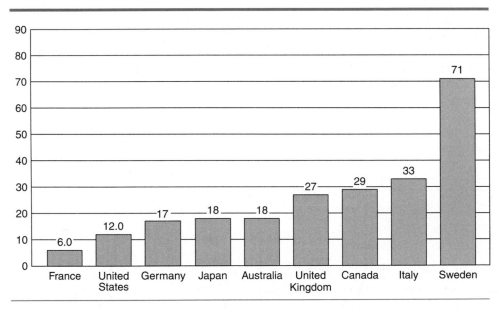

Figure 3
Union Membership as a Percentage of Labor Force, Selected Industrial Countries, 2008
Source: Author's Internet search.

Jobs: Exportable and Nonexportable

There is work that must be done in the United States, and there is work that can be done abroad. If we import a good or service, then obviously it can be produced in another country. Since the mid-20th century, four main groups of unionized workers have lost their jobs to foreigners—those in the auto, steel, textile, and apparel industries. Clearly, we can import cars, steel, textiles, and clothing.

One thing we can't import is trucking deliveries. And that service is dominated by the International Brotherhood of Teamsters. Why do these folks earn well over $20 an hour, while millions of other Americans work just as hard for only $8 or $9 an hour?

How much someone is paid comes down to the supply of labor and the demand for that labor. But when that labor must be used locally, then that supply is limited to those currently residing in the United States.

Fifty years ago our largest unions were industrial and craft unions, most of whose members worked in manufacturing. Now, as you can see from glancing back at Table 1, a majority of our union members are service workers. And more to the point, their jobs are relatively safe from foreign competition.

The Economic Power of Labor Unions

Labor is the capital of our working man.

—Grover Cleveland,
U.S. President

Many people accuse unions of being monopolies. Indeed, they were prosecuted under the Sherman Antitrust Act during the first two decades of this century. In a sense, of course, unions *are* monopolies. For example, the painters', plumbers', carpenters', longshoremen's, and teamsters' trades are nearly 100 percent unionized. Aren't these monopolies?

We define a monopoly as the seller of a good or service for which there are no close substitutes. Of course, labor is not really a good or service but rather a factor that helps produce a good or service. But if we brush aside that technicality, then for all intents and purposes unions *are* sometimes monopolies.

Unions have two ways of asserting power: inclusion and exclusion.

Unions have two basic ways of exerting power. They can take in as members virtually everyone who works in a particular craft or industry. This is the *method of inclusion,* and it could give the union a monopoly. Examples are the United Steel Workers, the United Auto and Aerospace Workers, and the Teamsters.

A second way of exerting power, which is quite common in the building trades, is the *principle of exclusion.* You don't take in just anyone. There are tests, you might need experience, and believe it or not, it probably wouldn't hurt to know someone—preferably a close relative like a father or an uncle—who happens to be an influential member of the union. By keeping people out, you keep down the supply of carpenters, plumbers, bricklayers, and electricians, and amazingly, wages go all the way up.

Let's see what the principles of inclusion and exclusion look like graphically. In Figure 4A we have the inclusive union, generally a large industrial union such as the United Steel Workers. The union tries to obtain a high standard wage from U.S. Steel (now part of USX), Nucor, Republic, and the other companies. But at a high wage rate, the companies will hire fewer workers than they would have hired at lower wages.

Figure 4

Inclusive and Exclusive Unions
For both inclusive unions (see panel A), like the large industrial unions, and exclusive unions (see panel B), more typically craft unions, the wage rate is set by supply and demand.

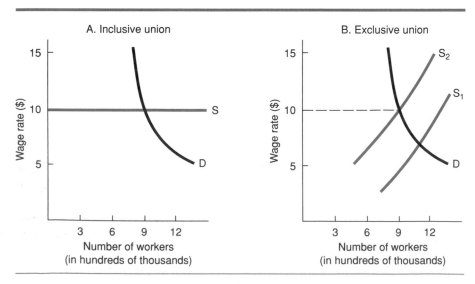

We get the same results from the exclusive union (see Figure 4B). This time, however, the union has restricted the supply of workers by allowing only certain people into its ranks. It's clear, then, that both exclusion and inclusion will lead to higher wages.

Do unionized workers earn more than workers who are not members of labor unions? The answer is "yes." Next question: How much more per hour do unionized workers earn than nonunionized workers? In 2009, among full-time wage and salary workers, union members had median weekly earnings of $908, while those who were not represented by unions had median weekly earnings of just $710. Unionization may explain most of this earnings differential, but so too does variation in the distribution of union members and nonunion employees by occupation, industry, firm size, and geographic region. A Michigan auto worker, for example, earns a lot more than a Mississippi farm laborer.

Are unions too powerful? Public opinion is divided on this issue, but before we even attempt to answer this question, we should look at the other side of the coin. Are large corporations too powerful?

The Economic Power of Large Employers

We've seen that workers, who were once powerless to bargain individually with huge corporate employers, have formed unions that have become quite powerful. Let's consider an extreme case of corporate power, that of monopsony. The seller of a product for which there are no close substitutes is a monopolist. *Monopsony is the market situation in which there is only a single buyer for a product.* The most common kind of monopsony is a labor market where there is only a single employer. At one time or another General Electric in Schenectady, New York; textile producer J. P. Stevens in several towns in the South; and the military bases in various towns around the country have completely dominated the local job markets. Sometimes 60 to 80 percent of the jobs in these areas have been provided by a single employer. Technically, a monopsonist is a single buyer, but these towns came pretty close. Bentonville, Arkansas, home of Walmart, had a population of 35,526 in 2008. Walmart headquarters has 12,000 employees. There are an additional 3,000 people employed in the four Walmart stores located in Bentonville.

The case of monopsony

Winston-Salem, North Carolina, home of R. J. Reynolds, was a typical company town. Because the company paid double or triple the local average manufacturing wage, they were able to support restaurants, dry cleaners, day care and other service industries. Dean Foust and Brian Grow described the company town atmosphere in *BusinessWeek:*

> Reynolds could be like a stern father—for years it banned long hair and frowned on divorce—but that didn't bother locals who earned as much as $60,000 a year at the company's factory in nearby Tobaccoville. "I've gotten a lot of checks over the years from customers that they'd stamped with the words 'Tobacco Pays My Bills,'" says Penny Terry, who runs a furniture store near the plant.[6]

But in response to declining demand for cigarettes, and rising competition from discount cigarette makers using cheaper foreign tobacco, R. J. Reynolds began laying off workers. By 2010, it was down to just a few hundred employees in Winston-Salem, from 14,000 in 1983.

In this chapter we are concerned with the monopsonist as the dominant employer in a locality, but a monopsonist, in more general terms, faces the entire supply curve of anything being sold—labor, other resources, or any good or service. Perhaps the prime example today exists in Japan's Toyota City, with its rings of auto supplier firms radiating outward from the Toyota Motor Company headquarters. This city of 350,000 is a prime example of a company town, where nearly everyone is employed, directly or indirectly, by the same company.

In the Soviet Union, hundreds of company towns, called *monotowns,* grew around a single plant or factory. Even today, two decades after the disappearance of the Soviet

---

[6]Dean Foust and Brian Grow, "Blues for a Company Town," *BusinessWeek,* October 6, 2003, p. 56.

Professional Sports as Monopsonies

If you happen to be a professional athlete, you probably don't have many prospective employers to whom you can sell your services. Take baseball. If you're a really good prospect, the chances are you'll be drafted by one of the major-league teams, and if you're *really* good, you'll work your way up to the big leagues. But then you'll have to play for the team that drafted you for another five years before you may become a free agent and sell your services to other teams willing to bid on them.

Professional football had virtually no free agency until 1993. Until then if you were one of the better players in the National Football League, you were virtually tied to your team for your entire career, unless you were traded to another team. Every 8 or 10 years a rival league would spring up and a bidding war would ensue, driving up salaries. In the 1960s there was the American Football League, which later merged with the National Football

League. In the 1970s we had the World Football League, and in the 1980s the United States Football League. These two leagues folded, but not before they pushed up salary levels in the National Football League.

The National Basketball Association, which has dominated professional basketball since the 1940s, eventually merged with the newer American Basketball Association, but not until a costly bidding war had raised salaries into the millions.

Today the professional baseball, football, and basketball leagues have pure monopsony power. So, too, does professional hockey, which endured labor stoppages before the playoffs in 1992 and for the entire 1994–95 and 2004–05 seasons. Although professional athletes are handsomely paid, and although they do enjoy some degree of free-agent power, their salaries would be even higher if there were more bidders for their services.

Union, there are about 450 monotowns scattered across Russia. In addition to being the single employer, these town-forming enterprises are responsible for providing all social services and amenities—from clinics and schools to heat, water, and electricity—for populations ranging from 5,000 to 700,000.

The monopsonist faces the entire supply curve of labor.

The monopsonist faces the entire supply curve of labor. Because that curve sweeps upward to the right (that is, to induce more people to work more, you have to pay them a higher wage rate), the monopsonist who wants to hire more workers will have to offer a higher wage rate. The best-known monopsonists these days are professional baseball, football, and basketball leagues (see the box, "Professional Sports as Monopsonies").

When a union that controls the supply of labor is opposed by an employer that controls the demand for labor, we have a bilateral monopoly. Using that term loosely, we may call several labor markets bilateral monopolies: auto workers, professional baseball players, teachers in most large school districts, and aerospace workers. Like the very competitive oligopolists we talked about a few chapters back, a union dealing with a monopsony employer knows that any move it makes will invite a countermove by the firm. And vice versa. At the bargaining table, who ends up with what depends largely on the relative power on both sides.

Collective Bargaining

The main arena

Collective bargaining is the main arena of the power struggle between labor and management. In general, labor tries to secure substantial increases in wages, fringe benefits, and perhaps better working conditions. Management, of course, offers considerably less than labor wants. And so they bargain. But backing up their bargaining power are their two ultimate weapons: for labor, it is the strike; for management, it is the ability to take a strike.

The strike and the ability to take a strike are the ultimate weapons.

Strikes, Lockouts, and Givebacks

The lockout

Some observers say the lockout is management's ultimate weapon. That's like saying that if labor's ultimate weapon is to punch management in the nose, management can

Lockout on the Docks

In the fall of 2002, 10,500 members of the International Longshore and Warehouse Union were locked out of their jobs at 29 West Coast ports after engaging in a month-long work slowdown. After 11 days, President George W. Bush invoked the 80-day cooling-off period of the Taft-Hartley Act (for the first time in 24 years), the ports were reopened, and less than two months later, both sides resolved their dispute and signed a six-year contract.

During the lockout, the economy was losing about $1 billion a day, and would have been losing considerably more if the lockout had lasted longer. Automobile assembly lines, dependent on just-in-time deliveries, had begun shutting down, and retailers were worried about having the inventory needed to stock their shelves for the Christmas shopping season.

The crux of the dispute was over the introduction of information technology such as bar-codes, which would greatly improve efficiency, but lead to the loss of 400 clerical jobs. In the agreement, in exchange for the loss of these jobs, the union extracted a guarantee of lifetime employment for all the 1,600 current clerks. In addition, the longshoremen, who earned an average of $100,000 a year, received an 11 percent pay increase over the life of the contract.

beat labor to the punch, so to speak, by punching *itself* in the nose. If a strike hurts the company by cutting off production, so does a lockout. But in 2002 when the West Coast longshoremen staged a work slowdown, the port operators felt they had no choice but to enforce a lockout (see the box, "Lockout on the Docks").

No, the ultimate weapon of management is the ability to take a strike. To carry my analogy further, a good fighter must be able to take a punch. Perhaps in other fields the term *glass jaw* or *canvas back* might be laudatory, but not in boxing—and not in collective bargaining. If the union knows management cannot withstand a strike, it will certainly push much harder for a favorable settlement.

The ability to take a strike, of course, varies from firm to firm and from industry to industry. Generally, manufacturing fares better than services because the manufacturer can build up inventories in anticipation of a strike. On the rare occasions when the Taft-Hartley Act is invoked by the president, such a company can add even more to its stockpiles during the 80-day halt of the strike. As a strike wears on, orders can be filled from this large inventory. Also, delivery times can be stretched out from the normal two months to three or four months. When the strike is over, workers can be put on overtime and extra workers temporarily hired to help build up the depleted inventories and fill any backlog of orders.

Firms in service industries are less able to take a strike than those in manufacturing because they do not have an inventory to help them cushion the effects of lost production. An airline, an insurance company, a bank, a computer firm, or a real estate company cannot make up lost sales because their competitors will have picked up the slack.

A diversified firm, particularly a large conglomerate, can ride out a strike more easily than can the firm that produces a single good or service. A strike will affect only one or two divisions; the others will keep operating. Similarly, a large firm has a better chance of surviving a strike than a small firm does because it has greater financial resources. Finally, a multinational corporation might simply shift operations to another country in the event of a strike.

All this brilliant analysis notwithstanding, one can occasionally draw exactly the opposite conclusion about negotiating strength varying with the ability to take a strike. It's like the rhetorical question "Would you hit a person wearing glasses?" Then, of course, you put on a pair of glasses.

What does this have to do with the ability to take a strike? I'm glad you asked. If you worked for a company that might go under, would *you* call for a strike? You'd probably win the strike and be out of a job. That's why the United Auto Workers did not dare call a strike in the 1970s and early 1980s, although they could have easily defeated Chrysler. To carry this a bit further, if a company like Chrysler is financially weak, you won't ask for much of a wage increase. In fact, during the 1981–82 recession, some

Which firms and industries can best withstand a strike?

COLAs

Productivity increases

Pattern-setting wage increases

Grievance procedure

The focal point of negotiations is generally the wage increase.

Job security and seniority

unions actually negotiated not only no wage increases but even wage reductions. Saving jobs, especially during the economic doldrums of the early 1990s, has often led to wage reductions.

Productivity increases are a key issue because they provide the basis for pay increases. If workers produce more, they have a good argument for increased pay; and if more is produced, the company can afford to pay more. Unfortunately, productivity—output per labor hour—is not often measured accurately. A union might argue that productivity is rising 4 percent a year, and management might just as reasonably counter that the figure is only 2 percent.

The United Steelworkers have taken a very cooperative approach towards collective bargaining, helping to restructure the ailing U.S. steel industry. In 2003, it helped create a plan to revitalize Goodyear Tire & Rubber Co., the nation's largest tire maker, which had lost $1.5 billion the previous year, and a large slice of its market share to rivals selling cheap tires made in low-wage countries.

The union appeared to have just two options—either allow Goodyear to replace some of its 14 U.S. plants with ones in Asia, or to call a strike that might force the company into bankruptcy. But the United Steelworkers came up with a third choice—slash labor costs by $1.15 billion over three years and cut 3,000 jobs in exchange for Goodyear's promise to keep—and invest in—12 of its 14 U.S. factories and to limit imports from its factories in Brazil and Asia. In addition to the job cuts, USW members won't get a raise for three years. But this may have been a small price for the thousands of workers who will be able to keep their $22 an hour jobs.

Finally, there's the issue of pattern-setting wage increases. For example, after the uniform services (police, fire, and sanitation) negotiations are completed in New York, the city then begins negotiations with the other municipal unions. The bargaining teams for those unions do not want to go back to their members with less than the other guys got. It's as simple as that. During periods of rapid inflation, with the added pressure of keeping up with the rising cost of living, the unions sometimes view the pattern-setting settlements as minimums that must be exceeded. This tends to create still newer pattern setters, which themselves become goals to be surpassed.

The Collective Bargaining Agreement

Collective bargaining negotiations will end with either an agreement or a strike. The collective bargaining agreement is a contract running from a page or two up to several hundred pages. The first key provision is wages and hours. The second is job security and seniority. Other areas often covered include grievance procedures, working conditions, and the role of the union in the day-to-day running of the firm. Also spelled out in the contract are health benefits, the number of paid holidays, paid sick leave and personal leave days, and vacation days.

The focal point of the negotiations is generally the amount by which wage rates will be increased. In fact, progress reports on the negotiations generally refer to the latest wage offer. Everything else gets lumped together as "other issues."

Job security and seniority are also important contract provisions. Generally, the last people hired are the first to be laid off. Seniority is often the most important criterion for promotion as well. This has tended to pit older, more experienced workers against younger workers, but a union negotiating team will almost always regard seniority as sacrosanct, especially because older workers tend to dominate most unions.

Company officials typically dislike union wage scales and seniority provisions because they require everyone to be paid at the same rate regardless of individual productivity differences. Furthermore, officials are legally bound to lay off the least senior workers during bad economic times—times when it would make more sense to lay off the least efficient workers. Union officials counter that it would be arbitrary and unfair to use any criterion other than seniority as the basis for wage rates, promotion, and order of layoffs.

Health care benefits were not an especially contentious issue until the 1990s. But with rapidly rising medical insurance costs, many companies began to demand that their employees pay a higher proportion of these costs. Unions strongly resisted this "give-back," and the issue came to a head during the 2007 contract negotiations between the United Auto Workers and the Big Three Detroit automobile companies. The negotiators reached a historic agreement under which the union agreed to take over the health care insurance obligation for hundreds of thousands of employees and retirees. In exchange, the companies will contribute tens of billions of dollars.

Another important provision in many contracts is the grievance procedure, which is spelled out step-by-step. For example, an assembly line worker whose supervisor yelled at her might first have to go to her shop steward, who then talks to the supervisor. If the grievance is not settled at that level, it might go to the chief steward and the head of the department. Beyond that, the contract may specify two or three still higher levels. However, most grievances are settled at the steward–supervisor level.

The Strike

Very few strikes have disrupted the U.S. economy. Since the passage of the Taft-Hartley Act in 1947, only two have caused major economic disruption: the 1959 steel strike and the United Auto Workers' strike against General Motors in 1970.

Show me a country in which there are no strikes and I'll show you that country in which there is no liberty.

—Samuel Gompers

Figure 5 provides a historical record of work time lost to strikes. Since the late 1980s, we have never lost as much as one-tenth of one percent of work time because of strikes.

Very few strikes have disrupted our economy.

The American economy, despite some acrimonious collective bargaining, rarely experiences major strikes. Israel, South Korea, Canada, and Spain lost more than twice as much work time due to labor disputes.

Until very recently in China, workers were not allowed to form unions or to strike. A docile, poorly paid labor force was used to attract tens of thousands of foreign manufacturers.

But in the spring of 2010 two major strikes were permitted, both of which led to large wage increases. About a dozen suicides among workers at the Taiwanese owned Foxconn, a huge producer of electronics, set off a strike which was settled only after the company agreed to double wages to about $300 a month.

A series of strikes and walkouts at Honda, the Japanese auto company, also led to large wage increases. Still, Honda was able to counter the power of the strikers by bringing in replacement workers—a tactic that several American firms had employed over the last couple of decades in the United States.

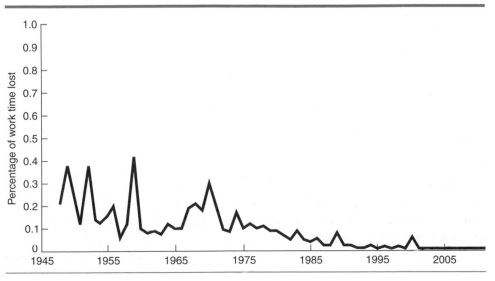

Figure 5

Work Time Lost because of Strikes, 1945–2009
From 1946 through 1970, strikes often resulted in very substantial losses of labor hours. Since 1970, there has been a marked decline in hours lost, and since the mid-1970s, we have never had a year in which those losses amounted to even one-tenth of one percent of total work time.
Source: U.S. Department of Labor, *Monthly Labor Review,* various issues.

To get the most current figures on work stoppages, go to www.stats.bls.gov. Use A-Z Index at upper right. Click on W, go to Work Stoppages, then Archived Major Work Stoppages, and then Major Work Stoppages.

Averting Strikes: Mediation and Arbitration

Collective bargaining is the basic way of averting strikes. The two sides sit down together and, after some tough bargaining, hammer out an agreement that each can live with.

But what if they can't reach an agreement? Or what if they can't even agree to sit down together in the same room? In those cases, a mediator or an arbitrator may be called in, either by the parties themselves or by the federal government.

A mediator is literally a go-between, who tries to speed up the process of negotiations, getting each side to give a little more and take a little less. Often he or she sits down with each side separately and then, when an agreement seems possible, gets both sides together for what is, the mediator hopes, the final bargaining session.

The mediator does not have the power to impose a settlement but can play a valuable role as an expediter. The job of an arbitrator is to impose settlements. This takes the decision out of the hands of labor and management, making arbitration a situation both sides usually want to avoid. Under compulsory arbitration, a labor contract or law actually stipulates that if the two parties cannot reach an agreement, an arbitrator will make the decision.

Will You Ever Be a Member of a Labor Union?

Fifty years ago most families had at least one union member. People were very reluctant to cross picket lines. And powerful unions like the Teamsters and the Longshoremen could shut down much of the economy by going out on strike.

Unless you end up working in the public sector, the chances are very slight that you will ever join a union. From kindergarten through the high school, it's very likely that your teachers were union members. And the chances are, the professors at your college are also unionized. So if you end up teaching, then there's probably a union card in your future.

If you happen to have a family tree handy, what would you learn by researching who in your family was ever a union member? I suspect that as you moved from your great grandparents' generation to your grandparents,' and then to that of your parents and their siblings, you'd find fewer and fewer union members. Unless, of course, many of your family members have been government employees.

Current Issue: The Card Check Law

In each session of Congress since 2005, a bill has been introduced to alter the process of union organizing. Formally called the *Employee Free Choice Act,* it would make it much easier for unions to organize. When 50 percent plus one employee signed authorization cards proffered by union organizers, the union would then represent that workplace.

Once the needed signatures were secured, the employer would be required to enter into collective bargaining with the union. If the company and the union did not reach an agreement within 90 days, either party could refer the matter to the National Mediation and Conciliation Service. If a deal were not reached within 30 days, either side could refer the matter to a federal arbitration panel.

Before you decide whether or not the card check law should be passed, you might want to hear from one of its strongest opponents, the U.S. Chamber of Commerce, and one of its strongest proponents, Kate Bronfenbrenner, the director of labor research at the Cornell School of Labor and Industrial Relations.

The main argument by the Chamber of Commerce against the card check is that secret-ballot elections would be replaced by a process that would be open to abuse by union organizers, "who would simply ask workers to sign a card. Any worker who refused could be asked over and over again, and even be repeatedly visited by union organizers in their homes."[7]

The Chamber is also very unhappy with the arbitration provision, which, it claims, takes the power of reaching a collective bargaining agreement away from the employees and the employer, and places it in the hands of a government decision maker.

Essentially, then, the Chamber asks, why replace a democratic process which works reasonably well, with one which not only stacks the deck in favor of the union, but leaves employees open to potential badgering and abuse by union organizers?

Bronfenbrenner, who conducted a study of 1,004 National Labor Relations Board (NLRB) union certification elections that took place between 1999 and 2003, reached very different conclusions from those of the Chamber:

- In the NLRB election process, it is standard practice for workers to be subjected to threats, interrogation, harassment, surveillance, and retaliation for union activity.

- Of the unions that *did* win elections, 52 percent were still without a contract a year later, and 37 percent were still without a contract two years after an election.

- In 34 percent of the union-won elections, companies fired employees for union activity; in 57 percent, employers threatened to shut down all or part of their facilities; and in 47 percent, employers threatened to cut wages and benefits.[8]

A recent study by researchers at the University of Illinois–Chicago found that 91 percent of employers required employees to attend one-on-one meetings with their supervisors during organizing drives. "The study also found that 51 percent of employers facing union drives have tried to influence worker voting through favoritism or bribery, such as suddenly providing a bonus or raising wages; 49 percent have threatened to close a work site; and 30 percent have fired pro-union workers."[9]

As is the case with most highly politicized issues, both sides present strong cases. Having heard their arguments, are you for or against the card check bill? If you feel strongly—one way or the other—then let your Congressperson and U.S. Senator know your opinion.

___

on the web

To find the most recent card check developments, go to www.google.com or www.bing.com and type in "Employee Free Choice Act" along with the current year.

___

Questions for Further Thought and Discussion

1. Which key provisions of the Taft-Hartley Act persuaded union leaders that the law was antilabor?

2. What are the basic provisions of a collective bargaining agreement?

3. Explain the differences between mediation and arbitration.

4. Explain how a monopsonist operates in the labor market, and illustrate your explanation with an example.

___

[7] www.uschamber.com/wfi/cardcheckbasics.htm

[8] Kate Bronfenbrenner, "NO HOLDS BARRED: The Intensification of Employer Opposition to Organizing," *EPI Briefing Paper #235* (Economic Policy Institute: Washington, D.C., May 20, 2009), Executive Summary.

[9] www.KansasCity.com

5. On average, do unionized workers earn higher wages than comparable nonunion workers? Why?

6. How do you account for the declining membership in labor unions?

7. *Practical Application:* Was President George W. Bush right in invoking the Taft-Hartley Act to end the 2002 lockout of the longshoremen?

8. *Practical Application:* Unions have long been advocating a law that would permit a card check to be used to determine if a union should represent the workers at a company. Explain why you favor or oppose such a law.

9. *Practical Application:* Union membership as a percentage of the labor force has been declining for decades. Why has it been so hard for union leaders to reverse this trend? What two political measures would help increase union membership?

Workbook for Chapter 15 \text{Mc Graw Hill} **connect** |ECONOMICS

Name _____   Date _____

Multiple-Choice Questions

Circle the letter that corresponds to the best answer.

1. Unions have _____. (LO5)
    a) increased wages
    b) decreased wages
    c) had no effect on wages

2. Which statement is true about labor unions in the United States? (LO1)
    a) They have always been very popular.
    b) They did not gain widespread acceptance until the 1940s.
    c) They have never gained widespread acceptance.
    d) None of these statements is true.

3. Which is the most accurate statement? (LO2, 5)
    a) Collective bargaining is almost always between the two parties of a bilateral monopoly.
    b) Monopsonies are illegal under the Taft-Hartley Act.
    c) The United States has a lower percentage of its work force unionized than most other industrial nations.
    d) Most physicians are now members of labor unions.

4. The American Federation of Labor became the nation's predominant labor organization in _____. (LO1)
    a) the early 19th century
    b) the 1880s
    c) the early 20th century
    d) the 1940s

5. The AFL has always been basically interested in _____. (LO1)
    a) better wages, hours, and working conditions
    b) the formation of small producers' cooperatives
    c) the creation of true socialism
    d) none of the above

6. The act that supported union organizing was the _____. (LO2)
    a) National Labor Relations Act
    b) Taft-Hartley Act
    c) Landrum-Griffin Act
    d) Sherman Antitrust Act

7. Employers' rights were protected in the _____. (LO2)
    a) National Labor Relations Act
    b) Taft-Hartley Act
    c) Clayton Act
    d) Sherman Antitrust Act

8. Jurisdictional disputes and secondary boycotts are prohibited under the _____ Act. (LO2)
    a) National Labor Relations   c) Clayton
    b) Taft-Hartley   d) Sherman Antitrust

9. Limits on takeovers of locals by national unions and a listing of the financial responsibilities of union officials were provisions of the _____ Act. (LO2)
    a) National Labor Relations   c) Clayton
    b) Taft-Hartley   d) Sherman Antitrust

10. Under a(n) _____ shop, an employer may hire only union members. (LO2, 5)
    a) closed   c) open
    b) union

11. Right-to-work laws promote the formation of _____. (LO2)
    a) closed shops   c) open shops
    b) union shops

12. In 1935 the _____. (LO3)
    a) AFL was organizing along industry lines and the CIO was organizing along craft lines
    b) AFL was organizing along craft lines and the CIO was organizing along industry lines
    c) AFL and the CIO were both organizing along craft lines
    d) AFL and the CIO were both organizing along industry lines

13. The AFL and CIO split up in _____ and got back together in _____. (LO1)
    a) 1915, 1935
    c) 1955, 1975
    b) 1935, 1955
    d) 1975, 1985

14. The only prolabor name among the following is _____. (LO2)
    a) Sherman
    c) Taft-Hartley
    b) Clayton
    d) Wagner

15. Which statement is true? (LO5)
    a) No union is a monopoly.
    b) Some unions are monopolies.
    c) All unions are monopolies.

16. Which statement is true with respect to the two basic ways unions have of exerting power? (LO5)
    a) Only inclusion leads to higher wages.
    b) Only exclusion leads to higher wages.
    c) Both inclusion and exclusion lead to higher wages.
    d) Neither inclusion nor exclusion leads to higher wages.

17. A monopsony is _____. (LO5)
    a) the only seller of a product for which there are no close substitutes
    b) the only buyer of a product for which there are no close substitutes
    c) both the seller and the buyer of a product for which there are no close substitutes
    d) neither the seller nor the buyer of a product for which there are no close substitutes

18. Each of the following companies except _____ was once a monopsony. (LO5)
    a) General Electric
    c) R. J. Reynolds
    b) J. P. Stevens
    d) AT&T

19. The ultimate weapon that management can use against unions is _____. (LO6, 5)
    a) collective bargaining
    b) the strike
    c) the ability to take (or withstand) a strike
    d) the lockout

20. The firm with the least ability to withstand a strike would be a __ _____. (LO6, 5)
    a) manufacturing firm
    b) service firm
    c) diversified firm

21. A collective bargaining negotiation is _____. (LO6)
    a) solely a test of power
    b) solely a presentation and discussion of real issues
    c) both a test of power and a presentation and discussion of real issues
    d) neither a test of power nor a presentation and discussion of real issues

22. Pattern-setting wage increases tend to be viewed as _____. (LO6)
    a) minimums by unions engaged in subsequent bargaining
    b) maximums by unions engaged in subsequent bargaining
    c) irrelevant by unions engaged in subsequent bargaining

23. Collective bargaining negotiations _____ end with a strike. (LO6, 5)
    a) always
    c) occasionally
    b) usually
    d) never

24. The two key areas covered by provisions of collective bargaining agreements are _____. (LO6)
    a) wages and hours, and job security and seniority
    b) wages and hours, and working conditions
    c) job security and seniority, and working conditions

25. The job of a(n) _____ is to impose a settlement. (LO6, 5)
    a) arbitrator
    b) mediator
    c) collective bargaining team leader

26. Most strikes _____. (LO5)
    a) cause widespread economic disruption
    b) cause little economic disruption
    c) cause no economic disruption

27. Which group of workers would be the easiest for a union to organize? (LO2, 4, 5)

   a) Employees at a Walmart store

   b) Employees of a county government

   c) Employees at a Honda plant in Ohio

   d) Employees at a textile mill in North Carolina

28. You would most likely be a union member if you

   _____. (LO2, 4, 5)

   a) were a teacher

   b) lived in the South

   c) worked for Walmart

   d) were a corporate executive

29. Which is the most accurate statement? (LO3, 4)

   a) Within 10 years there will be no manufacturing jobs in the United States.

   b) In general, it is harder to export service jobs than manufacturing jobs.

   c) A higher percentage of private employees than government employees are unionized.

   d) The employees of Walmart are among the highest paid retail workers in the United States.

30. Which is the most accurate statement? (LO4, 5)

   a) In recent years the United States has experienced relative labor peace.

   b) The last few years have been excellent ones for American labor unions.

   c) Labor union membership today is at an all-time low.

   d) Most nations have lost less time to strikes (per thousand workers) than the United States.

31. Which statement is true? (LO5, 6)

   a) In good economic times, employers demand more givebacks from labor unions than in bad economic times.

   b) We have not had a major strike in over ten years.

   c) The United States is one of the most heavily unionized nations in the world.

   d) There are at least five unions with at least one million members.

32. You would most likely be a union member if you

   lived in _____. (LO5)

   a) the United States   d) Germany

   b) Japan   e) Sweden

   c) Canada

33. Which of the following is the most accurate statement? (LO1, 4)

   a) Every large labor union is a member of the AFL–CIO.

   b) Labor union membership rose in 2007.

   c) Government employees are less unionized than private employees.

   d) On average, union members earn about the same wages as people who are not union members.

34. About 1 out of every _____ American workers is a member of a labor union. (LO1, 4)

   a) 2   d) 8

   b) 3   e) 12

   c) 6

35. Which of the following is the most accurate statement about the card check law? (LO7)

   a) It would make it easier for unions to organize workers.

   b) It would make it harder for unions to organize workers.

   c) It is opposed by unions.

   d) Its strongest advocate is the U.S. Chamber of Commerce.

Fill-In Questions

1. The two most important pieces of labor legislation were the _____ Act and the _____ Act. (LO2)

2. The apparatus for conducting union representation elections was set up under the _____ _____ Act. (LO2)

3. The _____ Act put the force of the federal government behind collective bargaining. (LO2)

4. Jurisdictional disputes and secondary boycotts are prohibited under the _____ Act. (LO2)

5. Under the _____ shop, an employer may hire only union members. (LO2)

6. Under the _____ shop, no one is forced to join the union. (LO2)

7. Industrial unions are organized along _____ lines, while craft unions are organized along _____ lines. (LO1, 3)

8. The biggest spurt in union membership occurred during the decade of the _____. (LO1)

9. The conflict within the AFL over whether to organize on a craft basis or an industrial basis led to _____ _____. (LO1, 3)

10. Unions have two basic ways of exerting power. They are to (1) _____ and (2) _____. (LO5)

11. A monopsony is _____ _____. (LO5)

12. _____ is the main arena of the power struggle between labor and management. (LO6)

13. The ultimate weapon for labor is _____, while the ultimate weapon for management is _____. (LO6, 5)

14. At collective bargaining sessions, management operates under two main constraints: (1) _____ and (2) _____. (LO6)

15. Collective bargaining negotiations will end with either _____ or _____. (LO6, 5)

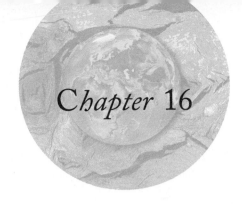

Chapter 16

Labor Markets and Wage Rates

In the United States, as well as in most other countries, there is a wide disparity in income. People like Giorgio Armani, Tom Clancy, Stephen King, Tom Hanks, Madonna, Alex Rodriguez, David Letterman, Jay Leno, and the presidents of major corporations, as well as heart surgeons and even the writers of best-selling economics textbooks, make millions of dollars a year.

Two thousand nine was a very good year for Oprah Winfrey, who pulled in $275 million. Producer and director Steven Spielberg ($150 million) and champion golfer, Tiger Woods ($110 million) also did very nicely. More than one hundred professional athletes earned over $10 million. You probably never heard of David Tepper, a Wall Street hedge fund manager, who took home $4 billion (That's not a misprint!). The managers of six other hedge funds each took home over $1 billion in 2009. But the typical American wage-earner was paid between $25,000 and $35,000.

Why do people earn such widely varying incomes? There are several reasons for this disparity, but the bottom line remains the same. You guessed it: supply and demand.

on the web

If you want to find out how much any major celebrity earned last year, go to www.forbes.com and type "celebrity 100" in the search box.

LEARNING OBJECTIVES

After reading this chapter you should be able to:

1. Distinguish among the various groups constituting the supply of labor.
2. Interpret the backward-bending individual labor supply curve.
3. Discuss the factors influencing the demand for labor.
4. Explain and analyze how the wage rate is determined by supply and demand.
5. Analyze the relationship between high wage rates and economic rent.
6. Differentiate between real wages and money wages and calculate real wages.
7. Define and distinguish between the minimum wage and the living wage.
8. Explain the effects of employment discrimination on wages.
9. Discuss the education gap between the rich and the poor.

The Supply of Labor

Noncompeting Groups

There are various classes, or strata, of labor. There is skilled labor, which includes carpenters, plumbers, machinists, computer programmers, printers, schoolteachers, and airline pilots. There is semiskilled labor, such as assembly-line workers, file clerks, short-order cooks, receptionists, and supermarket checkers. Finally, there is unskilled labor, which includes freight handlers, dishwashers, porters, janitors, and gas station attendants.

In a sense, there are thousands of noncompeting groups. But that doesn't mean there's no overlap or that people with one skill do not compete for jobs with those who have other skills. In fact, an employer is often faced with the decision to hire either a skilled worker for high pay or a lower-paid trainee. College administrators are especially sensitive to the disparities in the salaries earned by senior professors and newly hired PhDs. A full professor with 20 years experience often earns three times as much as an assistant professor just starting out. To save their schools a bundle of money, some college presidents—including my own—have offered senior professors buyouts they can't refuse.

If the opportunities arise in certain fields—professional sports, engineering, accounting, computer programming, medicine—people will go through the necessary training and compete for jobs. If there are large numbers of relatively high-paying jobs, people currently in those fields will eventually be joined by huge numbers of competitors.

In still another sense, we are all competitors in the same employment pool. Certain skills are partially substitutable for other skills. One 100-word-per-minute typist is a perfect substitute for another 100-word-per-minute typist; but an electrician who can type 20 words per minute is only a partial substitute. Similarly, a plumber's assistant is a partial substitute for a plumber, and a file clerk is an even more partial substitute for a plumber's assistant.

In the long run most of us can learn to do many different jobs. In some cases it takes just a few hours, but it takes many years to learn other skills. In the short run, however, we are all partial substitutes for one another. The question is, how partial?

There *are* noncompeting groups, but these distinctions tend to blur in the long run. To the degree that there is a good deal of labor mobility—the ability to change occupations and/or geographic locations—there is less demarcation among the nation's various occupational groups.

The Theory of the Dual Labor Market

Obviously, we are not all in the same labor market, primarily because we are separated by skill, ability, and training. A more radical theory than that of noncompeting groups places the entire labor force into two broad categories: the primary and secondary labor markets.

The primary market has most of the good jobs, which not only pay well but offer good opportunities for advancement. Examples of such jobs include the skilled crafts, management, the professions, and virtually all the other jobs requiring college degrees. (See the box, "Are You in the Primary Market or in the Secondary Market?")

The secondary market consists of all the jobs that are left over. The pay is low, and there is little chance for advancement. Often the jobs are temporary, and the people who hold them are called "disposable workers." These jobs include work in laundries, hospitals, fast-food chains, and clothing factories or spraying pesticides, stripping hotel beds, shampooing carpets, and scrubbing toilets. These positions are often filled by minority group members, women, and immigrants.

In *Nickel and Dimed,* Barbara Ehrenreich describes her experiences working in the secondary job market as a waitress, a hotel maid, a cleaning woman, a nursing home aide, and a Walmart sales clerk. Here is her description of her downtime at her waitress job:

> Managers can sit—for hours at a time if they want—but it's their job to see that no one else ever does, even when there's nothing to do, and this is why, for servers, slow times can be as exhausting as rushes. You start dragging out each little chore because if the manager on duty catches you in an idle moment he will give you something far nastier to

Are You in the Primary Market or in the Secondary Market?

Thirty years ago, you could graduate from high school, get married, have kids, and have a decent life in a blue-collar town.

—Gary Bauer, president of the Family Research Council (quoted in *BusinessWeek*, March 13, 1995, p. 74)

Median Annual Earnings by Amount of Education, 2009	
Some high school	$23,608
High school diploma	32,552
Some college or Associate degree	37,752
College degree	53,300
Advanced degree	69,056

Source: U.S. Bureau of Labor Statistics.

As you can see from the table, a person's average earnings rises with her level of education. Someone with an advanced degree earns about three times what a high school dropout earns. And the income of a college graduate is more than $20,000 higher than that of a high school graduate.

Does this mean that a college degree will almost double your earnings? Increasingly, the answer is no.

A diploma remains a *necessary* condition for a person to move from the secondary to the primary labor market. But that diploma is no longer a *sufficient* condition. You not only need a college degree, but you also need to be educated (the two are not necessarily synonymous)—and maybe a little lucky or well-connected. However, if you *don't* have a college degree, your chances of ever getting a job in the primary market are nil—unless, of course, your parents own the company.

do. So I wipe, I clean, I consolidate catsup bottles and recheck the cheesecake supply, even tour the tables to make sure the customer evaluation forms are all standing perkily in their places—wondering all the time how many calories I burn in these strictly theatrical exercises. In desperation, I even take the desserts out of their glass display case and freshen them up with whipped cream and bright new maraschino cherries; anything to look busy. When, on a particularly dead afternoon, Stu finds me glancing at a *USA Today* a customer has left behind, he assigns me to vacuum the entire floor with the broken vacuum cleaner, which has a handle only two feet long, and the only way to do that without incurring orthopedic damage is to proceed from spot to spot on your knees.[1]

Barbara Ehrenreich

The dual labor market theory is a class theory of employment. The rich stay rich, and the poor stay poor. The college degree seems to be a dividing line, a line that is seldom crossed by those from poorer economic backgrounds (see the box, "A College Degree Is the Ticket out of Poverty").

The rich stay rich, and the poor stay poor.

One problem with this theory is that it doesn't account for the huge middle level of occupations—police officers, post office supervisors, noncommissioned military officers, executive and legal secretaries, store managers, clerical supervisors, and noncollege-graduate managerial positions in insurance, banking, and retailing. But the theory *does* support the contention that there are noncompeting groups in the labor market. The only question is, how many?

The Backward-Bending Individual Labor Supply Curve

When we talk about the supply of labor, I ask my students whether they would be willing to do clerical work for $8 an hour. Nobody would. How about $15 an hour? A lot of hands go up. And at $100 an hour, everyone volunteers.

This demonstrates the *substitution effect*. As the wage rate rises, people are willing to substitute more work for leisure time because leisure time is becoming more expensive. Imagine if an hour of leisure time cost you $100! Suppose the wage rate were increased to $1,000 an hour. Now an hour of leisure time would cost you $1,000! That's a lot of money to give up for just one hour of watching TV, playing bingo, or hanging around the shopping mall.

The substitution effect

---

[1]Barbara Ehrenreich, *Nickel and Dimed* (New York: Henry Holt, 2001), pp. 22–23.

A College Degree Is the Ticket out of Poverty

If you grow up in a poor family, but manage to get a college degree, it's very unlikely that you'll still be poor. But that door to the middle class is closing. In 1979 students from the richest 25 percent of American homes were four times as likely to attend college as those from the poorest 25 percent; by 1994 they were ten times as likely. Why? The main reason is that since 1979 the cost of going to college has gone up twice as fast as the rate of inflation.

To make matters still worse, Pell Grants, which help the children of the poor and working class to attend college, and covered 84 percent of the cost of attending a four-year public college in 1979, now cover just one-third the cost. The only way that most low-income students can afford college is to work long hours at part-time jobs, while attending a 2-year, rather than a 4-year school.

At an elite university, you are 25 times more likely to run into a rich student than a poor one. As educator Terry Hartle has put it, "Smart poor kids go to college at the same rate as stupid rich kids."

Let's look at the record. *BusinessWeek* published these findings:

A mere 4.5 percent of those from the bottom quartile of income brackets get a degree by age 24, according to an analysis of Census Bureau data by Thomas G. Mortenson, who publishes an education research newsletter in Oskaloosa, Iowa. About 12 percent of students in the next quartile get a BA, while 25 percent of those in the third quartile do. In the top quarter, meanwhile, 51 percent of students finish college.*

*Aaron Bernstein, "A British Solution to America's College Tuition Problem," *BusinessWeek*, February 9, 2004, p. 72.

Something else is happening as your wage rate keeps getting higher. You're making all this money. You're rich! You're making $1,000 an hour. But if you keep working more and more hours, when are you going to be able to spend your money? When are you going to have time to see your family and friends? And when are you going to have time to sleep?

At some point, as your wage rate continues to rise, you will say to yourself, "I want more leisure time for myself, if only so that I'll be able to spend some of my money." Now you're willing to give up some income in exchange for more leisure time. We call this the *income effect*.

The income effect

How many hours would you work picking up money?

Let's see how the substitution and income effects work for *you*. How would you like a job picking pennies up off the floor? You get to keep all the pennies you pick up. What's the catch? There *is* no catch. Just tell me how many hours per week you'd be willing to work.

Of course some people would not stoop so low as to take a job picking up pennies. How about nickels? Dimes? Quarters? Half-dollars? How about dollar bills? All right, I'll even let you pick up five-dollar bills. What I want to know is how many hours per week you would be willing to work picking up each of these denominations of coins and bills.

Write down your answers. Then compare them to mine in Table 1. Of course, there *is* no "right" answer. Everyone has his or her own schedule of hours of willingness to work.

TABLE 1 Hypothetical Work Schedule Picking Up Money

Type of Money	Hours per Week
Pennies	35
Nickels	50
Dimes	58
Quarters	61
Half-dollars	63
Dollar bills	65
Five-dollar bills	62

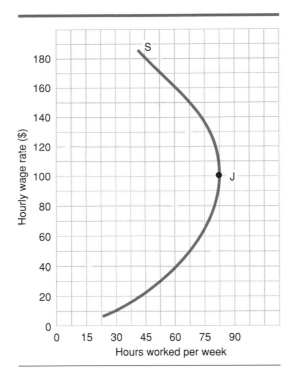

Figure 1
Hypothetical Labor Supply Curve
A person will be willing to work an increasing amount of hours per week as the hour wage rate goes up. But at some point (point J) he will begin to cut back on his hours as the wage rate continues to rise. Up to point J he is substituting extra work for leisure time. Beyond point J the curve bends backward as the income effect outweighs the substitution effect and this person is willing to trade away some money for more leisure time.

Most people would work more hours to pick up nickels than they would to pick up pennies. And more hours to pick up dimes than to pick up nickels. That's the substitution effect at work: They're substituting more work for leisure time. But at some point their hours reach a maximum. In this example, people would work 65 hours to pick up dollar bills. Beyond that point, the income effect will outweigh the substitution effect, as they give up some income in exchange for more leisure time.

Turning to Figure 1, we see that as the wage rate rises from very low levels to higher and higher levels, people substitute extra work for leisure time. That's the substitution effect. And it happens up to point J. Beyond point J the curve begins to move upward to the left as the wage rate continues to rise. That's the income effect.

To summarize: The substitution effect means that you trade away leisure time for more money, and the income effect means that you trade away some money for more leisure time. At wage rates below point J on the curve, the substitution effect outweighs the income effect. At point J the two effects just offset each other. Above J the income effect outweighs the substitution effect.

We call curve S in Figure 1 the labor supply curve. Perhaps the typical individual will work a maximum of 80 hours a week.

Do you recall that the chapter "Demand in the Factor Market" introduced a different substitution effect? For example, if the price of labor went up, business firms would tend to substitute capital or land for some of their now more expensive workers. So *that* substitution effect described substituting one resource for another. In *this* chapter the substitution effect describes how, as wage rates rise, people are willing to substitute more work for leisure time. Economists are usually good at giving the same concept two or three different names. In the case of the substitution effect, however, we've given the same name to two different concepts.

The Market Supply of Labor

In theory the market supply curve of labor, like the individual curve shown in Figure 1, should also be backward bending. The horizontal axis, showing hours worked per week, though, would be about 150 million times as long, reflecting all the people in our labor force. But the size of our labor force is not a constant. At very low wage rates some people would retire early, younger workers would return to school, and some people

Figure 2
Hypothetical Labor Market
Supply

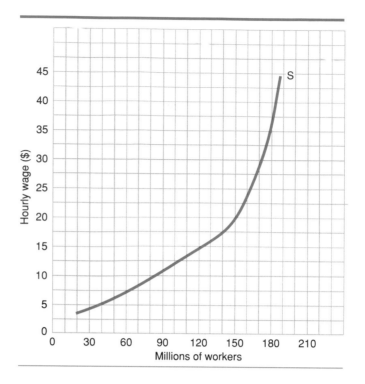

would opt out of the labor force to take care of their families. Similarly, at very high wage rates, some workers would put off retirement and recent retirees would rejoin the labor force, students would drop out of school to take jobs, and homemakers would find it made economic sense to take jobs, while paying others to care for their families.

All of these factors would make the shape of the market supply curve somewhat different from the backward bending individual supply curve. Instead of reaching its point of inflection at $100 (point J in Figure 1), that point would be put off until a somewhat higher hourly wage rate. In addition, there is the very practical consideration that our average wage rate will not come close to $100 any time in the foreseeable future (unless, of course, we experience a very heavy bout of inflation).

So what does the market supply curve of labor actually look like? As you see in Figure 2, it slopes upward to the right, just like nearly all the supply curves you've seen before. If we extended the vertical axis, which measures hourly wages, high enough, say to $150 an hour, or, possibly to $200 an hour, would the labor market supply curve bend backwards upon itself?

The answer is yes. You don't see that happening, then, in Figure 2, simply because it makes no practical sense to have the graph go that high, since the average hourly wage rate for most American workers today is under $20.

The Demand for Labor

The Marginal Revenue Product Schedule

You may have noticed that I have been trying to impress on you the idea that the wage rate is determined by two factors, supply and demand. We just covered supply. Demand is the firm's MRP schedule for labor.[2] In the more general sense, the demand for a particular type of labor is the sum of all the firms' MRP schedules.

Demand for labor is represented by the MRP schedule.

Like nearly all demand curves we've encountered, the market demand curve for labor, shown in Figure 3, slopes downward to the right. It conforms to *the law of demand,* a concept first introduced in Chapter 3: *When the price of a good is lowered, more of it is demanded; when it is raised, less is demanded.* Because every firm's MRP curve slopes downward to

---

[2]We covered MRP two chapters back in "Demand in the Factor Market."

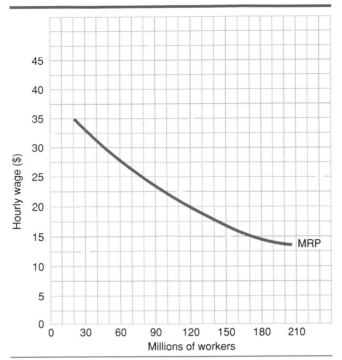

Figure 3
Hypothetical Labor Marginal Revenue Product Curve

*We have gone from average hours worked per week to millions of hours worked per week to reflect the total labor market with millions of people selling their labor.

the right (as the wage rate, or price of labor, declines), it follows that the general demand curve for labor, which is the sum of these curves, also slopes downward to the right.

We may ask what determines the demand for labor or, more specifically, the MRP schedule of each firm. Remember that the demand for each factor of production—land, labor, capital—is a derived demand. It is derived from the demand for the final product.

Firms hire labor because that labor produces a final product, which is then sold. Not all labor is identical. Some people are more productive because they are better trained, more skilled, or have more natural ability.

Obviously, workers who are more productive will be more in demand and better paid than less productive workers. The more highly skilled machinist and the better basketball player will usually earn more than their less productive colleagues. Some people become more productive because of education and training, some because of work experience, and, of course, some are just born with greater natural ability.

Closely related to worker productivity are specialized skills possessed by some workers, which also influence the demand for labor. Generally, the highly skilled worker or the highly trained specialist will earn higher wages than the person with less developed skills. Specialists in medicine and dentistry, in law, and in engineering are usually among the best paid practitioners of their professions. This is especially true when their skills are in relatively high demand in relation to their supply.

Specialized skills

Finally, some workers are in demand because of the natural abilities they possess. Obvious examples abound in show business and professional athletics. A little later we'll consider the special cases of David Letterman and Willie Mays, when we introduce the concept of economic rent.

Nonhomogeneous Jobs and Compensating Pay Differentials

Still another factor accounting for different wage rates is worker preference with respect to working hours and conditions. Those willing to work longer hours, night shifts, and weekends will usually earn higher wages than will those who work the standard Monday-to-Friday, nine-to-five workweek; those who work under unsafe conditions earn higher wages as well. Pay differentials are institutionalized, for example, for window washers who work above the 20th floor.

Pay differentials adjust for harder, more unpleasant, less convenient work.

Harder, more unpleasant, or less convenient work is usually somewhat better paid than the more conventional occupations. Night workers and those who work overtime get pay differentials. The out-of-town salesman is better paid than his home territory counterpart, while the sandhog who builds tunnels is given much shorter hours and higher pay than most other construction workers.

These wage differentials are called *compensating differences* because employers need to provide these pay differentials to get certain job slots filled. Some workers holding these jobs refer to these compensating differences as "combat pay." Like troops receiving extra pay for being in places where people are shooting at them, sufficient pay incentives will persuade some workers to take on more hazardous, unpleasant, or strenuous work.

More than a century ago John Stuart Mill took a diametrically opposite view of how well people were paid to do undesirable work:

> The really exhausting and the really repulsive labours, instead of being better paid than others, are almost invariably paid the worst of all . . . The hardships and the earnings, instead of being directly proportional, as in any just arrangements of society they would be, are generally in an inverse ratio to one another.[3]

How do we get people to pick up our garbage?

Do you happen to know the year in which the Rev. Martin Luther King, Jr., was assassinated? It was 1968. And in which city? Memphis. What was King doing in Memphis? He was leading a strike of sanitation workers. The Memphis sanitation workers were predominantly black, and they were paid little more than minimum wage. Because there was so much employment discrimination against blacks, especially in the South, many black men were forced into doing this undesirable work at very low wages.

But the situation was different in New York City. Not only were sanitation workers relatively well paid, but few were black or Hispanic. In fact, for years public school teachers complained that garbage men were paid more than *they* were. So New York got its garbage picked up by paying white men very well to do it; Memphis got *its* garbage picked up by not allowing black or Hispanic men to do more desirable types of work.

How does our society get its dirty work done? By paying people enough to make it worth their while? Or by calling on oppressed minorities to work as migrant farm laborers, bedpan orderlies, janitors, dishwashers, and launderers? This disturbing question may be argued persuasively from either side.

on the web

If you're interested in the job prospects in a specific occupation, an excellent source of information is U.S. Department of Labor's *Occupational Outlook Handbook*. Go to www.stats.bls.gov/emp. Click on "Career Outlook Information," and then on "Occupational Outlook Handbook (OHH), 2009–2010 Edition (or, if available, 2010–2011 Edition).

Another very useful website is www.payscale.com. You can find out, for example, how much graduates of Dartmouth and MIT earn in comparison to those of Michigan State and Merced College.

Determination of the Wage Rate: Supply and Demand

Here's what we've all been waiting for. You'll find it right there in Figure 4.

Much of this course is based on a simple law: the law of supply and demand. When quantity demanded is equal to quantity supplied, we've got our price. In this case the price of labor, or the wage rate, is $17.50 an hour. But remember, this is only a *hypothetical* wage rate. How much is the *actual* wage rate? A lot lower? In many cases, yes. It all depends on the type of work you do and on the demand and supply schedules in each of hundreds, or even thousands, of job markets.

---

[3]John Stuart Mill, *Principles of Political Economy*, ed. H. Ashley, p. 388.

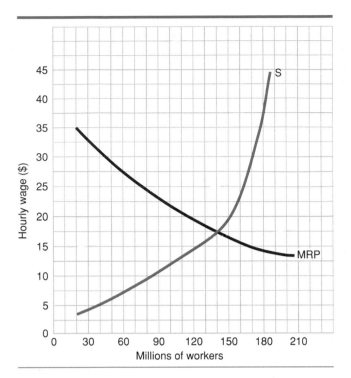

Figure 4

Hypothetical Labor Market
Demand and Supply
The wage rate is set by the
intersection of the general demand
and supply curves for labor. In this
case the wage rate is $17.50 an
hour.

From the mid–1940s through the mid–1960s, our nation had a very high birth rate. Over the next two decades more than 45 million baby boomers will be retiring. How will this affect wage rates?

I'll bet you said it would raise them. And you'd be right. You can see that by just glancing at Figure 5, which shows that a decline in the supply of labor pushes up the wage rate, assuming no change in the demand for labor.[4]

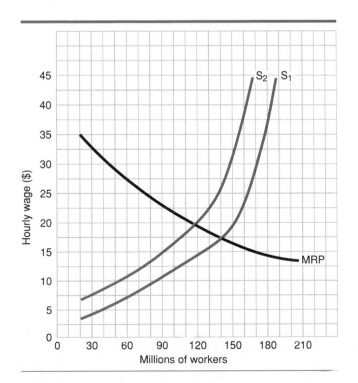

Figure 5

Hypothetical Labor Market:
Decrease in Supply
A decrease in the supply of labor
results in an increase in the wage
rate from $17.50 to $20.

---

[4]Actually, the labor supply won't fall over the next 20 years, but unless there is a huge flood of immigrants, it will rise much more slowly than it has been over the last 20 years.

And here's more good news for you. The retirement of the baby boomers will free up a large number of high paying jobs. So despite all the gloom and doom you've encountered elsewhere in this book, your long-term job prospects may indeed be quite bright.

High Wage Rates and Economic Rent

In the early 1950s, when the Giants still played baseball at New York's Polo Grounds, Willie Mays joined the team as a young rookie and quickly established himself as the most exciting player in the game. Like most ballplayers of his generation, Mays came from an economically deprived background and was eventually earning unheard-of sums of money.

Lou Gehrig, the star first baseman on the great 1920s and 1930s Yankee teams, and Willie Mays, who began his long career as the New York Giants centerfielder in 1951, had an interest in common—besides being elected to the baseball Hall of Fame. Both loved playing ball so much that in their spare time, they played stickball in the street with the neighborhood kids. On the off-chance that you're not familiar with stickball, all you need is a broom handle and a rubber (Spaldeen) ball, and you can play it on a side street where there isn't too much traffic.

Professional baseball, football, basketball, hockey, tennis, and other sports give a few thousand people a chance to make a living playing kids' games. Although they negotiate for huge salaries, many, like Willie Mays, would have been willing to play for a lot less. Maybe it's a chance to prolong one's childhood for a few more years. Perhaps that's what gave Roger Kahn the idea for the title of his story of the 1953 Brooklyn Dodgers, *The Boys of Summer.*

Whenever a person gets paid more than the minimum she would be willing to accept, we call the excess over the minimum *economic rent.* For example, I might be willing to accept just $20,000 to be an economics professor. As I am now collecting a salary of $950,000, my economic rent is $930,000.

In January 1998 the ABC, CBS, and Fox networks agreed to collectively pay $17.6 billion for the rights to broadcast National Football League games for the next eight years. Question: What effect did this deal have on the players' salaries and on their economic rent? Obviously it raised both salaries and economic rent.

How much does David Letterman make? Although Mr. Letterman asked me not to disclose his exact earnings, it is estimated at $30 million a year. I will try to put aside my personal misgivings about a mere show business personality earning even more than I do.

It all comes back to supply and demand.

We come back again to supply and demand. There may be thousands of would-be comics occasionally getting a gig here and there, but there are perhaps half a dozen really good ones. Thus, we have a graph like that in Figure 6, in which the wage rate comes to $30 million.

Now David Letterman probably could scrape by on $10 million a year if he really had to. If that were his secret bottom line—if he was really willing to work for that paltry sum—his economic rent would be some $30 million.

Is David Letterman overpaid? The question boils down to supply and demand. Good stand-up comedians, great athletes, cosmetic surgeons, and authors capable of writing best-sellers are all in relatively short supply. If supply is relatively low in relation to demand, the resulting wage rate will be high.

These explanations as to why a tiny fraction of our population makes so much more than the rest of us, cloaked in such terms as *marginal revenue product* and *economic rent,* may still leave us wondering if these folks are *really* worth such huge incomes. For another view, see the box, "Winner-Take-All Markets."

on the web

How much are others earning who do the same work you do? Go to www.payscroll.com, fill out your job title and city, and then learn how much money people make at different jobs.

Winner-Take-All Markets

Why do the chief executive officers of America's largest corporations earn, on average, nearly 400 times the wages of the average production worker? Was Apple CEO Steve Jobs really worth the $647 million he took home in 2006? Did Ray Irani, CEO of Occidental Petroleum, earn every penny of the $322 million he was paid? The heads of America's 500 biggest companies received an aggregate 38 percent pay raise in 2006. Eight made over $100 million.

Robert Frank and Philip Cook note that top corporate executives in the United States, unlike their foreign counterparts, are relatively free to move from firm to firm, going to the highest bidder, in what the authors call "winner-take-all markets." These are markets in which a handful of top performers walk away with the lion's share of total rewards. This payoff structure has always been common in entertainment and professional sports, but in recent years it has permeated many other fields—law, journalism, consulting, investment banking, corporate management, design, fashion, even the hallowed halls of academe.* The star system is distorting American society by diverting talented young people into competition that most will lose.

---

*Robert Frank, "Talent and the Winner-All Society," *The American Prospect,* Spring 1994, p. 95. See also, Robert Frank and Philip Cook, *The Winner-Take-All Society* (New York: Free Press, 1995).

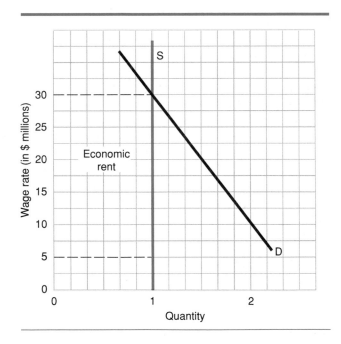

Figure 6
Determination of Economic Rent by Supply and Demand
How much of David Letterman's earnings are economic rent? If his earnings of $30 million are set by supply and demand, then his economic rent would depend on the minimum wage he would be willing to accept. For instance, if that were $5 million, then his economic rent would be $25 million.

Real Wages versus Money Wages

How do American wages stack up against those of other industrial countries? Until the late 1970s or early 1980s this country paid higher wages than any other nation. But as you can see in Figure 7, a few countries have overtaken us.

American wages versus wages in other industrial countries

If you were offered a job today at a salary of, say, $100,000, you probably would be inclined to take it. But what if you were locked into that salary for life? Isn't it conceivable that by the time you reach middle age, $100,000 won't buy all that much? With the cost of living quadrupling since 1970, who knows what will happen to prices over the next 20 or 30 years? By real wages, economists mean what you can actually buy with your wages. If the rate of inflation were 10 percent a year, you'd need a 10 percent

What are real wages?

Figure 7

Hourly Wage and Fringe
Benefits in Manufacturing,
Selected Countries, 2007
Back in the 1970s and 1980s, U.S.
workers led the world in wages and
fringe benefits, but today, we are
no longer number one. Norway,
Germany, Britain, and Canada have
recently passed us. In addition,
workers in relatively poorer
countries, especially in the newly
industrial countries in Western Asia,
have been closing the wage gap.
Source: Bureau of Labor Statistics.

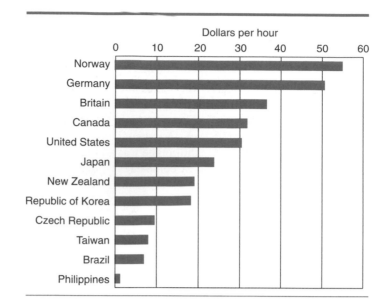

pay raise each year just to maintain your standard of living. And a person who earned $100,000 in 1970 would need about $400,000 today to continue living the same lifestyle.

Our main measure of inflation is the consumer price index (CPI), which tells us the percent by which the price level rose since a base year. We always set the CPI at 100 for the base year. If it rose from 100 in 1972, the base year, to 135 in 1999, by what percent did the CPI rise? It rose by 35 percent.

We're going to be working out a couple of problems. Doing so requires being able to calculate percentage changes. If you'd like a quick review of calculating percentage changes, please work your way through the accompanying box.

Suppose your wage rate rises from $5 an hour in 1993 to $8.40 an hour in 1999. Meanwhile, the consumer price index rises from 100 in 1993 (the base year) to 120 in 1999 (the current year). How much is your real hourly wage in 1999, and by what percentage has it increased since 1993?

Solution:

$$\text{Real wages (current year)} = \frac{\text{Money wages (current year)}}{\text{CPI (current year)}} \times 100$$

$$= \frac{\$8.40}{120} \times 100$$

$$= \$.07 \times 100$$

$$= \$7$$

We found, then, that your real wage rate is $7 an hour in 1999. For the second part of the problem we want to find the percentage increase in real wages from 1993 to 1999. We just found real wages of $7 for 1999. How much were real wages in 1993? There's only one choice—$5, which was given. Because 1993 was the base year, we're

Quick Review of Calculating Percentage Changes

If you were earning $12 an hour and got a raise to $15 an hour, by what percentage did your wage rate go up? To solve this problem we write down the formula:

$$\text{Percentage change} = \frac{\text{Change}}{\text{Original number}}$$

When our pay rises from $12 to $15, by how much did it rise?

It rose by $3. Next question: How much pay were you making before your pay increase?

You were making $12, so the change is $3 and the original number is $12. Let's plug them into the formula and solve:

$$\text{Percentage change} = \frac{\text{Change}}{\text{Original number}}$$

$$= \frac{\$3}{\$12}$$

$$= \frac{1}{4}$$

$$= .25$$

$$= 25\%$$

Here's one more for you to work out. Find the percentage increase in your pay if you get a raise from $8 to $12.

Solution:

$$\text{Percentage change} = \frac{\text{Change}}{\text{Original number}}$$

$$= \frac{\$4}{\$8}$$

$$= \frac{1}{2}$$

$$= .50$$

$$= 50\%$$

comparing what an hour's wages bought you in 1993 to what an hour's wages buy you in 1999.

So what is the percentage change when we go from $5 to $7?

Solution:

$$\text{Percentage change} = \frac{\text{Change}}{\text{Original number}}$$

$$= \frac{\$2}{\$5}$$

$$= .4$$

$$= 40\%$$

When we convert a decimal to a percentage, we move the decimal point two places to the right and add a percentage sign: $.4 = .40 = .40.\% = 40\%$.

Here's the next problem. Mr. Zitnik, who was earning $20,000 in 1994, received several promotions and is earning $32,500 in 1997. Over this same period the CPI rose to 125. Assume that 1994 was the base year. How much are Mr. Zitnik's real wages in

1997, and by what percentage did they change since 1994? Work out your solution to both parts of the problem right here, and then check your work.

Solution:

$$\text{Real wages (1997)} = \frac{\text{Money wages (1997)}}{\text{CPI (1997)}} \times 100$$

$$= \frac{\$32,500}{125} \times 100$$

$$= \$260 \times 100$$

$$= \$26,000$$

$$\text{Percentage change} = \frac{\text{Change}}{\text{Original number}}$$

$$= \frac{\$6,000}{\$20,000}$$

$$= .30$$

$$= 30\%$$

What has happened to real wages in the United States since the 1970s? Have they gone up or down? Most people's real wages went down. You'll see that immediately when you look at Figure 8. This graph shows what's happened to real wages and money wages since 1973. Money wages rose steadily while real wages remain stuck below $9 (in 1982–1984 dollars).

How many times have you heard someone say "time is money"? In the accompanying box, we'll see exactly how many minutes the average American needs to work to pay for a gallon of gasoline.

Let's take a closer look at Figure 8. Basically real average hourly earnings fell between 1973 and 1993, hitting a low in the mid-1990s about 17 percent below their 1973 peak. Since then, real wages rose again, but in early 2008 were still 9 percent less than

Figure 8

Real Wage Rate and Money Wage Rate, 1972–2007
Since 1973 money wages have quintupled, but real wages are actually lower today than they were in 1973.

Source: Economic Report of the President, 2008; www.bls.gov.

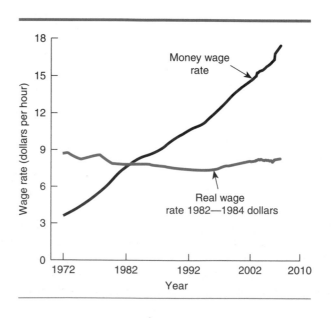

The 10-Minute Gallon

We are used to thinking about the price of gas in terms of dollars and cents. But since we need to work for our money, it makes sense to ask, "How many minutes do we need to work to pay for a gallon of gas?" Figure A shows that since 1998, a gallon of gas cost anywhere from just over five minutes to about 14 and a half minutes.

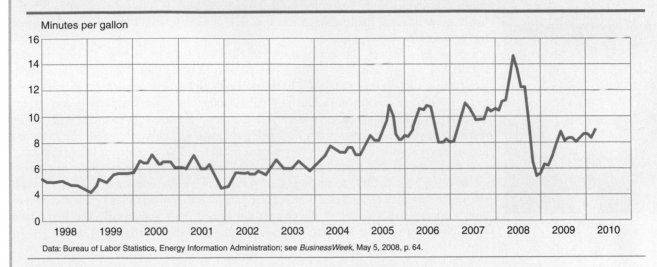

Data: Bureau of Labor Statistics, Energy Information Administration; see *BusinessWeek*, May 5, 2008, p. 64.

Figure A

The Number of Minutes the Average American Works to Pay for a Gallon of Gas
The chart is based on hourly pay for production workers, who make up some four-fifths of private nonfarm payrolls.

in 1973. *Think* about it. Never before in our history have real wages fallen over such an extended period of time. And yet, even though this period was marked by six recessions, real per capita GDP actually doubled. We need to ask two questions: (1) Why did real wages fall? And (2) How did families manage to keep up their standard of living?

Real wages cannot grow unless productivity grows. But productivity growth slowed from the late 1970s through the mid-1990s from an annual average of well over 2 percent to barely 1 percent. Meanwhile factories were closing left and right as our relatively high-paying manufacturing jobs went to Mexico, Japan, Southeast Asia, and China. In 1973, two out of seven Americans worked in manufacturing, but by 1996, just one in seven did.

So where did people find jobs? They found them in the relatively lower paying service sector, which, incidentally, was less likely than manufacturing to be unionized. Today, with 1.4 million employees, Walmart is the largest employer in America. In 2007 it paid its sales clerks an average hour wage of less than $10, and as we noted in the previous chapter, not one employee was a union member.

As you can observe in Figure 2 of the previous chapter, the unionization rate of private sector employment fell by more than two-thirds between 1973 and 2007. Unionized workers generally earn at least 20 percent more than their nonunionized counterparts.

Another factor holding down real wages has been rapidly increasing health care premiums, which are paid by the employers of over 60 percent of the labor force. In effect, then, the money that would have otherwise gone towards pay increases was eaten up by rising health care costs.

Finally we have the effects of globalization, which has depressed American wages in two ways. As we've already noted, millions of high-paying manufacturing jobs have migrated to low-wage countries. But perhaps even more important, tens of millions of American workers are, directly or indirectly, competing with much lower paid workers in China, India, Mexico, and other low-wage countries. Even doctors and lawyers are learning that since the advent of high-speed worldwide communications, much of their work can be performed abroad. Everyone in the labor force should be asking herself or himself, Will my employer soon find a way to give my job to someone in another country who will do it for one-fifth my salary?

As the forces of globalization proceed, the wages in all the richer countries may be depressed by what has been termed, "the race to the bottom." As a growing number of workers in these countries find themselves competing with much lower paid workers in the less developed countries, will their real wages decline? Has this process already taken hold? Look again at the real wage rate line in Figure 8. It would appear that the race to the bottom has already begun.

Now let's answer our second question: How did families manage to keep up their standard of living? Mainly by having formerly stay-at-home moms going out and getting jobs to help support their families. Elizabeth Warren and Amelia Warren Tyagi believe that most two-income families are actually worse off today than their one-income counterparts were in the 1970s. They observe that "Today, after an average two-income family makes its house payments, car payments, insurance payments, and childcare payments, they have less money left over, even though they have a second, full-time earner in the workplace."[5]

That's the middle class. They're managing, but barely. The people *really* hurting are the working poor. In 2007 some 30 million Americans, nearly one out of every four workers, made less than $9 an hour, which placed them and their families below the poverty line, a concept we'll define in the chapter after next. Beth Schulman's *The Betrayal of Work* describes who the working poor are and the jobs they perform:

> They are nursing home workers and home health-care workers who care for our mothers and fathers, yet make so little income that many qualify for food stamps. They are poultry processing workers who bone and package the chicken we eat for our dinner, yet are not allowed to leave the line to go to the bathroom. They are retail store workers who help us in department stores, grocery stores and convenience stores, but can't get enough hours or benefits to support themselves without working at least two jobs. They are hotel workers who ensure that the rooms we sleep in on our business trips and family vacations are clean, but who have no sick days or funeral leave or vacation time. They are janitorial workers who empty our wastebaskets after dark but who have no childcare. They are catfish workers who process the fish we enjoy, but must work with injured wrists from continuous motion on the line. They are 1-800 call-center workers who answer our requests and take our orders while under constant management surveillance. And they are childcare workers who educate and care for our children while their own live in poverty.[6]

Our opulent lifestyle is subsidized by the low-wage work performed by tens of millions of Americans, not to mention tens of millions of foreign workers earning even less. Barbara Ehrenreich and Beth Schulman believe these workers should be better paid, even though this would raise prices. What do *you* think?

The Minimum Wage and the Living Wage

The Minimum Wage Rate: 1938 to the Present

The Fair Labor Standards Act

In 1938 Congress passed the Fair Labor Standards Act calling for a 25-cent-an-hour minimum wage (raised to 30 cents in 1939), a standard workweek of 44 hours (reduced to 40 hours in 1940), and the payment of time and a half for overtime. You know, of course, that 25 cents bought a lot more in 1938 than it does today.

Since then the minimum wage has been raised periodically, but these raises have not kept pace with inflation. In 1991 it reached $4.25, $5.15 in 1997, and finally, $7.25 in

Beth Schulman

We have thousands and thousands of people working on full-time jobs, with part-time incomes.

—Martin Luther King, Jr.

---

[5]Elizabeth Warren and Amelia Warren Tyagi, *The Two-Income Trap* (New York: Basic Books, 2003), pp. 51–52.

[6]Beth Schulman, *The Betrayal of Work* (New York: The New Press, 2003), pp. 5–6.

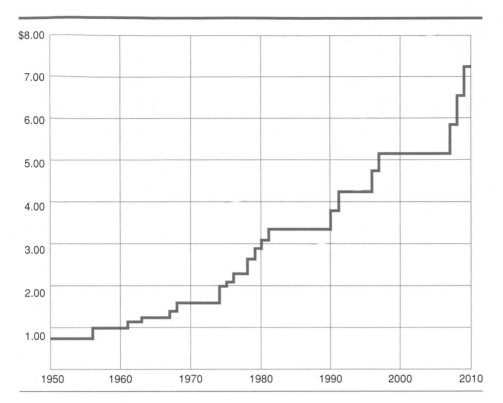

Figure 9
U.S. Minimum Hourly Wage, 1950–2010
The minimum wage is raised periodically, but in recent decades it has not kept up with inflation. Between 1997 and 2007 it was not raised at all.
Source: U.S. Bureau of Labor Statistics, *Employment and Earnings,* January 2010. www.bls.gov/cps.home.htm

mid-2009 (see Figure 9). Most Americans earn a lot more than the minimum wage, but when the minimum wage was raised in 3 steps between 2007 and 2009, about 6 million workers got substantial pay raises. In addition, as a ripple effect, perhaps 10 million others who were earning $7.25 or slightly more also got pay raises.

Should There Be a Minimum Wage Rate?

According to many conservative economists, the minimum wage law hurts the very people it is supposed to help—young workers, the unskilled, and those whose productivity is low. These economists use marginal revenue product analysis (which we covered a couple of chapters back) to support their claim that the basic effect of the minimum wage is to cause millions of marginal workers to be unemployed. And they point to the high teenage unemployment rate as their proof.

Many younger workers are familiar with the catch–22 of job interviews: "Come back when you have some experience." Where are you supposed to get that experience before you land your first job? The conservative economists would help younger workers get that experience by suspending the minimum wage. Once they acquired the requisite experience, they would be able to get jobs that pay at least the minimum wage.

This raises another issue. My students—many of whom staff the fast-food emporiums of America—claim that were the minimum wage lower this would just be an excuse to pay them even less. In fact, the whole attack on the minimum wage is suspect on the same grounds.

So which side is right? Is it the conservatives who believe that some employers would hire fewer people if the minimum hourly wage is set too high? Or is it those who maintain that without a legal minimum hourly wage, we would return to the old sweatshop conditions of the 1930s? To help us decide, let's look at the two graphs shown in Figure 10.

In both Panel A and Panel B, the equilibrium wage rate is $6, while the minimum legal wage is $7.25. According to the information in panel A, then, if the minimum legal wage were raised from the equilibrium level of $6 to $7.25, how many people would lose their jobs?

Conservatives: The minimum wage law hurts the very people it is supposed to help.

To fix the minimum of wages is to exclude from labour many workmen who would otherwise have been employed; it is to aggravate the distress you wish to relieve.

—Jeremy Bentham, *A Manual of Political Economy*

To "help" teenagers, President Reagan proposed lowering their minimum wage to $2.50 an hour.

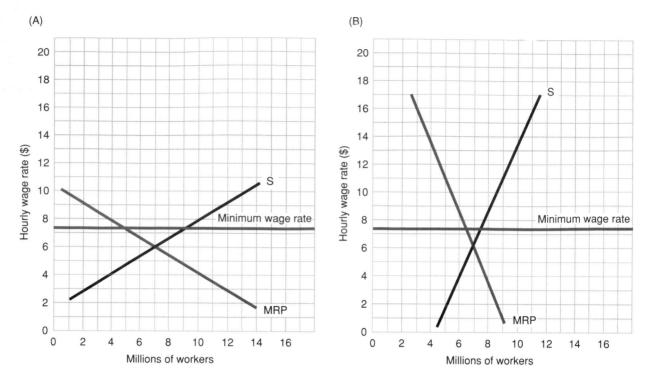

Figure 10

How much does the minimum wage lower employment?

If the minimum wage is set above equilibrium, it will lower employment. If the demand for labor and the supply of labor are elastic (see Panel A), employment will be greatly reduced. If the demand for labor and the supply of labor are inelastic (see Panel B), there will be a relatively small reduction in employment.

Four million people would lose their jobs. As you'll notice, we've gone from 9 million people working to just 5 million. Moving right along, in Panel B, if the wage rate were raised from $6 to $7.25, how many people would lose their jobs?

The answer is 1 million. Why do so many more people lose their jobs when the minimum wage is raised in Panel A than in Panel B?

Panel A has much more elastic demand and supply curves than panel B. Indeed, the more elastic the demand and supply for labor, the more people will lose their jobs when the minimum legal wage is raised. OK, so which panel better describes how our economy is operating?

The correct answer is that we don't know. The conservatives would certainly say that Panel A is more accurate, so that even a small rise in the minimum wage rate would cause millions of workers to lose their jobs. The proponents of a higher minimum wage would say that Panel B is more accurate.

But *this* much is clear: If the minimum wage were raised above the equilibrium wage, *some* unemployment would result. *Some* employers, especially restaurants and other small businesses, would lay off some of their unskilled workers. But how *many?* No one knows the answer to *that* question.

Many states set their own minimum hourly wage rates, which can be somewhat higher than the federal rate. For example, Washington state has a minimum wage almost three dollars an hour higher than its neighbor, Idaho. Are Washington businesses flocking to Idaho or laying off workers? No, but many Idaho teenagers are crossing the state line to work in fast-food restaurants in Washington.

A widely cited study by Alan Krueger of Princeton and David Card of Berkeley focused on the effect of a 1990 minimum wage hike in New Jersey on unemployment in that state and neighboring Pennsylvania. They found that "employment actually expanded in New Jersey relative to Pennsylvania, where the minimum wage was constant."[7] In additional studies that they conducted using data from other states, Card and Krueger found a positive correlation between a higher minimum wage and employment.

Does this mean that we could raise the minimum wage to, say, $15 or $20 an hour, without causing substantial unemployment? Definitely not! But we *may* conclude that the increases in the federal and state minimum wage rates in recent decades have *not* resulted in any appreciable increases in unemployment.

Who earns the minimum wage? In 2009 nearly 3 million Americans did. They included hamburger flippers, gas station attendants, garment workers, salesclerks, and janitors. About two-thirds were adults, while most of the rest were teenage members of low-income families for whom the wages were an important source of income.

The minimum wage was raised during the Great Recession of 2007–2009. Some economists believe that this raise increased unemployment. Professor Rajeev Dhawan, director of Georgia State University's Economic Forecasting Center, stated that, "Wherever you have the higher unemployment rates, that's where the business conditions are bad—and that's where a minimum wage increase will have an impact on the negative side." But Representative George Miller (D-CA), who authored the 2007 minimum wage legislation, countered that, "A higher minimum wage helps working families' budgets and results in increased spending on local business, which is good for everyone."[8]

Whether or not you believe that a substantial increase in the minimum wage during a bad recession raises unemployment, one thing *is* certain. Economists will be debating this question for years to come. To throw in my own two cents, I believe that the minimum wage increase *has* raised unemployment. The big question is: By how much?

How does our minimum wage compare with those of other advanced economies? As you can see from Figure 11, ours is pretty close to the bottom of the heap. Only Spain and Korea—two traditionally poorer countries—have lower minimum hourly wage rates.

The Living Wage

The living wage is a minimum hourly wage rate that must be paid to employees of major contractors doing business with over 150 municipalities and countries. But nationwide, only about 150,000 workers are covered; about one-third are in New York City. In a few

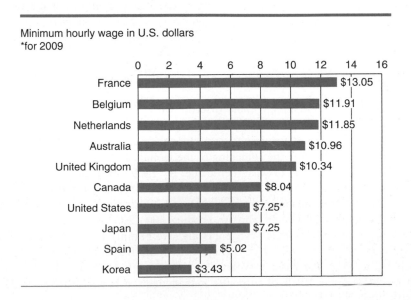

Minimum hourly wage in U.S. dollars
*for 2009

France	$13.05
Belgium	$11.91
Netherlands	$11.85
Australia	$10.96
United Kingdom	$10.34
Canada	$8.04
United States	$7.25*
Japan	$7.25
Spain	$5.02
Korea	$3.43

Figure 11
Minimum Hourly Wage in Selected Industrial Countries, 2008

---

[7]David Card and Alan Krueger, *Myth and Measurement: The New Economics of the Minimum Wage* (Princeton University Press, 1995), p. 66.

[8]CBS News, Associated Press, "Minimum Wage Hike Raises Recession Fears." www.cbsnews.com/stories/2009/0724/business/main5185628.shtml?tag=topnews.

cities, like Santa Fe, New Mexico, the living wage must also be paid to city employees. In most cases, the stipulated hourly rate is between $7.50 and $10.00. Other major cities with living wage laws include Boston, Cincinnati, Los Angeles, Baltimore, Chicago, Minneapolis, Denver, and San Francisco.

Maryland became the first state in the nation to pass a living wage law. Passed in 2007, the law requires most employers with state contracts to pay their workers a minimum hourly amount—$11.30 in the Baltimore–Washington corridor and $8.50 in the rural counties, where wages and prices are usually lower.

A study of 36 cities by David Neumark of Michigan State University found that while such laws did tend to reduce employment somewhat among low-wage workers, they also resulted in a moderate decline in urban poverty. Although more localities will soon be passing living wage laws, it is quite unlikely that they will cover even 1 percent of the U.S. labor force.

In the chapter before this, we saw how labor unions, largely by restricting the supply of labor, have raised the wages of their members. And in this chapter, we saw how the federal minimum wage as well as local living wage laws have placed a floor under wages. These are two instances of interference with the functioning of the market forces of supply and demand. But at best, about 20 percent of our labor force is affected by unions, the minimum wage, or the living wage. So our bottom line remains the same: The wage rate is determined mainly by supply and demand.

The Effects of Employment Discrimination on Wages

The civil rights movement of the 1960s and the women's liberation movement of the 1970s had a profound impact on the nation's workplace. As late as the 1960s, the job ads of newspapers were divided into two sections—male and female. Employment agencies had not-so-secret numerical codes. For instance, an employer with a job opening for a secretary might call to ask for a 1, which meant WASP (White Anglo-Saxon Protestant). It was understood, of course, that this was a woman's job. "Send me a 4" meant that an African American was needed for some menial job.

People from many different groups were discriminated against, but the two largest targets were women and African Americans. And if you happened to be an African American woman, then, of course, you had two strikes against you before you even came to bat.

Employment Discrimination against Women

In Chapter 2 we saw how employment discrimination leads to a misallocation of our economy's resources. One out of every two members of our workforce is a woman, so let's try to get some idea of how much employment discrimination affects their wages.

Back in 1972, just before the launching of the women's liberation movement, women made, on average, 58 percent of what men made. By 2009 they made 77 percent. Clearly there's been substantial progress. Professions that had been largely closed to women—medicine, law, corporate management, and public administration—are now almost gender blind. But the number of women who are Fortune 500 CEOs is still just 15—including seven who are Fortune 100 CEOs—Angela Braly (Well Point), Lynn Eisenhans (Sunoco), Ellen Kullman (Du Pont), Indra Nooyi (PepsiCo), Irene Rosenfeld (Kraft Foods), Mary Sammona (Rite Aid), and Patricia Woertz (Archer Daniels Midland). Until many more women reach the upper levels of corporate management, it is apparent that a glass ceiling is still in place.

Perhaps the best measure of the absence of employment discrimination is the degree to which there is equal pay for equal work. How does the pay of women stack up against that of their male counterparts in various jobs? Not all that well according to the numbers in Figure 12.

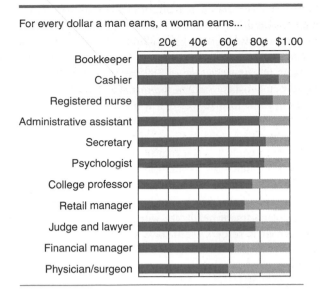

For every dollar a man earns, a woman earns...

Figure 12

Unequal Pay for Equal Work
Source: Betsy Morris, "How Corporate America Is Betraying Women," *Fortune,* January 10, 2005; Bureau of Labor Statistics; Census Bureau; *The New York Times,* Section 4, p. 4, March 1, 2009.

You'll see that for each of the 11 jobs listed, women earn less than their male colleagues. Please look at the listings vertically, first starting at the top and reading down. Now read them again, this time starting at the bottom.

Did you notice a pattern? Please take a minute to summarize your observation right here. You can probably do it in just a couple of sentences.

Here's *my* observation: Only in the lower paying jobs do both sexes earn roughly the same. The further up the pay scale and the higher the education, the wider the earnings gap. The top five or six professions listed—bookkeeper, cashier, administrative assistant, registered nurse, secretary, and, possibly, psychologist—are what may be termed "women's jobs," because most of these jobs are held by women. Traditionally women's jobs have paid more poorly than other jobs. Interestingly, even in *these* jobs, women are paid somewhat less than men. But when we get into jobs traditionally closed to women—judge and lawyer, financial manager, and physician and surgeon—the pay differential between women and men becomes much more pronounced. According to the American Bar Association, women in 2008 made up almost half of all associates, but only 18.3 percent of partners.

The field of work with the highest proportion of female workers is kindergarten and preschool teaching. Women hold 98 percent of these particular jobs, but a man in this job typically earns $5,000 more than a woman.

Are there any jobs in which women earn more than men? Yes—financial analysts, postal service clerks, special education teachers, speech pathologist, radiation therapist, library worker, and biological technician. Female sales engineers make 43 percent more than their male counterparts, while female statisticians earn 35 percent more. But these jobs are rare exceptions to the rule: Men earn more than women doing the same work.

In recent years women have filed numerous sex discrimination suits. Although sexual harassment suits have gotten the most attention, the suits against employment discrimination have yielded the best financial results:

- Boeing agreed to pay $73 million to settle a class-action suit brought by female employees who asserted that they were paid less than men and not promoted as quickly.

- Morgan Stanley agreed to a $100-million-plus settlement to a class-action that made similar allegations.

- Nine hundred women who filed a sex discrimination suit against Merrill Lynch were paid over $100 million.

- UBS, Europe's largest bank, was ordered by a federal jury in New York to pay Laura Zubulake $29 million for mistreating her for being a woman, and then firing her after she complained to the Equal Employment Opportunity Commission.

In the mother of all class-action sex discrimination suits, Walmart is being sued on behalf of 2 million current and past women employees. Women make up more than two-thirds of the company's hourly workers, but hold only about one-third of the store manager jobs. In addition, women earn substantially less than men in similar jobs. For example, women store managers made an average of $89,280 a year, $16,400 less than men.

While working as an assistant Sam's Club manager in Riverside, California, Stephanie Odle said she was surprised to discover that a male assistant manager at the store was making $60,000 a year, $23,000 more than she was earning.

"I was outraged," Ms. Odle said. "When I went to the district manager, he first goes, 'Stephanie, that assistant manager has a family and two children to support.' I told him, 'I'm a single mother and I have a 6-month-old child to support.'"[9]

Women are only 10 percent of the regional vice presidents, 10 percent of the district managers, and 14 percent of the store managers. And yet 89.5 percent of the cashiers and 79 percent of the department heads are women. Is there a glass ceiling at Walmart? Perhaps when the lawsuit is settled, we'll have a definitive answer.

Employment Discrimination against African Americans

Like women, African Americans have made spectacular employment advances in recent decades. An interesting project would be to watch tapes of TV shows from the 1950s and compare them to current programming. Back in Chapter 2, we discussed the racial employment barriers that had been in place for centuries.

Despite their fantastic employment gains, African American men earn just 75 percent of what white men earn, while African American women earn only 67 percent. Incidentally Hispanic Americans fare even worse. Compared to white men's earnings, Hispanic men earn 68 percent and Hispanic women earn 61 percent.

In 1999 Franklin Raines became the first African American to head a major American corporation when he was named the CEO of the mortgage-financing giant, Fannie Mae. He was soon joined by four others—Barry Rand (Avis); Kenneth Chenault (American Express); Stanley O'Neal (Merrill Lynch); and Richard Parsons (AOL Time Warner). In 2006 Ron Williams became the CEO of Aetna. But still more spectacular were the appointments by President George W. Bush of Colin Powell as his first secretary of state, and of Powell's successor, Condolezza Rice.

Conclusion

May we conclude that employment discrimination fully explains the wage differentials that we have just noted? What about work experience, educational attainment, and, in the case of most women, the impact on career advancement of taking years off for child rearing?

It goes well beyond the scope of this book, not to mention the competence of the author, to discuss the degree to which sex discrimination accounts for the differences in the earnings of women and men. That said, I strongly suspect that sexual discrimination is alive and well in the American workplace.

Current Issue: The Education Gap

Societies are almost always divided between the "haves" and the "have-nots." Generally the haves have much more money, a much higher standard of living, and much greater social standing than the have-nots.

That has always been the case in our country, even back in colonial times. But today, increasingly, the great divide between the haves and the have-nots is a college degree.

---

[9]Steven Greenhouse, "Wal-Mart Sex Discrimination Suit Is Granted Class-Action Status," *The New York Times*, June 23, 2004, p. C8.

A college degree provides entrée to the primary job market. And, as it happens, college graduates, on average, earn almost twice as much as high school graduates. And people with professional degrees—for example, MBAs, CPAs, lawyers—earn almost 50 percent more than what a college graduate earns.

So it makes sense for children to study hard and get good grades from elementary school through college and graduate school. But then one must consider the odds of getting a college degree, which seem to be determined largely by family background. If your family has an income of over $90,000, your chances of getting a college degree by the age of 24 are 1 in 2. A child in a family earning $35,000 to $61,000 has a 1 in 10 chance. But if your family earns less than $35,000, you've got just a 1 in 17 chance of getting a college degree by the time you're 24.

Why don't more poor teenagers attend college? Could it be the colleges' stringent entrance requirements? While high school graduates from all economic backgrounds face daunting odds to get accepted by the nation's 100 or so most selective schools, there are, at the other end of the academic spectrum, perhaps one-third of our colleges that will take anyone with a high school diploma, or an 18-year-old birth certificate.

Money has become a growing problem, but most students willing to hold down a part-time job can attend at least a local community college. In addition, Ivy League and other elite colleges are increasingly offering free educations to qualified students who otherwise could not afford to attend.

New York Times columnist David Brooks believes that cultural differences between educated, relatively rich parents and less educated, relatively poor parents, largely determine whether or not their children will go to college. Just as elementary, middle, and high schools often have tracking systems for the college bound, and for the educationally left-behinds, there is a parallel tracking system among families. Brooks summed it all up in these two sentences: "Educated parents not only pass down economic resources to their children, they pass down expectations, habits, knowledge and cognitive abilities. Pretty soon you end up with a hereditary meritocratic class that reinforces itself generation after generation."[10]

Do you agree that there is, then, an educational tracking system, not just within schools, but within families? And do you believe that our society can be dichotomized between those with college degrees and those without? If you do, then you're clearly hoping to end up a "have" rather than a "have-not."

Questions for Further Thought and Discussion

1. Are you in the primary labor market or the secondary labor market? Use your answer to show how these markets differ.

2. Explain why the backward-bending labor supply curve has this shape.

3. What is economic rent? Make up an example that illustrates this concept.

4. What is the most important factor underlying the long-run increase in average real wage rates in the United States?

5. *Practical Application:* Should there be a minimum wage rate for teenagers? Present both sides of the issue.

6. *Practical Application:* List the jobs held by your friends and family members that are in (a) the primary labor market and (b) the secondary labor market.

7. *Practical Application:* List the pros and cons of raising the minimum wage.

8. *Web Activity:* How much will you earn when you graduate? Go to www.payscale.com and after answering a series of questions about which college you are attending, your major, and your job skills, you will get an estimate of your future earnings.

---

[10]David Brooks, "The Education Gap," *The New York Times,* September 25, 2005, Section 4, p. 11.

W*orkbook* for Chapter 16 Mc Graw Hill connect |ECONOMICS

Name _____   Date _____

Multiple-Choice Questions

Circle the letter that corresponds to the best answer.

1. According to the backward-bending supply curve, as the hourly wage rate increases from 0 to $10,000 the number of hours worked per week by the average person will _____. (LO2)
   a) be constant
   b) decrease, then increase
   c) increase, then decrease
   d) increase steadily
   e) decrease steadily

2. The demand for labor in a particular market is _____. (LO3)
   a) the sum of all the individual labor supply curves
   b) the sum of all the firms' MRP curves
   c) the sum of all the individual labor supply curves and all the firms' MRP curves
   d) none of these

3. Which statement is true? (LO3, 6)
   a) Differences in wage rates are explained entirely by differences in productivity.
   b) Differences in wage rates are explained entirely by differences in education and training.
   c) Differences in wage rates are explained entirely by whom you know (rather than what you know).
   d) None of these statements is true.

4. The possibility of earning economic rent is great if _____. (LO5)
   a) the supply of a factor is very high relative to demand
   b) the demand for a factor is very high relative to supply
   c) both demand for a factor and supply of a factor are high
   d) both demand for a factor and supply of a factor are low

5. If Tiffany Kuehn is earning $200,000 a year today and she were to earn $400,000 a year 10 years from today, her _____. (LO6)
   a) real wages and money wages will both have increased
   b) real wages and money wages will both have decreased
   c) real wages will have increased
   d) money wages will have increased

6. Which job would pay the highest real wages over the last 20 years? One that paid _____. (LO6)
   a) twice the minimum wage rate
   b) a fixed wage of $10 an hour
   c) a starting hourly wage of $10 with raises adjusted to the Consumer Price Index
   d) exactly the real average hourly wage rate in 1982 dollars

7. Conservative economists believe the minimum wage law _____. (LO7)
   a) helps all workers equally
   b) hurts all workers equally
   c) hurts teenagers more than other workers
   d) helps teenagers more than other workers

8. Which statement is the most accurate? (LO7)
   a) The federal minimum wage rate is indexed to the rate of inflation: Each year it's raised equal to the rate of inflation during the previous year.
   b) Over 10 million Americans are covered by a living wage law.
   c) There is considerable disagreement as to whether the federal minimum wage helps the unskilled workers more than it hurts them.
   d) Very few people's wage rates are actually determined by supply and demand.

9. If the minimum wage were eliminated, the employment of marginal workers would _____. (LO7)
   a) rise a lot
   b) rise a little
   c) stay exactly the same
   d) fall a little
   e) fall a lot
   f) fall by an indeterminate amount
   g) rise by an indeterminate amount

10. The living wage set by municipalities tends to be _____. (LO7)
    a) higher than the federal minimum wage
    b) lower than the federal minimum wage
    c) about the same as the federal minimum wage

11. When the minimum wage is abolished, the wage rate for marginal workers will _____. (LO7)
    a) fall and employment will fall
    b) fall and employment will rise
    c) rise and employment will rise
    d) rise and employment will fall

12. Which statement is true? (LO1, 3)
    a) Over time the distinctions among noncompeting groups tend to blur.
    b) Over time the distinctions among noncompeting groups tend to become sharper.
    c) Over time there is no tendency for the distinctions among noncompeting groups to change.

13. Which statement is true? (LO1, 3)
    a) The primary job market has most of the good jobs.
    b) The secondary job market has most of the good jobs.
    c) Neither the primary nor the secondary job market has the best jobs.
    d) None of these statements is true.

14. According to the theory of the backward-bending labor supply curve, _____. (LO1)
    a) first the substitution effect sets in, then the income effect
    b) first the income effect sets in, then the substitution effect
    c) the substitution effect and the income effect set in at the same time
    d) there is neither a substitution effect nor an income effect

15. Which statement is true about incomes in the United States? (LO5)
    a) Almost everyone earns about the same income.
    b) Almost everyone is either very rich or very poor.
    c) There is a wide disparity in income.
    d) None of these statements is true.

16. Which statement(s) is/are true? (LO1, 3, 9)

    Statement I: A college diploma is still a necessary condition for a person moving from the secondary to the primary labor market, but that diploma is no longer a sufficient condition.

    Statement II: Professional basketball (especially the National Basketball Association) is an example of a winner-take-all market.

    a) Statement I is true and statement II is false.
    b) Statement II is true and statement I is false.
    c) Both statements are true.
    d) Both statements are false.

17. On average, (LO1, 3, 9)
    a) people with professional degrees earn about twice as much as high school dropouts.
    b) college graduates earn about four times as much as high school graduates.
    c) high school dropouts earn less than $20,000 a year.
    d) people with college degrees earn about $100,000 a year.

18. Which statement is true? (LO1, 7, 9)
    a) The minimum wage has kept up with the rate of inflation.
    b) Average real hourly earnings are much higher today than they were in 1973.
    c) A college degree is definitely not a ticket out of poverty since so many college graduates are poor.
    d) Over half of the college students whose parents' incomes are in the top quartile finish college.

19. Which statement is true? (LO7)
    a) The average hourly wage in the United States is $5.15 an hour.
    b) If the minimum wage rate were lowered, more unskilled workers would find jobs.
    c) The hourly wage rate in the United States is higher than that in any other country.
    d) Many cities have laws requiring most private employers to pay a "living wage."

20. Compared with 1973 the nominal hourly wage rate is _____ and the real hourly wage rate is _____. (LO6)

a) higher, higher
b) lower, lower
c) higher, lower
d) lower, higher

21. Which statement about production workers is true? (LO6)

a) They earn more in the U.S. than anywhere else in the world.
b) They earn more in the U.S. than almost anywhere else in the world.
c) They earn about the same in the U.S. as in most other countries.
d) They earn less in the U.S. than in most other countries.

22. Beth Schulman makes the point that workers in nursing homes, retail stores, hotels, and child care are (LO7)

a) well paid considering that their work is not very important.
b) lucky they have jobs at all.
c) doing important work, but not being paid enough money.
d) not well paid, but generally well regarded by their employers.

23. _____ a minimum wage rate higher than the federal minimum wage rate. (LO7)

a) All states have
b) Most states have
c) A few states have
d) No state has

24. Which statement is true? (LO7)

a) The federal minimum wage has ensured that virtually everyone employed full-time earns enough to support a family above the poverty line.
b) The federal minimum hourly wage rate will be raised to $7.25 in 2009.
c) The federal minimum wage rate is raised each year to keep up with the rate of inflation.
d) The federal minimum wage was last raised in 2003.

25. Which is the most accurate statement? (LO6)

a) The fall in real wages between 1973 and 1993 was the longest in our history.
b) Although real wages fell between 1973 and 1993, by 2007 they were the highest they have ever been.

c) Real wages fell in the 1970s and 1980s, and money wages fell even more.
d) The period between 1973 and 1993 was a period of rising real wages.

26. Which statement is true? (LO8)

a) Only 10 percent of the Fortune 500 corporations are headed by either women or African American men.
b) In most occupations, women earn about the same as men.
c) The wage gap between women and men has closed somewhat over the last 40 years.
d) Each of these statements is true.
e) None of these statements is true.

27. Which is the most accurate statement? (LO8)

a) Employment discrimination has been almost entirely wiped out over the last few decades.
b) The glass ceiling no longer exists.
c) Nearly everyone agrees that Walmart is an equal opportunity employer.
d) Women have won huge settlements in sex discrimination suits against their employers.

28. A woman is most likely to earn as much as a man in the same occupation if she is a _____. (LO8)

a) cashier
b) lawyer
c) college professor
d) physician

29. Which one of these groups has the lowest earnings? (LO8)

a) Hispanic women
b) Hispanic men
c) African American women
d) African American men

30. Which job paid the highest real wages over the last 20 years? One that paid _____. (LO4, 7)

a) twice the minimum wage rate
b) a fixed wage of $10 an hour
c) a starting hourly wage of $10 with raises adjusted to the consumer price index (CPI)
d) exactly the real average hourly wage rate in 1982 dollars

Fill-In Questions

1. The dual labor market consists of a _____ market and a _____ market. (LO1, 3)

2. The substitution effect (on the backward-bending labor supply curve) takes place when _____ _____.
   The income effect takes place when _____ _____. (LO2)

3. At very low wage rates the _____ effect outweighs the _____ effect; at very high wage rates the _____ effect outweighs the _____ effect. (LO2)

4. The wage rate is always determined by two factors: _____ and _____. (LO4)

5. Economic rent is _____. (LO4)

6. By real wages, economists mean what you can _____. (LO6)

7. If we abolished the minimum wage law, employment of low-wage workers would _____. (LO7)

8. If the minimum wage were eliminated, wages would definitely _____ for some marginal workers, and the employment of marginal workers would definitely _____. (LO7)

9. If the minimum wage were abolished, there would be a substantial increase in the employment of marginal workers only if the MRP for marginal labor was very_____ and the supply of marginal labor was very _____. (LO7)

Problems

1. Ms. Spielvogel was paid $400 a week in 1987, the base year. By 1995 she was earning $900 a week. If the consumer price index was at 180 in 1995, how much were Ms. Spielvogel's real wages that year, and by what percentage had they changed? (LO6)

2. Karryn Bilski made $2,400,000 in 2001, the base year. By 2004 she was earning $3,600,000. If the CPI rose to 120 by 2004, how much were her real wages that year, and by what percentage had they changed? (LO6)

Refer to Figure 1 to answer Problems 3 and 4.

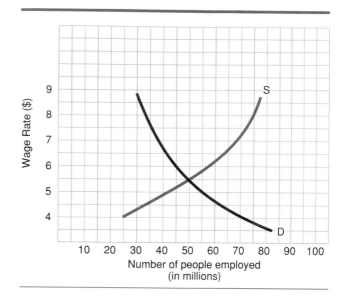

Figure 1

3. An increase in the minimum wage to $6 would cause _____ million people to lose their jobs. (LO7)

4. An increase in the minimum wage to $7 would cause _____ million people to lose their jobs. (LO7)

5. Mr. Dostievsky earned $40,000 in 1999, the base year. By 2006 he was earning $80,000. If the consumer price index was at 160 in 2006, how much would Mr. Dostievsky's real wages be that year, and by what percentage would they have changed? (LO6)

Chapter 17

Rent, Interest, and Profit

B ack in Chapter 2 we introduced the four economic resources—labor, land, capital, and entrepreneurial ability. Now we have finally gotten around to discussing how these resources are compensated. The last chapter discussed labor markets and wage rates.

We're now ready to tackle the payments to the remaining three factors of production—land, capital, and entrepreneurial ability. As you might have expected, rent and interest are determined by supply and demand. Profits, however, are determined somewhat differently.

LEARNING OBJECTIVES

After reading this chapter you should be able to:

1. Define land and how rent is determined.
2. Define and illustrate economic rent.
3. Demonstrate whether prices are high because rents are high, or whether rents are high because prices are high.
4. Define capital and how the interest rate is determined.

5. Explain and calculate the present value of future income.
6. List and discuss how profits are determined.
7. Name and discuss the theories of profit.
8. Discuss usury, and payday and fringe lenders.

Rent

What Is Land?

Land is a resource or a factor of production. The owner of land is paid rent for allowing its use in the production process. The amount of rent paid for a piece of land is based on the supply of that land and the demand for that land.

This raises four questions: (1) Exactly what *is* land? (2) How does one piece of land differ from another? (3) How is the supply of land derived? (4) How is the demand for land derived?

Exactly What Is Land? Land is land. An acre of land in Lake Forest, Illinois, an affluent Chicago suburb, is a suitable site for building a home. A half acre in downtown Los Angeles could be used for an office building, and 160 acres in Kansas might do well for growing wheat. How land is used depends on its location, its fertility, and whether it possesses any valuable minerals.

Sometimes we confuse land with what is built on it. A plot of land with apartment houses, stores, or office buildings will bring a lot more rent than a plot that lies vacant.

Sometimes we confuse land with what is built on it.

395

But, strictly speaking (in economic terms), we pay rent on the land itself. We'll call the payments on buildings and other capital goods a form of interest, which we'll cover in the next part of this chapter.

How Does One Piece of Land Differ from Another?   As I just noted, a plot of land may have a few alternative uses. If it is used at all, it will be used by the highest bidder—the one willing to pay the most for it. For example, real estate developers bought up hundreds of dairy farms in central New Jersey over the last two decades. The developers made these farmers offers they could not refuse. In effect, then, the land was worth more as housing sites than as farms.

The basic way in which one piece of land differs from another is location. Only four plots of land can be located at the four corners of one of the most expensive pieces of real estate in the world, Fifth Avenue and 57th Street in Manhattan. Land that is just off this intersection is nearly as expensive. Land near airports, near highway interchanges, in shopping malls, or in the downtown sections of cities is more expensive than less desirably located land.

How Is the Supply of Land Derived?   The supply of land is virtually fixed. Aside from the efforts of the Dutch to reclaim small parcels of land from the North Sea, and relatively minor dredging and draining projects around the world, about one-quarter of the earth's surface is land. Until we're ready for interplanetary travel, everything we've got to work with is on the earth's surface. To go one step further, at any given location there's a fixed amount of land.

Of course, we can make more efficient use of that land. In cities, for example, we build straight up so that thousands of people can work on just one acre. Unfortunately, we've been unable to duplicate this feat in the suburbs because of the extensive acreage we've found it necessary to devote to parking lots.

There is finite amount of land.

Any way we slice it, we have a finite amount of land. In economics we say the supply of land is fixed. We represent the supply of land as a vertical line, such as the one in Figure 1. We're lumping all land together in that graph, but technically there are tens of thousands of different supplies of land because each location differs from every other location.

The demand for land is derived from a firm's MRP curve.

How Is the Demand for Land Derived?   The demand for land, like the demand for labor and capital, is derived from a firm's MRP curve. The land will go to the highest

Figure 1

Determination of Rent
The demand for rent is the MRP schedule of the highest bidder for a specific plot of land. The supply of that land is fixed, so its supply curve is perfectly inelastic. The rent, like the price of anything else, is set by supply and demand.

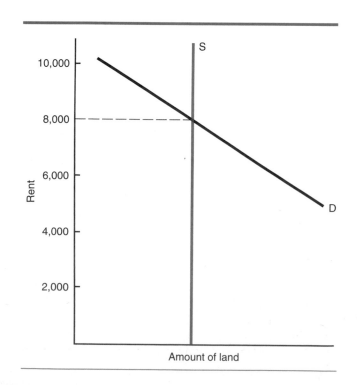

bidder; the demand curve in Figure 1 represents the MRP schedule of the firm willing to pay the most for the land.

Why does the demand curve for land slope downward to the right? You may remember that a firm's MRP curve declines with output because its marginal physical product declines with output (due to diminishing returns). In addition, if the firm is an imperfect competitor, it must lower its price to increase sales, thereby further depressing MRP as output expands.

How Is Rent Determined?

You do not have to be a great economist to answer the question of how rent is determined. It is determined by the law of supply and demand. In Figure 1, we find that rent is $8,000.

Just to make sure you've got this straight, if the demand for land were D₁ in Figure 2, how much would the rent be?

Did you say $120,000? Good! If demand for land rose to D₂, how much would rent be?

Was your answer $160,000? All right, then. Did you notice that when the demand for land rises, the rent goes up as well? This is exactly what you'd expect under the law of supply and demand.

There is one peculiarity, though. You've noticed that the supply of land is fixed, or perfectly inelastic. Because supply doesn't change, changes in price are brought about by changes in demand.

We can use this information to analyze rents charged on three different plots of land. Suppose plot 1 is 100 miles from the nearest city and is not in demand for any use. How much rent does it bring?

It brings nothing because no one wants to use it. It's what we call marginal land. Suppose someone sets up a store on this land with the permission of the landlord but pays no rent. Very few people shop in this store because it's in the middle of nowhere. If the store owner's capital costs are $10,000, the cost of his labor is $20,000, and his sales are $30,000, he will make zero economic profits.

Now we'll move on to plot 2, just 30 miles from the center of town. This store also has capital costs of $10,000 and labor costs of $20,000, but its sales are $45,000. Guess how much rent this store owner will pay?

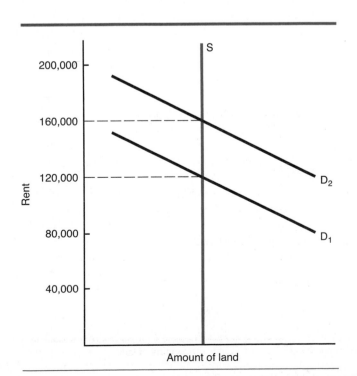

Figure 2

Increase in Demand for Land

Since the supply of land is perfectly inelastic, an increase in demand is reflected entirely in an increase in price (and not an increase in the quantity of land).

She will pay $15,000. You see, business is so good at this location that if the rent were anything less than $15,000, the guy who built his store on the marginal (or free) land in the boondocks would have bid $15,000. The location of the land closer to town, where so many more potential customers pass by, makes plot 2 worth $15,000 to at least one firm.

Finally, we have plot 3, right in the center of town where people pass by in droves. How much rent will someone pay for this plot? It will bring much more than $15,000. If the costs of capital are $10,000, the costs of labor $20,000, and sales $100,000, how much will this land rent for?

It will rent for $70,000. If it were renting for less, someone would come along and offer the landlord $70,000. The owner of the store on plot 1 certainly would; and so would the owner of the store on plot 2.

Now I'd like you to try this one on for size. Suppose costs remain the same, but sales on plot 1 rise to $40,000. Will the owner of plot 1 pay any rent? How much? He will pay $10,000 in rent.

If sales on plot 2 rise to $55,000, how much rent will it bring? It will bring $25,000. If sales on plot 3 rise to $110,000, how much rent will it bring? It will bring $80,000. To summarize, location is the basic differentiating factor in the rents of various plots of land, and the demand for each piece of land determines how much rent is paid.

Economic Rent

Payment in excess of what people would be willing to accept is economic rent.

In the last chapter, I introduced the concept of economic rent, the amount of money certain people are paid beyond what they would be willing to work for. For example, baseball players who love the sport, like the legendary Willie Mays, are willing to play for a lot less than they're paid, and perhaps David Letterman would actually accept a measly $5 million a year instead of whatever it is that he earns. The surplus is called economic rent.

Should landlords be paid anything at all?

Economic rent, then, is the payment above the minimum necessary to attract this resource to the market. Rent paid to landlords (exclusive of any payment for buildings and property improvements) is, by definition, economic rent.

We may ask whether landlords should indeed be paid any rent at all for their land. After all, the land was always there; it certainly wasn't created by the landlords. (See the box, "Who Created the Land?") Whether they expropriated it, inherited it, or even purchased it, the land really belongs to society. More than 120 years ago a man named Henry George even started a single-tax movement whose objective was to finance government solely by taxing land rent. George reasoned that the land did not really belong to the landlords and the payment of rent did not increase production (because the land is there for the taking), so why not tax away this unearned surplus?

In his best-selling book, *Progress and Poverty* (1879), George observed that as the frontier closed and the nation's population continued to rise very rapidly, the demand for land was growing. But the supply was fixed, or, as you've seen in Figure 2, perfectly inelastic. The landlords were reaping huge returns for merely holding land.

Henry George, American economist

What Henry George overlooked

Although this tax proposal has been criticized on several counts,[1] it does have considerable merit. A tax on land would raise revenue, and such a tax would fall largely on unproductive resource owners.

But Henry George overlooked an important attribute of rent: As the price for the use of land, it serves as a guidance mechanism, directing the most productive (that is, highest-paying) enterprises to the most desirable (that is, expensive) land. Because the most desirable locations bring the highest rents, they are inevitably occupied by the highest bidders. If we taxed away these rents, we might conceivably have some effect on the

---

[1]It would raise only a small fraction of needed government revenue; landlords sometimes improve the land; and rent on land is not the only kind of income that is unearned.

Who Created the Land?

Do you remember the very first words of the Bible? "In the beginning God created the heaven and the earth" (Genesis 1:1). This raises an interesting question. Why do landlords get to charge rent on this land? If you have ever posed this question, let's look at Leviticus (25:23): "The land shall not be sold for ever: for the land is mine; for ye are strangers and sojourners with me."

Pierre-Joseph Proudhon carried this reasoning to its logical conclusion: "Who is entitled to the rent of land? The producer of the land without doubt. Who made the land? God. Then, proprietor, retire!" Just to sum things up, Proudhon asked himself this question: What is property? His answer? "Property is theft!"

A very strong current in economic thought denies the landlord's claim to rent. However, the problem we have had since being banished from the Garden of Eden is that we need to deal with scarcity, and rent is an excellent means of efficiently allocating the use of scarce land.

Pierre-Joseph Proudhon, French journalist

allocation of land. For instance, if I owned a plot of land in midtown San Francisco and all my rent were taxed away, I might just as soon rent it to a candy store as to a fancy boutique.

Are Prices High because Rents Are High, or Are Rents High because Prices Are High?

How many times have you gone into a store in a high-rent district and been overwhelmed by the prices? Didn't you say to yourself, "Their prices are high because the owner has to pay such a high rent"? Fair enough. A store situated in an expensive area has to charge high prices to make enough money to pay its greedy landlord.

We're going to digress for a couple of minutes and a couple of centuries because this same question came up in early 19th-century England. David Ricardo, the great economist, set the record straight: "Corn is not high because a rent is paid, but a rent is paid because corn is high."[2]

The price of corn (and wheat) was high because there was a great demand for it caused by the Napoleonic Wars. Because the supply of farmland in England was entirely under cultivation (and therefore fixed), a rise in the demand for corn raised the demand (or the MRP) for farmland, thereby driving up rents.

Now, back to the present. You've seen that stores in expensive neighborhoods charge high prices and pay high rents. But *why* do they pay high rents? Because they outbid all the other prospective tenants. Why did they bid so high? Because they wanted the desirable location. Stores located in busy shopping areas pay much higher rents than do stores in less busy areas. Why? Because their locations are so desirable that their rents are bid up.

David Ricardo, English economist

Do certain stores charge high prices because they have to pay high rents?

---

[2]David Ricardo, *The Principles of Political Economy and Taxation,* ed. L. Reynolds and W. Fellner (Burr Ridge, IL: Richard D. Irwin, 1963), p. 34.

Now we'll look at the same question from the other side. Suppose a store happens to pay a low rent—say a mom-and-pop grocery not far from where you live. How do its prices compare with supermarket prices? They're higher, right? But you'd expect them to be lower, if low rents lead to low prices.

High rents don't cause high prices.

Here's the final word. High rents don't cause high prices. Desirable locations attract many prospective renters, who bid up rents because they believe they will get a lot of business. In other words, following Ricardo's analysis, rents are high because the demand for the final product—and consequently the derived demand—is high.

Interest

What Is Capital?

Capital consists of office buildings, factories, stores, machinery and equipment, computer systems, and other synthetic goods used in the production process. When we invest, we are spending money on new capital. When we build an office park, a shopping mall, or an assembly line, or when we purchase new office equipment, we are engaged in investment.

Economists feel good when they can think in terms of stocks and flows. The stock of capital increases by means of a flow of investment. Suppose you have half a glass of water; that's your capital stock. You can fill up that glass by letting tap water flow into it; that's your investment flow. When you've filled your glass, you have doubled your capital stock.

To use a machine example, say you have a capital stock of four machines. You buy two more. That's your investment for the year. Now you have a capital stock of six machines.

How Is the Interest Rate Determined?

The law of supply and demand

You guessed it! The interest rate is determined by the law of supply and demand. Figure 3 shows this.

The demand for capital is the firm's MRP schedule for capital. As we've seen, MRP curves always slope downward to the right.

Figure 3
Determination of the Interest Rate
The interest rate is determined by the demand for loanable funds and the supply of loanable funds.

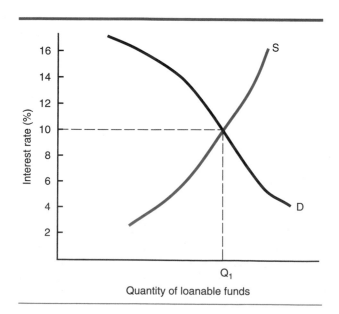

Usury in Ancient Times

Mosaic laws in the book of Deuteronomy strictly forbid not only usury (lending money at exorbitant interest rates), but even the taking of any interest. In those days loans were made mainly for charitable purposes, so the prohibition made a great deal of sense.

Aristotle considered the charging of interest to be the most unnatural method of accumulating wealth:

*The most hated sort, and with the greatest reason, is usury, which makes a gain out of money itself, and not from the natural objects of it. For money was intended to be used in exchange, but not to increase at interest . . . Of all modes of getting wealth this is the most unnatural.**

These same views continued to be reflected in the rules of the Church, which prevailed until the end of the Middle Ages. With the rise of commerce, however, the basic purpose of most loans changed, and the prohibitions against taking interest were dropped. But what constitutes a "fair" rate of interest on consumer loans continues to be debated to this day.

Unlike Christians and Jews, Muslims to this day follow the stricture of the Koran, that one neither gives nor receives interest. However, banks in Islamic countries do have ways of getting around this inconvenience. Suppose you wanted to buy a Toyota Camry. Your bank would buy it from the dealer, for $18,000, and you buy your car from

Aristotle, Greek philosopher

your bank for $21,000, paid out in monthly installments over three years.[†]

Islamic banking avoids using the term "interest," but the mark-up—in this case, $3,000—that is paid to the bank certainly looks and smells a lot like interest.

---

*Aristotle, *Politics*, ii, p. 1258.
[†]See Jerry Useem, "Banking on Allah," *Fortune*, June 10, 2002, p. 155.

The supply of loanable funds, however, unlike the supply of land (which is perfectly inelastic), slopes upward to the right. You may remember that the backward-bending labor supply curve of the previous chapter slopes upward to the right, until, at extremely high wage rates, it bends backward.

Why does the supply of loanable funds or savings slope upward to the right? Because the amount of money people save is somewhat responsive to interest rates. The higher the interest paid, the more people will save.

Interest Rates and Consumer Loans

Do high interest rates deter borrowing for consumer loans? Obviously they do. And do the banks charge too much on credit card loans? They *do?* Then maybe a legal ceiling should be placed on the interest that may be charged on these and other loans.

Although there is no federal law on the books, many states have what are called usury laws, which place legal ceilings on the interest rates that may be charged on certain types of loans. (See the box, "Usury in Ancient Times.") Usury is defined as charging "an unconscionable or exorbitant rate of interest." Usury laws are intended to curb this greedy practice. But, as the old saying goes, the road to hell is paved with good intentions.

Usury laws, however popular with the public, drive many economists wild. Why? There are two reasons. First, these laws may hurt the very people they are intended to help by creating a shortage of loanable funds. This is illustrated in Figure 4, which we'll look at in a minute.

Do banks charge too much interest on credit card loans?

Usury laws place limits on how much interest may be charged.

Figure 4

Interest Rate Ceiling
An interest rate ceiling is set at 16 percent, well below the equilibrium level of 24 percent. How much is the resulting shortage of loanable funds? Since, at 16 percent, $550 billion in loanable funds is demanded but only $200 billion is supplied, the shortage is $350 billion. What would be the best way to eliminate that shortage of loanable funds? Answer: Eliminate the 16 percent interest rate ceiling and allow the interest rate to rise to its equilibrium level of 24 percent.

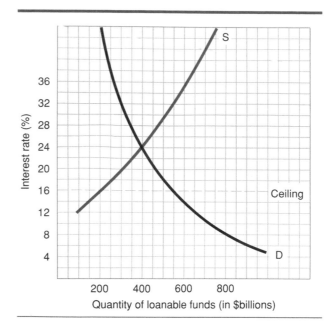

A second reason why economists love to hate usury laws is that these laws blatantly interfere with the price mechanism, more familiarly known as the law of supply and demand. Prices signal the buyers and sellers in the market. When prices are low buyers try to buy more, and when they're high sellers offer more of their goods or services for sale. Because the interest rate is the price of money, a high price signals sellers to provide more loanable funds, while discouraging borrowers from borrowing. A high enough interest rate would completely eliminate the shortage of loanable funds.

Let's look at Figure 4 to see how the price mechanism would work. First, if there *were* a legal ceiling on interest rates of 16 percent, there would be a shortage of how much? It looks to me like $350 billion ($550 billion demanded −$200 billion supplied). And how much is the equilibrium interest rate? That's right—it's 24 percent. So if we eliminated the interest ceiling, the interest rate would quickly rise to 24 percent, and the shortage would be eliminated.

Usury laws are price ceilings.

You may recall our discussion of price ceilings and price floors in the chapter titled "Supply and Demand." Usury laws are price ceilings because they prevent the interest rates from rising to their equilibrium levels. In other words, usury laws place an upper limit on interest rates. Consequently, there are a lot more borrowers in the market than lenders, which creates a shortage of loanable funds.

So how exactly do usury laws hurt borrowers? They hurt the borrowers with relatively poor credit ratings. For example, if the interest rate were fixed at 16 percent, lenders would be willing to lend out only about $200 billion, all of which would go to people they considered the most creditworthy borrowers. The rest of us would be completely left out. Some of us would go to consumer finance companies (for example, Household Finance, Seaboard Finance, and Beneficial Finance); these might not be covered by usury laws and could therefore charge higher interest rates. Or we might go to loan sharks who often charge a straight 10 percent interest—that's 10 percent a week! So the next time you think you're paying an arm and a leg in interest on a bank credit card, consider the alternative.

While I'm still up on my soapbox, I'd like to make the connection between usury laws and other legal obstacles to the price mechanism. Farm price supports, or price floors, are one such obstacle. In the last chapter we discussed the minimum wage law, another price floor. Wage and price controls were mentioned a few times in the earlier chapters of *Economics* and *Macroeconomics*. Still another legal interference with the law of supply and demand is rent control, which puts a ceiling on how much rent landlords may charge for apartments.

Economists dislike the laws that set up these obstacles because they interfere with the price mechanism and often end up harming the very people they were intended to help. That said, a case can be made for each one of these laws. And while in general most economists would prefer not to tamper with the forces of supply and demand, many of us are prepared to make certain exceptions. My own predilection is for minimum wage laws, which I believe do a lot more good than harm. Another exception I'd make is to place a cap on so-called "payday loans" (see Current Issue: "Subprime, Fringe, and Payday Lending" at end of this chapter). The issue comes down to making judgment calls. But those judgment calls are yours—not mine.

Price ceilings and price floors interfere with the price mechanism.

on the web

How much interest would *you* have to pay to borrow money? Go to www.bankrate.com and type in your zip code.

The Present Value of Future Income

Economists are fond of saying that a dollar today is worth more than a dollar you will have in the future. Why? Inflation?

While it's true that most of us have never known anything *but* inflation in our lifetimes, a dollar today would be worth more than a future dollar even if there were no inflation. If no inflation were expected in the future, lenders would charge borrowers what we call the real rate of interest.[3]

A dollar today is worth more than a dollar you will have in the future.

Let's say you have a dollar today and no inflation is expected over the next year. If you can get 5 percent interest by loaning out your dollar, that means one year from now you will have $1.05. On the other side of the coin, so to speak, the person who borrows the dollar from you today is willing to pay you $1.05 in one year. Why, then, is a dollar today worth more than a future dollar? Because it can be lent out to earn interest.

Waiting necessarily commands a price.

—Gustav Cassel,
The Nature and Necessity of Interest

Next question. If a dollar today is worth more than a future dollar, how *much* more is it worth? If the interest rate were 8 percent, how much would $100 today be worth in terms of dollars you will have one year from now?

The correct answer is $108. Naturally, we have a formula to figure these problems out.

The present value of a dollar received one year from now is $1/(1 + r)$, when r is the interest rate. Substitute .08 for r (remember 8 percent is equivalent to the decimal .08) in the formula, and see what you get.

Present value of a dollar received n years from now =
$$\frac{1}{(1 + r)^n}$$

Did you get 92.59 cents? (The actual answer is 92.592592592, with the three numbers repeating themselves ad infinitum.) So a dollar one year from now would be worth only 92.59 cents today.

What if the interest rate were 5 percent? How much would a dollar received one year from now be worth today?

Solution: $\dfrac{1}{1 + r} = \dfrac{1}{1.05} = 95.24$ cents

We'll do one more—when the interest rate is 12 percent.

Solution: $\dfrac{1}{1 + r} = \dfrac{1}{1.12} = 89.29$ cents

---

[3]During times of inflation, the expected inflation rate is factored into the interest rates charged to borrowers. You may recall this from the section headed "Anticipated and Unanticipated Inflation" in Chapter 10 of *Economics* and *Macroeconomics*.

We can say, then, that when the interest rate rises, the present value of future dollars will decline; when the interest rate falls, the present value of dollars held in the future will rise.

We can use a general formula for the present value of dollars held any number of years into the future:

$$\text{Present value of a dollar received } n \text{ years from now} = \frac{1}{(1 + r)^n}$$

Remember that time is money.
—Benjamin Franklin

If you're uncomfortable with algebra, don't worry. Once you plug in the numbers for r and n, it's no longer algebra, but just arithmetic.

The letter n is an exponent. It tells us to multiply what's inside the parentheses by itself n times. If the numbers inside the parentheses are $(1 + .12)$ and n is 3, what should we do? We should multiply $1.12 \times 1.12 \times 1.12$.

Now we'll work out a couple of problems using the formula. If the interest rate is 6 percent and you will be paid a dollar in two years, what is the present value of that dollar? Work it out to the nearest cent right here:

Solution: $$\frac{1}{(1 + r)^n} = \frac{1}{(1.06)^2} = \frac{1}{(1.06) \times (1.06)} = \frac{1}{1.1236} = 89 \text{ cents}$$

Let's recap, and then we'll work out one more problem. The higher the interest rate, the lower the present value. And the longer you must wait for your money, the less it is worth to you today. Another way of looking at these relationships is to see what a rising interest rate and a rising waiting period do to the denominator of the formula. Clearly they raise it, which lowers the present value of the asset.

What is the present value of $1,000 that will be paid to you in three years if the interest rate is 5 percent? Work it out to the nearest cent.

Solution: $$\text{Percent value} = \$1,000 \times \frac{1}{(1 + r)^n}$$

$$= \$1,000 \times \frac{1}{(1.05)^3}$$

$$= \$1,000 \times \frac{1}{(1.05)(1.05)(1.05)}$$

$$= \$1,000 \times \frac{1}{1.157625}$$

$$= \$1,000 \times .863838$$

$$= \$863.84$$

Now that I've put you through all those moves computing present value, I'm going to show you a shortcut. You may be able to find a table like the one in the box, "How Much Is $100 Received in the Future Worth to You Today?" Or if you have a really good pocket calculator, you should be able to find present value a lot faster. But if n is only 1 or 2, then I'm sure you can work out most problems with our handy formula in just a minute or two.

The Internal Revue Service now offers informants who turn in tax cheats 15 to 30 percent of whatever money the government recovers. Many of the potential informants

How Much Is $100 Received in the Future Worth to You Today?

This may not be a question people commonly ask you, but it is an interesting one, at least to economists. First, you may give a general answer: less than $100. But how *much* less than $100? That depends on two factors—when you will receive that $100 and what the interest rate is. The table here gives us a lot of answers.

So, what is the present value of $100 received four years from now if the interest rate is 12 percent? It's $63.55. And how much is the present value of $100 received in 15 years if the interest rate is 6 percent? It's $41.73.

Are you ready for a couple of generalizations? All right, then, here they come. First, as the interest rate rises, the present value declines. Second, as your years of waiting for your money increase, the present value declines. To generalize, the present value of a future dollar payment is inversely related to both the interest rate and how long you have to wait for your money.

Suppose you've just won $10,000,000. Exactly how much is that $10,000,000 actually worth? I hate to tell you, but it's worth a lot less than $10,000,000. You'll still take it? OK, then, let's get some idea of how much you actually won.

First you'll have to pay federal income tax, and very likely, state income tax as well. Let's say that the government takes a 40 percent slice, leaving you with $6 million. Still not too shabby.

Now comes the fun part—figuring out the present value of the $6 million. You'll probably get paid in annual installments, say over 20 years. That would come to $300,000 a year. Suppose that you receive your first installment one year after you win. Its present value would depend on the going rate of interest. The higher that is, the lower the present value of your payments.

If the interest rate were 4 percent can you figure out the present value of your first year's payment?

It would be $288,450. (Using the table, multiply $300,000 by 0.9615.) How much is the present value of 20th payment?

That comes to just $136,920 ($300,000 × 0.4564). What if the interest rate were 12 percent? See if you can find the present value of the first payment and then the 20th payment.

Solution: The first payment comes to $267,870.

The 20th payment comes to $31,110.

So it turns out that how much money you actually won, at least in terms of present value, depends largely on the going rate of interest. The higher the interest rate, the lower the present value.

Years in the Future	2 Percent	4 Percent	6 Percent	8 Percent	12 Percent
1	98.04	96.15	94.34	92.59	89.29
2	96.12	92.46	89.00	85.73	79.72
3	94.23	88.90	83.96	79.38	71.18
4	92.39	85.48	79.21	73.50	63.55
5	90.57	82.19	74.73	68.06	56.74
6	88.80	79.03	70.50	63.02	50.66
7	87.06	75.99	66.51	58.35	45.23
8	85.35	73.07	62.74	54.03	40.39
9	83.68	70.26	59.19	50.02	36.06
10	82.03	67.56	55.84	46.32	32.20
15	74.30	55.53	41.73	31.52	18.27
20	67.30	45.64	31.18	21.45	10.37

are current or former employees of large corporations, who hope to ultimately collect tens or even hundreds of millions of dollars from this program.

But whistle blowers have two main problems. The payoff is uncertain, and it may be years before they will see any of this money. In the meanwhile, they may find themselves out of a job. Into the breach have stepped a variety of hedge funds, private equity groups, and other big investors, who are willing to buy a percentage of future IRS payments in exchange for a smaller amount upfront to the whistle blowers. And as we well know, a dollar in hand is worth more than a dollar that will be received sometime in the future.

Profits

Profits, the last topic of this chapter, does not lend itself to any mathematical formulas or computations. Indeed, except for some problems at the end of this chapter, you have seen the last of the mathematical computations you will be asked to perform in this book. The entire study of profits, unlike that of rent and interest, is hotly debated by economists, politicians, and social critics. Let's begin by looking at how profits are determined and how large they are, and then I'll outline a few theories of profits.

How Are Profits Determined?

Profits are considered a residual left after payment of rent, interest, and wages.

Until now I've been saying that the law of supply and demand determines the price of just about everything. Now I'm going to have to change my tune. Economists treat profits as a residual left to the entrepreneur after rent, interest, and wages have been paid. One could argue that because these three resource payments are determined by supply and demand, then what's left over, profits, are indirectly determined by supply and demand.

What do *you* think? Does that sound plausible? Should we just leave it at that? Profits are indirectly determined by supply and demand?

Considering that this section goes on for another few pages, apparently *I'm* not too thrilled with leaving it at that. After all, if profits are the catalytic agent, the prime motivating factor, the ultimate reward for the entrepreneur, surely we can do better than to treat them as a mere residual. True, the business firm must pay rent, interest, and wages, and it may keep any remaining profits, but surely profits are a little more exciting than that, if I may be so bold.

How Large Are Profits?

What do we know about profits so far? At the beginning of Chapter 3, we talked about their role as an economic incentive under capitalism. The lure of profits is what gets business firms to produce the huge array of goods and services that provide the industrial countries of the world with such high standards of living.

We also know that economists derive profits somewhat differently from the way accountants derive them. Both subtract explicit costs (out-of-pocket or dollar costs, such as wages and salaries, cost of materials, fuel, electricity, rent, insurance, and advertising) from sales. But economists also subtract implicit costs (opportunity costs of additional resources used, such as the wages the owner of the firm and family members could have earned working elsewhere, and interest on money tied up in the firm that could have been earned by investing it elsewhere). Subtracting both explicit and implicit costs from sales means that economic profits are somewhat lower than accounting profits.

Large corporations have no implicit costs, but the majority of the nation's 4 million corporations are very small businesses with substantial implicit costs.

In 2009 corporate profits before taxes were $997 billion, and proprietors' income was $1,041 billion. Profits, then, were a total of $2,638 billion of a national income of $12,288 billion paid to all the factors of production, or 16.6 percent.

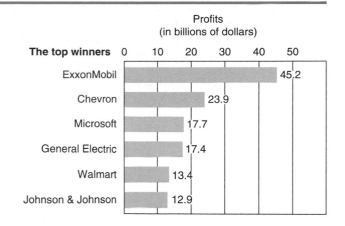

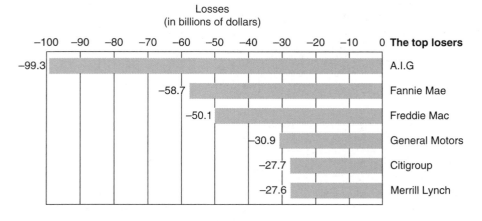

Figure 5

The Top Corporate Winners and Losers of 2008

As you can see, the losses sustained by the top losers greatly exceeded the profits earned by the top winners.

Source: www.fortune.com

Profits and Losses during the Great Recession

2008 was not a good year for corporate profits. As we sunk into the worst economic downturn since the Great Depression, corporate profits plunged—and much more to the point—corporate losses rose exponentially. The extent of these losses is shown in Figures 5 and 6.

From just glancing at Figure 5, you can see that the biggest losers lost a lot more than the largest corporate earners. A.I.G., which was bailed out by the Federal Reserve and the Treasury (see Chapter 14 of *Economics* and *Macroeconomics*), managed to lose just under $100 billion, which is an all-time record. Virtually no company could have sustained such a huge loss and stayed in business without massive government aid. General Motors, along with Chrysler, also lost huge amounts of money during the recession; both were bailed out by the Treasury.

Theories of Profit

Economic profit is the payment for entrepreneurial ability—whatever *that* is. The entrepreneur is rewarded for recognizing a profit opportunity and taking advantage of it. There are four somewhat overlapping theories of how the entrepreneur earns a profit: (1) as a risk taker; (2) as an innovator; (3) as a monopolist; and (4) as an exploiter of labor. We'll take up each in turn.

Capitalism without bankruptcy is like Christianity without hell.

—Frank Borman,
Astronaut and business executive

Figure 6

Declining Fortunes: 2004–2008
More than a quarter of our nation's largest corporations lost money in 2008. Losses in 2008 were more than 10 times greater than those of 2006.

Source: http://money.cnn.com/magazines/fortune/fortune500/2009/

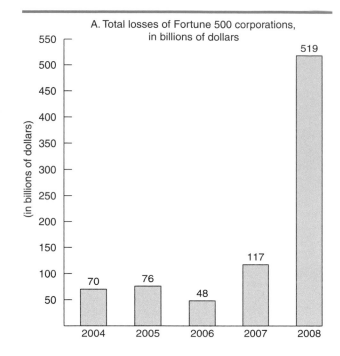

A. Total losses of Fortune 500 corporations, in billions of dollars

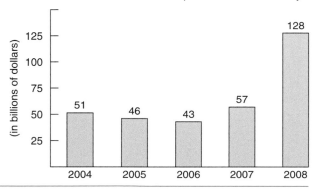

B. Number of Fortune 500 corporations that lost money

To win you have to risk loss.

—Jean-Claude Killy,
Professional skier

To get people to make risky investments, offer them high rates of return.

If you're not a risk taker, you should get the hell out of business.

—Steven J.Ross
former chairman, Time Warner

Profit is the result of risks wisely selected.

—Frederick Barnard Hawley

The Entrepreneur as a Risk Taker   Have you ever played the lottery? Did you ever hit the number? The $5 or $10 that most lottery players spend each week is a very risky "investment." Why do it? Because the payoff is so high. And if you don't play, then you can't even *dream* of winning.

The only way to get people to make risky investments is to offer high rates of return. In general, the riskier the investment, the higher the average rate of return. I mean, would *you* play the lottery if your chance of winning were one in a million and the payoff were 10 percent of your investment? Or 100 percent? Or even 1,000 percent?

Not too many folks are drilling for oil in the United States these days, but at one time you could hardly move without running into an oil well in wide stretches of Texas, Oklahoma, and a few other Southwestern states. Wildcatters may do all kinds of geological surveys and probability studies, or they may just trust dumb luck. Either way, you're taking one big risk when you start drilling down 5,000 feet or more. You're spending tens of thousands of dollars and you're either going to hit a gusher or you're going to come up dry. But as they say, nothing ventured, nothing gained.

According to Frank Knight's classic *Risk, Uncertainty, and Profit,* all economic profit is linked with uncertainty. Think of the telephone, the television, the automobile, and the airplane. Who knew for certain that they would work technologically and catch on commercially? Think of the wildcat oil-well drillers. These people took risks and

Jay Sorensen, Inventor, Innovator, and Entrepreneur

Jay Sorensen's inspiration came when he was sitting in a coffee house and managed to spill coffee on his lap. Here's what happened next (as described in a CNN/Money online article).*

> "It got me thinking that there had to be a better way," said Sorensen, who began to notice that other coffee-house patrons were holding steaming cups between their thumb and forefingers to avoid burning their hands.
>
> Sorensen's solution? A cardboard sleeve that would fit around the coffee cups.
>
> He developed the idea, then offered it to Starbucks. The then-nascent chain wanted exclusive rights and it was "dragging its feet" about the product. So Sorensen went out on his own, putting his last finances on the line to found his company, Java Jacket.
>
> "At that point I had about six months of living expenses," he said.
>
> Sorensen borrowed $3,000 from his parents to hire a patent attorney, and he ended up piling up credit card debt to have 100,000 coffee cup jackets made from waffled, recycled cardboard.
>
> "I had to pay for the order up front," he recalls. "It seemed like a ton at the time."

> The day he picked up the prototypes in his pickup truck, Sorensen returned to the cafe where he had originally spilled the coffee on his lap. He had no appointment but was told he could see the owner if he was willing to wait a bit.
>
> While he waited, he read about a coffee trade show to be held a week later. He had no money to attend. A few minutes later he was introduced to the cafe owner, who immediately bought some jackets.
>
> "He was kind enough to ask, 'Do you need a check now?' I said, 'Sure, that'd be nice,'" laughs Sorensen. He promptly used the money to attend the trade show, where he got orders from 150 cafes. His wife, Colleen—now company CEO—followed up with hand-written notes and a sample sleeve to the other 3,500 trade-show attendees.
>
> The efforts paid off big time. Today, the family-owned company sells between 20 million and 25 million sleeves a month, including neighborhood cafes to national chains.

*Leslie Haggin Geary, CNN/Money Staff Writer, "From Rags to Riches," http://money.cnn.com/2003/05/21/pf/saving/dreams_q_ragsriches/index/htm

made huge fortunes, but a lot of other people took risks and failed. As many rich Texans have long been fond of saying, money is just a way of keeping score.

Frank Knight saw profit as the reward for risk bearing. And those profits, while relatively uncertain and unstable, are also much higher than the normal profits earned by the owners of mainstream business enterprises.

The Entrepreneur as an Innovator We need to distinguish between invention and innovation. An invention is a new idea, a new product, or a new way of producing things. An innovation is the act of putting the invention to practical use. Sometimes the inventor comes up with something commercially feasible, but for one reason or another—usually a shortage of capital—does not market it. The Wright brothers, for example, never made a penny from commercial air flight, although Alexander Graham Bell, of all people, tried to steal their ideas.

Jay Sorensen is an inventor, an innovator, and an entrepreneur. The story in the accompanying box describes how he got his inspiration and how he followed through. As Thomas Edison put it, invention is 2 percent inspiration and 98 percent perspiration.

Joseph Schumpeter, one of the foremost business cycle theorists, stressed the pre-eminence of innovation as the basis for economic advance.

Frank Knight, American economist

Distinction between invention and innovation

Schumpeter's theory of innovation

> Whenever a new production function has been set up successfully and the trade beholds the new thing done and its major problems solved, it becomes much easier for other people to do the same thing and even to improve upon it. In fact, they are driven to copying it if they can, and some people will do so forthwith. It should be observed that it becomes

Which Theory of Profits Do We Apply?

Can you imagine what would happen if a pharmaceutical company came up with a drug that really *did* promote substantial hair growth? Its marketers would probably use the advertising slogan "Gone today, hair tomorrow." Or what if the company discovered a drug that reversed the aging process? Or how about a company that produced a drug that really did allow us to lose weight while eating as much as we wanted?

Now try to imagine what would happen to the profits of a company that discovered a miracle drug that grew hair, reversed the aging process, *and* helped us lose weight.

Which theory of profits do we apply to this example? Innovation? Certainly this company is an innovator. Monopoly? Until its patent runs out, the firm has a monopoly. Is the firm being rewarded for being a risk taker? I think we can argue that it took the risk of spending millions on research that might pay off big—but might not pay off at all.

So we can't neatly pigeonhole this entrepreneurial profit in any of these three categories. But if you *had* to pick one, which one would you pick? Which one would I pick? I'd have to go with profit as a reward for innovation, but it's not an easy call.

Joseph Schumpeter, American economist

Distinction between capitalist and entrepreneur

Natural scarcities versus contrived scarcities

easier to do the same thing, but also to do similar things in similar lines—either subsidiary or competitive ones—while certain innovations, such as the steam engine, directly affect a wide variety of industries. . . . Innovations do not remain isolated events, and are not evenly distributed in time, but. . . . on the contrary they tend to cluster, to come about in bunches, simply because some, and then most, firms follow in the wake of successful innovation.[4]

Schumpeter went on to say that "risk bearing is no part of the entrepreneurial function."[5] That's done by the capitalist who puts up the money. If the entrepreneur himself puts up the money, then he bears the risk of losing it as a capitalist, not as an entrepreneur. Finally, Schumpeter notes that in a purely competitive economy, profit "is the premium put upon successful innovation in capitalist society and is temporary by nature: it will vanish in the subsequent process of competition and adaption."[6]

If we distinguish, then, between the capitalist and the entrepreneur, the reward for entrepreneurship would be profits due to innovation. The capitalist's return would be interest, not profits. The capitalist's interest rate would depend on the risk.

So far we've depicted the entrepreneur as a risk taker and an innovator. No more Mr. Nice Guy. From here on, we'll see the entrepreneur cast in the role of economic villain.

The Entrepreneur as a Monopolist   Do the monopolist and the oligopolist, for that matter, make a profit? They sure do! In the previous chapters devoted to these kinds of firms, we concluded that they were able to make profits because of a shortage of competition. If this shortage of competitors is due to hard work, foresight, and innovation, one could hardly complain about the evils of big business.

Still, we need to make a distinction between "natural scarcities" and "contrived scarcities." A firm that develops a technology before anyone else (as IBM and Xerox both did) or one that possesses a unique location (as does the owner of land at a busy intersection) is the beneficiary of a natural scarcity and consequently earns monopoly profits.

Then there are the other guys, who have created or are able to take advantage of a contrived scarcity. The controllers of patents and those who own or have cornered the market on a vital resource (DeBeers diamonds, the National Football League) will almost always restrict output so they can earn monopoly profits. These are the economic bad guys because they are holding output below the levels at which the public wishes to purchase. (See the box, "Which Theory of Profits Do We Apply?")

[4]Joseph A. Schumpeter, *Business Cycles* (New York: McGraw-Hill, 1964), p. 75.
[5]Ibid., p. 79.
[6]Ibid., pp. 79–80.

The Entrepreneur as an Exploiter of Labor   Karl Marx based his theory of profits on the supposition that the capitalist exploits the worker. To illustrate this relationship, we'll take a simple numerical example. Suppose a worker needs to work 12 hours a day to have enough money to buy food. But suppose he could produce this food in just six hours working for the capitalist. The reason he can produce so much food is because he uses the capitalist's machinery.

Marxist exploitation theory

The worker produces enough food for two people in 12 hours. The capitalist gives him just enough wages to buy one day's food and keeps the other day's food for himself. Thus, a capitalist's role is to exploit his employees. Not bad work if you can get it.

Marx calls the expropriation of the proceeds of six hours of labor time "surplus value." The capitalist uses this to buy more capital. Then he will be able to exploit even more workers.

Surplus value

Capital, then, comes from the surplus value that has been stolen from the worker, and that surplus value represents the capitalist's profit.

Conclusion

What does all of this add up to? Which theory of profits is correct? Well, you know my style by now. I ask you what you think, I let you sweat for a while, and then, finally, I reveal the truth to you. I'll give you some time to go back over each of the four theories of profit. Imagine we're playing a couple of minutes of music while the clock is ticking away. OK—time's up! What's your answer?

Whichever answer you chose is right because there is a lot of truth in each of the four theories—even the Marxist theory. After all, more than 1 billion Chinese can't all be completely wrong! Furthermore, it's undeniable that monopolists *do* make profits. And surely there are plenty of profits earned by innovators and risk takers.

What we may conclude, then, is that everybody's right. And we may conclude that nobody has a monopoly on the truth.

Current Issue: Subprime,[7] Fringe, and Payday Lending

The poorer you are, the harder it is to borrow money. And because poor people are not great credit risks, they are forced to pay high, and sometimes exorbitant, interest rates. Late night TV is flooded with ads that always seem to say, "Bad credit? No problem." You can get a "subprime loan." The only problem is that you'll have to pay between 15 and 30 percent interest as well as additional high fees. Since 1995 the subprime lending business has more than quadrupled to well over $300 billion a year, and has attracted some of the nation's largest banks, including Citibank and Wells Fargo.

H & R Block, Jackson Hewlitt, and many other tax preparation firms issue tax refund anticipation loans, mainly to the working poor. The loans typically are issued for flat fees, often $78 or $88, which usually equate to annual interest rates of more than 100 percent, and sometimes as much as 1,500 percent.

But if you're *really* poor, your only credit option may be "fringe lending." So-called payday stores, often operating out of pawnshops and liquor stores, charge interest rates as high as 800 percent. Basically you're getting a loan until payday, but since you're strapped for cash in the first place, chances are you won't be able to pay off your loan without taking out still another one. Once you're hooked, you'll be paying sky-high interest rates, and falling deeper in debt.

---

[7]Large creditworthy corporate borrowers pay the prime interest rate, which may be 2 or 3 percentage points below mortgage rates. But subprime borrowers, who have less than splendid credit ratings, may pay 6 or 8 times prime rate. The prime interest rate is discussed in Chapter 13 of *Economics* and *Macroeconomics*.

Surrounding nearly all of our nation's hundreds of military bases you'll find a multitude of payday lenders like *Moneyback, Checkmate,* or even those with official-sounding names like *Military Financial Network.* All are quite happy to extend military personnel and their families instant no-questions-asked loans to tide them over until payday. What could be *bad?*

Say you wanted to borrow $500 until payday, less than two weeks from now. No problem. Just write out a check for $575, which we promise not to cash until payday, and you'll walk out of here with $500 cash. That comes to an annual interest rate of over 390 percent, and that's just for starters. If you were short $500 two weeks before *this* payday, and you're starting out the *next* pay period $575 behind . . . well, you can see where this is going. A month from now you'll be back for a bigger loan, and before long you'll owe thousands of dollars in interest on that original $500 loan you never really got out from under.

Until 2007 at least a quarter of all military families did business with high-cost instant lenders. Many became trapped in a spiral of borrowing that not only ruined their finances, but distracted them from their duties, and even destroyed their careers. Alarmed that troops preoccupied with their financial troubles might be distracted from their wartime duties, Congress finally acted by prohibiting payday loans to active duty service personnel and their families effective October 1, 2007, while capping interest rates on other unsecured consumer loans at a 36 percent annual percentage rate.[8] The law has effectively closed down payday operations around military bases.

Despite this setback, the practice of payday lending is alive and well in the 35 states that permit it. There were about 500 payday loan locations in 1990; today there are about 22,000. These guys are certainly better than loan sharks—at least they won't break your legs.

Questions for Further Thought and Discussion

1. Are prices high because rents are high, or are rents high because prices are high? Use an example to illustrate your answer.

2. What are usury laws? Why do economists hate them?

3. Explain why a dollar today is worth more than a dollar you will have in the future.

4. Why is the supply of loanable funds upward sloping? Why is the demand for loanable funds downward sloping?

5. Outline the main theories of profits. Which one(s) do you subscribe to?

6. *Practical Application:* Would you consider becoming a payday lender? List the reason why you would and why you would not.

7. *Practical Application:* As a financial officer of a large corporation, you find that it has been underpaying the Internal Revenue Service by tens of millions of dollars a year. As a whistle blower, you will probably receive a payment of $10 million within a few years. If a large investor offers to pay you a substantial amount of money today in exchange for your future award from the IRS, what would be the minimum amount for which you would settle? Explain how you arrived at that figure.

8. *Web Activity:* Which were the five most profitable corporations in 2009, and how much profit did each of them earn? Go to www.fortune.com

9. *Web Activity:* What is the present value of $10,000 10 years from today if the interest rate is 10 percent? You can find the answer in about five seconds by going to www.moneychimp.com/calculator/present_value_calculator.htm

---

[8]Michael A. Stegman, "Payday Lending," *Journal of Economic Perspectives* 21, No. 1 (Winter 2007), p.174.

Workbook for Chapter 17 ![McGraw Hill] connect | ECONOMICS

Name _____   Date _____

Multiple-Choice Questions

Circle the letter that corresponds to the best answer.

1. Which statement is true? (LO1)
   a) All land has the same economic value.
   b) The most important factor affecting rent is location.
   c) The economic value of a plot of land is determined exclusively by the raw materials it contains.
   d) None of these statements is true.

2. The supply of land _____. (LO1)
   a) is fixed
   b) varies from time to time
   c) rises with demand
   d) is higher in urban areas than in rural areas

3. Land is most efficiently used in _____. (LO1)
   a) cities
   b) suburban areas
   c) rural areas

4. The rent on a particular piece of land is based on _____. (LO1)
   a) the supply of land
   b) the buildings located on that land
   c) the MRP schedule of the highest bidder
   d) the MRP schedule of the lowest bidder

5. When the demand for a plot of land rises, _____. (LO1)
   a) its supply will fall   c) its price will fall
   b) its supply will rise   d) its price will rise

6. The supply of land is _____. (LO1)
   a) perfectly elastic   c) relatively elastic
   b) perfectly inelastic   d) variable in elasticity

7. Rent on marginal land is _____. (LO1)
   a) very high   c) zero
   b) above zero   d) negative

8. Each of the following is a valid criticism of Henry George's ideas except that _____. (LO1)
   a) a tax on land would raise only a small fraction of needed government revenue
   b) landlords sometimes improve the land
   c) like rent, other kinds of income are unearned
   d) a tax on land would result in a decrease in the supply of land

9. Which statement is true? (LO3)
   a) Prices are high because rents are high.
   b) Rents are high because prices are high.
   c) David Ricardo believed high rents would drive English farmers out of business.
   d) None of these statements is true.

10. As interest rates rise _____. (LO4)
    a) more borrowing will be undertaken
    b) less borrowing will be undertaken
    c) there is no change in the level of borrowing

11. In the Middle Ages the taking of interest was forbidden to _____. (LO4, 8)
    a) both Jews and Christians, but not Muslims
    b) both Christians and Muslims, but not Jews
    c) both Jews and Muslims, but not Christians
    d) Jews, Christians, and Muslims

12. A clothing store on fashionable Rodeo Drive charges more for the same clothes than another store in less fashionable Compton. Why does the first store charge more? (LO3)
    a) They have to pay a higher rent.
    b) They know their customers can afford to pay more.
    c) They advertise more.
    d) Because they can.

13. If there were no inflation, a dollar today would be worth _____. (LO5)
    a) exactly the same as a dollar received in the future
    b) more than a dollar received in the future
    c) less than a dollar received in the future

14. Which statement is true? (LO6)

    a) Profits are determined by supply and demand.

    b) Profits are solely a reward for risk taking and innovation.

    c) Profits are derived solely from the exploitation of workers.

    d) None of these statements is true.

15. Which statement is true? (LO6)

    a) Profits are about one-quarter of GDP.

    b) Profits are about 1 percent of GDP.

    c) Accounting profits are larger than economic profits.

    d) None of these statements is true.

16. Which economist believes all profits are linked with uncertainty and risk? (LO6, 7)

    a) Frank Knight   c) Karl Marx

    b) Joseph Schumpeter   d) John Maynard Keynes

17. "Innovations do not remain isolated events, and are not evenly distributed in time, but . . . on the contrary they tend to cluster, to come about in bunches, simply because some, and then most, firms follow in the wake of successful innovation." Who made this statement? (LO6, 7)

    a) Frank Knight   c) Karl Marx

    b) Joseph Schumpeter   d) John Maynard Keynes

Use Figure 1 to answer questions 18 through 20.

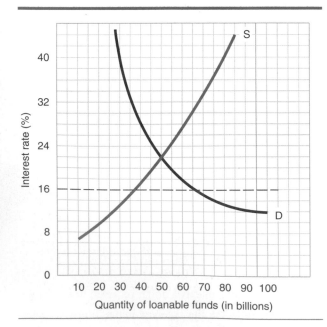

Figure 1

18. The horizontal dotted line is _____. (LO4)

    a) a price ceiling

    b) a price floor

    c) either a price ceiling or a price floor

    d) neither a price ceiling nor a price floor

19. If there were no usury law, the interest rate would be _____ percent. (LO4, 8)

    a) 16   d) 22

    b) 18   e) 24

    c) 20

20. With the usury law in effect there is a _____ of _____ billion. (LO4, 8)

    a) shortage, $28   c) shortage, $56

    b) surplus, $28   d) surplus, $56

21. The present value of a dollar declines as _____. (LO5)

    a) the interest rate declines and the number of years you wait for your money declines

    b) the interest rate rises and the number of years you wait for your money rises

    c) the interest rate declines and the number of years you wait for your money rises

    d) the interest rate rises and the number of years you wait for your money declines

22. Which statement is true? (LO2)

    a) Only the owners of labor can earn an economic rent.

    b) Only the owners of land can earn an economic rent.

    c) Both the owners of land and labor can earn an economic rent.

    d) Neither the owners of land nor the owners of labor can earn an economic rent.

23. Which statement is true? (LO4, 8)

    a) At different times in history Jews, Christians, and Moslems were forbidden to charge interest.

    b) Jews have never been forbidden to charge interest.

    c) Christians have never been forbidden to charge interest.

    d) Moslems have never been forbidden to charge interest.

24. For a usury law to be effective, it must set the interest rate ceiling _____. (LO4, 8)
   a) above the equilibrium rate of interest
   b) below the equilibrium rate of interest
   c) at exactly the equilibrium rate of interest

25. Which of the following is the most accurate statement about payday lenders? (LO8)
   a) Virtually all of them operate illegally.
   b) Payday lending operations prey primarily on military service members and their families.
   c) They charge extremely high interest rates.
   d) They are very useful to low-income families, because they force the families to save.

26. If you took out a payday loan, you could expect to pay an annual interest rate of _____. (LO8)
   a) less than 5 percent
   b) between 5 and 10 percent
   c) between 10 and 30 percent
   d) between 30 and 100 percent
   e) over 100 percent

27. The practice of usury _____. (LO8)
   a) is illegal in the United States
   b) is legal in some states and illegal in others
   c) is legal only if borrowers are in the military service
   d) was approved of by most major religions until just a few centuries ago

28. These lenders avoid using the term "interest," but their borrowers still do pay a charge for borrowing money. This would be considered _____ lending. (LO4, 8)
   a) Islamic   c) fringe
   b) payday   d) subprime

29. Why do Starbucks customers at busy downtown locations in major cities pay more for a cup of coffee than they would at less busy locations? (LO3)
   a) Starbucks coffee is better than that of any other company.
   b) They are willing to pay more for the convenience of Starbucks' location.
   c) Starbucks must pay more rent than stores located in less expensive neighborhoods.
   d) The lines are always shorter at Starbucks because of their higher prices.

30. Which statement is true? (LO5)
   a) A dollar today is worth more than a future dollar because of inflation.
   b) A dollar in the future is generally worth more than a dollar today.
   c) There is no way to determine whether a future dollar is worth more or less than a dollar today.
   d) A dollar today is worth more than a dollar in the future.

31. Which one of the following is the most accurate statement? (LO6)
   a) In 2008 more of the Fortune 500 earned a profit than lost money.
   b) About the same number of the Fortune 500 lost money in 2008 as in 2004.
   c) The total losses among the Fortune 500 in 2008 were twice as great as the losses in 2007.
   d) Only a handful of large corporations made a profit in 2008.

Fill-In Questions

1. The amount of rent paid for a piece of land is based on the _____ and the _____. (LO3)

2. In economic terms, we pay rent only on _____ _____. (LO1)

3. Plots of land are differentiated mainly with respect to _____. (LO1)

4. The amount of land in the world is virtually _____. (LO1)

5. In a demand and supply graph for land, supply is represented by a(n) _____ line. (LO3)

6. The main thing Henry George advocated was a _____. (LO1, 3)

7. An important attribute of rent overlooked by Henry George was its role as a _____, directing the most productive enterprises to the _____. (LO3)

8. Rent is high because _____ _____. (LO3)

9. We can add to our stock of _____ by means of a flow of _____. (LO4)

10. The interest rate is determined by the law of _____ and _____. (LO4)

11. If the interest rate were 7 percent, $100 today would be worth _____ in dollars you will have one year from now. (LO5)

12. If interest rates fall, the present value of future dollars will _____. (LO5)

13. Economists treat profits as a _____ left to the entrepreneur after _____, _____, and _____ have been paid. (LO6, 7)

Problems

1. If the interest rate is 10 percent and a dollar will be paid to you in three years, what is the present value of that dollar (to the nearest 10th of a cent)? (LO5)

2. What is the present value of $10,000 that will be paid to you in four years if the interest rate is 8 percent? Work it out to the nearest cent. (LO5)

3. If the interest rate is 12 percent and a dollar will be paid to you in four years, what is the present value of that dollar (to the nearest cent)? (LO5)

4. Which has a higher present value? (a) $100 in 10 years when the interest rate is 2 percent or (b) $100 in 3 years when the interest rate is 8 percent? (LO5)

5. Which would you rather have? (a) $1,000 in 6 years if the interest rate is 4 percent or (b) $1,000 in 3 years if the interest rate is 8 percent? (LO5)

6. Which is worth more? (a) $100 today or (b) $300 in 15 years if the interest rate is 8 percent? (LO5)

7. Which is worth more? (a) $500 today or (b) $1,000 in 9 years if the interest rate is 8 percent? (LO5)

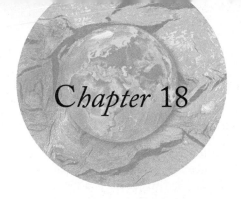

Chapter 18

Income Distribution and Poverty

The economic history of the United States has been one of tremendous growth, a rising standard of living, and a home in the suburbs for most American families. But income has not been distributed evenly, and tens of millions of Americans have been left far behind. Indeed, poverty amid plenty has been one of the basic failures of our society.

Fifth Avenue is the eastern border of New York's Central Park. More than a dozen billionaires have Fifth Avenue addresses, living in duplexes and triplexes with great views of the park. Many homeless people also have Fifth Avenue addresses, but they live in cardboard boxes just inside the park.

Visit any welfare office and you'll see dozens of very poor children waiting with their mothers for a worker to see them about their cases. But these children are rich compared to the children you'll find picking through garbage in the outlying areas of most large South American cities. Go out at night and you'll find children sleeping on the sidewalks.

This chapter is divided into two parts: income distribution and poverty. If income were distributed evenly, every American would have an income of $40,000 a year—that's every man, woman, and child—and there would be no poverty. In fact, if income were distributed evenly, there would be virtually nothing to say about income distribution and poverty, and this chapter would not have been written.

The forces of a capitalist society, if left unchecked, tend to make the rich richer and the poor poorer.

—Jawaharlal Nehru

LEARNING OBJECTIVES

After reading this chapter you should be able to:

1. Measure the inequality of income distribution in the United States.
2. Distinguish between the distribution of income and the distribution of wealth.
3. List and discuss what determines how income is distributed.
4. Define and discuss poverty in the United States.
5. Name and discuss the groups of people who are poor.
6. List the main government transfer programs to help the poor.
7. Explain the main causes of poverty.
8. Differentiate between the liberal and conservative theories of poverty.
9. Discuss and assess the solutions to poverty.
10. Judge whether welfare reform has been successful.
11. Assess your chances of ever being poor.

Income Distribution in the United States

The Poor, the Middle Class, and the Rich

I've been rich and I've been poor; rich is better.
—Sophie Tucker

How unequal is income distribution in the United States? To answer this question, we must first answer three subsidiary questions: How unequal are the incomes of (1) the poor and the rich, (2) blacks, whites, and Hispanics and (3) males and females? There are no big surprises here. The rich make more money than the poor; whites make more than blacks; and men make more money than women. The question is, How *much* more?

Do you know what a quintile is? I'll bet no one ever asked you *that* before. A quinquennial is an event that occurs every five years; a quintuplet is one of five babies born at the same time. A *quintile* is one-fifth, just like a quarter is one-fourth. We'll use this term to measure income distribution.

Who is rich, who is middle class, and who is poor?

The poor are in the lowest quintile, the middle class in the next three quintiles, and the rich in the upper quintile. Is it accurate to say that 20 percent of our population is poor, 60 percent is middle class, and 20 percent is rich? Probably not. But because social scientists can't agree about where to draw the dividing lines between the poor and the middle class and between the middle class and the rich, this arbitrary arrangement is as good as any other. And besides, we get to deal with nice round numbers—20, 60, and 20.

Table 1 lists the dividing lines between quintiles. If your family's income is below $20,712, then it is in the lowest quintile of household income. If it's above $100,240, it's in the highest quintile. And just in case you're interested, if your family's income is above $180,000, then it's in the top 5 percent.

TABLE 1	U.S. Household Income, by Quintile, 2006	
		Upper Income Limit
Lowest quintile		$20,712
Second quintile		37,400*
Third quintile		59,500*
Fourth quintile		100,240
Top quintile		

*Author's estimates
Source: www.census.gov

The Lorenz curve

Now we're going to analyze a Lorenz curve, named for M. O. Lorenz, who drew the first one in 1905. Let's begin by looking at the axes of Figure 1. On the horizontal axis we have the percentage of households, beginning with the poor (0 percent to 20 percent), running through the middle class (20 percent to 80 percent), and ending with the rich (80 percent to 100 percent). The vertical axis shows the cumulative share of income earned by these households.

Figure 1 has just two lines. The straight line that runs diagonally from the lower left to the upper right is the line of perfect equality. You'll notice that the poorest 20 percent of the households receive exactly 20 percent of the income, and that 40 percent of the households receive exactly 40 percent of the income. In other words, every household in the country makes exactly the same amount of money.

The curve to the right of the straight diagonal line is the Lorenz curve, which tells us how income is actually distributed. What percent of income does the poorest 20 percent of all households receive? And how much does the next poorest 20 percent receive? Put your answers here:

Lowest fifth:

Second fifth:

HELP

Finding the Percentage of Income Share of the Quintiles in Figure 1

The lowest quintile receives 5 percent of all income. Right? How much does the second quintile get? It gets 7.5 percent. Where did we get that number? What is the percentage share of income earned by the lowest 40 percent of households? It looks like 12.5 percent—right? Now if the bottom quintile earns 5 percent, and the lowest two quintiles earn a total of 12.5 percent, how much do households in the second-lowest quintile earn? They earn 7.5 percent (12.5 percent − 5 percent).

Next question: How much is the cumulative percentage share of income of the lower 60 percent of households? It comes to 25 percent. So how much is the third

quintile's income share? It's 12.5 percent (25 percent − 12.5 percent). In other words, we take the lower 60 percent of households' share (25 percent) and subtract from it the combined share of the lower two quintiles (12.5 percent).

The lower 80 percent receives 40 percent of income. From that, we subtract the income share of the lower 60 percent (25 percent), which leaves the fourth quintile with a 15 percent income share. One more quintile to go—the highest quintile. If 100 percent of all households receive 100 percent of all income and the lowest 80 percent of all households receive a total of 40 percent, what's left for the top quintile? You got it—60 percent.

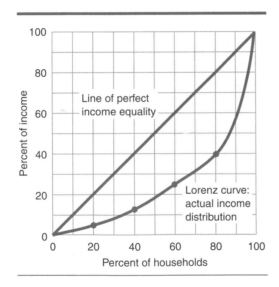

Figure 1

Hypothetical Lorenz Curve
The line of perfect income equality shows that any given percent of households receives that same percent of income. For example, the lowest 20 percent of all households would receive 20 percent of the income. Every household would receive the same income: There would be no rich or poor. The Lorenz curve shows the actual income distribution. In this particular example, the poorest 20 percent of all households receive about 5 percent of all income, while the richest fifth receives 60 percent.

Third fifth:

Fourth fifth:

Highest fifth:

The lowest fifth receives just 5 percent of all income; the second fifth receives 7.5 percent; the third fifth receives 12.5 percent; the fourth fifth receives 15 percent; and the highest fifth receives 60 percent. (If you don't know how I got these numbers, please read the box, "Finding the Percentage of Income Share of the Quintiles in Figure 1.")

What do you think of *that* income distribution? Not very equal, is it? You'll notice the Lorenz curve is pretty far to the right of the diagonal line. That diagonal is the line of perfect equality, so the farther the Lorenz curve is from it, the less equal the distribution of income becomes.

Do you know what I forgot to do? I forgot to define the Lorenz curve. Do *you* want to take a stab at a definition? Here's mine: *A Lorenz curve shows the cumulative share of income earned by each quintile of households.*

Definition of the Lorenz curve

Figure 2

Lorenz Curve of Income
Distribution of the United
States, 2008
Would you say that the United
States has an equal distribution of
income? No? I would agree. OK,
what percentage of all income is
received by those in the poorest
20 percent of all households, and
what percentage of all income is
received by those in the richest
20 percent of all households?
The poorest 20 percent received
3.4 percent of all income; the richest
20 percent received over 50 percent
of all income.
Source: U.S. Bureau of the Census,
Current Population Reports, Series P-60.
Issued August 2009.

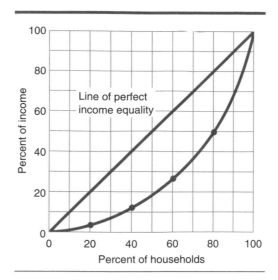

How does our own income distribution look? It's plotted for you in Figure 2. Once again, figure out the distribution of income, and write your answers here:

Lowest fifth:

Second fifth:

Third fifth:

Fourth fifth:

Highest fifth:

Check your answers against those in the right-hand column of Table 2. Your figures don't have to match mine exactly because we're both making our own observations from the graph.

It doesn't take a rocket scientist to figure out that income distribution was more uneven early in the 21st century than it was in the late 1960s. We know that changes in our tax laws have been a major factor. Income tax rates and taxes on capital gains were cut, especially for the rich, while payroll tax rates were raised, taking a large bite out of the incomes of the working poor, the working class, and the lower middle class. Indeed, about 75 percent of all Americans pay more today in payroll taxes than they do in personal income tax.

The rich also reaped huge capital gains since the 1980s, largely from increases in stock prices, real estate, and investments in their own businesses. During this same period the average hourly wage rate (adjusted for inflation) has not risen. Meanwhile the relatively high-

TABLE 2	Percentages of Total Income before Taxes Received by Each Fifth of American Families, 1968 and 2008	
Income Rank	1968	2008
Lowest fifth	5.6%	3.4%
Second fifth	12.4	8.6
Third fifth	17.7	14.7
Fourth fifth	23.7	23.3
Highest fifth	40.5	50.0

Note: 1968 figures don't add to 100.0 because of rounding.
Source: See Figure 2.

paying manufacturing sector has been shedding hundreds of thousands of jobs almost every year, while employment in the relatively low-paying service sector has been rising rapidly.

Now, let's compare the distribution of income in 2008 with that in 1968. Has income become *more* evenly distributed or *less* evenly distributed? A society in which the poorest fifth of the population gets just 3.4 percent of the income and the richest fifth gets half has a very uneven distribution of income. Since 1968, the top fifth's share of income rose from 40.5 percent to 50.0 percent, whereas the share of the lower three-fifths declined from 35.7 percent to 26.7 percent. In short, then, the rich are getting richer and the poor are getting poorer.

When it is said that our income is unevenly distributed, we need to ask: relative to what standard? Obviously it is unevenly distributed relative to the line of perfect income equality in Figure 2. It is less evenly distributed relative to its distribution in the late 1960s.

How well off is the typical American family? Probably the best way to measure that is by finding the median, or middle income, of all families. Imagine if we could list all American household incomes in ascending order. Half of all families would have incomes above the median and the other half would have incomes below the median. How much would the median income be? By glancing at the left bar in Figure 3 you'll find the answer for our median income in 2008. How much was it?

Has income become more equally distributed since 1968?

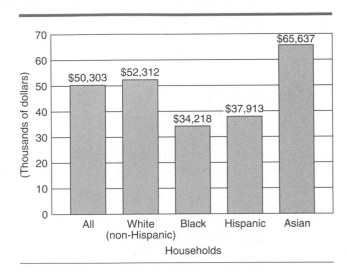

***Figure* 3**

Median Household Income, by Selected Characteristics, 2008
The median household income in 2008 was $50,303. Half of all households earned less than $50,303 and half earned more than $50,303. Median household income for white and Asian households was higher than the overall median; it was lower for black and Hispanic households than the overall median.
Source: See Figure 2.

It came to exactly $50,303. Of course some folks did better than others. Asian-American families did the best, with a median income of $65,637; black families did the worst, earning a median income of just $34,218.

Now let's see how our overall median income fared over time. The record since 1967 is presented in Figure 4. You'll notice from its title that we're looking at "Real Median Household Income," which is measured in 2008 dollars (in other words, dollars of constant purchasing power). So the typical family earned $40,300 in 1967, and just over $50,000 in 2008—an increase of about 20 percent.

Between 1967 and 2008 median family income increased by nearly one quarter. At the beginning of this period, just one-third of all married women with children were working. By 2008 nearly two-thirds of them had jobs. Indeed, the increase in median family income between 1967 and 2008 is explained entirely by the fact that tens of millions of married women with children went out and got jobs.

We know, of course, that over this period, the quality of goods and services improved substantially, and many new ones became available. So the typical American family is much better off than it was back in 1968.

If you glance again at Figure 4, you'll notice the shaded areas designating periods of recession. It's no surprise that during each of the recessions over the last 40 years, real median household income declined. But take a look at the years immediately following the previous two recessions. It appears likely, then, that real median family income will decline from 2007—when the Great Recession began—perhaps through 2010 or even 2011. As you'll notice, real median income continued to fall well after every previous recession ended.

Figure 4

Real Median Household Income: 1967 to 2008, in 2008 Dollars
Median household income—the level at which half of all households earn more money and half earn less—was about 25 percent higher in 2008 than it was in the late 1990s.

Note: The data points are placed at the midpoints of the respective years. Median household income data are not available before 1967.

Source: U.S. Census Bureau, Current Population Survey, 1968 to 2009 Annual Social and Economic Supplements.

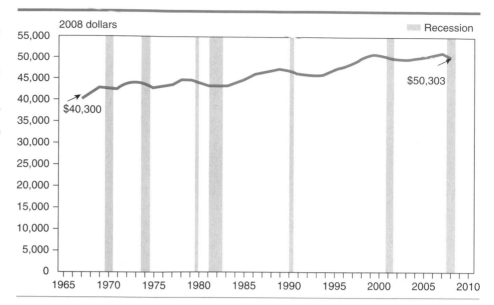

The global divide between the rich and the poor is much more apparent in the area of consumption spending. The richest 20 percent of humanity consumes 86 percent of all goods and services, while the poorest fifth consumes just 1.3 percent. In other words, when we look at the consumption rate of all the people on this planet, someone in the richest fifth consumes about 66 times as much as someone in the poorest fifth.

Distribution of Wealth in the United States

Every year *Forbes* magazine compiles a list of America's richest 400 men and women. To have made this list in 2009 you needed a net worth, or total wealth, of at least $950 million—down from $1.3 billion in 2007.

Who made *Forbes* magazine's top 10 list of American billionaires? It's shown in Table 3. It should come as no surprise that Bill Gates heads the list, and some of the other names should also be familiar.

The rich are different from you and me.

—F. Scott Fitzgerald

Yes, they are different. They have more money.

—Ernest Hemingway

Let's make sure we're clear on the difference between wealth and income. Your income this year includes your annual wages or salary, as well as any interest, dividends, profits,

TABLE 3 The Forbes 2009 Top 10 List of American Billionaires*

Name and Rank	Main Source of Income	Net Worth (in $ billions)
1. William H. Gates, III	Microsoft (cofounder)	$53
2. Warren E. Buffett	Berkshire Hathaway / Stock market	47
3. Lawrence J. Ellison	Oracle (founder)	28
4. Christy Walton & family	Walmart (inheritor)	22.5
5. Jim C. Walton	Walmart (inheritor)	20.7
6. Alice Walton	Walmart (inheritor)	20.6
7. S. Robson Walton	Walmart (inheritor)	19.8
8. Michael Bloomberg	Bloomberg LP (founder)	18.0
9. Sergey Brin	Google (cofounder)	17.5
Larry Page	Google (cofounder)	17.5
Charles Koch	Koch Industries inheritor	17.5
David Koch	Koch Industries inheritor	17.5
10. Steven Ballmer	Microsoft	14.5

*One thing stands out when we look at this list of the nation's richest people. Six of them inherited their wealth.
Source: www.forbes.com/lists/2010/10/billionaires-2010_The-Worlds-Billionaires_Rank.html

rent, and government transfer payments you received (for example, Social Security benefits, unemployment insurance benefits). Wealth includes housing and other real estate, checking and savings accounts, certificates of deposit, stocks and bonds, and other valuable assets. One reason for the greater concentration of wealth in the hands of the rich is the slashing of federal income tax rates paid by the very rich. In 1981 the top tax bracket was 70 percent; today it is 35 percent. But the main reason why the distribution of wealth in America is becoming less equal is because the distribution of income is becoming less equal. In summary, the rich are getting richer and the poor are getting poorer.

There is inherited wealth in this country and also inherited poverty.
—President John F. Kennedy

on the web

Here's *Forbes* magazine's list of the 400 richest Americans: www.forbes.com/richlist Each year *Forbes* updates this list. If you keep looking, who knows? Maybe your name will turn up.

Distribution of Income: Equity and Efficiency

First we'll consider what a fair and just distribution of income would be, and then we'll talk about how income distribution affects the efficient operation of our economy.

Is it fair that some people earn hundreds of millions of dollars a year while others don't make enough to put food on the table and a roof over their heads? Shouldn't we be a more egalitarian society, where no one is superrich or dirt poor? Or should we go even further and ensure that we all earn approximately the same income?

There is widespread agreement that it's good for the rich to give some of their money to the poor. After all, the tens of millions of Americans who give to charity each year can't all be wrong. And if the government uses some of our tax dollars to help the truly needy, that too is something that most of us could support.

OK, so would it be such a bad thing for a rich guy to fork over a buck or two to a poor guy? After all, that money would mean a whole lot more to the poor guy, while the rich guy would hardly miss it. But what if we carry this redistribution scheme to its logical conclusion? Let's have everyone who's earning more than the average income give his surplus to those earning less. When we've finished, we'll all have exactly the same income. I have just stated the utilitarian case for equality.

What do *you* think? Is this fair? What about the people who worked hard for their money, putting in hours of overtime, holding down two jobs, and never seeing their families or friends? And what about the lazy bums who don't even bother looking for a job because they know they'll have exactly the same income as the working stiffs?

So much for a fair and just distribution of income. How does income distribution affect our economic efficiency? Well, for starters, what would an equal distribution of income do to work incentives? Would *you* work hard if you'd end up with exactly the same income as a lot of people who just sat at home and waited for their checks? Two of the things that make our economy go are the carrot and the stick. The carrot is all the money you can make by working hard. And the stick is that if you don't work, you don't eat.

Another incentive that would suffer is the incentive to save. Considering that the interest you'd get from your savings would be divided among everyone, why bother to save at all? Why invest, for that matter? Why bother to engage in any productive activities whatsoever, when we'll all end up with the same income no matter what we do?

Of course, if we were to pursue this reasoning to its logical conclusion, we would end up with very little output (because only a few workaholics would still be producing) and therefore very little real income.

So what should we do? Neither extreme seems desirable. Complete income equality would rob us of our productive incentives. And substantial income inequality would mean a great deal of human suffering, because many of the poor would not be able to afford even the basic necessities of life.

Whatever the means of income redistribution, the ends are always the same—to take from the rich and give to the poor. Robin Hood may not have won favor with the Sheriff of Nottingham or with the rich people he robbed, but most folks agree that the

Poverty is an anomaly to rich people; it is very difficult to make out why people who want dinner do not ring the bell.
—Walter Bagehot

Short of genius, a rich man cannot imagine poverty.
—Charles Péguy

How does income distribution affect our economic efficiency?

rich—*and* the middle class—should give some of their money to the poor. The only question is, how much?

What Determines Income Distribution?

About two-thirds of all personal income is earned in wages and salaries, so we'll concentrate on the factors causing these incomes to vary so widely. And then we'll take a look at property income, which accounts for a little less than one-quarter of all personal income. Finally, we'll look at government transfer payments, which account for the rest.

Differences in Wages and Salaries   We saw in the chapter, "Labor Markets and Wages Rates," that wage rates are determined by the forces of supply and demand. Demand is the marginal revenue product schedule for a particular line of work, and supply is the people willing and able to do this work.

Intelligence, skills, education, and training all enhance the demand for particular individuals. But increasingly, members of our labor force are competing not only against one another, but against workers all over the world. In a widely used example, hospitals are electronically sending MRIs to India where they are read and interpreted by Indian physicians, who work for just a fraction of the wages paid to American doctors. Our high-tech, globalizing world is enlarging the supply of labor for certain jobs, and consequently, depressing wage rates.

Property Income   As you might have suspected, most property income goes to the rich. These payments are in the form of rent, interest, dividends, and profits (which include capital gains). The two largest sources of wealth, exclusive of inheritance, have been the fortunes made in the stock market and the starting up of new companies (see Table 3).

Property income may also be derived from ownership of stocks, bonds, bank deposits, and other assets. Because the poor and the working class hold little property, little (if any) of their income comes from this source. The Tax Policy Center has determined that families with incomes of less than $50,000 derived just 3 percent of their income from capital gains and dividends; families with incomes in excess of $10 million received 61.4 percent of their incomes from those sources.

Income from Government Transfer Payments   In addition to wages, salaries, and property income, some people receive government transfer payments. For retirees, Social Security benefits may be their main means of support. For most people collecting unemployment benefits, these checks are usually their sole means of support. And public assistance recipients all depend on these benefits plus food stamps for most or all of their income.

As you can see in Figure 5, Social Security, Medicare, and Medicaid are the big three of federal income transfer programs. Although the poor benefit from all three, only Medicaid spending is "means tested."

Why do some people earn more than others?

Why does a college graduate earn more than a grade school dropout?

Some people's money is merited. And other people's money is inherited.

—Ogden Nash

Figure 5

Federal Income Transfer Programs, Fiscal Year 2009
Social Security, Medicare, and Medicaid account for nearly 80 percent of all federal transfers. Welfare benefits are just 4 percent.
Source: Office of Management and Budget.

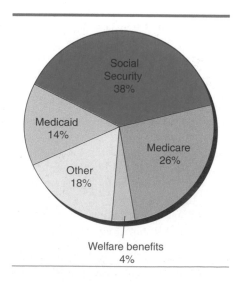

Poverty in America

I still have the audacity to believe that people everywhere can have three meals a day.

–The Reverend Martin Luther King, Jr.–

The poor will never cease out of the land.

—Moses, *Deuteronomy*, 15:11

Poverty Defined

There are two basic ways to define poverty—as a relative concept and as an absolute concept. By defining the poor as the lowest income quintile (that is, the lowest 20 percent) in the nation, we're saying that this group of people is poor relative to the rest of the population.

The relative concept of poverty

There are a couple of problems with this definition. First, suppose everyone's standard of living quadrupled from one year to the next. We'd *still* be calling those in the lowest quintile poor, even though most of the "poor" would be living better this year than the entire middle class lived last year. Although Jesus *did* say, "For ye have the poor always with you" (Matthew 26:11), *these* poor people would be driving late-model cars, living in nice houses, and eating in fancy restaurants three or four nights a week.

Viewed over time, poverty is clearly a relative concept. Nearly 90 percent of Americans living in 1900 would fall below the poverty line as it is defined today.

A second difficulty with the concept of relative poverty is that the lowest income quintile in the United States and other relatively rich countries is infinitely better off than the average citizens of the world's poorest nations. In Bangladesh, Ethiopia, Mali, and Zambia, most people struggle to survive on maybe $200 or $300 a year. Even our homeless population fares considerably better than that.

What about the absolute concept of poverty? Well, there's one basic problem here, too. Who gets to determine the dividing line between poor and not poor, and how is that determination reached? The best approach is to set up a minimum basic standard of living and figure out how much it costs to maintain that standard from year to year. So far, so good. Who gets to set up this basic living standard, and what goods and services should go into it?

The absolute concept of poverty

Just how bad is the problem of poverty in the rest of the world? One-third of the world's people have no access to electricity and nearly two-thirds have never made a phone call (see box, "The Price of Safe Drinking Water"). Almost half of the world lives on less than $2 a day. There is general agreement that the world's greatest concentration of poverty is in sub-Saharan Africa. According to Cornell's International Labour Organization more than three-quarters of the population in 14 countries lives on less than $2 a day—Nigeria, Mali, Madagascar, Zambia, India, Burkina Faso, Niger, Pakistan, Gambia, Central African Republic, Nepal, Mozambique, Bangladesh, and Ethiopia.

A better measure of economic well-being for the poor would be their level of consumer spending. In the Labor Department's latest Consumer Expenditures Survey (2003), the average reported income for the bottom quintile of households was just $8,201, but reported consumption outlays were $18,492. How do we explain how the poor can spend more than twice their incomes? Clearly, most poor people don't report their entire incomes. And then, too, they are going deeper into debt each year. Whatever the full explanation, the poor are obviously better off than the official poverty level would indicate.

The most widely used poverty standard in the United States is the official poverty line calculated each year by the U.S. Bureau of the Census. Its estimate is based on the assumption that poor families spend about one-third of their incomes on food. Each year it calculates the minimum food budget for a family of four for one week, multiplies that figure by 52 for the family's annual food budget, and then triples that figure to get the official poverty line. In 2008 that line was set at $22,025 for a family of four.[1]

Can a family of four live on $22,000? It all depends on what you mean by "live." Is it enough to put food on the table, clothes on your back, and a roof over your head?

The official poverty line

---

[1] When this method of calculating poverty was devised in the early 1960s, food accounted for 24 percent of the average family budget (not 33 percent); today food accounts for just 10 percent.

The Price of Safe Drinking Water

Americans, on average, drink over 25 gallons of bottled water a year. And globally, bottled water is now a $50-billion industry. At the other end of the economic spectrum, more than one billion of the world's poor people lack reliable access to safe drinking water. Writing in *The New York Times,* Tom Standage noted that "The World Health Organization estimates that at any given time, around half the people in the developing world are suffering from diseases associated with inadequate water or sanitation, which kill around a million people a year."*

Newsweek reports that "More than one billion people worldwide lack access to safe drinking water and 6,000 people die each day of waterborne diseases like typhoid, cholera, and dysentery."†

So while the world's relatively affluent folks think nothing of shelling out a dollar for a bottle of water—rather than drink perfectly adequate tap water—over one billion people don't have any safe drinking water at all. What would it take to provide them with clean water? The International Water Management Institute estimates that clean water could be provided to everyone on earth for an outlay of $1.7 billion a year beyond current spending on water projects. But despite the best efforts of rock star Bono and hundreds of other advocates, the world's rich countries have not given sufficient help.

Perhaps $1.7 billion seems like a lot of money, so let's break that down to nickels. Worldwide we buy 50 billion bottles of water. How much money would we raise if we paid a nickel deposit on each bottle of water we purchased? Go ahead and do the math.

We would raise $2.5 billion. Wouldn't *you* be willing to pay a nickel each time you bought a bottle of water for such a worthy cause? Still, you may remember the response of Queen Marie Antoinette during the days just before the French Revolution when told that the people had no bread. "Let them eat cake!" she declared. And so, when we're told that over one billion poor people don't have safe drinking water, we say, "Let them drink *bottled* water!"

---

*Tom Standage, "Bad to the Last Drop," *The New York Times,* August 1, 2005. See online at www.globalpolicy.org/component/article/218-injustice-and-inequality/46547.html
†Jennie Yabroff, "Water for the World," *Newsweek,* June 18, 2007, p. 20.

In some parts of the country, the answer is yes. In the more expensive cities such as New York, Boston, and San Francisco, as well as in many suburban communities, especially in the Northeast, $22,000 won't provide even the bare necessities, largely because of relatively high rents.

Once the poverty line has been established, we can find the poverty rate by dividing the number of poor people by the total population of the country. So the poverty rate is the percentage of Americans who are poor. In 2008 our poverty rate was 13.2, which means that 13.2 percent of Americans were poor.

The Census Bureau has been tracking the poverty rate since 1959. As you can observe in Figure 6, there was a sharp decline throughout the 1960s and early 1970s. In 1973 the rate bottomed out at about half the 1960 rate. The main causes of the decline were the prosperity of the 1960s and the War on Poverty conducted by the administration of President Lyndon Johnson. The federal government spent tens of billions of dollars on education, job training, and the creation of government jobs for millions of poor people.

You'll notice the shaded parts of Figure 6, which indicate periods of recession. Usually the poverty rate rises during recessions and falls again once we've recovered. Because of the Great Recession, our poverty rate in 2008 hit an 11-year high.

The poverty rate would be substantially lower if we counted the value of in-kind benefits.

Some conservative critics point out that the poverty rate would be substantially lower if we counted the value of noncash, or in-kind, benefits given to the poor by the government. These include Medicaid, housing subsidies, low-rent public housing, food stamps, and school lunches. If these in-kind benefits were counted, the poverty rate would have been about 3 percentage points lower than the reported rate of 13.2 percent.

Poverty is a relative term. When compared to the average American, those living below the poverty line have a much lower standard of living. But that standard of living usually includes at least one large screen TV and, very possibly, a cell phone and a computer. Over 70 percent of the poor own cars and 46 percent own their own homes. Not only do the American poor live much, much better than the poor in Africa, Asia, and Latin America, but they also live about as well as the average American did just

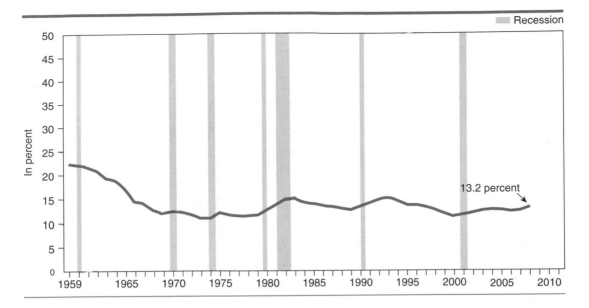

Figure 6

U.S. Poverty Rate: Percentage of Individuals below the Poverty Line, 1959–2008

The poverty rate was cut in half between 1960 and 1973, largely because of President Lyndon Johnson's war on poverty, much of which was continued and even expanded under President Richard Nixon. It remained above 12 percent from 1980, began falling steadily since 1993, and finally got below 12 percent in 1999. However, it began rising again in 2001, reaching 12.7 in 2004, then falling to 12.3 in 2006, and rising to 13.2 in 2008.

Note: The data points are placed at the midpoints of the respective years.

Source: U.S. Census Bureau, Current Population Survey, 1960 to 2007 Annual Social and Economic Supplements. U.S. Census Bureau, Current Population Reports, PV 60–233 Income, Poverty, and Health Insurance Coverage in the United States: 2006, issued August 2007.

decades ago. Michael Cox, of the Dallas Federal Reserve Bank, found that the material possessions of Americans at the poverty line in 2000 roughly equaled those of middle-income Americans in 1971.[2]

on the web

How does your income compare with those of the other 6.7 billion people in the world? Go to www.globalrichlist.com, type in your annual income (without the dollar sign) and make sure it's classified in the appropriate currency.

Who Are the Poor?

Who *are* the poor? Old people? Traditionally, people older than 65 have had a much higher poverty rate than the general population, but the advent of Medicare, higher Social Security benefits, and supplementary Social Security benefits over the last three decades has reduced the poverty rate for older Americans to well below the overall rate. The proportion of retirees living in poverty has fallen from 35 percent in 1960 to just 9.7 percent in 2008.

Are most poor people black? No, most poor people are white. It *is* true that almost one out of four blacks is poor, but only 13 percent of our population is black. So about one quarter of the poor is black. Figure 7 shows the relative poverty rates for white, black, Hispanic, and Asian Americans. The poverty rates for both blacks and Hispanics is almost triple the poverty rate for non-Hispanic whites.

If you happen to be a member of a female-headed household with children, your chances of being poor are more than two out of five. But if your family has any children

Most poor people are white.

God must love the poor—he made so many of them.

—Abraham Lincoln

[2]See W. Michael Cox and Richard Alms, "Defining Poverty Up," *Wall Street Journal,* November 2, 1999, p. A26.

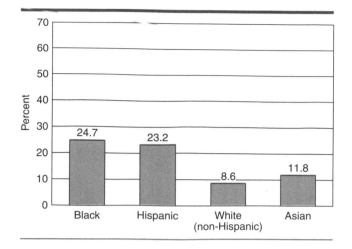

Figure 7

Poverty Rates by Race, 2008
The poverty rates of blacks and Hispanics are both more than double that for whites.
Source: U.S. Bureau of the Census.

under six (with no husband present) then you have a better than one chance in two of living below the poverty line.

Where do the poor live? Although they are scattered throughout the nation, until recently the largest concentration of poor people was in large- and medium-sized cities. But according to the results of a 2005 Brookings Institution survey, there were 1.2 million more poor people living in the suburbs than in the cities. Most of the suburban poor live in the Midwest and the South.[3]

The working poor

All the people employed at or just above the minimum wage could be considered the working poor. Most of them receive little or no government benefits, yet somehow manage to make ends meet from paycheck to paycheck. But even if they don't get one cent from the government, they are still part of our poverty problem.

The long-term unemployed

Finally, there are the chronically (long-term) unemployed and the discouraged workers. Although the U.S. unemployment rate was relatively low from the mid-1990s until the Great Recession of 2007–2009, this measure does not take into account the millions of Americans who have been out of work for years. The official unemployment statistics count only those who have actively sought employment; people who have given up looking for jobs are not included. And at the very bottom of the economic barrel are the homeless (see the box, "The Homeless").

Child Poverty

Perhaps the most striking thing about poverty in America is how it affects children. Particularly hard hit by poverty are black children and Hispanic children (see Figure 8). Of children who grew up in long-term poverty—those poor for a least nine years during their childhood—about 80 percent were black. "Children are our future" may be a cliché, but they are nevertheless a future that we neglect at our peril.

It is said that a society may be judged by how it treats its children. In 2008 19 percent of American children lived in poverty. It is astounding that a nation as rich as ours can permit this to happen.

The Organization for Economic Cooperation and Development (OECD) is a group of 24 of most of the world's richest nations. UNICEF (the United Nations Children's Fund) did a study in 2008 which measured the degree of child poverty in each of the OECD countries. Child poverty was defined as the percent of children under 18 in households with earnings of less than 50 percent of the national median income. For the United States, that came to under $24,100.

How well did we do? Would you believe that the United States had a child poverty rate of 22.5 percent—by far the highest rate among all 24 OECD countries?

---

[3]See Peg Tyre and Matthew Philips, "Poor Among Plenty," *Newsweek,* February 12, 2007, p. 54.

The Homeless

The law, in its majestic equality, forbids the rich as well as the poor to sleep under bridges, to beg in the streets, and to steal bread.

—Anatole France—

We've created a lot of $6-an-hour jobs and not much $6-an-hour housing.

—John Donahue—

Chicago Coalition for the Homeless

There have always been homeless people in America—the hobo jungles of the Depression era, the skid rows (or skid roads, as they are known in the West), and, of course, the isolated shopping-bag ladies and other folks who lived out on the street, in doorways, or in train stations. But now there are literally millions of them. In a nation of some 310 million people, between 2 and 3 million are homeless.

A convergence of four trends has multiplied the number of homeless people who congregate in all our large cities. Since World War II the number of entry-level factory jobs almost disappeared from every large city. Meanwhile, the availability of cheap housing (basically furnished rooms) has also declined as the cities'

more dilapidated neighborhoods were demolished to make way for urban renewal projects.

A third trend has been gentrification, which has pushed rents through the roof, so to speak, in New York, San Francisco, Boston, Chicago, and most other major cities. Finally, the deinstitutionalization of the mentally ill over the last two and a half decades (without the promised halfway houses to treat and shelter them) has further added to the homeless population.

The U.S. Department of Health and Human Services estimates that one-third of the homeless are mentally ill and that half of the homeless are alcoholics or drug addicts. The Veteran's Administration estimates that nearly 200,000 veterans of various wars are homeless on any given night, many as a result of substance abuse. "Veterans, who represent only 11% of the civilian adult population, comprise 26% of the homeless population," says a report by the Homelessness Research Institute.*

Interestingly, about one-quarter of the homeless work full time, according to the U.S. Conference of Mayors. The problem for them is being trapped between jobs that pay too little and housing that costs too much.

*See *Time*, November 19, 2007, p. 21.

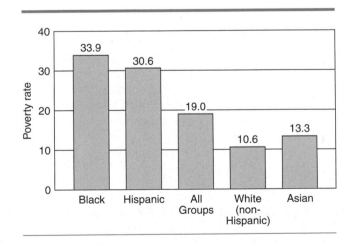

F*igure* 8

Children under 18 below Poverty Level by Race and Hispanic Origin, 2008

The child poverty rate is more than three times as high for black children as for white children. More than 1 in 3 black children live in poverty.

Source: Bureau of Labor Statistics and Bureau of the Census, *CPS Annual Demographic Survey.*

(See Figure 9.) Four nations—Belgium, Finland, Norway, and Sweden—had rates well under 5 percent. And another four—Denmark, the Czech Republic, France, and the Netherlands—all were well below 10 percent.

How do we interpret these results? While we cannot conclude that poor American children are much worse off than poor children in *all* of the OECD countries, they certainly are worse off than those in *most* of them. Because our median family income is higher than those of most other OECD countries, it would be reasonable to assume that poor American children are no worse off than poor children in countries like Poland, Spain, Greece, or the Czech Republic.

Figure 9

Child Poverty Rates in Selected Countries: Children Living in Households with Income Less than 50 Percent of the National Median Income, 2007–2008
Of the countries shown here, the United States has the highest rate of child poverty. Note that this measure is somewhat different from defining the childhood poverty rate as the percentage of children in families living below the official poverty line shown in Figure 8.
Source: UNICEF.

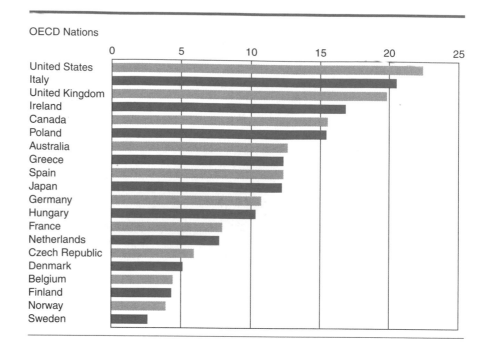

But this study actually highlights a strong dichotomy within our country. If 22.5 percent of our children are members of families earning less than $24,100, then clearly the standard of living of poor American children is very low compared to that of middle-class and rich American children.

Perhaps the most troubling statistic is that 53.3 percent of all American children under six in a family headed by a female lived in poverty in 2008. But just 11.0 percent of the children under six living in married-couple families are poor. Using this information, Katherine Boo draws an interesting conclusion: ". . . for children a two-parent household is the most effective antipoverty program we know. Three out of four white children are born to such households. Only one in three black children is."[4]

Large-scale, high-rise, low-income public housing projects have been especially good breeding grounds for this culture of poverty. In these neighborhoods at least three-quarters of the families are on welfare, most of the girls get pregnant before they are 18, and there is a great degree of drug dependency and an extremely high rate of violent crime. The gangs are the real authority in the ghetto, according to Nicholas Lemann. The gang "forces kids through physical terror, to give up school and work and become professional criminals."[5] To some degree this phenomenon has evolved in poor Hispanic and non-Hispanic white neighborhoods as well.

A decent provision for the poor is a true test of civilization.
—Samuel Johnson

The Main Government Transfer Programs

Until the 1930s, the poor depended on help from friends and family, and failing that, from private charities. But when millions of otherwise respectable middle class and working class Americans were thrown out of work during the Great Depression, they demanded that the federal government provide them with some means of support, whether jobs, welfare payments, or any other programs that would keep the wolf from the door. Today, of course, the government continues to provide most of the help given to the poor, but private charities also continue to help as well.

---

[4]Katherine Boo, "The Black Gender Gap," *The Atlantic Monthly,* January/February 2003, p. 107.
[5]Nicholas Lemann, "The Origins of the Underclass," *The Atlantic Monthly,* June 1986, p. 39.

Support Our Troops

We noted in the last chapter how our military bases were surrounded by payday lenders, only too happy to extend our service men and women and their spouses short-term loans at exorbitant interest rates. But these companies are just symptoms of an underlying problem, not the cause. The problem is that we don't pay our troops enough to keep their heads above water. Hundreds of thousands of military families live from paycheck to paycheck, leaving them at the mercy of these predatory lenders.

In a book describing hunger in America, Loretta Schwartz-Nobel wrote a chapter entitled, "From Front Lines to Food Lines." Here's how she explains why so many military families run into financial problems:

Advocates for the military families consistently point out that the acute problem comes when an enlisted man marries and has children. That is partly because there is no additional food allowance for the family of an enlisted man, and also because housing allowances are never enough to cover the costs of housing, food and all the other added expenses of families. In fact, they usually aren't even enough to cope with housing expenses alone. As a result, families who are living in areas with high rents often end up moving forty or fifty miles away from their duty stations to areas where housing is less expensive and more available. But even that has a downside, because it means that now they have to maintain both a car and costly insurance.

If they live in military housing, the government pays for their utilities, but if they live off base, the utilities are often a large additional expense. Unfortunately, many bases have very little housing and extremely long waiting lists. *

Most of those joining the military are hoping for a step up on the economic ladder. How well paid *are* the members of our armed forces? In 2008 a private first class with less than two year's active service earned $1,534.20 a month before taxes ($18,410.40 on an annual basis). That income leaves a family of four well below the poverty line of $22,025.

Here's an excerpt from an article entitled, "Thousands of US Military Families Live in Poverty," by Brian Mann.

Ms. Levesque runs a food pantry in Watertown, New York, a short drive from the Fort Drum Army base. She says Army families make up 20 percent of the people who come in, looking for free meals and supplies. "The military kind of has a 'we take care of our own' motto, which you realize that they kind of don't," she said. "And there are a lot of people who fall through the cracks and need the assistance who aren't getting it."

Ms. Levesque speaks from experience, as a social service worker, but also as the wife of a soldier. Her husband, an army specialist, brings home roughly $1,300 a month after taxes—not enough to pay for rent, food, utilities and other necessities. "I have always worked two jobs," said Amy Levesque. "And my husband, he's in the military plus he has a nighttime job. Luckily we don't have any children. With children, it would be very difficult." [†]

There's another side to this issue. Since the draft was ended in 1974, almost 90 percent of the volunteers have been members of poor and working-class families. For these youngsters, joining the military usually provides more promising economic prospects than they would have enjoyed in civilian life. "Be the best you can be," is presumably better than you could have been "on the outside." So despite the shortcomings just enumerated in this box, for most new recruits, joining the service actually raises their economic well-being.

---

*Loretta Schwartz-Nobel, *Growing Up Empty: The Hunger Epidemic in America* (New York: HarperCollins, 2002), pp. 99–100.

[†]*Source:* www.globalpolicy.org/component/article/218-injustice-and-inequality/46509.html

The poor are not invisible. The people lined up outside food pantries or inside check cashing stores are usually living below the poverty line or pretty close to it, but you might be surprised to learn that some of them are in military families. Their economic situation is described in the box, "Support Our Troops."

The Social Security Act of 1935 set up three major programs: Social Security, unemployment insurance, and public assistance. Taxes paid by workers and their employers financed the first two programs. Public assistance, which was intended to help families experiencing temporary economic distress, was the only means-tested program. To obtain public assistance (or relief, as it was then called), you needed to demonstrate that your income or means of support was insufficient to cover your basic needs.

The Social Security Act of 1935

Helping the Poor Get Money Back from the IRS

In a column in *Newsweek*, Bob Burke tells how he organized a program to help poor families get substantial tax refunds.

One day I had an idea. I knew the federal government had tax credits to ease the burden on working-poor families, but the process for claiming these credits was simply too complicated for most to get the assistance they had coming. I came up with a plan: I would gather a group of business professionals to offer free tax-preparation services. We'd meet at the school on Saturday mornings and get the word out in the community that we were there to help.

. . .

After about an hour, these volunteers usually had the pleasant task of informing a hardworking,

low-income family that they would receive thousands of dollars back from the Internal Revenue Service. All that without a commercial tax-preparation service's taking out a big chunk.

I vividly remember when a single mother of two, who hadn't earned enough in three years to file a return, burst into tears when I told her that the IRS had withheld too much from her paychecks and owed her $10,000. She said she would use the money to fix the leaky roof on her house. Others were equally emotional, making plans to pay overdue bills, buy clothes and school supplies for their children or even move to a safer neighborhood.

Source: Bob Burke, "Helping the Needy Crack the Tax Code," *Newsweek*, April 26, 2004, p. 15.

Can you name our biggest antipoverty program? The one that lifts more people out of poverty than any other government program?

Amazingly, the correct answer is Social Security. After all, Social Security is *not* an antipoverty program, but that's just being picky. The fact is, if it were not for Social Security, close to one out of every two Americans over 65 would be living below the poverty line. And for two-thirds of the elderly, Social Security supplies more than half their income. So we can say that while Social Security is not an antipoverty program per se, it certainly has that effect.

Medicare and Medicaid

Two major programs, Medicare and Medicaid, were added in the mid-1960s under President Johnson's Great Society program. Medicare, which is really a supplement to Social Security, provides retirees and their families with free or very low-cost medical care. Free medical care is provided to the poor under Medicaid.

The food stamp program, which also began in the 1960s, enabled the very poor as well as the working poor to buy enough food. Like Medicare and Medicaid, it has expanded tremendously since the late 1960s. But until the mid-1990s, just 40 percent of those eligible were actually on the rolls. This changed as the presidential administrations of Bill Clinton and George W. Bush helped erase the program's stigma and made the enrollment process easier. Today, one in eight Americans, and one in four children receive food stamps.

About two-thirds of those eligible are now covered. Benefits average about $130 a month for each person in a household. During the recession of 2007–2009, the number of people receiving benefits rose from 26 million to 39 million. About half of all Americans receive food stamps, at least briefly, by the time they turn 20. Among black children, the figure is 90 percent.

Still another very important form of aid to the working poor is the earned income tax credit, which is written into our Internal Revenue Code. Those eligible, instead of *paying* income tax, actually receive what amounts to a refund check from the Internal Revenue Service. The purpose of the earned income tax credit is to encourage the poor to work by supplementing their earnings. The program supplements their earnings by as much as $2 an hour. Some of the recipients of the earned income tax credit not only get a full refund on the income taxes that were withheld from their paychecks all year but, in addition, they may receive a once-a-year payment of up to a couple of thousand dollars. Over 20 million Americans receive the credit, with about 5 million gaining enough to rise above the poverty line (see the box, "Helping the Poor Get Money Back from the IRS").

Still, millions of eligible low-wage workers are either unaware of this program or cannot figure out how to apply. The earned income tax credit is popular with liberals because it provides a substantial amount of income to the poor, and it is also popular with conservatives because only families with a working member are eligible. Today it is, by far, the biggest single federal policy targeting the poor. In addition, about a dozen states have also introduced their own EITC programs that supplement the federal credit.

Have these programs worked? Yes, they have. Each has accomplished what it was set up to do. But there are three major problems: (1) their costs have gone through the roof; (2) they have fostered a permanent dependency on government support among millions of poor families; and (3) they have not ended poverty.

Public assistance has been the greatest disappointment. Intended to provide "temporary relief," public assistance instead engendered a permanent dependence in millions of families.

One misconception about welfare mothers is that they keep having more and more children so that they can collect bigger checks. Indeed, many states no longer increase the size of a welfare grant if more children are born into a family. In actuality, 72 percent of all welfare families have only one or two children.

A welfare culture evolved over decades, giving rise to second-, third-, and fourth-generation welfare families. Typically, teenage girls become pregnant, keep their babies, go on welfare, do not marry, and have no hope of becoming self-supporting. In a sense, the young mothers are provided with surrogate husbands in the form of public assistance checks. Eventually their children grow up, become teenage parents themselves, and continue the welfare pattern through another generation.

The welfare culture

The number of people receiving public assistance remained remarkably steady—at about 11 million—from 1975 through 1992, but the welfare rolls shot up from 11 million in mid-1993 to a peak of 14.4 million in March 1994 (see Figure 10 near the end of this chapter). The main reason for this increase was the recession of 1990–91. By early 1994, the benefits of the subsequent economic expansion finally began to reach people at the bottom of the economic ladder, and the welfare rolls began to decline. Another important factor was that many states have restricted eligibility for welfare. And then, too, the passage of the Welfare Reform Act—which we'll discuss near the end of the chapter—was perhaps the main reason why so many mothers found work and left welfare.

The words of one welfare mother are especially poignant: "I'm sorry I got myself into this and my children into this. And I don't know how to get them out of it. If I don't get them away from here, they're going to end up dead, in jail, or like me."[6]

Theories of the Causes of Poverty

Any theory of poverty must take into account our entire socioeconomic system, how it is set up, how it is run, and who gets what. Poor people live on the margin or even beyond the system. They are basically superfluous and rarely have much impact on the system. They are an unfortunate presence, by-products that have been discarded but are grudgingly tolerated by society's "productive" members.

At least a dozen theories of poverty have attracted support, and each has at least *some* apparent validity. But because there are so many different poverty groups, no single theory can have universal applicability. We'll begin by briefly outlining a few theories, and then we'll look at the two with the largest number of adherents: the conservative and liberal theories.

The Poor Are Lazy   This theory was popular through most of the 19th century and right up to the time of the Great Depression. God's chosen people, who were destined to go to heaven, worked hard all their lives and were rewarded by attaining great earthly

---

[6]See Celia W. Dugger, "On the Edge of Survival: Single Mothers on Welfare," *The New York Times,* July 6, 1992, p. B6.

riches. And the poor? Well, you can figure out for yourself where they were headed. This theory went down the tubes when the Great Depression hit and millions of relatively affluent Americans were thrown out of work, lost their life savings, and had to ask the government for handouts.

The Heritage of Slavery   Because blacks were brought here in chains and held back for three centuries by slavery and a feudal sharecropping system in the South, the current poverty of many blacks can be explained by centuries of oppression. Not only were blacks systematically excluded from all but the most menial jobs, but they were denied the educational opportunities open to almost all other Americans. Mortgage loans, restaurant meals, hotel and motel lodging, union membership, and apartment rentals were routinely denied. In effect, then, blacks were systematically excluded from the nation's economic mainstream until the 1960s. Is it any wonder, ask adherents of this theory, that after so many years of oppression both during and after slavery, so many blacks still find themselves mired in poverty?

Full-time working women have earned 60 percent of what full-time working men earned.

Employment Discrimination   Employment discrimination has been especially strong in holding down the incomes of women, blacks, Hispanics, and other minorities. The fact that women working full-time have generally earned about three-quarters of what their male counterparts have earned clearly points toward discrimination. Similar figures for blacks and Hispanics arouse the same suspicion.

But other factors have also contributed to these wage differentials—education, training, and experience, and, in the case of many women, the years taken off work to raise children. Social scientists generally believe that about half of these wage differentials result from employment discrimination and the other half from other factors. As more employment opportunities become available to women and to minorities, we may see a narrowing of wage differentials. Meanwhile, employment discrimination has obviously been playing a major role in the poverty of women, blacks, Hispanics, and other minorities.

Black Male Joblessness   Back in 1970, about 33 percent of all black families were headed by women. By the mid-1990s, the number had jumped to over 60 percent. The growing perception of a permanent welfare population of single black mothers and their children has raised the question of where are the young black males who got them pregnant? In college? Playing major-league ball? Probably not.

Only half of all black males aged 16 to 64 are employed.

While more than four-fifths of all white males aged 20 to 44 are employed, only about half of their black counterparts have jobs. What are the rest of them doing? Some are officially unemployed, and some are "discouraged workers" who have stopped looking for work. And where are the rest of these guys? Some may be working in the underground economy—in either the legal or illegal sector. And others have just slipped through the cracks.

William A. Darity, Jr., and Samuel L. Myers, Jr., argue that "black men are being excluded from the emerging economic order; they are socially unwanted, superfluous, and marginal." Consequently there is a shrinking pool of marriageable black men. This growing marginality has led to drug abuse, violent crime, incarceration, and a high death rate, further depleting the ranks of marriageable young black men. Cutting welfare benefits, Darity and Myers observe, will do nothing to lower the number of black female-headed households, because the underlying problem is finding meaningful employment for millions of black men.[7]

The absence of eligible males does explain why there are so many single young black women, but it doesn't explain why these women are having so many children.

---

[7]William A. Darity, Jr., and Samuel L. Myers, Jr., "Family Structure and the Marginalization of Black Men: Policy Implications," presented at the American Economic Association Meetings, Washington, DC, January 1995.

Some conservatives, most notably Charles Murray,[8] believe that they allow themselves to get pregnant because they want to get on welfare. However, substantial research indicates that although public assistance is the main source of support once these girls give birth, peer pressure, the wish to go through the rite of passage into womanhood, and the desire for something to love are the real motivating factors.[9]

Let's pause here for a minute to catch our breath. We've been talking for a while about the causes of what is mainly black poverty. Keep in mind that most poor people are white. But when we distinguish between short-term poverty and a permanent underclass, we are talking mainly about a problem that has affected blacks, who constitute about 60 percent of the long-term poor.

Poverty Breeds Poverty   Poverty itself generally breeds poverty. Before birth an infant may suffer from poor prenatal care or even acquire an addiction to drugs, particularly crack. During childhood inadequate nutrition and a lack of medical and dental care also take their tolls. An unsafe—or even violent—environment, emotional deprivation, and a broken home also militate against a good childhood. This situation makes it extremely difficult to do well in school, so the easiest course is to give up.

Inadequate Human Capital   Human capital is defined as the acquired skills of an individual—education, training, and work habits. People who grew up poor usually had poor home learning environments, attended poor schools, dropped out before graduation, acquired little useful work experience, did not develop good work habits, and have poorly developed communication skills. In sum, they are virtually unemployable in today's economy.

The Conservative View versus the Liberal View

Now we're ready for the Super Bowl of poverty theory debate—the conservatives versus the liberals. Representing the conservative view will be Charles Murray, whose book *Losing Ground* depicts overly generous public assistance programs as perpetuating a dependent underclass. William Julius Wilson is perhaps the most prominent of Murray's liberal critics, so he'll represent their view.[10]

The conservatives and the liberals agree completely on ends—getting the long-term poor off welfare and into self-supporting employment—but they disagree completely on the appropriate means. Basically, the liberals favor the carrot approach, while the conservatives advocate the stick.

The conservatives and liberals agree on ends but disagree on means.

During the Great Depression, President Franklin Roosevelt's New Deal program attempted to lift one-third of all Americans out of poverty. Poverty wasn't rediscovered until the 1960s,[11] and the response was President Lyndon Johnson's Great Society program. Did this program and its extension through the 1970s actually help alleviate poverty? Here's Murray's response:

Did the Great Society program help alleviate poverty?

> In 1968, as Lyndon Johnson left office, 13 percent of Americans were poor, using the official definition. Over the next 12 years, our expenditures on social welfare quadrupled. And, in 1980, the percentage of poor Americans was—13 percent.[12]

---

[8]Charles Murray, *Losing Ground: American Social Policy, 1950–1980* (New York: Basic Books, 1984).

[9]P. Cutright, "Illegitimacy and Income Supplements," *Studies in Public Welfare,* paper no. 12, prepared for the use of the Subcommittee on Fiscal Policy of the Joint Economic Committee. Congress of the United States (Washington, DC: Government Printing Office, 1973); C. R. Winegarden, "The Fertility of AFDC Women: An Economic Analysis," *Journal of Economics and Business* 26 (1974), pp. 159–66; William Julius Wilson, *When Work Disappears* (New York: Knopf, 1996), pp. 107–9.

[10]Wilson would probably reject any label, but his views are supported by nearly all liberals.

[11]Interest was sparked by Michael Harrington's book, *The Other America* (New York: MacMillan, 1962).

[12]Murray, *Losing Ground,* p. 8.

Charles Murray, American economist

Murray draws this conclusion: By showering so much money on the poor, the government robbed them of their incentive to work. Using the archetypal couple, Harold and Phyllis, showed how in 1960 Harold would have gone out and gotten a minimum-wage job to support Phyllis and their newborn baby. But 10 years later the couple would be better off receiving public assistance and food stamps, living together without getting married, and having Harold work periodically. Why work steadily at an unpleasant, dead-end job, asks Murray, when you can fall back on welfare, food stamps, unemployment insurance, and other government benefit programs?

All of this sounds perfectly logical, but Murray's logic was shot full of holes by his critics. We'll start with welfare spending. Although payments *did* increase from 1968 to 1980, when we adjust them for inflation these payments actually decreased between 1972 and 1980. William Julius Wilson really lowers the boom:

> The evidence does not sustain Murray's contentions. First, countries with far more generous social welfare programs than the United States—Germany, Denmark, France, Sweden, and Great Britain—all have sharply lower rates of teenage births and teenage crime.
>
> Second, if welfare benefits figured in the decision to have a baby, more babies would be born in states with relatively high levels of welfare payments. But careful state-by-state comparisons show no evidence that [public assistance] influences childbearing decisions; sex and childbearing among teenagers do not seem to be a product of careful economic analysis.[13]

Another problem with Murray's analysis is that the unemployment rate doubled between 1968 and 1980, yet the poverty rate remained constant. Why? Because of all the social programs that were in place—unemployment insurance, public assistance, food stamps, and Medicaid, among others. Although there was substantial economic growth throughout most of the 1970s, this growth was insufficient to absorb all of the housewives and baby boomers who had entered the labor market.

Murray blamed the antipoverty programs for increasing poverty. Liberals would say he really had it backward: These programs prevented a bad situation from getting worse. During a time of rising unemployment, particularly among black males, it was actually a triumph of social policy to keep the poverty rate from rising.

All of this said, Murray's thesis should not be dismissed out of hand. There *are* plenty of people out there who choose welfare as the easy way out. Even more to the point, a culture of poverty *has* developed during the last four decades. Had he said that the largesse of the federal government had induced a sizable minority of the poor to succumb to the joys of living on the dole, he would have had a valid point. Murray simply overstated his case.

Decades ago, when I was a case worker for the New York City Welfare Department, I saw hundreds of thick case folders documenting the lives of second-, third-, and fourth-generation welfare families, consisting of scores of people, virtually all of whom had spent most or all of their lives dependent on public assistance. Had Murray confined his theory to this group, he would have had the support of the large majority of those working directly with the welfare population. Again, there *is* no valid general theory of the causes of welfare dependency.

In his landmark work *The Truly Disadvantaged,* Wilson begins by describing the black ghettos as they were more than 40 years ago. Sure there was crime, but it was still safe to walk the streets at night. And sure there was joblessness, but nothing like what there has been these last 30 years. Then he goes on to describe other social problems:

> There were single-parent families, but they were a small minority of all black families and tended to be incorporated within extended family networks and to be headed not by unwed teenagers and young adult women but by middle-aged women who usually were widowed, separated, or divorced. There were welfare recipients, but only a very small percentage of

Forty years ago the ghettos were a lot kinder and gentler places to live.

---

[13]William Julius Wilson, Introduction to Lisbeth B. Schorr and Daniel Schorr, *Within Our Reach* (New York: Doubleday, 1989), p. xxv.

the families could be said to be welfare-dependent. In short, unlike the present period, inner-city communities prior to 1960 exhibited the features of social organization—including a sense of community, positive neighborhood identification, and explicit norms and sanctions against aberrant behavior.[14]

William Julius Wilson, American sociologist

So what happened? What happened was the civil rights revolution led by Martin Luther King, Jr., in the early 1960s and the subsequent legislation that lowered racial housing and employment barriers. Until then the big-city ghettos had been socioeconomically integrated. But this quickly changed by the late 60s as millions of blacks, who had been penned up in the ghettos, were finally able to move out. They moved into the houses and apartments that had been vacated by the whites who had fled to the suburbs.

How did this outward migration affect those who were left behind?

The exodus of middle- and working-class families from many ghetto neighborhoods removes an important "social buffer" that could deflect the full impact of the kind of prolonged and increasing joblessness that plagued inner-city neighborhoods in the 1970s and early 1980s. . . . Even if the truly disadvantaged segments of an inner-city area experience a significant increase in long-term joblessness, the basic institutions in that area (churches, schools, stores, recreational facilities, etc.) would remain viable if much of the base of their support comes from the more economically stable and secure families. Moreover, the very presence of these families during such periods provides mainstream role models that help keep alive the perception that education is meaningful, that steady employment is a viable alternative to welfare, and that family stability is the norm, not the exception.[15]

The outward migration of middle- and working-class blacks had a significant impact on those left behind.

This isolation makes it harder to find a job; few ghetto dwellers are tied into the job network. And because few relatives or neighbors have steady work, tardiness and absenteeism are not considered aberrant behavior. Consequently, those who do find jobs seldom hold them very long.

So the key is jobs—or rather the lack of them:

Lack of jobs is the key.

The black delay in marriage and the lower rate of remarriage, each associated with high percentages of out-of-wedlock births in female-headed households, can be directly tied to the employment status of black males. Indeed, black women, especially young black women, are confronting a shrinking pool of "marriageable" (that is, economically stable) men.[16]

The migration of black middle- and working-class families from the ghettos removed the key social constraint against crime. And the erection of huge, high-rise, low-income public housing projects further destroyed the remaining sense of community. Place together a large number of female-headed families with a large number of teenage children (who commit more crime than any other population group) and you've got the recipe for not only high crime rates but almost complete social breakdown.

Wilson's thesis is a direct repudiation of Murray's, which blames public assistance and other social programs for the emergence of the permanent black underclass. Wilson finds no evidence to support that contention. Instead, he blames a whole range of social and economic forces, including past employment discrimination.

Solutions

All poor people have one thing in common: They don't have nearly enough money. Or, in the words of the great wit, Finley Peter Dunne, "One of the strangest things about life is that the poor, who need the money the most, are the very ones that never have it."

The best way to help poor people is to not be one of them.

—Reverend Ike,
New York City preacher

---

[14]William Julius Wilson, *The Truly Disadvantaged* (Chicago: University of Chicago Press, 1987), p. 3.
[15]Ibid., p. 56.
[16]Ibid., p. 145.

The basic liberal solution—in addition to combating employment discrimination—is to provide the poor with better education and training, and with millions of government jobs. The conservatives have placed their faith in providing the poor with jobs mainly in the private sector. But the basic strain running through conservative thought about welfare recipients may be summed up in just three little words: Cut 'em off. A solution with widespread support, workfare, combines the liberal carrot of training and jobs with the conservative stick of cutting off the benefits of those who refuse to seek training or work.

The Conservative Solutions   To end the poor's dependency on government largesse, Charles Murray would simply pull the plug on the life-support system:

> [Scrap] the entire welfare and income-support structure for working-aged persons, including [public assistance], medicaid, food stamps, unemployment insurance, workers' compensation, subsidized housing, disability insurance, and the rest. It would leave the working-aged person with no recourse whatsoever except the job market, family members, friends, and public or private locally funded services.[17]

The Liberal Solutions   While the conservatives claim the government has done too much for the poor, the liberals believe much too little has been done. Barbara Ehrenreich, for example, points out that an increasing number of jobs do not pay enough to subsist on.[18] The solution? Government jobs.

Jobs, jobs, jobs

Government jobs doing what? Jobs rebuilding the nation's crumbling highways and bridges, and staffing hospitals, schools, libraries, and day care centers. Jobs rebuilding dilapidated inner-city housing and cleaning up toxic waste dumps. In the 1930s, the Works Progress Administration (WPA) of the New Deal employed millions of Americans building highways, airports, bridges, parks, and school buildings. Much of this infrastructure is badly in need of repair. In addition we need millions of people to staff day care centers, libraries, and after-school programs. Why not create a labor-intensive, minimum-wage public service jobs program of last resort for today's low-skilled and jobless workers?[19]

But some liberals acknowledge that even a massive jobs program won't get *all* of the poor off the dole. Remember that nearly all people receiving public assistance are women with young children.

Our country will need to go beyond providing jobs if we are to succeed in greatly reducing poverty. The lives of those in the permanent underclass are filled with hopelessness and despair. The lack of jobs put most of these families into this predicament, but it will take more than jobs, three or four generations later, to get them out of it.

More is needed than providing jobs.

Dr. David Rogers, president of the Robert Wood Johnson Foundation, remarked that "human misery is generally the result of, or accompanied by, a great untidy basketful of intertwined and interconnected circumstances and happenings"[20] that all need attention if a problem is to be solved. This point was amplified by Lisbeth and Daniel Schorr in their landmark work *Within Our Reach:*

> The mother who cannot respond appropriately to a child's evolving needs while simultaneously coping with unemployment, an abusive husband or boyfriend, an apartment without hot water, insufficient money for food, and her own memories of past neglect—even a mother who is stressed to the breaking point can be helped by a neighborhood agency that provides day care, counseling, and the support that convinces her that she is not helpless and alone.[21]

---

[17]Murray, *Losing Ground,* pp. 227–28.

[18]Barbara Ehrenreich, *Nickel and Dimed* (New York: Henry Holt, 2001); Beth Schulman, *The Betrayal of Work* (New York: The New Press, 2003).

[19]See William Julius Wilson, *When Work Disappears* (New York: Knopf, 1996), pp. 225–38; and Sheldon Danziger and Peter Gottschalk, *America Unequal* (Cambridge, MA: Harvard University Press, 1995), p. 174.

[20]Robert Wood Johnson Foundation, *Annual Report,* 1984.

[21]Lisbeth B. Schorr and Daniel Schorr, *Within Our Reach* (New York: Doubleday, 1989), p. 151.

Welfare Reform: The Personal Responsibility and Work Opportunity Reconciliation Act of 1996   This was the most significant piece of welfare legislation since the Social Security Act of 1935. These are its main provisions:

- The federal guarantee of cash assistance for poor children is ended.

- The head of every welfare family would have to work within two years or the family would lose benefits.

- After receiving welfare for two months adults must find jobs or perform community service.

- Lifetime welfare benefits would be limited to five years. (Hardship exemptions would be available to 20 percent of families. These families would continue receiving public assistance.)

- Each state receives a lump sum to run its own welfare and work programs.

- Up to 20 percent of those on public assistance—the ones who are least employable—will be allowed to remain on the rolls beyond the time limit.

We have ended welfare as we know it.
—President Bill Clinton

For the first time since 1935 the federal government no longer guaranteed support to all of America's children. Critics have pointed out that the law required some 4 million mothers, nearly all with little education and poor job skills, to somehow go out and find jobs that would support their families. And most significantly, the law created no new jobs, paid for no training programs, and made no provision for additional free or low-cost day care facilities.

The trouble with being poor is that it takes up all your time.
—Willem de Kooning

Around the time that Congress had passed and President Clinton had signed the Welfare Reform Act there were dire predictions that when families were thrown off public assistance, we would see children starving in the streets. But a study by Kathryn Edin and Laura Lein found that virtually all poor single mothers—whether working or receiving public assistance—were supplementing their income with money from a support network of relatives, boyfriends, or the absent fathers of their children.[22]

Has welfare reform been successful? The answer is yes—and no. In March 1994, the welfare rolls stood at a peak of 14.4 million recipients. (See Figure 10.) The rolls,

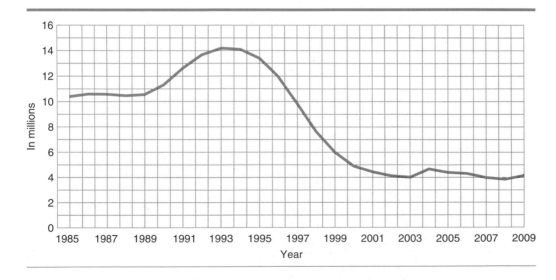

F*igure* **10**

Recipients of Temporary Assistance for Needy Families, 1985–2009
After climbing from 1989 through 1993, the welfare rolls declined every year. The decline was especially sharp between 1994 and 1999.
Source: Statistical Abstract of the United States, 2009; U.S. Department of Health & Human Services, www.acf.hhs.gov.

---

[22]Kathryn Edin and Laura Lein, *Making Ends Meet* (Ithaca, NY: Cornell University Press, 1997).

Going the Extra Mile

President Ronald Reagan used to refer to "Welfare Queens"—women who lived high off the hog on their welfare checks and made no effort to support themselves or their children. While there are indeed still some "Welfare Queens," most of the women on welfare are either working, very actively looking for work, or are being trained for some form of work. In order to work, poor single mothers not only have to find jobs, find transportation to those jobs, but they have to arrange child care as well. This is what six Greenwood Mississippi women must go through every working day:

Six Leflore County mothers are picked up in vans at 3 a.m. for a ride to jobs in faraway chicken

processing plants where they earn about $6 an hour, or $12,000 a year. With stops to deliver children to sitters, the trip takes three or four hours.

The women still collect a welfare check because the pay does not lift them above the poverty line, and the state pays for their child care and the van, and gives them $5 a day for lunch and a $3,000 bonus for working for two years.*

*Peter T. Kilborn, "Recession Is Stretching the Limit on Welfare Benefits," The New York Times, December 9, 2001.

which began falling in 1994, continued to fall steadily through the next 9 years, reaching 4 million in 2003. (See the box, "Going the Extra Mile.") Since then between 3.8 and 4.8 million Americans have been receiving public assistance.

The current mantra is "work first," the policy of putting people to work without detours through training and education. So far, the state strategies appear to be paying off, since recipients have fled the welfare rolls in record numbers, but there have been serious problems. The wages earned by former welfare mothers average about $8 an hour, and 75 percent of them also lacked medical benefits. About one-third of those who left the rolls were back on welfare within a year.

Douglas J. Besharov, who teaches at the University of Maryland School of Public Policy and is a resident scholar at the conservative American Enterprise Institute, has summarized what has happened to the single mothers who left the welfare roles in the wake of welfare reform:

> . . . the best estimates are that only about 40 percent to 50 percent of mothers who left welfare have steady, full-time jobs. Another 15 percent or so work part time. According to surveys in various states, these mothers are earning about $8 an hour. That's about $16,000 a year for full-time employment. It is their story that the supporters of welfare reform celebrate, but $16,000 is not a lot of money, especially for a mother with two children.[23]

Despite the worst job market in 70 years, millions of single mothers are expected to find jobs that will support their families. Among families living below the poverty level with working mothers, child care absorbs about one third of household income.

Recognizing the need for subsidized childcare, the federal government now provides $7 billion a year to be used in state run programs. But in a time of tremendous budgetary pressure, about half the states cut hundreds of thousands of subsidized child-care slots in 2008, 2009, and 2010. Today just 1.6 million children—a small fraction of those eligible—receive subsidized child care.

Unable to secure affordable child care, thousands of single working mothers have been pushed out of the labor force and onto the public assistance rolls. It would appear then that welfare reform without adequate provision for child care has left many poor families between a rock and a hard place.

[23]Douglas J. Besharov, "End Welfare Lite As We Know It," The New York Times, August 15, 2006, p. A19.

Current Issue: Will You Ever Be Poor?

What are the chances that your income will fall below the poverty line for at least a year? Most Americans experience more than a year of poverty sometime after their 20th birthday. We're not talking about college or graduate student poverty. Indeed you can greatly increase your chances of experiencing some poverty if you don't have a high school diploma. And if you're black, then you stand more than 9 chances out of 10 of being poor for more than a year sometime during your adulthood.

Where do these numbers come from? They come from an ongoing study, the Panel Study of Income Dynamics, which has been following the same individuals and households every year since 1968. These 18,000 individuals from 4,800 households are tracked annually, and children born into these families are also included. Any dropouts are replaced by families with similar characteristics.[24]

TABLE 4 The Cumulative Percentage of Americans Who Experience at Least a Year of Poverty, by Race

	Cumulative Percentage	
Age	Black	White
20	29.7	6.9
35	61.6	25.6
55	79.3	38.3
75	91.0	52.6

Source: Data from Panel Study of Income Dynamics. Computations from Rank, op. cit., p. 96.

Table 4 shows the cumulative percentage of poverty by race for various age groups. Interestingly a majority of whites experiences a bout of poverty by the age of 75. But some 91 percent of all blacks spend at least a year of their lives below the poverty line.

See if you happen to know the answer to *this* question: Who would more likely be poor—a black person or a high school dropout? You can figure out the answer for yourself by glancing at Tables 4 and 5.

TABLE 5 The Cumulative Percentage of Americans Who Experience at Least a Year of Poverty, by Education

	Cumulative Percentage	
Age	Less than 12 years	12 years or more
20	12.4	8.6
35	41.5	29.1
55	60.5	39.2
75	75.3	48.0

Source: Data from Panel Study of Income Dynamics. Computations from Rank, op. cit., p. 96.

Comparing the cumulative percentages at each age, you should note that the chances of a black person being poor are much greater than that of a high school dropout. In

[24]See Mark Robert Rank, *One Nation, Underprivileged* (New York: Oxford University Press, 2004), pp. 90–91.

other words race is a much better predictor of one's lifetime prospects of being poor than a high school diploma.

Despite the fact that your income may fall below the poverty line, you probably won't ever be truly poor. The reason is that you'll be able to fall back on your accumulated wealth, especially your home. As you know, tens of millions of Americans have taken out home equity loans, which they use to finance their children's educations, major consumption purchases, and sometimes just to maintain a lifestyle that requires spending more than their current income. So if your income *does* fall below the poverty for a year or two, or possibly even longer, you will probably manage quite well by taking out a home equity loan, digging into your savings, borrowing from your retirement plan, or, if worst comes to worse, maxing out your credit cards.

Middle class people generally have a built-in safety net to help them through bad times. But the truly poor, who were described in great detail through most of this chapter, have few resources to fall back on in bad times. Indeed, for most of them, the bad times may well be the norm. So over the next 50 years, I'd like you to keep a record of how many years your income falls below the poverty line. If that never happens, then you've beaten the odds.

Questions for Further Thought and Discussion

1. What's the difference between the distribution of income and the distribution of wealth? Describe the distribution of income and the distribution of wealth in the United States.

2. Discuss the basic determinants of income distribution.

3. Who are the poor in the United States? A few population groups have very high incidences of poverty. Explain why people in each of these groups tend to be poor.

4. There are several theories of the causes of poverty. Why can't a single theory explain all the poverty in the United States?

5. Compare and contrast the conservative and liberal views of poverty.

6. What has happened to the welfare rolls since the mid-1990s? What are the causes of this trend?

7. *Practical Application:* What steps would you take to cut our poverty rate in half?

8. *Web Activity:* Are you eligible for the Earned Income Tax Credit? Find out at www.hrblock/taxes/tax_tips/calculators/index.html and click on Earned Income Credit or www.wwwebtax.com/credits/earned_income_credit.htm

9. *Web Activity:* Do you want to be a billionaire? Aside from inheriting money, in which three industries or economic sectors have our 100 richest billionaires made their fortunes? Go to www.forbes.com/richlist

Workbook for Chapter 18

Name _____   Date _____

Multiple-Choice Questions

Circle the letter that corresponds to the best answer.

1. Most social scientists define the poor as being the lowest _____ percent of our income recipients. (LO4)
   a) 10
   b) 20
   c) 3
   d) 40
   e) 50

2. Which is the most accurate statement? (LO7)
   a) Although there are several theories of poverty, it is possible to formulate just one theory which completely explains 99 percent of all poverty in the United States.
   b) There are at least a dozen theories of poverty, and each has at least some apparent validity.
   c) Poverty can be explained largely by employment discrimination.
   d) Poverty is no longer a major socioeconomic problem in the United States.

3. The Darity-Myers thesis is an attempt to explain _____. (LO7)
   a) black poverty
   b) the poverty of the elderly
   c) worldwide poverty
   d) the permanent underclass

4. An equal distribution of income would _____. (LO1)
   a) hurt both the work incentive and the incentive to save
   b) hurt neither the work incentive nor the incentive to save
   c) hurt the work incentive but not the incentive to save
   d) hurt the incentive to save but not the work incentive

5. Doctors earn more than people in other professions basically because _____. (LO2, 3)
   a) they need to be compensated for all those years they spent in school
   b) they are in short supply relative to the demand for their services
   c) it costs a lot more to be a doctor—office expenses, support staff, and malpractice insurance—than it does to be in almost any other profession
   d) doctors put in longer hours than most other people

6. To keep a family of four at the poverty line a person working a 40-hour week would need to earn about _____ an hour. (LO4)
   a) $7
   b) $9
   c) $11
   d) $13
   e) $15

7. Compared to their levels in 2003, the poverty line has _____ and the minimum hourly wage has _____. (LO4)
   a) gone up, gone up
   b) stayed the same, stayed the same
   c) gone up, stayed the same
   d) stayed the same, gone up

8. Women working full-time earn a little more than _____ percent of what is earned by their male counterparts. (LO1, 2)
   a) 33
   b) 50
   c) 75
   d) 100

9. Each of the following is a major source of great wealth except _____. (LO2)
   a) earning large salaries
   b) starting up new companies
   c) real estate
   d) inheritance

10. Which is not aimed solely at the poor? (LO6)
    a) Food stamps
    b) Public assistance
    c) Social Security
    d) Medicaid

11. Which statement is true? (LO7, 9)
    a) Very few poor people hold jobs.
    b) The main reason for poverty is that some people refuse to work.
    c) A person holding a minimum wage job could raise her family out of poverty.
    d) There are millions of people whose jobs don't pay enough to support their families.

12. Which statement is false? (LO5)
    a) About three-fourths of the poor are single mothers and their children.
    b) About half of the poor are elderly.
    c) People living in the South are more likely to be poor than those living in the rest of the country.
    d) None of these statements is false.

13. About _____ million Americans are homeless. (LO5)
    a) 2 to 3   d) 20 to 25
    b) 6 to 8   e) 40 to 50
    c) 12 to 15

14. Which statement is true? (LO5)
    a) Most poor people are black.
    b) Most black people are poor.
    c) People over age 65 have a higher poverty rate than the overall rate for Americans.
    d) None of these statements is true.

15. Darity and Myers predict that _____. (LO7)
    a) welfare reform will lead to a sharp decline in the number of black families living below the poverty line
    b) cutting welfare benefits will increase the ranks of marriageable young black men
    c) the underlying cause of poverty is too much government intervention
    d) there will be an increasing number of black families headed by females

16. "The exodus of middle- and working-class families from many ghetto neighborhoods removes an important 'social buffer'" was said by _____. (LO7)
    a) Nicholas Lemann
    b) Charles Murray
    c) Barbara Ehrenreich
    d) William Julius Wilson

17. Which statement is true? (LO5)
    a) Virtually none of the homeless have jobs.
    b) Many of the homeless are mentally ill.
    c) The homeless are concentrated in a few large cities.
    d) None of these statements is true.

18. Nearly one out of every _____ children lives in poverty. (LO5)
    a) two   c) five
    b) three   d) nine

19. Social scientists believe _____ the differential between what women and men earn can be explained by employment discrimination. (LO3)
    a) almost all of
    b) about half of
    c) only a small part of

20. Which statement is false? (LO7, 9)
    a) Poverty breeds poverty.
    b) Poor people have low human capital.
    c) The liberals and conservatives disagree on how to get people off the welfare rolls and into self-supporting jobs.
    d) None of these statements is false.

21. It would not be reasonable to say that poor people are _____. (LO5)
    a) grudgingly tolerated by society's "productive" members
    b) largely superfluous to our socioeconomic system
    c) basically self-supporting
    d) poor for a variety of reasons

22. Which one of the following statements is false? (LO6, 7)

   a) The poor pay higher prices to buy groceries, furniture, and appliances.

   b) Low-income families can pay over $500 more for the same car bought by a higher-income household.

   c) The poor pay higher interest rates than people with higher incomes.

   d) Very few poor people can claim the earned income tax credit.

23. The earned income tax credit is _____. (LO6)

   a) a form of welfare

   b) a refund check paid to the working poor by the Internal Revenue Service

   c) a very minor form of government aid to the poor

   d) opposed by both liberals and conservatives

24. The superrich get most of their income from _____. (LO3)

   a) rent, interest, and profits

   b) wages

   c) illegal transactions

   d) real estate investments

25. The richest fifth of all American families receives _____ percent of our total income. (LO1)

   a) almost 35   c) more than 60

   b) about 50   d) more than 75

26. Which of the following is the most accurate statement? (LO5)

   a) The standard of living of poor American children is very low compared to that of middle-class American children.

   b) Poor children in the United States are much worse off than poor children in virtually all other OECD countries.

   c) Poor children in the United States are much better off than poor children in virtually all other OECD countries.

   d) There is no way to compare the degree of child poverty in the United States with the degree of child poverty in other economically advanced countries.

27. Between 1968 and 2008, the percentage share of total income grew for the _____. (LO1, 3)

   a) lowest two quintiles

   b) the middle three quintiles

   c) the highest quintile

   d) the highest quintile and the lowest quintile

28. Between 1968 and 2008, our income distribution has _____. (LO1)

   a) became more equal

   b) stayed about the same

   c) became less equal

29. Real median family income in the U.S. has _____. (LO1, 2)

   a) grown each year since 2000

   b) declined each year since 2000

   c) risen by about 20 percent since the late 1960s

   d) become lower today than it was in 1975

30. Which of the following statements is the most accurate? (LO5, 6)

   a) The welfare rolls today are much lower than they were in 1996.

   b) About 1 in 8 Americans lives below the poverty line.

   c) Without Social Security benefits, at least 75 percent of all senior citizens would be poor.

   d) The Welfare Reform Act of 1996 has cut the poverty rate by almost 60 percent.

31. Which statement is true? (LO2)

   a) All of the 10 richest Americans inherited their fortunes.

   b) In order to make the top ten list of American billionaires, you need a fortune of over $15 billion.

   c) The two richest families in the United States today are the Rockefellers and the Fords.

   d) Most of the 10 richest Americans own large manufacturing companies.

32. Which is the most accurate statement? (LO4, 5)

   a) Although there are poor children in the U.S., our child poverty problem is not nearly as bad as that of most other rich countries.

   b) The reason so many people in poor countries still don't have safe drinking water is that it would cost at least $50 billion a year to provide it.

   c) Poor people in the U.S. spend more than double their reported incomes.

   d) Although some war veterans are poor, virtually none is homeless because of the efforts of the Veteran's Administration to find them housing.

33. Which statement is true? (LO1, 2)
    a) If we redistributed income every year so that everyone would get the same amount, this would hurt the efficiency of our economy.
    b) Virtually everyone agrees that we should redistribute most of the income received by the rich to the poor.
    c) The poor get a great deal more satisfaction from each additional dollar of income than the rich.
    d) There is no relationship between the distribution of income and economic incentives.

34. The largest government program aimed exclusively at helping the poor is _____. (LO6)
    a) the earned income tax credit
    b) public assistance
    c) food stamps
    d) Social Security

35. Which one of the following people would most likely experience at least a year of poverty after her or his 20th birthday? (LO5)
    a) A high school dropout
    b) A black person
    c) A white person
    d) A college dropout

36. Which statement is true? (LO6, 10)
    a) Most of the nation's poor receive welfare benefits.
    b) Since the Welfare Reform Act of 1996, no new welfare cases have been accepted.
    c) More people than ever are receiving welfare benefits.
    d) Most single mothers who have recently left the welfare rolls remain poor.

37. Which statement is true? (LO6, 9)
    a) Over 90 percent of the families receiving public assistance are headed by people who are employed.
    b) Nearly 90 percent of those in the workforce earn at least $10 an hour.
    c) The welfare rolls are much lower today than they were in 1994.
    d) If every adult on welfare were willing to work, we could cut the number of welfare families by over 75 percent.

38. Which one of the following is the most accurate statement? (LO4)
    a) Our poverty rate is somewhat higher today than it was in 1999.
    b) Our poverty rate is over 15 percent.
    c) If it were not for the 2007–2009 recession, our poverty rate would probably be below 10 percent.
    d) Our poverty rate is currently at an all-time low.

39. What would be the most effective way of raising people out of poverty? (LO9)
    a) Cut off welfare payments to every family with at least one adult member between the ages of 18 and 64.
    b) Raise the minimum hourly wage.
    c) Eliminate the earned income tax credit.
    d) Have the government put welfare recipients to work at minimum wage jobs.

40. Which one of the following statements is the most accurate? (LO9)
    a) Our nation provides cradle-to-grave security for our military personnel and their families.
    b) Because of the relative high pay and benefits provided by the military, very few military families run into financial problems.
    c) No military family lives below the poverty line.
    d) Some military families depend on food pantries.

41. Which one of these is the most accurate statement about real median family income? (LO1, 2)
    a) It has declined steadily over the last five years.
    b) It has fallen during nearly every recession since the 1960s.
    c) It is about twice as high as it was in 1970.
    d) It increased steadily since 2000.

42. Which is the most accurate statement? (LO6)
    a) Because of the efforts of the Veterans Administration, only a handful of veterans are homeless.
    b) Most military families have to get by on food stamps and help from food pantries and soup kitchens.
    c) Military pay is high enough to keep virtually all military families well above the official poverty line.
    d) Although nearly all of our leading politicians wear American flag lapel pins, they do not provide enough economic support to our troops, so many military families are in severe financial difficulty.

43. Who made this statement? "I still have the audacity to believe that people everywhere can have three meals a day." (LO4, 8)
   a) Charles Murray
   b) William Julius Wilson
   c) Barbara Bush (mother of President George W. Bush)
   d) Martin Luther King, Jr.
   e) Lisbeth B. Schorr

44. Which one of the following statements is *false?* (LO5)
   a) Nearly half of all poor Americans own their own homes.
   b) A poor person today has roughly the same standard of living as a middle-income person 30 years ago.
   c) The reported consumption spending of people in the lowest income quintile is about twice their reported income.
   d) The standard of living of American's poor is comparable to that of most of the rest of the world's poor people.

45. Who would most likely receive food stamps before the age of 20? (LO6)
   a) A white person
   b) A black person
   c) An Asian-American person
   d) A person who grew up in a two-parent household

46. Which is the most accurate statement? (LO6, 10)
   a) Most poor people receive public assistance (formerly called welfare).
   b) Public assistance has been discontinued.
   c) The number of people receiving public assistance is less than one-third as high as it was in 1993.
   d) Because of the 2007–2009 recession, the public assistance rolls have reached an all-time high.

47. Which statement best reflects the views of Charles Murray? (LO8)
   a) The main cause of poverty can be traced to the heritage of slavery.
   b) Poverty is caused largely by government antipoverty programs.
   c) Poverty can be substantially reduced by providing government jobs to all who want to work.
   d) The prime cause of poverty is that poor people are basically lazy.

48. Which one of the following people would stand the least chance of being poor during her or his lifetime? (LO 11)
   a) Someone with less than 12 years of education
   b) Someone with more than 12 years of education
   c) Someone white
   d) Someone black

Fill-In Questions

1. The richest 1 percent of our population owns over _____ percent of our wealth. (LO2)

2. The two biggest benefit programs aimed solely at the poor are _____ and _____. (LO6)

3. About one out of every _____ black Americans is poor. (LO4)

4. About _____ percent of all poor people are black. (LO4)

5. The basic problem with the absolute concept of poverty is finding the _____. (LO4)

6. The poverty line is set by the _____. (LO4)

7. The richest quintile of humanity spends about _____ times as much on consumption as the world's poorest quintile. (LO1)

Problems

Use Figure 1 to answer problems 1 through 4. (LO1)

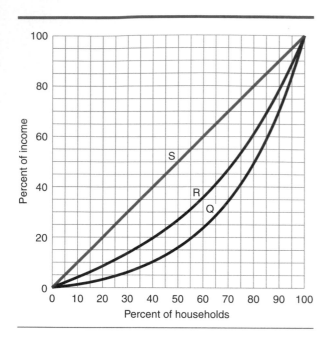

Figure 1

1. How much is the percentage of income received by the lowest quintile on line R?

2. How much is the percentage of income earned by the highest quintile on Lorenz curve Q?

3. How much is the percentage of income received by the highest quintile on line R?

4. How much is the percentage of income received by the middle three quintiles on line S?

Chapter 19

International Trade

More and more of our imports come from overseas.
—President George W. Bush

H uge container ships steam into Seattle every day loaded with shoes, clothing, textiles, furniture, TVs, and cameras that were made in Asia. On their return trip these same ships leave half empty, bearing chemicals, meat, grain, as well as hay, scrap metal, and scrap paper. These cargoes vividly illustrate our relationship with our Asian trading partners: We buy what they make, but they don't buy that much of what we make.

Trillions of dollars' worth of business in international trade is conducted every year. Certain trading nations—Japan, the United Kingdom, Singapore, the Netherlands, Korea, and Taiwan among them—draw their economic lifeblood from foreign trade, while others, such as the United States, France, Germany, Russia, and China, are relatively self-sufficient. Yet even the United States has become increasingly dependent on imported TVs, apparel, textiles, steel, compact cars, oil, and other goods.

How this trade is conducted is the subject of this chapter; how it is financed is the subject of the next. The thread that runs through international trade and finance is specialization and exchange. If all the nations of the world were self-sufficient, there would be no international trade and little need for international finance. But if that were to happen, the world would have a much lower standard of living.

LEARNING OBJECTIVES

After reading this chapter you should be able to:

1. Summarize the history of U.S. trade.
2. Explain the relationship between specialization and exchange.
3. Define and differentiate between absolute advantage and comparative advantage.
4. List and evaluate the arguments for protection.
5. Compare the advantages and disadvantages of tariffs versus quotas.
6. List and discuss the causes of our trade imbalance.
7. Compare the causes of our trade deficits with Japan and China.
8. Differentiate between free trade in word and in deed.
9. Explain how we can reduce our trade deficit.
10. Evaluate the pros and cons of a "Buy American" policy.
11. List and discuss the effects of globalization on our economy.

America is being flooded with imports, and millions of workers are being thrown out of work. Americans are buying not just foreign-made cameras and DVD players, but also foreign-made steel, textiles, apparel, personal computers, cars, and toys. But why worry? After all, the world is now a global village, and we all buy from and sell to each other. Why should we buy something from an American firm when we can get a better deal from a foreign firm?

International trade is really good for everyone. As consumers, we are able to purchase a whole array of goods and services that would not have otherwise been available—at least, not at such low prices. Hence, we can thank international trade for much of our high standard of living. As producers, we are able to sell a great deal of our output abroad, thereby increasing our employment and profits. So far, so good. The only trouble is that during the last two decades or so, we have been buying a lot more from foreigners than they have been buying from us.

So what do we *do*? Do we throw up protective tariff barriers to keep out lower-priced foreign imports? Or, like the old Avis rent-a-car commercials, do we just try harder? After a brief history of U.S. trade, in Part II of the chapter we'll consider the theory of international trade, why such trade is so wonderful, and why we should not do anything to impede its flow. In Part III we'll take a closer look at the practice of international trade and try to zero in on the causes of our trade imbalance and what we can do to redress it. And then, in Part IV, we'll look at why we've been running huge trade deficits with Japan and China.

Part I: A Brief History of U.S. Trade

The United States did not always run large trade deficits. Indeed, we ran surpluses for virtually the entire first three-quarters of the 20th century. Let's look at that record, and at U.S. government trade policy over the years.

U.S. Trade before 1975

We ran trade surpluses before 1975 and deficits after 1975.

Why 1975? Because that's the last year we ran a trade surplus. Until 1971 the United States had run a surplus nearly every year of the 20th century.

Until the early 1900s we were primarily an agricultural nation, exporting cotton and grain to Europe in exchange for manufactured goods. These included not just consumer goods—shoes, clothing, books, and furniture—but also a great deal of machinery and equipment for our growing industrial sector. We ran relatively small trade deficits through most of the 19th century.

But once we had become a powerful industrial nation, by the turn of the 20th century, we had not only less need of European manufactures but we were now exporting our own manufactured goods. With the outbreak of World War I in 1914, we added armaments to our growing list of exports, as our trade surpluses mounted. In the 1920s we inundated the world with Model T Fords, as well as a host of other American vehicles, along with radios, phonographs, toasters, waffle irons, and other consumer appliances.

The Great Depression of the 1930s depressed not only worldwide production of goods and services but their export as well. Our trade surpluses increased in the 1940s, with the advent of World War II, when, once again, we shipped huge quantities of food and armaments to England, the Soviet Union, China, and our other allies. It took 15 years for the world's other leading industrial powers to recover from the devastation of the war, during which time we supplied the world from our cornucopia of manufacturing and agricultural products. During this period, and well into the 1960s, we continued running substantial trade surpluses.

U.S. Trade since 1975

We faced increasing trade competition in the 1960s.

By the early 1960s Japan and the industrial nations of Western Europe had rebuilt their factories and stemmed the flood of American imports. Later in that decade these nations, especially Japan, were exporting cars, TVs, cameras, and other consumer goods to the United States and going head-to-head with American manufacturers throughout the world. By the late 1970s our trade deficits were mounting (see Figure 1). Although these deficits rose and fell over the years, by 1984 they crossed the $100 billion mark.

In the late 1990s, our trade deficit really took off. Some of the contributing factors were the high U.S. dollar (which made our exports more expensive and our imports cheaper), our rapid economic growth, which expanded our demand for foreign goods and services, and our insatiable appetite for foreign consumer goods.

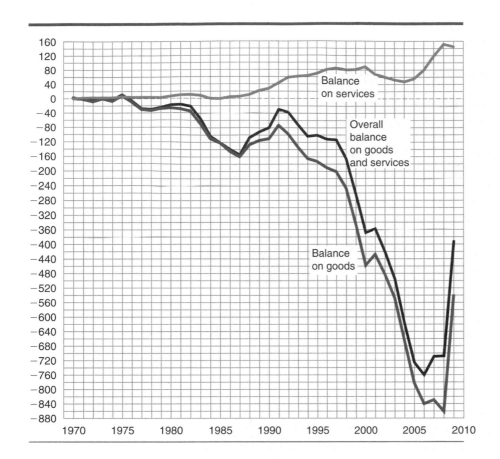

Figure 1

U.S. Balance of Trade in Goods and Services, and Overall Balance, 1970–2009 (in billions of dollars)

Since the late 1980s we have been running a large and growing surplus on services. Our balance on goods, which has been negative since the mid-1970s, has grown much worse since 1991.

Sources: Economic Report of the President, 1985–2010; Economic Indicators, April 2010.

Our service sector has had a positive balance since the mid-1980s, but it has been increasingly overwhelmed by our huge and growing negative balance of trade in goods. The major contributors to our positive service balance include education, financial, travel, medical, and legal services, royalties and license fees, operational leasing, and film and television video rentals and sales.

Back in 1960 just 4 percent of the cars Americans purchased and 6 percent of our TVs, radios, and other consumer electronics were built outside the United States. Also, we imported just 5 percent of our steel and 3 percent of our machine tools. Today all of our TVs, nearly all of our other consumer electronics, and over one-quarter of our cars are imported. And today we import two thirds of our oil, compared to just 15 percent in 1960.

Table 1 provides a snapshot view of our imports, exports, and balance of trade in 2009. As you can see, we imported $537 billion more in goods than we exported. Services

TABLE 1	U.S. Balance of Trade, 2009*
	(in billions of dollars)
Goods	
Imports	−$1,572
Exports	+ 1,035
Balance of goods	− 537
Services	
Imports	−$380
Exports	+ 525
Balance of services	+ 145
Balance of trade*	− 392

*Numbers may not add up exactly because of rounding.

continued to be the one bright spot of our trade balance, since we exported $145 billion more than we imported.

The Effect of the Great Recession on Our Balance of Trade

As you'll notice from the middle line in Figure 1, our trade deficit—the overall balance on goods and services—fell by over $300 billion from 2008 to 2009. Why did it fall so sharply, and—even more important—will this be a permanent decline? As we shall see, the answer to the first question will help answer the second.

The Great Recession of 2007–2009 affected not just our own country, but nearly all our major trading partners. As consumption and production fell, all these nations curbed their imports. And, of course, by definition, as worldwide imports fell, worldwide exports fell by exactly the same amount.

Consumption and production declined somewhat faster in the United States than it did in the rest of the economically advanced nations. Consequently our demand for imported goods and services fell more than the demand for our exports. What happened, then, in 2009, was that our imports fell much more than our exports, and our trade deficit declined substantially.

Our trade deficit also fell during the recessions of 1990–91and 2001, but during the Great Recession of 2007–2009 it fell much more sharply. In the late spring of 2010, with a financial crisis brewing in Europe—and with the fall of the euro—it appeared that for the rest of the year our exports to Europe would lag. If our own economic recovery continued, then it appeared likely that our trade deficit would shoot back up again.

So how likely will our relatively low trade deficits be permanent? As the world continues to recover from the Great Recession, our imports and our exports will increase. And unless our recovery is relatively slow—compared to those of our trading partners—we can expect that our trade deficit will climb steadily over the next few years.

on the web

How big was our trade deficit last month? Go to www.census.gov/indicator/www/ustrade.html

U.S. Government Trade Policy

We can get a snapshot view of this policy over the last two centuries by glancing at Figure 2. The relatively high tariffs through most of the 19th century and during the Great Depression reflected the political climate of those times.

A century of high protective tariffs

Back in Chapter 1 we talked about the high protective tariff being a cause of the Civil War. How did that come to be? Initially the tariff was purely a revenue-raising device, but after the War of 1812 war-born industries found it impossible to meet British competition, and the tariff took on a protective tinge. In 1816 the first protective tariff was adopted, followed in 1828 by the "Tariff of Abominations." But to whom was this tariff so abominable? To the South, which was primarily an agrarian economy, exporting cotton and importing manufactured goods. Of course the industrial Northern manufacturers wanted the South to buy their own goods rather than import them from Europe. However the South, allied with the Western states joining the union, was able to induce Congress to progressively lower tariffs until the Civil War. Note that, in 1861, when the 11 states of the Confederacy withdrew from the union, tariffs went right back up once more. Business-oriented Republican administrations kept them high until the Underwood Tariff of 1913, which, incidentally, was passed by a Southern-dominated Democratic Congress.

Again, during the Great Depression, virtually every industrial power, beset with massive unemployment, raised its tariffs to keep out foreign goods. Of course, since everyone was doing this, world trade dwindled to a fraction of what it had been in the 1920s. While certain jobs were protected, others, mainly in the export sector, were lost. Economists believe that these high tariffs, especially the Smoot-Hawley Tariff of 1930, made the depression a lot worse than it might have otherwise been.

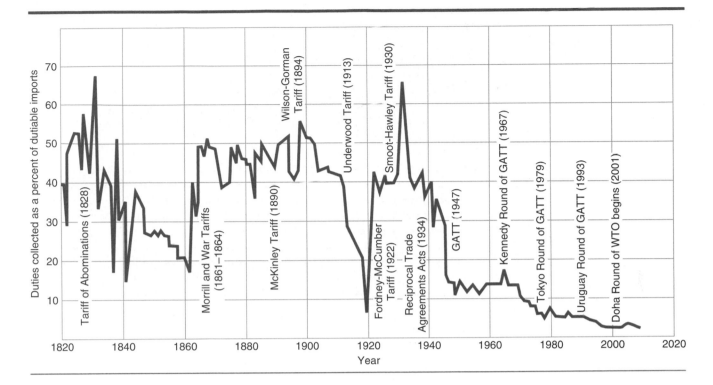

Figure 2
U.S. Tariffs, 1820–2009
Although tariffs fluctuated widely from the 1820s through the early 1930s, there has been a strong downward trend. Today tariffs average less than 5 percent of the price of our imported durable goods.
Source: U.S. Department of Commerce.

The GATT (General Agreement on Trade and Tariffs) treaty of 1947 began a downward trend in tariffs all around the world, leading to the formation of the World Trade Organization, which was set up to further facilitate world trade. GATT and the World Trade Organization were discussed in Chapter 8 of *Economics* and *Macroeconomics*.

A downward trend in tariffs since 1947

on the web

You can find our imports, exports, and trade deficit for the most recent three years at www.bea.gov. Click on "Survey of Current Business" at the left, then go to "National Data," "National Income and Product Accounts," NIPA tables, and finally, "Gross Domestic Product." It's much less complicated than it sounds.

Part II: The Theory of International Trade

Since 1992 our trade deficit has ballooned from just $30 billion to hundreds of billions. What can we do to reverse this trend? Should we restrict this profusion of imports, or should we listen to the reasoning of the economics profession, which is nearly unanimous in arguing for free trade?

If we will not buy, we cannot sell.
—President William McKinley

Specialization and Trade

The basis for international trade is specialization. Different nations specialize in the production of those goods and services for which their resources are best suited. An individual who attempts to be entirely self-sufficient would have to make her own nails, grow her own food, spin her own cloth, sew her own clothes, make her own tools, ad

Specialization is the basis for international trade.

infinitum. It is much easier and a lot cheaper to work at one particular job or specialty and use one's earnings to buy those nails, food, clothes, and so on.

What makes sense individually also makes sense internationally. Thus, just as it pays for individuals to specialize and trade, it pays for nations to do so. And that's exactly what we do: On a national basis we specialize and trade. But it would be impossible to do this unless there were a big enough market in which to buy and sell the goods and services we produce. Of course, the United States has long been the world's largest national market.

It pays for nations to specialize, just as it pays for individuals.

Adam Smith recognized the advantages of foreign trade more than two centuries ago when he wrote:

> If a foreign country can supply us with a commodity cheaper than we ourselves can make it, better buy it of them with some part of the produce of our own industry, employed in a way in which we have some advantage. The general industry of the country . . . will not thereby be diminished . . . but only left to find out the way in which it can be employed with the greatest advantage.[1]

Smith's argument provides the basis for international trade. Country A specializes in making the products that it can make most cheaply. Country B does the same. When they trade, each country will be better off than they would have been if they didn't specialize and trade.

Absolute Advantage

Let us say that workers in Brazil can produce more cell phones per hour than workers in Argentina. But Argentinian workers can turn out more PlayStations per hour than can Brazilian workers. We would say, then, that Brazilian workers have an absolute advantage in producing cell phones, while Argentinian workers have an absolute advantage in producing PlayStations. *Absolute advantage is the ability of a country to produce a good using fewer resources than another country.*

Common sense tells us that Brazil should trade some of its PlayStations for some of Argentina's cell phones. But the basis for trade is not absolute advantage, but comparative advantage. This concept shows us just how much two countries can gain by trading.

The propensity to truck, barter and exchange one thing for another is common to all men, and to be found in no other race of animals.

—Adam Smith

Comparative Advantage

Back in Chapter 2 we introduced production possibility curves, which showed how much a country could produce if its output were limited to just two goods. Now we'll look at the production possibilities frontiers of Peru and Pakistan (see Figure 3).

Notice that the production possibilities frontiers of Peru and Pakistan are straight lines, rather than the curves we had in Chapter 2. To keep things simple, let's assume that the resources used to produce corn are equally suitable for producing cameras. That enables us to have straight-line production possibility frontiers, which will help us demonstrate the law of comparative advantage.

Peru can produce two bushels of corn for every camera it makes. And Pakistan can produce one bushel of corn for every two cameras it makes. Are you ready for the million dollar question? OK, here's the question: Should Pakistan and Peru trade with each other?

What's your answer? If you said "yes," then you're right! That's because both nations are better off by trading than by not trading. Pakistan gains by trading cameras to Peru for corn; Peru gains by trading corn to Pakistan for cameras. So both nations gain by trading.

Let's go back to the concept of opportunity cost. What is Pakistan's opportunity cost of producing two cameras? In other words, to produce two cameras, what does Pakistan give up?

The answer is one bushel of corn. Now what is the opportunity cost of growing two bushels of corn for Peru?

---

[1]Adam Smith, *The Wealth of Nations,* vol. 1, ed. Edwin Cannan (London: University Paperbacks by Methuen, 1961), pp. 478–79.

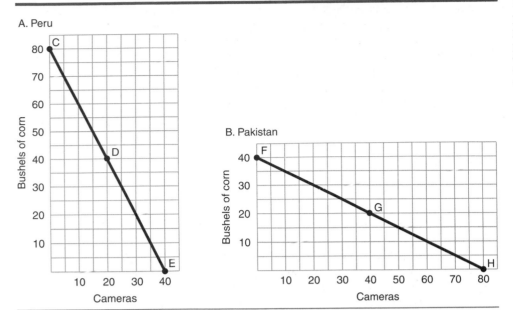

Figure 3

Production Possibilities Curves
Peru, operating at full capacity, can produce 80 bushels of corn or 40 cameras. Pakistan, operating at full capacity, can produce 40 bushels of corn or 80 cameras.

Peru's opportunity cost is one camera. Now we're ready for the law of comparative advantage. *The law of comparative advantage states that total output is greatest when each product is made by the country that has the lowest opportunity cost.* If the relative opportunity costs of producing goods (what must be given up in one good in order to get another good) differ between two countries, there are potential gains from trade.

Please glance back at Figure 3. You'll notice that Peru produces at point D (40 bushels of corn and 20 cameras). Pakistan is at point G (20 bushels of corn and 40 cameras). Table 2 restates points D and G.

TABLE 2	Production and Consumption of Corn and Cameras before Specialization and Trade	
	Pakistan	Peru
Bushels of corn	20	40
Cameras	40	20

We know that Pakistan can gain by trading cameras for corn, while Peru can gain by trading corn for cameras. So let's have Pakistan specialize in the production of cameras, placing it at point H of Figure 3. Meanwhile Peru, which now specializes in growing corn, will produce at point C of Figure 3. Table 3 restates points C and H.

Now Peru and Pakistan can trade. Let's assume the terms of trade are one camera for one bushel of corn. Pakistan will send Peru 40 cameras in exchange for 40 bushels of corn. This brings us to Table 4.

TABLE 3	Production of Corn and Cameras after Specialization	
	Pakistan	Peru
Bushels of corn	0	80
Cameras	80	0

TABLE 4	Consumption of Corn and Cameras after Trade	
	Pakistan	Peru
Bushels of corn	40	40
Cameras	40	40

It should be pretty obvious that both countries gained by specializing and trading. Just compare the numbers in Table 2 with those in Table 4. Pakistan gained 20 bushels of corn and Peru gained 20 cameras.

Let's work out another comparative advantage example. If France used all its resources, it could turn out 10 cars or 20 flat screen TVs, while Spain, using all its resources could turn out 5 cars or 15 TVs.

Which country has a comparative advantage in building cars, and which country has a comparative advantage in building TVs? Write your answers here:

_____ has a comparative advantage building cars.

_____ has a comparative advantage building TVs.

Solution: The opportunity cost to France of producing one car would be two TVs. The opportunity cost to Spain of producing one car would be three TVs. So France has a comparative advantage building cars and Spain has a comparative advantage building TVs.

Suppose the terms of trade were five TVs for two cars. Why would it pay for France to trade two cars in exchange for five TVs?

Solution: If France produced both cars and TVs, for every five TVs it made, it would be making two and a half less cars. But if France traded with Spain, she could produce just two cars and get five TVs in exchange.

Next question: Why would it pay for Spain to trade five TVs for two cars?

Solution: If Spain produced both cars and TVs, for every two cars she made, Spain would be making six less TVs. But if Spain traded with France, she could produce just five TVs and get two cars in exchange. If you'd like a little more practice, see the box, "How Comparative Advantage Leads to Gains from Specialization and Trade."

You probably never heard of the renowned facelift surgeon Dr. Khorsheed, but he is a legend in his own country, not just for his splendid work, but because of the great illustration he provides of the law of comparative advantage (see the box, "To Facelift or to File: *That* Is the Question").

Absolute Advantage versus Comparative Advantage

One of the things economists are fond of saying is that you can't compare apples and oranges. Here's a corollary: You can't compare absolute advantage and comparative advantage. The words may not exactly trip off your tongue, but still they ring true. Let's see why.

First, what *is* absolute advantage? It means that one country is better than another at producing some good or service (that is, it can produce it more cheaply). For example, the United States enjoys an absolute advantage over Japan in building commercial aircraft. But the Japanese enjoy an absolute advantage over the United States in making cameras. They can turn out cameras at a lower cost than we can, while we can build planes at a lower cost than the Japanese can.

So absolute advantage is a comparison of the cost of production in two different countries. What about comparative advantage? Let me quote myself: "The law of comparative advantage states that total output is greatest when each product is made by the country that has the lowest opportunity cost."

How Comparative Advantage Leads to Gains from Specialization and Trade

Just glance at Figure A and answer this question: Which country should specialize in producing telescopes and which country should specialize in producing microscopes?

Solution: If Canada used all its resources, it could produce either 60 telescopes or 30 microscopes. The opportunity cost of producing one microscope would be two telescopes. If Belgium used all its resources it could produce either 30 telescopes or 90 microscopes. The opportunity cost of producing one telescope would be three microscopes.

Clearly, then, Canada should specialize in making telescopes and Belgium should specialize in making microscopes.

If one microscope could be traded for one telescope, let's see how Canada would gain by trading its telescopes for Belgium's microscopes.

If Canada didn't specialize and trade, the opportunity cost for every microscope it produced would be not producing two telescopes. But it can now trade one telescope and receive in return one microscope. It's better to give up one telescope in exchange for one microscope than to give up two telescopes for one microscope (by producing both rather than specializing and trading).

Now let's see how Belgium gains from trading its microscopes for Canada's telescopes. If Belgium didn't trade, the opportunity cost of producing one telescope would be three microscopes. But if Belgium specialized in making microscopes, it would give up just one microscope in exchange for one telescope.

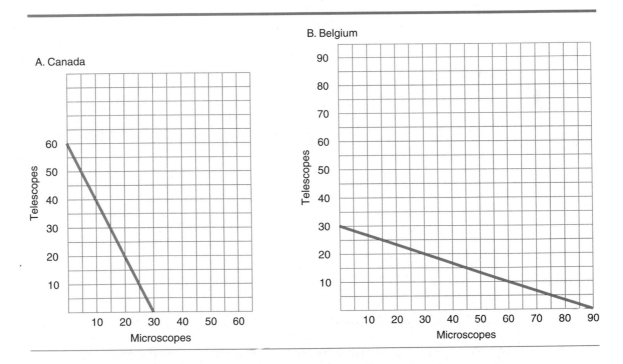

Figure A

Production Possibilities Curves

Operating at full capacity, Canada can produce 60 telescopes or 30 microscopes. Operating at full capacity, Belgium can produce 30 telescopes or 90 microscopes.

So we can say that as long as the relative opportunity costs of producing goods differ among nations, there are potential gains from trade even if one country has an absolute advantage in producing everything. Therefore *absolute* advantage is not necessary for trade to take place, but *comparative* advantage is.

To Facelift or to File: That *Is the Question*

Fereydoon Khorsheed is known in his country as the Michaelangelo of facelifts. He can do two a day at $3,000 a pop. The only problem is that he has to spend half the day doing paperwork, leaving him time to perform just one operation. So he hires Ashok Desai for $200 a day to deal with insurance companies, to do billing, filing, scheduling, and to keep the books. Now he is free to spend his entire working time doing facelifts, and his earnings double to $6,000 a day.

A perfectionist, Dr. Khorsheed soon discovers that it takes Mr. Desai a full day to do what he, Dr. Khorsheed, did in just half a day.

Question: Who has an absolute advantage in doing paperwork and who has an absolute advantage in doing facelifts?

Answer: Dr. Khorsheed has an absolute advantage in both endeavors. Mr. Desai can't do facelifts at all, and Dr. Khorsheed is twice as fast at paperwork.

Next question: Should Dr. Khorsheed fire Mr. Desai and do the paperwork himself?

Answer: Clearly not. He now earns $6,000 doing facelifts, pays Mr. Desai $200, leaving a net income of $5,800. If Dr. Khorsheed did paperwork for half the day, he'd have time for only one facelift and earn just $3,000.

So while Dr. Khorsheed is both a better facelifter and a better paperworker, it pays for him to specialize in facelifting, in which he has a comparative advantage, and leave the paperwork to Mr. Desai.

"The Gains from Trade" box summarizes most of what we've covered over the last 5 pages. I guarantee that when you have worked your way through this discussion, you will have become a great advocate of free trade.

The Arguments for Protection

> *America's gargantuan trade deficit is a weight around American workers' necks that is pulling them into a cycle of debt, bankruptcy and low-wage service jobs.*
>
> –Richard Trumka–
> AFL–CIO secretary-treasurer

As America continues to hemorrhage manufacturing jobs, there is a growing outcry for protection against the flood of foreign imports. But American consumers are virtually addicted to Japanese cars, South Korean TVs, Chinese microwave ovens, and hundreds of other manufactured goods from all over the world. How do we justify taxing or excluding so many things that so many Americans want to buy?

Four main arguments for protection

Four main arguments have been made for protection. Each seems plausible and strikes a responsive chord in the minds of the American public. But under closer examination, all four are essentially pleas by special interest groups for protection against more efficient competitors.

Does our dependence on foreign suppliers make us vulnerable in time of war?

(1) The National Security Argument   Originally this argument may have been advanced by American watchmakers, who warned the country not to become dependent on Swiss watchmakers because in the event of war Americans would not be able to make the timing devices for explosives without Swiss expertise. Yet during one long, drawn-out war, World War II, the United States was able to develop synthetics, notably rubber, to replace the supplies of raw materials that were cut off. And the Germans were able to convert coal into oil. It would appear, then, that the Swiss watch argument may have been somewhat overstated.

If our country were involved in a limited war, it is conceivable that our oil supplies from the Mideast might be cut off (although no American president would stand by passively while this happened), but we could probably replace these imports by producing more oil ourselves and by drawing on our strategic oil reserve. When Iraqi forces invaded Kuwait in 1990 President George Bush was able to put together an international coalition that quickly

The Gains from Trade

Let's look at the gains from trade, this time from a somewhat different prospective. By just glancing at Table A, you should easily be able to answer these questions:

1. Which country has an absolute advantage in producing shoes and which country has an absolute advantage in producing soybeans?

2. Which country has a comparative advantage in producing shoes and which country has a comparative advantage in producing soybeans?

Did you write down your answers? Please do that now. OK, let's see if we got the same answers:

1. The United States has an absolute advantage in producing both shoes and soybeans.

2. The United States has a comparative advantage in producing soybeans, while China enjoys a comparative advantage in producing shoes.

So it will pay for the United States to trade soybeans for Chinese shoes. And, of course, it will pay for the Chinese to trade their shoes for our soybeans.

I'd like to take credit for this example, but it actually appeared in the Federal Reserve Bank of Dallas's 2003 annual report. As we'll see, trade expands the economic pies of both China and the United States, leaving the consumers of both nations much better off than before they traded. That, indeed, is the reason why economists love free trade.

Table B shows China and the U.S. before and after trade. Before trade, China produced 500 pairs of shoes and the United States produced 300 pairs. After trade, China produced all the shoes—all 2,000 pairs. So total shoe production after trade rose from 800 pairs to 2,000 pairs.

Now let's see what happened to soybean production, which is shown in Table B. Before trade, the U.S. produced 4,000 bushels, while China produced 3,000. After trade the U.S. produced 10,000 bushels, while China did not produce any soybeans. So total output of soybeans rose from 7,000 before trade to 10,000 after trade.

Because trade enabled the U.S. to specialize in soybean production, and China to specialize in shoe production, the total output of both goods rose very substantially.

At the bottom of Table B, we have consumption of shoes and soybeans in both countries. Trade enabled China to increase its consumption of shoes from 500 pairs

Table A Hypothetical Labor Force and Output, U.S. and China*

	CHINA	UNITED STATES
Labor Force	500	100
Output per Worker		
Shoes (pairs)	4	5
Soybeans (bushels)	8	100

Table B Hypothetical Employment, Production, and Consumption, U.S. and China*

	CHINA		UNITED STATES	
	No Trade	Free Trade	No Trade	Free Trade
Employment				
Shoes	125	500	60	0
Soybeans	375	0	40	100
Production				
Shoes	500	2,000	300	0
Soybeans	3,000	0	4,000	10,000
Consumption				
Shoes	500	1,500	300	500
Soybeans	3,000	5,000	4,000	5,000

to 1,500 pairs. In the U.S., shoe consumption rose from 300 pairs to 500. Similarly, soybean consumption rose from 3,000 bushels to 5,000 in China, while in the U.S. it rose from 4,000 to 5,000.

Let's sum up. China enjoyed a comparative advantage in producing shoes, while the U.S. had a comparative advantage in producing soybeans. By specializing in the good each nation produced most efficiently, and then trading for the other good, both nations were much better off.

---

*Table A and Table B are reproduced from the 2003 Annual Report of the Federal Reserve Bank of Dallas, p. 16.

Sweatshop Labor

Sweatshop employees put in very long hours under very poor working conditions for very low pay. Most of the clothing and footwear we import is produced by sweatshops. Reebok, Nike, Liz Claiborne, the Gap, J.C. Penney, Sears-Kmart, Walmart, Disney, and Target are some of the leading sellers of goods made in sweatshops in Asia and Latin America.

In El Salvador alone, 200 factories make clothing for the American market. In 1995, conditions were so bad in her factory, a contractor for the Gap, Abigail Martinez, helped lead a strike that got the Gap's attention. This is a *New York Times* then-and-now account:

Six years ago, Abigail Martinez earned 55 cents an hour sewing cotton tops and khaki pants. Back then, she says, workers were made to spend 18-hour days in an unventilated factory with undrinkable water. Employees who displeased the bosses were denied bathroom breaks or occasionally made to sweep outside all morning in the broiling sun.

Today, she and other workers have coffee breaks and lunch on an outdoor terrace cafeteria. Bathrooms are unlocked, the factory is breezy and clean, and employees can complain to a board of independent monitors if they feel abused.

The changes are a result of efforts by Gap, the big clothing chain, to improve working conditions at this independent factory, one of many that supply its clothes.

Yet Ms. Martinez today earns 60 cents an hour, only 5 cents more than six years ago.

But consider the alternative. If Abigail Martinez quits, will she get a better job? And if wages in El Salvador were to rise, the Gap and other foreign clothing firms would move to another low-wage country.

In 2003 *BusinessWeek* reported that a dozen companies belonging to the Fair Labor Association (www.fairlabor.org) made public labor audits of the overseas factories that produce their products. Among their findings were that workers were forced to do overtime and work seven straight days, there were arbitrary firings, very limited drinking water, widespread sexual harassment, dirty toilets, no sick leave, and no pay stubs.

Sources: Leslie Kaufman and David Gonzalez, "Labor Standards Clash with Global Reality," *The New York Times,* April 24, 2001, p. A1; Aaron Bernstein, "Sweatshops: Finally, Airing the Dirty Linen," *Business-Week,* June 23, 2003, p. 100.

defeated Iraq. And if there were a third world war we would certainly not have to worry about a cutoff of needed war material because the war would last only a few minutes.

If the national security argument is applied only to limited or local wars rather than to worldwide wars, it is possible that we do need to maintain certain defense-related industries. A justification that the United States should make its own aircraft, ordnance (bombs and artillery shells), and nuclear submarines might well be valid on a national security basis. But these industries have done extremely well in international markets and are hardly in need of protection.

Are American industries still infant industries?

(2) The Infant Industry Argument   In the late 18th century American manufacturers clamored for protection against "unfair" British competition. British manufacturers were "dumping" their products on our shores. By pricing their goods below cost, the British would drive infant American manufacturers out of business. Once their American competition was out of the way, the British companies would jack up their prices.

Whatever validity this reasoning once had has long since vanished. American manufactured products are no longer produced by infant industries being swamped by foreign giants. About the best that can be said is that some of our infant industries never matured, while others went well beyond the point of maturity and actually attained senility. Perhaps a senile industry argument might be more applicable to such stalwarts as steel, textiles, clothing, and automobiles.

How can the United States compete against countries that pay sweatshop wages?

(3) The Low-Wage Argument   The reasoning here is best summed up by this question: How can American workers compete with foreigners who are paid sweatshop wages (see box)? Certain goods and services are very labor intensive (that is, labor constitutes most or nearly all of the resource costs). Clothing manufacturing, domestic work, rice cultivation, most kinds of assembly-line work, and repetitive clerical work are examples. There is no reason for American firms to compete with foreign firms to provide these goods and services.

Why *are* certain workers paid higher wage rates than others? Why *are* some countries high-wage countries, while others are low-wage countries? In general, high-wage workers produce more than low-wage workers. The main reason workers in high-wage countries produce more is that they have more capital with which to work than do workers in low-wage countries.

Why are some countries high-wage countries, while others are low-wage countries?

And so labor was paid more in the United States than almost anywhere else in the world during the three decades following World War II because we had more capital (plant and equipment) per worker than any other country. But as other countries succeeded in rebuilding and adding to their capital, our advantage disappeared.

The low-wage countries of Asia, Africa, and Latin America have a competitive advantage. So do the high-capital countries of Japan, the United States, Canada, and the European Union. Why not combine the best of both worlds—low wages and high capital?

That's just what multinational corporations have done around the world. Just across the Rio Grande in northern Mexico, thousands of factories churn out everything from cars and refrigerators to water beds and garage-door openers; they then ship most of these goods back into the United States. The factories are called *maquiladoras,* from the Mexican word for handwork. The workers are seldom paid much more than $1 an hour, less than a quarter of the U.S. minimum wage of $7.25.

The question, then, is how to deal with low-wage competition. The answer is to deal with it the way we always have. We have always imported labor-intensive goods—sugar, handmade rugs, wood carvings, even Chinese back scratchers—because they were cheap. By specializing in the production of goods and services in which we excel, we can use the proceeds to buy the goods and services produced by people who work for very low wages.

(4) The Employment Argument   Hasn't the flood of imports thrown millions of Americans out of work? There is no denying that hundreds of thousands of workers in each of the industries with stiff foreign competition—autos, steel, textiles, clothing, consumer electronics, and petroleum—have lost their jobs due to this competition. If we had restricted our imports of these goods by means of tariffs or quotas, most of these jobs could have been saved.

But the governments of our foreign competitors would have reciprocated by restricting our exports. Furthermore, a nation pays for its imports by selling its exports. By curbing our imports, we will be depriving other nations of the earnings they need to buy our exports. In sum, if we restrict our imports, our exports will go down as well.

If we restrict our imports, our exports will decline.

The jobs we save in steel, autos, textiles, clothing, consumer electronics, and petroleum will be lost in our traditional export industries—machinery, office equipment, aircraft, chemicals, computer software, and agricultural products. From an economic standpoint, this would involve a considerable loss because we would be shifting production from our relatively efficient export industries to our relatively inefficient import industries. Is that any way to run an economy?

Nevertheless, you may ask about the human cost. What happens to the workers who are thrown out of work by foreign competition? Should their employers help them or should the government? And what can be done to help them? Ideally, these displaced workers should be retrained and possibly relocated to work in our relatively efficient industries. Those who cannot be retrained or cannot move should be given some form of work, if only to keep them off the welfare rolls.

What about the workers who lose their jobs because of imports?

Who should help these displaced workers adjust? In a sense, their employers are responsible because these people were loyal and productive employees for perhaps 20 or 30 years. Often, however, the companies that should bear most of the responsibility for helping their employees are hardly in a position to do so. After all, they wouldn't be laying off workers if business were good to begin with.

Does the United States Win or Lose from Globalization?

There is no question that the forces of globalization have raised the living standards of all trading nations. Worldwide competition has forced every trading nation to become much more efficient. American firms must compete not only against each other, but increasingly against their counterparts based all over the world.

Ask yourself this question: Am I better off today than my parents were when they were my age? Just look at the huge array of consumer goods the average person enjoys today that did not even exist 25 or 30 years ago. Nearly all of them—personal computers, cell phones, DVD players, iPods, PlayStations, BlackBerry devices, for example—are imported from abroad. Had globalization not progressed as quickly, some of these goods would not have been available to the average American.

No one has ever disputed that globalization has made some people winners and others losers. As consumers, of course, we're all winners, but how many of us have already lost our jobs or will lose them over the next few years?

So far most of the work sent abroad has been labor-intensive and lower skilled, so the job losses were limited to blue-collar factory workers. As long as we're specializing in high skilled work, and have plenty of it, the job losses are confined to our most poorly educated and low skilled workers.

But now we are seeing more and more offshoring of so-called white-collar jobs, which are performed by nearly half our workforce. Today that brainpower can zip around the world at low cost, and a global labor market for skilled workers seems to be emerging for the first time—and has the potential to upset traditional notions of national specialization.

What if blue- and white-collar employees alike are thrown into the global labor pool? Tens of millions of workers could end up losing more than they gain in lower prices.

Let's take a closer look at globalization's job losers. Just 30 percent of laid-off workers earn the same or more after three years. In fact only 68 percent even hold a job at that point, while the rest are unemployed, retired, or just not in the labor force. On average, those reemployed earn 10 percent less than they did on their old jobs.

You might not even need to lose your job to be adversely affected by globalization. What if you found yourself competing against much lower-paid foreign professionals, like many of today's radiologists, programmers, and software writers? Or what if you found yourself in a profession being crowded by thousands of laid-off Americans? All you would need would be a simple supply and demand graph to show you that your wage rate would be going down.

Ten years ago economists were virtually unanimous in extolling the advantages of globalization. But now, a growing minority is not so sure. While there's no holding back the tide of globalization, one can wonder if there isn't more we could do to ensure that all of our economic boats rise with the tide.

That leaves the party of last resort: the federal government. What does the federal government do for workers who are displaced by foreign competition? Not very much. These workers receive extended unemployment benefits, are eligible for job retraining, and may receive some moving expenses. But the bottom line is that a middle-aged worker who loses her $20-an-hour job will probably not find another one that pays close to that, and government programs will not begin to compensate for this loss (see box, "Does the United States Win or Lose from Globalization?").

Tariffs or Quotas

Although economists are loathe to be in such a situation, suppose it came down to choosing between the two main forms of protection: tariffs and import quotas. Which would be better? Or, more accurately, which is the lesser of two evils?

A tariff is a tax on imports.

A tariff is a tax on imports. Throughout most of U.S. history until World War I, the tariff was our main source of federal revenue. The United States, which has lower tariffs than most other countries, charges less than 5 percent of the value of most imports.

A quota is a limit on the import of certain goods.

A quota is a limit on the import of certain goods. Sometimes this is a legal limit (as in the case of steel, apparel, textiles and sugar), and sometimes it is a "voluntary" limit (as was the case with cars from Japan). In the early and mid-1980s the Japanese limited their export of cars to the United States to fewer than 2.5 million a year, but only because of the threat of more stringent legal limits in the form of higher tariffs.

We have long maintained textile import quotas, which, in recent years, have been especially effective in keeping out low-priced Chinese textiles. Although the quotas on Chinese textiles were ostensibly removed on New Year's day of 2005, American textile producers were able to get nearly half reinstated later in the year. In addition we persuaded the Chinese to voluntarily adhere to quotas.

Both tariffs and quotas raise the price that consumers in the importing country must pay. However, there are three important differences in the effects of tariffs and quotas.

First, the federal government receives the proceeds of a tariff. Under import quotas there *are* no tax revenues.

Second, a tariff affects all foreign sellers equally, but import quotas are directed against particular sellers on an arbitrary basis. For example, in 1986 various Japanese car manufacturers had widely varying quotas, but the import of South Korean Hyundais was unrestricted.

A third difference involves relative efficiency. Efficient foreign producers will be able to pay a uniform tariff that less efficient producers will not be able to meet. But arbitrary import quotas may allow relatively inefficient foreign producers to send us their goods while keeping out those of their more efficient competitors. This comes down to somewhat higher prices for the American consumer because less efficient producers will charge higher prices than more efficient producers.

Figure 4 illustrates the effects of a tariff. A $50 tariff on cameras raises the price of a camera from $200 to about $245. And it causes the quantity purchased to fall from 2.25 million to 2.1 million.

Incidentally, a tariff, like any other excise tax, causes a decrease in supply—that is, a smaller quantity is supplied at every possible price. The effect of taxes on supply was discussed at length near the end of the elasticities of demand and supply chapter in *Economics* and *Microeconomics*.

To summarize, tariffs are better than quotas, but free trade is best. In the long run, the American consumer must pay for trade restrictions in the form of higher prices.

Tariffs are better than quotas, but free trade is best.

Conclusion

The case for free trade is one of the cornerstones of economics. (See the box, "Petition of the Candlemakers to Shut Out the Sun.") Economics is all about the efficient allocation of scarce resources, so there is no reason why this efficient allocation should not be

No nation was ever ruined by trade.

—Benjamin Franklin

Figure 4

A Tariff Lowers Supply
This $50 tariff lowers supply from S_1 to S_2. Price rises from $200 to about $245, and quantity purchased falls from 2.25 million to 2.1 million. We move from equilibrium point E_1 to E_2. The tariff of $50 is the vertical distance between S_1 and S_2.

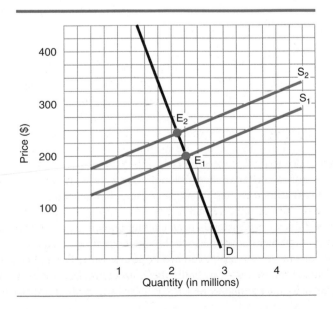

Petition of the Candlemakers to Shut Out the Sun

The case of protection against "unfair" competition was extended to its absurd conclusion by Frédéric Bastiat, a mid-19th-century French economist who wrote an imagined petition to the Chamber of Deputies. Parts of that petition follow.

We are suffering from the intolerable competition of a foreign rival, placed, it would seem, in a condition so far superior to ours for the production of light, that he absolutely inundates our national market with it at a price fabulously reduced. The moment he shows himself, our trade leaves us—all consumers apply to him, and a branch of native industry, having countless ramifications, is all at once rendered completely stagnant. This rival . . . is no other than the Sun. What we pray for is, that it may please you to pass a law ordering the shutting up of all windows, skylights, dormerwindows, outside and inside shutters, curtains, blinds, bull's eyes; in a word, of all openings, holes, chinks, clefts, and fissures, by or through which the light of the sun has been in use to enter houses . . .*

Frédéric Bastiat,
19th-century French economist

*Frédéric Bastiat, *Economic Sophisms* (Edinburgh: Oliver and Boyd, Tweeddale Court, 1873), pp. 49–53.

applied beyond national boundaries. A baseball team that has more pitchers than it knows what to do with but needs a good-hitting shortstop will trade that extra pitcher or two for the shortstop. It will trade with a team that has an extra shortstop but needs more pitching. This trade will help both teams.

International trade helps every country; we all have higher living standards because of it. To the degree that we can remove the tariffs, import quotas, and other impediments to free trade, we will all be better off.

It has been estimated that lower-priced imports kept the rate of inflation one or two points below what it would otherwise have been since the mid-1980s. This is still another important reason for not restricting imports.

Imports pressure American companies to become more efficient. It is obvious, for example, that Toyota, Nissan, Honda, and the other Japanese automakers drove Detroit to make far better cars with far fewer workers than it used to. Indeed, our annual productivity gains of 10 percent would have been inconceivable without the spur of Japanese competition. Our chemical, steel, pharmaceutical, computer, textile, apparel, commercial aircraft, machine tool, paper copier, and semiconductor industries have all been spurred to much higher levels of efficiency by their foreign competitors.

None of this is to deny that there are problems. The millions of workers who have lost their jobs due to foreign competition cannot be expected to cheerfully make personal sacrifices in the interest of the greater national economic well-being. In the long run we may all be better off if there is worldwide free trade, but, as John Maynard Keynes once noted, "In the long run we are all dead."

The economics profession nearly unanimously backs free trade.

While the economics profession is nearly unanimous in advocating free trade, there is nearly complete disagreement over what to do about our huge trade deficit. If we do nothing, as fervent free traders advocate, can we count on our trade imbalance to eventually correct itself? Or will foreigners—especially the Japanese and Chinese—continue to outsell us? These are just two of the questions I'll try to answer in the third part of this chapter.

Part III: The Practice of International Trade

What Are the Causes of Our Trade Imbalance?

Here are the top five reasons for our huge and growing trade imbalance.

(1) We Have Become a Nation of Consumption Junkies The United States is the world's greatest consumption superpower. Today we are borrowing over $2 billion a day from foreigners to finance our consumption habit. Most Americans believe that somehow we're entitled to all these goods and services, even if we need to borrow to pay for them.

We are notoriously poor savers. Indeed since 2005 we have not been able to save even 1 percent of our disposable personal income. If you're not saving, it's hard to invest. Luckily foreign savers have been picking up the slack by lending us hundreds of billions of dollars a year. But this windfall will not continue indefinitely.

We are consuming more than we are producing, borrowing more than we are saving, and spending more than we are earning.

—Murray Weidenbaum

(2) Huge Oil Imports Because we are so dependent on gasoline for transportation, we import two thirds of our oil. And yet, we pay just a fraction of what the citizens of other industrial nations pay for gasoline. As our domestic production of oil continues to decline, our dependency on oil imports will keep growing. In 2009 the cost of our oil imports, driven by tight global supplies and high prices, reached a record high of $350 billion, accounting for nearly our entire trade deficit.

Why are we so dependent on oil imports? Until the 1960s, as the world's leading producer, we needed to import no more than 15 percent of our oil. But American production peaked in 1970, and as our need for oil grew rapidly with suburbanization, we had to import more and more. Today we must get two-thirds of our oil from abroad.

Other major industrial countries, most notably Japan and the members of the European Union, were better able to deal with their need for oil, even though few produced much of their own. None had anything like the suburban sprawl of the United States, so their citizens were not nearly as dependent on automobile transportation. And then too, unlike Americans, their citizens were willing to pay $3 or $4 a gallon in taxes, which provided a powerful incentive to conserve gasoline.

(3) Our Failing Educational System The American educational system, once second to none, is now second to practically everyone's. The illiterate high school graduate is no longer the rare exception, and about one-third of all college freshmen need remedial work in the three Rs—reading, writing, and arithmetic. Nearly every college—even the Ivy League schools—has special classes for students unprepared to do college work. In test after test, Americans rank at or near the bottom of the industrial countries.

Half our high school math and science teachers are unqualified to teach those subjects. In Florida and in Massachusetts, thousands of teachers failed exams testing them on the very subject matter they had been hired to teach. No wonder that our educational system turns out one million functional illiterates every year—not exactly job candidates for today's high-tech economy.

An attempt to correct some of the problems of our failing educational system was made by President George W. Bush when he got Congress to pass the "Leave No Child Behind" law, which mandated testing of children at different grade levels to ensure that all children would meet certain national educational standards. Though this legislation was passed with widespread bipartisan support, its implementation has proven very controversial, and widespread opposition has arisen from state and local educational establishments.

While we're on the subject, what do you think of *this* educational reform? Every teacher must pass an 8th grade reading test and every math teacher must pass a test

Our schools are turning out students who cannot read or write.

covering the math that she or he teaches. Whenever this idea is proposed, you can't imagine the opposition it generates from teachers' unions and other interest groups.

Most of the science, math, and computer graduate students receiving PhDs in our universities are foreigners, more and more of whom are returning home, mainly to China, India, and other Asian countries. As our manufacturing base erodes, we are losing our cutting-edge intellectual superiority in product design, software engineering, and other vital fields. Today, most patent applications are made by foreigners, and in the not too distant future, the term "Made in America" may become an anachronism.

(4) The Role of Multinationals   Before the 1960s the vast low-wage workforces of the world's poorer nations were no threat to the workers in the high-wage economies like the United States. Our workers were many times more productive than those in the poorer nations because they had so much more capital to work with.

More capital, higher productivity, and higher wages

All of this began to change in the 1960s as multinational corporations began to move their manufacturing operations offshore to take advantage of this low-wage labor pool. By providing these workers with sufficient plant and equipment, the multinationals were able to increase their productivity to the level of American assembly-line workers.

The hollow corporation

The term *hollow corporation* gained currency in the last two decades as more and more companies put their names on imported goods. These companies' sole function is to sell such goods as the Dodge Colt or the Panasonic TV, both of which are made in Japan. Yet our import business is not dominated by firms that market goods for foreign producers, but rather by our own multinational corporations that have shifted most of their production overseas. Joel Kurtzman describes their operations:

> These multinationals have transformed themselves from producers of goods to importers and marketers of goods made overseas by their foreign divisions and affiliates. Because so many of our imports come to us in the form of trade between the different divisions of American multinationals, the balance-of-payments deficit has become structurally integrated into our economy.[2]

(5) Relative Growth Rate   So far we've talked about all our deficiencies contributing to our balance of trade deficit. But even our virtues seem to contribute to that deficit. Between 1995 and 2007 we have had one of the highest rates of economic growth in the industrialized world. Countries with high economic growth rates import more goods and services than they would have if they had low growth rates.

(6) Our Shrinking Manufacturing Base   Still another reason for our huge and growing trade imbalance is that since the 1960s we've lost a good part of our manufacturing base as American companies shipped production and jobs abroad. Cars, steel, consumer electronics, computers, textiles, and clothing were once among our leading exports, but millions of jobs in those industries have disappeared. Still, for decades, our chemical industry seemed largely immune from foreign competition. No more. Although that industry will certainly not disappear any time soon, it may be fighting a losing battle against foreign competitors who can undersell us (see the box, "The Chemical Industry in Decline").

In recent years the U.S. dollar has been high relative to the currencies of our trading partners—most notably to the Chinese yuan. Consequently the prices of our exports have been higher, and we sold less to foreigners than if the dollar had been lower. Similarly, the prices of our imports have been higher, and we have been buying more from foreigners than if the dollar were lower. We'll address this issue at length in the next chapter.

---

[2]Joel Kurtzman, *The Decline and Crash of the American Economy* (New York: W. W. Norton, 1988), p. 131.

The Chemical Industry in Decline

Through the late 1990s, the United States led the world in making chemicals, with the largest market, the latest technology, and the best know-how. And U.S. plants had a natural advantage thanks to an abundant supply of cheap natural gas, a building block for plastics, fertilizers, and even pharmaceuticals. Today none of that is true. U.S. natural gas prices are the highest in the world, while the bigger, faster growing markets are overseas. And new facilities in the developing world are as sophisticated and productive as those in the United States.

Some 120 chemical plants are being built around the world with price tags of $1 billion or more. Only one of those plants will be in the United States, but 50 are being built in China. The reason: It's becoming much too costly to produce chemicals in the United States.

As chemical production facilities close across the United States—Dow Chemical has closed over 25 percent of its plants since the new millennium—the next casualty will be the engineers and scientists doing workaday research. In 2004, Du Pont opened a lab in Shanghai that has grown into a basic research center with 200 scientists.

Our balance of trade in chemicals had long been one of our economic mainstays. As recently as 1997 we had a $20 billion surplus. But just six years later that surplus became a $10 billion deficit.

Our $500 billion chemical industry will not disappear overnight, but its demise is emblematic of the decline and fall of the entire American manufacturing sector. And with respect to our trade deficit, our chemical industry, instead of holding down the deficit, is becoming a major contributor.

Part IV: Our Trade Deficit with Japan and China

For most of the 1980s and 1990s, Japan was our fiercest trade competitor. In addition, year after year we ran huge trade deficits with that country. In the long run, however, our largest trade deficits are with China, which overtook Japan in 2000. (See Figure 5.)

Many goods once made elsewhere in Asia—in Japan, Taiwan, Singapore, South Korea—are now produced in foreign-owned factories that have been moved to China. So our growing deficit with China is partially offset by declining deficits with other Asian nations.

Japanese Trading Practices

The American economy has long been, by far, the largest in the world. But in the years after World War II, as the only major nation with an undamaged economy, we produced half the world's manufactured goods. Our economy had been built on the dual foundations of mass production and mass consumption. Basically we mass produced consumer goods, which were then sold to the vast American market.

The Japanese economic infrastructure had been largely destroyed by our relentless bombings during the war. And even if the Japanese had somehow been able to produce low-cost consumer goods, their market was not only much smaller than the American market, but much, much poorer. So the Japanese government and business leaders developed a strategy to rebuild their economy. They would flood the rich American market with very cheap, low-end consumer goods, and then move up the economic feeding chain, eventually producing black and white TVs, color TVs, motorcycles, and cars.

The Japanese compete not just on the basis of price but on the basis of product quality. They have taken our system of mass production one step further, turning out a wide range of customized variations, while we continue to concentrate largely on single standardized products.

The Japanese compete on the basis of price and quality.

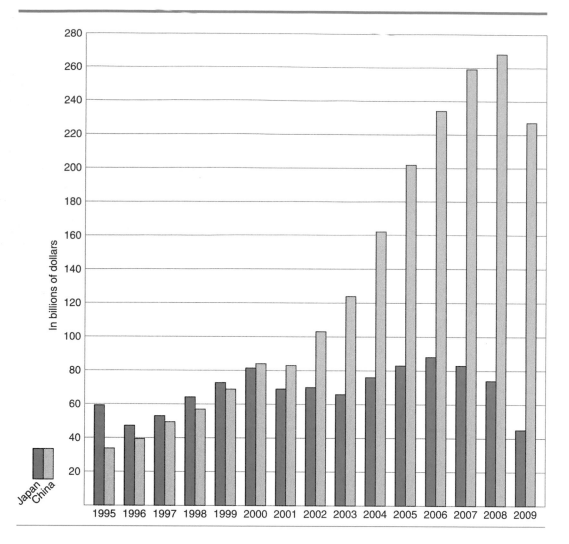

Figure 5

U.S. Trade Deficit with Japan and China, 1995–2009
Our deficit with China grew steadily since 1990 and has surpassed our deficit with Japan.
Source: U.S. Dept. of Census.

Our Trade Deficit with China

When we began trading with China in the mid-1970s, after President Richard Nixon's historic trip to open relations with that nation, American exporters had great hopes that the world's most populous nation would eventually become the world's largest consumer market. Three decades later, toys, athletic shoes, clothing, textiles, and other relatively low-price manufactured goods are flooding into the United States, along with an increasing stream of higher-priced goods such as tools, auto parts, electronic gear, microwave ovens, and personal computers. Although U.S. exports to China are growing rapidly, our exports are less than one-fourth of our imports.

Why are we importing so much from China? Mainly because U.S. retailers are seeking the cheapest goods available and finding them in China. Walmart Stores imported $27 billion worth of goods in 2009; and Target, Sears-Kmart, Toys 'R' Us, and other giant retailers also found that the price was right in China.

One of the big trade issues between China and the United States is that thousands of Chinese factories, many controlled by top officers of the Chinese army, have been making unauthorized, or knock-off, copies of American movies, CDs, and most important, computer software. Days after the premier of the latest *Terminator* film in the U.S., pirate copies were on sale throughout China. More than 90 percent of the movies, music, and software are illegal copies sold at a fraction of the original price.

It's bad enough that the Chinese are pirating American goods and services and selling them in their own country. But now they're taking their piracy a step further. In 2005, the U.S. Patent and Trademark Office said that 66 percent of the counterfeit goods seized at American borders now come from China, up from just 16 percent five years before. Indeed Chinese-made fakes are so good that bogus Duracell batteries, Oral-B toothbrushes, and pretend Prestobarba disposable razors are sold all over the world. And the U.S. Chamber of Commerce says that Chinese piracy and counterfeiting have cost American industry over $200 billion a year.

Our trade deficits with China have been running over $200 billion a year since 2005. These are the largest deficits ever recorded by one country with another country. But closer inspection reveals that our trade deficit with China is grossly overstated. Most often "made in China" is actually made elsewhere—by multinational companies in Japan, South Korea, Taiwan, and the United States, that are using China as the final assembly station in their vast global production networks. Indeed, about 60 percent of this country's exports are controlled by foreign companies. A Barbie doll may cost $20, but China gets only about 35 cents of that. In recent years, however, the Chinese government has insisted that increasing proportions of its manufactured goods actually be made in China. For example, solar panels—of which China is the leading producer—must have at least 75 percent Chinese content.

While China had a huge trade surplus with the United States, it also had a huge trade deficit with the rest of Asia in 2009. What were the Chinese importing? Much of their imports were components of television sets, cars, refrigerators, microwave ovens, and other consumer electronics. When these products were assembled and shipped out as final products, China's exports appeared to be much greater than they actually were. Consequently its trade surplus with the United States was greatly exaggerated.

Since the beginning of the new millennium we have lost over 5 million manufacturing jobs. Some of these losses may be attributed to China, but probably other nations and certainly the huge multinational corporations—many of which are based in the United States—should bear much more of the blame. And it is the American consumer who has benefited the most from the flood of low-cost goods that were assembled, if not made, in China.

Trading with China and Japan: More Differences than Similarities

There is one striking similarity between the Japanese and Chinese development models. Both were pulled by the engine provided by the huge American market. After World War II, the only consumers who had the money to buy Japanese exports were the Americans. So the Japanese economic recovery plan was, essentially, a no-brainer. Close the much smaller Japanese home market to American producers, while selling the bulk of their manufactures to the rich Americans.

When the Chinese launched their industrial development plan in the early 1980s, they followed a similar strategy—create an export platform on the East China coast to sell cheap manufactured goods to the rich Americans, and, to a lesser degree, to the rich consumers of Western Europe and Japan. The Chinese, unlike the Japanese before them, had a relatively open economy. Foreign manufacturers were more than welcome to set up shop in China.

Was the Chinese market closed to foreigners? *What* market? Few Chinese consumers had the money to buy relatively expensive imported goods. But as Chinese economic development really began to take off, and relatively cheap Chinese manufactured products flooded the world, the American consumer could no longer finance this expansion. No problem. The Chinese government simply lent Americans' much of the money we needed each year to finance our huge and growing trade deficit.

During the Japanese industrial revival of the 1950s and 1960s, their manufacturers went head-to-head with ours. In the production of black and white TVs, and later, color TVs, the Japanese built on our technology, undersold American manufacturers in the vast American market, while the Japanese market remained closed to American TVs. As a result, American TV manufacturers were driven out of business.

Our trading position with Japan is very much like a colony and a colonial power. Our trading relationship with the Chinese is very different. We send airplanes, computers, movies, compact disks, cars, cigarettes, power-generating equipment, and computer software in exchanges for toys, clothing, shoes, and low-end consumer electronics. Much of what they're sending to us used to come from Japan back in the 1950s. "Made in Japan" has been replaced by "Made in China."

Our huge trade deficit with China will probably continue to grow, but even more importantly, its entire nature is rapidly evolving. We have long assumed this division of labor: The Chinese would focus on lower-skill sectors, while the United States would dominate the knowledge-intensive industries. But as Harvard economist Richard B. Freeman observed, "What is stunning about China is that for the first time we have a huge, poor country that can compete both with very low wages and in high tech. Combine the two, and America has a problem."

So far the hardest hit industries have been those that were destined to migrate to low-cost nations anyway. But now China is moving into more advanced industries where America remains competitive, adding state-of-the-art capacity in motor vehicles, specialty steel, petrochemicals, and microchips. In other words, the United States has been losing its lead in the knowledge economy, while China evolves from our sweatshop to our competitor.

Japanese gains in the production of semiconductors, machine tools, steel, autos, TVs, and VCRs led directly to the loss of millions of well-paying American jobs. Although Chinese products may compete on a broader scale with American goods in the future, Chinese exports so far have generally not translated into major job losses in the United States. China's leading exports are products that have not been produced in large quantity by American factories for more than a decade.

The Chinese, like the Japanese before them, have insisted on licensing agreements and large-scale transfer of technology as the price for agreeing to imports. These agreements, of course, lead to the eventual elimination of imports from the United States. However, the Chinese have taken this process one step further. Sometimes, instead of entering into licensing agreements, Chinese factories simply manufacture pirated versions, or knock-offs, of American videos, CDs, computer software, and designer apparel.

From the mid-1980s through the mid-1990s we engaged in a good deal of Japan-bashing, blaming that country for our growing trade deficit. To a large degree our complaints were justified. Not only were our manufacturing jobs migrating to Japan, but the Japanese market was largely closed to American exports.

In recent years we have shifted much of the blame to China, with whom we now run our largest trade deficit (see Figure 5). But the nature of our trade deficit with China today is not, in any sense, like our deficit with Japan two decades ago. Japan was competing in businesses that were at the heart of the American economy. But our imports from China—clothing, toys, shoes, textiles, TVs, and consumer electronics—are mainly merchandise we stopped making here decades ago. Furthermore, China is remarkably open to trade. Between 1995 and 2005, our exports to China almost quadrupled. In coming years, this rapid growth will continue as the Chinese consumer market continues its rapid expansion.

My own prediction is that by 2015, not only will we be running still larger trade deficits with China, but we will be importing more than a million very low-priced Chinese cars each year. By then China bashing may have been elevated from an art form to the national sport.

Final Word

Two major issues have been raised in this chapter. First, that there are clear advantages to free trade. And second, that the United States, which has been a strong free trade advocate, has been running large and growing trade deficits. Let's take one more look at both issues.

Free Trade in Word and Deed

Going back to the early 1980s, every president has strongly advocated the principle of free trade and has helped reduce tariffs and other trade barriers throughout the world. Robert Zoellick, the chief trade negotiator during the first term of President George W. Bush, pushed various proposals within the World Trade Organization to lower tariffs and export subsidies, as well as to remove all barriers to the free flow of goods and services across national borders. European Union members, most notably France, have refused to lower subsidies.

Members of the European Union called our free trade advocacy hypocritical when in March 2002, President Bush raised tariffs on imported steel. In fact they brought a case against the United States before the World Trade Court. In December 2003, President Bush rescinded the tariffs.

Like his immediate predecessor, President Barack Obama has advocated free trade, at least in principle. But just eight months after taking office, he imposed a 35 percent tariff on Chinese tires. This was done at the behest of the United Steelworkers Union after the U.S. International Trade Commission ruled that a huge increase in tire imports had cost an estimated 5,000 workers their jobs.

A second deviation from our free trade policy is our huge agricultural subsidies—averaging almost $20 billion a year. The world's poorer nations, where up to 90 percent of the labor force is engaged in agriculture, have demanded that the United States, the European Union, and other rich nations abolish these subsidies, which, clearly, make it impossible for the poorer nations to sell their agricultural goods on the world market (see the box, "Farm Subsidies and the Poorer Nations").

On balance, the United States has long been a free trading nation. Zoellick was very active in negotiating free trade agreements with Singapore, Chile, South Africa,

Farm Subsidies and the Poorer Nations

The world richest countries provide over $300 billion in subsidies to their farmers. These subsidies enable farmers from the United States, the European Union, Canada, and Australia to export much of their output at artificially low prices. The farmers of the world's poorer nations cannot match these low prices, so they are largely shut out of world agricultural markets. Consequently these nations cannot export their agricultural surpluses and get foreign exchange.

Mexico is the world's birthplace of corn. But after the signing of the North American Free Trade Agreement (NAFTA) in 1994, American farmers flooded the Mexican market with low-priced corn. Since then, the price of Mexican corn fell more than 70 percent, severely reducing the incomes of the 15 million Mexicans who depend on corn for their livelihood.

Of the $20 billion a year that American taxpayers shell out in farm subsidies, more than $10 billion goes to corn farmers. This allows them to sell their corn at prices far below what it cost them to produce it. In effect, then, the American taxpayer has subsidized the shipment of cheap corn to Mexico, where it has pushed the poorest farmers out of business.

Japan's subsidies are 59 percent of the value of production, while those of the European Union are 34 percent of production and in the United States they are 21 percent. Will these nations agree to lower or eliminate these subsidies? Probably not in *our* lifetime. It would be political suicide. Imagine what would happen to all those senators and representatives from the farm states, not to mention all those presidential electoral votes.

and other countries. Our $20 billion in agricultural subsidies are just 6 percent of the annual subsidies provided to farmers in the world's richest countries.

Reducing Our Trade Deficit

No man is an island, entire of itself.

— John Donne

To reduce our overall trade deficit we need to make a combination of four things happen. First, we need to maintain our high rate of productivity growth and keep improving the quality of American goods and services. Second, we need to lower our dependence on oil imports, perhaps by raising the federal tax on gasoline. Third, we must reduce our rapidly rising deficit with China. And finally, we need to face up to the fact that we are a nation of consumption junkies. In sum, we consume much more than we produce, and have done so by running up a multitrillion dollar tab.

Perhaps our best hope to reduce our trade deficit lies with the rapidly expanding Internet, which makes it much easier to provide services of all types—banking, education, consulting, retailing, and even gambling—through websites that are globally accessible. Since the United States has long had a positive trade balance in services, there is good reason to expect the Internet to continue pushing up our export of services.

Current Issue 1: Buy American?

Our nation has long been committed to free trade, but a growing number of Americans believe that we need to curb our imports, largely to keep jobs from being offshored as well as to preserve our economic independence. For much of the time since World War II, Japanese consumers willingly paid more for domestically produced goods than they would have for foreign imports. They did this not just to help Japanese manufacturers through their long recovery from the devastation caused by American bombing during the war, but also in the sometimes misguided belief that somehow Japanese products better met their needs. This practice was best exemplified by the widely accepted claim that Japanese-made skis were better suited than imported skis for the unique Japanese snow.

But the American consumer has never been very susceptible to calls for patriotic buying. Even during the era of bad national feeling toward the French for opposing our 2003 invasion of Iraq, about the best we could do to punish the French was to refer to french fries as "freedom fries." Take *that,* you ingrates! And after all we did for you during World War II! More significantly, during 2003 our imports from France actually went up.

Perhaps a better case for economic nationalism could be made against Saudi Arabia. We now import two thirds of our oil, and that country has long been one of our largest suppliers. Although 15 of the 19 plane hijackers on 9/11 were Saudis, we never considered curbing oil imports from that country, let alone going to war.

Today there's a good deal of China bashing for running $200 billion trade surpluses with us, flooding our stores with low-cost TVs, DVD players, microwave ovens, toys, furniture, and textiles. But all that bad feeling toward the Chinese has not hurt business at Walmart, which sells more Chinese exports than any other company in the world. Back in the early 1970s, when we began running large trade deficits with Japan, our leading Japan basher was Treasury Secretary John Connally, who declared that as far as he was concerned, the Japanese could sit in their Toyotas on the docks of Yokohoma, watching their Sony TVs. Still, through the next two decades, our trade deficit with Japan continued to mount.

The bottom line is that Americans are consumers first, while paying just lip service to economic nationalism. No nation of economic nationalists would run up our long string of record-setting trade deficits. So pass the freedom fries and, in the words of the old Beach Boys song, "I better turn on the lights, so we can ride my Honda tonight."

Current Issue 2: Globalization

While globalization is a relatively new term, it is a process which has been going on for hundreds of years. But it has sped up over the last three decades as we have been moving from hundreds of national economies to a worldwide economy.

A decline in shipping costs, vast improvements in communications, the opening and development of the Chinese economy, and the end of the Cold War have all accelerated the pace of globalization. As a result, billions of people around the globe have become active participants in a free enterprise world economy.

We can define globalization as the unimpeded flow of goods and services, labor, and capital across national borders. It ensures a more efficient allocation of resources, which is what economics is all about.

What makes globalization so controversial is the offshoring of millions of jobs and the decimation of our manufacturing base. In theory, these jobs will be replaced by others—mainly high value-added and high-tech jobs. There's just one problem: we are still waiting for those jobs to be created. And in the meanwhile, hundreds of thousands of high-tech jobs have been offshored.

Those living in the Midwest have seen firsthand how our industrial heartland turned into a rust belt. But that rust belt extends well beyond the borders of Wisconsin, Michigan, Illinois, Indiana, and Ohio. It also runs through most of western and central Pennsylvania, much of upstate New York, as well as the old textile towns of the southeastern states and the steel mills of Birmingham.

Trying to reverse the forces of globalization would be no more successful than trying to hold back the tides. The American consumer buys imported goods if they are at least as good as domestic goods and are cheaper. American business firms shift production overseas if they can cut costs. And finally, foreign savers invest their money in the United States when they can earn a higher return here than elsewhere.

But globalization is one tide that has not raised all boats. As Senator John McCain told Michigan voters during his 2008 presidential campaign: all those automotive industry jobs would not be coming back. Indeed, just a few months later General Motors and Chrysler went bankrupt.

The question we must answer is not how to stop, or even slow, globalization; rather, it is how to best deal with its consequences. Clearly we cannot bring back the millions of manufacturing jobs that have migrated to low-wage countries.

Perhaps the most promising effort so far is sending hundreds of thousands of laid-off blue collar workers to local community colleges to be trained for jobs in expanding industries such as renewable energy and health care. For example, three out of five nurses are educated at community colleges. But until hiring picks up, perhaps in 2011, it won't be clear if retraining will have much of an impact.

One may ask if, on the whole, globalization has been good or bad for the American economy. The easy answer is that it has been a great boon to consumers, but a disaster to workers whose jobs have been offshored. My view is that while most Americans are better off because of globalization, it has contributed substantially to our long-term economic decline. I believe that America is a fading economic power, and, at the end of the next—and last—chapter, I've summed up the reasons for such a pessimistic prognosis.

Questions for Further Thought and Discussion

1. Explain what comparative advantage is. Make up an example to illustrate this concept.
2. What is wrong with having tariffs and quotas? Which is the lesser of the two evils, and why?
3. Explain why globalization is good for the United States. What are the drawbacks of globalization for our economy?

4. What would you suggest we do to reduce our trade deficit?

5. We run huge trade imbalances with two countries. Explain the cause of the imbalances.

6. Should we be worried about our trade deficit? Explain why or why not.

7. What is the economist's case for free trade?

8. *Practical Application:* Can you think of any valid reason for tariff protection? Try to make a case for it.

9. *Web Activity:* How much were our imports, exports, and trade deficit during the last year? Go to www.bea.gov, click on "Survey of Current Business" at the left, then go to "National Data," "National Income and Product Accounts," NIPA tables, and finally, "Gross Domestic Product."

Workbook for Chapter 19 connect ECONOMICS

Name _____ Date _____

Multiple-Choice Questions

Circle the letter that corresponds to the best answer.

1. Our balance of trade _____. (LO2)
   a) has always been positive
   b) turned negative in the mid-1970s
   c) turned negative in the mid-1980s
   d) has always been negative

2. Which makes the most sense economically? (LO2)
   a) Individual self-sufficiency
   b) National self-sufficiency
   c) National specialization
   d) None of these

3. Which statement do you agree with? (LO6, 9)
   a) There are several problems causing our huge trade deficit; there are no easy solutions to these problems.
   b) We could quickly eliminate our trade deficit by raising tariffs.
   c) The main reason we have a large trade deficit is that foreigners refuse to buy American goods and services.
   d) The main reason for our large trade deficit is our relatively low rate of economic growth.

4. The Chinese economic expansion since the early 1980s and the Japanese economic expansion from the late 1940s through the 1980s were _____. (LO7)
   a) virtually identical
   b) both dependent on the American market
   c) based in the economic principles of Karl Marx
   d) based on closing their domestic markets to American goods and services

5. Which statement is false? (LO3)
   a) No nation will engage in trade with another nation unless it will gain by that trade.
   b) The terms of trade will fall somewhere between the domestic exchange equations of the two trading nations.
   c) Most economists advocate free trade.
   d) None of these statements is false.

6. Our largest trade deficit is with _____. (LO7)
   a) Japan   d) Mexico
   b) Canada   e) Germany
   c) China

7. Which one of the following does NOT contribute to our huge trade deficit? (LO6)
   a) Our failing educational system
   b) Our high defense spending
   c) Our high saving rate
   d) Our huge oil imports

8. The least applicable argument for protecting American industry from foreign competition would be the _____ argument. (LO4)
   a) national security   c) low-wage
   b) infant industry   d) employment

9. Imports would be lowered by _____. (LO5)
   a) tariffs only
   b) import quotas only
   c) both tariffs and import quotas
   d) neither tariffs nor import quotas

10. Of these three choices—tariffs, quotas, and free trade—economists like _____ the most and _____ the least. (LO5)
    a) tariffs, quotas   d) free trade, quotas
    b) tariffs, free trade   e) quotas, free trade
    c) free trade, tariffs   f) quotas, tariffs

11. Our biggest annual trade deficit in our history was more than _____ billion. (LO2)
    a) $300
    b) $400
    c) $500
    d) $600
    e) $700

12. Which country regularly counterfeits American goods and services, a practice which costs American industry over $200 billion a year? (LO6)
    a) Mexico
    b) Canada
    c) China
    d) Japan

13. Which would be the most accurate statement with respect to our chemical industry? (LO6)
    a) It is on the decline and now contributes to our balance of trade deficit.
    b) It is large and growing.
    c) It generally provides a trade surplus of about $20 billion a year.
    d) It will almost completely disappear by the year 2015.

14. Which one of these statements is the most accurate? (LO8)
    a) Globalization, on balance, has been very bad for the U.S. economy.
    b) All the effects of globalization have been very good for the U.S. economy.
    c) The best way to reduce our trade deficit is for Congress to pass a law requiring that we buy only American products.
    d) Each of our recent presidents has basically supported the concept of free trade.

15. Our trade deficit with China in 2009 was _____. (LO7)
    a) under $100 billion
    b) between $100 billion and $150 billion
    c) between $150 billion and $200 billion
    d) over $200 billion

16. Statement 1: Our trade deficit with China is larger than our trade deficit with Japan.
    Statement 2: Americans pay lower taxes on gasoline than do the citizens of most of the nations in Western Europe. (LO7)
    a) Statement 1 is true, and statement 2 is false.
    b) Statement 2 is true, and statement 1 is false.
    c) Both statements are true.
    d) Both statements are false.

17. Of the following, our imports of _____ contribute most to our trade deficit. (LO6)
    a) oil
    b) clothing
    c) textiles
    d) consumer electronics

18. Which of the following would best describe our trading relationship with China five years from now? (LO7)
    a) Our trade deficit will be higher and we will be importing a higher proportion of "low-skill" products.
    b) Our trade deficit will be higher and we will be importing a higher proportion of "high-skill" products.
    c) Our trade deficit will be lower and we will be importing a higher proportion of "low-skill" products.
    d) Our trade deficit will be lower and we will be importing a higher proportion of "high-skill" products.

19. Which statement is the most accurate? (LO1, 2)
    a) Globalization has made some people winners and others losers.
    b) Globalization has been good for everyone involved.
    c) Globalization has been bad for everyone involved.
    d) Virtually all economists believe that globalization has almost no downside.

20. Which statement is true about how globalization has affected American workers? (LO4, 1)
    a) The only jobs that have been lost or will be lost are blue-collar factory jobs.
    b) Most workers who have lost their jobs because of globalization have ended up in better paying jobs.
    c) Until now a relatively high proportion of Americans perform high-skill, well paying jobs, while a relatively high proportion of Chinese perform low-skill, poorly paying jobs.
    d) Globalization cannot be considered a threat to the livelihoods of highly-skilled, well paid American workers.

21. Which is the most accurate statement? (LO1)

    a) The United States can be described as a purely free trading nation.

    b) The United States is one of the most protectionist nations in the world.

    c) The rich nations provide hundreds of billions of dollars in agricultural subsidies to the poorer nations.

    d) The United States provides smaller agricultural subsidies than does Japan and the European Union.

22. Which statement is true? (LO3)

    a) Comparative advantage is not necessary for trade to take place, but absolute advantage is.

    b) Absolute advantage is not necessary for trade to take place, but comparative advantage is.

    c) Both absolute and comparative advantage are necessary for trade to take place.

    d) Neither absolute nor comparative advantage are necessary for trade to take place.

23. Which statement is true? (LO4)

    a) There are basically no arguments that can be made on behalf of trade protection.

    b) The arguments for trade protection are more valid than the arguments for free trade.

    c) The United States has had a record of fully supporting free trade since the early 20th century.

    d) Much of what we import has been produced by "sweatshop labor."

24. In order for trade between two countries to take place, _____. (LO3)

    a) absolute advantage is necessary

    b) comparative advantage is necessary

    c) both absolute and comparative advantage are necessary

    d) neither absolute nor comparative advantage is necessary

25. Which of the following is the most accurate statement? (LO2, 10)

    a) Americans are very willing to buy domestically produced goods, even if they are more expensive than imported goods.

    b) We import more foreign goods than we did 40 years ago, but merchandise imports are still about the same percentage of our GDP.

    c) In the decades following World War II, the Japanese consumer has strongly favored domestically manufactured goods over imports.

    d) France paid a high economic price when many Americans switched from french fries to freedom fries.

26. Which one of the following statements is the most accurate? (LO11)

    a) Our economy would be much better off if the entire globalization process were reversed.

    b) The globalization process creates billions of winners and no losers.

    c) The process of globalization could easily be reversed if Congress and the president were willing to act.

    d) Globalization ensures a more efficient allocation of resources throughout the world.

27. What accounts for the sharp fall in our trade deficit in 2009? (LO1)

    a) Our imports fell more than our exports.

    b) Our exports fell more than our imports.

    c) The recession was much worse in the rest of the world than in the U.S.

    d) The American consumer made a much greater effort to buy American products to keep jobs in the United States.

Fill-In Questions

1. The basis for international trade is _____. (LO2)

Use Figure 1 to answer questions 2 and 3.

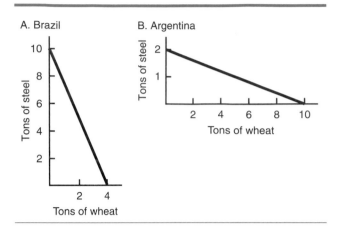

A. Brazil   B. Argentina

Figure 1

2. Brazil is better at producing _____ than at producing _____.
   Argentina is better at producing _____ than at producing _____. (LO3)

3. If 1 ton of steel could be traded for 1 ton of wheat, Brazil would trade its _____ for Argentina's _____. (LO3)

4. _____ is the country with which we have the largest trade imbalance. (LO6, 7)

5. It would greatly reduce our trade deficit the most if we could curb our import of _____. (LO6)

6. Our trade deficit in 2009 was $ _____. (LO2, 6)

7. If our trade deficit with China and Japan were 0, our total trade deficit would be reduced by almost $ _____ billion.

8. The law of comparative advantage states that total output is greatest when each product is made by the country that has the _____. (LO3)

9. A tariff is a tax on _____; a quota is a limit on _____. (LO5)

10. _____ was the last year in which we ran a trade surplus. (LO2)

Problems

Assume Bolivia and Chile use the same amount of resources to produce tin and copper. Figure 2 represents their production possibilities curves. Use it to answer problems 1 through 4.

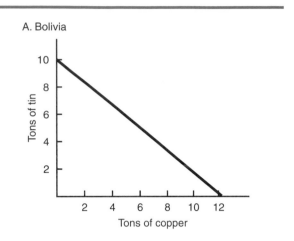

A. Bolivia

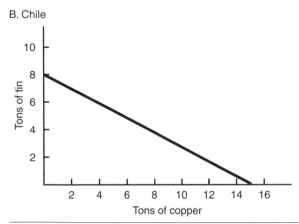

B. Chile

Figure 2

1. Bolivia has a comparative advantage in the production of which metal? (LO3)

2. Chile has a comparative advantage in the production of which metal? (LO3)

3. Bolivia will trade _____ for _____. (LO3)

4. Chile will trade _____ for _____. (LO3)

Chapter 20

International Finance

The United States is the world's largest economy and the world's largest trading nation. We import more than any other nation and we also run the world's largest negative trade balance—averaging over $700 billion between 2005 and 2008.

How do we finance all this trading, and how do we finance our negative balance in trade? International trade is just one part of international finance. The other part encompasses foreign investment, capital inflows and outflows, exchange rates, and other international transactions, as well as the finance of international trade.

One consequence of our mounting trade deficits is that foreigners are buying up American assets. How much of America is foreign owned today, and will most of this country one day be owned by foreigners? Will foreigners soon have enough financial leverage to influence—or even dictate—our economic and foreign policies? Stay tuned, and by the end of the chapter you will learn the answers to these important questions.

LEARNING OBJECTIVES

After reading this chapter you should be able to:

1. Explain how international trade is financed.
2. Define and measure our balance of payments.
3. List and discuss the different exchange rate systems.
4. Summarize how we became a debtor nation.
5. Explain American exceptionality from a historical perspective.

The Mechanics of International Finance

Think of international trade and finance as an extension of our nation's economic activities beyond our borders. Instead of buying microchips from a firm in California, we buy them from a firm in Japan. Instead of selling Cadillacs in Miami, we sell them in Rio de Janeiro. And rather than building a factory in Chicago, we build one in China.

Financing International Trade

When an American importer buys $2 million of wine from a French merchant, how does she pay? In dollars? In euros? In gold? Gold is used only by governments, and then only on very rare occasions, to settle international transactions. Dollars, although sometimes acceptable as an international currency, are not as useful as euros to the

TABLE 1 U.S. Balance of Payments, 2009*
*(in $ billions)**

Current Account	(billions of dollars)
Exports of goods and services	+1,560
Imports of goods and services	−1,952
Net investment income	+ 89
Net transfers	− 118
Current account balance	− 421
Capital Account	
Foreign investment in the U.S.	+435
U.S. investment abroad	−237
Statistical discrepancy	−184
Capital account balance	+421

*Numbers may not add up due to rounding.
Source: *Survey of Current Business,* April 2010; *Economic Indicators,* April 2010.

French wine merchant. After all, the merchant will have to pay his employees and suppliers in euros.

There's no problem exchanging dollars for euros in either the United States or France. Many banks in New York have plenty of euros on hand, and virtually every bank in the country can get euros (as well as other foreign currencies) within a day or two. In Paris and every other French city, dollars are readily available from banks and storefront foreign exchange dealers. On any given day—actually, at any given minute—there is a market exchange rate of euros for dollars; all you need to do is find the right teller and you can exchange your dollars for euros or euros for dollars within minutes.

Financing international trade is part of the economic flow of money and credit that crosses international boundaries every day. For the rest of this chapter we'll see where these funds are going and, in particular, how the United States is involved. We'll begin with the U.S. balance of payments, which provides an accounting of our country's international financial transactions.

The Balance of Payments

Often our balance of payments is confused with our balance of trade. Actually, the balance of trade is a major part of the balance of payments. *The entire flow of U.S. dollars and foreign currencies into and out of the country constitutes the balance of payments,* while the trade balance is just the difference between our imports and our exports.

The balance of payments consists of two parts. First is *the current account, which summarizes all the goods and services produced during the current year that we buy from or sell to foreigners.* The second part is *the capital account, which records the long-term transactions that we conduct with foreigners.* The total of the current and capital accounts will always be zero; that is, our balance of payments never has a deficit or a surplus. When we look at these accounts in more detail, the picture should become clearer.

Table 1 shows the U.S. balance of payments in 2009. The great villain of the piece is our huge trade deficit. Next we have income from investments. From the early 20th century to the early 1980s the United States had a substantial net investment income because Americans invested much more abroad than foreigners invested in the

The balance of payments has two parts: the current account and the capital account.

Sending Money Home

My maternal grandmother, the oldest of eight children, grew up in a small town in Russia, not far from the Black Sea. While still a teenager she was sent to America where she would work in a garment factory, saving up money to send for her younger siblings, one-by-one. Together, they earned enough within a few years to bring the entire family to America. This was a familiar family saga in the decades before the restrictive immigration laws were passed in the 1920s, intended to restrict the influx of "undesirables" from Eastern and Southern Europe.

Today recent immigrants cannot easily send for their families, but they do provide them with substantial support by regularly wiring them money. If you'll glance at Table 1, you'll notice that $118 billion in net transfers was sent abroad in 2009. About three-quarters of those funds were remittances sent by recent immigrants to their families back home.

Here's the deal: We hire immigrants to harvest our crops, tend our lawns, take care of our children, staff our restaurants, clean our offices and homes, and pay them minimum, or even sub-minimum wages, often off the books. They live as cheaply as possible, scrimping and saving so they can send money home to their parents and children, often providing the sole means of support for their families. To sum up: These folks perform low-wage work that most Americans won't do themselves, and then send home a large part of their wages.

United States. Since then foreigners have been investing more in the U.S. than we have been investing abroad, so eventually those investments will earn more income than ours. In other words, in the not-too-distant future, net investment income will turn negative. Finally, we have net transfers, which include foreign aid, military spending abroad, remittances to relatives living abroad, and pensions paid to Americans living abroad.

I think that our net unilateral transfers abroad may be even larger than the −$118 billion listed in Table 1. (See the box, "Sending Money Home.") This was sent mainly by recent immigrants to their families in Mexico, the Caribbean, and to Central and South America.

Our balance on the current account is a clear indicator of how we're doing. A negative balance on the current account of −$421 billion means that we went $421 billion deeper into debt with foreigners.

When we add up the numbers that go into our current account, it is easy to see why this figure is negative and why our current account deficit has been growing in recent years. (See Figure 1.) But what international finance takes away with one hand, it pays back with the other. Thus, by definition, our current account deficit is balanced by our capital account surplus.

Our current account deficit is balanced by our capital account surplus.

Although our balance of payments every year, by definition, is zero, foreigners are buying up more and more of our country. So it is tempting to refer to our current account deficit as our balance of payments deficit (I've slipped a few times myself). Please remember that our huge current account deficit is offset by our capital account surplus.

The way it works is that we buy much more from foreigners than they buy from us. In effect, they lend or give us the money to make up the difference between our imports and our exports. It would not be an exaggeration to say that we borrow so much from foreigners to finance our current account deficits that we sell them pieces of the American rock, so to speak. Those pieces consist mainly of corporate stock and real estate, but they also lend us hundreds of billions of dollars each year in the form of purchases of corporate and government bonds and other debt instruments. Unless we can reduce our deficit in the trade of goods and services, our current account deficit will keep growing, and foreigners will have little choice but to keep sending most of those dollars back here to buy up more and more of our assets.

As you can see from Figure 2, our current account deficit as a percentage of GDP has been rising very rapidly since the early 1990s. In 2006 we were borrowing 6.2 percent of our GDP from foreigners, but by 2009 it has fallen back to just 2.9 percent. The main

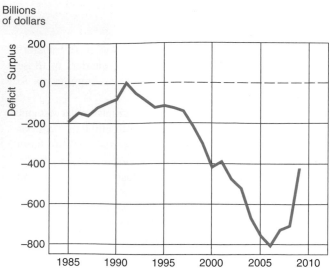

Figure 1

U.S. Current Account Surpluses and Deficits, 1985–2009

Since 1991 our negative balance on current account grew steadily, topping $800 billion in 2006. But it peaked in 2006 and fell precipitously in 2009, to just $421 billion.

Source: Economic Report of the President, 2009; *Economic Indicators,* March 2010.

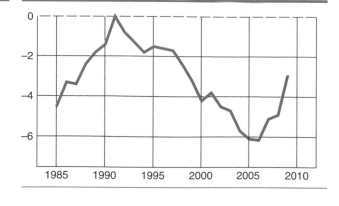

Figure 2

U.S. Current Account Deficit or Surplus as a Percentage of GDP, 1985–2009

In 1991 we ran a tiny surplus—$3 billion—on our current account. But in subsequent years we ran mounting deficits. By 2005 our current account deficit was 6.3 percent of GDP.

Source: Economic Report of the President, 2006.

reason for this decline was that our trade deficit fell sharply in 2009—a byproduct of the Great Recession.

Figure 3 shows how our current account deficit as a percentage of GDP compared with that of other major trading nations. China and Germany had huge current account surpluses. But the United States, along with Australia, ran relatively large deficits as a percentage of GDP.

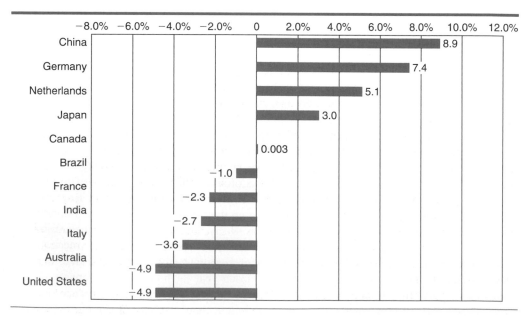

Figure 3

Current Account Deficit or Surplus as Percentage of GDP, Selected Countries, 2008

Among these countries, the United States and Australia are running the largest current account deficits relative to their GDPs.

Source: OECD.

Exchange Rate Systems

The basis for international finance is the exchange of well over 100 national currencies. Until the 1930s the world's currencies were based on gold. Since then a relatively free-floating exchange rate system has evolved. Under this system exchange rates are determined largely by the forces of supply and demand. In other words, how many yen, yuan, euros, or pounds you can get for your dollars is determined largely by the impersonal forces of the market.

An exchange rate is the price of a country's currency in terms of another currency. If you received 100 Japanese yen for $1, then you could say that a yen is worth one cent. And if a British pound were exchanged for $2, then you could say that a dollar is worth half a pound. In April 2010, you needed about 75 euros (the euro is the official currency of Germany, France, Italy, and nine other European countries) to get $100. So a euro was worth about $1.33.

There are three fairly distinct periods in the recent history of exchange rates. First, we'll examine the period before 1944, when most of the world was on the gold standard. Second, we'll look at the period from 1944 to 1973, when international finance was based on fixed exchange rates. Finally, we shall review the period from 1973 to the present, when we have had relatively freely floating exchange rates.

Three distinct periods

The Gold Standard

There has been some talk in recent years about a return to the gold standard, but it's not going to happen. Exactly what *is* the gold standard, what are its advantages, and what are its disadvantages? Funny you should ask.

Exactly what is the gold standard?

A nation is on the gold standard when it defines its currency in terms of gold. Until 1933 the U.S. dollar was worth 1/23 of an ounce of gold. In other words, you could buy an ounce of gold from the Treasury for $23 or sell this department an ounce for $23. Paper money was fully convertible into gold. If you gave the Treasury $23, you would get one ounce of gold—no ifs, ands, or buts. In 1933, we raised the price of gold to $35 an ounce, which meant a dollar was worth 1/35 of an ounce of gold.

To be on the gold standard, a nation must maintain a fixed ratio between its gold stock and its money supply. That way, when the gold stock rises, so does the money supply. Should gold leave the country, the money supply declines.

That brings us to the third and last requirement of the gold standard: There must be no barriers to the free flow of gold into and out of the country.

When we put all these things together, we have the gold standard. The nation's money supply, which is based on gold, is tied to the money supply of every other nation on the gold standard. It is the closest the world has ever come to an international currency. This system worked quite well until World War I, when most of the belligerents temporarily went off the gold standard because many of their citizens were hoarding gold and trying to ship it off to neutral nations.

Ideally, here is how the gold standard works. When Country A exports as much as it imports from Country B, no gold is transferred. But when Country A imports more than it exports, it has to ship the difference, in gold, to the trading partners with whom it has trade deficits.

How the gold standard works

Suppose the United States had to ship 1 million ounces of gold to other countries. This would lower our gold stock and, consequently, our money supply. When our money supply declined, so would our price level. This would make our goods cheaper relative to foreign goods. Our imports would decline and our exports would rise because foreigners would find American imports cheaper than their own goods.

What we had, then, was a self-correcting mechanism. A negative balance of trade caused an outflow of gold, a lower money supply, lower prices, and ultimately, fewer

A self-correcting mechanism

imports and more exports. Thus, under the gold standard, negative trade balances eliminated themselves.

After World War I the nations that had left the gold standard returned to the fold, but some nations' currencies were overvalued (relative to their price in gold) while others' currencies were undervalued. Adjustments were difficult because the nations whose currency was overvalued would have faced a gold drain and, consequently, lower prices and lower wages. But wages and prices are rarely downwardly flexible.

An alternative was to devalue—that is, lower the price of money in relation to gold. For example, a 10 percent devaluation would mean that instead of getting 10 British pounds for an ounce of gold, you now get 11. As the Great Depression spread, one nation after another devaluated, and within a few years virtually everyone was off the gold standard.

Evaluation of the gold standard

Let's step back for a moment and evaluate the gold standard. It *did* work for a long time, automatically eliminating trade surpluses and deficits. And it *did* stimulate international trade by removing the uncertainty of fluctuating exchange rates.

But the gold standard has a downside. First, it will work only when the gold supply increases as quickly as the world's need for money. By the early 20th century this was no longer the case. Second, it will work only if participating nations are willing to accept the periodic inflation and unemployment that accompany the elimination of trade imbalances. In today's world political leaders must pay far more attention to their domestic constituencies than to their trading partners. Finally, strict adherence to the gold standard would render monetary policy utterly ineffective. If gold were flowing into the United States, the Federal Reserve would be powerless to slow the rate of monetary growth and the ensuing inflation. And if there were an outflow of gold, the Federal Reserve would be unable to slow the decline in the money supply and thereby prevent the advent of a recession.

With the breakdown of the gold standard in the 1930s, protectionism returned as one nation after another raised tariff barriers higher and higher. Devaluation followed devaluation until the entire structure of international trade and finance was near complete collapse. Then came World War II—and with it, a great revival of economic activity. While the war was still raging, the Bretton Woods conference was called to set up a system of international finance that would lend some stability to how exchange rates were set.

The Gold Exchange Standard, 1944–73

Fixed exchange rates

The Bretton Woods (New Hampshire) conference set up the International Monetary Fund (IMF) to supervise a system of fixed exchange rates, all of which were based on the U.S. dollar, which was based on gold. The dollar was defined as being worth 1/35 of an ounce of gold, so gold was $35 an ounce, and dollars were convertible into gold at that price.

Other currencies were convertible into dollars at fixed prices, so these currencies were indirectly convertible into gold. But this was short of a gold standard because the money supplies of these nations were not tied to gold and no longer would trade deficits or surpluses automatically eliminate themselves. If a nation ran consistent trade deficits, it could devalue its currency relative to the dollar. A devaluation of 10 percent or less could be done without the IMF's permission (larger cuts required permission).

The new system functioned well for 25 years after World War II. The United States ran almost continual balance-of-payment deficits during the 1950s and 1960s, which eventually led to an international financial crisis in 1971. But until that year these deficits contributed to international liquidity. This is because U.S. dollars as well as gold were held as reserves for international payments by virtually every country in the world but the United States.

Why were U.S. dollars so acceptable?

Why were U.S. dollars acceptable to other nations? First, the United States held the largest stock of gold in the world and stood ready to sell that gold at $35 an ounce to the central banks of all nations. Second, the American economy was by far the largest and strongest in the world.

By the late 1960s, as our gold stock dwindled and as foreign governments found themselves with increasing stocks of dollars, these nations began to ask some embarrassing questions. If the United States continued to run balance-of-payments deficits, would we be able to redeem the dollars they were holding for gold at $35 an ounce? Would the United States be forced to devalue the dollar, thus making other countries' dollar holdings less valuable?

The Freely Floating Exchange Rate System, 1973 to the Present

To return to 1971, when our payments deficits finally forced us to abandon the gold exchange standard—and forced the rest of the world off as well—the IMF needed to set up a new system fast, and that system was, in computer terminology, a default system.

We were back to the old system that economists fondly refer to as the law of supply and demand. How does it apply to foreign exchange? The same way it applies to everything else.

Figure 4 shows hypothetical supply and demand curves for British pounds. Inferring from these curves, you can get 2 dollars for 1 pound.

Who sets this exchange rate? Basically, the forces of supply and demand do. The question then is, Where does the supply and demand for pounds come from?

The demand curve for pounds represents the desire of Americans to exchange their dollars for pounds. Why do they want pounds? To buy British goods and services, stocks, bonds, real estate, and other assets.

Likewise, the supply curve of pounds represents the desire of British citizens to purchase American goods, services, and financial assets.

Now we get to the beauty of the law of supply and demand. The point at which the two curves cross tells us the exchange rate of pounds and dollars. In Figure 4 we have a rate of 2 dollars for 1 pound.

With freely floating exchange rates, currencies will sometimes *depreciate* in value relative to other currencies. If the pound, for instance, depreciates with respect to the euro, it may fall from one pound equals 1.5 euros to one pound equals 1.4 euros. *Depreciation of a currency occurs when one currency becomes cheaper in terms of another currency.* Similarly, a currency can *appreciate* in value relative to another currency. Before appreciation 125 yen equaled one euro, but after the yen appreciated 120 yen

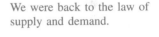

We were back to the law of supply and demand.

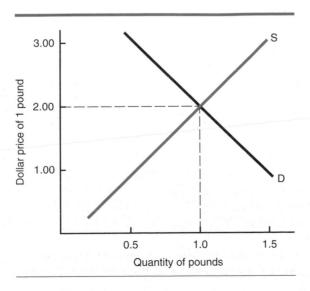

Figure 4

Hypothetical Demand for and Supply of British Pounds
How is the exchange rate set between dollars and pounds? It is set by the forces of demand and supply.

equaled one euro. *Appreciation of a currency occurs when one currency becomes more expensive in terms of another currency.* Whenever one currency depreciates, another currency must appreciate.

We don't have completely free-floating exchange rates.

If we had completely free-floating exchange rates (that is, no government interference), the market forces of supply and demand would set the exchange rates. To a large degree, this is what happens; but governments do intervene, although usually for just a limited time. In other words, government intervention may temporarily influence exchange rates, but exchange rates are set by the forces of supply and demand in the long run.

China is the big exception to the freely floating exchange rate system. For many years the Chinese government tied its currency to the dollar at the rate of 8.28 yuan to the dollar. By the new millennium it was clear that the yuan was undervalued and that if it was allowed to float freely, fewer yuan would be exchanged for each dollar. Finally, since the summer of 2005 the Chinese government has allowed the yuan to very slowly appreciate against the dollar—a topic we'll return to later in this chapter. But it does not appear that future appreciations of the yuan will substantially reduce our trade deficit with China. Indeed it reached an all-time world record of $268 billion in 2008. As *The Economist* observed:

> America's trade deficit is due mainly to excessive spending and inadequate saving, not to unfair Chinese competition. If China has contributed to America's deficit it is not through its undervalued exchange rate, but by holding down bond yields and so fuelling excessive household borrowing and spending. From this point of view, global monetary policy is now made in Beijing, not Washington.[1]

How have the Chinese managed to manipulate the exchange rate of the yuan against the dollar? Because it runs huge trade surpluses with the United States, the Chinese government uses its surplus dollars to buy dollar-denominated securities, largely U.S. government bonds. Maintaining an undervalued yuan, it has been able to make Chinese exports more attractive to American consumers by keeping down their prices.

Three factors influence the exchange rates between countries. The most important factor is the relative price levels of the two countries. If American goods are relatively cheap compared to German goods, there will be a relatively low demand for euros and a relatively high supply of euros. In other words, everyone—Germans and Americans—wants dollars to buy American goods.

A second factor is the relative growth rates of the American and German economies. Whichever is growing faster generates a greater demand for imports. If the American economy is growing faster, it will raise the demand for euros (to be used to buy imported goods from Germany) while decreasing the supply of euros (the Germans will hold more euros and fewer dollars because they are not buying many American goods).

The third and final factor is the relative level of interest rates in the two countries. If the interest rates are higher in Germany than they are in the United States, American investors will want to take advantage of the higher rates by buying German securities. They will sell their dollars for euros, driving up the price of euros. In effect, then, the demand for euros will rise and their supply will decline.

Figure 5 shows five important exchange rates. If the weighted-average exchange value of the U.S. dollar in Panel A confuses you, then help is on the way. You'll find it in the box, "Interpreting the Top Line in Figure 5."

Because of our record trade deficits with China, officials of the Bush and Obama administrations, as well as many members of Congress, demanded that the Chinese government allow the yuan to appreciate at a faster pace against the dollar. At its present pace, the dollar will not depreciate to 6 yuan before the end of 2013.

----

[1]*The Economist*, July 30, 2005, p. 11.

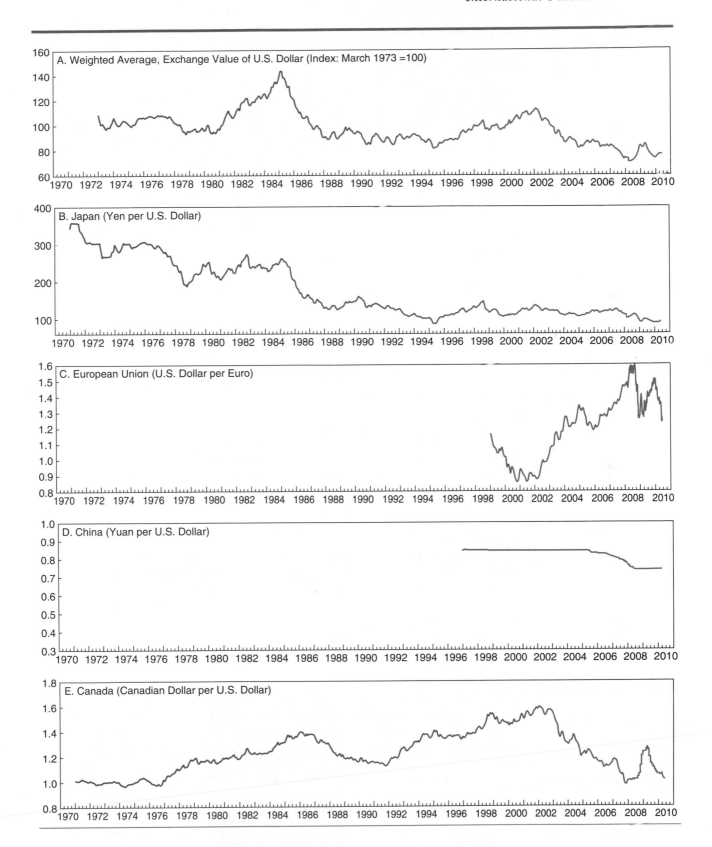

Figure 5

International Exchange Rates, 1972–2010

The value of the U.S. dollar in relation to the yen, the yuan, and other currencies has fluctuated rather
widely over the last four decades. To a large degree the dollar has appreciated and depreciated relative to all
other major currencies, moving up in value in the early 1980s, down in the later 1980s, up in the late 1990s,
and down again in the new millennium.

Source: Business Cycle Indicators, April 2010.

The graph line in Panel A of Figure 5 shows how the U.S. dollar has fluctuated against other major currencies since 1972. When the line rises, that means the dollar has risen in value against a weighted average of 10 major foreign currencies. What does this mean in plain English?

First, a weighted average of currencies is similar to your grade point average. If you're really curious about how weighted averages are constructed, look at the box "Construction of the Consumer Price Index" in Chapter 10 in *Economics* and *Macroeconomics*.

Figure 5 charts an index of the dollar's relationship to other major currencies, with a base of March 1973. Let's say that in March 1973 a dollar traded for 50 francs. We set that base year at 100. Suppose the index rose to 200 a few years later. Then you might be able to get 100 francs for your dollar.*

The index did rise from 95 in 1980 to just over 140 in 1985; so the dollar rose by about 60 percent. What did this mean to American consumers? It meant that on the average they could get about 60 percent more foreign currency for their dollars than they could have just five years before.

Interpreting the Top Line in Figure 5

Suppose a Honda Accord cost 1,000,000 yen in 1985. If 250 yen exchanged for one dollar, the car cost an American $4,000 (1,000,000/250). By 1988 you could get only 125 yen for your dollar. If that new Accord still cost 1,000,000 yen, how many dollars did you need to buy it? Don't wait for me to tell you. I'd like you to work out the answer here:

Here's the solution: 1,000,000/125 = $8,000.

When the dollar rises in value, foreign goods become cheaper; at the same time American goods become more expensive to foreigners. What do you think this does to our trade balance? That's right—it makes it worse. Since the late 1980s the index has generally fluctuated within a range of 80 to 100.

*This is, of course, an oversimplification, because the dollar will not have risen by 100 percent against every currency during this period. It will have risen by more than 100 percent against some and by less than 100 percent against others.

Let's see how the dollar stacks up against the currencies of our leading trading partners as of April 8, 2010. Figure 6 tells us how many euros, pounds, yen, and other foreign currencies we could have gotten for a dollar.

Suppose you bought a Volkswagen Beetle for 9,500 euros. How much would that come to in dollars and cents?

Solution: First, note that, since the exchange rate in Figure 6 is 0.75 euros for a dollar, the number of dollars you need to pay is more than the number of euros. To find the answer (to the nearest dollar), divide the 9,500 euros by the exchange rate of 0.75.

$$\frac{9,500}{0.75} = \$12,667$$

Figure 6

Exchange Rates: Foreign Currency per American Dollar, April 8, 2010

How many Mexican pesos would you get for a dollar? You would get 12.2 pesos. Can you figure out how many dollars (actually how many cents) you would get for a peso? You would get 8.2 cents. Exchange rates fluctuate from minute to minute, and they are usually calibrated to hundredths, or even thousandths of a cent.

Source: The Federal Reserve, www. federalreserve.gov

$1 Will Buy

1.77 Brazilian reals
0.65 British pounds
1.00 Canadian dollars
6.83 Chinese yuan
0.75 euros
44.4 Indian rupees
93.4 Japanese yen
12.2 Mexican pesos
7.27 South African rand
1121.0 South Korean won
1.07 Swiss francs

To convert U.S. dollars into euros, yen, yuan, and other currencies, go to www.x-rates. com/calculator.html

How Well Do Freely Floating (Flexible) Exchange Rates Work?

Until 1973 most countries had fixed exchange rates because they feared flexible rates-would fluctuate wildly. Has that happened since 1973? While there certainly have been some ups and downs, most notably with the dollar, we can still say so far, so good.

So far, so good.

The Euro

On January 1, 1999, most of Western Europe introduced a single currency, the euro. (See Panel C, Figure 5.) The European Monetary Union has 17 members—Austria, Belgium, Cyprus, Estonia, Finland, France, Germany, Greece, Ireland, Italy, Luxembourg, Malta, Netherlands, Portugal, Slovakia, Slovenia, and Spain. Flying into Spain from Finland now involves no more hassle than the hop from Chicago to New York. No need to show a passport and—thanks to the euro—no need for the traveler to change money or grapple with baffling prices.

Imagine if the United States were divided into 50 states, each with its own currency. Think how hard it would be to do business. Not only would exchange rates change, literally from minute to minute, but, since business payments are often made 30 or 60 days after delivery, you might end up paying 5 or 10 percent more—or less—than the contractual price. This added element of uncertainty would make it much harder to do business. So, what the members of the euro area are doing, then, is attempting to move toward a unified market with a single currency, just like the one we've long enjoyed in the United States.

The Yen and the Yuan

As we noted in the previous chapter, our two biggest trade deficits are with China and Japan. And, as it happens, the Chinese and Japanese monetary authorities have kept the value of their currencies low against the dollar. Indeed the Chinese yuan (also called the renminbi) has been pegged at 8.28 from 1998 until mid-2005 when it was finally allowed to appreciate, albeit at a very slow pace (see Figure 5, Panel D). It was estimated that in the spring of 2010 the yuan was still artificially undervalued by as much as 40 percent against the dollar. This has made Chinese goods and services cheaper to American consumers and American goods and services more expensive to Chinese consumers. Between mid-2005 and mid-2008 the yuan rose 21 percent against the dollar. But then, in July 2008, China informally repegged the yuan at 6.83 to the dollar. After almost two years of intense pressure from the United States and its other major trading partners, at the end of June 2010 the Chinese central bank announced that it would once again allow the yuan to appreciate against a basket of other currencies, including the dollar. However, it was expected that the ensuing appreciation would be no faster than it had been from 2005 through 2008.

Japan, too, extremely concerned about falling exports, has kept the yen artificially low against the dollar, making its exports to the U.S. cheaper and American imports more expensive. Japan has long been one of our major trading partners, so the exchange rate between the yen and the dollar is very closely watched. What would happen to the number of yen you could get for a dollar if the supply of dollars rose and the demand for dollars fell?

You should be able to figure that out very easily. In Figure 7, we show the question in graphic form, and as we can see, in this particular case, the dollar fell from 100 yen to 80 yen.

Figure 7

Hypothetical Supply of and Demand for Dollars Relative to Yen

If the supply of dollars outside the United States were to go up from S_1 to S_2 while the demand for dollars went down from D_1 to D_2 what would happen to the price of the dollar relative to yen? It would go down, in this case from 100 yen to 80 yen.

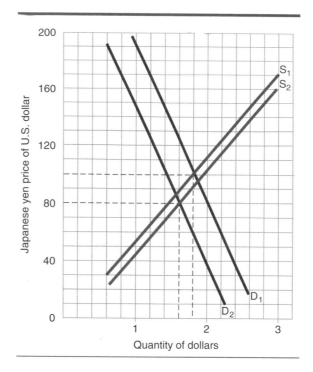

The chances are you've never heard of the hamburger standard or the Big Mac index, but you're about to. Begun by *The Economist* as a tongue-in-cheek effort to see if the dollar was undervalued or overvalued, the hamburger standard has actually taken on a life of its own (see the box, "The Hamburger Standard").

The Falling Dollar and the U.S. Trade Deficit

If foreigners have to pay higher prices, they will buy fewer of our exports. For example, if the dollar appreciates against the euro, from say, 0.8 euros to the dollar to 1.2 euros to the dollar, that would make our goods and services 50 percent more expensive to the French, the Germans, the Italians, and all the other Europeans buying our exports. So an appreciating dollar would tend to lower our exports.

Similarly, an appreciating dollar would tend to raise our imports from France, Germany, Italy, and other countries using the euro. Before the dollar appreciated, you might have had to pay $10 for a bottle of European wine; but after it appreciated from 0.8 euros to 1.2 euros, you would pay just $6.67. As the law of demand tells us, *when the price of a good is lowered, more of it is demanded.*

So if the U.S. dollar appreciates, our exports tend to fall and our imports tend to rise. And what happens when the dollar depreciates? You *guessed* it! Our exports tend to fall and our imports tend to rise.

So what has been happening to the dollar since January 2002? Let's go to the video tape—or, in this case, the top chart in Figure 5. From January 2002 through March 2008, the dollar depreciated 37 percent against a weighted average of currencies.

OK, so others things being equal, what would you expect to have happened to our trade deficit over this period? You would have expected it to fall. *Did it?* The answer is yes and no. Table 2 (on page 492) lists our trade deficits from 2001 through 2009. You'll notice that our trade deficit more than doubled between 2001 and 2006, and then, in 2007 it finally declined.

Apparently the lower dollar eventually *did* push down our trade deficit in 2007, making our exports cheaper and our imports more expensive. But why did our depreciating dollar take so long to reduce our trade deficit? There are two fairly obvious answers. First, two of our leading trading partners, China and Japan, were very actively buying up U.S. Treasury securities to prop up the dollar, all the while holding down the value of their

The Hamburger Standard

Suppose you were addicted to Big Macs, so no matter where you were in the world, you would rush to MacDonald's for dinner. If you did this in the United States in January 2010, a Big Mac would have cost you, on average, $3.58. If you had been in China, after you changed your dollars into yuan, that same Big Mac would have cost you just $1.83 (see chart). But in Switzerland, after changing your dollars into Swiss francs, you would have had to shell out $6.30—and in Norway, you would have had to shell out seven dollars and two cents in Norwegian krone.

The Big Mac index was created by *The Economist* to determine whether or not the dollar was overvalued or undervalued. If it were overvalued with respect to another currency, then you would be getting a bargain when you exchanged your dollars for that currency. You'd certainly have gotten a bargain in China when you exchanged your dollars for yuan and bought that Big Mac for the equivalent of just $1.83. That same hamburger would have cost you $3.58 in the United States. Indeed, we could say that the yuan was undervalued with respect to the dollar. By the same logic, you would not have gotten your money's worth in Norway, paying the equivalent of $7.02 for your Big Mac. We could say that the Swiss franc was overvalued with respect to the dollar.

See if you can figure out by what percent the Norwegian krone is *over*valued relative to the dollar. Be sure to write down your answer.

Solution: It's overvalued by 93 percent. Here's the math: You're overpaying by $3.44 ($7.02 − $3.58).

$$\frac{\$3.44}{\$3.58} = 0.93 = 93\%$$

One last question. By what percent is the Chinese yuan *under*valued relative to the dollar?

Solution: It's undervalued by 49 percent. You're underpaying by $1.75. $\frac{\$1.75}{\$3.58} = 0.49 = 49\%$

Published two or three times a year by *The Economist,* The Big Mac index is intended as a light-hearted guide to whether currencies are at their "correct level."

> . . . in the long run, exchange rates should move toward rates that would equalise the prices of an identical basket of goods and services in any two countries. To put it simply: a dollar should buy the same everywhere. Our basket is a MacDonald's Big Mac, produced locally to roughly the same recipe in 118 countries.*

---

*"Economic focus/McCurrencies," *The Economist,* June 11, 2005.
Source: The Economist, February 1, 2007.

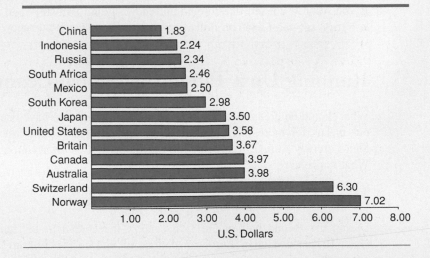

The Hamburger Standard: The Price of a Big Mac in Selected Countries
Source: The Economist, January 6, 2010.

own currencies relative to the dollar. In other words, while the dollar was depreciating against the euro, the British pound, and the Canadian dollar, it was not depreciating against the yuan and the yen.

The second reason why the depreciating dollar did not push down our trade deficit before 2007 was that foreign sellers were willing to accept lower prices and profits in

TABLE 2	U.S. Trade Deficit, 2001–2009

(in billions of dollars)

Year	Deficit
2001	$371
2002	427
2003	504
2004	619
2005	723
2006	769
2007	714
2008	708
2009	392

Source: Economic Report of the President, 2010; Survey of Current Business, March 2010.

order to protect their share of the world's largest consumer market. This view is summarized by *New Yorker* financial columnist, James Surowiecki:

> But what's most interesting is that foreign companies have essentially chosen to protect U.S. consumers from the effects of the weak dollar. They have resisted increasing prices here, accepting lower profit margins in order to maintain their market share. The American market is too big and too important for them to run the risk of losing customers, and, because it's so competitive, they generally can't raise prices without losing market share. So high-end television sets, foreign beer, and luxury cars have all remained relatively affordable, even though the dollars we buy them with are worth much less than they were a few years ago.[2]

on the web

How much can you get for one U.S. dollar in yen, yuan, euros, and other currencies? Go to www.federalreserve.gov/releases and then click on foreign exchange rates—daily. If you want to convert one foreign currency, say the British pound, into another foreign currency, say the Canadian dollar, go to http://oanda.com/currency/converter

Running Up a Tab in the Global Economy

What should be pretty clear by now is that, as a nation, we have been living well beyond our means for more than 25 years—and that the party can't last forever. The United States quickly shifted from being the world's largest creditor nation to the largest debtor. What happened?

From Largest Creditor to Largest Debtor

During the second half of the 19th century the United States borrowed heavily from Great Britain and other European nations to finance the building of railroads and the construction of much of our plant and equipment. Our country was a classic debtor nation, importing manufactured goods, exporting agricultural products, and borrowing capital in order to industrialize.

On the eve of World War I with the process of industrialization largely completed, we finally became a creditor nation. In 1914 foreigners owed us more than we owed them. The assets Americans held in foreign countries—factories, real estate, office buildings, corporate stock and bonds, and government bonds—were greater than the

During World War I the United States became the world's leading creditor nation.

[2]James Surowiecki, "The Financial Page Greenback Blues," *The New Yorker,* October 8, 2007, p. 38.

assets foreigners held in the United States. Our creditor status rose substantially during the war as we loaned the Allies billions of dollars. We became the world's leading creditor nation, a position we held until 1982.

How did we lose this position and fall into debt, quickly becoming the world's largest debtor? How could the largest, most productive economy in the world—a nation with low unemployment and stable prices—manage to run up such a huge tab?

The main reason for this turnaround was our large and growing trade deficits. As a nation we are living for today and not worrying about what will happen tomorrow. To say that, as a people, Americans are world-class consumers would not be an exaggeration. "Born to shop" and "shop till you drop" are apt descriptions of tens of millions of American consumers.

You can see the trend in foreign assets in the United States and U.S. assets abroad by looking at Figure 8. In 1985 we became a net debtor nation, and since that year,

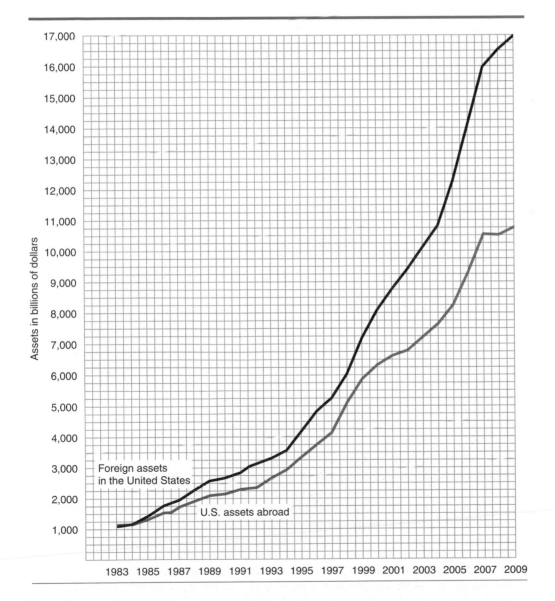

Figure 8

U.S. Assets Abroad and Foreign Assets in the United States, 1983–2009

In the mid-1980s we went from being a creditor nation to a debtor nation. Almost each year since 1985 the gap between foreign assets in the United States and U.S. assets abroad has kept growing. By the end of 2009 this gap had reached over $6 trillion.

Sources: Economic Report of the President, 2009; *Survey of Current Business,* March 2010.

foreign investment in the United States has far outstripped our investment abroad. These trends will continue into the foreseeable future as foreigners continue accumulating dollars—mainly because of our huge trade deficits—and using them to buy up our assets.

And yet, American investors are earning more interest, dividends, and profits on their investments abroad than were foreigner investors on their investments in the United States. How could that be? William Cline provides a succinct explanation:

> The large and liquid U.S. asset market, with its legal guarantees and (despite Enron) transparency, make the United States the natural place for foreign investors to place the lower-risk spectrum of their portfolios. Conversely, U.S. investors will tend to seek foreign assets to obtain the higher-risk, higher-return spectrum of their portfolios.[3]

If we add up all the assets that Americans own abroad and subtract the assets that foreigners own in the United States we would get the U.S. stock of net foreign assets. Looking at Figure 8, you can see that the U.S. stock of net foreign assets has been negative since the mid-1980s, and that it began to grow very rapidly at around the beginning of the 21st century.

In 2000 Americans owned about $6.2 trillion in foreign assets, while foreigners owned about $8 trillion in American assets—a gap of $1.8 trillion. By 2009 this gap grew to $6.3 trillion, when the American stock of assets held abroad was $10.7 trillion and the stock of assets foreigners held in the U.S. was nearly $17 trillion. So during this nine-year period, our stock of net foreign assets shot up from −$1.8 trillion to −$6.3 trillion. Even if our current account deficit were to keep falling over the next 10 years, the gap between what we own abroad and what foreigners own in the United States will continue to rise.

Something's gotta give. Most likely the dollar's decline, which began in 2002, will continue, perhaps for years. This will make our exports cheaper, so foreigners will buy more from us. Similarly, the lower-valued dollar will make imported goods and services more expensive, so we'll import less. As the dollar falls—note that I said "as" and not "if"—our exports will rise, our imports will fall, and so our trade deficit will shrink.

But a declining dollar, as Paul Krugman notes, makes foreign investment in dollar-denominated assets much less attractive, thereby slowing the inflow of foreign investment:

> Right now foreign investors are willing to hold 10-year U.S. government bonds, even though they pay only a slightly higher interest rate than their European counterparts. Those investors seem to believe, in other words, that today's strong dollar will persist for another 10 years. But the size of our trade deficit makes that unlikely. So foreign investors, and therefore the value of the dollar, are arguably doing a Wile E. Coyote—one of these days they will look down, realize that they have already walked over the edge of the cliff, and plunge.[4]

Well over $1 trillion of our currency remains abroad where it circulates as a medium of exchange. The Federal Reserve estimates that over two-thirds of all the U.S. currency being printed is eventually used as unofficial legal tender in China, Russia, Mexico, Romania, Bolivia, the Philippines, Tajikistan, Vietnam, and dozens of other countries. Lithuania, Argentina, and Brazil have formally pegged their currencies to the dollar, while many others have done so informally. In effect, then, much of the world is unofficially on the dollar standard.

The U.S. dollar is actually the official currency of more than two dozen countries, the largest of which are Ecuador, El Salvador, Guatemala, and Panama. And several others, including Mexico and Argentina, have been considering dollarization.

---

[3]William R. Cline, *The United States as a Debtor Nation* (Washington, DC: Institute for International Economics, 2005).

[4]Paul Krugman, "Deficit Attention Disorder," *The New York Times*, March 26, 2000, section 4, p. 17.

The Role of Drug Money

There are no hard figures or even reliable estimates on the amount of money sent abroad to pay for cocaine and heroin imports. But considering that the United States is clearly the world's leading drug importer, it is reasonable to say that more than $30 billion a year is sent abroad to drug growers and traffickers. The transfer of funds is done by cash or electronically through the worldwide banking network and is not easy to trace.

How does this affect our balance-of-payments deficit? It doesn't, except that we often run "statistical discrepancies" that sometimes run to over $80 billion. Now where could all that money be coming from? And where could it be going?

Some of it is coming back into the United States to purchase legitimate businesses, some to buy luxury condominiums along South Florida's "Gold Coast," and some may even be going to buy up part of the national debt. The point is, however reprehensible the drug dealers are, the economic effect of their transactions is similar to the effects of any other imports. The bottom line is that Americans are buying today's pleasures with tomorrow's income.

Laura D'Andrea Tyson, Dean of the London Business School, explains how the de facto dollar standard works:

> In a dollar-standard world, global growth fuels the demand for liquid dollar assets, and the United States can provide these assets, whether in the form of currency, government securities, or private securities, with no well-defined time frame for net repayment. As a result, the United States seems to enjoy a virtually unlimited line of credit denominated in its own currency with the rest of the world. This credit finances America's large and growing current-account deficit. The United States benefits from this arrangement because it can consume much more than it produces. But the rest of the world also benefits both because it gets the dollar holdings it requires and because the United States uses the credit to import goods and services and serve as the world's growth engine.[5]

Laura D'Andrea Tyson, Dean of the London School of Economics

As long as we can maintain a low inflation rate and currency stability, the world may continue to accept our dollars in exchange for a multitude of goods and services. We're certainly getting a great deal. We get to buy hundreds of billions of dollars' worth of stuff each year and pay for it just by printing money.

The foreign saver has a strong voice in setting the interest rates—not just for U.S. government securities but indirectly for other interest rates as well. As our dependence on funds from abroad grows, we are abdicating not just our role as the world's leading economic power but our economic sovereignty. As time goes by, decisions affecting the American economy will be made not in New York and Washington but in Tokyo, London, Beijing, Frankfurt, and other financial capitals outside the United States.

The U.S. Treasury depends on the foreign saver to finance the deficit.

As a nation we are living for today and not worrying about what will happen tomorrow. "America has thrown itself a party and billed the tab to the future," says Harvard economist Benjamin Friedman.[6] But all parties must end sometime, and someone is going to be left with a mess to clean up. (See the box, "The Role of Drug Money," for a discussion of another aspect of our living for today.)

We are living for today and not worrying about tomorrow.

Living beyond Our Means

The root cause of our problems has been that we as a nation have been consuming more than we have been producing, spending more than we have been earning, or, in short, living for today without providing for tomorrow. In the 19th century, when this country also

---

[5]Laura D'Andrea Tyson, "In the Dollar We (and All Other Nations) Trust," *BusinessWeek,* October 28, 2002, p. 26. Dr. Tyson was Chair of the President's Council of Economic Advisors, 1993–95.

[6]Benjamin M. Friedman, *Day of Reckoning* (New York: Random House, 1988), p. 4.

ran up a large international debt, we were financing capital expansion. This investment in the future enabled us to vastly expand our production and quickly pay off our debt.

Today we are following a radically different course. We are not borrowing from abroad to finance capital expansion but rather to pay for a massive spending spree. What are we buying? We're buying consumer electronics, cars, designer clothes, and oil.

America has become a nation of consumption junkies. This is not, in itself, such a terrible thing if we supported our habit. But we can't. So we ask foreigners to indulge us. And so far they have—at a price. We've been giving them IOUs in the form of U.S. dollars, and more and more, foreigners have been cashing them in for pieces of America. It seems as though everyone—the British, the Japanese, the Dutch, the Canadians, the Chinese, the Germans—owns a piece of the rock.

Since the early 1980s we've seen a massive recycling of dollars. As our trade deficits rose, the dollars we sent abroad were lent back to us as foreigners took advantage of our relatively high interest rates to purchase Treasury securities and corporate bonds. But they have increasingly been using their dollar stash to buy up pieces of America in the form of real estate and corporate stock. One might say foreigners are now not just America's creditors but its owners as well. *The Economist* summed up our current account dilemma:

> Just as an individual cannot pile on credit-card debt forever, so a country cannot increase the burden of its foreign debt indefinitely. Eventually, interest on the accumulated debt would use all the economy's resources, leaving nothing for domestic spending.[7]

We are a nation of consumption junkies.

We are selling off the rock—piece by piece.

A Codependent Relationship

China, and to a lesser degree, Japan and a few other East Asian countries, are locked into a codependent relationship with the United States. As long as we keep buying from them, even though we're running huge bilateral trade deficits, they continue to finance those deficits by lending us money. Indeed, China and Japan alone not only finance over half our trade deficit, but over half our federal budget deficit as well.

This is a great deal for us, because we get to consume much more than we produce. Why are these nations so nice to us? Because the huge American market enables them to expand production and job creation beyond what their own populations can consume. In addition, these Asian nations are so eager to keep their goods inexpensive, that they are willing to buy hundreds of billions of dollars in U.S. Treasury securities each year to prevent the dollar from depreciating too quickly.

Had the central banks of China, Japan, and America's other major Asian trading partners not made these purchases, the market forces of supply and demand would have driven the dollar well below its current level. A lower dollar would have made our imports more expensive and our exports cheaper, helping to reduce our trade deficit. But our codependent relationships with these nations precluded that from happening.

The Economist summarized the consequences of our codependent relationships with our Asian trading partners:

> The Asian central banks are masking market signals; America's current-account deficit reflects insufficient saving by households and an excessive budget deficit. Normally, investors would demand higher bond yields to compensate them for the increased risk, thereby giving the government a warning as well as an incentive to borrow less. But Asia's buying of Treasury bonds, with little regard for risk and return is keeping yields artificially low, which makes pruning the budget seem less urgent. At the same time low interest rates prolong America's unhealthy consumer spending and borrowing binge.[8]

The United States borrows almost $2 billion a day from foreigners, largely to finance our trade deficit, but much of this money is also used to finance the federal budget

[7]"The Price of Profligacy," *The Economist*, September 20, 2003, p. 7.
[8]"A Fair Exchange?" in *The Economist*, October 2, 2004, p. 16.

deficit as well. The Japanese and Chinese governments are the largest holders of U.S. government securities. Together they are keeping us financially afloat.

This arrangement has operated smoothly as we began running larger and larger trade and budget deficits, with the salutary effect of holding down our interest rates. Presumably it will continue into the foreseeable future because we, the Chinese, and the Japanese have too much to lose by upsetting the financial apple cart. But the time may come, perhaps five or ten years down the road, when our foreign creditors strongly disagree with some policy of the American government.

I won't even speculate as to what might set off such a conflict, but increasingly, we will have to take into account the opinions of our creditors. Most alarming, each year, we are digging ourselves into a deeper and deeper financial hole.

Why We Need to Worry about the Current Account Deficit

Ours is the world's largest economy, our rate of productivity growth is quite high, and we are on the cutting edge of the latest technology. So why worry about our current account deficit?

Countries that use American dollars for their currency as well as countries that hold U.S. government securities as assets have somewhat limited needs and will reach a point when they don't need any more dollars or U.S. Treasury debt. And as we continue selling off our nation's assets and debt to foreigners, they will reach the limit of how much they are willing to hold.

When that happens, foreigners will demand fewer dollars, the dollar will depreciate in value, foreigners holding American assets will suffer tremendous losses, and Americans will find that they have to pay a lot more for imported goods. Our living standard will fall, and we'll probably have a really bad recession or even a depression.

Today we still have a choice. We can bring our current account deficit under control or we can pay the consequences a few years from now. My guess is that we'll let things keep drifting until it's too late. In the meanwhile, keep your eye on the current account deficit.

Editorial: American Exceptionality

Toward the end of the main section of daily newspapers, you'll find the editorial page. Here's where the editors get a chance to say what they *really* think. This may surprise readers, who find plenty of opinions expressed in news articles. But economics textbook authors are held to a higher standard. We are expected to present both sides of most controversial economic issues. So while our personal viewpoints may well show through, we really do make a strong effort to be, in the words of Fox News, "fair and balanced."

In this last section of the last chapter, I'd like to shift gears, going from neutral to fast forward. Let me tell you what I *really* think about the American economy and where it's headed.

For a century we've been the world's largest economy, and for most of this time we have enjoyed the highest standard of living in history. There has long been a strong belief in American exceptionalism, perhaps best expressed by this line from our hymn, *America the Beautiful,* "God shed his grace on thee."

Since the implosion of the Soviet Union in 1991, we have been the world's only superpower. Indeed we spend nearly as much on armaments as the rest of the world combined. There are some who see parallels between our recent military record and those of the Roman, the Spanish, and the British empires. In fact, one can easily make the case that our empire is not only in decline, but may soon begin to fall apart.

There are many people, both in this country and abroad, who believe that, like the Romans, the Spanish, and the British before them, the Americans have built a huge empire to serve its economic interests. And like the *Pax Britannica* that lasted a century from the end of the Napoleonic Wars in 1815 to the beginning of World War I in 1914, we too have used our military might to impose what has been termed a "New World Order." And what would be the coin of our realm? You *guessed* it! The U.S. dollar! Bill Bonner and Addison Wiggin describe the economic workings of this American empire, and how it differs from its predecessors.

> America provides a *pax dollarium* for nearly the entire world. But the United States does not take direct tribute from its vassal states and dependent territories for providing this service. Instead, it borrows from them. Living standards rise in the United States. But they are rising on borrowed money, not on stolen money. The big difference is that America's vassal states can stop lending at any time. If they care to, they can even dump their current loans on the open market destroying the U.S. dollar and forcing interest rates so high that a recession—or depression—is practically guaranteed. What is worse, the longer the present system continues, the worse off Americans are.[9]

Let's look at the facts:

- Our federal budget deficits are well over $1 trillion.
- We have been running huge trade deficits for over a decade.
- Our defense spending is growing at an unsustainable pace, while our military is stretched to the breaking point.
- We are living well beyond our means, depending on the kindness of foreigners.
- We have lost most of our manufacturing base and are now losing our innovative edge as well.
- Americans have one of the lowest savings rate of all nations.
- American students have among the lowest scores on international tests.
- We import two-thirds of our oil.
- We spend almost twice as much per capita on health care than most other economically advanced nations.
- The United States is the only economically advanced nation without a high-speed railway system.

Considered individually, none of these facts is too alarming, but what conclusions do you reach when you look at the entire package? What trends do you see? Do you think our nation can sustain this course indefinitely?

No one disputes that by early in the 20th century we had built the greatest economy in the history of the world. Six factors, reinforcing one another, and unique to our nation, largely accounted for the rise of our economy:

1. Universal free public education.
2. A world-class local, interurban, and national public transportation network.
3. The development of mass production.
4. The development of mass consumption.
5. The building of a huge manufacturing base.
6. Maintaining our cutting-edge technology.

Today, not only are these factors no longer unique to our nation, but some of our economic rivals have caught up to, and surpassed us. Less than a century ago we were a lean and mean rising industrial power. We ran the world's most efficient economy. Today, we still are, by far, the world's largest economic power. But unless we begin to make far more efficient use of our resources, we will quickly become a fading economic superpower.

By nature economists are usually pessimists. That's why economics has long been called "the dismal science." So here we have the United States at the top of its economic

---

[9]Bill Bonner and Addison Wiggin, *Empire of Debt* (Hoboken, NJ: John Wiley and Sons, 2005), p. 40.

game, the unchallenged leader of the world, and I'm suggesting that our game is almost up, that we've been building up to a great fall.

One of the endearing characteristics of economics is that different people can look at the same set of facts and reach diametrically opposed conclusions. I've concluded that we are headed for an economic collapse—a collapse that will certainly come sometime in the next two or three decades. But you might have looked at these same facts and concluded that the best is yet to come. Hopefully we'll both live long enough to see which one of us is right.

Questions for Further Thought and Discussion

1. What is meant by our balance of payments? Explain what current account and capital account are.

2. What is the gold standard? How does it work?

3. Why does the dollar fluctuate with other currencies?

4. How did the United States go from being the world's largest creditor nation to the world's largest debtor?

5. Can there be a deficit on Current Account and a deficit on Capital Account at the same time? Explain.

6. For several months before your vacation trip to Germany you find that the exchange rate for the dollar has increased relative to the euro. Are you pleased or saddened? Explain.

7. If the dollar depreciates relative to the Japanese yen, will the Sony DVD player you wanted become more or less expensive? What effect will this have on the number of Sony DVD players that Americans buy?

8. Explain why a currency depreciation leads to an improvement in a nation's balance of trade.

9. What is a foreign exchange rate? Provide a few examples.

10. How is the exchange rate determined in a freely floating rate system?

11. Who demands Japanese yen? Who supplies yen?

12. *Practical Application:* Foreigners are buying up hundreds of billions of dollars a year in American assets. In what ways should this be a matter of concern to Americans?

13. *Practical Application:* Anne Hilbert has been hired by a Washington think tank to predict the trend over the next decade in the weighted average exchange value of the U.S. dollar. Its record from 1972 through early 2010 is shown in Figure 5 (A); she needs to provide evidence to back up her conclusion.

14. *Web Activity:* Jennifer Saxton bought a microwave oven made in China for $200. How much would she have paid in Chinese yuan? Go to www.x-rates.com/calculator.html

15. *Web Activity:* Melissa Larmon bought a German camera for 300 euros. How much would she have paid in U.S. dollars? Go to www.x-rates.com/calculator.html

Workbook for Chapter 20

Name _____   Date _____

Multiple-Choice Questions

Circle the letter that corresponds to the best answer.

1. We became a debtor nation in _____. (LO4)
   a) 1975   c) 1985
   b) 1980   d) 1990

2. In 2009 our net foreign debt was over $ _____ trillion. (LO4)
   a) two   c) six   e) ten
   b) four   d) eight

3. Which one of the following is the most accurate statement? (LO5)
   a) The American empire, like the Romans, the Spanish, and the British before us, uses its military might to force other nations to provide us with low-cost goods.
   b) No one would ever suggest that there is such a thing as an American empire.
   c) We have become very dependent on our trading partners, who have been willing to accept U.S. dollars to finance our trade deficits.
   d) Although our international trade position has deteriorated in recent years, we can continue on this course indefinitely.

4. During the 1980s, _____. (LO4)
   a) both American investment abroad and foreign investment in the United States increased
   b) both American investment abroad and foreign investment in the United States decreased
   c) American investment abroad increased and foreign investment in the United States decreased
   d) American investment abroad decreased and foreign investment in the United States increased

5. The world's leading debtor nation is _____. (LO4)
   a) Argentina   c) Mexico
   b) Brazil   d) the United States

6. Which statement is true? (LO4)
   a) Foreigners own most of the assets in the United States.
   b) We own more assets in foreign countries than foreigners own in the United States.
   c) Foreigners are driving up interest rates in the United States.
   d) None of these statements is true.

7. Which one of the following statement is the most accurate? (LO4)
   a) As a percentage of GDP, the United States has the highest current account surplus of any nation.
   b) As a percentage of GDP, the United States has the highest current account deficit of any nation.
   c) As a percentage of GDP, our current account deficit is roughly the same as it was 10 years ago.
   d) Our current account deficit is rising at an unsustainable pace.

8. An American importer of Italian shoes would pay in _____. (LO1)
   a) dollars   c) euros
   b) gold   d) lira

9. The total of our current and capital accounts _____. (LO2)
   a) will always be zero
   b) will always be negative
   c) will always be positive
   d) may be positive or negative

10. In recent years we bought _____ from foreigners than they bought from us, and we invested _____ in foreign countries than foreigners invested in the United States. (LO2, 4)
    a) more, more   c) less, more
    b) less, less   d) more, less

11. Today international finance is based on
    _____. (LO3)
    a) the gold standard
    b) mainly a relatively free-floating exchange rate system
    c) fixed rates of exchange

12. The international gold standard worked well until
    _____. (LO3)
    a) World War I   c) 1968
    b) 1940   d) 1975

13. If we were on an international gold standard,
    _____. (LO3)
    a) inflations would be eliminated
    b) recessions would be eliminated
    c) trade deficits and surpluses would be eliminated
    d) no nation would ever have to devaluate its currency

14. Which of the following is false? (LO3)
    a) The gold standard will work only when the gold supply increases as quickly as the world's need for money.
    b) The gold standard will work only if all nations agree to devaluate their currencies simultaneously.
    c) The gold standard will work only if participating nations are willing to accept periodic inflation.
    d) The gold standard will work only if participating nations are willing to accept periodic unemployment.

15. The gold exchange standard was in effect from
    _____. (LO3)
    a) 1900 to 1944   c) 1955 to 1980
    b) 1944 to 1973   d) 1973 to the present

16. The United States began to consistently run current account deficits since _____. (LO1, 4)
    a) 1961   d) 1991
    b) 1971   e) 2001
    c) 1981

17. Today currency exchange rates are set mainly by
    _____. (LO3)
    a) the International Monetary Fund
    b) the U.S. Treasury
    c) bilateral agreements between trading nations
    d) supply and demand

18. The most important influence on the exchange rate between two countries is _____. (LO3)
    a) the relative price levels of the two countries
    b) the relative growth rates of the two countries
    c) the relative level of interest rates in both countries
    d) the relative wage rates of both countries

19. Devaluation would tend to _____. (LO3)
    a) make the devaluating country's goods cheaper
    b) make the devaluating country's goods more expensive
    c) have no effect on the value of the devaluating country's goods

20. Which is the most accurate statement? (LO3, 4)
    a) Since the euro was introduced it has lost almost half its value.
    b) The euro has facilitated trade among the members of the euro zone.
    c) The euro is now the world's most important reserve currency.
    d) The euro circulates as currency in most of the countries of the world.

21. The main reason why we are the world's largest debtor nation is _____. (LO4)
    a) our military spending
    b) our trade deficit
    c) inflation
    d) high taxes

22. Which is the most accurate statement? (LO2)
    a) Since our current account deficit is matched by our capital account surplus, we have no problem with respect to our international transactions.
    b) Foreigners invest all the dollars they receive from our capital account deficit to buy American assets.
    c) Our current account deficits are declining and should disappear before the year 2015.
    d) A declining dollar makes foreign investment in dollar-denominated assets much less attractive to foreigners.

23. Which of these is the most accurate statement? (LO4)
    a) There is no basis for the claim that the United States is living beyond its means.
    b) Our current account deficit is not a serious problem.
    c) Our trade deficit is a major economic problem.
    d) Since 2002 the dollar has been rising against most major currencies.

24. If you were going to spend time in Italy, France, and Germany, you would be paying for things with

_____. (LO1)

a) lira, francs, and marks

b) dollars

c) euros

d) gold

25. Which is the most accurate statement? (LO2)

a) Our balance on the current account is negative.

b) Since our balance of payments is always zero, there is little to worry about.

c) The income Americans receive from their foreign investments is much greater than the income foreigners receive for their American investments.

d) Because our imports are much greater than our exports, the federal government is forced to make up the difference.

26. Suppose the world was on the gold standard. If Peru ran persistent trade deficits, _____. (LO3)

a) Peru would be able to continue doing so with no consequences

b) Peru's money stock would decline, its prices would fall, and its trade deficit disappear

c) Peru would soon suffer from inflation

d) Peru would raise tariffs and prohibit the shipment of gold from the country

27. Suppose that in the year 2014 we run a trade deficit of $900 billion. Our current account deficit would be

about _____ billion. (LO4)

a) $600   d) $1,000

b) $800   e) $1,200

c) $900

28. The most accurate statement would be: (LO4)

a) The current account deficit is high, but falling.

b) The current account deficit will bankrupt us by 2020.

c) If our trade deficit begins falling, the current account deficit will fall.

d) Our trade deficit is much higher than our current account deficit.

29. According to the "Big Mac Index,"

_____. (LO3)

a) the U.S. dollar is too highly valued relative to virtually all other currencies

b) the U.S. dollar is valued too low relative to virtually all other currencies

c) you will be able to buy a Big Mac much more cheaply in China or Russia than in the United States

d) you will have to pay much more for a Big Mac in China or Russia than you would in the United States

30. Which is the most accurate statement? In early 2008 there was strong evidence that the _____. (LO3)

a) yuan and yen were overvalued against the dollar

b) yuan and yen were undervalued against the dollar

c) yuan was undervalued against the yen

d) yen was undervalued against the yuan

31. Running mounting current account deficits is analogous to _____. (LO4)

a) running up debt on a credit card

b) taking money out of one pocket and putting it in another

c) owing money to ourselves

d) borrowing money that never has to be repaid

32. If a Japanese DVD player priced at 12,000 yen can be purchased for $60, the exchange rate is (LO3)

a) 200 yen per dollar.   d) 200 dollars per yen.

b) 20 yen per dollar.   e) none of the above.

c) 20 dollars per yen.

33. Suppose that last month the U.S. dollar was trading on the foreign-exchange market at 0.85 euros per dollar. Today the U.S. dollar is trading at 0.88 euros per dollar. (LO3)

a) The dollar has depreciated and the euro has appreciated.

b) The euro has depreciated and the dollar has appreciated.

c) Both the euro and the dollar have appreciated.

d) Neither the euro nor the dollar have depreciated.

Fill-In Questions

1. The entire flow of U.S. dollars and foreign currencies into and out of the country constitutes our _____. (LO2)

2. Most all the dollars that foreigners have earned from trading with the United States have been _____ in the form of _____ _____. (LO2)

3. The basis for international finance is the exchange of _____. (LO1)

4. A nation is on the gold standard when it _____ _____. (LO3)

5. To be on the gold standard, a nation must maintain a fixed ratio between its gold stock and _____ _____. (LO3)

6. Under the gold standard, if country J imports more than it exports, it has to ship _____ _____ to the trading partners with whom it has trade deficits. This will depress country J's _____, and its price level will _____. (LO3)

7. Under the gold standard, if country K's price level declines, its imports will _____ and its exports will _____. (LO3)

8. Today exchange rates are set by _____ and _____. (LO3)

9. If Tim Matray wanted to buy wine from a French merchant, he would pay her with _____. (LO1)

10. The main difference between our being a debtor nation in the 19th century and our being a debtor nation since the early 1980s was that in the 19th century we ran up a debt by buying _____ goods; since the early 1980s we have run up a debt buying _____ goods. (LO4)

Problems

Use the exchange rates listed in Figure 6 of the chapter to find how much it would cost in U.S. dollars and cents to make the purchases listed in problems 1–4.

1. A Toyota Corolla priced at 1.4 million yen. (LO3)

2. A carton of Canadian paper priced at $9.00 Canadian. (LO3)

3. A British book priced at 12 pounds. (LO3)

4. A German camera priced at 250 euros. (LO3)

Use the exchange rates listed in Figure 6 to find how much it would cost in the currency specified to make the purchases listed in problems 5–8.

5. A DVD priced at $10 is sold in Mexico City. (LO3)

6. Windows Vista priced at $100 is sold in China. (LO3)

7. A Cadillac priced at $20,000 is sold in London. (LO3)

8. A bottle of Viagra priced at $40 is sold in Berlin. (LO3)

9. A country had exports of $100 billion, imports of $90 billion, net transfers from abroad of −$10 billion, and −$5 billion of net income from foreign investments. What is the country's current account balance? (LO3)

10. Brazil ran a current account deficit of $55 billion. What is its balance on the capital account? (LO3)

11. If you could buy a market basket of goods and services in the United States for $1,000 and those same goods and services cost you $1,200 after you converted your dollars into euros, (a) is the euro undervalued or overvalued relative to the dollar? (b) by what percent? (LO3)

12. If you could buy a market basket of goods and services in the United States for $10,000 and those same goods and services cost you $7,000 in Russia after you converted your dollars into rubles, (a) is the ruble undervalued or overvalued relative to the dollar? (b) by what percent? (LO3)

Glossary

a

Ability-to-Pay Principle The amount of taxes that people pay should be based on their ability to pay (that is, their incomes).

Absolute Advantage The ability of a country to produce a good at a lower cost than its trading partners.

Accelerator Principle If sales or consumption is rising at a constant rate, gross investment will stay the same; if sales rise at a decreasing rate, both gross investment and GDP will fall.

Accounting Profit Sales minus explicit cost. Implicit costs are not considered.

Aggregate Demand The sum of all expenditures for goods and services.

Aggregate Demand Curve Curve showing planned purchase rates for all goods and services in the economy at various price levels.

Aggregate Supply The nation's total output of goods and services.

Aggregate Supply Curve Curve showing the level of real GDP produced at different price levels during a time period, *ceteris paribus*.

Allocative Efficiency Occurs when no resources are wasted; it is not possible to make any person better off without making someone else worse off.

Anticipated Inflation The rate of inflation that we believe will occur; when it does, we are in a situation of fully anticipated inflation.

Antitrust Laws These laws, including the Sherman and Clayton acts, attempted to enforce competition and to control the corporate merger movement.

Appreciation An increase in the value of a currency in terms of other currencies.

Arbitration An arbitrator imposes a settlement on labor and management if they cannot reach a collective bargaining agreement.

Asset Something that is owned by or owed to an individual or a business firm.

Asset Demand Holding money as a store of value instead of other assets such as stocks, bonds, savings accounts, certificates of deposit, or gold.

Automatic Stabilizers Programs such as unemployment insurance benefits and taxes that are already on the books to help alleviate recessions and hold down the rate of inflation.

Autonomous Consumption The minimum amount that people will spend on the necessities of life.

Average Fixed Cost Fixed cost divided by output.

Average Propensity to Consume The percentage of disposable income that is spent; consumption divided by disposable income.

Average Propensity to Save The percentage of disposable income that is saved; saving divided by disposable income.

Average Tax Rate The percentage of taxable income that is paid in taxes; taxes paid divided by taxable income.

Average Total Cost (ATC) Total cost divided by output.

Average Variable Cost (AVC) Variable cost divided by output.

b

Backward-Bending Labor Supply Curve As the wage rate rises, more and more people are willing to work longer and longer hours up to a point. They will then substitute more leisure time for higher earnings.

Balanced Budget When federal tax receipts equal federal government spending.

Balance of Payments The entire flow of U.S. dollars and foreign currencies into and out of the country.

Balance of Trade The difference between the value of our imports and our exports.

Balance on Capital Account A category that itemizes changes in foreign asset holdings in one nation and that nation's asset holdings abroad.

Balance on Current Account A category that itemizes a nation's imports and exports of goods and services, income receipts and payments on investment, and unilateral transfers.

Bank A commercial bank or thrift institution that offers checkable deposits.

Bank Run Attempts by many depositors to withdraw their money out of fear that that bank was failing, or that all banks were failing.

Barrier to Entry Anything that prevents the entry of new firms into an industry.

Barter The exchange of one good or service for another good or service; a trade.

Base Year The year with which other years are compared when an index is constructed: for example, a price index.

Benefits-Received Principle The amount of taxes people pay should be based on the benefits they receive from the government.

Board of Governors The Federal Reserve System's governing body.

Bonds (See Government Bonds or Corporate Bonds.)

Boom Period of prolonged economic expansion.

Break-Even Point The low point on the firm's average total cost curve. If the price is below this point, the firm will go out of business in the long run.

Budget Deficit When federal tax receipts are less than federal government spending.

Budget Surplus When federal tax receipts are greater than federal government spending.

Business Cycle   Increases and decreases in the level of business activity that occur at irregular intervals and last for varying lengths of time.

Business Firm   A company that produces goods and services for sale to individual consumers, other firms, or the government.

C

CPI   (See Consumer Price Index.)

Capital   All means of production (mainly plant and equipment) created by people.

Capital Account   The section of a nation's international balance of payments statement in which the foreign purchases of that nation's assets and that nation's purchases of assets abroad are recorded.

Capitalism   An economic system in which most economic decisions are made by private owners and most of the means of production are privately owned.

Capital/Output Ratio   The ratio of capital stock to GDP.

Cartel   A group of firms behaving like a monopoly.

Central Bank   A bank whose chief function is the control of the nation's money supply.

Certificate of Deposit (CD)   A time deposit (almost always of $500 or more) with a fixed maturity date offered by banks and other financial institutions.

Change in Demand   A change in the quantity demanded of a good or service at at least one price that is caused by factors other than a change in the price of that good or service.

Change in Supply   A change in the quantity supplied of a good or service at at least one price that is caused by factors other than a change in the price of that good or service.

Checkable-Deposit   Any deposit in a commercial bank or thrift institution against which a check may be written.

Check Clearing   The process by which money is transferred from the checking accounts of the writers of checks to the checking accounts of the recipients of the checks.

Circular Flow Model   Goods and services flow from business firms to households in exchange for consumer expenditures, while resources flow from households to business firms in exchange for resource payments.

Classical Economics   Laissez-faire economics. Our economy, if left free from government interference, tends toward full employment. The prevalent school of economics from about 1800 to 1930.

Closed Economy   An economy which does little or no trading, or has any other interactions with other economies.

Closed Shop   An employer may hire only union members; outlawed under the Taft-Hartley Act.

Collective Bargaining   Negotiations between union and management to obtain agreements on wages, working conditions, and other issues.

Collusion   The practice of firms to negotiate price and/or market share decisions that limit competition in a market.

Commercial Bank   A firm that engages in the business of banking, accepting deposits, offering checking accounts, and making loans.

Communism   An economic system characterized by collective ownership of most resources and central planning.

Comparative Advantage   Total output is greatest when each product is made by the country that has the lowest opportunity cost.

Competition   Rivalry among business firms for resources and customers.

Complementary Goods   Goods and services that are used together; when the price of one falls, the demand for the other rises (and conversely).

Concentration Ratio   The percentage share of industry sales by the four leading firms.

Conglomerate Merger   Merger between two companies in unrelated industries.

Constant-Cost Industry   An industry whose total output can be increased without an increase in long-run-per-unit costs; an industry whose long-run supply curve is flat.

Constant Dollars   Dollars expressed in terms of real purchasing power, using a particular year as the base of comparison, in contrast to current dollars.

Constant Returns to Scale   Cost per unit of production are the same for any output.

Consumer Price Index   The most important measure of inflation. This tells us the percentage rise in the price level since the base year, which is set at 100; represented by CPI.

Consumer Surplus   The difference between what you pay for some good or service and what you would have been willing to pay.

Consumption   The expenditure by individuals on durable goods, nondurable goods, and services; represented by C.

Consumption Function   As income rises, consumption rises, but not as quickly.

Consumption Schedule   A schedule of the amounts that people plan to spend for consumer goods and services at different levels of disposable income.

Contraction   The downturn of the business cycle, when real GDP is declining.

Contractionary Fiscal Policy   To fight inflation, the federal government raises taxes and/or cuts spending.

Contractionary Monetary Policy   To fight inflation, the Federal Reserve decreases the money supply.

Corporate Bonds   This is a debt of the corporation. Bondholders have loaned money to the company and are its creditors.

Corporate Stock   Share in a corporation. The stockholders own the corporation.

Corporation   A business firm that is a legal person. Its chief advantage is that each owner's liability is limited to the amount of money he or she invested in the company.

Cost-of-Living Adjustments (COLAs)   Clauses in contracts that allow for increases in wages, Social Security benefits, and other payments to take account of changes in the cost of living.

Cost-Push Inflation   Rising costs of doing business push up prices.

Craft Unions   Labor unions composed of workers who engage in a particular trade or have a particular skill.

Credit Unions   Financial institution cooperatives made up of depositors with a common affiliation.

Creeping Inflation   A relatively low rate of inflation, such as the rate of less than 4 percent in the United States in recent years.

Cross Elasticity of Demand This measures the responsiveness of the demand for good A to a change in the price of good B, indicating how much more or less of good A is purchased as the price of good B changes.

Crowding-In Effect An increase in private sector spending stimulated by federal budget deficits financed by U.S. Treasury borrowing.

Crowding-Out Effect Large federal budget deficits are financed by Treasury borrowing, which then crowds private borrowers out of financial markets and drives up interest rates.

Crude Quantity Theory of Money The belief that changes in the money supply are directly proportional to changes in the price level.

Currency Coins and paper money that serve as a medium of exchange.

Current Account The section of a nation's international balance of payments that records its exports and imports of goods and services, its net investment income, and its net transfers.

Cyclical Unemployment When people are out of work because the economy is operating below the full-employment level. It rises sharply during recessions.

d

Decreasing Cost Industry An industry in which an increase in output leads to a reduction in the long-run average cost, such that the long-run industry supply curve slopes downward.

Deficit (See Budget Deficit.)

Deflation A decline in the price level for at least two years.

Demand A schedule of quantities of a good or service that people will buy at different prices; represented by D.

Demand Curve A graphical representation of the demand schedule showing the inverse relationship between price and quantity demanded.

Demand Deposit A deposit in a commercial bank or other financial intermediary against which checks may be written.

Demand for Money This represents the inverse relationship between the level of money balances and the price of holding money balances.

Demand, Law of When the price of a good is lowered, more of it is demanded; when the price is raised, less is demanded.

Demand-Pull Inflation Inflation caused primarily by an increase in aggregate demand: too many dollars chasing too few goods.

Demand Schedule A schedule of quantities of a good or service that people are willing to buy at different prices.

Depository Institutions Deregulation and Monetary Control Act of 1980 This made all depository institutions subject to the Federal Reserve's legal reserve requirements and allowed all depository institutions to issue checking deposits.

Depreciation A fall in the price of a nation's currency relative to foreign currencies.

Depression A deep and prolonged business downturn; the last one occurred in the 1930s.

Deregulation The process of converting a regulated firm or industry into an unregulated firm or industry.

Derived Demand Demand for resources derived from demand for the final product.

Devaluation Government policy that lowers the nation's exchange rate so that its currency is worth less than it had been relative to foreign currencies.

Diminishing Marginal Utility Declining utility, or satisfaction, derived from each additional unit consumed of a particular good or service.

Diminishing Returns, Law of If units of a resource are added to a fixed proportion of other resources, marginal output will eventually decline.

Direct Tax Tax on a particular person. Most important are federal personal income tax and payroll (Social Security) tax.

Discounting The method by which the present value of a future sum or a future stream of sums is obtained.

Discount Rate The interest rate charged by the Federal Reserve to depository institutions.

Discouraged Workers People without jobs who have given up looking for work.

Discretionary Fiscal Policy Changes in government spending and taxes to promote full employment, price stability, and economic growth.

Diseconomies of Scale An increase in average total cost as output rises.

Disequilibrium When aggregate demand does not equal aggregate supply.

Disinflation Occurs when the rate of inflation declines.

Disposable Income Aftertax income. Term applies to individuals and to the nation.

Dissaving When consumption is greater than disposable income; negative saving.

Dividends The part of corporate profits paid to its shareholders.

Division of Labor The provision of specialized jobs.

Durable Goods Things that last at least a year or two.

e

E-commerce Buying and selling on the Internet.

Economic Cost Explicit costs plus implicit costs.

Economic Goods Goods that are scarce, for which the quantity demanded exceeds the quantity supplied at a zero price.

Economic Growth An outward shift of the production possibilities frontier brought about by an increase in available resources and/or a technological improvement.

Economic Problem When we have limited resources available to fulfill society's relatively limitless wants.

Economic Profit Sales minus explicit costs and implicit costs.

Economic Rent The excess payment to a resource above what it is necessary to pay to secure its use.

Economics The efficient allocation of the scarce means of production toward the satisfaction of human wants.

Economies of Scale Reductions in average total cost as output rises.

Efficiency Conditions under which maximum output is produced with a given level of inputs.

Elasticity of Demand Measures the change in quantity demanded in response to a change in price.

Elasticity of Supply Measures the change in quantity supplied in response to a change in price.

Entitlement Programs Government programs such as Social Security, Medicare, Medicaid, and food stamps, that guarantee particular levels of cash or noncash benefits to those who fit the programs' criteria.

Entrepreneurial Ability Ability to recognize a business opportunity and successfully set up a business firm to take advantage of it.

Equation of Exchange Shows the relationship among four variables: M (the money supply), V (velocity of circulation), P (the price level), and Q (the quantity of goods and services produced). MV = PQ.

Equilibrium When aggregate demand equals aggregate supply.

Equilibrium Point Point at which quantity demanded equals quantity supplied; where demand and supply curves cross.

Equilibrium Price The price at which quantity demand is equal to quantity supplied.

Equilibrium Quantity The quantity bought and sold at the equilibrium price.

Euro The common currency in most of Western Europe.

European Union (EU) An organization of European nations that has reduced trade barriers among themselves.

Excess Reserves The difference between actual reserves and required reserves.

Exchange The process of trading one thing for another.

Exchange Rates The price of foreign currency; for example, how many dollars we must give up in exchange for marks, yen, and pounds.

Excise Tax A sales tax levied on a particular good or service; for example, gasoline and cigarette taxes.

Expansionary Fiscal Policy To fight recessions, the federal government lowers taxes and/or raises spending.

Expansionary Monetary Policy To fight recessions, the Federal Reserve increases the money supply.

Expected Rate of Profit Expected profits divided by money invested.

Expenditures Approach A way of computing GDP by adding up the dollar value at current market prices of all final goods and services.

Explicit Costs Dollar costs incurred by business firms, such as wages, rent, and interest.

Exports Goods and services produced in a nation and sold to customers in other nations.

Externality A consequence of an economic activity, such as pollution, that affects third parties.

FDIC (See Federal Deposit Insurance Corporation.)

Factors of Production The resources of land, labor, capital, and entrepreneurial ability.

Featherbedding Any labor practice that forces employers to use more workers than they would otherwise employ; a make-work program.

Federal Deposit Insurance Corporation Insures bank deposits up to $100,000.

Federal Funds Rate The interest rate banks and other depository institutions charge one another on overnight loans made out of their excess reserves.

Federal Open Market Committee (FOMC) The principal decision-making body of the Federal Reserve, conducting open market operations.

Federal Reserve Note Paper money issued by the Federal Reserve.

Federal Reserve System Central bank of the United States, whose main job is to control our rate of monetary growth.

Federal Trade Commission (FTC) Works to prevent false and deceptive advertising and has a role in approving or disapproving mergers.

Fiat Money Paper money that is not backed by or convertible into any good; it is money because the government says it is money.

Financial Intermediaries Firms that accept deposits from savers and use those deposits to make loans to borrowers.

Firm A business that employs resources to produce a good or service for profit and owns and operate one or more plants.

Fiscal Policy Manipulation of the federal budget to attain price stability, relatively full employment, and a satisfactory rate of economic growth.

Fiscal Year Budget year. U.S. federal budget fiscal year begins on October 1.

Fixed Costs These stay the same no matter how much output changes.

Fixed Exchange Rate A rate determined by government and then maintained by buying and selling quantities of its own currency on the foreign exchange market.

Floating Exchange Rate An exchange rate determined by the demand for and the supply of a nation's currency.

Foreign Exchange Market A market in which currencies of different nations are bought and sold.

Foreign Exchange Rate The price of one currency in terms of another.

Fractional Reserve Banking A system in which depository institutions held reserves that are less than the amount of total deposits.

Free Trade The absence of artificial (government) barriers to trade among individuals and firms in different nations.

Frictional Unemployment Refers to people who are between jobs or just entering or reentering the labor market.

Fringe Benefits Nonwage compensation, mainly medical insurance, that workers receive from employers.

Full Employment When a society's resources are all being used with maximum efficiency.

Full-Employment GDP That level of spending (or aggregate demand) that will result in full employment.

Future Value The amount of money in the future that an amount of money today will yield, at current interest rates.

Game Theory The study of how people behave in strategic situations.

GATT (General Agreement on Tariffs and Trade) An agreement to negotiate reductions in tariffs and other trade barriers.

GDP (See Gross Domestic Product.)

GDP Deflator A price index used to measure price changes in the items that go into GDP.

GDP Gap The amount of production by which potential GDP exceeds actual GDP.

Globalization   The integration of national economies into a worldwide economy.

Gold Standard   A historical system of fixed exchange rates in which nations defined their currency in terms of gold, maintained a fixed relationship between their stock of gold and their money supplies, and allowed gold to be freely exported and imported.

Government Bonds   Long-term debt of the federal government.

Government Expenditures   Federal, state, and local government outlays for goods and services, including transfer payments.

Government Failure   Misallocation of resources in the public sector.

Government Purchases   All goods and services bought by the federal, state, and local governments.

Government Transfer Payment   (See Transfer Payment.)

Gross Domestic Product (GDP)   The nation's expenditure on all the goods and services produced in the country during the year at market prices; represented by GDP.

Gross Investment   A company's total investment in plant, equipment, and inventory. Also, a nation's plant, equipment, inventory, and residential housing investment.

h

Herfindahl-Hirschman Index   A measure of concentration calculated as the sum of the squares of the market share of each firm in an industry.

Horizontal Merger   Conventional merger between two firms in the same industry.

Household   An economic unit of one or more persons living under one roof.

Human Capital   The accumulation of knowledge and skills that make a worker productive.

Hyperinflation   Runaway inflation; in the United States, double-digit inflation.

i

Imperfect Competition   All market structures except perfect competition; includes monopoly, oligopoly, and monopolistic competition.

Implicit Costs   The firm's opportunity costs of using resources owned or provided by the owner.

Imports   Goods and services bought by people in one country that are produced in other countries.

Income   A flow of money to households.

Income Approach   Method of finding GDP by adding all the incomes earned in the production of final goods and services.

Income Effect   A person's willingness to give up some income in exchange for more leisure time.

Income Elasticity of Demand   The ratio of the percentage change in the quantity demanded of a good to a percentage change in consumer income. It measures the responsiveness of consumer purchases to changes in income.

Incomes Policy   Wage controls, price controls, and tax incentives used to try to control inflation.

Increasing Costs, Law of   As the output of a good expands, the opportunity cost of producing additional units of this good increases.

Increasing Returns   An increase in firm's output by a larger percentage than the percentage increase in its inputs.

Increasing Returns to Scale   A situation in which a firm's minimum long-run average total cost decreases as the level of output rises.

Indexation   The automatic correction by contract or law to a dollar amount to allow for inflation.

Indirect Tax   Tax on a thing rather than on a particular person; for example, sales tax.

Induced Consumption   Spending induced by changes in the level of income.

Industrial Union   A union representing all the workers in a single industry, regardless of each worker's skill or craft.

Inelastic Demand   A demand relationship in which a given percentage change in price results in a smaller percentage change in quantity sold.

Inelastic Supply   A supply relationship in which a given percentage change in price results in a smaller percentage change in quantity supplied.

Inferior Goods   Goods for which demands decrease when people's incomes rise.

Inflation   A general rise in the price level.

Inflationary Gap   Occurs when equilibrium GDP is greater than full-employment GDP.

Innovation   An idea that eventually takes the form of new, applied technology or a new production process.

Interest   The cost of borrowed funds.

Interest Rate   Interest paid divided by amount borrowed.

Interlocking Directorates   When one person serves on the boards of at least two competing firms.

Intermediate Goods   Goods used to produce other goods.

International Monetary Fund (IMF)   An organization of over 150 nations set up as a lender of last resort, especially to nations that had otherwise been planning to devalue their currency, or were in financial crisis.

Inventories   Goods that have been produced but remain unsold.

Inventory Investment   Changes in the stocks of finished goods and raw materials that firms keep in reserve to meet orders.

Investment   The purchase or construction of any new plant, equipment, or residential housing, or the accumulation of inventory; represented by I.

j

Jurisdictional Dispute   A dispute involving two or more unions over which should represent the workers in a particular shop or plant.

k

Keynesian Economics   As formulated by John Maynard Keynes, this school believed the private economy was inherently unstable and that government intervention was necessary to prevent recessions from becoming depressions.

Kinked Demand Curve   The demand curve for the cutthroat oligopolist, which is based on the assumption that competitors will match a price cut, but will not match a price increase.

l

Labor   The work and time for which employees are paid.

Labor Force   The total number of employed and unemployed people.

Labor Union   Worker organization that seeks to secure economic benefits for its members.

Laffer Curve   Shows that at very high tax rates, very few people will work and pay taxes; therefore government revenue will rise as tax rates are lowered.

Laissez-Faire   The philosophy that the private economy should function without any government interference.

Land   Natural resources used to produce goods and services.

Law of Demand   An increase in a product's price will reduce the quantity of it demanded, and conversely for a decrease in price.

Law of Diminishing (Marginal) Returns   The observation that, after some point, successive equal-sized increases of a resource, added to fixed factors of other resources, will result in smaller increases in output.

Law of Diminishing Marginal Utility   As we consume increasing amounts of a good or service, we derive diminishing utility, or satisfaction, from each additional unit consumed.

Law of Increasing Costs   As the output of one good expands, the opportunity cost of producing additional units of this good increases.

Law of Supply   An increase in the price of a product will increase the quantity of it supplied; and conversely for a decrease in price.

Legal Reserves   Reserves that depository institutions are allowed by law to claim as reserves; vault cash and deposits held at Federal Reserve district banks.

Legal Tender   Coins and paper money officially declared to be acceptable for the settlement of financial debts.

Less Developed Countries (LDCs)   Economies in Asia, Africa, and Latin America with relatively low per capita incomes.

Leveraged Buyouts   A primarily debt-financed purchase of a controlling interest of a corporation's stock.

Limited Liability   The liability of the owners of a corporation is limited to the value of the shares in the firm that they own.

Liquidity   Money or things that can be quickly and easily converted into money with little or no loss of value.

Liquidity Preference   The demand for money.

Liquidity Trap   At very low interest rates, said John Maynard Keynes, people will neither lend out their money nor put it in the bank, but will simply hold it.

Loanable Funds   The supply of money that savers have made available to borrowers.

Long Run   When all costs become variable costs and firms can enter or leave the industry.

Long-Run Equilibrium   The intersection of the AD and LRAS curves, when wages and prices have adjusted to their final equilibrium levels.

Lorenz Curve   Data plotted to show the percentage of income enjoyed by each percentage of households, ranked according to their income.

m

M   The money supply—currency, checking deposits, and checklike deposits (identical to M1).

M1   Currency, checking deposits, and checklike deposits.

M2   M1 plus savings deposits, small-denomination time deposits, and money market mutual funds.

M3   M2 plus large-denomination time deposits.

Macroeconomics   The part of economics concerned with the economy as a whole, dealing with huge aggregates like national output, employment, the money supply, bank deposits, and government spending.

Malthusian Theory of Population   Population tends to grow in a geometric progression (1, 2, 4, 8, 16), while food production tends to grow in an arithmetic progression (1, 2, 3, 4, 5).

Margin Requirement   The maximum percentage of the cost of a stock purchase that can be borrowed from a bank, stockbroker, or any other financial institution, with stock offered as collateral; this percentage is set by the Federal Reserve.

Marginal Cost (MC)   The cost of producing one additional unit of output.

Marginal Physical Product (MPP)   The additional output produced by one more unit of input.

Marginal Propensity to Consume (MPC)   Change in consumption divided by change in income.

Marginal Propensity to Save (MPS)   Change in saving divided by change in income.

Marginal Revenue (MR)   The revenue derived from selling one additional unit of output.

Marginal Revenue Product (MRP)   The demand for a resource, based on that resource's marginal output and the price at which it is sold.

Marginal Tax Rate   Additional taxes paid divided by taxable income.

Marginal Utility   The additional utility derived from consuming one more unit of some good or service.

Market   Any place where buyers and sellers exchange goods and services.

Market Failure   A less than efficient allocation of resources.

Market Period   A period during which sellers are unable to change quantity offered for sale in response to a change in price.

Maximum Profit Point   A firm will always produce at this point; marginal cost equals marginal revenue.

MC = MR Rule   For a firm to maximize its profits, marginal cost must equal marginal revenue.

Measure of Economic Welfare   A measure developed by James Tobin and William Nordhaus that modifies GDP by excluding "economic bads" and "regrettable necessities" and adding household, unreported, and illegal production.

Mediation   A third party acts as a go-between for labor and management during collective bargaining.

Medium of Exchange   Items sellers generally accept and buyers generally use to pay for a good or service; the primary job of money.

Merchandise Trade Balance   The difference between the value of merchandise exports and the value of merchandise imports.

Merger   Two or more firms combining to form a single firm.

Microeconomics   The part of economics concerned with individual units such as firms and households and with individual markets, particular prices, and specific goods and services.

Minimum Wage   An hourly wage floor set by government that firms must pay their workers.

Mixed Economy   An economy in which production and distribution is done partly by the private sector and partly by the government.

Monetarism   A school of economics that places paramount importance on money as the key determinant of the level of prices, income, and employment.

Monetary Policy   Control of the rate of monetary growth by the Board of Governors of the Federal Reserve.

Monetary Rule   The money supply may grow at a specified annual percentage rate, generally about 3–4 percent.

Money   Main job is to be a medium of exchange; also serves as a standard of value and a store of value.

Money Multiplier   The amount of money the banking system generates with each dollar of reserves.

Money Supply   Currency, checking deposits, and checklike deposits (M or M1).

Money Wages   The current dollar amount of a person's wages.

Monopolistic Competition   An industry that has many firms producing a differentiated product.

Monopoly   An industry in which one firm produces all the output. The good or service produced has no close substitutes.

Monopsony   A market in which a single buyer has no rivals.

Moral Hazard   The condition that exists when one party to a transaction changes his behavior in a way that is hidden from and costly to the other party.

Multinational Corporation   A corporation doing business in more than one country; often it owns production facilities in at least one country and sells in many countries.

Multiplier   Any change in spending (C, I, or G) will set off a chain reaction leading to a multiplied change in GDP. Equation is $1/(1 - \text{MPC})$.

n

NDP   (See Net Domestic Product.)

National Debt   (See Public Debt.)

National Income   Net domestic product minus indirect business taxes.

Natural Monopoly   An industry in which a single firm can provide cheaper service than could several competing firms.

Negative Income Tax   Cash payments by the government to the poor—an income tax in reverse. The cash payments decrease as income levels increase.

Net Domestic Product   The sum of consumption, net investment, government purchases, and net exports.

Net Domestic Product (NDP)   GDP minus depreciation.

Net Exports   One country's exports to other countries minus its imports from other countries.

Net Investment   Gross investment minus depreciation.

Net Productivity of Capital   The expected annual profit rate.

Net Worth   The difference between assets and liabilities.

Nominal GDP   The value of the final goods and services produced in a given year valued at that year's prices.

Nominal Interest Rate   The real interest rate plus the inflation rate.

Nominal Wages   (See Money Wages.)

Noncompeting Groups   Various strata of labor that do not compete for jobs; for example, doctors and secretaries, skilled and unskilled workers.

Nondurable Goods   Goods that are expected to last or be used for less than one year.

Normal Good   A good whose demand varies directly with income; nearly all goods are normal goods.

Normal Profits   The return to the businessowners for the opportunity cost of their implicit inputs.

North American Free Trade Agreement (NAFTA)   A free trade area consisting of the United States, Canada, and Mexico.

o

Offshoring   Work that had been performed at home is sent abroad.

Oligopoly   An industry with just a few firms.

Oligopsony   A market in which there are only a few buyers.

Open Economy   An economy linked to the rest of the world through international trade.

Open-Market Operations   The purchase or sale of Treasury securities by the Federal Reserve; main monetary policy weapon.

Open Shop   When no one is forced to join a union even though the union represents all the workers in contract negotiations.

Opportunity Cost   The forgone value of what you give up when you make a choice.

Output Effect   When the price of any resource rises, the cost of production rises, which, in turn, lowers the supply of the final product. When supply falls, price rises, consequently reducing output.

p

P   The price level, or the average price of all goods and services produced during the current year.

Paradox of Thrift   If everyone tries to save more, they will all end up saving less.

Partnership   A business firm owned by two or more people.

Payroll Tax   (See Social Security Tax.)

Per Capita Income   A nation's total income per person.

Per Capita Real GDP   Real GDP divided by population.

Perfect Competition   An industry with so many firms that no one firm has any influence over price, and firms produce an identical product.

Perfectly Elastic Demand Curve   A perfectly horizontal demand curve; the firm can sell as much as it wishes at that price.

Perfectly Elastic Supply Curve   A perfectly horizontal supply curve; the slightest decrease in price causes the quantity supplied to fall to zero.

Perfectly Inelastic Demand Curve   A perfectly vertical demand curve; no matter what the price is, the quantity demanded remains the same.

Perfectly Inelastic Supply Curve   A perfectly vertical supply curve; quantity supplied remains constant no matter what happens to price.

Permanent Income Hypothesis   Formulated by Milton Friedman, it states that the strongest influence on consumption is one's estimated lifetime income.

Personal Income   Income received by household, including both earned income and transfer payments.

Phillips Curve   Curve showing inverse relationship between the unemployment rate and the rate of inflation.

Plant   A store, factory, office, or other physical establishment that performs one or more functions in the production, fabrication, and sales of goods and services.

Poverty   A situation in which the basic needs of an individual or family exceed the means to satisfy them.

Poverty Rate   The percentage of the population with incomes below the official poverty line established by the federal government.

Present Value   The value today of the stream of expected future annual income that a property generates.

Price   The amount of money needed to buy a particular good, service, or resource.

Price Ceiling   Government-imposed maximum legal price.

Price Discrimination   Occurs when a seller charges two or more prices for the same good or service.

Price Elasticity of Demand   (See Elasticity of Demand.)

Price Elasticity of Supply   (See Elasticity of Supply.)

Price Floor   Government-imposed minimum price (used almost exclusively to keep agricultural commodity prices up).

Price Index   An index number that shows how the weighted average price of a market basket of goods changes through time.

Price Leadership   One firm, often the dominant firm in an oligopolistic industry, raises or lowers price, and the other firms quickly match the new price.

Price Level   A measure of prices in a given month or year in relation to prices in a base year.

Price Support   Government-created price floor for a good or service.

Price System   Mechanism that allocates resources, goods, and services based on supply and demand.

Prime Rate   Rate of interest that banks charge their most creditworthy customers.

Producer Surplus   The difference between what sellers receive for a good or service and the minimum price for which they would have sold the good or service.

Product Differentiation   The distinction between or among goods and services made in the minds of buyers.

Production   Any good or service for which people are willing to pay.

Production Function   A technological relationship expressing the maximum quantity of a good attainable from different combinations of factor inputs.

Production Possibilities Curve   The potential total output combinations of any two goods for an economy.

Production Possibilities Frontier   A curve representing a hypothetical model of a two-product economy operating at full employment.

Productivity   Output per unit of input; efficiency with which resources are used.

Profit   The difference between total revenue and total cost.

Progressive Tax   Places greater burden on those with best ability to pay and little or no burden on the poor (for example, federal personal income tax).

Proportional Tax   A tax whose burden falls equally among the rich, the middle class, and the poor.

Proprietorship   An unincorporated business firm owned by just one person.

Protective Tariff   A tariff designed to shield domestic producers of a good or service from the competition of foreign producers.

Public Debt   The amount of federal securities outstanding, which represents what the federal government owes (the accumulation of federal deficits minus surpluses over the last two centuries).

Public Goods   Goods or services produced by the government; they can be jointly consumed by many individuals simultaneously at no additional cost and with no reduction in quality or quantity.

q

Q   Output, or number of goods and services produced during the current year.

Quantity Theory of Money   Crude version: Changes in the money supply cause proportional changes in the price level. Sophisticated version: If we are well below full employment, an increase in M will lead to an increase in output. If we are close to full employment, an increase in M will lead mainly to an increase in P.

Quotas   Numerical limits imposed on the quantity of a specific good that may be imported.

r

Rational Expectations Theory   This is based on three assumptions: (1) that individuals and business firms learn through experience to anticipate the consequences of changes in monetary and fiscal policy; (2) that they act immediately to protect their economic interests; and (3) that all resource and product markets are purely competitive.

Real Balance Effect   The influence a change in household purchasing power has on the quantity of real GDP that consumers are willing to buy.

Real GDP   GDP corrected for inflation; actual production.

Real Income   Income adjusted for price changes.

Real Interest Rate   Nominal interest rate minus inflation rate.

Real Wages   Nominal wages corrected for inflation.

Recession   A decline in real GDP for two consecutive quarters.

Recessionary Gap   This occurs when equilibrium GDP is less than full-employment GDP.

Recovery   Phase of business cycle during which real GDP increases from trough level to level of previous peak.

Regressive Tax   Falls more heavily on the poor than on the rich; for example, Social Security tax.

Rent   (See Economic Rent.)

Rent Control   Government-set price ceiling on rent.

Required Reserve Ratio   Percentage of deposits that must be held as vault cash and reserve deposits by all depository institutions.

Required Reserves   Minimum vault cash or reserves; held at the Federal Reserve District Bank.

Reserves   Vault cash and deposits of banks held by Federal Reserve district banks.

Resources   Land, labor, capital, and entrepreneurial ability used to produce goods and services.

Retained Earnings   Earnings that a corporation keeps for investment in plant and equipment or for other purposes, rather than distributed to shareholders.

Right-to-Work Laws   Under the Taft-Hartley Act, states are permitted to pass these laws, which prohibit the union shop. (Union membership cannot be made a condition of securing employment.)

Rule of Reason   Mere size is no offense. Market conduct rather than market share should determine whether antitrust laws have been violated.

S

Saving   Disposable income not spent for consumer goods; equal to disposable income minus personal consumption expenditures.

Saving Function   As income rises, saving rises, but not as quickly.

Say's Law   Supply creates its own demand.

Scarcity   The inability of an economy to generate enough goods and services to satisfy all human wants.

Seasonal Unemployment   Unemployment resulting from the seasonal pattern of work in certain industries, with workers regularly laid off during the slow season and rehired during the busy season.

Secondary Boycott   A boycott of products or a company that sells the products of a company that is being struck.

Sherman Act   The federal antitrust law enacted in 1890 that prohibited monopolization and conspiracies to restrain trade.

Shortage   The amount by which the quantity demanded of a product exceeds the quantity supplied at a particular (below-equilibrium) price.

Short Run   The length of time it takes all fixed costs to become variable costs.

Shut Down   Cessation of a firm's operations as output falls to zero.

Shut-Down Point   The low point on the firm's average variable cost curve. If price is below the shut-down point, the firm will shut down in the short run.

Socialism   An economic system in which the government owns most of the productive resources except labor; it usually involves the redistribution of income.

Social Security   The U.S. social insurance program financed by a federal payroll tax that provides disability, retirement, and death benefits.

Social Security Tax   A tax paid equally by employee and employer, based on employee's wages. Most proceeds are used to pay Social Security retirement and Medicare benefits.

Sole Proprietorship   An unincorporated business firm owned by one person.

Specialization   Division of productive activities so that no one is self-sufficient.

Stagflation   A period of either recession or stagnation accompanied by inflation.

Stock   (See Corporate Stock.)

Strike   When a collective bargaining agreement cannot be reached, a union calls for a work stoppage to last until an agreement is reached.

Structural Unemployment   When people are out of work for a couple of years or longer.

Substitute Goods   Products or services that can be used in place of each other. When the price of one falls, the demand for the other falls, and conversely with an increase of price.

Substitution Effect   If the price of a resource, say labor, goes up, business firms tend to substitute capital or land for some of their now-expensive workers. Also, the substitution of more hours of work for leisure time as the wage rate rises.

Supply   A schedule of quantities that people will sell at different prices.

Supply, Law of   When the price of a good is lowered, less of it is supplied; when the price is raised, more is supplied.

Supply-Side Economics   Main tenets: economic role of federal government is too large; high tax rates and government regulations hurt the incentives of individuals and business firms to produce goods and services.

Surplus   The amount by which the quantity supplied of a product exceeds the quantity demanded at a specific (above-equilibrium) price.

Surplus Value   A Marxian term: the amount by which the value of a worker's daily output exceeds the worker's daily wage.

t

Tariff   A tax on imported goods.

Terms of Trade   The ratio of exchange between an imported good and an exported good.

Time Deposit   A deposit in a financial institution that requires notice of withdrawal or must be left for some fixed period of time.

Total Cost   The sum of fixed and variable costs.

Total Revenue   The price of a good or service multiplied by the number of units sold.

Trade Deficit   The amount by which the value of a nation's imports exceed the value of its exports.

Transactions Demand for Money   The demand for money by individuals and business firms to pay for day-to-day expenses.

Transfer Payment Payment by one branch of government to another or to an individual. Largest transfer payment is Social Security.

Transmission Mechanism The series of changes brought about by a change in monetary policy that ultimately changes the level of GDP.

u

Unanticipated Inflation A rate of inflation that is either higher or lower than expected.

Underemployment Failure to use our resources efficiently. A situation in which workers are employed in positions requiring less skill and education than they have or other resources are employed in their most productive use.

Underground Economy Unreported or illegal production of goods and services that is not counted in GDP.

Unemployment The total number of people over 16 who are ready, willing, and able to work, who have been unsuccessfully seeking employment.

Unemployment Rate Number of unemployed divided by the labor force.

Union Shop All employees must join the union, usually within 30 days after they are hired.

U.S. Treasury Securities Bonds, bills, and notes that the Treasury issues when it borrows.

Utility The satisfaction you derive from a good or service that you purchase. How much utility you derive is measured by how much you would be willing to pay.

v

Variable Costs These vary with output. When output rises, variable costs rise; when output declines, variable costs fall.

Velocity (V) The number of times per year each dollar in the money supply is spent.

Vertical Merger The joining of two firms engaged in different parts of an industrial process, or the joining of a manufacturer and a retailer.

w

Wage The price paid for the use or services of labor per unit of time.

Wage and Price Controls Rules established by the government that either place a ceiling on wages and prices or limit their rate of increase.

Wealth Anything that has value because it produces income or could produce income.

Workfare A plan that requires welfare recipients to accept jobs or to enter training programs.

World Trade Organization (WTO) The successor organization to GATT, which handles all trade disputes among member nations.

Photo Credits

Index

Page numbers followed by n refer to notes.

Economies of being established, 250–251
Economies of scale
    as barrier to entry, 248
    characteristics, 185–186
    in communication, 186
    definition, 34
    in entertainment, 186
    justification for natural monopoly, 252
    long-run average total cost curve, 194
    overcoming, 251
    and plant size, 193
Economist, 320, 490, 491, 496
Economists
    debate on minimum wage, 383–385
    on free trade, 464
    on full employment, 29
    opposition to rent control, 81
    on trade deficits, 464
Economizing, 26
Economy/Economies
    capitalism, 63–64
    circular flow model, 54–55
    communism, 64–65
    competition, 52–53
    Congressional earmarks, 68
    equity and efficiency, 53–54
    fall of communist system, 66
    fascism, 65
    government failure, 59–61
    invisible hand theory, 51–52
    legal systems and, 55
    and market failure, 56–59
    national vs. global, 17–18
    price mechanism, 52
    private sector, 49
    productive efficiency, 37
    public sector, 49
    role of capital, 61–63
    role of government, 55–56
    socialism, 65–66
    supply and demand as guidance
        system, 71
    transformation in China, 66–68
    trust, 53
Eden, Kathryn, 439
Edgar Thompson steel works, 5
Edison, Thomas A., 27
Edmunds.com, 103
Education; *see also* College education;
        Public education
    and annual earnings, 369
    effect of GI Bill of Rights, 13
    as government failure, 60
    relation to wage rates, 388–389
Efficiency
    definition, 213, 228
    in economics, 53–54
    effect of imports, 464
    in income distribution, 423–424
    monopolistic vs. perfect competition, 268
    peak, 213

prices, profit and, 228
profitable output, 213–214
review of, 214–215
of tariffs and quotas, 463
Ehrenreich, Barbara, 368–369, 382,
        438, 444, 447
80-day cooling-off period, 357
    in Taft-Hartley Act, 349
Einstein, Albert, 59
Eisenhans, Lynn, 386
Eisenhower, Dwight D., 13–14, 21, 22,
        23, 24, 262, 325
Elastic demand
    contributing factors, 135
    determining, 133–135
    and price changes, 127–128
    and total revenue, 137–138
Elasticity
    cross elasticity of demand, 140–141
    estimating, 125–141
    formula, 126, 127
    income elasticity of demand, 138–140
    perfect, 128–130
    relative, 130
    of straight-line demand curve, 132
    and total revenue, 137–138
Elasticity of demand
    definition, 125
    over time, 135
    price elasticity, 126–133
    and product uses, 135
    for selected goods, 134
Elasticity of supply, 125
Electric power, 7
Electric utilities, 107
Eli Lilly, 252, 324
Ellison, Lawrence J., 26, 422
El Paso, 284
EMI Group, 317
Emissions rights trading, 58
Employee Free Choice Act, 360–361
Employers
    ability to handle strikes, 357
    economic power of, 355–356
    and Taft-Hartley Act, 348–349
    unfair labor practices, 348
Employment
    class theory of, 369
    decline in 2008–2009, 12
    effect of minimum wage, 383–385
    by sector 1940–2010, 50
Employment argument for protectionism,
        461–462
Employment discrimination
    African Americans, 374
    cause of poverty, 434
    effect on wages
        African Americans, 388
        women, 386–388
    minorities, 29
    women, 29–30

Engels, Friedrich, 64
England, factory conditions in 19th
        century, 62–63
Enron Corporation, 284, 323, 324, 494
Entertainment, economies of scale in, 186
Entrepreneurial ability, as economic
        resource, 26, 27
Entrepreneurial climate, 27
Entrepreneurs, 27
    versus capitalists, 410
    self-interest of, 51
    theories of profit
        exploitation of labor, 411
        innovation, 409–410
        monopolist, 410
        risk takers, 408–409
Environmental issues, and automobiles, 14
Environmental Protection Agency, 58
Equal Employment Opportunity
        Commission, 387
Equal pay for equal work, 386–387
Equilibrium in supply and demand,
        111–113
Equilibrium price
    and change in supply and demand, 95
    definition, 74
    effect of price ceilings or floors,
        79–83
    finding, 111–113
    and market price, 74–75
    below market price, 112
    and shifts in supply and demand,
        74–79, 114–115
    with simultaneous supply and demand
        shifts, 116–117
    and surpluses or shortages, 74–75,
        112–113
Equilibrium quantity
    and change in supply and demand, 95
    demanded and supplied, 111–113
    finding, 111–113
    and shifts in supply and demand,
        75–79, 114–115
    with simultaneous supply and demand
        shifts, 116–117
Equilibrium wage, 384
Equity
    in economics, 53–54
    in income distribution, 423–424
Ernst & Young, 317
Esar, Evan, 277
ESSO, 313
Estate tax, 147
Euro
    adoption and use, 489
    and dollar, 480
    per U.S. dollar, 487
Europe, postwar capital formation, 63
European Commission, 290
    antitrust enforcement, 317–318
European Monetary Union, 489

McGraw Hill **connect**™
|ECONOMICS

Less managing. More teaching. Greater learning.

INSTRUCTORS...

Would you like your **students** to show up for class **more prepared**?
(Let's face it, class is much more fun if everyone is engaged and prepared...)

Want an **easy way to assign** homework online and track student **progress**?
(Less time grading means more time teaching...)

Want an **instant view** of student or class performance? *(No more wondering if students understand...)*

Need to **collect data and generate reports** required for administration or accreditation? *(Say goodbye to manually tracking student learning outcomes...)*

Want to **record and post your lectures** for students to view online?

With **McGraw-Hill's** *Connect*™ *Plus Economics*,

INSTRUCTORS GET:

- Simple **assignment management,** allowing you to spend more time teaching.
- **Auto-graded** assignments, quizzes, and tests.
- **Detailed Visual Reporting** where student and section results can be viewed and analyzed.
- Sophisticated **online testing** capability.
- A **filtering and reporting** function that allows you to easily assign and report on materials that are correlated to accreditation standards, learning outcomes, and Bloom's taxonomy.
- An easy-to-use **lecture capture** tool.
- The option to **upload course documents** for student access.

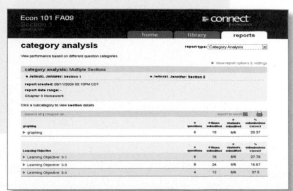

STUDENTS...

Want to get **better grades**? *(Who doesn't?)*

Prefer to do your **homework online**? *(After all, you are online anyway...)*

Need **a better way** to **study** before the big test?

(A little peace of mind is a good thing...)

With **McGraw-Hill's *Connect™ Plus Economics*,**

STUDENTS GET:

- **Easy online access** to homework, tests, and quizzes assigned by your instructor.

- **Immediate feedback** on how you're doing. (No more wishing you could call your instructor at 1 a.m.)

- **Quick access** to lectures, practice materials, eBook, and more. (All the material you need to be successful is right at your fingertips.)

- A Self-Quiz and Study tool that **assesses your knowledge** and **recommends** specific readings, supplemental study materials, and additional practice work.*

Available with select McGraw-Hill titles.

Want an online, **searchable version** of your textbook?

Wish your textbook could be **available online** while you're doing your assignments?

Connect™ Plus Economics eBook

If you choose to use *Connect™ Plus Economics*, you have an affordable and searchable online version of your book integrated with your other online tools.

Connect™ Plus Economics eBook offers features like:

- Topic search
- Direct links from assignments
- Adjustable text size
- Jump to page number
- Print by section

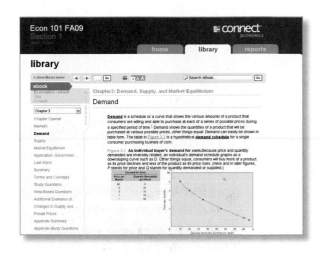

Want to get more **value** from your textbook purchase?

Think learning economics should be a bit more **interesting**?

Check out the STUDENT RESOURCES section under the *Connect™* Library tab.

Here you'll find a wealth of resources designed to help you achieve your goals in the course. Every student has different needs, so explore the STUDENT RESOURCES to find the materials best suited to you.

LABOR FORCE PARTICIPATION[1] RATE, SELECTED YEARS, 1950–2009

Year	Males	Females
1950	85.3	33.3
1955	84.5	35.4
1960	83.3	37.7
1965	80.7	39.3
1970	79.7	43.3
1975	77.9	46.3
1980	77.4	51.5
1985	76.3	54.5
1990	76.4	57.5
1995	75.0	58.9
2000	74.8	59.9
2005	73.3	59.3
2007	73.2	59.3
2009	72.0	59.2

[1]Civilian labor force as percent of civilian noninstitutional population.

UNEMPLOYMENT RATE, SELECTED YEARS, 1975–2009

Year	White	Black	Hispanic
1950	—	—	—
1955	—	—	—
1960	—	—	—
1965	—	—	—
1970	—	—	—
1975	7.8	14.8	12.2
1980	6.3	14.3	10.1
1985	6.2	15.1	10.5
1990	4.8	11.4	8.2
1995	4.9	10.4	9.3
2000	3.5	7.6	5.7
2005	4.4	10.0	6.0
2007	4.1	8.3	5.6
2009	8.5	14.8	12.1

AVERAGE HOURLY EARNINGS, PRIVATE EMPLOYEES, 1964–2009

Year	Current Dollars	1982 Dollars
1964	$2.53	$7.86
1965	2.63	8.04
1966	2.73	8.13
1967	2.85	8.21
1968	3.02	8.37
1969	3.22	8.45
1970	3.40	8.46
1971	3.63	8.64
1972	3.90	8.99
1973	4.14	8.98
1974	4.43	8.65
1975	4.73	8.48
1976	5.06	8.58
1977	5.44	8.66
1978	5.87	8.67
1979	6.33	8.40
1980	6.84	7.99
1981	7.43	7.88
1982	7.86	7.86
1983	8.19	7.95
1984	8.48	7.95
1985	8.73	7.91
1986	8.92	7.96
1987	9.13	7.86
1988	9.43	7.81
1989	9.80	7.75

Year	Current Dollars	1982 Dollars
1990	10.19	7.66
1991	10.50	7.58
1992	10.75	7.55
1993	11.03	7.52
1994	11.32	7.53
1995	11.64	7.53
1996	12.03	7.57
1997	12.49	7.68
1998	13.01	7.89
1999	13.49	8.01
2000	14.02	8.04
2001	14.54	8.12
2002	14.97	8.25
2003	15.37	8.28
2004	15.69	8.24
2005	16.13	8.18
2006	16.76	8.24
2007	17.43	8.33
2008	18.08	8.30
2009	18.62	8.60